JOURNAL FOR STAR WISDOM 2014

JOURNAL FOR STAR WISDOM

2014

Edited by Robert Powell

EDITORIAL BOARD

William Bento
Brian Gray
Claudia McLaren Lainson
Lacquanna Paul
Robert Schiappacasse

Lindisfarne Books

LINDISFARNE BOOKS
AN IMPRINT OF STEINERBOOKS/ANTHROPOSOPHIC PRESS, INC.
610 Main Street, Suite 1
Great Barrington, MA, 01230
www.steinerbooks.org

Journal for Star Wisdom 2014 © 2013 by Robert Powell. All contributions are used by permission of the authors. All rights reserved. No part of this publication may be reproduced, stored in a retrieval system, or transmitted in any form or by any means, electronic, mechanical, photocopying, recording, or otherwise without the prior written permission of the publisher.

With grateful acknowledgment to Peter Treadgold (1943–2005), who wrote the Astrofire program (available from the Sophia Foundation), with which the ephemeris pages in the *Journal for Star Wisdom* are computed each year.

Disclaimer: The views expressed in the articles published in the *Journal for Star Wisdom* are the sole responsibility of the authors of these articles and do not necessarily reflect those of the editorial board of the *Journal for Star Wisdom*.

DESIGN: WILLIAM JENS JENSEN

ISBN: 978-1-58420-149-6 (paperback)

ISBN: 978-1-58420-150-2 (eBook)

CONTENTS

Preface	9
The Rose of the World (*Rosa Mira*) by Daniel Andreev	14
Editorial Foreword by Robert Powell	18
Working with the *Journal for Star Wisdom*	21
2014 and the Coming of the Kalki Avatar by Robert Powell	22
The Bodhisattva Who Will Become the Maitreya Buddha by Estelle Isaacson	36
Finding Jerusalem, part 2 by David Tresemer	38
Corporate Personhood: The Touch of Neptune by David Tresemer	41
Reuniting Psyche with Astro-Logos: A Study in the Light of the Uranus–Pluto Cycle by William Bento	54
A Brief Note on Mirandola and Ficino by David Tresemer and Robert Schiappacasse	71
Evolutionary Streams Accompanying Christ's Descent by Paul Marx	72
Zodiacs and Calendars: Controversy about Guidance from the Heavens by David Tresemer	78
Where on Earth Is the Zodiac?...and Other Concerns of Astro-Gaiasophy by Brian Gray	84
Working with the Star Calendar by Robert Powell	107
Symbols Used in Charts	109
Time	110
Introduction to the Commentaries 2014: Kashyapa in the Light of Pentecost by Claudia Mclaren Lainson	113

Commentaries and Ephemerides: January–December 2014
   by Claudia Mclaren Lainson
   with Monthly Astronomical Sky Watch by Sally Nurney
	120

Glossary	218
References	225
About the Contributors	228

ASTROSOPHY

The Sophia Foundation was founded and exists to help usher in the new Age of Sophia and the corresponding Sophianic culture, the Rose of the World, prophesied by Daniel Andreev and other spiritual teachers. Part of the work of the Sophia Foundation is the cultivation of a new star wisdom, *Astro-Sophia* (Astrosophy), now arising in our time in response to the descent of Sophia, who is the bearer of Divine Wisdom, just as Christ (the Logos, or the Lamb) is the bearer of Divine Love. Like the star wisdom of antiquity, Astrosophy is sidereal, which means "of the stars." Astrosophy, inspired by Divine Sophia, descending from stellar heights, directs our consciousness toward the glory and majesty of the starry heavens, to encompass the entire celestial sphere of our cosmos and, beyond this, to the galactic realm—the realm that Daniel Andreev referred to as "the heights of our universe"—from which Sophia is descending on her path of approach into our cosmos. Sophia draws our attention not only to the star mysteries of the heights, but also to the cosmic mysteries connected with Christ's deeds of redemption wrought two thousand years ago. To penetrate these mysteries is the purpose of the yearly *Journal for Star Wisdom*.

U

For information about Astrosophy/Choreocosmos/Cosmic Dance workshops
Contact the Sophia Foundation:
525 Gough St. #103, San Francisco, CA 94102
(415) 522-1150; sophia@sophiafoundation.org;
www.sophiafoundation.org

PREFACE

Robert Powell, Ph.D.

This is the fifth edition of the *Journal for Star Wisdom*, which is intended as a help to all people interested in the new star wisdom of astrosophy and in the cosmic dimension of Christianity, which began with the star of the magi. The calendar comprises an ephemeris page for each month of the year computed with the help of Peter Treadgold's Astrofire computer program, and a monthly commentary by Claudia McLaren Lainson (with Sally Nurney). The monthly commentary relates the geocentric and heliocentric planetary movements to events in the life of Jesus Christ.

Jesus Christ united the levels of the earthly personality (geocentric = Earth-centered) and the higher self (heliocentric = Sun-centered) in so far as he was the most highly evolved earthly personality (Jesus) embodying the Higher Self (Christ) of all existence, the Divine "I AM." To see the life of Jesus Christ in relation to the world of stars opens the door to a profound experience of the cosmos, giving rise to a new star wisdom (astrosophy) that is the Spiritual Science of Cosmic Christianity.

The *Journal for Star Wisdom* is scientific, resting upon a solid mathematical-astronomical foundation and also upon a secure chronology of the life of Jesus Christ, and at the same time it is spiritual, aspiring to the higher dimension of existence that is expressed outwardly in the world of stars. The scientific and the spiritual come together in the sidereal zodiac that originated with the Babylonians and was used by the three magi who beheld the star of Bethlehem and came to pay homage to Jesus a few months after his birth. In continuity of spirit with the origins of Cosmic Christianity with the three magi, the sidereal zodiac is the frame of reference used for the computation of the geocentric and heliocentric planetary movements that are commented upon in the light of the life of Jesus Christ in the *Journal for Star Wisdom*.

Thus, all zodiacal longitudes indicated in the text and presented in the following calendar are in terms of the sidereal zodiac, which has to be distinguished from the tropical zodiac in widespread use in contemporary astrology in the West. The tropical zodiac was introduced into astrology in the middle of the second century AD by the Greek astronomer Claudius Ptolemy. Prior to this the sidereal zodiac was in use. Such was the influence of Ptolemy upon the Western astrological tradition that the tropical zodiac became substituted for the sidereal zodiac used by the Babylonians, Egyptians, and early Greek astrologers. Yet the astrological tradition in India was not influenced by Ptolemy, and so the sidereal zodiac is still used to this day by Hindu astrologers.

The sidereal zodiac originated with the Babylonians in the sixth to fifth centuries BC and was defined by them in relation to certain bright stars. For example, Aldebaran ("the Bull's eye") is located in the middle of the sidereal sign/constellation of the Bull at 15° Taurus, and Antares ("the Scorpion's heart") is in the middle of the sidereal sign/constellation of the Scorpion at 15° Scorpio. The sidereal signs, each 30° long, coincide closely with the twelve astronomical zodiacal constellations of the same name, whereas the signs of the tropical zodiac, since they are defined in relation to the vernal point, now have little or no relationship to the corresponding zodiacal constellations. This is because the vernal point, the zodiacal location of the sun on March 20/21, shifts slowly backward through the sidereal zodiac at a rate of 1° in seventy-two years ("the precession of the equinoxes"). When Ptolemy introduced the tropical zodiac into astrology, there was an almost exact coincidence between the tropical and the sidereal zodiac, as the vernal point, which is defined to be 0° Aries in the tropical zodiac, was at 1° Aries in the sidereal zodiac in the middle of the second century AD. Thus, there was only 1° difference between the two zodiacs. So, it made hardly any difference to Ptolemy or his contemporaries to use the tropical zodiac instead of the sidereal zodiac. But now—the vernal point, on account of precession, having shifted back from 1° Aries to 5° Pisces—there is a 25° difference and so there is virtually no correspondence between the two. Without going into further detail concerning the complex issue of the zodiac, as shown in the *Hermetic Astrology* trilogy, the sidereal zodiac is the zodiac used by the three magi, who were the last representatives of the true star wisdom of antiquity. For this reason the sidereal zodiac is used throughout the *Journal for Star Wisdom*.

Readers interested in exploring the scientific (astronomical and chronological) foundations of Cosmic Christianity are referred to the works listed below under "Literature." The *Chronicle of the Living Christ: Foundations of Cosmic Christianity,* listed on the next page, is an indispensable source of reference (abbreviated *Chron.*) for the *Journal for Star Wisdom,* as, too, are the four Gospels (Matthew = Mt.; Mark = Mk.; Luke = Lk.; John = Jn.). The chronology of the life of Jesus Christ rests upon the description of his daily life by Anne Catherine Emmerich in her four-volume work *The Life of Jesus Christ* (abbreviated *LJC*). Further details concerning the *Journal for Star Wisdom* and how to work with it on a daily basis may be found in the general introduction to the *Christian Star Calendar.* The general introduction explains all the features of the *Journal for Star Wisdom*. The new edition, published 2003, includes sections on the megastars (stars of great luminosity) and on the 36 decans (10° subdivisions of the twelve signs of the zodiac) in relation to their planetary rulers and to the extra-zodiacal constellations, those constellations above or below the circle of the twelve constellations/signs of the zodiac. Further material on the decans, including examples of historical personalities born in the various decans, and also a wealth of other material on the signs of the sidereal zodiac, is to be found in *Cosmic Dances of the Zodiac,* listed below. Also foundational is *History of the Zodiac,* published by Sophia Academic Press, listed below under "Works by Robert Powell."

LITERATURE

(See also "References" section)

General Introduction to the Christian Star Calendar: A Key to Understanding, 2nd ed. Palo Alto, CA: Sophia Foundation, 2003.

Bento, William, Robert Schiappacasse, and David Tresemer, *Signs in the Heavens: A Message for our Time*. Boulder: StarHouse, 2000.

Emmerich, Anne Catherine, *Visions of the Life of Jesus Christ* (new edition, with material by Robert Powell). San Rafael, CA: LogoSophia, 2012.

Paul, Lacquanna, and Robert Powell, *Cosmic Dances of the Planets*. San Rafael, CA: Sophia Foundation Press, 2007.

———, *Cosmic Dances of the Zodiac*. San Rafael, CA: Sophia Foundation Press, 2007.

Smith, Edward, *The Burning Bush: An Anthroposophical Commentary on the Bible*. Great Barrington, MA: SteinerBooks, 1997.

Steiner, Rudolf, *Astronomy and Astrology. Finding a Relationship to the Cosmos*. London: Rudolf Steiner Press, 2009.

Sucher, Willi, *Cosmic Christianity and the Changing Countenance of Cosmology*. Great Barrington, MA: SteinerBooks, 1993. *Isis Sophia* and other works by Willi Sucher are available from the Astrosophy Research Center, PO Box 13, Meadow Vista, CA 95722.

Tidball, Charles S., and Robert Powell, *Jesus, Lazarus, and the Messiah: Unveiling Three Christian Mysteries*. Great Barrington, MA: SteinerBooks, 2005. This book offers a penetrating study of the Christ mysteries against the background of *Chronicle of the Living Christ* and contains two chapters by Robert Powell on the Apostle John and John the Evangelist (Lazarus).

Tresemer, David (with Robert Schiappacasse), *Star Wisdom & Rudolf Steiner: A Life Seen Through the Oracle of the Solar Cross*. Great Barrington, MA: SteinerBooks, 2007.

ASTROSOPHICAL WORKS BY ROBERT POWELL, PH.D.

Starcrafts *(formerly Astro Communication Services, or ACS):*
History of the Houses (1997).
History of the Planets (1989).
The Zodiac: A Historical Survey (1984).
www.acspublications.com
www.astrocom.com
Business Address:
Starcrafts Publishing
334 Calef Hwy.
Epping, NH 03042
Phone: 603-734-4300
Fax: 603-734-4311
Contact maria@starcraftseast.com

SteinerBooks:
Orders: (703) 661-1594; www.steinerbooks.org;
PO Box 960, Herndon, VA 20172.

The Astrological Revolution: Unveiling the Science of the Stars as a Science of Reincarnation and Karma, coauthor Kevin Dann (Great Barrington, MA: SteinerBooks, 2010). After reestablishing the sidereal zodiac as a basis for astrology that penetrates the mystery of the stars' relationship to human destiny, the reader is invited to discover the astrological significance of the totality of the vast sphere of stars surrounding the Earth. This book points to the astrological significance of the entire celestial sphere, including all the stars and constellations beyond the twelve zodiacal signs. This discovery is revealed by the study of megastars, illustrating how they show up in an extraordinary way in Christ's healing miracles by aligning with the Sun at the time of those events. This book offers a spiritual, yet scientific, path toward a new relationship to the stars.

Christian Hermetic Astrology: The Star of the Magi and the Life of Christ (Great Barrington, MA: SteinerBooks, 1998). Twenty-five discourses set in the "Temple of the Sun," where Hermes and his pupils gather to meditate on the Birth, the Miracles, and the Passion of Jesus Christ. The discourses offer a series of meditative contemplations on the deeds of Christ in relation to the mysteries of the cosmos. They are an expression of the age-old hermetic mystery wisdom of the ancient Egyptian sage, Hermes Trismegistus. This book offers a meditative approach to the cosmic correspondences between major events in the life of Christ and the heavenly configurations at that time 2,000 years ago.

Chronicle of the Living Christ: Foundations of Cosmic Christianity (Great Barrington, MA: SteinerBooks, 1996). An account of the life of Christ, day by day, throughout most of the 3½ years of his ministry, including the horoscopes of conception, birth, and death of Jesus, Mary, and John the Baptist, together with a wealth of material relating to a new star wisdom focused on the life of Christ. This work provides the chronological basis for *Christian Hermetic Astrology* and the *Journal for Star Wisdom*.

Elijah Come Again: A Prophet for our Time: A Scientific Approach to Reincarnation (Great Barrington, MA: Steiner Books, 2009). By way of horoscope comparisons from conception–birth–death in one incarnation to conception–birth–death in the next, this work establishes scientifically two basic astrosophical research findings. These are: the importance 1) of the sidereal zodiac and 2) of the heliocentric positions of the planets. Also, for the first time, the identity of the "saintly nun" is revealed, of whom Rudolf Steiner spoke in a conversation with Marie von Sivers about tracing Novalis's karmic background. The focus throughout the book is on the Elijah individuality in his various incarnations, and is based solidly on Rudolf Steiner's indications. It also can be read as a karmic biography by anyone who chooses to omit the astrosophical material.

Journal for Star Wisdom (Great Barrington, MA: SteinerBooks, annual). Edited by Robert Powell and others in the StarFire research group: A guide to the correspondences of Christ in the stellar and etheric world. Includes articles of interest, a complete sidereal ephemeris and aspectarian, geocentric and heliocentric. Published yearly in November for the coming year. According to Rudolf Steiner, every step taken by Christ during his ministry between the baptism in the Jordan and the resurrection was in harmony with, and an expression of, the cosmos. The journal is concerned with these heavenly correspondences during the life of Christ. It is intended to help provide a foundation for Cosmic Christianity, the cosmic dimension of Christianity. It is this dimension that has been missing from Christianity in its 2,000-year history. A starting point is to contemplate the movements of the Sun, Moon, and planets against the background of the zodiacal constellations (sidereal signs) today in relation to corresponding stellar events during the life of Christ. This opens the possibility of attuning to the life of Christ in the etheric cosmos in a living way.

Sophia Foundation Press and Sophia Academic Press Publications

Books available from Amazon.com
JamesWetmore@mac.com
www.logosophia.com

History of the Zodiac (San Rafael, CA: Sophia Academic Press, 2007). Book version of Robert Powell's Ph.D. thesis on the *History of the Zodiac*. This penetrating study of the *History of the Zodiac* restores the sidereal zodiac to its rightful place as the original zodiac, tracing it back to fifth-century-BC. Babylonians. Available in paperback and hard cover.

Hermetic Astrology: Volume 1, Astrology and Reincarnation (San Rafael, CA: Sophia Foundation Press, 2007). This book seeks to give the ancient science of the stars a scientific basis. This new foundation for astrology based on research into reincarnation and karma (destiny) is the primary focus. It includes numerous reincarnation examples, the study of which reveals the existence of certain astrological "laws" of reincarnation, on the basis of which it is evident that the ancient sidereal zodiac is the authentic astrological zodiac, and that the heliocentric movements of the planets are of great significance. Foundational for the new star wisdom of astrosophy.

Hermetic Astrology: Volume 2, Astrological Biography (San Rafael, CA: Sophia Foundation Press, 2007). Concerned with karmic relationships and the unfolding of destiny in seven-year periods through one's life. The seven-year rhythm underlies the human being's astrological biography, which can be studied in relation to the movements of the Sun, Moon, and planets around the sidereal zodiac between conception and birth. The "rule of Hermes" is used to determine the moment of conception.

Sign of the Son of Man in the Heavens: Sophia and the New Star Wisdom (San Rafael, CA: Sophia Foundation Press, 2008). Revised and expanded with new material, this edition deals with a new wisdom of stars in the light of Divine Sophia. It is intended as a help in our time, when we are called on to be extremely wakeful during the period leading up to the end of the Mayan calendar in 2012.

Cosmic Dances of the Zodiac (San Rafael, CA: Sophia Foundation Press, 2007) coauthor Lacquanna Paul. Study material describing the twelve signs of the zodiac and their forms and gestures in cosmic dance, with diagrams, including a wealth of information on the twelve signs and the 36 decans (the subdivision of the signs into decans, or 10° sectors, corresponding to constellations above and below the zodiac).

Cosmic Dances of the Planets (San Rafael, CA: Sophia Foundation Press, 2007), coauthor Lacquanna Paul. Study material describing the seven classical planets and their forms and gestures in cosmic dance, with diagrams, including much information on the planets.

American Federation of Astrologers (AFA) Publications

PO Box 22040, Tempe, AZ 85285.

The Sidereal Zodiac, coauthor Peter Treadgold (Tempe, AZ: AFA, 1985). A *History of the Zodiac* (sidereal, tropical, Hindu, astronomical) and a formal definition of the sidereal zodiac with the star Aldebaran ("the Bull's Eye") at 15° Taurus. This is an abbreviated version of *History of the Zodiac.*

Rudolf Steiner College Press Publications

9200 Fair Oaks Blvd., Fair Oaks, CA 95628

The Christ Mystery: Reflections on the Second Coming (Fair Oaks, CA: Rudolf Steiner College Press, 1999). The fruit of many years of reflecting on the Second Coming and its cosmological aspects. Looks at the approaching trial of humanity and the challenges of living in apocalyptic times, against the background of "great signs in the heavens."

The Sophia Foundation

525 Gough St. #103, San Francisco, CA 94102; distributes many of the books listed here and other works by Robert Powell.
Tel: (415) 522-1150
sophia@sophiafoundation.org
www.sophiafoundation.org

Computer Program for Charts and Ephemerides, with grateful acknowledgment to Peter Treadgold, who wrote the computer program *Astrofire* (with research module, star catalog of over 4,000 stars, and database of birth and death charts of historical personalities), capable of printing geocentric and heliocentric/hermetic sidereal charts and ephemerides throughout history. The hermetic charts, based on the

Preface

astronomical system of the Danish astronomer Tycho Brahe, are called "Tychonic" charts in the program. This program can:

- compute birth charts in a large variety of systems (tropical, sidereal, geocentric, heliocentric, hermetic);
- calculate conception charts using the hermetic rule, in turn applying it for correction of the birth time;
- produce charts for the period between conception and birth;
- print out an "astrological biography" for the whole of lifework with the geocentric, heliocentric (and even lemniscatory) planetary system;
- work with the sidereal zodiac according to the definition of your choice (Babylonian sidereal, Indian sidereal, unequal-division astronomical, etc.);
- work with planetary aspects with orbs of your choice.

The program includes eight house systems and a variety of chart formats. The program also includes an ephemeris program with a search facility. The geocentric/heliocentric sidereal ephemeris pages in the yearly *Journal for Star Wisdom* are produced by *Astrofire*. This program runs under Microsoft Windows. Those interested in *Astrofire* may contact:

The Sophia Foundation
525 Gough St. #103, San Francisco, CA 94102
Tel: (415) 522-1150
sophia@sophiafoundation.org
www.sophiafoundation.org

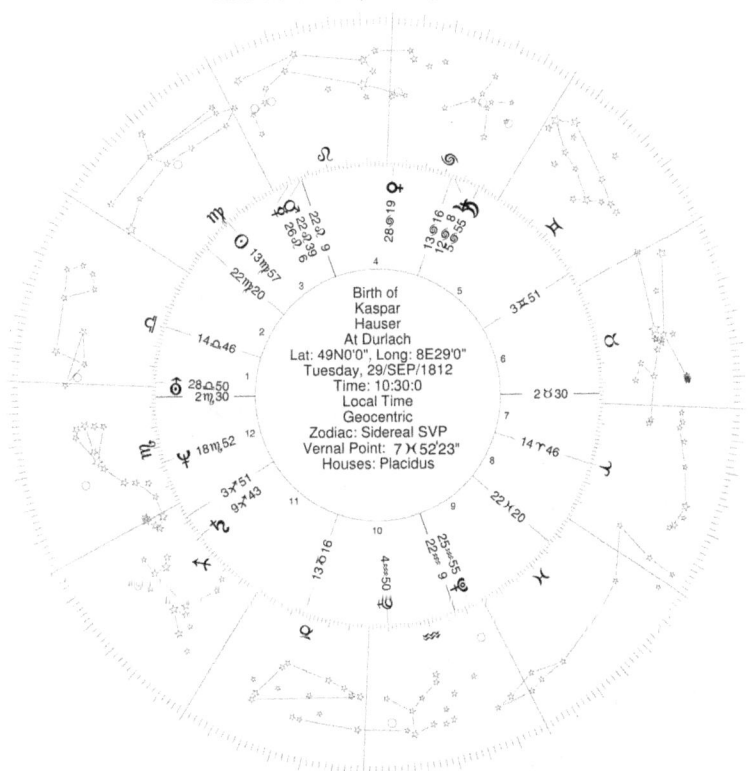

A horoscope generated by the Astrofire program

THE ROSE OF THE WORLD (*ROSA MIRA*)
Daniel Andreev

By warning about the coming Antichrist and pointing him out and unmasking him when he appears, by cultivating unshakable faith within human hearts and a grasp of the meta-historical perspectives and global spiritual prospects within human minds...[we help Sophia bring to birth the new culture of love and wisdom called by Daniel Andreev the "Rose of the World."]...[Sophia's] birth in one of the *zatomis* will be mirrored not only by the Rose of the World; feminine power and its role in contemporary life are increasing everywhere. It is that circumstance, above all, that is giving rise to worldwide peace movements, an abhorrence of bloodshed, disillusion over coercive methods of change, an increase in woman's role in society proper, an ever-growing tenderness and concern for children, and a burning hunger for beauty and love. We are entering an age when the female soul will become ever purer and broader, when an ever-greater number of women will become profound inspirers, sensitive mothers, wise counselors, and far-sighted leaders. It will be an age when the feminine in humanity will manifest with unprecedented strength, striking a perfect balance with masculine impulses. See, you who have eyes.[1]

{These words are those of Daniel Andreev (1906–1959), the great prophet of the coming Age of Sophia and the corresponding Sophianic culture he called the "Rose of the World." In this quote, *zatomis* refers to a heavenly realm within the Earth's etheric aura. Andreev refers to Sophia as *Zventa-Sventana*, "Holiest of the Holy."]

A mysterious event is taking place in the meta-history of contemporary times: new divine-creative energy is emanating into our cosmos. Since ancient times the loftiest hearts and most subtle minds have anticipated this event that is now taking place. The first link in the chain of events—events so important that they can be compared only to the incarnation of the Logos—occurred at the turn of the nineteenth century. This was an emanation of the energy of the Virgin Mother, an emanation that was not amorphous, as it had been before in human history [at Pentecost, when there was an emanation of Sophia into the Virgin Mary], but incomparably intensified by the personal aspect it assumed. A great God-born monad descended from the heights of the universe into our cosmos (ibid., p. 356).

[The words of the great Russian seer, Daniel Andreev, are prophetic. As indicated in *The Most Holy Trinosophia*,[2] he points to the descent of Sophia and the resulting Sophianic world culture, the Rose of the World, in a most inspiring way.]

She is to be born in a body of enlightened ether.... There She is, our hope and joy, Light and Divine Beauty! For Her birth will be mirrored in our history as something that our grandchildren and great-grandchildren will witness: the founding of the Rose of the World, its spread throughout the world, and...the assumption by the Rose of the World of supreme authority over the entire Earth (ibid., p. 357).

[The Sophia Foundation was founded and exists to help usher in the new Age of Sophia and the corresponding Sophianic culture, the Rose of the World, prophesied by Daniel Andreev and other spiritual teachers.

---

1 Daniel Andreev, *The Rose of the World*, p. 358. Words in brackets [ ] here and in the following text are added by Robert Powell.

2 Robert Powell, *The Most Holy Trinosophia: The New Revelation of the Divine Feminine.*

As quoted at the beginning, "warning about the coming Antichrist and pointing him out and unmasking him when he appears" is important. As discussed in the article "In Memory of Willi Sucher" (*Journal for Star Wisdom 2010*).

Humanity's encounter with the Antichrist is part of the initiation trial of humanity as a whole crossing the threshold. The external aspect of this initiation trial is the meeting with the Antichrist as the embodiment of the sum-total of humanity's negative karma, *the double of humankind as a whole*. The inner aspect is the encounter with Christ or the Archangel Michael as the Guardian of the Threshold. The result of successfully passing through this initiation trial is the opening up of conscious awareness of the angelic realm. This is one aspect of the great event at the culmination of the process of humankind as a whole crossing the threshold. Another aspect of this culmination is depicted in the article on World Pentecost.[3]

More than anyone else, Daniel Andreev, as prophet of the coming Sophia culture, the Rose of the World, had a visionary experience of the coming of the Antichrist. His words concerning this are not in the English edition of the *Rose of the World*. Because of the importance of Daniel Andreev's vision of the coming of the Antichrist, his words about this appeared for the first time in English in this journal.

The German translation of Daniel Andreev's book *Rosa Mira: Rose of the World*, in three volumes, comprises a translation of the *whole* original Russian text, whereas the English edition corresponds to volume 1 of the three German volumes.[4]]

THE PREPARATION OF HUMAN BEINGS FOR THE COMING ANTILOGOS

Certainly, humanity has not lacked warnings. Not only the *New Testament* but also the *Qur'an* and even the *Mahabharata* have warned us in the distant past. Have spiritual seers in the East and in the West not proclaimed the Antichrist as an unavoidable evil? All leaders of the Rose of the World will concentrate their forces upon the work of warning about this monster.... This bearer of a dark mission will probably not truly grasp whom he serves and for whom he prepares the way. With all his intellectual genius, his mind will be completely closed to anything of a mystical nature.... He will be greeted enthusiastically: "There he is! The one for whom we have been waiting!" He will show his true force only much later, when the "savior" holds the entire power in his hands....

Is it a matter of a human being? Yes and no. On several occasions [in *Rosa Mira*] I have indicated that this individual was incarnated as a Roman emperor and how, over the centuries and from life to life, he became enveloped in demonic substance. Concerning this monad, whom Gagtungr [Ahriman, or Satan] himself has kidnapped...enough has been said about his previous incarnation [as Stalin] in Russia.... [In that incarnation,] the forces of providence hindered [Satan's attempt] to make of him a dark, universal genius.

[Now, in 1958, he is being prepared] for the successful fulfillment of the historic role of the Antichrist. Stalin's tyrannical genius and his ability to control hypnotically the will of others is well known.... [When he reincarnates as the Antichrist,] he will have at his disposal an enormous capacity for work and a multitude of talents.... He will be uniquely and terribly beautiful. From his facial characteristics, it will be difficult to place him in any particular race or nation. Rather, he will be seen as a representative of the collective of humanity.... [At a certain point in his life, he will undergo a transformation.] His transformation will be noticed by people immediately, yet they will be unable to recognize the meaning or the "how" [of this transformation]. The external appearance of the transformed one will remain virtually unchanged. However, a terrible and frightening energy will proceed from him...Anyone who touches him will receive an electric shock. An invincible hypnotic force [will proceed from him].... The disturbing influence [on spiritually striving human beings] and upon the entire population set in motion by the transformation of the Antilogos will be extraordinary....

---

3 See Robert Powell, *Prophecy–Phenomena–Hope*.
4 The following translation from German into English is by RP.

After a rigged vote, he—the miracle worker—will crown himself.... Humanity will be divided [into those who accept him as world ruler] and those who refuse to acknowledge the usurper.... Of course, force will be used against anyone who refuses to follow the Antichrist. Dark miracles will increasingly occur, shattering the consciousness of people to the very roots of their being. For many, Christ's miracles will pale into insignificance. Crazy enthusiasm will roll in waves across the world.... Eventually, the Antilogos will hold the sole rulership of the planet in his hands. Yet, the true and highest leaders will not subject themselves to this usurper. This will also be the case for millions, perhaps hundreds of millions, of people in every country of the world.

The age of persecution commences. From year to year, they become increasingly extensive, methodical, [and] cruel. Here, the cunning Gagtungr [Ahriman/Satan] even makes use of the heroic protest of the masses. The candidate for the Antichrist who had failed...who had taken his life at the end of World War II,[1] advances now to become the self-appointed leader of the rebels in the struggle against the world ruler.... His thoroughly dark movement will draw the hearts of many into a spiral of raging wickedness and senseless hatred.... Christ's significance will continually be weakened. Then his name will be denied—and finally enveloped in silence....

Shock and terror will take hold of many. Millions of those who had previously distanced themselves from religious matters, who occupied themselves primarily with concerns in their own little world or with artistic pursuits or scientific research, will sense that an irrevocable and very dangerous choice confronts them. In the face of this, even torture and execution pale.... Countless people will turn away from this offspring of hell...from the dark miracles and the charm of the superman, as well as from his immeasurable intelligence and frighteningly cynical wickedness.... The majority of people will fall away from God and allow themselves to be led astray by Gagtungr's protégée....

Stalin wanted not only to be feared; he also wanted to be loved. The Antichrist, however, has need of only one thing: the conviction that everyone [should hold] without exception, [to] believe in his superiority and [to] subject themselves to him without hesitation....

When [during the reign of the Antichrist] the machine civilization begins its total assault on Nature, the entire landscape of the Earth's surface will be transformed into a complete Anti-Nature.... Nature, having become inwardly empty and outwardly crippled, will no longer awaken aesthetic or pantheistic feelings....

Certainly, too, during the complete rule of the tyrant, there will be many whose innermost life will rebel against the senseless existence under the Antichrist. However, psychic control will stifle such thoughts as they arise, and only a few will succeed in acquiring a system of psychic self-defense to protect them from being physically destroyed....

All written or other testimonies that could be dangerous for the Antichrist will be destroyed....

[The suffering of human beings gives nourishment (*gavvach*) to the demons.]... No world wars, revolutions, or repressions, no mass spilling of blood, could have produced *gavvach* in such amounts.... In fact, even humanity in its demonized aspect will not satisfy the Antichrist. He needs humanity as his source of *gavvach*.... [However] even in the most sinful soul, an inextinguishable spark of conscience gleams. However, despair, increasing ignorance, and sheer boredom with life will also take hold of many people, and this will lead to their rejection by the Antichrist. Of what use to him is the intellectual paralysis that sets in after such excesses of despair? Such people are hardly suited to the further development of demonic science and technology or to the conquest of the cosmos or the satanizing of the world....

---

[1] Daniel Andreev depicts the two main candidates for the Antichrist in their twentieth-century incarnations: Adolf Hitler and Joseph Stalin. In those incarnations, they competed with each other to become the most evil. In the following incarnation, the most evil one would become the vessel for the incarnation of the Antichrist. According to Daniel Andreev, Joseph Stalin outdid Adolf Hitler to become the chosen one, the prince of darkness. —R. POWELL

[After the Antichrist's death] the world state will rapidly collapse, and only drastic measures will hinder anarchy in various parts of the world.... "And there appears a great sign in heaven: a woman clothed with the Sun" [Revelation 12:1]. Who is the *woman clothed with the Sun?* It is *Sventa-Sventana* [Sophia], embraced by the planetary Logos and chosen to give birth to the Great Spirit of the Second Aeon. The reflection of this event in world history is the Rose of the World, whose utmost striving before, during, and after the time of the Antichrist prepares humanity to become a vessel for the Great Spirit.... An unimaginable jubilation will take hold of this and other worlds as humanity passes through a great, light-filled transformation.

The prince of darkness will terrify human beings.... Christ, however, will take on as many forms as there are conscious beings on Earth to behold him. He will adapt himself to everyone and will converse with all. His forms will simultaneously yield an image in an unimaginable way: *One who appears in heaven surrounded by unspeakable glory.* There will not be a single being on Earth who will not see the Son of God and hear his Word.[2]

[These words by Daniel Andreev are prophetic. They were written shortly before his death in 1959. Now, more than fifty years later, not only is the encounter with the Son of God possible, but also the possibility of hearing his Word. Today, we can experience this meeting with the Son of God in the realm of life forces, also known as the *etheric realm*. This is the most important event that anyone in earthly existence can experience. This spiritual event is the initiatory aspect of human encounters with the Antichrist and the initiation trial for humanity as a whole crossing the threshold.

An example of this spiritual event is related in an account of a young woman of her initiatory experience in meeting Christ as the Greater Guardian of the threshold. Her name is Estelle Isaacson.[3] This description of her meeting with Christ in the etheric realm—with the etheric Christ, to use Rudolf Steiner's expression—can be a source of inspiration to everyone. She describes how she came to this experience of the etheric Christ through meditating on Christ's experiences during the night prior to the Mystery of Golgotha, the night in the Garden of Gethsemane.]

My focus was again turned to Gethsemane. I entered the light of his deed in the garden and a state of ecstasy—an ineffable, unutterable ecstasy. The light of Christ in Gethsemane enveloped the Earth. Up to that point, I had never merged with such light. My heart soared in ecstasy, lifted into another realm of spirit. I exclaimed, *"This is Life! This is Life eternal, the Life of the world. This is Love! This is eternal Love, which knows no boundaries, for it has penetrated everything in the Earth. It lives within the Earth as an eternal promise of redemption. His love is eternal; His love is free for all who will accept it!"*

Christ then gave me a message for all: *"Love one another and love the Earth. Send your love to your fellow beings and into the Earth that the Earth may be lifted up on wings of peace. There is a body of the Earth, which is a body of love; this is My body that I gave to the Earth. You become one with the body of love by doing works of love, by cultivating feelings of love and by thinking thoughts of love. I invite all to become one with Me in this body of love. I call you home; My arms are around you. Return to love. Remember love. For where love is there am I; and because I desire to have you in My heart, I ask you to love one another, that I may be in you and you in Me. Look for Me to come to you for I am coming and shall gather you to myself and you shall be safely folded in Me because you are precious in My sight; and My sight is ever upon you. Return to Me."*

I then gazed upon him, embracing all of the cosmos. With his arms outstretched across the expanse of Heaven, his voice penetrating the depths of my heart with these words: "I AM eternally here!"

---

2 Daniil Andrejew, *Rosa Mira: Die Weltrose*, vol. 3, pp. 202–226.
3 Estelle Isaacson is the author of *Through the Eyes of Mary Magdalene*. (2 vols.).

EDITORIAL FOREWORD

Robert Powell, Ph.D.

The *Journal for Star Wisdom* (formerly *Christian Star Calendar*) has appeared every year since 1991. From the beginning the central feature has been the calendar comprising the monthly ephemeris pages together with commentaries drawing attention to the Christ events remembered by the ongoing cosmic events. The significance of following the Christ events in relation to daily astronomical events is an important foundation for the new star wisdom of astrosophy.[1] This new star wisdom is arising in our time in response to the second coming of Christ—known as his return in the etheric realm of life forces—as a path of communing with Christ in his life body (ether body). It should also be mentioned that, with the onset of the second coming of Christ during the course of the twentieth century, Christ is now the Lord of Karma, and this is important to take into consideration in the development of a new relationship of humanity to the stars in our time, particularly with respect to the horoscope as an expression of human karma or destiny.

The events of Christ's life lived two thousand years ago are inscribed into his ether body, and to meditate upon these events at times when they are cosmically remembered is a way of drawing near to Christ. The recently updated version of my article "Subnature and the Second Coming" (in *The Inner Life of the Earth*[2]) outlines the background to contemporary events as a confrontation between good and evil in relation to Christ's descent at this time through the sub-earthly realms and also gives an overview of the various cosmic rhythms unfolding in relation to his second coming, including the thirty-three-and-one-third-year rhythm of his ether body.

The *Journal for Star Wisdom* encourages the reader to engage in the practice of stargazing, which is fundamental to the development of the new star wisdom of astrosophy. One of the foundations of astrosophy lies in the science of astronomy, providing the new star wisdom with a secure scientific foundation, which moreover, can be brought into the realm of experience through the practice of stargazing. In astrosophy there is no longer a separation between astronomy and astrology. For example, when in the *Journal for Star Wisdom* it is indicated that currently Mars in the heavens is at 15° Taurus then, assuming that Mars is visible, the red planet can be seen in conjunction with Aldebaran marking the Bull's eye at the center of the constellation of Taurus, whose longitude, as the central star in this constellation, is 15° Taurus. In astrosophy, the astrological fact of Mars at 15° Taurus is identical with the astronomical reality of Mars' location at the

---

[1] There are many different approaches to astrosophy and not all use the equal-division sidereal zodiac that forms the basis of the approach followed in the *Journal for Star Wisdom*. All references to the zodiac and to planetary positions in the zodiac in the *Journal for Star Wisdom* are in terms of the sidereal zodiac as defined in my book *History of the Zodiac*. Moreover, in astrosophy there are different chronologies of the life of Christ, and the chronology that forms the basis of the approach followed in the *Journal for Star Wisdom* is set forth in my book *Chronicle of the Living Christ*. Thus, all references to planetary positions at the Christ events in the *Journal for Star Wisdom* are in terms of the scientifically established chronology of the life of Christ set forth in my book *Chronicle of the Living Christ*.

[2] O'Leary (ed.), *The Inner Life of the Earth*, pp. 69–141.

center of the constellation of Taurus. Astrosophy thus relates to sense-perceptible reality and to the Divine "background of existence" (the spiritual hierarchies)[3] underlying this reality, whereas astrology is generally practiced in such a way that there is a split between astrology and astronomy (in this example, modern astrology, which uses the tropical zodiac rather than the equal-division sidereal zodiac used in astrosophy, would say that Mars is "in Gemini"). The historical background as to how this separation between astronomy and astrology arose is described in my book *History of the Zodiac*.[4]

The present issue of the *Journal for Star Wisdom* is the twenty-third, but is the fifth published under the new title, as the first eighteen issues were published under the title *Christian Star Calendar*. By way of explanation concerning the new title: this publication is intended as an outreach from the StarFire research group (an astrosophy group) that meets yearly in Boulder, Colorado (sometimes in Fair Oaks, California); see the website www.StarWisdom.org.[5] The *Journal for Star Wisdom* is intended as an organ for the development of the new star wisdom of astrosophy. This was also the purpose of the *Christian Star Calendar*. However, there the focus, at least, initially, was primarily on the calendar—the monthly ephemeris and commentaries. In the course of time, more and more research articles on the new star wisdom of astrosophy came to be published in the *Christian Star Calendar*. A point was reached where it became clear that the publication is more of a journal than a calendar, although the calendar continues to play an important role. It is therefore a natural transition from the *Christian Star Calendar* to the *Journal for Star Wisdom*.

As referred to in my article in this issue of the *Journal for Star Wisdom*, perhaps the greatest prophecy of our time—one that is little known, but that is the reason for the existence of this journal, and is a source of tremendous spiritual light—is Rudolf Steiner's prophecy from the year 1910, just over one hundred years ago. On January 12, 1910, he prophesied that the second coming of Christ would begin in 1933, an event called "Christ's appearance in the etheric realm"—not a return in a physical body but in an etheric (life) body, the realm of life forces. Here with my translation of Marie Steiner's notes from this important, hitherto unpublished lecture:

3000 BC: Kali Yuga commenced and lasted until 1899—a time of great transition.

1933: human beings will appear with clairvoyant faculties, which they will develop naturally. At this time, which we are approaching, the newly beginning clairvoyant faculties have to be satisfied, to experience what they [human beings] should do with them.

I am with you always, even unto the end of the world.

Christ will appear in an etheric form. The physical Christ became the Spirit of the Earth—this was the midpoint, the balance, of Earth evolution.

5th Letter of the Ap(ocalypse): I will come again; however, take heed that you do not fail to recognize me.

2,500 years is the time that humanity has to develop again the gifts of clairvoyance. Around 1933 the Gospels must be recognized in their spiritual meaning such that they have worked preparing for Christ. Otherwise untold confusion of the soul will be caused.

---

3 According to Rudolf Steiner, the constellations are the abode of the first hierarchy, called Seraphim, Cherubim, and Thrones. The movement of the planets takes place against the background of the zodiacal constellations, which—considered as the abode of the first hierarchy—form the Divine "background of existence" in the heavens. "Suppose you wanted to point to some particular [group of] Thrones, Cherubim and Seraphim, one denotes them by a particular constellation. It is like a signpost. In that direction over there are the [group of] Thrones, Cherubim and Seraphim known as the Twins, over there [the group of Thrones, Cherubim and Seraphim known as] the Lion, etc." (Steiner, *The Spiritual Hierarchies*, p. 99; words in brackets added by RP).

4 Robert Powell, *History of the Zodiac*.

5 Other astrosophy websites are www.sophiafoundation.org and www.astrogeographia.org.

Around 1933 there will be some representatives of black magical schools, who will falsely proclaim a physical Christ.

Each time that he becomes perceptible, Christ is perceptible for other faculties.[1]

This was Rudolf Steiner's greatest prophecy: the second coming of Christ, which he called the appearance of Christ in the etheric realm, beginning in 1933. It is this event, the presence of the etheric Christ, lasting from 1933 for 2,500 years (until 4433), that is pivotal for the approach to astrosophy (star wisdom) outlined in the *Journal for Star Wisdom*.

In conclusion I would like to express gratitude to our publisher, Gene Gollogly of SteinerBooks, and to the able assistance of Jens Jensen of SteinerBooks, for making this fourth issue of the *Journal for Star Wisdom* available, and to all those who have contributed to make this issue possible, in particular to our authors for presenting their research articles as contributions to the foundations of the new star wisdom of astrosophy, and to all our readers who ultimately are the reason for the existence of the *Journal for Star Wisdom*.

---

[1] Translated from the first page of Marie Steiner's notes, recently published in German for the first time in *Der Europäer*, vol. 14, December/January 2009/2010, p. 3.

To starry realms,
To the dwelling places of Gods,
Turns the Spirit gaze of my soul.

From starry realms,
From the dwelling places of Gods,
Streams Spirit power into my soul.

For starry realms,
For the dwelling places of Gods,
Lives my Spirit heart through my soul.
—RUDOLF STEINER

WORKING WITH THE
JOURNAL FOR STAR WISDOM

The listing of major planetary events each month is intended as a stimulus toward attunement with the Universal Christ, the Logos, whose being encompasses the entire galaxy. The deeds of the historical Christ wrought two thousand years ago are of eternal significance—inscribed into the cosmos—and they resonate with the movements of the heavenly bodies, especially when certain alignments or planetary configurations occur bearing a resemblance with those prevailing at the time of events in the life of Jesus Christ. With the rare astronomical event of the transit of Venus across the face of the Sun that took place June 8, 2004, at exactly the zodiacal degree (23° Taurus), where the Sun stood at Christ's Ascension, a new impulse was given from divine-spiritual realms for the further unfolding of star wisdom, *Astro-Sophia*.

The calendar may be found beginning on page 120. It comprises ephemeris pages for the twelve months of the year with accompanying monthly commentaries on the astronomical events listed on the ephemeris pages. Indications regarding the similarity of contemporary planetary configurations with those at events in the life of Christ are given in the lower part of the monthly commentaries, and the upper part gives a commentary on the notable astronomical occurrences each month. Unless otherwise stated, all astronomical indications regarding visibility mean "visible to the naked eye." See the note concerning time on the page preceding the monthly commentaries.

With this calendar, astronomy and astrology, which were a unity in the ancient star wisdom of the Egyptians and Babylonians, are reunited and provide a foundation for astrosophy, the all-encompassing star wisdom, *Astro-Sophia*, an expression of Sophia and referred to in the Revelation of John as the "Bride of the Lamb."

2014 AND THE COMING OF THE KALKI AVATAR

Robert Powell

As described below, a new 600-year cultural rhythm is due to begin in the year 2014, and this coincides with the prophesied date of the coming of a great leader of humanity, the Kalki Avatar.[1] Kalki is awaited in Hinduism as the coming Avatar—after Rama, Krishna, and Buddha or Balarama (the brother of Krishna), who are regarded as the seventh, eighth, and ninth Avatars. In the Hindu tradition Kalki (also Kalkin or Kalaki) is the name of the tenth and final Avatar of Vishnu, the Maintainer, the second Person of the Hindu *Trimurti*, corresponding to the Son in the Holy Trinity. The prophecy quoted below indicates that Kalki will come at the end of *Kali Yuga*. The name Kalki denotes the *Annihilator of Ignorance*. He is said to be the ruler of the realm of Shambhala, the lost paradise at the heart of Mother Earth.[2] As Kalki, Vishnu will descend to annihilate ignorance and restore the golden age of virtue, *Satya Yuga*. It is imagined that he will come on a white horse, wielding a flaming sword with which to destroy wickedness and restore righteousness to the earth. His is a two-edged sword—for the good, and against evil. He is the same as the Maitreya Buddha (*Maitreya*, "bearer of goodness"), the successor of Gautama Buddha, who is awaited in the Buddhist tradition.[3]

The source for this prophecy is the *S'rîmad Bhâgavatam* (also known as the *Bhâgavata Purâna*), which is one of the most important sacred books of India. It is arranged in twelve so-called cantos, and comprises 335 chapters with a total of about 18,000 verses. It stresses the prime importance of the *maintaining* aspect of God personified by the transcendental form of *Vishnu*. According to tradition, the writer of this work was Vyâsadeva (Vyâsa), also known as Bâdarâyana. He is said to have compiled the Vedas and also the great epic poem entitled the *Mahâbhârata*, of which the *Bhagavad Gîtâ* is the most important part. Vyâsa also wrote the Purânas as well as the *Brahma-sûtra*.

Given that one possible date forecast for the emergence of the Kalki Avatar as the bearer of a new and mighty impulse for the evolution of the earth and humanity is July 27, 2014—see below—this coincides, within twenty months, with the date of the end of the Maya calendar on December 21, 2012. On this account, bearing in mind the elucidation in chapter 6 of *Christ and the Maya Calendar* concerning the dating of *Kali Yuga* in relation to the Maya Calendar,[4] where the beginning of the transition—from a "modified Hindu perspective"—of the *Kali Yuga* ("Dark Age") to the New Age of *Satya Yuga* ("Age of Light") is equated with December 21, 2012, it seems fitting

---

1 Powell, "Subnature & the Second Coming," in O'Leary (ed.), *The Inner Life of the Earth*, pp. 116–118. The emergence of the true Kalki Avatar in 2014 is being preempted from various quarters—one example being Sri Kalki Bhagavan, the self-styled "Living Avatar".
2 Concerning Shambhala, see Powell, *Cultivating Inner Radiance and the Body of Immortality*, pp. 26–27, 146–148, 167.
3 Anonymous, *Meditations on the Tarot*, p. 614: "Since it is a question of the work of the fusion of revelation and knowledge, of spirituality and intellectuality, it is a matter throughout of the fusion of the Avatar principle with the Buddha principle. In other words, the Kalki Avatar awaited by the Hindus and the Maitreya Buddha awaited by the Buddhists will manifest in a single personality. On the historical plane the Maitreya Buddha and the Kalki Avatar will be one."
4 Powell & Dann, *Christ and the Maya Calendar*, chap. 6.

to look at the prophecy concerning the coming of the Kalki Avatar. For the Kalki Avatar, like Christ, is a bearer of the Mystery of Love.

> When the Supreme Lord has appeared on earth as Kalki, the maintainer of religion, *Satya Yuga* will begin, and human society will bring forth progeny in the mode of goodness…When the Moon, the Sun, and Brhaspati (Jupiter) are together in the constellation Karkata (Cancer), and all three enter simultaneously into the lunar mansion Pushya—at that exact moment the age of *Satya*, or *Krita*, will begin. (*S'rîmad Bhâgavatam* 12.2.22, 24)

Thus, when the Sun, Moon, and Jupiter are in conjunction in the Hindu lunar *nakshatra* Pushya (4°–17° Cancer in the sidereal zodiac), the emergence of the Kalki Avatar, the "bearer of goodness," is expected. It is in this lunar mansion that the beautiful star cluster known as the Beehive (Greek: *Praesepe*), Jupiter's place of exaltation, is to be found.[5] Evidently the Hindu sages attributed something special to Jupiter's location in this part of the zodiac: a special impulse of the Good comes to expression here.

One historical possibility of this conjunction, the prophesied conjunction of the Sun, Moon, and Jupiter in Pushya, will take place on July 27, 2014—shortly after what could possibly be designated as the start of the historical 3½ years of the earthly rule of the Antichrist—also known as the time of the "incarnation of Ahriman" (see below: **The 3½ Years**). If it is indeed true that this rule, denoted by the incarnation of Ahriman into his human vessel (Mr. X), began around the summer solstice 2013, it follows that the 3½ years of Antichrist's reign as world ruler is expected to end shortly after the winter solstice of 2016, in which case the emergence of the Kalki Avatar during this 3½-year period takes on an extraordinary significance. Against this background, the conjunction on July 27, 2014 may signify the emergence of the Kalki Avatar to inaugurate a new spiritual era when something of the impulse of goodness, connected with the work of the Kalki Avatar, might be expected to begin to stream in as a counterbalance to the evil of the Antichrist. For the Kalki Avatar is the teacher of morality (goodness) and is the chosen vessel for the second Person of the Godhead (Vishnu in the Hindu tradition; Christ in the Christian tradition) to spearhead the overcoming of the evil of the Antichrist. The Kalki Avatar's possible emergence in 2014 could manifest in a new spiritual impulse along the lines of strengthening moral consciousness, empowering deeds of sacred magic, as indicated in the quote later in this article from *S'rîmad Bhâgavatam* 12; 2; 16-23. The Kalki Avatar, also known as the "maintainer of religion," works in particular with sacred magic for the renewal of true religion.

Against a background of astrosophical research, as mentioned, the potential advent of the Maitreya Buddha/Kalki Avatar individuality[6] in 2014 coincides with an indication by Rudolf Steiner in connection with the 600-year rhythm of culture. This rhythm (as discussed in *Hermetic Astrology*, volume I) is actually the half-rhythm of the 1,199-year Venus rhythm, the time it takes for the "Venus pentagram" to rotate once (moving retrograde) through all twelve signs of the sidereal zodiac.[7] This period of almost exactly 1,200 years is the length of time that elapses between the start of a new zodiacal age and the beginning of the new cultural epoch corresponding to that age. For example, the *Age of Pisces*, which began when the vernal point on account of the *precession of the equinoxes* shifted retrograde from Aries into Pisces, started in the year 215,

---

5   The exact location of Praesepe, which denotes the place of exaltation of Jupiter in the zodiac, is 12°39' Cancer—see Powell & Bowden, *Astrogeographia*, pp. 35–41.

6   As indicated in footnote 3, "On the historical plane the Maitreya Buddha and the Kalki Avatar will be one." As I have described in *Hermetic Astrology I*, following Steiner, the Bodhisattva known as the Maitreya individuality, generally incarnates once in every century and will continue to do so for about 2,500 years, until around the year AD 4443, when he will incarnate as the Maitreya Buddha. This is the approximate date, then, which is referred to in the statement, "On the historical plane the Maitreya Buddha and the Kalki Avatar will be one." Thus, in speaking of the Maitreya Buddha/Kalki Avatar individuality, it is a matter of the Bodhisattva who will become the Maitreya Buddha/Kalki Avatar around the year 4443.

7   Powell, *Hermetic Astrology I*, pp. 58–66; this edition, available from Amazon.com, is a reprint of the 1987 edition; see chap. 3.

reckoned to be the birth year of the Prophet Mani, the founder of Manichaeism. In 1414 (1,199 years later), the corresponding *Piscean cultural epoch* commenced, birthing the Renaissance in Europe. It is striking that the great individuality of Joan of Arc, who was born in 1412 immediately preceding this date of 1414, emerged near the beginning of the new cultural epoch as a leading figure in the shaping of the unfolding new epoch, the fifth since the destruction of Atlantis. Looking at the half-period, going back 600 years from 1414, we arrive at 814, the year of Charlemagne's death[1] and the beginning of a new era in Europe, when the monastic schools started to flourish. Going forward 600 years from 1414, we reach 2014—the present time. Concerning this date of 2014, Rudolf Steiner indicated prophetically in 1911, "We are living today at the beginning of a period of transition before the onset of the next 600-year *wave of culture*, when something *entirely new* is pressing in upon us, when the Christ impulse is to be enriched by something new."[2]

Here it is clear that 600 years is the half period of the 1,199-year rhythm of the Venus pentagram. Steiner describes the 600-year period as a *cultural wave*. Evidently, two *cultural waves*, each 600 years long, elapse between the beginning of a zodiacal age and the start of the corresponding cultural epoch.

Applied to the Piscean Age, the first cultural wave of 600 years was from 215 to 814, the year of the death of Charlemagne (Carolingian Renaissance), and the second cultural wave of 600 years lasted from 814 to 1414 (flourishing of the monastic schools in Europe). Adding another 600 years, we arrive at 2014 as the start of a new cultural wave.

Given that 2014 begins a new 600-year cultural wave, it is possible that a spiritual leader such as the Kalki Avatar could emerge at this time as a bearer of the impulse for the new wave of culture as a seed impulse for the next 600 years. It is a matter of a new culture being seeded during this challenging time of the reign of the Antichrist and his False Prophet. However, that reign will come to an end, as Steiner indicates in his discussion of "the fall of the Beast and of the False Prophet."[3] As mentioned above, one possibility is that "the fall of the Beast," i.e., the end of the reign of the Antichrist, will be shortly after the winter solstice of 2016.

This is further elucidated in connection with the thesis developed in chapter 6 of *Christ and the Maya Calendar*.[4] Although, according to Steiner, the *Kali Yuga* ended and the *Satya Yuga* ("New Age of Light") began in 1899, evidently there was a 113-year transition period until the end of the Maya calendar in 2012, so that the full flowering of the New Age, *Satya Yuga*, only truly began around the time of the winter solstice of the year 2012. The coming of the Kalki Avatar in 2014 could thus be seen as fulfilling the inauguration of this New Age. In this light, let us consider the following words by way of attunement to the prophecy of the activity of the Kalki Avatar in our time as the transmitter of the power of goodness that our modern world is in need of now, more than ever before:

> By the time the age of *Kali* ends...religious principles will be ruined...so-called religion will be mostly atheistic...the occupations of men will be stealing, lying and needless violence, and all the social classes will be reduced to the lowest level.... Family ties will extend no further than the immediate bonds of marriage...homes will be devoid of piety, and all human beings will have become like asses. At that time, the Supreme personality of the Godhead will appear on the earth. Acting with the power of pure spiritual goodness, he will rescue eternal religion.... Lord Kalki will appear in...the great soul of *Vishnuyasha*....[5] When

---

1 The year 814 was also the start of the period of the Archangel Raphael (814–1169) connected with the 355-year rhythm of the planet Mercury and this was the time of the founding of the Mysteries of the Holy Grail associated with the figure of Parzival, whom Rudolf Steiner brings into connection with the time of Charlemagne.

2 Steiner, *Background to the Gospel of St. Mark*, p. 153 (italics by RP).

3 Steiner, *The Book of Revelation and the Work of the Priest*, pp. 154–156.

4 Powell & Dann, *Christ and the Maya Calendar*.

5 *Vishnuyasha* is the Hindu name in the *S'rîmad Bhâgavatam* for the human being who will be the bearer of the Kalki Avatar, and for the Kalki Avatar to emerge in 2014, it follows that

2014 and the Coming of the Kalki Avatar

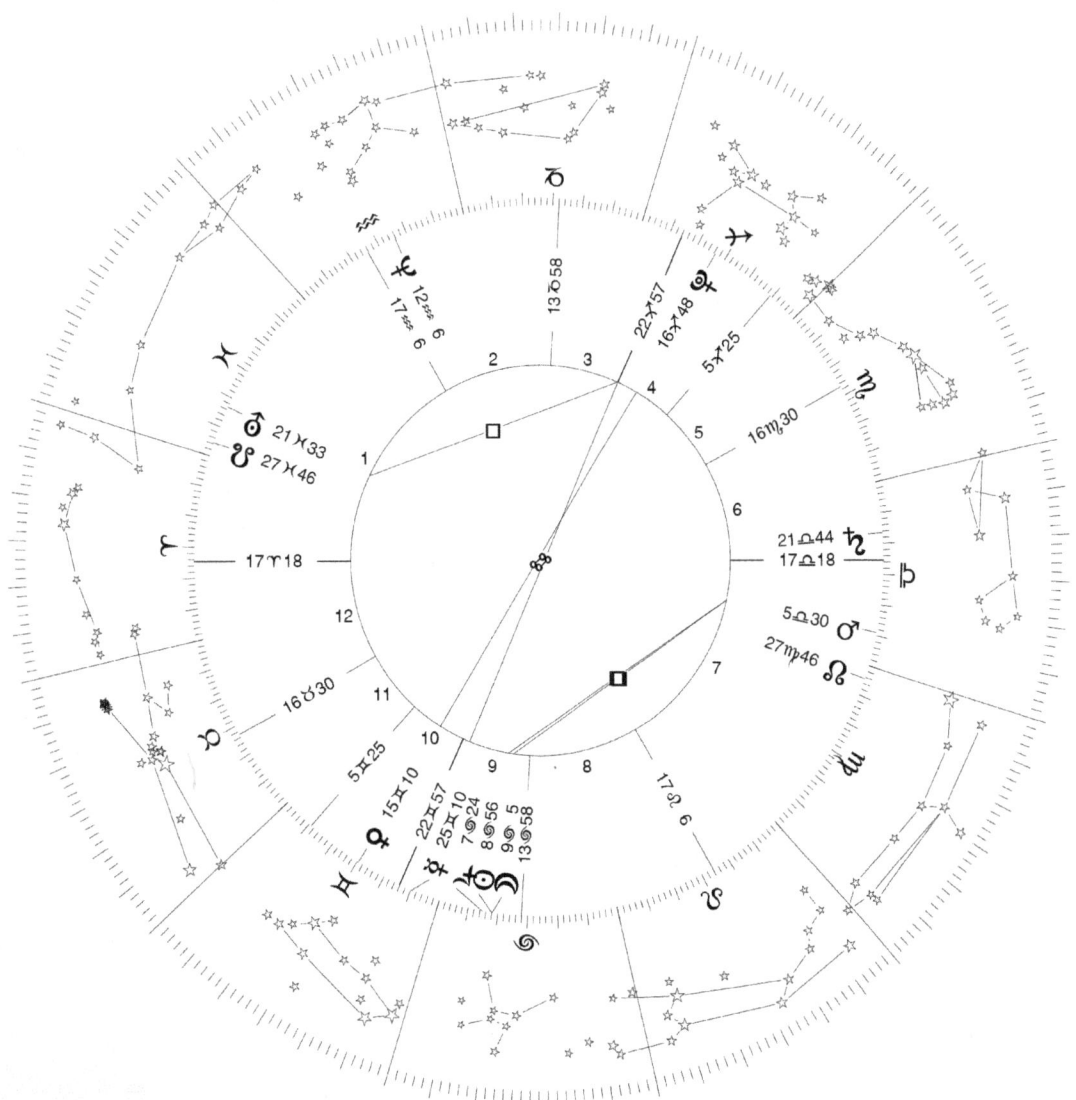

Birth of Kalki Avatar - Geocentric
At London, United Kingdom, Latitude 51N30', Longitude 0W10'
Date: Sunday, 27/JUL/2014, Gregorian
Time: 0: 0, Time Zone GMD
Sidereal Time 19:17:34, Vernal Point 5♓ 3'24", House System: Placidus
Zodiac: Sidereal SVP, Aspect set: Conjunction/Square/Opposition

the Supreme Lord has appeared on earth as Kalki, the maintainer of religion, *Satya Yuga* will begin, and human society will bring forth progeny in the mode of goodness. (*S'rîmad Bhâgavatam* 12; 2; 16–23)

Let us return now to consider the identity of the Kalki Avatar/Maitreya Buddha individuality. When he was asked if he was the Maitreya Bodhisattva individuality,[6] whom he had spoken of as having been incarnated on the Earth about 100 years before Christ as Jeshu ben Pandira, the teacher of the Essenes, Rudolf Steiner replied that he was not—and that he had no connection with Jeshu ben Pandira, meaning that he (Rudolf Steiner) had not been incarnated as Jeshu ben Pandira.[7] Moreover, Steiner deflected attention

---

Vishnuyasha must already be in incarnation.

6 According to Steiner, the Maitreya Bodhisattva individuality, as the successor to Gautama Buddha, incarnates in almost every century to prepare for his final, culminating incarnation as the Maitreya Buddha in about 2,500 years; see footnote 6.

7 In footnote 155, p. 169, of Meyer and Vreede, *The*

from himself as a Bodhisattva by pointing to the Bodhisattva who would come after him, whom he said would be the *actual herald of Christ in his etheric form*.[1] Steiner indicated that this Bodhisattva incarnated at the "beginning of the century"—signifying the beginning of the twentieth century—and he also indicated that this Bodhisattva would emerge ("become noticeable") in the 1930s.[2] It is also reportedly said that this Bodhisattva would be connected with the Anthroposophical Society and that one would be able to recognize him by the fact that he would speak of the return of Christ in the etheric.

These indications offer a few pointers concerning the identity of this Bodhisattva.[3]

Further, Rudolf Steiner wrote toward the end of his life about his "possible successor," whom he never named, however, because he died before the time had come when he would have been able to do so.[4] It is important to understand that when he used the expression *successor*, this was by no means an arbitrary term. He was using it in a very specific way, as it is used in the Bodhisattva circle—for example, when Gautama Buddha pointed to Kashyapa as his successor, thus indicating that he would be the next Buddha, the Maitreya Buddha. The term *successor* has a very specific meaning in the Bodhisattva circle. When Rudolf Steiner used that expression, he was speaking as a Bodhisattva—one of the circle of the great teachers of humanity—who was going to name his "possible successor." But that was not possible because of Rudolf Steiner's premature death. Nevertheless, this important indication implies that this Bodhisattva—the successor of Rudolf Steiner—is the one who on the one hand was destined to proclaim from 1933 onward the event of Christ's coming in an etheric form and on the other hand who in about 2,500 years time will become the next Buddha, the Maitreya Buddha, referred to as the *Bearer of the Good*.

It was Rudolf Steiner's mission as a Bodhisattva[5] to bring *Spiritual Science*, i.e., to bring the great spiritual truths of existence to expression for our present-day culture. For a deeper level of understanding, *truth* is the mission of science

---

Bodhisattva Question, Meyer notes that Walter Vegelahn (1880–1959) was one of the stenographers who recorded more than 500 lectures of Rudolf Steiner from 1903 on. Among these was the Berne cycle, *The Gospel of St. Matthew*. Shortly before his death in 1959, he stated, in October 1958, to a visitor in Berlin: "It was in Berne that Rudolf Steiner spoke about the Bodhisattva. The members were curious to know whom Dr. Steiner had in mind with this statement. They put their heads together and chose the most suitable among them, Günther Wagner, to approach Dr. Steiner about it. Steiner's answer was: 'I am not the one.' At the following meeting, Dr. Steiner gave a report of all that had happened during the previous months and mentioned also the Berne lectures. While doing so he interrupted what he was saying by an aside: 'I wish to add in parenthesis to all those, who are ever ready to invent incarnations from their fantasy, that in my own individuality I have no connection with Jeshu ben Pandira.'" The communication of this important fact (from a member of the Rudolf Steiner *Nachlassverwaltung* [literary estate administration]), was given to the author [Meyer] by the person who received it, to whom he is very grateful (words in brackets by RP).

1   Steiner emphasized that Jeshu ben Pandira reincarnated in the 20th century as a great Bodhisattva individuality to fulfill the lofty mission of proclaiming Christ's coming in the etheric realm, beginning around 1933. In Steiner's own words on the reincarnation of the Bodhisattva Jeshu ben Pandira in the 20th century: "*He will be the actual herald of Christ in his etheric form*" (from a lecture on Jeshu ben Pandira, Leipzig, Nov. 4, 1911).

2   Powell, "Rudolf Steiner, Valentin Tomberg, and the Return of Christ in the Etheric"; www.sophiafoundation.org > articles. My research indicates that the emergence of this Bodhisattva individuality began around 1933.

3   Powell, "Valentin Tomberg Symposium 2009 Report: Valentin Tomberg and the Bodhisattva of the 20th Century"—www.sophiafoundation.org>articles.

4   Steiner used this expression when he formulated Statute 7 of the Anthroposophical Society: "The establishment of the School of Spiritual Science is, to begin with, in the hands of Steiner, who will appoint his collaborators and his possible successor" (from a 1925 pamphlet of the Anthroposophical Society in Great Britain).

5   That Rudolf Steiner was an incarnation of a great Bodhisattva individuality, one of the twelve great teachers of humanity, is *absolutely certain*, as I will show—based on statements made by Steiner himself—in a forthcoming publication. Within the Bodhisattva circle Steiner occupies a very special position at the "right-hand" of Christ.

as a whole. However, as Rudolf Steiner pointed out, science has unfortunately become taken hold of—not universally, but by and large, at least to a certain extent—by dark forces, thus becoming a vehicle for the permeation of our culture and civilization with untruths about the human being and the world. One example of such an untruth or inverted idea—one that is widespread and widely believed—is the Darwinian thesis that human beings are descended from the apes, when in reality human beings are a class of beings unto themselves, and therefore the "missing link" will never be found, because there is no "missing link" between apes and human beings.[6] Many other examples of this kind of untruth put forward with conviction by modern science could be given.

Rudolf Steiner's mission was to work in the scientific field—expanding upon it—to bring for humankind the truths about the human being's true spiritual nature and spiritual origin, including how to apply these truths in practical life. He then pointed to his successor as the *bearer of goodness*, the teacher of morality, the teacher of righteousness, who had been incarnated as Jeshu ben Pandira, the teacher of the Essenes, about 100 years before Christ. Rudolf Steiner identified Jeshu ben Pandira as an earlier incarnation of this Bodhisattva who was known to the Essenes as the *teacher of righteousness*—the teacher of the good.[7] Further, from Rudolf Steiner's indications we can go back some four centuries prior to the incarnation as Jeshu ben Pandira (about 100 BC) to the incarnation of this same individuality as Kashyapa at the time of Gautama Buddha (sixth to fifth centuries BC).[8] And we can go back further still to the incarnation of this individuality as Abraham (second millennium BC), who was the founder of the chosen people, the people of Israel, the people who were to prepare for the coming of Christ in a physical body.[9] Abraham–Kashyapa–Jeshu ben Pandira, who will be the future Maitreya Buddha, the Bearer of the Good, is destined to be the transmitter of the impulse of Christ in his second coming and on into the far-distant future. Christ *is* the Good, and the Bearer of the Good is, in a certain respect, a Christ Bearer.

Given the background of the incarnation as Abraham, the founder of Ancient Israel, as another indication for the identity of this successor to Rudolf Steiner, it is evident that it is a matter of someone who undoubtedly bears inwardly a panoramic overview over the Old Testament comprising the history of Ancient Israel. Moreover, as the bearer of the principle and impulse of goodness, this Bodhisattva is clearly intimately connected with Christ, having a profound relationship with everything that is expressed in the New Testament and in the Book of Revelation. When we contemplate the deep connection of this reincarnated Abraham–Kashyapa–Jeshu ben Pandira individuality with the mysteries of the Bible, we see a relationship between Rudolf Steiner and his successor as expressed in the relationship between truth and goodness.

With the Maitreya individuality, the primary focus is on the Good. We can think of this as expressing something of the difference in orientation between Gautama Buddha and the Maitreya Buddha. Gautama Buddha brought the impulse of focusing on helping individuals to become better

---

6   For a deeper discussion, see Powell, *Cultivating Inner Radiance and the Body of Immortality*, chap. 5.

7   Steiner held two lectures about Jeshu ben Pandira in Leipzig on Nov. 4–5, 1911; for a summary, see page 1 of the article, Powell, "Valentin Tomberg Symposium 2009 Report: Valentin Tomberg and the Bodhisattva of the 20th Century," www.sophiafoundation.org>articles.

8   See my article "Kashyapa and the Proclamation of Christ in the Etheric," *Starlight* vol. 11, no. 1 (Easter 2011) available as a free download from the Sophia Foundation website; www.sophiafoundation.org.

9   In his lecture in Karlsruhe, Jan. 25, 1910, Steiner implicitly identifies Abraham as the individuality whose mission it will be to prepare humanity for the vision of Christ in his etheric body, when he says, in the context of Christ's second coming: "And it will be known that just as Abraham preceded Christ as a preparer, he also takes over the mission, after Christ's coming, of being a helper in his work" (*The True Nature of the Second Coming*). This is just one of many statements by Steiner about Abraham as the individuality who will be the *actual proclaimer* of Christ's coming in the etheric realm—in other words, the Jeshu ben Pandira inviduality.

human beings through the eightfold path, through developing virtue. Here a difference with the Maitreya Buddha is revealed, especially when we consider the image associated with him—or, rather, with the Kalki Avatar—riding on a white horse, with a two-edged sword issuing from his mouth. What are the two edges of his sword? One is for the good, and the other is for the fight against evil. This belongs to the impulse of the Maitreya Buddha/Kalki Avatar individuality, whose mission takes account of the fact that in the post-Christian era there is a fight, a great battle between good and evil—this being the theme of the Apocalypse.

Since we are free beings, we do not *have* to take part in this battle unless called to do so. It is very important to know that taking up the battle with evil is a *calling* and, in fact, it would be foolhardy for someone to try to undertake anything in the battle with evil unless that person felt a definite calling to do so. In this connection there are some inspiring words of Valentin Tomberg (1900-1973) from his *Studies on the Apocalypse*, where he draws our attention to what this battle is about. He talks about the forces that are working against the true Christ impulse in the world, indicating that even in nominally Christian countries to a certain extent Christianity has been done away with in business, politics, and the realm of science. It is a matter of "the banishment of Christianity from all areas of life." In referring to Christianity, he is speaking here of *true Christianity arising from the Christ impulse.*

> The banishment of Christianity from all areas of life goes on and on, and the realities of the physical world arrange themselves in stronger and stronger opposition to Christianity and in opposition to the love-filled light of wisdom that is just as essential to the human soul as are sunlight and warmth to a plant.[1]

Here he is saying that Christ and Sophia, love and wisdom, are as essential to the human soul as sunlight and warmth to the plant, and that we see in the world more and more how this possibility is excluded.

From this view of Christianity, the human world is empty and cold. Indeed the realities of the physical world of humanity are gradually developing in a way that Christianity has been reduced. What Christian truth can manifest in present-day life—that is, without having to protect itself everywhere through compromise? Only in the *word* can the Christ impulse become a reality among the people of today. This is important because it is the essential impulse of the Maitreya, who, as the Bearer of the Good, is destined to bring to manifestation the power of the word as a force for the Good.

True Christianity today has the same opportunity as does the word to live in the world without becoming adulterated and falsified by compromise; it is a time of great testing. The vast and powerful realities of today's "Chastel Merveille" [the expression for the anti-Grail castle, the castle of Klingsor, which is active in the world at this time] are opposed only by the word and nothing else at all. The millions of Christians cannot and must not be arrayed to do battle with the organized antichristian millions. Antichristian forces cannot and must not be fought with the use of their own weapons. Power, number, and organization—all are opposed only by the word borne by the human voice. The test is this: Despite everything, we must never say, "These are mere words; they are not the realities." Rather, because they can be only words, the *whole* reality of the Christ impulse must be experienced *in* them.[2]

In his *Studies of the Apocalypse* just quoted from, Valentin Tomberg has much more to say about this (referred to in the Book of Revelation), where he points out that there is a "little strength" against the "colossal power" which is arrayed against the Good. This "little strength" is referred to in these words of Christ:

> I know your deeds. See, I have placed before you an open door that no one can shut. I know that you have little strength, yet you have kept my word and have not denied my name. (Rev. 3:8)

---

1 Tomberg, *Christ and Sophia*, p. 343.

2 Ibid.

Here it is clearly indicated that we have to side with the *little strength* against the great strength of untruth and evil in the world, i.e., we have to align ourselves with the power of the word. And, moreover, we must refrain from denying the name of Christ. This means on the one hand that we are called upon to uphold the true ideals of the Christ impulse in spite of the great power of external realities that are currently arrayed against them. And on the other hand the appeal made here is not to deny the name of Christ, since this would essentially be tantamount to excluding the power of the Good itself—as Christ *is* the Good.

The faculty of the *word* and that of *moral logic* (keeping the word and not denying the name) will be most highly developed at the beginning of the sixth epoch, that of Philadelphia [Revelation 3:7], when the Maitreya Buddha, the "Bringer of Goodness," will appear. The special task of the Maitreya is to develop what has "little strength"—the *word* and the *thought*—into a power that will regain a position in the world that allows a cultural community to evolve. The moral force of the word will live and work so powerfully in the Maitreya that human beings will be stopped and will experience a spiritual conversion...through the magical, moral influence of the word. Thoughts will no longer merely explain the nature of goodness, but actually transmit it. The Maitreya Buddha will not merely show goodness; he will awaken it in the soul.[3]

Through an astronomical understanding of the prophecy made in the *S'rîmad Bhâgavatam* referred to above, it would appear that the year 2014 could signify the time of emergence of the Kalki Avatar/Maitreya Buddha individuality in a new incarnation, his twenty-first-century incarnation. Bearing in mind Steiner's indication that this individuality incarnates in almost every century, this sequence of incarnations leads to the culminating incarnation in about 2,500 years, when he will attain Buddhahood and no longer incarnate on the Earth but continue to work from spiritual realms for the good of humanity and the Earth's evolution.

In the words of Rudolf Steiner quoted earlier, "We are living today at the beginning of a period of transition before the onset of the next 600 year wave of culture, when something *entirely new* is pressing in upon us, when the Christ impulse is to be enriched by something new."[4] What is meant here by *something entirely new*? In the same lecture Rudolf Steiner elucidates that it is the stream of Buddhism in a new form, enlivened by the Christ impulse, that is the "something new." And given that Kashyapa, the future Maitreya Buddha, is the successor of Gautama Buddha, it is abundantly clear that it is the Abraham-Kashyapa-Jeshu ben Pandira-Maitreya Buddha/Kalki Avatar individuality—the "bringer of the Good"—who is the one to spearhead the stream of Buddhism in a new form, enlivened by the Christ impulse. Thus we see how the prophecy of Rudolf Steiner relating to the year 2014 emerges in a remarkable way in light of the ancient prophecy made in the *S'rîmad Bhâgavatam*.

For purposes of astrosophical study I am including the horoscope of the possible date of emergence of the Kalki Avatar on July 27, 2014, where it can be seen that the New Moon (conjunction of Sun and Moon at 9° Cancer) is in conjunction with Jupiter (7½° Cancer)—all in the nakshatra Pushya, which extends from 4° Cancer to 17° Cancer (see horoscope and see also the entry for July 27 in the commentaries in this issue of the journal). It is also interesting, according to this horoscope, that at this time the position of Pluto in Sagittarius is transiting the position of the Sun in Sagittarius at the birth of Jesus of Nazareth, whose birth is described in the Gospel of Luke, and also that Pluto is close to where it was located at the historical events of Christ's Ascension and Pentecost. Moreover, in this horoscope Saturn is located at its place of exaltation in the zodiac, in conjunction with the brightest star, the alpha star, in Libra. The conjunction of Saturn with this star[5]—referred to

---

3 Ibid, p. 345.

4 Steiner, *Background to the Gospel of St. Mark*, 1968, p. 153.

5 Powell & Bowden, *Astrogeographia*, p. 37, gives the exact location of the alpha star of Libra, Zubenelgenubi, as 20°17' Libra; see the table of exaltations of the planets on page 37 of that book.

as Saturn's *exaltation*—was seen as the most powerful location of Saturn in the entire zodiac:

> In the case of the exaltation of Saturn at 21° Libra, the Babylonians saw that Saturn was exalted when it appeared in conjunction with the star Zubenelgenubi, the brightest star in Libra, marking the south-western end of the beam of the Balance. The exact degree of this star is 20½° Libra, so the exaltation should be corrected from 21° to 20½° Libra. In this case the original specification of the exaltation of Saturn—the star Zubenelgenubi—was (after the introduction of the zodiac) equated with the zodiacal longitude of 21° Libra.[1]

Given the longstanding association of Saturn with righteousness, taken together with the Scales of Libra denoting the symbol of the law in the legal profession, that this position was seen as Saturn's exaltation is understandable. In this connection it is interesting to consider that the Maitreya individuality, in his incarnation as Jeshu ben Pandira, the teacher of the Essenes, was referred to as the *teacher of righteousness*. It is this quality of righteousness that is lacking at this time of the reign of the Antichrist, who is referred to by St. Paul as the *man of lawlessness*.

> Concerning the coming of our Lord Jesus Christ and our being gathered to him... Don't let anyone deceive you in any way, for that day will not come until the rebellion occurs and the man of lawlessness is revealed, the man doomed to destruction. He will oppose and will exalt himself over everything that is called God or is worshiped, so that he sets himself up in God's temple, proclaiming himself to be God....
>
> The secret power of lawlessness is already at work; but the one who now holds it back will continue to do so until he is taken out of the way. And then the lawless one will be revealed, whom the Lord Jesus will overthrow with the breath of his mouth and destroy by the splendor of his coming. The coming of the lawless one will be in accordance with how Satan works. He will use all sorts of displays of power through signs and wonders that serve the lie, and all the ways that wickedness deceives those who are perishing. They perish because they refused to love the truth and so be saved. For this reason God sends them a powerful delusion so that they will believe the lie and so that all will be condemned who have not believed the truth but have delighted in wickedness.
>
> But we ought always to thank God for you, brothers and sisters loved by the Lord, because from the beginning God chose you to be saved through the sanctifying work of the Spirit and through belief in the truth. He called you to this through our gospel, that you might share in the glory of our Lord Jesus Christ.
>
> So then, brothers and sisters, stand firm and hold fast to the teachings we passed on to you, whether by word of mouth or by letter.
>
> May our Lord Jesus Christ himself and God our Father, who loved us and by his grace gave us eternal encouragement and good hope, encourage your hearts and strengthen you in every good deed and word. (2 Thes. 2:1–17, NIV)

A man of righteousness—according to the research presented here: the Abraham-Kashyapa-Jeshu ben Pandira-Maitreya Buddha/Kalki Avatar individuality—is prophesied to arise at this time of the reign of the man of lawlessness. The contrast of righteousness and iniquity is spoken of by Christ in Matthew 13 in connection with his second coming, his return as the Son of Man in great power and glory accompanied by angels: "The Son of Man will send out his angels, and they will weed out of his kingdom everything that causes sin and all who do evil. They will throw them into the blazing furnace, where there will be weeping and gnashing of teeth. Then the righteous will shine like the sun in the kingdom of their Father. Whoever has ears, let them hear" (Matt. 13:41–43, NIV).

If the research presented in this article is accurate, the time referred to by St. Paul, when Christ will overthrow the Antichrist "with the breath of his mouth and destroy by the splendor of his

---

For the Babylonians, each planet has a particular location in the zodiac, usually designated by its conjunction with a particular star or star cluster, where is it most powerful. This location where a planet is most powerful in the zodiac is referred to as the planet's *exaltation*.

1 Ibid, p. 34.

coming" will be shortly after the winter solstice of 2016, at the end of the 3½-year reign of the prince of darkness. In the words of the Russian poet and seer, Daniel Andreev:

> The prince of darkness will terrify human beings.... Christ, however, will take on as many forms as there are consciousnesses on Earth to behold him. He will adapt himself to everyone, and will converse with all. His forms, in an unimaginable way, will simultaneously yield an image: *One who appears in heaven surrounded by unspeakable glory.* There will not be a single being on Earth who will not see the Son of God and hear his Word.[2]

The 3½ Years

Regarding the 3½ years referred to above: the 3½ years of the rule of the Antichrist is a theme that has been addressed in my book *Prophecy–Phenomena–Hope: The Real Meaning of 2012* and also in the book, written together with Kevin Dann, *Christ and the Maya Calendar: 2012 and the Coming of the Antichrist*. As I have shown scientifically in an earlier book, *Chronicle of the Living Christ*, the length of Christ's ministry from the baptism to the resurrection was 3½ years or 1,290 days (this is actually twelve days longer than the exact period of 3½ years amounting to 1278 days). A period of three years and six months is mentioned in Luke 4:25, which, as discussed in *Chronicle of the Living Christ*, can be interpreted in relation to the 3½ years of Christ's ministry. On the other hand, two periods of approximately 3½ years are referred to in the Book of Daniel 12:11-12—an initial period of 1290 days and a subsequent period of 1335 days. As described in *Prophecy–Phenomena–Hope*, pages 59-65, this evidently refers to the preparatory 3½ years and the culminating 3½ years of the Antichrist's rule, which is characterized in these words in the Book of Revelation: "And the beast...was allowed to exercise authority for forty-two months" (13:5).[3]

In the "end times" discourse of Jesus to the disciples in the Gospel of Matthew, the same expression—the "abomination of desolation"—is referred to (Matthew 24:15) as in Daniel 12:11. This is a clear reference to the presence of the Antichrist—in particular, to the desolation wrought by what Vladimir Soloviev calls the "Antichrist's army."[4] A modern-day scenario of the significance of these words of the Prophet Daniel for our time emerges in considering the invasion of one country after another by the "world army" of the Antichrist, leaving behind untold death, misery, and desolation—the "abomination of desolation"—in the wake of each invasion.[5]

For those readers unfamiliar with the background depicted in my aforementioned books, the term "Antichrist" in the Christian tradition, *and as it is used here in this article*, is the same as what Rudolf Steiner refers to as the *incarnation of Ahriman*. From Rudolf Steiner's indications, a parallel can be drawn between the incarnation of Christ in Jesus, which lasted for 1290 days, and the incarnation of Ahriman in a human being (Mr. X), lasting for 3½ years. This is a vast and complex theme, which cannot be discussed here in any detail. However, the quotes from Daniel Andreev's article "Rose of the World" earlier in this journal give some helpful indications—helpful for our understanding of the present time of the

---

2 Quoted from Powell, *Prophecy–Phenomena–Hope*, p. 89.
3 Why has a 3½-year period been granted to the Antichrist, the incarnated Ahriman? This obviously has to do with the fact of the 3½ years of Christ's ministry, that the Antichrist is being granted the same period of time in his attempt to win over—away from Christ—all human beings to his side. For an understanding concerning the long-standing conflict between Christ and Ahriman, see Powell & Dann, *Christ and the Maya Calendar*.
4 "A Short Story of the Anti-Christ," in Soloviev, *War, Progress, and the End of History*, originally published in 1900.
5 For a graphic depiction of what the "abomination of desolation" looks like (http://www.informationclearinghouse.info/article33166.htm) see the second video (19 minutes) for the revealing of one aspect of the world as it is taking shape with the use of high-tech weapons against defenseless civilians, where Ahriman is feeding from the immense suffering that these innocent men, women, and children are undergoing. His goal is to maximize human suffering. The "abomination of desolation" amounts to the creation of "Hell on Earth."

Comparison Chart

Outer - Geocentric
Event of Incarnation of Ahriman 1
At Washington, District of Columbia, Dist 0, Latitude 38N53', Longitude 77W2'
Date: Wednesday, 19/JUN/2013, Gregorian
Time: 11:10, Time Zone EDT
Sidereal Time 3:53:52, Vernal Point 5 ♓ 4'20"

Inner - Geocentric
Birth of Joseph Stalin (V. !)
At Gori/Tiflis/Georgia, Latitude 42N00', Longitude 44E05'
Date: Wednesday, 6/DEC/1878, Julian
Time: 3:39, Local Time
Sidereal Time 9:24:50, Vernal Point 6 ♓ 56'58"

House System: Placidus, Zodiac: Sidereal SVP
Aspect set: Conjunction/Square/Opposition

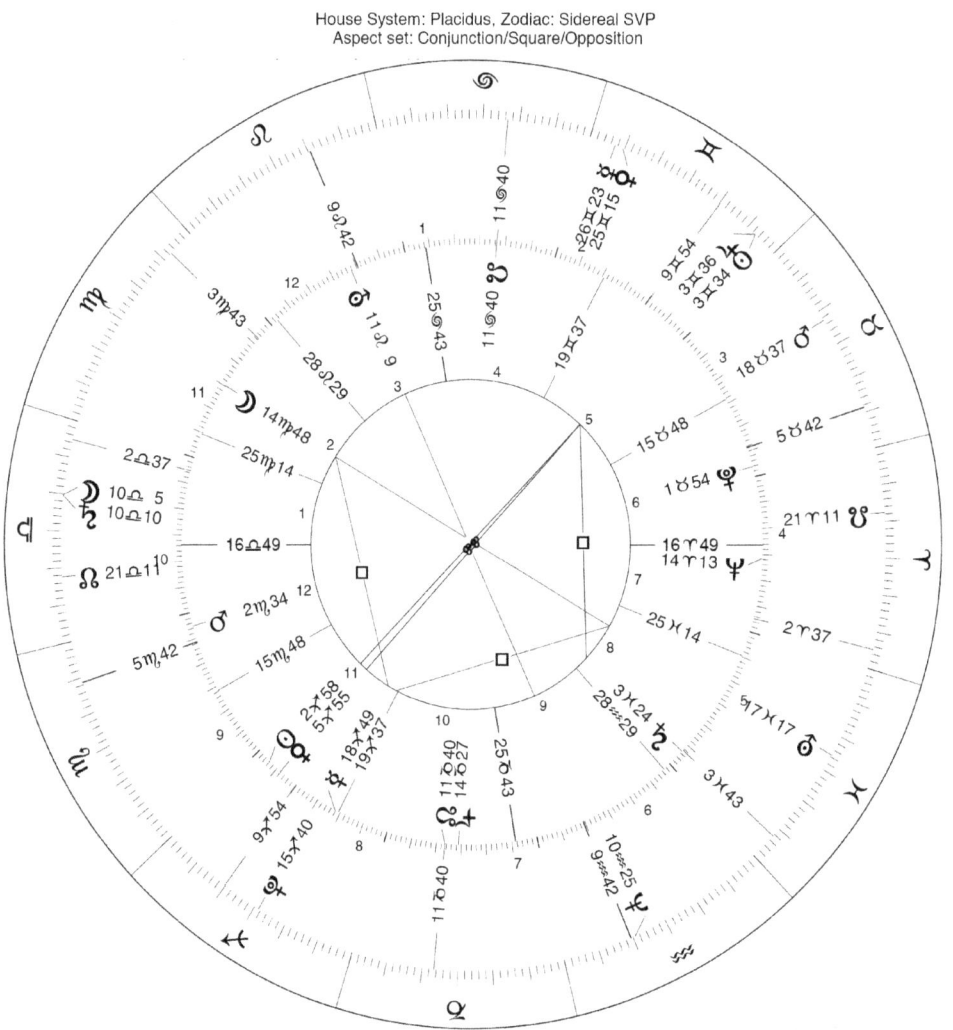

Antichrist's activity in the world—including the indication that in his previous incarnation Mr. X was Joseph Stalin (1878–1953). It is this indication, combined with spiritual research, which was helpful in determining a possible date for the onset of the 3½-year period of the incarnation of Ahriman, commencing around June 19, 2013; see the horoscope comparing the planetary configuration on this date with the birth horoscope of Stalin.

It can be seen from this horoscope comparison that the conjunction of the Sun and Jupiter on June 19, 2013, is opposite the conjunction of the Sun and Venus at the birth of Stalin. Moreover, we see that the Sun at Stalin's birth was in conjunction with the galactic center (2° Sagittarius). Although, with little or no justification, most modern astronomers think of the galactic center as a *supermassive black hole*, this great center is called by Daniel Andreev, on the basis of a mystical vision he had of the galactic center, the *Divine Heart at the center of our galaxy*.[1] On June 19, 2013, the galactic center was opposed by the conjunction of the Sun and Jupiter. Normally, of course, this configuration would not indicate something gravely negative. It is only in the context of Stalin's reincarnation as

---
1 Andreev, *The Rose of the World*.

Mr. X, the vessel for Ahriman's incarnation, in conjunction with the spiritual research that I was able to make in following the return of the soul of Stalin into incarnation, which led me to the date June 19, 2013.

How to identify Mr. X on the world stage? "Ahriman promotes the illusion, the lie...Ahriman lives upon lies; he is a spirit of untruth, the father of lies."[2] Much of what was put forward by Stalin was a lie, including his official date of birth. So it is with Mr. X: his date and place of birth—indeed, much of his "official biography"—are nothing but a web of lies. The lie—and, correspondingly, deception—is one indicator of this individual. Another is Ahriman's quest for power, whereby his goal is to guide his protégé, Mr. X, to the highest seat of power—to rule the world as a kind of "world emperor."[3]

Yet another indicator: Whereas the incarnated Christ laid down his life for humanity and the Earth, the incarnated Ahriman seeks to rule the world by abrogating to himself the right to be able to kill anyone on the Earth or to imprison them indefinitely, as Stalin did when he sent millions of Russians to the Soviet forced labor camp system known as the Gulag. And just as one of Stalin's primary focuses was the "kill list," which identified those he and others (of his close advisors) wanted to be killed, it can also be expected—as a karmic signature—that the Antichrist will also oversee a secret kill list in our time.[4]

Yet another indicator: This has to do with his *world army*, which wreaks death and destruction—the *abomination of desolation*—wherever it goes. Moreover, whereas Christ is the protector and nurturer of life on Earth, Ahriman seeks to replace divine creation with his own creation: artificial or virtual reality on the level of human consciousness, and genetically manipulated organisms on the level of the plant and animal kingdoms.

And still another indicator: the mission of humanity—in and through Christ—is to bring to realization freedom and love. Freedom is a most precious gift. Christ leaves us free. In freedom we are able to come to love in the spirit of the three aspects of love taught by Christ:

1. Love the Lord your God with all your heart and with all your soul and with all your strength and with all your mind;
2. Love your neighbor as yourself (Luke 10:27);
3. Love your enemies (Matt. 5:44).

In contrast, an indicator of the Antichrist—in the guise of "protecting" human beings—is to direct against humankind a regime embodying the opposite of freedom and love. In this regime of the Antichrist, instead of the freedom of each individual being respected, the goal is to spy on everyone—to the degree that this is technologically possible in our digital age—by gathering communications of human beings around the globe. One of the consequences of the global spying apparatus is to create an atmosphere of suspicion and mistrust and to stifle the unfolding of love.

In relation to the preceding indications regarding the Antichrist, as Daniel Andreev writes, "Only much later, when the 'savior' holds the entire power in his hands, will he show his true force." (from page 15 in this issue). From these indications, it is evident that the choice now confronting every human being on the planet at this time is: Christ or Antichrist—this means that either we submit

---

2 See http://www.bibliotecapleyades.net/biblianazar/ahriman01.htm; Robert S. Mason's website, "The Advent of Ahriman."

3 Anonymous, *Meditations on the Tarot*, chap. 4, has much to say about the "post" of emperor. For example, it was the striving of Napoleon, and later Hitler, to seize the post of emperor in their quest for ultimate power—to rule over the whole world.

4 Stalin is held responsible for the death of millions of Russians and Ukrainians. "The consensus figure for those that Joseph Stalin murdered when he ruled the Soviet Union is 20,000,000.... The figure comes from the book by Robert Conquest, *The Great Terror: Stalin's Purge of the Thirties* (Macmillan 1968).... As for Stalin, when the holes in Conquest's estimates are filled in, I calculate that Stalin murdered about 43,000,000 citizens and foreigners, over twice Conquest's total. Therefore, the usual estimate of 20 million killed in Soviet democide is far off for the Soviet Union per se, and even less than half of the total Stalin alone murdered" (R. J. Rummel, Professor Emeritus, University of Hawaii; http://www.distributedrepublic.net/archives/2006/05/01/how-many-did-stalin-really-murder).

to the prince of darkness or we choose to align ourselves with the living Christ, now manifesting in the etheric realm.

In my book *Cultivating Inner Radiance and the Body of Immortality* I have outlined a path of practice for connecting with Christ in the etheric realm. There is a meditation by Valentin Tomberg, which forms the basis for one of the exercises in this book, which I would like to include in this article. From 1933 onward Valentin Tomberg stood in inner connection with the Christ in the etheric realm, and at Easter 1941 he communicated these words, indicating the name of the Etheric Christ as *AMEN*:

> The AMEN bears the World Word within as the Kingdom,
> And in the miracles and stages of the Passion wields the Power,
> And as the Risen One is the Glory.
> The Kingdom, the Power, and the Glory are united in Jesus Christ,
> And their fulfillment is the AMEN.
> His head is the Kingdom, embracing all the stars in the heavens.
> His breath is the Power to continue the work of creation, a breathing, radiant cross of light against the background of the starry heavens.
> And his limbs are the Glory of spirit-permeated substance, like a rainbow in the foreground.
> And the unity of the rainbow, the radiant cross of light, and the starry heavens is the all-encircling circle of the AMEN.[1]

"His breath is the Power"—and according to St. Paul, in the passage quoted earlier: "And then the lawless one will be revealed, whom the Lord Jesus will overthrow with the breath of his mouth and destroy by the splendor of his coming." This is the blessing referred to by the Old Testament prophet Daniel at the end of the trial of the second 3½-year period: "Blessed is he who waits, and comes to the 1,335 days" (Daniel 12:12). From June 19, 2013, it is 1290 days to December 29, 2016, or 1335 days to February 12, 2017—1290 days and 1335 days being the two periods mentioned by Daniel. Star wisdom is focused upon the glory of the starry heavens, of which—as indicated in the foregoing meditation—the head of the Etheric Christ is a manifestation: "His head is the Kingdom, embracing all the stars in the heavens."

Moreover, in the words of Daniel Andreev:

> Christ...will take on as many forms as there are consciousnesses on Earth to behold him. He will adapt himself to everyone, and will converse with all. His forms, in an unimaginable way, will simultaneously yield an image: *One who appears in heaven surrounded by unspeakable glory.* There will not be a single being on Earth who will not see the Son of God and hear his Word.[2]

Andreev's vision is in accordance with the words of the Book of Revelation: "Look, he is coming with the clouds, and every eye will see him" (Rev. 1:7).

And in the words of Rudolf Steiner:

> Understanding the Mystery of Golgotha is the only thing that enables us to experience the whole of nature morally. If one then gazes up at the clouds and sees the lightning flashing from them, one will then be able to behold Christ in his etheric form. With the "clouds," that is to say with the elements, he will appear in spirit form. This vision will one day appear to every person.[3]

The following brief description of the 3½ years of the Antichrist—considered as a trial that humankind is experiencing now—includes several aspects. The first year is a time of coming to experience the *dark night of the soul*, during which there is no reference point for an inner sense of knowing the reality of oneself other than Christ, who accompanies us through this trial. Without Christ, the dark night of the soul can be an experience of great fear and overwhelming loneliness. One has to become aware at this time that a great

---

1 Powell, *Cultivating Inner Radiance and the Body of Immortality*, pp. 39–40.

2 Quoted in Powell, *Prophecy–Phenomena–Hope*, p. 89.

3 Steiner, *"Freemasonry" and Ritual Work*, p. 374.

battle is being waged for one's soul—and for every soul—a battle that is being waged on a subtle level. Also, one has to become aware of snares being set by the adversary, the Antichrist, whose dark forces seek to desolate human beings. In this situation it is of supreme importance to *hold to Christ*. To do this one has to first win over one's soul completely from the dark forces. *One can do this only for oneself, and then one increasingly finds new love within the depths of the soul*. Further, one can turn to one's Guardian Angel, who is able to show one where one has gone astray from the true path—the true path being that of love.

In the second of the three years a great feeling of emptiness arises within human beings. There is a sense that everything is too difficult to comprehend. This is accompanied by increasing self-doubt and a sense of oppression. This can lead to the feeling that one is losing one's will. This is the experience of the void of the abyss, for it is the abyss separating the sensory realm from that of the spiritual at which one now stands. In contrast to the awareness of the battle for the soul being waged during the first year, the second year is characterized by the sense of being abandoned to oneself in a morass of nothingness, seeming like hell, accompanied by a sense of powerlessness. In this state of consciousness it is important to be aware that *there is something* within the nothingness. Then one can become aware of a flicker of light, and that underlying the light is the power of Christ's love—responding to one's own love for Christ. "Those who love me will keep my word, and my Father will love them, and we will come to them and make our home with them" (John 14:23). Then one will gradually come to know that there is no end to love, that Christ's love is enduring, and that he loves every human soul. The essence of the trial of nothingness in the second year is to lead one to the love within which enables one to find one's way out of the void. Underlying this is the realization that the world was created by love and that by the power of love it will be redeemed. Through the great love of Christ's sacrifice, he knows every human soul, and it is his love that is the lifeline that can lead the soul back to him.

During the third year of the great trial, through the *love born within* during the second year of the 3½ years of the Antichrist, inner darkness can gradually be overcome through the light of love. Nevertheless, dark beings still seek to hinder and discourage one, for they cannot abide the inner light within one's soul. In the midst of these new challenges, it is important to focus ever more upon Christ as the light, love, and life of the world. The challenge here is that it will seem as if Christ is gone. This is the challenge that historically the disciples underwent at Christ's Ascension when he disappeared before their eyes. It was necessary for them to go through this experience in order to come to Pentecost, when the disciples had the experience of the birth of Christ within and became transformed into apostles. Hitherto they had been disciples, learning from the Master. And now, through the birth of Christ within, they became apostles, empowered to go out into the world and to teach and heal in the name of Christ. Daniel Andreev's words quoted above, where he speaks of Christ appearing in heaven simultaneously to every human being on the planet, appearing in unspeakable glory, is the new Pentecost—what Steiner called the World Pentecost. This event denotes the end of the 3½ years of the Antichrist, because the Antichrist will be overthrown, cast down, by the World Pentecost manifestation of Christ in unspeakable glory in the heavens. This will be accompanied by the sight of a rainbow of colors emanating from Christ as he gradually draws closer and closer, bestowing upon human beings a sense of peace and unfathomable love. Christ is unfathomable mercy, who calls all human beings to return to him—to return to love.[4]

---

[4] The similarity between the stages of the trials during the 3½ years of the Antichrist and the three days of Mary Magdalene's initiation as described by Estelle Isaacson (*Through the Eyes of Mary Magdalene,* vol. 2, pp. 20–37) seems to indicate that there is a parallel between the two initiation processes. See also the forthcoming book by Robert Powell and Estelle Isaacson, *Gautama Buddha's Successor: A Force for Good in Our Time.*

THE BODHISATTVA WHO WILL BECOME THE MAITREYA BUDDHA

Estelle Isaacson

I saw the Bodhisattva appear radiantly sitting in a gesture of peaceful compassion. His robes were emanating pure white light and his head was golden—as if made of gold. He drew very near and then gave the following message:

Wisdom has brought you here today [February 12, 2013], to receive a message.

There is now present one of the twelve Bodhisattvas, one who is drawing near at this moment. This Bodhisattva is inhabiting—over-lighting—the community of which you are a part.

You shall not be without divine guidance or protection; for the Angels who serve the most Holy Ones are gathering around. They already know their work and have already been called. The Bodhisattvas are preparing for what is coming and the Angels that serve them are gathering for their work.

Your thoughts and meditations on the life of this Bodhisattva bring him ever closer to you. It is the one who shall appear as the Maitreya Buddha. He can already appear in his form of the Maitreya—the Bringer of the Good—to those who are prepared to receive him now.

There are forerunners who are called to work with him now—to prepare the way for him to manifest as the Maitreya Buddha in the future. For this great one to manifest himself as the "Bringer of the Good" requires the preparation of many souls. Just as a great cathedral requires even the simplest stonemason, the one who knows where to find the stone and is able to bring it out of the mountain so that a great cathedral can be erected according to the vision of the one who directs its creation—so also do those great souls (even Jesus Christ and the Buddha and others) need the preparation of many souls to help bring about the manifestation of their incarnation. Likewise it is so even with one who is great and powerful like the Maitreya Buddha. Thus he who shall be the Maitreya Buddha calls his servants and helpers; for them the Maitreya is already beginning to come now into being such that they can have a direct experience with him before he shall appear in his future incarnation on the Earth as the Maitreya Buddha.

This Being was indeed Father Abraham, and out of that incarnation as Abraham some three thousand years ago came the world's great religions that are now in conflict. A great war is coming out of the seed of Abraham. This can be seen as one religion fighting against another. The children of Israel shall rage against the children of Ishmael. And included in the house of Israel there is the religion of the Jews and also the Christian religion.

Even the Antichrist himself, in part, is of the line of Abraham—but only in part—for there is an element that does not come through Abraham.

Woe unto the children of Abraham.

The Maitreya shall work upon the Abrahamic stream.

It is possible through working directly with this being to bring about much good—to bring light to the conflict. In order for the Maitreya to manifest in the future, there must be a resolution between these streams: Israel and Ishmael.

What is happening now in the world, and what is coming this year is very important for the mission of the Maitreya Buddha. Those who succumb to fear are not able to work with the Maitreya. He is the bringer of the Good. He shall bring forth the Good through the raw materials available to him. He cannot take fears and weave them into paradise; he does not take violence and weave it into peace. He takes works of faith and weaves the greater good. He weaves in spiritual community that is gathered together out of love. He is not present in fear-based community. *He is the Good.* He brings the Good. He takes the smallest offerings and through these manifests the greater Good.

Some individuals have been chosen to receive these things now; they are some of the few who have created space in their own hearts for the Maitreya. Whereas Abraham's seed was great, the Maitreya's seed is young and his numbers are few. He looks the world over and finds a only very small number of souls whom he can call to his work.

If you think of him, you are called. If you love him, you are called. The words he has spoken in the past, in other lifetimes, are words of wisdom that you have been able to make your own.

Again, you must understand that the manifestation of a Great One requires much work to be done by many souls in preparation—and those who are called are also the bringers of the Good, for they shall help to bring the Maitreya; and it is through current world conflict that they are now able to hold to the Good and work in prayer and meditation with the Maitreya.

Meditate upon the Platonic virtues: wisdom, temperance, and courage, which together bring about righteousness. As you develop these three virtues in a greater way you will aid the work of the Maitreya, just like the stonemason who, stone by stone, was able to assist in building the great cathedral.

The Maitreya shall appear as a being formed out of wisdom-filled cosmic thoughts that have been born from human souls. He will receive his form as if woven out of the Cosmic Ether of the most righteous and benevolent human thoughts. He will have the power of the greatest and most righteous human thoughts. This is why when you strive to lift your thoughts to a higher plane, ennobling them, you are building up the body of the Maitreya—and he begins to manifest when enough human thoughts have become ennobled by the power of the Nine Beatitudes spoken by Christ at the Sermon on the Mount. Then shall the Maitreya appear in his full form and he shall utter the Word born out of the Cosmic Thoughts, and the Good shall instantly manifest.

He shall manifest the power of human thought. He will embody righteousness—it will *become* his form. He can manifest the Good in any situation, even now if there is one person who can think the thoughts of Goodness. You have opportunities now to put this into practice—to think the good thoughts even when you are tempted to do otherwise. You have the power to bring love to any situation, or to people who do not seem to merit it. See the challenges before you as opportunities and tests to practice bringing the love—bringing the Good. You will be inspired and you will be guided as long as you do not give in to fear. This is only a moment in eternity. This moment will be over soon. Your suffering will be the suffering of one who *loves*—not the suffering of one who has been overtaken by dark powers. You love, and this love will become a source of suffering. No matter what comes, continue to love!

It would be strengthening and wonderful to bring the Maitreya more fully into your community by holding times for prayers and meditations, studying his words—and in any other ways in which you are guided to do.

FINDING JERUSALEM, PART 2

David Tresemer, Ph.D.

WHAT IS AT THE CENTER?

Every body has an inside and an outside, separated by a surface. Though the containers of animate objects have different layers of influence or energy that separate what's on the inside from the outside, one of these layers, as in the skin of our bodies, appears more confident than others that what's inside has one quality, and outside another.

Every thing has a center, more pronounced for animate bodies. The periphery can be thought of as the furthest reach of what lives inside. If infinite in extent, the proxy for periphery becomes the skin. At the center lives an "essence" at the "core," from *"coeur"* in French and *"cor"* in Latin, both meaning heart, the heart at the center.

We have the idea that, if we can get to the heart of the matter, we will know the truth underlying the superficial chatter at the surface. We strive for this center. We feel a surge of heart when falling in love, and the heartache when falling out of love. The heart area hosts the fourth chakra, the central chakra of seven.

The body's center of gravity lies just inside the navel, not half of one's height and not at the heart. There are different kinds of centers revealing different kinds of essence.

You can't put your hand right into the center of something to feel it, or bring it out to view it. One seeks an epicenter, a place on the surface that reveals the center or at least a pathway to the center. In the human being, one might say that the umbilicus—the navel or belly button—is one such place historically. Interestingly, averaged over many human beings, the navel lies at the golden proportion, phi minus 1 times the total height (.618 x ht.).

Does the Earth have an epicenter? Many places have claimed to be the navel of the Earth. The ceremonial opening of a *sipapu* in the earthen floor of a kiva is experienced as such a route to the heart of the Earth. Is there then a *primary* epicenter to the heart of the Earth? The Abrahamic religions propose that this place is Jerusalem.

JERUSALEM

In "Finding Jerusalem, part 1," I examined the location of Jerusalem on the planet. On a sphere without orientation, no one point has a more special meaning than any other point. Our (nearly) spherical Earth is oriented by its rotation on its axis, giving us north and south poles and an equator. I found that the location of Jerusalem is on a latitude that relates strongly to the golden proportion, phi (1.618), a proportion evident in many processes of growing (and decaying). Note that its bid as "navel" of the Earth relates to the same phi proportion that locates the navel of the human body in relation to its height.

Following the phi spiral inward to the mathematical center of the Earth, I found that the center of generation of that spiral lay at a point (or best to think of it as a zone) approximately a quarter of the way out from the mathematical center. This could be seen as the source/heart for powers of generation.

I cautioned that the journey through Jerusalem as gateway to that heart of generative power must be done with great care. I will explain why.

THE BEST AND THE WORST

I have visited the Old City of Jerusalem a dozen times. Each time, I visited the site of Golgotha, the scene of the apparent death of Jesus Christ, an event sorely misunderstood when seen merely as an act of cruelty and violence against a spiritual teacher whose teaching threatened the political system of the time. I was alerted through Rudolf Steiner's teachings to the possibility that the highly charged blood of this man, having touched the Earth there, led to a fructification—a nourishment and empowerment—of the being of the Earth, as well as all who live upon it. He had lived through in a short period of time what we all live through over much longer periods of time—that is, maturation of the physical body into a spiritual reality—through our suffering of many mistakes and their healing, as well as through the aggression of others perpetrating mistakes upon us.

When you pass through the grand doors at the entry of the Holy Sepulcher and then ascend the steep stone stairs immediately to the right, you come to a low-roofed and dimly lit place focused on the rock upon which the cross supposedly stood. Atop that spot has been affixed various structures with a large silver donut-shaped device just over the rock, through which you can put your hand to touch the actual rock. Around it loom statues, ornaments, decorations, and fixtures of gold and silver flickering in the candlelight. The Greek Orthodox Church hosts that section of the Holy Sepulcher, and they patrol it with incense; the walls are black with smoke. They set devotees into an orderly line and sometimes tell people to quiet down. There is a throng of people at all hours—large groups of people from Eastern Europe, South America, and Africa, and individuals from around the world. The groups sing hymns in many languages and line up for the opportunity to put their hand through the hole.

I did that on my first visit, putting my hand through the hole and touching the rock. Then I recoiled. At that time I did not know why. Why would I recoil when the energy of the place was so electric? Above and through the din and the smoke, through the press of people exhausted by long travel yet lifted on the wings of expectation, with their mistuned yet sincere hymns and their strong smells, there was a very high tone that got my attention. Accompanying a group of others, I felt an upwelling of strength and attentiveness. I felt that I was a Templar, protecting others in their pilgrimage to this holy place, and thereby remembering my previous pilgrimages there, to this epicenter of the heart of the Earth. The supposed burial site inside that vast rambling building did not interest me (and since then, I have preferred the Garden Tomb as the true site—another story). I left several times to look at other parts of the building and soon returned to ascend the stairs to the place by the rock where this most astonishing event of spiritualized blood transmitted to the rock of the Earth had taken place. At one of my returns, three others from our group were there, and we spontaneously, and without speaking, stood in a formation—two of them who were marrying in the light of this extraordinary place and two, another man and myself, as Templar knights flanking the man and woman before the altar of light, witnessing their spiritual marriage and protecting their vulnerability. We had to be pulled away by the necessity of the tour schedule.

At my second and subsequent visits, without the same limits of time, I sat on a bench looking directly at the point of the rock (with its back to the railing toward the entrance ten feet below). As I had sunglasses, I put those on. I have found them helpful when you don't wish people to stare at you when your eyes are closed; people simply don't notice and go about their business.

During my second visit, I sat for two hours bathing in the increasing bliss of the light that emanated from that spot. The spiritual power was immense, sometimes with light that warmly embraced, sometimes with what felt like a nuclear bomb blast of love. It pulsed and erupted like a gushing spring of water, like a volcanic cauldron. I felt that this was perhaps the most powerful place on Earth. Many groups of devotees came and went, replaced by new groups. I was absorbed in my meditation, participating in the love that was freely offered by this event from two thousand years ago, that seemed to be happening in the present.

I then began to notice a disturbance in my meditation, as if some drunk at a bar a block away was shouting incoherently. Over the period of ten minutes I began to hear more clearly an unceasing cacophony of angry screaming and derisive laughter around the edges. As I listened, it became clearer and louder. With soft gaze I could see that a darkness of aggressive energy was attacking the light. The light pushed back easily yet about twelve to twenty feet away were angry prods and malicious jabs of a hugely destructive force.

I asked, "What is this!?" and heard a voice within: "Watch very closely." I began to see the process. People had come from all over the world. They were devoted and prayerful. They had struggled to buy tickets to travel here. Their reward would be that Jesus would take their mistakes, errors, pains, and tragedies—in other words, all their sins. That was the promise. He would clear the slate and transform their lives into something holy and wonderful. They lined up to take turns to dump all their sins through that hole in the silver donut onto the rock and onto Jesus. I could feel the hopes of families and friends left behind at homes all over the world weighing on each one of these devotees, the hopes that each of these people would come back clear and overflowing with blessings. The devotees at the place of crucifixion desperately wanted to dump all their negativity.

The accumulation over centuries of this shedding of sin had created this hall as being the most demonic place that I had ever visited. I watched people dump their stuff. Opened by their prayers and hymns, sticky bits of someone else's karma would affix to them. I saw people leave with more than they had come with.

This is perhaps one of the grandest illusions of Christianity—that Jesus will take our sins away. This is only partly true. Rudolf Steiner made the helpful distinction that Jesus will take away the "world karma" of our deeds—the part that ripples out to all of humanity, to the entire Earth, and into the future. But he will not take away the "personal karma," for in truth, that's our task. That's what helps us to grow and explore. That's what develops character and purpose. Leaving it behind somewhere actually makes life more difficult, as at some point we all have to retrieve our personal karma and actively work with it.

This fundamental misunderstanding about the nature of Jesus Christ and his role has made the epicenter of the heart of the world—the gateway through Jerusalem—into the best and the worst place, both at once. Extreme caution is advised at this first gate of seven into those inner realms. You have to focus on the light, which you will find in sheaths, the outermost being the coarsest as it protects against the thick black aggression. Stay with the innermost and most refined light.

Of course, you must substantiate my opinions with your own experiences; my purpose here is to caution you.

I will speak to the other gates in a subsequent *Journal*.

O Spirit of God...
Fill the hearts that seek Thee,
Seek Thee in deep longing,
Deep longing for health
For health and strong courage,

Strong courage that flows
  within our limbs,
Flows as a precious divine gift,
Divine gift from Thee,
O Spirit of God.
—RUDOLF STEINER

CORPORATE PERSONHOOD: THE TOUCH OF NEPTUNE

David Tresemer, Ph.D.

A recent decision of the United States Supreme Court has given unprecedented powers to corporations to fund political campaigns because it was agreed that corporations have the rights of persons. The case had the title Citizens United vs. Federal Election Commission, abbreviated the "Citizens United" case. I began to look at this case and its predecessors, and found a prominence of the planet Neptune. As many observers have noted the connection of Neptune dynamics with sweeping changes in ideological systems, this seemed to show the influence of Neptune at work.

It must be said from the outset that Citizens United does not represent the united view of the citizens of the United States of America. Therefore, though I find abbreviations unsatisfactory, even thorny, I will call this decision the CitUnDecision, as I find the thorn of an abbreviation useful to awaken me out of any thought that this represents the will of the people.

The CitUnDecision has made political office and its valued vote much more vulnerable to being purchased by this new form of person, a corporation—a phantom of group thinking fashioned by paperwork into a body (corpus).

Based on my researches into the connection between earthly matters and celestial, I queried how the CitUnDecision—including its predecessors and its consequences—can be seen in relation to celestial movements. This research identifies a few of those connections. Those who believe such connections impossible will pay no attention. Those who are open to interconnections between heaven and earth will be interested in the patterns shown here and therefore in how to respond.

The CitUnDecision has a history that we must understand. Human beings have worked together as teams and tribes for a very long time. Corporations were set up as a formal team or tribe in order to organize supporters as stockholders, to establish routines and patterns that outlive the individuals who set it up, and to protect the individual humans involved from responsibility and litigation. A corporation was originally permitted to exist by a special charter of the royalty or, in a democracy, by an elected government representing the constituents who elected it. The charter could be revoked at will by the grantor. In relatively recent times, the form of a corporation has been gaining power. Though human beings had to fight for centuries to establish recognition of human rights, corporations have swiftly expropriated these rights for their fictional existence. This expropriation threatens to eclipse the rights of human beings.

What is a Person?

A person is defined by the Declaration of Independence, and other early documents, and has with it a sense of rights that a government cannot or should not take away. Human beings, by their nature, "are endowed by their Creator with certain unalienable Rights, that among these are Life, Liberty and the pursuit of Happiness." This includes a sense of divinity. "Creator," elsewhere in the Declaration termed "Nature's God"—has granted a charter, so to speak, to all human beings equally.

Rudolf Steiner distinguished between three soul functions, thinking, feeling, and willing, which can be thought of in terms of a threefold social order: Life as a feature of the limbs and metabolism (the will working in the economic sphere), Liberty as a feature of the thinking sphere (culture), and Happiness as a feature of the feeling life (the social sphere). That's a helpful way to think of personhood, balanced in all three spheres, each function an endowment of the Creator.[1]

Other rights were established for persons in the Constitution of the United States and its amendments, which other nations have followed. The First Amendment guarantees free speech, the ability to speak one's mind openly. The first section of the Fourteenth Amendment defines "persons" and affirms their enjoyment of equal protection under the law.

The owners of corporations have sought to endow their creations with these same rights.

THE TURNING POINT

The key turning point on the personhood of corporations occurred in the Supreme Court case titled Santa Clara County vs. Southern Pacific Railroad Company, decided May 10, 1886.[2] The main purpose of the case was to determine if the railroad ought to pay taxes to Santa Clara County for the fences running alongside the railroad tracks. Normally, the decision would have determined a minor clarification to tax law, and then would have been filed away.

Customarily the arguments back and forth among the justices of the Supreme Court were observed by the Reporter of Decisions, who then summarized the main arguments for and against at the front of the final write-up in a kind of executive summary called a "headnote." The Reporter of Decisions was an important post, and the Reporter's salary was as high as that enjoyed by the justices.

In the Santa Clara case, the Reporter of Decisions, Bancroft Davis, went beyond his usual duties when he added the following in his headnote: "The court does not wish to hear argument on the question whether the provision in the Fourteenth Amendment to the Constitution, which forbids a State to deny to any person within its jurisdiction the equal protection of the laws, applies to these corporations. We are all of the opinion that it does."

Though it takes some concentration to untangle the double negative to see what the second sentence affirms, this case was picked up by the popular press as meaning that the Supreme Court had affirmed the right of a corporation to have the same rights as a person, in other words, that the Supreme Court had affirmed the language of the Fourteenth Amendment to include corporations, for the first time. The trouble was that the Supreme Court justices did not in fact argue about this, nor agree on the application of the Fourteenth Amendment. Nonetheless, Davis's summary became a precedent that liberated corporations from their servitude to states who originally had had the power of charter over them. It was as if the Frankenstein body had lain on the table for a while, added to here and there, but was suddenly brought to life with an electrical shock, and then took over the controls.[3]

---

1   Rudolf Steiner's central book of philosophy, *The Philosophy of Freedom* (or *Intuitive Thinking as a Spiritual Path*), links freedom with the sphere of thinking. The insertion of happiness in the Declaration of Independence may have come from Thomas Jefferson's reading of *The Nature of Things* by the Roman author Lucretius, rediscovered in 1417; it links happiness with the proper goal in the world as a member of society. (The source of "happiness" for the Declaration from Lucretius was suggested by Stephen Greenblatt in *The Swerve*.)

2   The text of the decision can be found at http://supreme.justia.com/us/118/394/case.html. The identification of the key importance of the Santa Clara case is widespread. The exposure of the mammoth misunderstanding at the root of that case is the brilliant contribution of Thom Hartmann in *Unequal Protection: How Corporations Became "People"—and How You Can Fight Back*. Though much of his presentation has found its way to Wikipedia, the book includes many other important aspects of this case.

3   In 1938, Justice Hugo Black wrote in a dissent, "In 1886, this Court in the case of *Santa Clara County v. Southern Pacific Railroad*, decided for the first time that the word *person* in the amendment did in some instances include corporations.... The history of the amendment proves that the people were told that its purpose was to protect weak and helpless human beings and were not told that it was

Astrological Approach

Before going to the chart for the Santa Clara case, I should explain the chart system that I use. It is sidereal, with the location determined by Aldebaran as center of the Bull (Taurus) and Antares as center of the Scorpion. This comes from the Babylonian sidereal system as determined from Robert Powell's research in *History of the Zodiac*.[4] This allows for historical research in relation to the fixed stars, as the locations don't move as in a tropical chart. In "Discovery of a Planet Named Neptune," I found that Neptune for the birth and death of the discoverers was closely connected to the Royal Stars of Persia, the five fixed stars that I follow in my research.[5] Indeed, for the births and deaths of the four people most connected with its discovery in 1846, as well as for the discovery event itself, all but one of those nine events showed Neptune connected with these stars, a statistically significant finding. One could ask if the discoverers found Neptune or did Neptune (in relation to the prime fixed stars) find them.

Most of the observations made in this paper concern aspects between planets and therefore it matters little if we use sidereal or tropical celestial approaches. However, we will see some of the prime fixed stars arise, including the Galactic Center, which is the largest concentration of suns in any direction, the invisible power generator

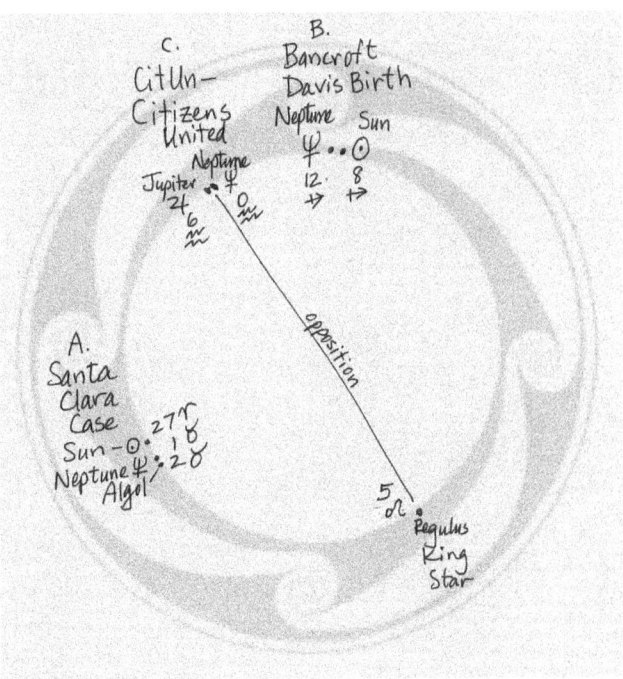

Figure 1: Neptune and Other Prominent Planets/Stars

that has come so strongly into the public eye in 2012 (when the Sun and Earth lay in an approximate line with the Galactic Center around December 21).[6]

Santa Clara Decision

The chart for that decision, given in full at the very end, and with features emphasized in figure 1, uses 10 a.m. as the time, which is customarily when decisions are announced by the Supreme Court. I will note three main points that will become important later:

1. Neptune (at 1°54' of the Bull, Taurus) conjunct the Sun (26°41' Ram, Aries), with Neptune in the Bull (Taurus) and the Sun at the end of the Ram (Aries), a 5° orb with Sun applying (drawing closer to Neptune in succeeding days). Perhaps we can see in this a focus of light (Sun) to make decisions (Sun in the Ram), putting an ideal (the idealism

---

intended to remove corporations in any fashion from the control of state governments.... The language of the [fourteenth] amendment itself does not support the theory that it was passed for the benefit of corporations" (from Connecticut General Life Insurance Company vs. Johnson; underline added).

4 Powell, *History of the Zodiac*. Powell has described this approach further in *The Astrological Revolution*, as well as in other books. This sidereal system is very close to other sidereal systems, including Vedic, though emphasizes the central pole between Aldebaran and Antares. Technically, it is the SVP (Synetic Vernal Point) from Neil Michelsen, *The American Sidereal Ephemeris*, both the 1976 and 2001 editions.

5 Tresemer, "Discovery of the Planet Named Neptune," *International Astrologer* (of the International Society for Astrological Research, ISAR), August 2012.

6 Though, as I showed in my *International Astrologer* (ISAR) article in 2010, this was hardly a unique event, nonetheless it excited the imagination of many people for a time.

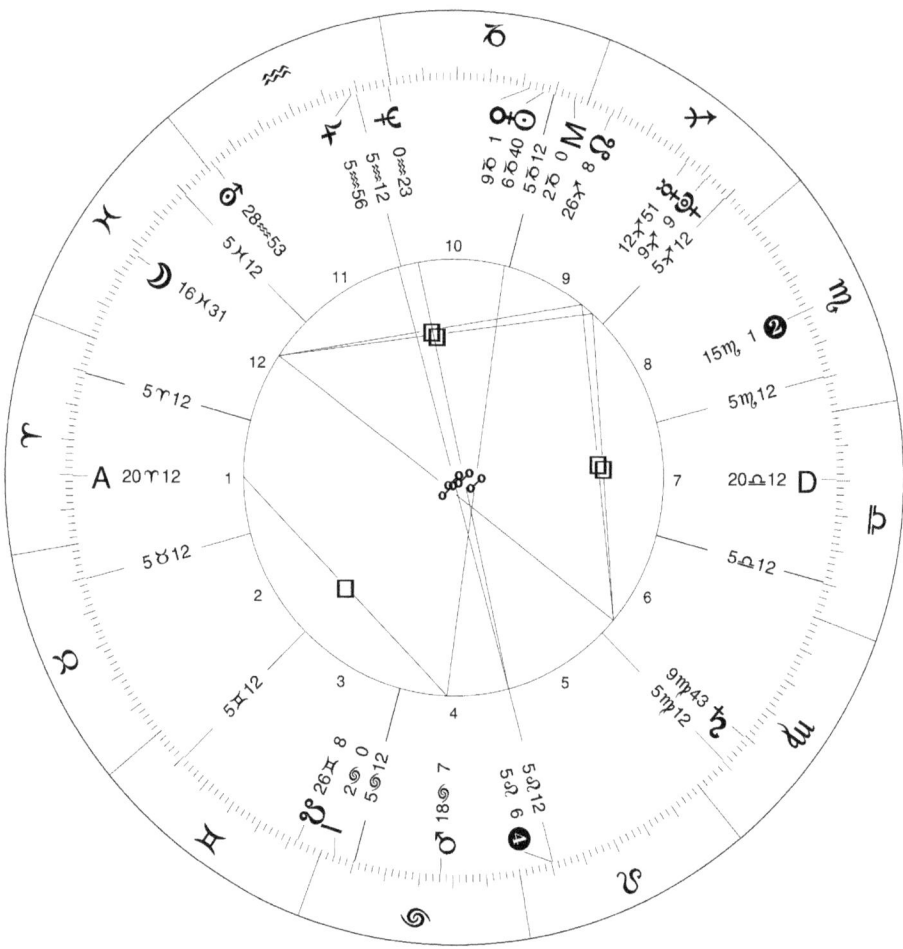

Santa Clara Case, May 10, 1886, 10 a.m.
(#2 indicates Antares directly opposite Aldebaran, #4 indicates Regulus)

of Aries) or ideology (Neptune) into matter (earth sign, Taurus). Though I like to use very tight orbs for historical research, I found this 5° orb recurring in my research on Neptune, and found it did not undermine the statistical significance when looking at the discoverers. In my view, the Sun conjunct any planet amplifies its effect.[1] Neptune's seems from research on world events to effect/inspire the creation of ideology and imaginations, to the extent of social upheaval, revolution, and even the forcing of ideology on others.[2] A poster of happy people doing hard work together on a Chinese communist farm shows the workings of Neptune—the image shapes our attention into the implied ideology of the image.

2. A T-square, that is three corners of a square occupied by a celestial player, between Uranus in Virgo, Saturn in the Twins (Gemini), and Venus in the Fishes (Pisces), in figure 2.

---

1 A point developed in my book, *The Venus Eclipse of the Sun 2012*.
2 See especially "The Signature of Neptune in World Events," *Journal for Star Wisdom 2013*, wherein Neptune when stimulated by conjunction with the prime fixed stars is shown to be related to a large number of revolutions, regime changes, and new ideologies. The wider orb was shown in Tresemer "Discovery," in relation to the discoverers of Neptune, as confirmed by a test for statistical significance. Liz Greene, *The Astrological Neptune and the Quest for Redemption*, is also a fount of wisdom about the phenomena found when Neptune is prominent, much in agreement with the findings of my research.

Whenever an astrologer observes a T-square, the astrologer pays particular attention to what moves into that empty fourth corner.

3. Neptune lay at 1°55' of the Bull (Taurus), conjunct to the star Algol (at 1°25' Taurus). My colleagues and I have written about this in *Signs in the Heavens*.[3] Algol is the star of Medusa, a mythological demon who turns good intentions into stone. Traditionally it is the most malefic star in the heavens. A traditional interpretation would be that no good can come of such a placement. Something was set in stone that ought not to have been, some kind of deadening empowered by the planet Neptune.

THE REPORTER OF DECISIONS

The popular press thought that the Supreme Court had affirmed the personhood of corporations. It can more accurately be understood as the work of the Reporter of Decisions, through a skillful "headnote" to the case.

The Reporter of Decisions was J. C. Bancroft Davis, a former president of the Newburgh and New York Railway Company, former ambassador to Germany, and former associate judge on the United States Court of Claims, thus a very qualified man. He was 63 years old at the hearing of the Santa Clara case. Some have rightly criticized his position in the Santa Clara case as a conflict of interest with his interests in railroads. He used an otherwise minor case to insert a change in law that the Supreme Court as a body had avoided.

Let us regard the birth of John Chandler Bancroft Davis on December 22, 1822.[4] As in the chart of the Santa Clara case, the Sun and Neptune are close to each other (in the 5° orb that we saw before) in the Archer (Sagittarius). That 5° orb between Sun and Neptune is also shown in figure 1. Uranus is there too. Mercury at 1°37' of

Figure 2: Santa Clara T-Square in Relation to Other Events

the Archer (Sagittarius) lies conjunct the Galactic Center at 2°6' of the Archer (Sagittarius). As the placement of a planet can mean that the energy from that part of the heavens becomes turbulent, we can ask what kind of turbulent communication (Mercury) can be coming from the center of our galaxy (behind Mercury). At the least one can expect a sense of communication from a much greater source functioning in Davis, even a sense of mission through his communication.

When comparing the chart for Davis's birth with the Santa Clara case, we see that Bancroft Davis was the right person in the right place at the right time. The location of Venus (7°49' Sagittarius), Sun (8°5' Sagittarius), Neptune (12°31' Sagittarius), and Uranus (14°49' Sagittarius) at Davis's birth completed the T-square (comprised of Uranus, Saturn, Venus between 10° and 13° of the other mutable signs) that existed at the Santa Clara case (see figure 2). In other words, in a square with three corners occupied and the fourth corner missing, the missing corner was filled to overflowing by the birth chart of the Reporter of Decisions. Bancroft Davis from his birth completed the T-square at the time of the Santa Clara "headnote."

---

3 Bento, Schiappacasse, and Tresemer, *Signs in the Heavens: A Message for Our Time*. A great circle with Algol in it meets at a perpendicular to the ecliptic plane at 1°25' Taurus.

4 Birth information from Wikipedia. As no time was given, I have used noon. Thus we must avoid interpretation of house placements.

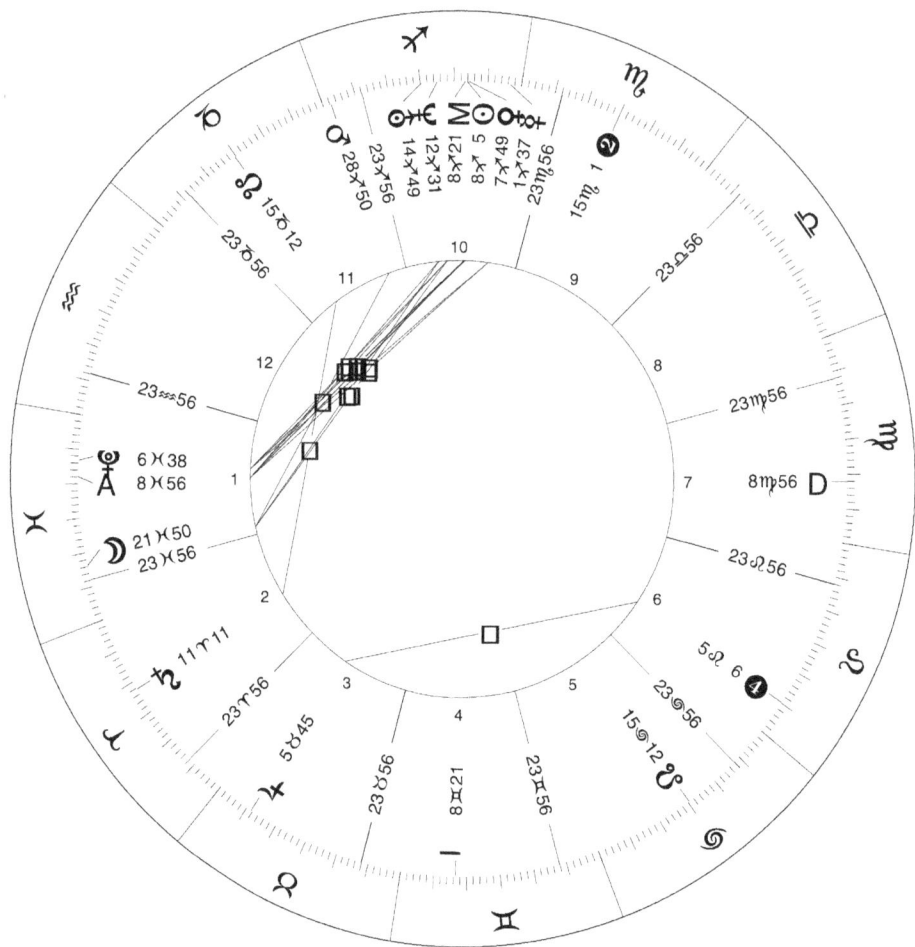

Birth of Bancroft Davis, December 22, 1822 (noon chart)
(#2 indicates Antares directly opposite Aldebaran, #4 indicates Regulus)

The 63-year-old had his moment of power, as if impelled to speak on behalf of the galaxy.[1]

Among those four planets that completed the T-square into a grand square, the most important in this context was Neptune. His ideology of what ought to happen fit into that open port so neatly, and led to the "headnote" that continues to work to unseat human persons as the only kind of persons.[2]

In *Unequal Protection*, Thom Hartmann points us to an influence on Davis: "The hand on the pen that did it [wrote that corporations could be considered persons under the Fourteenth Amendment] was that of the court reporter J. C. Bancroft Davis, aided and in all probability even persuaded or bought off by the same railroad barons who, through the money and the power of their railroad corporations, owned Justice Stephen J. Field."[3] Because the Chief Justice, Morrison Waite, was sickly, Justice Field had an inordinate effect on Davis. At Field's birth, Neptune lay conjunct the Galactic Center, the greatest concentration of suns in our galaxy; at his death, Neptune lay opposite to the Galactic Center.[4] Davis com-

---

1 Bancroft Davis continued as Reporter of Decisions until 1902 (age 79), and died in 1907 (Dec. 27, five days after his 85th birthday [Wikipedia]). No other incidents were reported in his time as Reporter of Decisions.

2 At the end of the article the horoscope of the Santa Clara decision is given in the inner wheel, and Davis's birth horoscope in the outer wheel. The aspect lines show only connections between charts, not within charts.

3 Hartmann, op. cit., 48.

4 Stephen J. Field was born in Haddam, Connecticut, on Nov. 4, 1816 (Neptune at 28°15' of Scorpio,

Corporate Personhood: The Touch of Neptune

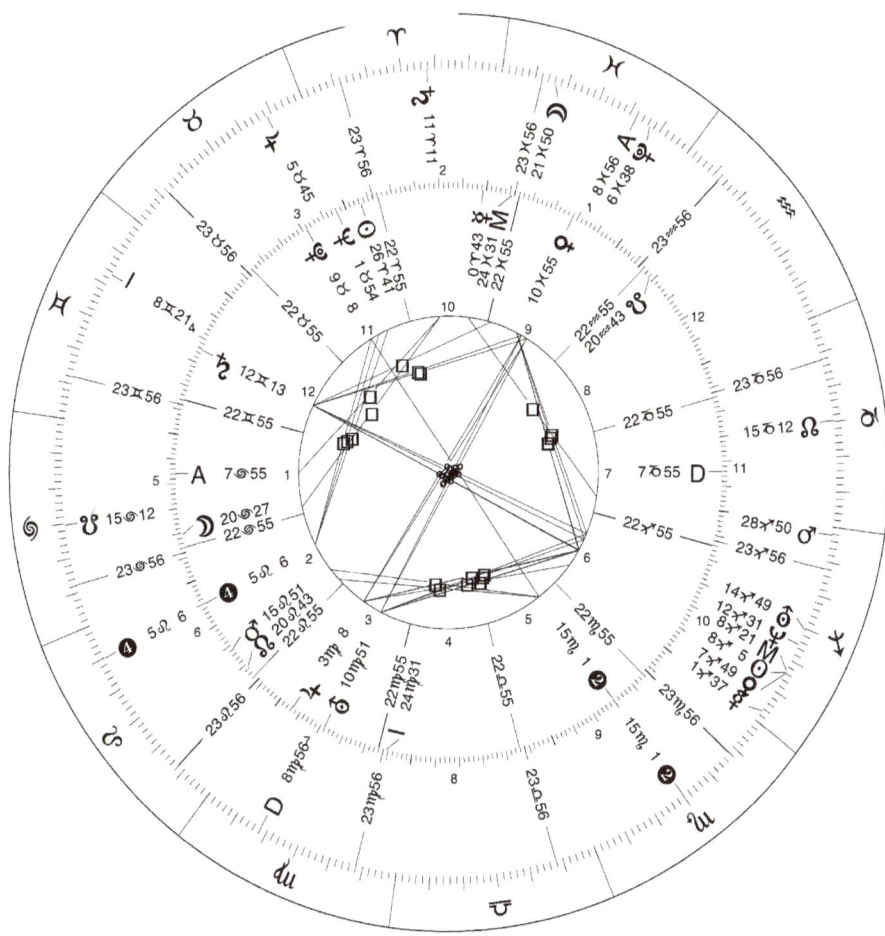

Comparison of Davis Birth (outer wheel) and Santa Clara Case (inner wheel)
(#2 indicates Antares directly opposite Aldebaran, #4 indicates Regulus)

municated (Mercury at the Galactic Center) what Field (Neptune at Galactic Center at birth and later in his legacy) had put into motion. Bancroft Davis's presence was the missing piece of a potential (his birth planets completing the T-square of the Santa Clara case) to deliver to the world a new ideology (Neptune). Though Thom Hartmann could speak about "the hand on the pen," and the man (Field) behind it, we can see that the planets and stars were also behind the hand on the pen. More accurately, we could say that the planets and stars helped create a resonant field wherein a human ideal could create a new ideology for the whole society.

During the case, the lawyers on behalf of the corporations were trying to lay claim to the Fourteenth Amendment. The defense against this by Delphin Delmas was brilliant, including his summary of the purpose of the Fourteenth Amendment:

> Its mission was to raise the humble, the downtrodden, and the oppressed to the level of the most exalted upon the broad plain of humanity—to make man the equal of man; but not to make the creature of the State—the bodiless, soulless, and mystic creature called a corporation—the equal of the creature of God.

---

conjunct the Galactic Center at 2°6' Sagittarius within 4°, and square to Pluto at 0°3' of Pisces). At his death on April 9, 1899, in Washington, D.C., Neptune lay at 29°2' of Taurus, opposite to the Galactic Center (within 4°), also opposite to Saturn at 0°18' Sagittarius, and opposite to Neptune at his birth. The bookends of his life showed Neptune obscuring or creating turbulence in the connection to the greatest concentration of suns at the Galactic Center. Birth data from Wikipedia, without time of day.

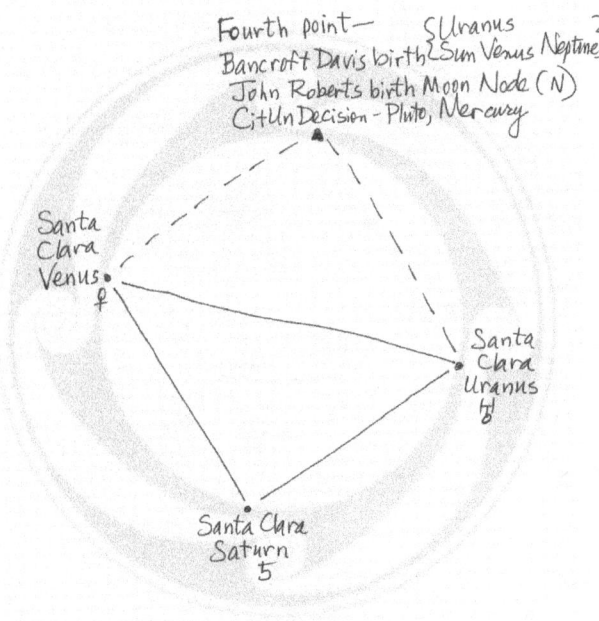

Figure 3. Neptune in Various Related Events

At Delmas's death—a picture of his legacy—Neptune lay conjunct the great star Regulus, the King (and Queen) Star. Delmas dared speak truth to power, to challenge the petty kings with the power of a truer king (figure 3).[1]

Lewis Powell

Some years later Lewis Powell became a Supreme Court judge. Though it was not revealed in the Senate hearings for his assumption of that post, in his career as a lawyer for corporations, he had written a manifesto of his philosophy stating that everything possible should be done to influence laws and courts to support the rights of corporations as people, even awarding them with rights outstripping those of natural persons. The program that he outlined had the attitude that this was for the good of the nation, of the people, and of all individuals; as some vociferous individuals might not be able to see this program's benefits, he recommended that it had to be done stealthily.[2] That memo was written on August 23, 1971, when Neptune at 6°0′ Scorpion was exactly square to the Sun at 5°32′ Lion which was in turn conjunct Regulus at 5°5′ Lion.[3] Thus we see emerging a repeated reference to the King Star, Regulus (figure 3). In this case, Neptune was in tension (square) with the Sun at the King Star laying groundwork for the 2010 CitUnDecision case.

Corporations and Free Speech

The most recent affirmation of corporations' rights as persons involves free speech. Free speech was ensured by the First Amendment to the Bill of Rights, adopted on December 15, 1791. Most people assumed that this related to the freedom of speech of natural persons. Over time, and in many cases, free speech has been claimed as a right by artificial persons, that is, by corporations.

In the CitUnDecision (recalling this as Citizens United vs. Federal Election Commission), on January 21, 2010, the Supreme Court (in a 5 to 4 decision) held that corporate funding of independent political broadcasts in candidate elections cannot be limited under the First Amendment, overruling previous decisions that limited such contributions.[4] The decision has generally been construed as recognizing corporations as persons deserving of free speech, and withdrawing all limits from that speech, furthermore affirming that money is speech. More important than

---

1 Delmas's speech was quoted in Hartmann, op. cit., 22. At Delmas's death on Aug. 1, 1928 (Wikipedia), Neptune (4°26′ Leo) lay conjunct the great star Regulus, the Heart of the Lion, one of the Royal Stars of Persia (5°5′ Leo). His speaking against the rise of corporate power was his regal legacy and what he spoke to the powers centered in Neptune.

2 Occasionally something slips out from those of this inclination, such as the statement by the then presidential candidate, Mitt Romney on Aug. 11, 2011, in Des Moines, Iowa: "Corporations are people, my friend."

3 Jeffrey Clements, *Corporations Are Not People: Why They Have More Rights than You Do and What You Can Do about It*, makes much of that memo and Lewis Powell's subsequent actions in service of corporations. Another fine analysis can be found in Jeffrey Toobin, "Money Unlimited," *New Yorker Magazine*, May 21, 2012, 36-47.

4 Text at http://supreme.justia.com/us/558/08-205/. The case was first argued on March 24, 2009, reargued on September 9, 2009, and decided on January 21, 2010. The books by Hartmann and Clements go into great detail.

the affirmation of free speech is the recognition of corporations as persons deserving of that free speech. In effect, the so-called "united citizens" were arguing that corporations should join their ranks and become citizens too. The name of this group is such a terrible misnomer that, whenever mentioned, slips through the implication that it represented the unified view of citizens. We have to remember that this does not represent the united opinion of the citizens!

On its own, the chart of the CitUnDecision (full chart at the end) does not reveal its underlying inspirations, though we might note that Neptune lies at the beginning of the Water-Carrier (Aquarius) and Uranus at the very end of the Water-Carrier, exactly at the eastern horizon. Neptune lay within 5° of opposition to the King Star, Regulus (at 5°5' Leo), the 5° orb again, this time affirming the rights of the petty kings, rather than Delmas's affirmation of the truly regal (figure 3).

However, much is revealed by comparing the CitUnDecision with the Santa Clara case, both at their final announcement (using the customary time of announcement as 10 a.m.). (The full chart appears at the end with the CitUnDecision on the outer wheel and the Santa Clara case on the inner wheel.)

What do we see about Neptune in this comparison?

- Neptune in 1886 (1°55' of the Bull, conjunct the dangerous star Algol) is closely square to Neptune in 2010 (0°28' of the Water-Carrier). The two events are linked with each other in relation to Neptune. Both are linked to the magical power of Medusa's eye to turn all who look upon it into stone.
- Both are linked to Regulus, the King Star, which in its true expression ennobles the human spirit. The CitUnDecision marks a major step backward for the ennoblement of the human spirit.
- Instead of Neptune conjunct the Sun, as in the Santa Clara case, we find Neptune at the CitUnDecision conjunct Jupiter, with the same 5° orb. What was spawned in 1886 now finds expansion (Jupiter). Both of these are in the 5° to 6° orb, which is wide for historical research, yet not so for reading individual charts. And this particular gap is repeated over and over again, recalling Marc Edmund Jones's recommendation to see orbs or gaps qualitatively rather than only quantitatively: Further apart does not only mean weaker, but also has a particular quality. Investigations of Neptune's relation to world events show that this approach is warranted.[5]

What about the T-square that Bancroft Davis' birth horoscope completed?

- That fourth point of the T-square in 1886 is indeed completed in the CitUnDecision by Mercury (12°48' Archer) and Pluto (9°9' Archer).

Thus there are several key interrelationships between "the first time" that corporations were treated as persons and the recent case expanding those powers.

What do we see about Neptune in this?

- The watery theme conventionally associated with Neptune comes through in the following complaint of a candidate for mayor in Los Angeles: "'The *flood of money* since [CitUnDecision] is *literally drowning out our voices*,' said Garcetti, who is running for mayor in 2013. 'If we're going to be moving forward in this country, we need less special interest money in the political process.'"[6]
- Relation to the Eye of Medusa, the star Algol, suggests that one follow the tale of Perseus's success in dealing with the demon witch,

---

[5] See especially Tresemer "The Signature of Neptune in World Events," op.cit. Jones's recommendation for any degree separation less than ten was to understand its quality rather than quantity.

[6] From http://latimesblogs.latimes.com/lanow/2011/12/corporate-personhood-la-constitutional-amendment.html?utm_source=feedburner&utm_medium=feed&utm_campaign=Feed%3A+lanowblog+%28L.A.+Now%29&utm_content=Google+Feedfetcher, viewed June 2012, italics added. The use of the word *literally* by the mayoral candidate asks us to see this as more than metaphor.

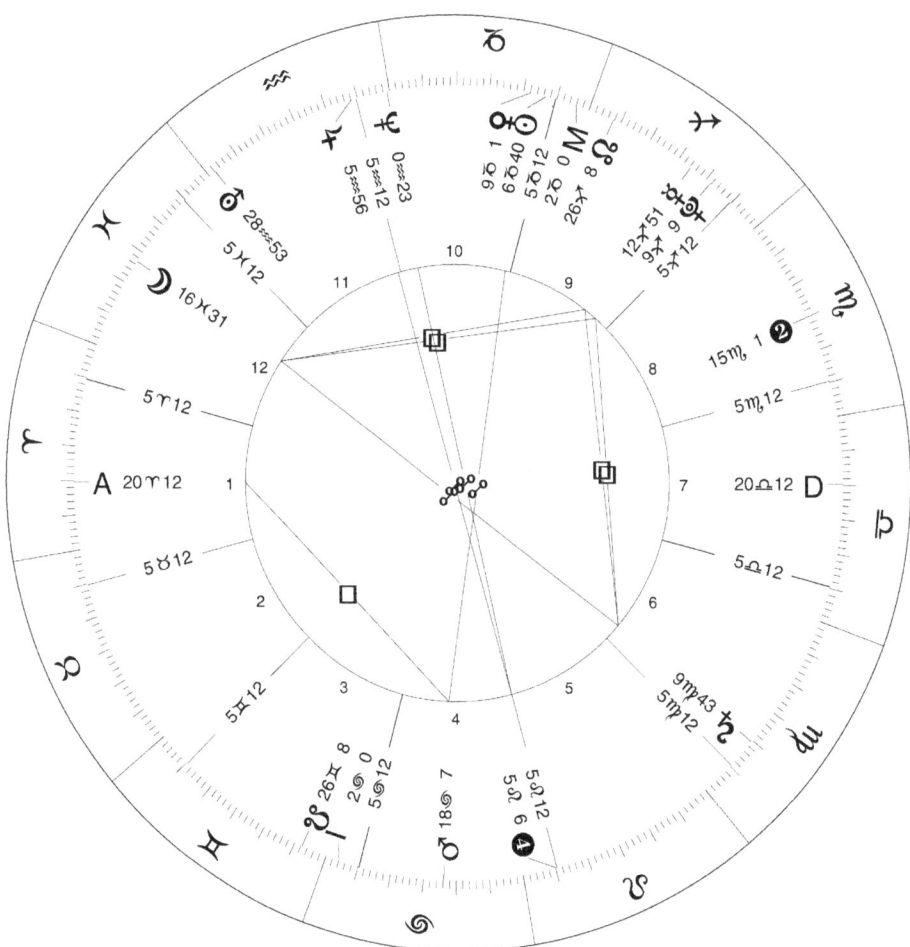

The CitUnDecision Chart, January 21, 2010, 10 a.m.
(#2 indicates Antares directly opposite Aldebaran, #4 indicates Regulus)

Medusa who can turn human beings to stone, that is, drive them back from living beings to lifeless mineral substance. As Perseus did, we must learn to see her in the cool reflection of a mirror and thus dispassionately. Following Perseus, we can move slowly backward until close enough to behead the demon and put the head with its hair of writhing snakes into a bag so that its gaze falls on no other. We must all come to be led by cool and systematic movements, as well as strong actions to cut away and cover the offending eyes of the demon of our time.

- Relation of Neptune to the King/Queen Star, Regulus, suggests that we should adopt a regal attitude—a high standard of moral demeanor, working on behalf of the whole community, which depends on the uprightness and leadership of its king/queen.

- Neptune as the concentration of ideological fervor to the extent of pushing others aside and setting into place what one feels is most important. I wondered after reviewing the births and deaths of the discoverers of Neptune, marveling that Neptune was prominent at the book-ends of their lives. I continue to marvel how Neptune comes into play in this instance when the battle over ideology has gone to new extremes.

The Key Person in the Case

Just as in the Santa Clara case, which had a right person in the right place at the right time, we have such a key figure in the CitUnDecision—not the

Corporate Personhood: The Touch of Neptune

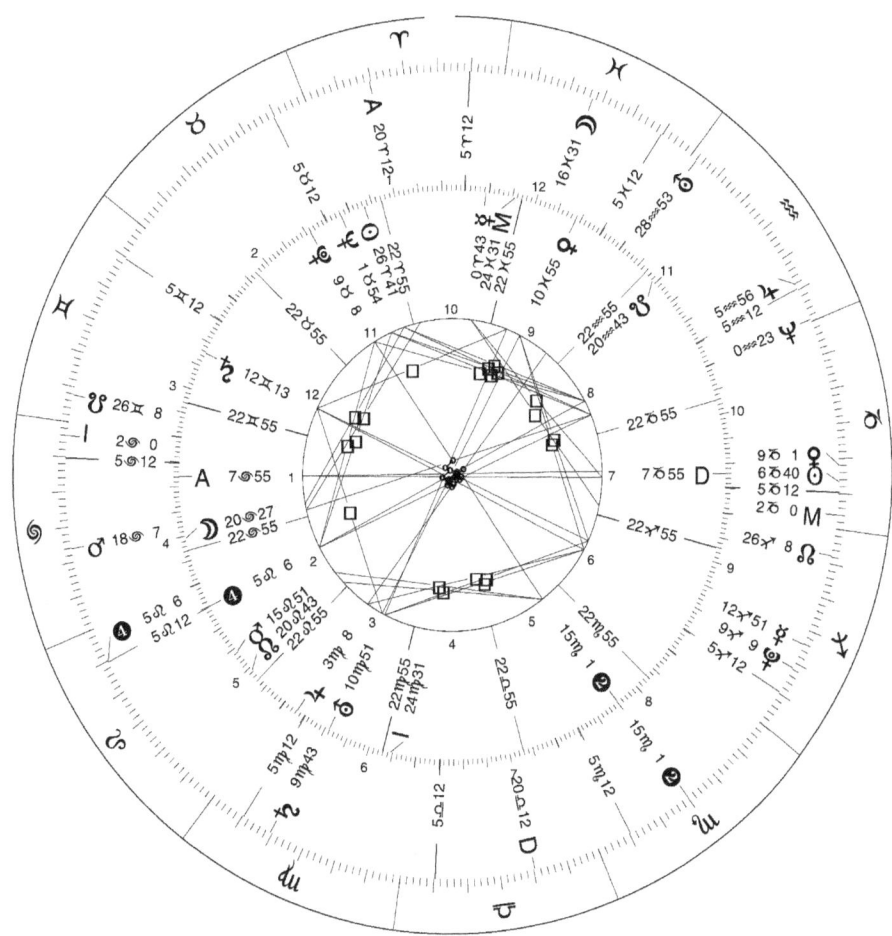

CitUnDecision (outer wheel) in comparison with Santa Clara Case (inner wheel)
(#2 indicates Antares directly opposite Aldebaran, #4 indicates Regulus)

Court Reporter this time, but rather the Chief Justice, John Roberts, Jr., who was very active in getting the CitUnDecision through his court. He was born on January 27, 1955 (noon chart, full chart at the end of this article).[1]

Just as Bancroft Davis had the Sun, Venus, Neptune, and Uranus at his birth filling the final point in the open T-square of the Santa Clara case (the T-square involving Uranus, Saturn, and Venus), so the Chief Justice had the North Moon Node (11°2' Sagittarius) on that same completion point (figure 2). The North Moon Node is traditionally understood as an indicator of the site of one's personal destiny, what one is here on earth to accomplish. This suggests that he was (and is) taking into the future this campaign that had a significant turning point in the Santa Clara case. Furthermore, that small area in Sagittarius becomes more important when we observe that the location of Pluto at the CitUnDecision was also nearby, at 9°9' Sagittarius. If one sees that the true fruit of the announcement of the Santa Clara case is the CitUnDecision, then one can see the quality of its fruit denoted by Pluto, god of riches and of the underworld.

The theme of Neptune comes round again—the location of Neptune in the CitUnDecision, at 0°23' Aquarius, lies conjunct to Chief Justice Roberts's birth-Mercury at 1°18' Aquarius. That position of Mercury is also square to Algol at 1°25' Taurus, the Eye of Medusa again. Roberts became the spokesperson (Mercury) for the new ideology (Neptune) that has been speaking through this entire series of events. Indeed he was the one who engineered that

---

1 John Roberts, Jr., Rodden databank ("X," no birth time).

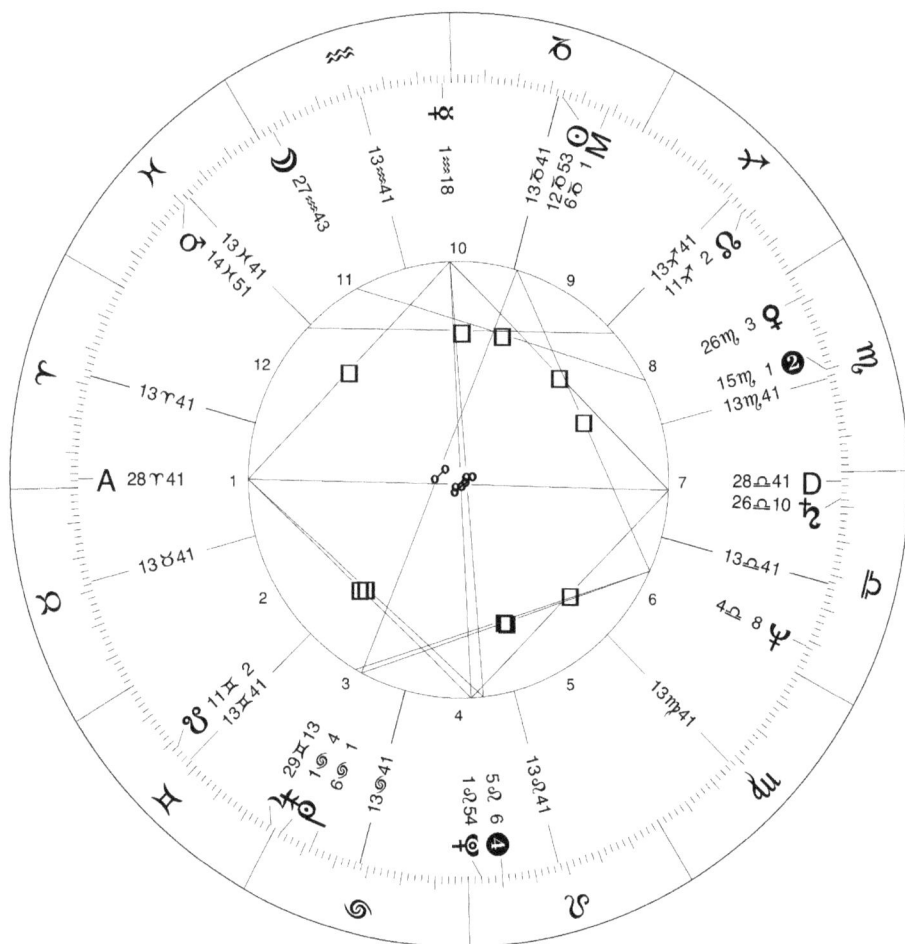

John Roberts Jr. Birth Chart (noon chart)
(#2 indicates Antares directly opposite Aldebaran, #4 indicates Regulus)

it be put into stone (an aspect of the mythology of Algol) as a decision of the Supreme Court.

THE TROUBLE WITH CORPORATIONS— TO WHOM DO THEY ANSWER?

Corporations are chartered within the laws of a state. In the past this meant that the corporation did its business in that state. It was its home. The state could dissolve the corporation, a power to the people promised in the Declaration of Independence.

In recent years, some states offered better deals for corporations to reside there. For a time Delaware hosted a very large proportion of the corporations in the United States. Now, however, many corporations are multi-local and multi-national, which has the effect of no home.

Imagine that each land mass and nation expresses the essence of an archangelic "folk soul," an ancient notion that Rudolf Steiner revived. In that case, every nation and country connects to the earth, to Nature, and to "Nature's God," the terms from the Declaration of Independence that began this process of defining personhood. Just as the "Creator" and "Nature's God" endow human beings with the rights of personhood, so can the state extend those powers to the fictions of corporations. But the power to endow has now been seized by the corporations themselves, who have disowned the land and authority of their creators and gone out on their own. Thus they are no longer beholden to their creators.

The trouble with corporations is that they do not die. Nor do they sleep, nor eat in a way that we can understand. They have none of the rhythms that characterize human beings. As collective thought forms created by many, they have become ghosts that seem to wield power over those who imagine that they are in control. Once carefully monitored by the people—and the folk souls—in the places where they operated, now they run rampant, with little mercy for the humans who spawned them, the humans who still need to eat and sleep ... and die. Corporations now gather huge sums of money to purchase the support of those politicians whose job had originally been meant to represent the people of an area, who in turn represented the folk souls guiding human relations with the Nature's God of a land. Corporations have, in effect, become a kind of folk soul of their own, mimicking the archangels, without the sense of responsibility held by that office.

Treating a corporation as a person, as a human being, has created a dangerous monster, a golem, a Frankenstein.[1] What was the servant is fast becoming a master. This entire exercise seems poised to prepare human beings for the step of recognizing that artificial intelligence has equal status to human beings. Then the spokespersons who had fought for recognition of inalienable rights will find those rights seized by aliens.

How can an individual respond to the rise of corporate power through the ruse of personhood, especially when one sees humans acting as spokespersons for planetary forces, especially powerful in the case of Bancroft Davis? One caution occurs when you think you're fated to be in the right place at the right time—in that situation, you must analyze your own birth circumstances (your birth chart), to see how much of this is your individuality speaking, and how might other influences be working through you.

Hartmann and Clement have recommendations for action that can be studied, suggestions for social action in relation to the hegemony of corporations. Already some states are fighting back with a constitutional amendment to restrict personhood to human persons, but will the elected officials who have benefited from corporate largesse vote in such a change?

Astrologically speaking, one can become aware of personal and world events when planets cross that fourth point in figure 2; for the Sun, this is December 26 to 28. One can also become aware of when the Sun moves past Neptune; for a 5° orb, this is February 17 to 28, 2014, and February 20 to March 3, 2015 (in opposition, August 21 to September 1, 2013, and August 23 to September 3, 2014).

The present study suggests that, most importantly, one identify the true folk souls rather than their artificial look-alikes, that is, to relate to the sacred powers of geography and particular places, to language, to national and community destiny—to the archangels—directly and with increasing intimacy. From this relationship comes the moral guidance and moral courage to act responsibly. Recommitment to the folk souls of our own regions will assist us to counter the rebellious activities of the inhuman folk souls of corporations.

With acknowledgement to the help of William Bento and Robert Schiappacasse. A different version of this research has been published by International Astrologer *(journal of the International Society for Astrological Research). More discussion on the Declaration and the Fourteenth Amendment may be found at www.StarWisdom.org > Research.*

---

1 From Martin Buber's terse appraisal in his proposal of "I–Thou" relations (human, warm, expansive, heartful) and "I–It" relations (mechanical, cold, contracted, functional, death-dealing): "The severed It of institutions is a golem." In Jewish legend, a golem is a clay figure brought to life by magic—not even a Frankenstein made of human parts. It moves and acts and haunts its creators (Buber, *I and Thou*, p. 93). The human parts necessary to make a Frankenstein would be the participants (or wage slaves) of the corporations.

REUNITING PSYCHE WITH ASTRO-LOGOS
A STUDY IN THE LIGHT OF THE URANUS–PLUTO CYCLE

William Bento, Ph.D.

INTRODUCTION TO THE TIMELINESS OF THE STUDY

In the *Journal of Transpersonal Psychology* (Nov. 2012), Stanislav Grof, MD, published his article "Revision and Re-Enchantment of Psychology: Legacy of Half a Century of Consciousness Research." Grof, a founder of the transpersonal psychology movement, is widely known for his use of psychedelic drugs and radical breathing techniques in what he termed a "holotropic" approach, as well as co-creating with his wife Christina, the concept of "spiritual emergency" to identify individuals undergoing disorientation due to unanticipated extraordinary states of consciousness. In the conclusion of this article, Grof emphasizes that the future of consciousness research relies on an inclusion and intimate relationship with archetypal psychology and astrology. This particular position assumed by Grof is bound to be a radical departure for most clinical psychiatrists and psychologists, including many transpersonalists.

This article strikes me as a timely clarion call for transdisciplinary efforts in the search for a paradigm that remains faithful to the roots of humanity's spiritual heritage, and yet gives hope for a new development of consciousness. For a reunion to occur between psyche and astro-logos, we must first reevaluate their respective origins and current states. By doing so we may find the necessary forces for a renewal of each and a union between the two that opens up a new way of thinking about the sources of spiritual activity innately present in every human soul. Such a discovery may re-empower the soul to overcome the enchantment of the materialistic paradigm from which we now all suffer.

It is my conviction that the spiritual scientific path laid out by Rudolf Steiner at the outset of the twentieth century provides an invaluable aid in this particular challenge of reuniting psyche with astro-logos. Through a historical and phenomenological perspective I intend to stress the value of this endeavor for our time. Although this study cannot convey every significant detail worth considering, important highlights mentioned in this study can serve to inspire others to enter into a dialogue that aims to raise consciousness about the meaningfulness of the axiom, "As above, so below," or to rephrase it for our particular context, "As the stars go, so does the soul turn."

Stanislav Grof along with Abraham Maslow (1908–1970) coined the phrase "Transpersonal Psychology" in 1965–1966 as a way of describing a unique discipline arising from the foundations of Humanistic Psychology. Although the specific term, *Transpersonal Psychology* was first used by William James (1842–1910) in 1905 in his notes preparing for a course in psychology at Harvard University, credit has historically been given to Grof and Maslow for their willingness to confront the metaphysical assumptions of a materialistically based psychology that was being questioned in the main halls of academia during the tumultuous times of the 1960s. The ground-shaking breakthrough innate to Transpersonal Psychology rested upon an embrace of what mainstream psychology termed *anomalous phenomena,* related to the mystical nature of consciousness, the multiple dimensions of the human psyche, and the validity of spirituality as an essential attribute for the human soul.

Transpersonal psychology is a school of psychology that studies the transpersonal, self-transcendent, and spiritual dimensions of the human experience. Transpersonal experiences may be defined as "experiences in which the sense of identity or self extends through and beyond (*trans*) the individual or personal to encompass wider aspects of humankind, life, psyche, or cosmos" (Walsh and Vaughan, 1993a). A short definition from the *Journal of Transpersonal Psychology* suggests that transpersonal psychology "is concerned with the study of humanity's highest potential and with the recognition, understanding, and realization of unitive, spiritual, and transcendent states of consciousness" (Lajoie and Shapiro, 1992).

Please note that these descriptions do not pertain to the often-used term *altered states of consciousness*. Although that term is often associated with transpersonal psychology, it is an inaccurate description, for altered states of consciousness can also refer to disorientation, impairment of intellectual functions, and subsequent amnesia. These states may be clinically important to investigate, but they lack therapeutic and heuristic potential. Grof has insisted on using the term *holotropic*, a word that literally means "oriented toward wholeness." In this respect *holotropic consciousness* is more apt a term to describe the intention of transpersonal psychology and the proposition that the human soul is connected to something much greater than itself.

A school of psychology that is quite in accord with transpersonal psychology is anthroposophic psychology (or *Psychosophy*, literally meaning "soul wisdom"), based on Rudolf Steiner's Spiritual Science. It has been more than a century since Steiner gave indications for Psychosophy. Its development has been slow compared to other psychological disciplines and approaches, yet its roots are deep and its time of emergence seems to be heralded by the recent founding of the International Federation of Anthroposophic Psychotherapists Association in Dornach, Switzerland, on September 15, 2012 (see bibliography for W. Bento, "A Report on the Medical Section Conference..." Sept. 13–16, 2012).

Within the anthroposophic psychology paradigm, the emphasis is shifted from mind to soul. For the anthroposophic psychotherapist, the word *soul* is not an abstraction or a romantic notion. It fires the imagination of the living expression of a spiritual being united with the stars that is undergoing the trials and tribulations of becoming human. The soul has at its core a vast repository memory of this ongoing becoming process. Soul has access to a past that is greater than one's own personal biography. It retains the sacred space for the "I" to be present and longs to receive the spirit's creative powers from the future so as to become a free co-creator in earthly and cosmic existence. Indeed, anthroposophic psychology rests on a cosmological foundation that embraces the unity of psyche and astro-logos. Distinct from the transpersonalist reliance on adopting perennial philosophical ideas, anthroposophic psychotherapists stand firmly in the knowledge and practice of Spiritual Science as developed by Rudolf Steiner. For the anthroposophic psychotherapist, it has become abundantly clear that the human soul has become a battleground. The enterprise of engaging in anthroposophic psychotherapy has the implicit task of preserving the dignity of the human being in the face of so much inhumanity. Between the primitive driving forces of animalism and the deceptive sway of demonic adversarial forces, the soul seeks a new dynamic state of balance—a state of being truly human.

INTRODUCTION TO THE URANUS–PLUTO CYCLE

The cycle of life is mirrored in the cycle of the planetary motions in the Heavens. Dane Rudhyar (1895–1985), a modern Renaissance man, described in his book, *The Lunation Cycle: A Key to Understanding Personality*, that astrology is a technique for the study of life cycles. The lunation cycle is one of our most archetypal of life cycles, albeit it involves two celestial lights—Sun and Moon—and not the planets. It refers to the synodic period of the Moon (from new moon to new moon), which lasts on an average 29 days 12 hours 44 minutes. Rudhyar describes the lunation cycle as "a cycle of transformations, a cycle of relatedness" between the psyche and the realm of planetary relationships.

> Spirit operates creatively only where relatedness is given a basic significance as a dynamic factor having a cyclic rhythm of its own; and as a spiritual evolution in man is polarized by

the need for total consciousness in selfhood, it follows that to live spiritually is to live in the consciousness of relationship. This means that it is essential for human beings to understand the cyclic nature and the cyclic laws of relationship; for only through such an understanding can the individuals adjust themselves to, and fully grow in spirit from, the experiences of relationship. Modern psychology is striving to give to the confused individuals of our day a deep, all-inclusive understanding of the values and meaning of relationship; and this, too, should be the goal of astrology (*astro-logos*). (Rudhyar, 1946, p. 18)

The Uranus–Pluto cycle is 127.30 years in length. To understand the meaning of its relatedness, a brief characterization of the nature of Uranus and Pluto should be given prior to giving definition to the cycle of Uranus–Pluto. To do this I shall draw upon Richard Tarnas's epochal book, *Cosmos and Psyche: Intimations of a New World View*, and the vast work of Rudolf Steiner, both sources I have been able to confirm as worthy and credible from my own forty-two years as a student and practitioner of the art and science of astrology.

From an astrological perspective, "the unanimous consensus among astrologers is that the planet Uranus is empirically associated with the principle of change, rebellion, freedom, liberation, reform and revolution, and the unexpected breakup of structures, with sudden surprises, revelations and awakenings, lightning-like flashes of insight…creativity and originality" (Tarnas, 2006). With regard to Pluto, which—despite astronomers' recent demotion of its classification from planet—is regarded by the astrological community as "associated with the principle of elemental power, depth, and intensity; with what compels, empowers and intensifies whatever it touches, sometimes to overwhelming and catastrophic extremes; with primordial instincts…destructive and regenerative, cathartic and transformative." (Tarnas, 2006).

From an anthroposophic viewpoint, Uranus can be related to what Steiner refers to in his book *Theosophy* as the fifth region in spiritland. It is from this region that the "spirit self" formulates and administrates incarnational intentions for a lifetime. Many esoteric and psychological schools know this "spirit self" as having the nature of the higher, true self. Steiner states in reference to the "spirit self" dwelling in the fifth region of spiritland:

> [The self] feels itself to be a member of the world's divine order, and the laws and limitations of earthly life do not touch its innermost being. The strength needed for everything that it carries out comes from the spiritual world. But this spiritual world is a unity, and those who live in it know that the eternal has worked to create the past. They are also able to determine their future direction in accordance with the eternal. (Steiner, 1994, pp. 144–145)

Most significant to an anthroposophic characterization of Uranus, as it is associated with the human being, is its potential to foster free-thinking (thinking independent from sense perceptions) and to ignite imaginative capacities within the soul life. From a transpersonal view this relates to the imaginal mind, which lives in a world of possibilities. As a soul capacity Uranus engenders the ability to see both the laws for transformation and the means to facilitate creative changes needed for self-development, as well as global development.

Steiner's view of the seventh region of spiritland can easily be related to the planet Pluto. Beyond the mythical correspondence made with Pluto as a sphere of the underworld or the realm of death and rebirth, there is the esoteric reality of the ever-transcendent nature of the human being, the Atman, or "spirit body" (formerly referred to as "spirit man"). Steiner sees the dwelling place of the "Spirit body" as being in the seventh region of spiritland. There the source of all life is known, including the deep and seemingly unfathomable riddles of human karma and destiny. "Spirit body" understands the laws of reincarnation as the essential guiding principles for spiritual development. Most significant to an anthroposophic characterization of Pluto, as it is associated with the human being, is its potential to purify the will to do the good in the face of evil, and to awaken intuitive and prophetic capacities within the soul life.

Tarnas describes the Uranus–Pluto cycle from an archetypal-mythological view giving ample evidence to his interpretation by citing many historical revolutions in the cultural sphere, from the French Revolution to the Counter-Cultural Movement of the 1960s (Tarnas, 2006, pp. 141–205). It is a fascinating documentation of the correlation between the cycle of Uranus–Pluto with the Promethean (ascribed to Uranus) and Dionysian (ascribed to Pluto) archetypal powers with the shaping of the human psyche through radical changes of prevailing paradigms. In his research, Tarnas followed the Uranus–Pluto cycle through major aspects between them (conjunctions = 0°, oppositions = 180°, and squares = 90° or 270°). For the purposes of this study I shall replicate this procedure, but focus on a subtle yet universal theme of the Uranus–Pluto cycle (i.e., the evolutionary development of soul consciousness to obtain the cosmic consciousness associated with the planetary cycles). It is deeply related to the longing in the human soul (psyche) to reunite with the unitive experience of the cosmos—an essential distinguishing trait found in the development of transpersonal psychology, as well as an ancient cardinal objective of astrology (astro-logos) for millennia.

As we unfold the cycles of Uranus–Pluto from the time of consciousness soul (beginning, according to Steiner, in 1413 CE) to the present, we shall see patterns of paradigmatic shifts of worldviews; we shall see how perceptions that the human being has of itself and its existence change. The consciousness soul Age demands an awakening to the true sense of Self and a courageous willingness to discern and confront evil. In Rudolf Steiner's prophetic statements and sobering assessments of the unfolding of this age, it is made clear that humanity is in need of greater capacities of cognition to rightly understand the supersensible world (known to many transpersonalists as the imaginal reality). Steiner expresses an urgent need for a greater certainty of the territory that is fast approaching every post-modern human being, a territory known as the threshold between the physical/earthly world and the spiritual world. This study is being undertaken to give some insights into what is emerging in our time as significant factors contributing to a new paradigm, and specifically to reaffirm the often forgotten relatedness between the True Self and the Starry World.

Although the following table contains five cycles of Uranus–Pluto, it is not possible to give a detailed account of all aspects in this period extending from 1450 to 2083. However, a reading of Richard Tarnas's book *Cosmos and Psyche: Intimations of a New World View* (2006) will provide the reader with many significant insights as to the nature of this planetary cycle. The focus for this study shall be primarily upon the first conjunction and waxing square of Uranus–Pluto, covering the period of 1450 to 1507, with the fifth conjunction and waxing square of Uranus–Pluto, covering the period of 1960 to 2020. The author's premise is that the seeds for a new world order laid out in the first Uranus–Pluto cycle are germinating in the fifth Uranus–Pluto cycle that is now underway. Furthermore, the author contends that no new and progressive healthy world order is possible without a recovery of the intimate relatedness of the human soul (psyche) with the planetary revolutions of the heavens (astro-logos). Finally, the author encourages the reader to place his or her own experiences into the context of the study, for each of us are living through the germination period of a new culture. There is no wish to state that we are repeating the historical events of the Renaissance, but there are two implicit aims to have the reader grasp: 1) the thematic issues that are common to the Renaissance; and 2) to sense the challenging and exciting prospects of being in the midst of a major paradigmatic change for humankind.

HISTORICAL ROOTS OF THE URANUS–PLUTO CYCLE OF THE CONSCIOUSNESS SOUL AGE

Prior to taking our starting point for this study with the first Uranus–Pluto conjunction in the period of 1450 to 1461 we shall examine the background out of which the cultural and spiritual impulses that flowed into the conjunction were rooted. Immediately we shall find ourselves examining the genesis

The Uranus–Pluto Cycle in the Consciousness Soul Age

Aspects: 4 Cardinal Major Aspects of 5 Cycles of Uranus–Pluto	Exact Alignment: Less than 1°	Orb Values: Degree Distance=Conjunctions Oppositions are 15° Squares are 10°
Opposition prior to 1413 commencement of consciousness soul age	1398–1399	1392–1404
First waning square of consciousness soul age	1422–1423	1418–1428
First conjunction	1455–1456	1450–1461
Waxing square	1496–1500	1489–1507
Opposition	1538–1540	1533–1545
Waning square	1566–1567	1563–1570
Second conjunction	1597–1598	1592–1602
Waxing square	1623–1624	1620–1627
Opposition	1648–1649	1643–1654
Waning square	1678–1680	1674–1683
Third conjunction	1710–1711	1705–1716
Waxing square	1755–1758	1749–1764
Opposition	1792–1794	1787–1798
Waning square	1820–1821	1816–1824
Fourth conjunction	1850–1851	1845–1856
Waxing square	1876–1877	1873–1880
Opposition	1901–1902	1896–1907
Waning square	1932–1934	1928–1937
Fifth conjunction	1965–1966	1960–1972
Waxing square	2012–2015	2007–2020
Opposition	2046–2048	2041–2053
Waning square	2077–2080	2073–2083

of the Renaissance as it began in the region of Florence, Italy, and the emergence of the esoteric fraternity of the Rosicrucian Order founded by Christian Rosenkreutz between 1407 and 1414. In the cultural phenomenon of the Renaissance we can imagine the flourishing of the *world soul*, and in the Rosicrucian Order we can sense humanity's relatedness with the *spiritual world*. Although the author will present these two impulses as distinct streams shaping the consciousness soul Age, it should not be understood as separate but as complimentary streams—two streams working toward one aim, the birthing of a new world view.

Cultural Stream

At the outset of the consciousness soul age in 1413 CE, the Medici family became bankers to the papacy, which signified a position of economic dominance throughout Europe. Cosimo de Giovanni de Medici (1389–1564), known as the Elder, accompanied the Antipope John XXIII to the Council of Constance in 1415 and returned to Florence in the same year to be named the "Priore of the Republic." His influence upon shaping the Renaissance culture, politics, and economics is second to none. He used his vast wealth of 150,000 gold florins (equivalent to 30 million US dollars in today's market) to direct the affairs of Florence and northern Italy. Although he did not hold official public office, all political questions were resolved in his home. Most significant to our study is Cosimo's role as a patron of the arts and the founding of the Florentine Platonic Academy. He was patron to the Palazzo Medici and to the architectural wonder of Santa Maria del Fiora (Duomo) designed and built by Brunelleschi. He also sponsored the artists Fra Angelico, Fra Filippo Lippi, and Donatello. Cosimo had a deep love and interest in the wisdom books of the ancient cultures. His vision was to make Florence the center of wisdom for the new age, and in that respect he financed the rediscovery of philosophical and esoteric tracts from Rome, Greece, Egypt, and the Middle East. He established the Bibliotheca Medicea Laurenziana in Florence in 1444. Later, he commissioned a young sixteen-year-old lad named Marsilio Ficino to translate the many works of Plato from Greek into Latin. Cosimo, in the annals of history, epitomizes the humanistic responsibility of the civic duty that comes with wealth.

Although Cosimo founded the Florentine Platonic Academy in 1440, it was not until the 1450s that Marsilio Ficino emerged as the undisputed teacher of the Academy at Careggi. His lectures and philosophical letters of that time, wherein he often drew upon the four sects of philosophy (Platonists, Aristotelians, Stoics, and Epicureans), brought him wide acclaim. In this period Uranus and Pluto were conjunct in the sign of the Crab, intimating a radical shift in the worldview of the time. All things material in the hands of the gifted were transformed into works of art dedicated to the glory of the Divine. Reevaluations of the path to the Divine were experienced as disruptive, causing the stronghold of the Church grave consternation. What was once wisdom transmitted by word of mouth or symbolic and sacred visual works of art became materialized into print, the book. The Gutenberg press with its metal plates made books more and more accessible to the masses. This time of a new dispensation of knowledge and wisdom was symbolically captured in Ghiberti's completion of the "Gates of Paradise" at the Florence Baptistery in 1452.

Marsilio Ficino may well have been the last individual in the 5,000-year period of Kali Yuga, which ended in 1899, to have fully understood and articulated the intimate relatedness between psyche and astro-logos. For this reason alone, Ficino can be considered the quintessential Renaissance individual. He, like his father, was a physician, but his professional competency knew no bounds. He was also a philosopher, musician, poet, theologian/priest, astrologer, and a person of profound and beautiful letters. Historians have unanimously recognized Ficino's genius for his translations of and commentaries on Plato, Plotinus, and the Hermetic Corpus. Ficino's great legacy is his defense of the immortality of the soul and its innate natural appetite to be united with the movements of the planets in the Heavenly sky above. The *Platonic Theology*, written between 1469 and 1474, subtitled *On the Immortality of Souls*, expresses both his deep understanding of a theory of theology and a practice of sacred psychology.

Allen and Hankins convey Ficino's sentiment regarding the nature of the soul in the first chapter of his *Platonic Theology*:

> Were the soul not immortal, no creature would be more miserable than man.... Man alone never rests in his present habit of living: he alone is a pilgrim in these regions and cannot rest on the journey as long as he aspires to his celestial homeland, which all of us see. (2001–2006, 1.1, vol. 1, pp.14–15)

Ficino did not ascribe to a dualism of body and mind as later formulated by René Descartes (1596–1650), but saw the threefold nature of the body, soul, and spirit as the fundamental reality in which the human being shares existence both with the material world and with the divine, the soul being the mediator between the two. Like his fellow Florentine Dante (1265–1321), author of the world classic literary work *The Divine Comedy*, Ficino advocated that love, not wisdom, links all things together. For him love flows first from God into existing things and in the human soul becomes "spirit," the power that binds human beings to one another. Ficino's conception of love was intimately linked with the experience of beauty.

> The splendor of the highest good is refulgent in individual things, and where it blazes the more fittingly, there it especially attracts someone gazing upon it, excites his consideration, seizes and occupies him as he approaches, and compels him both to venerate such splendor as the divinity beyond all others, and to strive for nothing else but to lay aside his former nature and to become that splendor itself. Once this attraction has taken place the soul burns with a divine radiance that is reflected in the man (or woman) of beauty as in a mirror, and (then) caught up by that radiance secretly as by a hook, he is drawn upward in order to become God. And God would be a 'wicked tyrant' if he implanted in human beings this aspiration without allowing the possibility of its eventual fulfillment. (Allen and Hankins, 2001–2006, 14.14, vol. 4, 222–223)

The Polish Rider *(Christian Rosenkreutz)* by Rembrandt or Willem Drost, c. 1650

Spiritual Stream

Shortly prior to this remarkable transition time in human history defined by the Renaissance in Florence, an extraordinary initiation of the first soul to be initiated by the Christ (Lazarus–John) arrived on the world stage, albeit hidden from public view. This individual was the legendary Christian Rosenkreutz (CR), who was the last descendant of the Germelshausen, a German family of nobility that embraced Albigensian (i.e., Cathar) doctrines, combining Gnostic and Christian beliefs. For their beliefs the whole family, excluding Christian Rosenkreutz, was put to death. Legend has it that he was four or five years old at the time and then was taken into a monastery where he was educated. When still "in his growing years," CR set out, accompanied by a monk, on a pilgrimage to the Holy Land. The monk died in Cyprus and CR then went on to study in Damascus. He left there having acquired great medical knowledge and skill and proceeded to "Damkar" in Arabia where he learned of the secrets of nature from a group of wise men who had been expecting him. They also taught him Arabic, astrology, physics, and mathematics. Prior to his departure from Arabia he was introduced to the Book M, which contained the secrets of the universe. His travels led him to Egypt where he

Marsilio Ficino, Cosimo de Medici, and Pico della Mirandola

studied botany and zoology. At the Fez he learned magic and the Cabala. These journeys and the learning he acquired, prepared CR to inaugurate the modern pathway into the spiritual world. As he journeyed and gathered the esoteric knowledge existent at the time, in the heavens Uranus formed the last waning square to Pluto. It was as though CR was destined to prepare the new age on the foundation of the perennial wisdom of the ages past. He eventually returned to Germany at approximately the age of twenty-nine and a half (Saturn return time) in 1407. Christian Rosenkruetz then assembled seven disciples and founded the Fraternity of the Rosy Cross. Under his direction a Temple called *Sanctus Spiritus* (House of the Holy Spirit) was built. Approximately at the same time that Cosimo de Giovanni de Medici assumed his leadership role in Florence Italy, Christian Rosenkreutz was teaching the initiatory principles of Christian Hermeticism and the secrets of alchemy to his disciples of the Rosy Cross, thus setting the foundations for a spiritual path suitable to the consciousness soul Age.

By the time of the Uranus–Pluto conjunction of 1455 to 1456, the Fraternity of the Rosy Cross had been well established throughout Europe. There is no better account of its teachings and its mission than Rudolf Steiner's twenty lectures, *The Temple Legend* (1985), in Berlin from May 23, 1904, to January 2, 1906, and the thirteen lectures compiled as *Esoteric Christianity and the Mission of Christian Rosenkreutz* (1984) from September 17, 1911, to December 18, 1912.

THE WAXING SQUARE OF URANUS TO PLUTO: 1489–1507

Cultural Stream

During this period of time the influences flowing out of the Florentine Platonic Academy were reaching its peak. Marsilio Ficino's students—Leonardo da Vinci, Michelangelo, Raphael, Sandro Boticelli, Lorenzo de Medici, Angelo Polziano, Leon Battista Alberti, Cristoforo Landino, and Pico della Mirandola—were at their prime. This group was as prolific a group of creative geniuses the world has ever known. Under Ficino's tutelage and his fervent passionate vision for a transformed culture based on an esoteric Christianity, great immemorial works of art and literature were created.

Ordained as a priest in the Catholic Church in 1473, Ficino later became a canon of Santa Maria del Fiore, Brunelleschi's famous domed cathedral of Florence. From this time forward he tirelessly sustained three professions—physician, priest, and philosopher—tending to healing and giving guidance for the body, soul, and spirit. The Academy was for him a circle of Platonic friends to whom for decades he wrote the most loving and moving letters. His qualification for being a friend was written in one of his letters to a German friend and correspondent, Martin Prenninger in 1491: "Know that all of my friends are indeed well-tested both with respect to their intellectual talent and their character. I have never considered anyone a friend unless I also determined that he had joined literary learning together with uprightness of character" (Ficino, M., 1985, p.45).

In 1489, Ficino published his most controversial works in the eyes of the Church, *Three Books on Life*. Book 1 was *On Caring for the Health of Students*. It begins with Doctor Ficino describing the nine guides of scholars. An excerpted passage of chapter 1 gives a sense for how Ficino was able to integrate disciplines through his vast knowledge of the ancient mysteries and convey his teachings in a very practical manner.

> Those who begin that bitter, arduous and long journey that leads with assiduous labor to the highest temple of the nine Muses, find they need guides for the journey. The first of these are the three in heaven who lead us, then the three in the soul, and finally the three on earth. In heaven, Mercury either compels us or exhorts us, making us begin the journey by inquiring about the Muses. Mercury is in charge of all inquiry. Then Apollo lights up with a rich splendor both the souls that seek and the things that are sought; so that we find whatever we seek carefully. Then comes most gracious Venus, mother of the Muses. With her nourishing and happy rays she constructs everything and decorates it so that whatever had been sought at Mercury's instigation, and whatever had been found with Apollo's showing it, is now surrounded with her marvelous and salutary pleasure. Venus always makes one love it and enjoy it. Then there are the three guides of the journey in the soul: an ardent and stable will, acumen of the mind, and a tenacious memory. Finally, the three on earth: a father who is prudent, a teacher who is excellent, and a doctor who is brilliant. (Ficino, 1980, p. 3; trans. revised)

In book 2, *How to Prolong your Life,* he points to the need for prudent judgment: "Long life is not only a matter of what the Fates have put in store for us from the beginning, but something our diligence takes care of as well. The astrologers admit this, too." Book 3, *On Making your Life Agree with the Heavens,* addresses the individual human soul and its relatedness to the *Anima Mundi*, the Soul of the World, as it is seen in the motions of the planets against the background of the zodiac.

In his *Three Books of Life,* Ficino provides his students with an exhaustive manual on the theory and practice of a cosmologically based spiritual psychology. A cursory read of Ficino's writings indicates how deeply connected he was with the great initiates of the previous ages. It was not only the pervasive references to astrological principles that drew negative attention from the Church but Ficino's explicit directions for ritualized activation of occult properties of certain stars that could be drawn down from the heavens and utilized on Earth. In his defense, Ficino quoted from the *Hermetic Corpus* that Hermes Trismegistus (thrice great, owing to his stature as king, philosopher, and priest) taught that in order to capture the power of any of the stars, ritual magic must be executed. Ficino particularly considered Hermes as his model for an ideal teacher, along with Zoroaster, who he praised as the "seer of the wisdom of the stars."

Spiritual Stream:

Christian Rosenkreutz died in 1484 at the age of 106. Much of his actual teaching does not come directly to us from any of his writing but through members of the Rosicrucian Order. The three Rosicrucian Manifestos, published early in the seventeenth century, reveal much of what we know of his life and work. The first of these manifestos was *Fama Fraternitatis Rosae Crucis* (1614); the second was *Confessio Fraternitatis* (1615); and the last was *The Chymical Wedding of Christian Rosenkreutz* (1616). These three manifestos announced the Dawn of a New Age and proclaimed a universal reform of science, religion, and society based on the wisdom of Christian Hermeticism. It is not out of the question to infer that the New Age being referred to in the Rosicrucian manifestos is characteristically the same as what Steiner calls "the consciousness soul age."

Given that Christian Rosenkreutz was not on the Earth during the time of the Uranus waxing square to Pluto (1496–1500), one wonders what might have been the Rosicrucians' response to this celestial sign. In my own deliberation, I have read and reread Steiner's lecture of Epiphany, 1924, in Dornach, Switzerland (Steiner, 1964), to understand how the death of Christian Rosenkreutz may have signified a new relationship between him and the remaining members of the Rosicrucian Order. Steiner describes a mystic, meditative, pious mood of soul that was developed within the close circle around Christian Rosenkreutz. Of the original seven who formed allegiance to Christian Rosenkreutz, three were able to enter the spiritual world under certain conditions, and the other four were capable of translating what the three were able to bring from their experiences in the spiritual world. In this particular lecture I believe there is a possibility of understanding something of the nature that may have occurred with the Rosicrucians around the time of the Uranus waxing square to Pluto.

> There were at such times, in their external bodily nature, wonderful, lovely, and beautiful radiance in their countenances, which shone like the Sun; and they wrote down, in symbols, revelations that they received from the spiritual world. These symbolic revelations were the first pictures that revealed to the Rosicrucians what it behooved them to know of the spiritual world. The pictures contained a kind of philosophy, a kind of theology and a kind of medicine.... These brothers, whose destiny it was to bring the symbols from the spiritual world, could write them down only when they returned again into ordinary consciousness: "We have been among the stars and among the spirits of the stars, and have found the old teachers of the occult knowledge." (Steiner, 1965, pp. 38–39; trans. revised)

Steiner goes on to say, "What had been thus received from the spiritual world in symbols was afterward communicated to small groups organized by the first Rosicrucians." As is the case in most cultural phenomena groups of various differing dispositions, some attempted to duplicate this experience without the prerequisite preparation, particularly mediums and astrologers. It then became very difficult to weed out the charlatans from the original Rosicrucians. Beside the very genuine mystical, meditative, and pious mood of soul the Rosicrucians also possessed a quality of brotherhood born out of their interdependence, which was not easily replicable. In this regard Steiner remarked that the Rosicrucians gradually felt "how in the evolution of humanity toward freedom the bond between humanity and the gods would be completely severed were it not kept whole by this kind of brotherhood, in which one looks to the other, in which one in fact depends on the other."

As charlatanry grew more pervasive at the end of the fifteenth century, the laity could not determine whether revelations were good or evil. With this uncertainty and the widespread anxiety that accompanied it, an intense fear of all knowledge became a predominant secular position. This was exemplified in the figure of Girolamo Savonrola (1452–1498), the Florentine Dominican friar and priest who prophesied that Florence would become the New Jerusalem. His own apocalyptic visions and his vehement passions against the Medici family and the Platonic Academy led him to inaugurate the "bonfire of vanities" in 1495, an event in which he burned all artistic works and books that did not meet his puritanical, dogmatic standards. This is a key example of the kind of fear that swept through Europe just as the waxing square of Uranus to Pluto was becoming exact. It was an expression of a cultural paradigm crisis between the emerging new Renaissance and an old culture of religious fundamentalism and scholasticism.

This clash between an emerging new view and a recalcitrant old view is characteristic of the waxing squares of Uranus–Pluto, and can be experienced in our current Uranus–Pluto waxing square.

Another significant figure on the world stage at this time was Pico della Mirandola (1463–1494), a student of Marsilio Ficino and acquainted with Rosicrucian groups throughout Europe. He wrote *The Oration on the Dignity of Man* in 1496 and set the direction for Humanism. His oration praising the moral philosophies of antiquity and proclaiming the right of freedom for every human being flew in the face of Church dogma. Mirandola asserted that every human being is endowed with a soul longing to pursue universal wisdom (Mirandola, P. D., 1956). Steiner indicated in a lecture on January 6, 1924, that Mirandola held the view that what happens on Earth depends on the stars, yet he advocated that human beings have to take into account only the immediate cause on Earth. This peculiar standpoint of Mirandola awakened a deep intuitive recognition that it was time for humanity to renounce "blind faith" in knowledge transmitted through ancient mysteries and learn to discover it anew.

This renunciation of mystery wisdom publicly stated by Mirandola had its counterpart in a Rosicrucian ritual arranged for the purpose of offering up human knowledge of the stars. This solemn and profound ritual, Steiner states, was held in the second half of the fifteenth century. However, there is the distinct possibility that it occurred some years after the death of Christian Rosenkreutz and may indeed have been directed by him from across the threshold. Steiner described the ritual in the following way.

> Men stood before a kind of altar and said, "We resolve to feel at this moment responsible not only for ourselves, our community, or our nation, or even only for the people of our time; we resolve to feel responsible for everyone who has ever lived on Earth; we resolve to feel that we belong to the whole of humankind. Moreover, we feel that what has really happened with human beings is that they have deserted the rank of the fourth hierarchy [of spiritual beings] and have descended too deeply into matter; and so that human beings may be able to return to the rank of the fourth hierarchy and be able to find for themselves, of their own free will, what the gods in earlier times tried to find for and with humankind, let the higher knowledge now be offered up for a season!" (Steiner, 1965, p. 44; trans. revised)

This particular ritual with its renunciation of the "higher knowledge," or star wisdom, cannot be underestimated. Knowledge of the intimate relatedness between the human soul and the cyclic nature of planetary movements in the heavens—with its lawfulness in determining the weight of karma and the direction of the destiny for humankind—is now something that individuals of consciousness soul age must rediscover. The two burning questions are: How are we to rediscover this mystery wisdom that explicates the relationship between the stars and the development of the soul? And how are we to know the duration of the season the Rosicrucians referred to in such a unique way?

BACKGROUND AND CONTEXT TO THE FIFTH URANUS–PLUTO CYCLE

Although it is not possible to give a full account of all the factors leading up to the Uranus–Pluto conjunction of 1965 to 1966, the selective cultural and spiritual events of the previous Uranus–Pluto opposition of 1901 to 1902 and the Uranus–Pluto waning square of 1932 to 1934 should provide sufficient historical context to follow the thread of what began in the fifteenth century as a movement of consciousness toward a new world order, particularly in relation to the rediscovery of the intimate kinship between soul wisdom and star wisdom.

Just prior to the exact opposition of Uranus–Pluto, the dark age of Kali Yuga came to an end. Steiner revealed that this end occurred in 1899 and heralded a new possibility for humanity to gain access to the spiritual world. In the period of the exact conjunction (1901–1902), two significant advocates of transpersonal realities emerged on the public stage—William James and Rudolf Steiner. James published his epochal work, *The Varieties of Religious Experience*, in 1902. In it he gave pragmatic phenomenological evidence to his psychological concept of the "Wider Self," the self beyond the personal and embedded in a mystical unity with the world or, as James put it, "in touch with God" (James, 1892). Steiner was at the same time laying foundations for the Anthroposophical Society, based on his continued prolific research in the development of Spiritual Science. During the exact conjunction, he delivered the lectures *Christianity as Mystical Fact and the Mysteries of*

Antiquity (1901–1902), as well as ten lectures in 1900, later published as *Mysticism at the Dawn of the Modern Age* (now *Mystics after Modernism: Discovering the Seeds of a New Science in the Renaissance*).

Owing to the enormous cultural influence of Sigmund Freud's psychoanalysis, which reached acclaim after his publication *The Interpretations of Dreams* (1900), history books refer to him as the father of modern psychology. However, what is often overlooked is William James's radical departure from behaviorism and psychoanalytic approaches, which formed the prevailing schools of psychology at the time. James fostered a transpersonal view of the psyche as a viable alternative to pursue. As a pragmatic phenomenologist James opened the door to the spiritual dimensions within the human psyche. Simultaneously, Steiner was mapping the territory beyond the threshold and giving the human being a method for doing spiritual investigation into the psyche that was not symbolic or archetypal but meditatively experiential. Weeks after James's death, Steiner gave his seminal four 1910 lectures on Psychosophy, published in *A Psychology of Body, Soul, and Spirit: Anthroposophy, Psychosophy, Pneumatosophy*. The lectures on Psychosophy were also grounded in a phenomenological inquiry.

According to Steiner's clairvoyant and prophetic vision, the return of the Christ in the etheric realm was scheduled to occur in 1933 (Steiner, 1998). This time fell in the middle of the exact Uranus–Pluto waning square of 1932 to 1934. This can be considered one of the most remarkable spiritual events of the twentieth century. The counter-event on Earth was Adolf Hitler's rise to power in Nazi Germany. The deep crisis in the human psyche precipitated by these two events could not have been graver for the unfolding of the twentieth century.

Expanding our research into the Uranus–Pluto waning square period from 1928 to 1937, we discover key contributions to humanity's endeavor to safeguard humanness and to reunite psyche with astro-logos. The Humanistic movement in psychology—generated by a need to address the uniquely human issues such as self, self-worth, self-actualization, creativity, love, hope, and resilience—began in the late 1930s by Carl Rogers (1902–1987) and Abraham Maslow. On the transpersonal psychological front, Carl Gustav Jung (1875–1961) had emancipated himself from the psychoanalytical school and began to advance his own psychiatric approach with a clear emphasis on transpersonal dimensions. In 1932, he gave his radical lectures *The Psychology of Kundalini Yoga*, followed by his publications *Modern Man's Search of a Soul* (1933) and *The Archetypes and the Collective Unconscious* (1934). Jung's openness to investigating the wisdom of the East and to translating its universal symbolism and practices into a spiritually oriented psychotherapy earned him the stature as a modern Western shaman. His approach to so-called "depth psychology" placed him as an individual ahead of his time. Jung's pioneering research into the spiritual technologies of the East, his adamant search to give validity to the reality of soul, and his unveiling of the archetypes that have shaped the human psyche throughout the ages gave the seekers of the counter-cultural sixties a compass to journey into the transcendent and immanent realities of the spirit.

In the field of modern astrology, Alice Bailey (1880–1949), Theosophist, occult teacher and author of numerous books on the subject of ageless wisdom, petitioned Dane Rudhyar to write about his insights into the esoteric and psychological ramifications of a modern astrology. Rudhyar responded affirmatively with his book *The Astrology of Personality: A Reformulation of Astrological Concepts and Ideals, in Terms of Contemporary Psychology and Philosophy* (1936). During this same period, Alice Bailey wrote her own treatise titled *Esoteric Psychology* (1936–1942) and *Esoteric Astrology* (1951).

THE URANUS–PLUTO CONJUNCTION OF 1965 TO 1966

The counter-cultural revolution of the 1960s was potentized not only by a memory of the Italian Renaissance 510 years earlier, but also by a celestial aspect of Uranus–Pluto in the Lion opposite Saturn in the Water-Carrier. The virtues of the

Lion (compassion as a capacity for liberating suffering) and the virtues of the Water-Carrier (discretion as a capacity for developing meditative strength) were clearly evident in the phenomena that flowed throughout the sixties. In the universities across the US and Europe, urgent and compelling cases were emerging against the "establishment." This term referred to any institution wielding authority in society. A new society was being envisioned and celebrated in the arts, music, literature, and so on. Not too dissimilar from Cosimo de Medici's vision to harvest the wisdom of antiquity and place them into service for building a new Europe, many significant leaders of the counter-cultural revolt turned toward the East to find the spiritual nourishment felt to be lacking in the West. From the Beatles' adoption of Transcendental Meditation to Richard Alpert's (later Ram Dass) and Alan Watts' (1915–1973) immersion in Hindu, Buddhist, and Zen practices, the sixties witnessed a profusion of Eastern spirituality coopted by young and old.

Developmental Markers in the Field of Psychology

Humanistic psychology had become a fashionable approach for those seeking an alternative for engaging in self-development, yet it did not facilitate a deeper understanding of the extraordinary states of consciousness that was so prevalent in spiritual practices. With this recognition in mind, Stanislav Grof and Abraham Maslow gave birth to the transpersonal psychology school around 1966, later formalized in 1975 as the Institute for Transpersonal Psychology (now renamed Sofia University). Amid the sixties revolutionary era, a resurgence of Carl Jung's work was embraced and popularized by comparative mythologist and cultural anthropologist Joseph Campbell (1904–1987). In the heart of the Uranus–Pluto conjunction, Roberto Assagioli (1884–1974), founder of Psychosynthesis, received recognition in the English-speaking world as one of the early pioneers of transpersonal psychology along with Carl Jung. Roberto Assagioli's studies in Theosophy and other arcane disciplines informed his approach for a holistic psychology capable of mapping the psyche and encouraging the recipient of psychotherapy to embrace all aspects of one's personality. *Psychosynthesis: A Collection of Basic Writings by Roberto Assagioli* (1965) was published in English and received by many leaders of alternative approaches to self-development, particularly in the San Francisco Bay area. In these writings, Assagioli describes the distinction between his approach and Jung's.

> Perhaps the best way to state our differences is with a diagram of the psychic functions. Jung differentiates four functions: sensation, feeling, thought, and intuition. Psychosynthesis says that Jung's four functions do not provide for a complete description of the psychological life. Our view can be visualized like this: We hold that outside imagination or fantasy is a distinct function. There is also a group of functions that impels us toward action in the outside world. This group includes instincts, tendencies, impulses, desires, and aspirations. And here we come to one of the central foundations of Psychosynthesis: There is a fundamental difference between drives, impulses, desires, and the will. In the human condition there are frequent conflicts between desire and will. And we will place the will in a central position at the heart of self-consciousness or the Ego. (Assagioli, 1965, p. 46)

Assagioli's formulation is, in fact, much closer to Steiner's basic ideas of the psyche than to Jung's, particularly in relation to placing "the will in a central position at the heart of self-consciousness, or the 'I.'" It remains a mystery and an apparent lost opportunity that Steiner's Spiritual Science for the modern human search for soul was not better known to the seekers of a transpersonal ontology.

Developmental Markers in the Field of Astrology

During this period of the 1960s, the interest in astrology was infectious. Bookstore shelves were stocked with astrological texts of all sorts. Dane Rudyhar's *Astrology For New Minds: A Non-dualistic Harmonic Approach to Astrological Charts and to the Relation Between Man and the*

Universe (1969) typified the search of many contemporary astrologers to find the links between astrology and psychology. Another important contributor to the elevation of astrology's status as a reputable philosophical and psychological metric for the human psyche was Marc Edmund Jones (1888–1980), a fellow Theosophist and friend of Dane Rudhyar. It must also be stated that, as in the mid-fifteenth century, there were a great deal of misguided attempts to claim possession of a prophetic wisdom of astrology that, unfortunately, were less than authentic and more charlatan in nature. Despite this unfortunate shadow in astrology's development, there were thousands of individuals who took up a sincere interest in learning more about the fundamental concepts of astrology and just as many who saw astrology as a significant guide for inner development. It became for many a spiritual technique for expanding one's awareness of self and the world.

In the ranks of the anthroposophic movement, there was an individual who took Steiner's plea to develop a new star wisdom quite seriously. Willi Sucher (1902–1985) became quite convinced that the task was his to pursue. During the Uranus–Pluto waning square (1932–1934), he became a coworker with Elizabeth Vreede (1879–1943), leader of the Mathematics and Astronomy Section of the School for Spiritual Science founded by Rudolf Steiner. Few individuals were able to really understand or support Sucher in his research, but he remained faithful to the task for many decades. In 1965, Sucher began to write monthly letters to a circle of faithful interested parties. The seven years of these monthly letters became the basis of his approach to a new star wisdom (Astrosophy), later published as *Practical Approaches Towards a New Astronomy* (1972–1974). Infused with anthroposophic concepts and grand cosmic imaginations of the spiritual hierarchies working into the lives of individuals and historic events, Sucher's approach established a radical departure from geocentric tropical astrology. He introduced a heliocentric view with a focus on the stars as they appeared in the constellations. For Sucher, the landscape of the soul life, with all its impulses of karma and destiny, was mapped out in the movement of the planets, from conception to birth. Thus the static idea of a soul being imprinted with a fixed set of traits was replaced with a dynamic view of a soul undergoing various opportunities for transformations whose goal is to attain a degree of freedom and to meet karma and destiny with a greater consciousness. Sucher was able to open up fields of investigation that are still being researched by the many contributors of the *Journal for Star Wisdom*.

On a personal note, the author, as one of Willi Sucher's students from 1975 to 1985, asked him on one occasion about the circumstances surrounding his writing the first monthly letter in the fall season of 1965. Sucher's response was delivered in his characteristic gentle, humble, and gracious manner. To paraphrase him he said, "I was studying the Uranus–Pluto conjunctions in history and felt a rising certainty that it was the spiritual signature of the Rosicrucians. One evening in this mood of certainty, I felt I 'heard' Christian Rosenkreutz say to me, 'It is time to write letters to friends defining the approach of modern human beings to a new star wisdom.' And so the next morning I began to write the letters."

This particular intimate communication has lived in my soul like a quiet flame upon an altar. I have come to view this time as a major historical esoteric moment, a time when the season mentioned by the Rosicrucians who offered up star wisdom in the second half of the fifteenth century had come to an end. I remained convinced that the season referred to by the Rosicrucians ended with the Uranus–Pluto conjunction of 1965 and 1966, and that a new season inaugurated by Sucher's work and being carried forward by the friends who contribute to the *Journal for Star Wisdom* is upon us.

THE URANUS–PLUTO WAXING SQUARE OF 2011 TO 2015

Within this period and its extended time frame defined by the 10° orb (2007–2020), many foreboding and promising prophecies have dominated the cultural landscape. The accelerated rate of advancement in scientific theories and technologies; its impact on changing societal values; the down-turn of economic solvency and its provoking angst for the individual and collective soul of everyone on the globe; and the fatigue of politics and its resultant disempowerment to make any significant change in safeguarding the rights of individuals and in alleviating the tensions between nations, all give evidence to the growing concerns provoked by the many apocalyptic prophecies.

Yet, on the other hand, the reevaluation of science's core concepts about the evolution and nature of the universe, earth, and humanity give hope to the discovery of empirical evidence to the wisdom of the ancients and thereby foster optimism in creating a more wholesome and dynamic paradigm for humanity's future. There are far too many recent phenomena to cite in relation to this overall characterization of our present time. In lieu of doing so, the author encourages the reader to merely search the Internet and its databases for newsworthy events from 2007 to the present. A brief survey will reveal the wide and numerous varieties of events that have transpired, and have left an indelible mark on the course of human history, as we know it.

Journal for Star Wisdom has been published through varying publishers from 1991 to the present. The primary authors of the content of the *Journal* have been Robert Powell, its editor, and the *Starfire Research Group*, active since 1982.

In the twenty-three years of this journal, there have been many articles demonstrating the nature and approach to a new star wisdom, sharing important research results from its application, and providing resources for its readership to follow the meaningfulness of the starry world in relation to the phenomenal signs of the time. The latter refers to both cultural life and the individual soul experiences that range the gamut from fear to hope.

For brevity's sake the author will cite just a few of the major themes that have been addressed in the journal publications.

1. The Reappearance of the Christ in the Etheric World;
2. The Possibility of a World Pentecost;
3. The Pending Incarnation of Ahriman;
4. The Controversial Maya Calendar Prophecy of December 21, 2012;
5. The Possibility of the Reincarnation of the Initiate Parzival–Mani;
6. The Dawning of the Age of Sophia.

Each of these themes touches upon deep esoteric content and deserve to be penetrated by examining the specific context in which they are embedded. However, this is not the space for such expositions. Back issues of the *Journal for Star Wisdom* are available and remain the best secondary sources to derive the meaningfulness of these themes for our time.

RELEVANCY OF THE SEARCH TO REUNITE PSYCHE WITH ASTRO-LOGOS

If our readers can reflect on all that has been selectively placed before them in this article, from the Renaissance to the present, then a return to the opening paragraphs of this article, addressing the timeliness of this study, may make more sense. For the most part, ardent students of Rudolf Steiner's Spiritual Science have ignored and, at times, dismissed the value of an anthroposophic psychology (intimately related to the discipline and goals of transpersonal psychology). The somewhat misplaced notion that knowledge of meditation exercises given by Steiner eliminates any need for a mindfulness practice of psychological awareness has hindered the development of an anthroposophic psychology. Robert Sardello, cofounder of the School for Spiritual Psychology and author of numerous books on the subject, has not only made this observation many times but has published it in the forward to *A Psychology of Body, Soul and Spirit* by Rudolf Steiner.

Although Sardello does not use the term *spiritual bypassing,* coined by Frances Vaughn and Roger Walsh in their book *Paths Beyond Ego* (1993b), it is precisely the phenomenon he describes and one I have long witnessed. It is not exclusive to anthroposophists, but quite endemic to all spiritual movements, both Eastern and Western.

Owing to the lack of recognition by mainstream schools of psychology regarding evidence of prenatal, perinatal, and postmortem states of consciousness, which are so much a part of the domain of transpersonal psychology, an unfortunate compartmentalization between extraordinary experiences and the human relationship to the starry world has persisted. However, the time has come for removing the veil that separates these two realms of existence and for seeing their true relatedness. The author's conviction is derived from a deep appreciation of Grof's published research in his books *Realms of the Human Unconscious* (1975), *Beyond the Brain* (1985), *The Adventure of Self-Discovery* (1987), and *Psychology of the Future* (2000). Grof articulates an interesting cartography of the human psyche, one that bursts through the barrier of postnatal biography, upon which psychoanalysis rests. He describes basic perinatal matrices (BPM) in four stages wherein consciousness is present. As radical as this breakthrough is, it still receives remarkably little attention. In this cartography of the psyche, Grof not only affirms Jung's discovery of a collective unconscious, but he also gives plausible evidence to "past-life memories," supporting Steiner's claims of the soul's development related to karma and reincarnation.

In the recent article by Grof in *The Journal of Transpersonal Psychology* (vol. 44, no. 2, 2012), he reveals the greatest surprise he has experienced during his fifty some years of conducting consciousness research—"discovery of the extraordinary predictive power of astrology." His collaboration with Richard Tarnas in studying individuals who were going through holotropic experiences in consciousness has resulted in an identification of planetary correspondences to each of the four stages of the basic perinatal matrices. The BPM I stage (prenatal unitive consciousness) is ascribed to the archetypal expression of Neptune, BPM II stage (first stage of birth process when uterus contracts and the cervix is not yet open) Grof ascribed to the archetypal expression of Saturn, BPM III stage (struggle of birthing after the uterine cervix dilates) he ascribed to the archetypal expression of Pluto, and lastly, BPM IV stage (memory of the emergence into the world, the birth experience itself) he ascribed to the archetypal expression of Uranus. Studying the positions of the transiting planets in relation to an individual's birth chart placements during holotropic experiences revealed many correspondences.

Another, less well-known published research from a transpersonal psychologist that provides evidence of the interrelationships between the psyche and the starry world is the author's *Somatic Psycho-diagnostic Approach to Personality Disorders: An Understanding of Personality through Spatial Orientation* (2009). In it, the author reveals his research into how movements into the three spatial planes are related to the zodiac and how dysfunctions in movement into these planes forms the basis of personality disorders. Equally significant to the study is the correlations made for each of the clinically identified personality disorders with one of twelve signs of the zodiac.

These research results in the field of transpersonal clinical psychology, demonstrating the intimate relatedness to the planets and stars, may well be the tip of the iceberg of a wealth of linkages between the psyche and astro-logos yet to be discovered. There is every good reason to believe that—just as the wisdom of the Rosicrucians and the imaginative and inspiring impulses of the Florentine Platonic Academy set the tone for a changing paradigm at the early stages of the consciousness soul age (the paradigm that replaced a geocentric worldview with a heliocentric worldview)—this time we are living in is setting the tone for a renewed esoteric activity flowing from the Rosicrucian stream and a revival of a culture of imaginations that has the power to move the soul toward wholeness. These possibilities become all the more palpable as we strive, in practical and therapeutic ways, to reunite the human psyche with the astro-logos of our cosmos. Through this endeavor we move a little closer to reclaiming our rightful place as the fourth hierarchy.

References

Allen, M. & Hankins, J. (ed. & tr.), 2001–2006. Marsilio Ficino. *Platonic Theology*, 6 vols. Cambridge, MA: Harvard University Press.

Assagioli, R. (1965). *Psychosynthesis: A Collection of Basic Writings by Roberto Assagioli*. New York: Penguin.

Bailey, A. (1951). *Esoteric Astrology*. New York: Lucis Publishing Company.

———. (1936–1942). *Esoteric Psychology*, vols.1–3. New York: Lucis Publishing Company.

Bento, W. (2009). "A Somatic Psycho-diagnostic Approach to Personality Disorders: An Understanding of Personality through Spatial Orientation." Köln: Lambert Academic.

———. (2012, Sept.). "A Report on the Medical Section Conference on Anthroposophic Psychiatry, Psychotherapy and Psychosomatics" (http://www.steinercollege.edu/report-on-the-international-medical-section-conference-2012).

Ficino, M. (1980). *The Book of Life*. Irving, TX: Spring.

———. (1975). *The Letters of Marsilio Ficino*, vol. 1. New York: Gingko.

Freud, S. (1997). *The Interpretations of Dreams*. Hertfordshire, UK: Wordsworth.

Grof, S. (1975). *Realms of the Human Unconscious: Observations from LSD Research*. New York: Viking Press.

———. (1985). *Beyond the Brain: Birth, Death and Transcendence in Psychotherapy*. Albany: SUNY.

———. (1987). *The Adventure of Self-Discovery*. Albany: SUNY.

———. (2000). *Psychology of the Future*. Albany: SUNY.

———. (2012). "Revision and Re-enchantment of Psychology: Legacy of a Half a Century of Consciousness Research." *Journal of Transpersonal Psychology*, vol. 44 (2), pp. 137–163.

James, W. (1902). *The Varieties in Religious Experience: A Study in Human Nature*. Edinburgh: Longman's Green.

———. (1985). *Psychology: The Briefer Course*. Notre Dame, IN: University of Notre Dame.

Jung, C. G. (1932). *The Psychology of Kundalini Yoga*. Princeton, NJ: Princeton University.

———. (1933). *Modern Man's Search for a Soul*. Orlando: Harcourt.

———. (1934). *The Archetypes and the Collective Unconscious*. Princeton, NJ: Princeton University.

Lajoie, D. H. & Shapiro, S. I. (1992). "Definitions of Transpersonal Psychology: The First Twenty-three Years." *Journal of Transpersonal Psychology*, vol. 24.

Mirandola, G. P. D. (1956). *Oration on the Dignity of Man*. Chicago: Gateway.

Powell, R. (ed.). *Journal for Star Wisdom*, 1991–2014. Great Barrington, MA: Lindisfarne.

Rudhyar, D. (1936). *The Astrology of Personality: A Reformulation of Astrological Concepts and Ideals in Terms of Contemporary Psychology and Philosophy*. New York: Lucis.

———. (1946, 1971). *The Lunation Cycle: A Key to Understanding Personality*. Berkeley: Shambala.

———. (1969). *Astrology For New Minds: A Non-dualistic Harmonic Approach to Astrological Charts and to the Relation Between Man and the Universe*. New York: ASI.

Steiner, R. (1965). *Rosicrucianism and Modern Initiation*. London, UK: Rudolf Steiner Press.

———. (1971). *Christianity as a Mystical Fact*. Blauvelt, NY: Rudolf Steiner Publications.

———. (1994). *Theosophy: An Introduction to the Spiritual Processes in Human Life and in the Cosmos*. Hudson, NY: Anthroposophic Press.

———. (1998). *The Book of Revelation: And the Work of the Priest*. London: Rudolf Steiner Press.

———. (1999). *A Psychology of Body, Soul, and Spirit: Anthroposophy, Psychosophy, Pneumatosophy*. Hudson, NY: Anthroposophic Press.

Sucher, W. (1972–74). *Practical Approaches Towards A New Astrosophy*. Meadow Vista, CA: Astrosophy Research Center.

Tarnas, R. (2006). *Cosmos and Psyche: Intimations of a New World View*. New York: Viking Press.

Walsh, R. & Vaughan, F. (1993a). "On Transpersonal Definitions." *The Journal of Transpersonal Psychology*, vol. 25 (2) 125–182.

———. (eds.) (1993b). *Paths Beyond Ego*. New York: Jeremy P. Tarcher/Putnam.

A BRIEF NOTE ON MIRANDOLA AND FICINO

David Tresemer and Robert Schiappacasse

In the article by William Bento, two important figures emerged as guidance for out time, blazing lights in the period immediately following the surge in consciousness soul for humanity (1413). This brief note recognizes a very few aspects of their legacy as shown by the date of death—what these beacons gave into the starry worlds, that would then serve humanity now and in the future.

On November 17, 1494, Giovanni Pico della Mirandola died in Florence, perhaps by poisoning. Even if his passing was not natural, it bore a powerful signature, for the Sun at his death lay conjunct with the star Antares, what we have come to call the Star of Death and Rebirth, a prominent star in the life of Mother Mary for example. This is one of the Royal Stars of Persia, and we have written about this more in our *Star Wisdom & Rudolf Steiner* (SteinerBooks, 2007).

Details: Sun at 16°36' of Scorpio and Antares at 15°1' of Scorpio.

On October 1, 1499, Marsilio Ficino died in Careggi. The Sun lay conjunct to Spica, another of the Royal Stars of Persia that we have come to call the Goddess Star. This is a powerful signature of connection with the wellsprings of feminine life-force for humanity, the picture in the stars of what lives in the Earth as Sophia.

Details: Sun at 29°4' Virgo, Spica at 29°6' Virgo, exact. Secondly, the Sun and Spica lay square to Neptune at 24°31' Sagittarius; Neptune's touch is elaborated in the *Journal for Star Wisdom* article on corporate personhood (with further references therein). Third, Ficino's death occurred during the Pluto–Uranus square spoken of in Bento's paper, Uranus at 4°36' Aquarius (closely opposite to the King Star, Regulus, at 5°5'Leo, another of the Royal Stars) and Pluto at 3°34' Scorpio. (The Pluto–Uranus square was 7° wide at Mirandola's death.)

The mark of these two forerunner individualities is summarized in Bento's paper. This note relates their legacy to the heavens, through the gestures of their deaths.

"It became clearer and clearer to me—as the outcome of many years of research—that in our epoch there is really something like a resurrection of the Astrology of the third epoch [the Egyptian–Babylonian period], but permeated now with the Christ Impulse. Today, we must search among the stars in a way different from the old ways. The stellar script must once more become something that speaks to us."
—RUDOLF STEINER (*Christ and the Spiritual World and the Search for the Holy Grail*, p. 106)

EVOLUTIONARY STREAMS ACCOMPANYING CHRIST'S DESCENT

Paul Marx

The descent of Christ from the Sun was accompanied by two evolutionary streams: an hereditary stream and a stream of Sun wisdom. Both were guided by Melchizedek, the highest initiate of our Earth Period.

The hereditary stream is known from the Gospels of Matthew and Luke and comprises forty-two generations from Abraham to the Solomon and Nathan Jesus children:

Abraham → Isaac → Jacob → Judah → David → Solomon/Nathan → Solomon Jesus/Nathan Jesus

Beginning earlier and then concurrent with the hereditary stream, there was a stream of Sun wisdom[1] that proceeded from Melchizedek to his pupil Zarathustra, who taught the wisdom of Ahura Mazda, the great Sun aura. Just as Venus and Mercury were ejected from the sun, this represented the Venus stage of a "streaming out" of Sun wisdom. Zarathustra's pupil, Hermes, gifted with his teacher's astral body, further disseminated Sun wisdom when he inaugurated the Egyptian civilization centered on the Sun god: Osiris. This represented the Mercury stage.

Another pupil of Zarathustra, Moses, gifted with his teacher's etheric body, received Sun wisdom indirectly as a memory. He converted it into Earth wisdom, notably the book: Genesis, by absorbing the teaching of Hermes during the first forty years of his life. He spent the next forty years as a disciple of Jethro, who instructed him in the Arabian mysteries in preparation for his role in receiving the Law from Yahweh. Jethro, who probably was instructed and given this task by Melchizedek, was a needed intermediary, for it was again necessary that Moses receive higher wisdom indirectly. He then could internalize this wisdom and be an example for the Israelites who established an internal consciousness of God (Yahweh) through their blood relationship with Abraham. The Moon-wisdom of Yahweh was the first stage of a return streaming of the Sun wisdom that originated from Melchizedek. This internalized wisdom continued to evolve through the religious rituals of the Israelites and reached a Mercury stage by the time of David. The Venus stage was reached during the Babylonian captivity when Zarathustra as Nazarthos taught Jewish scholars. It remained only for the subject of this wisdom stream to Incarnate and add the Eucharist to the teaching.

This Divine Plan required a special individual and a special people. That individual was Abraham who was born in Ur of the Chaldees, part of ancient Babylon. The people were the Israelites, who spiritually came into being at the time of God's covenant with Abraham (Gen. 15), through Abraham's faith and God's promise. Later, they physically came into being with the birth of Israel and his sons.

We know this from Exodus 12:40 where we are told the "children of Israel" were sojourners for 430 years. Then in Galatians 3:17 the period from Abraham's covenant to the Law of Moses is given as the same 430 years, so the sojourning began with the covenant. What must be kept in mind to avoid confusion over the length of the Egyptian Sojourn is that the Bible does not say all the Israelites' sojourning was in Egypt, only that the Israelites who lived in Egypt at the time of the Exodus had been sojourners for this period of time.

---

[1] Steiner, *According to Matthew*, Sept. 2, 1910.

We further know that Isaac was born twenty-five years after the covenant (Gen. 21:5) and Jacob was born when Isaac was sixty (Gen. 25:26). Then when Jacob entered Egypt to begin the sojourn of his people, he told the pharaoh that his "pilgrimage" had been 130 years, his lifespan until that time (Gen. 47:9). These three periods total 215 years, leaving the same number of years for the Egyptian Sojourn.

We pause here to consider the identity of the pharaoh who "exalted" Joseph and welcomed his kinsmen to begin a sojourn in Egypt. It would help to know the period of his reign. But if we knew that, we also would know when the Hebrew Exodus took place—215 years later. At the present time, this period of Hebrew history is clouded with uncertainty, which breeds controversy. One could say that the dating of the Exodus is the most controversial subject in the Bible today. It has led to a movement called biblical minimalism, which questions the very authenticity of the Bible as a chronicle of real events.

There are two principal schools of thought on when the Exodus took place. The first is based on an Egyptian timeline of pharaohs extending from Cleopatra back to the time of Hermes, around the beginning of the Kali Yuga in 3100 BC. This school accepts Ramesses II as the pharaoh who inaugurated the Israelite oppression—the forced labor of the Israelites in building the cities of Ramesses and Pithom.[2] This places the Exodus at the end of the nineteenth, the Ramesside Dynasty. The Egyptians were thorough in recording the reign of each of their pharaohs[3] and historians have assumed that the line of pharaohs was continuous, without a break. The Egyptian timeline[4] places the reign of Ramesses II between 1304 and 1237 BC and the nineteenth Dynasty circa 1320-1200 BC.

The second school is based on a Hebrew timeline anchored by a well-known historic event: when Nebuchadnezzar II and the Babylonians sacked Jerusalem in 586 BC. It's possible from this date to determine when the reign of Solomon took place by summing the reigns of the kings of Judah. It wouldn't have the accuracy of the 586 BC date because of overlapping reigns, but with the time of Solomon known, the period given by 1 Kings 6:1 (480 years) would establish an Exodus date with the same accuracy as the Solomon date. Solomon's reign is generally accepted to have begun between 970 and 960 BC, indicating a Hebrew Exodus between 1436 and 1446 BC.

On the continuous Egyptian timeline, this fifteenth century BC period correlates with the reign of Amenophis II, an eighteenth Dynasty pharaoh, a period much earlier than the oppression and the building of the cities, Ramesses and Pithom.

The seeming contradiction between the Hebrew and the Egyptian timelines could be resolved if there was an interregnum or break at some point in the Egyptian timeline. The Great Harris Papyrus housed at the British Museum in London offers an important clue. It was written at the beginning of the twentieth Dynasty and refers to a period of anarchy between the nineteenth and twentieth.

If an extensive period of anarchy began at the end of the nineteenth, the time of the Exodus, it would have provided a measure of protection for the Israelites as they began their new life, first in the Wilderness and then in Canaan, for as Bock points out, the Wilderness years were spent within borders that were part of Egypt.[5] The continuous chronology places the reign of the very forceful pharaoh, Ramesses III, within two years of the Exodus, a pharaoh likely to pursue an unarmed and vulnerable people. Moses, it seems, was aware of this divine protection when he proclaimed to the Israelites they had seen their last Egyptian the day they entered the Sinai desert (Ex. 14:13).

The interregnum is supported by two sets of biblical facts. First, the Bible records a cross-correlation between Egyptian and Hebrew chronologies at the time the pharaoh Sheshonq I (946–925 BC) invades Palestine (926 BC) and carries off treasures of the temple (1 Kings 14: 25–26). In the Bible he is

---

2 Kitchen, *On the Reliability of the Old Testament*, p. 254.
3 Waddell, *Manetho*.
4 Edwards, *Introductory Guide to the Egyptian Collections*, p. 244.

---

5 Bock, *Moses*, p. 87.

known as Shishak.[1] This occurred during the fifth year of the reign of Rehoboam (931–913 BC) who succeeded Solomon.

A second cross-correlation is recorded at the end of the reign of Josiah (639–609 BC). He was killed (2 Chron. 35:20-24) during a battle with the pharaoh Necho II (610–595 BC), a correlation that also helps to verify the continuity of the Egyptian timeline after the interregnum.

Secondly, the Bible allows us to account for most of the controversial 480 years of 1 Kings 6:1. Jephthah, one of the last judges, told the King of Ammon that his people had resided in Canaan and the trans-Jordan region for 300 years (Judg. 11:26). This number can be added to the forty Wilderness years and the seventy-six years of a united monarchy[2] for a total of 416 years.

Finally, through an indication provided by Willi Sucher, we can narrow even further the Exodus year.[3] With a dim recollection of Rudolf Steiner associating the Exodus with the Egyptian Sothis period, 1,461 years, Sucher arrived at a tentative 1437 BC Exodus year with some corrections to the Sothis period. He then looked for "cosmic happenings" around this date and found "In c. September 18, 1435 BC (helio), took place a Great Conjunction of Saturn and Jupiter, in c. 158.6° of the ecliptic then. This was an ancestor[4] event of the Great Conjunction of 6 BC, which I regard as the 'Star of the Three Kings', which they took as the signal." This date corrected became the ancestor Great Conjunction of 1436 BC, the Exodus year.

Because Moses' life was segmented by three forty year periods, the Exodus year Conjunction suggests that Great Conjunctions mark the other three notable events in Moses' life: his birth, exile, and death.

And by accepting 1436 BC as the Exodus year, the beginning of Solomon's reign can be narrowed to 960 BC, which, significantly, is the year of another ancestor Great Conjunction (Dec. 7). It also means we can return to the continuous Egyptian timeline before the interregnum and determine the pharaoh who welcomed the Israelites at the start of the Sojourn. Again, it is the eighteenth Dynasty pharaoh, Amenophis II (1678–1653 BC corrected) playing, this time, a different role. This comports with a period[5] when Egypt was "settled and prosperous." It was an ideal time for Egypt to take in an alien people.

The Hebrews enjoyed Egyptian hospitality until the death of Joseph in 1582 BC (during the famous Tutankhamun's reign) and for an additional 42 years. They lived during this time in Northern Egypt, on land east of the Nile delta known as Goshen. Because Egypt was governed from the southern city of Thebes, the Israelites attracted little attention. Then, however, a new Dynasty appeared, the nineteenth Ramesside Dynasty, whose rulers came from the Nile delta region and who preferred to govern from there. With no remembrance of Joseph, they considered the Israelites aliens who had overstayed their welcome, making them fair game to enslave. The heavy oppression began with the reign of the third dynastic pharaoh, Ramesses II, considered the greatest of Egyptian pharaohs because of his military prowess, his vast building program, and the longevity of his reign, sixty-six years.

With a Great Conjunction in sidereal Capricorn (November 27, 1516 BC, JC) heralding his birth, Moses was born during the reign of Ramesses II. It is here that Bock[6] questions the biblical account of his adoption as an infant: "The story of the abandonment of the newborn infant, as related in the Old Testament, remains full of riddles if it merely depicts the outer facts." And those facts are: the infant was known to have a Hebrew mother who

---

1 Kitchen, *On the Reliability of the Old Testament*, p. 461.
2 Ibid., p. 307.
3 Sucher, personal communication, June 21, 1972.
4 Great Conjunctions of Saturn and Jupiter appear in the same region of the zodiac every 60 years, displaced by 8°. Conjunctions that share this same-region attribute also share an ancestor to daughter relationship or, Conjunctions that are multiples of 60 years removed from the Three Kings Conjunction are all ancestor to it.

5 Edwards, *Introductory Guide to the Egyptian Collections*, p. 49.
6 Bock, *Moses*, p. 26.

didn't abandon her baby to the pharaoh's daughter but accompanied her baby to nurse him in the royal palace.

Those riddles would have remained unsolved except for the English writer, Joan Grant (1907–89), whose novels were autobiographies of past lives. Two of those lives were spent in ancient Egypt where she was connected with Egyptian royalty. In the first, she was a pharaoh's daughter and received instruction in past life remembrance, an ability she retained until the present day. In the second, she was the elder brother of Ramesses II and an eyewitness to the birth of Moses as recounted in her novel *So Moses Was Born*.[7]

Grant places the birth of Moses in the twenty-fourth year of Ramesses' reign. This allows an exact determination of the end of the nineteenth Dynasty based on the continuous Egyptian timeline of pharaohs: 1200 BC. Correlated with a 1436 BC Exodus year, this indicates an interregnum of 236 years.

It would be easy to dismiss a startling revelation made in her book were it not for its logical necessity, which will be forthcoming. Ramesses, it turns out, was the father of Moses by the young Hebrew girl who volunteered to nurse the infant boy. The chance encounter between Ramesses and Moses' mother was the consequence of a dream the older brother had and related to his brother, the pharaoh: he was soon to father a "Son of Horus," which for an Egyptian meant an initiate. Ramesses was pleased knowing this because he had wanted to re-establish a line of priest-pharaohs, a legacy long since lost because of the decadence overtaking Egypt.

The birth of Moses to a Hebrew girl presented a court-acceptance problem for the pharaoh—he couldn't simply bring the girl into the palace, make her a royal wife, and adopt her son as his heir, his older sons were sure to be jealous. A ruse was needed and it was the basis for the biblical story. If it could be arranged for Ramesses' unmarried daughter to find and adopt Moses, there would be little cause for jealousy. The mother, of whom Ramesses had grown fond, also could enter the palace as nurse to her son. The ruse worked as intended but it also symbolized something spiritual that occurred as Moses was enclosed in the basket: "The symbol of the Osiris chest as the initiation coffin is placed into the earliest destiny of Moses' life as a sign for the wondrous reawakening of an initiation undergone in a previous incarnation."[8]

The arranged adoption of Moses opened a mission-completing path for Moses, a path otherwise closed to a Hebrew boy in bondage. Even the pharaoh's daughter, the adoptive mother, could not accomplish what her father did for Moses' education, the scope of which Stephen revealed in Acts 7:22: "And Moses was instructed in all the wisdom of the Egyptians," a wisdom that was fundamentally a wisdom of Hermes, which was Moses' mission to receive in this manner and continue its evolution. According to Steiner: "As the earth thrust what it contained within it as moon, toward the sun, so the Earth wisdom of Moses had to go out to meet that of Hermes, who possessed in his astral sheath the direct wisdom of Zarathustra, and afterward had to carry on its own evolution."

By the time he was forty, Moses had completed the first part of his dual mission. It was marked by two events: the killing of an Egyptian overseer, which forced his exile, and another Great Conjunction, this time in sidereal Taurus (May 2, 1476 BC). Bock describes this transition point in Moses' life "as a slaying of the Egyptian within himself."

Moses spent his exile as a disciple of the priest Jethro in Midian, near the ancient site of Petra in southern Jordan. Moses was instructed by Jethro in the Arabian mysteries. Bock states[9]: "Just as a reabsorption of the Joseph element had been brought about through Moses' Egyptian initiation, so through his Arabian initiation, that of Ishmael was accomplished. The streams that had been excluded from the formation of the Israelite–Jewish hereditary line are now spiritually brought back from outside through the contributions they bestow on the enhancement of Israel's spiritual life and culture."

---

7 Grant, *So Moses Was Born*.

8 Bock, *Moses*, p. 30.

9 Ibid., p. 85.

Here Bock quotes Steiner:

> Moses found in the Ishmaelites, among whom there was Initiation of a certain kind, those attributes and qualities that had been transmitted to them through Hagar, qualities that were derived from Abraham, but in which were preserved many elements inherited from the ancient past. Out of the revelations he received from this branch of the Hebrew people, it became possible for Moses to make the revelation of Sinai intelligible to the Israelites. On Sinai, the ancient Hebrew people received back again, in the Mosaic Law, what had been cast out from their blood—they received it back from without.[1]

Paul disclosed this same secret (Gal. 4:25), where he equated the Law of Moses with Hagar: "Now Hagar is Mount Sinai in Arabia."

After forty years spent with Jethro, Moses returned to Egypt. His father had died two years after Moses dashed his hope for a priest-pharaoh heir. Moses' half-brother Merenptah had succeeded Ramesses and, in turn, was succeeded by his son Sethos II, who was the pharaoh Moses and Aaron faced when they demanded an end to the bondage of their people. At first it was refused and in the same way Abraham was aided when he faced a recalcitrant pharaoh (Gen.12:17), a series of psychosomatic plagues[2] was visited on the Egyptian people. Finally, Sethos gave permission for the Israelites to leave Egypt, which was not at the time of 1436 BC Conjunction, occurring too late in the year (Sept. 19) to mark a spring Exodus.

According to the Bible, the Exodus occurred in the Hebrew month of Abib (Exod. 13:4). This is when barley reaches a stage of ripeness called *abib*. We also know from the Bible that shortly before the Exodus, the barley had reached this stage (Exod. 9:31). And we know that barley, following its circadian rhythm, reaches this stage around the time of the vernal equinox, which occurred on April 3 (JC). The Hebrew month (and year) begins with the first new moon after abib, which provides two dates, March 21 and April 19. The corresponding Exodus dates are April 4 and May 3. April 4 can be ruled out by not allowing sufficient time for the barley as well as the wheat (Ex. 9:32) to be harvest-ready for the "unleavened bread." It seems probable, therefore, that the Hebrew Exodus began at midnight (Ex. 12:29–32) May 3, 1436 BC, with the light of a full moon.

The Israelites entered the Sinai desert by crossing the Sea of Reeds and not the Red Sea.[3] This would be in a direct line with their destination: Mt. Sinai, which was in Midian, near where Moses lived with Jethro.[4]

The Egyptian Sojourn was necessary to forge the identity of the Israelites as a distinct people. And the Oppression tested their fortitude in waiting for God's answer to their prayers, which they knew would come. For as Sucher contended, "The Exodus was not just a 'running away,' but was conducted out of a clairvoyant insight into the spiritual purpose of it in connection with the coming Incarnation, similar to what the Three Kings had."

Bock further explains the significance of the Exodus:

> When he led his people out of Egypt, Moses had carried away the secret of Osiris, who had ceased to reveal himself in Egypt. One who wanted to continue experiencing him had to depart from Egypt along with him. Moses and the people of Israel ventured into the desert to follow the vanishing god. When the Yahweh deity revealed himself to them in the pillar of cloud and fire, in the fiery lightning of Sinai, they encountered the same divine power that earlier had proclaimed itself to the Egyptians in the figure of Osiris. But just as we call the sunlight, when we see it mirrored by the moon, moonlight, so the Christ was called Yahweh or Jehovah. Hence, Yahweh is none other than the reflection of the Christ before he himself appeared on the Earth.[5]

The Giving of the Law was the first objective of the Exodus. It was marked by an ancestor Great Conjunction in sidereal Libra (Sept. 19, 1436 BC).

---

1   Steiner, *Deeper Secrets*, pp. 65f.
2   Bock, *Moses*, p. 52.
3   Ibid., p. 55.
4   Ibid., p. 68.
5   Ibid., p. 137

It represented the completion of the outward Earth stage and the first return-stage of the Sun wisdom. The ancestor Conjunction of 960 BC (Dec. 5) marked the completion of the Mercury-stage of the returning wisdom. David had died and Solomon was anointed King. Likewise, the ancestor Conjunction of 543 BC marked the completion of the Venus-stage when Zarathustra completed his teaching of Jewish scholars during the Babylonian Captivity. Finally, the Three Kings Conjunction of 7 BC (helio) heralded the coming Incarnation of the Solomon Jesus, the reincarnated Zarathustra, who took part in both evolutionary streams.

Melchizedek (Sun) →
Zarathustra (Sun: Venus stage) →
Hermes (Sun: Mercury stage) →
Moses I (Sun: Earth stage) →
Moses II (Moon) →
David (Mercury) →
Babylonian Captivity (Venus) →
Christ (Sun)

"If you lift your arm and point upward, you have up there the realm of particular Thrones, Cherubim, and Seraphim. If you move and again point upward, you would find other Thrones, Cherubim, and Seraphim above you.... Suppose you wanted to point to some particular Thrones, Cherubim, and Seraphim. They are by no means identical, like a group of twelve similar soldiers, for instance. They differ considerably from one another. Each bears its individual stamp, so that as one looks upward from various points, one sees quite separate beings. In order to locate particular Thrones, Cherubim, and Seraphim, one denotes them by a particular constellation. It is like a signpost. In that direction over there are the Thrones, Cherubim, and Seraphim known as the Twins, over there, the Lion, and so on. The constellations of the zodiac are more than mere signposts.... It is important to realize that, when we refer to the zodiac, we are speaking of spiritual beings."

— **Rudolf Steiner**, *Spiritual Hierarchies and the Physical World*, April 17, 1909

ZODIACS AND CALENDARS
CONTROVERSY ABOUT GUIDANCE FROM THE HEAVENS

David Tresemer

In the third century BCE, Hecateus of Abdera visited Thebes, including the remains of what we now call the Ramesseum, built nearly a thousand years before the historian's visit. Hecateus described the temple thoroughly, including this passage: "There, too, a gold circle was to be seen, three hundred and sixty-five cubits long and one cubit high." A cubit is the very portable measure of elbow to outstretched fingers. The Egyptians had standard measures for the cubit and every worker had a useful approximation from his own body. Hecateus explained: "Images for each day of the year were set out around this circle, one for every cubit: the rising and setting of the stars were recorded for each day, together with the signs with which those astral movements furnished the Egyptian astrologers." I have seen in Egypt the clay dolls used to represent each of the days in ancient temples. Each day was a demi-god with a unique job relating to the changing seasons of the year, beginning with the spring equinox, the tipping point of short days into long days; each day had a different balance of hours of light and dark, centering on the two days where the light and dark are equal, the equinoxes. The Egyptians loved tipping points, the sense of scales, for example, the weighing of one's deeds against the qualities of one's heart just after death.

Many features of that temple were last described by Hecateus. Now, as Shelley wrote about the great king Ramses (Oxymandias in Greek, thus the name of Shelley's poem), "Round the decay/Of that colossal Wreck, boundless and bare/ The lone and level sands stretch far away."

Two systems of time had been etched in stone, treated as a single measure of the rhythms of the year. One measured the procession of the days—each with its cubit in the temple—beginning the year at the spring equinox. The other system of time measured the occurrence of the stars, often in heliacal rising. Let me explain the heliacal phenomenon. All through the night, stars rise from the East. Then a thin band of orange heralds the coming Sun. You perhaps see a much beloved star rise, Sirius or the Pleiades, just before the sky brightens with the Sun's light. It's a brief moment of recognition before the twinkling star fades into the sky-brightness of the day. You look forward to see it increasingly clearly in the next days because they rise a little earlier than the Sun each day. Viewing heliacal rising is best done in the desert with clear skies and a broad horizon.

Though the connection between these two systems of time seemed reliable enough to carve into stone, they in fact diverge...slowly. In the 360° system given us by Zoroaster (which, adding five holy days, gives us the 365 of the year), the stars and seasonal days separate by one degree every 72 years. One really doesn't notice that in one's lifetime, nor even in a few generations. But over the decades, the stone calendar in the Ramesseum becomes unreliable. There are accounts of the dismay that this divergence caused the ancients who felt a disturbance to the regularity of the seasons as revealed in the stars.

Once we know we have two systems of time, we can appraise the different qualities that we gain from either one. We can call one the zodiac, which Zarathustra (also named Zoroaster and Zaratas—a story for another day) felt as living beings in the heavens, twelve of them, with thirty qualities of life-force (Zoë the root of zodiac) each. 12 x 30 gives us the 360 that we use both for time (our twelve-fold clock-face comes from that understanding) and space (the 360° of a circle). Zoroaster gave names to these living beings, such as the Bull, with its central star Aldebaran as the Eye of the Bull, what I have come to call the Star of Life and Abundance. Indeed, the map of the heavens was hinged on the main star of the Bull—Aldebaran—and of the Scorpion—Antares, Heart of the Scorpion, what I have come to call the Star of Death and Resurrection—both in the centers of those living beings, and exactly 180° apart. This system is the sidereal system, from "sidus," star—thus the star-based system, finding in the stars great living beings.

We can call the other system of time a seasonal calendar, based on the phenomena of longest day (summer solstice), shortest day (winter solstice), and equal day-light days (spring and autumn equinoxes), where the Earth's horizon is the frame of reference and not the stars. To an agricultural community, knowing where one is in the seasons of the year is all-important. One can even think of this as a weather calendar, but perhaps most simply as a day-length calendar. It is also called the tropical system, from *tropos*, turning. "To everything, turn, turn, turn, there is a season" (remember the song by the Byrds?). At the StarHouse in Boulder, Colorado, we celebrate the light-phenomena of equinoxes and solstices.[1] As Steiner recommended, "Celebrate the seasons!"

The trouble has been that some people have tried to hold on to the stone carvings observed by Hecateus that link the two systems of time. Some of the day-length calendar people have tried to say that the stars still appear as they were once seen. They have kept the names of the constellations, so that one can now hear, "The Eye of the Bull? Oh, that's now in the Twins, you know, Gemini. The Twins, you ask? Oh, they're now in the Crab." When you point to a planet visible near the Heart of the Scorpion, they say, "That planet is in Sagittarius."

As I recommend in *Star Wisdom & Rudolf Steiner*, it's fine to have names of the seasonal months—that is, from March 21 to April 21, and so on—but they should be season-based names, just as all indigenous peoples have had, what modern science calls phenology, noticing the regular changes of natural phenomena. Names such as "Month When Frost Settles on the Waters" or "Month When Kangaroo Apple Ripens" or "Month Beginning with Return of the Shearwaters" would elicit immediate nods of understanding from those who live in that area. Of course, "Month of Shortest Days" would define the relation to day-length that is the foundation for this system of time.[2]

When Ptolemy described the heavens in the second century, the great beings of the heavens—the Ram, Bull, Twins, Crab, and so on—coordinated with the seasonal calendar such that the first day of spring—vernal equinox, in the northern hemisphere—occurred near the first degree of the Ram (Aries). (This is, of course, reversed in the southern hemisphere.) He described this, and his work disappeared, then was picked up by the Muslim intellectuals, then found its way into Europe of the Middle Ages, who relied on Ptolemy's observation that the first day of spring occurred at the first degree of the Ram—because Ptolemy said so. Was this a mistaken reading of Ptolemy? Did Ptolemy really mean that what he observed in the second century should be true forever?

The divergence is now around 25°, nearly a whole sign of 30°. At one degree every 72 years, it takes 2160 years to move an entire sign. In a few thousand years, it will become very strange—when we start hearing that the Bull visible in the sky is "really" in the Lion and the Scorpion is "really" in the Water Bearer (Aquarius).

When I attended the United Astrology Conference (UAC, the largest of the international conferences that occurs every four years) in New Orleans in May 2012, one of the sub-themes amongst the

---

1 See www.TheStarHouse.org.

2 Elizabeth Vreede, for many years head of the Astronomical Section at Dornach, wrote, "We ought indeed to have two expressions, one for the twelvefold division of the year's cycle, the signs, and one for the configurations of stars visible in the sky, the real constellations of the zodiac." *Anthroposophy and Astrology*, p. 106. The native American approach for tropical astrology is given more thoroughly in *Star Wisdom and Rudolf Steiner*.

tropical astrologers was "Regulus is now moving into Virgo." As I normally practice sidereal astrology, based on what is often termed the "fixed" stars—Aldebaran, Antares, etc.—this caught me by surprise. Regulus—the Heart of the Lion, the King/Queen Star—sidereally at 5° of Leo—doesn't move in relation to the other constellations! But to those who identify the day-length calendar as their home, practically and spiritually, the fixed stars move; day-length is their home, its regular rhythms fixed and stable. Others feel more at home in the shining beings of light with whom they meditate in the heavens, finding pictures arise in their imagination from observing these great beings—in other words, in the tradition of Zarathustra. You have to choose: Do I find my Self, my soul, my home, in the regularity of the seasons unfolding—in day-length? Or do I find my Self, my soul, my home in the great beings of the heavens? In one's own lifetime these are correlated, changing the tiniest bit. But over time—over your personal lifetimes and in any historical research, including in one's reliance on the life of Christ and the Mystery of Golgotha for inspiration and support—one has to choose. Do you find the generative power of creation starting with the Earth and moving out into the heavens? Or do you find the generative power of creation starting with the heavens and coming into earthly life?[1]

You can choose both systems for different purposes, and some do pick on the tropical system as a hint to personality dynamics while relying on the sidereal understanding of the starry heavens for soul guidance. But controversies have now arisen about the "right" system, and that does tend to polarize all listeners. Unfortunately it turns many people away from the heavens altogether. If you would like to skip the controversy, go to the last section on naked eye astronomy.

Enter Dr. Adrian Anderson

Adrian Anderson's book *Living the Spiritual Year* was such a godsend, speaking with great depth of understanding of the breathing of the whole earth in relation to the seasons. I have used it intensively in my work, and am most grateful for it. It seems particularly important for the southern hemisphere—for the understanding of those "down under" as to right relations with the archangelic powers that come at different times of year, and for the education of the northern hemisphere about the contribution of the southern hemisphere to the health of the whole planet.

Recently Dr. Anderson has published two e-books that claim that the tropical system of time is the only right way to understand astrology. These books are *The Origin & Nature of the Tropical Zodiac: The Zodiac Signs: What They Are and Who Created Them* and the book *Rudolf Steiner, the Tropical Zodiac, and the Zodiac Ages*. The first is under his pen name, Damien Pryor.

I've shared my conclusions above—you have to educate yourself about this, as it's important! The issue concerns where you might find the resonance necessary for your own soul development. I would like to address certain claims in Anderson's writing so that his certainty in these matters is tempered by a wider view. They center on three questions:

- Is Robert Powell wrong?
- Did Steiner prefer the tropical system of time?
- How do I find my relationship to the heavens?

Is Robert Powell Wrong?

Robert Powell has written extensively about the zodiac, including *The History of the Zodiac*, which is a revision of his Ph.D. thesis at the Polish Academy of Sciences. More recently he wrote *The Astrological Revolution* about these issues, as well as a research paper, "The Bible of Astrology,"

---

1 In truth, everything moves, including the "fixed" stars in much slower "proper motion" around the Galactic Centre. The question is, what is more the stable home base and what the passing phenomena? It becomes a question of orientation—to what do you orient as your home? Steiner pictured this in *The Portal of Initiation*, scene 2, in which Johannes becomes profoundly disoriented: "And now [the process of coming to know himself] robs me of myself. I alter with the hours of the day, and change myself to night" (*The Four Mystery Plays*). He spirals into vertigo and horror because he has lost his bearings. The fundamental question of this paper: What gives you (your Self, your Soul) your most reliable bearings?

about Ptolemy's *Tetrabiblos* written in the second century.[2] Adrian Anderson criticizes "the incorrect writings of Powell" as an example of the wrong-headed siderealists by quoting a paper from the venerable tropical astrologer Robert Hand. Here is Hand's comment: "On page 10 of *The Zodiac: A Historical Survey* by Robert Powell, the author cites a passage from Neugebauer's *History of Ancient Mathematical Astronomy* [HAMA] as evidence for the Anonymous being a siderealist. Unfortunately the passage in question is one in which Neugebauer is dating this author and another author named Cleomedes to the 4th century by showing that their values for star positions are derived from correcting Ptolemy's positions using his precessional constant! One wonders how much of the evidence for the sidereal zodiac among the Greeks comes from similarly questionable research."[3] That's the critique from Hand. However, Powell's booklet, *The Zodiac: A Historical Survey*, is older (published 1984), rarer (as of this writing, Amazon lists it for $677.28), and briefer (32 pages) in comparison to his more recent works on this very topic, especially *History of the Zodiac* (224 pages), and also *The Astrological Revolution* (254 pages) and *Astrogeographia* (312 pages). Robert Hand's comments were based on Powell's much briefer and much older work, and Adrian Anderson has not kept up to date with the more thorough explanations. I recommended to both of them that they speak about the proper use of the Neugebauer material, but alas that didn't happen before these latest publications.

I have carefully studied Powell's research and writing, and chosen for most of my astrological work a direct connection with the stars. Indeed, in a recent article for *International Astrologer*, I presented a study of the discoverers of the planet Neptune. I found that all of the people most intimately involved with its discovery had at birth (the promise of a life) and at death (the legacy of a life) a strong connection between Neptune in the sky and one of the Royal Stars of Persia (which include Aldebaran, Antares, Regulus, and two others).[4] In a study of Steiner's birth, the centers of the fixed signs become very important, especially the axis between Aldebaran and Antares. During his life, whenever Jupiter crossed Antares, completing a four-sided square in his birth chart, astonishing breakthroughs occurred in Anthroposophy.[5]

I do find it interesting that Robert Hand's article, on which Adrian Anderson relies in order to reject Powell, ends like this:

> The tropical–sidereal controversy...was not a problem with which the ancients were seriously concerned. Given the limits of their computational accuracy, both systems would have given them the same results [as I explained, the two systems were nearly identical during the years of Ptolemy and the early astrologers]. This is a question that we have to solve for ourselves. An appeal to history will not work.

If we take Hand's advice, we must look elsewhere than to old quotes of ancient astrologers. However, you may wish to understand the roots of human consciousness in relation to the heavens by figuring out what was said—and more importantly, what was meant—by whom. Reference to the works cited makes a good beginning in that quest.

Did Rudolf Steiner Favor One System of Time over Another?

Adrian Anderson admits that Steiner understood the equal-size astrological signs, as they actually existed in the heavens, that is, sidereally. Steiner traced the course of the spring equinox through them over time. For example, on January 19, 1915, Steiner stated, "The time interval needed for the

---

2 Powell and Dann *The Astrological Revolution: Unveiling the Science of the Stars as a Science of Reincarnation and Karma*.

3 See http://cura.free.fr/quinq/01hand.html and Anderson's *The Origin and Nature of the Tropical Zodiac*.

4 More about the Royal Stars can be found in Tresemer (with Schiappacasse), *Star Wisdom & Rudolf Steiner*; and at www.StarWisdom.org. The Neptune article appears in *International Astrologer* of the International Society for Astrological Research, August 2012, pp. 74–80.

5 I wrote about these Jupiter transits in a paper for the *Journal of Anthroposophy in Australia*, and in various papers in the annual *Journal for Star Wisdom*.

Sun to progress from one constellation in the zodiac to the next is approximately 2,160 years, and this is important."[1] That's 72 years per degree, 2,160 years per sign, and 25,920 years to go fully around in the precession of the equinoxes due to the Earth's slow wobble on its axis.

Steiner also gave indications for biodynamic farmers that they relate to the presence of the stars as residences of living beings. Maria Thun interpreted this as following the constellations, which she viewed not of equal size.[2] Others, including the biodynamic calendar writer Brian Keats and the weather researcher Dennis Klocek, interpreted this as following the original sidereal signs (that is, the Eye of the Bull is still at the center of the Bull as one can observe), equal-sized, taking on the ancient Zarathustrian–Babylonian understanding of the heavens. The difference between Thun's sidereal unequal constellations and Keats' equal signs is really only a few degrees here and there, and they are both sidereal, star-oriented.

Adrian Anderson, however, says that Steiner preferred the tropical system for understanding human personalities, and that therefore Steiner was a tropical astrologer. He bases this on Steiner's comparison of the two albino children that came up in the question-answer period of the Curative Education course on July 5, 1924. Here was the scene: A question arose about two albino children. Elizabeth Vreede was attending and quickly drew up two charts in the main method available at the time, which was tropical. Steiner looked at the charts and spoke about them. The comments have far more to do with iron sulfide (about which he spoke on February 2 without reference to astrology), and the connection between Uranus and Neptune. The relationships between planets occur whether the approach is tropical or sidereal.

We can make a few observations. First, Steiner did not state a preference for tropical or sidereal in personality work, mostly because he made so little use of actual horoscopes. Second, the tropical mode for planetary positions was the only one known at the time—Elizabeth Vreede may have cast a tropical horoscope, because those planetary positions (ephemerides) were all that were available at that time. That dominance in the West was not altered until Cyril Fagan's work in the 1950s.[3] But look at Vreede's writings in *Anthroposophy and Astrology* and you will see that she emphasized the stars in the heavens where they actually lie—the phenomena themselves. She saw the primal harmony of the human being with Aries beginning on March 21 (northern hemisphere) destroyed when the two systems diverged:

> It *had* to be destroyed through the Christ impulse that had bound the cosmic forces to the earth...new forces were released. A short time after his earthly life Christ appeared under the symbol of a fish [vernal point in the Fishes (Pisces)], while formerly he was venerated as the good shepherd bearing the lamb, indeed, as himself the Lamb of God [vernal point in the Ram (Aries)].[4]

Thus the Turning Point of Time was indeed a turning point in relation to the heavens, as well—a meeting of 0° Aries and the equinox, which then diverged, releasing new energies.

Both Powell and Anderson go into great detail in books already mentioned, but the overwhelming sense I get is that the evidence from Steiner is sketchy, marginal, indirect, and emphasizing the importance of the great beings of the zodiac and of the hierarchies. Steiner made many references to the divine beings of the heavens.[5] However, very little has to do with individuals. He could have cast horoscopes for dozens of the people he spoke

---

1 *The Destinies of Individuals and of Nations*, p. 70. There are many small issues involving an understanding of exactly what Steiner meant by his star references. This one is clear. However, the analysis of the ages deserves a larger study beyond the scope of this paper.

2 The differences are not great—see Robert Powell's note on the boundaries of the zodiac in the Research section of www.StarWisdom.org.

3 The blockbuster was *Zodiacs: Old and New* and was substantiated with much more research in *Astrological Origins*. Fagan was President of the Irish Astrological Society in Dublin.

4 Vreede, *Anthroposophy and Astrology*, p. 105.

5 Rick Bobbette collected these, and it added up to three volumes!

about, but he did not. It has been left to us to unravel the "indications" to make them practical.

How Do I Find the Heavens?
Naked Eye Astronomy

Rather than become distracted by the conceptual controversies—which requires many more pages and footnotes—make a relationship with the actual stars in the heavens, those twinkling wonders that show themselves when you have left the city's glow. Don't let telescopes lure you into their greater detail because they obscure more than they reveal. And don't let tropical astrology confuse you that the Heart of the Lion is not in the Lion anymore, but rather has begun to penetrate the Virgin. Simply find a star and begin to contemplate it. Gaze at the star with warm interest. You don't even need to know its name, though if you discover a relationship with it, you might be interested later to learn some of its background, its resumé, so to speak. Beyond all the conceptual controversy, it comes down to this: Can you have a relationship with what Ramses set in stone and Hecateus admired—with the different beings who represent the days of the year (one of which is special to you as it's your birthday)[6] and with the stars that offer themselves in the sky for your warm interest? Can you find in one or both an inner sense of reverence and devotion to the divine beings of creation?

This article was initially printed in Journal for Anthroposophy in Australia, *2012*

---

[6] At www.StarWisdom.org, under "Your Solar Cross," we have given a recommendation on how to celebrate your birthday.

"The mission to which his birth called him [the birth of the Old Testament patriarch Jacob] was revealed to him through the realm of the angels...conscious perception of the angels came to him....The first stage...is attained when one enters conscious interaction with the beings of the angelic hierarchy.... [This] does not involve knowledge of universal laws, but entering conscious interaction with the beings who know the mysteries of birth. The true horoscope will not be reached by a path of calculation but through a path of interaction with suprasensory beings. What angels have imparted to humankind, that is the 'horoscope' in the true sense."
—Valentin Tomberg, *Christ and Sophia,* p. 47

WHERE ON EARTH IS THE ZODIAC?
AND OTHER CONCERNS OF ASTRO-GAIASOPHY

Brian Gray

"In my Father's house there are many dwellings; otherwise I would not have said to you: I go there to prepare a place for you." —John 14:2[1]

"Earth is a living organism. And just as human beings need air to live, so the Earth needs the spiritual light of the stars. It inhales this in order to live. And just as a person walks around on the Earth, so the Earth moves around in the cosmos. It dwells in the whole of the universe. The Earth is a living entity."[2]
—Rudolf Steiner, April 12, 1924, Dornach

"All fixed land swims and the stars hold it in position.... The continents swim.... They are held in position upon the Earth by the constellations. When the constellations change, the continents change, also. The old tellurians [Earth globes on a tilted axis to depict the seasons] and atlases properly included the constellations of the zodiac in relationship to the configuration of the Earth's surface. The continents are held from the periphery; the higher realms hold the parts of the Earth."[3]
—Rudolf Steiner, April 25, 1923, Stuttgart

S tar Wisdom becomes particularly meaningful when we discover where spiritual influences stream from the Stars to our living Earth, shaping and sustaining our cosmic/earthly existence. Star Wisdom and Earth Wisdom are deeply related. We live by the grace of spiritual beings dwelling in the Heavens and indwelling Mother Earth.

During this stage of evolution, when the wellbeing of our living Earth is sorely threatened by human ignorance, abuse, and excess, it is time for us to become aware of the dynamic spiritual relationships between the Stars and the Earth. Recognizing these interrelationships is crucially important for Human Wisdom to grow and flourish, and for us to participate creatively in shaping the future.

Star Wisdom (*Astro Sophia* or *Astrosophy*) encompasses the spirit, soul, and bodily wisdom of the heavens and of the deeds of spiritual Beings dwelling there. Earth Wisdom (*Gaia Sophia* or *Gaiasophy*) encompasses the spirit, soul, and bodily wisdom of the living Earth and of the Earth's place and mission in the cosmos. Human beings seeking correspondences between Star Wisdom and Earth Wisdom can be guided by *Astro-Gaia Sophia* (*Astro-Gaiasophy*). Astro-Gaia Sophia encompasses the correspondences between the *Wisdom of Star Beings (Astro Sophia)* and the *Wisdom of Mother Earth (Gaia Sophia)*.

Contemplating the mysteries of *Astro-Gaia Sophia* can expand our feelings of wonder and gratitude and stimulate our striving as upright human beings (*Anthropos*) to embrace and unite with all Wisdom (*Sophia*). Our quest to unite with *Anthropos Sophia* (Anthroposophy) can guide our striving to develop *Astro-Gaiasophy* (see figure 1). "The more spiritual knowledge flows into the evolution of humanity and the Earth, the greater the number of viable seeds will there be for the future."[4] The striving Human Being (*Anthropos*) can become a Mercurial mediator who embraces both Star Wisdom (Astrosophy) and Earth Wisdom (Gaiasophy) and creatively participates in the

---
1 Madsen, *The New Testament: A Rendering*, p. 248.
2 Steiner, *From Beetroot to Buddhism...* p. 127
3 Steiner, *Faculty Meetings with Rudolf Steiner*, pp. 617–618.

---
4 Steiner, *An Outline of Esoteric Science*, p. 397.

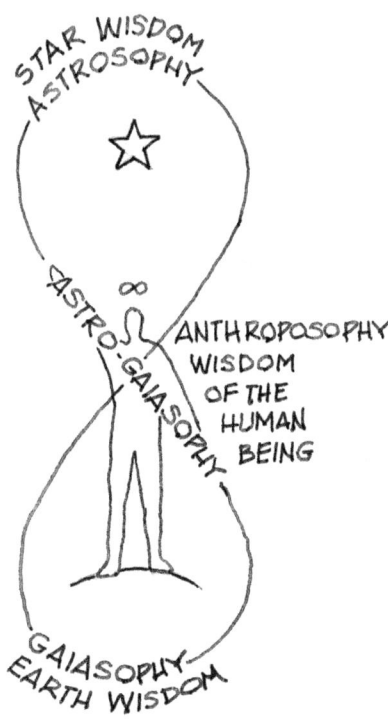

Figure 1

mysteries *Astro-Gaiasophy*. In this way *Astro-Gaiasophy* can become part of Wisdom of the Human Being (*Anthroposophy*). Human Wisdom (Anthroposophy) can then gradually be transformed into Love:

> Beginning with the Earth phase of evolution, the Wisdom of the Outer Cosmos becomes the Inner Wisdom in the Human Being. Internalized in this way, it becomes the seed of Love. Wisdom is the prerequisite for Love; Love is the result of Wisdom that has been reborn in the "I."[5]

Astro-Gaia Sophia beckoned me more than 30 years ago to awaken to her presence. She continually pours forth insights from the depths of her wisdom, yet her mysteries are so subtle that she may at times seem elusive. It takes time to prepare our souls to receive the seeds of her wisdom, and additional time for those seeds to grow and ripen. Astro-Gaia Sophia is present and active in the midst of all that we experience on Earth, yet she moves unseen among human beings. We long to awaken to her. Many paths lead toward her mysteries and many seekers today find clues about her activity. Astro-Gaia Sophia holds keys to the Wisdom of Macrocosm and Microcosm. The depths of her revelations open new perspectives and fill us with wonder and awe. While she generously bestows imaginations and inspirations, after pursuing her for three decades I have more *questions* than answers about her true nature. The words of Socrates best express my experience of her: "As for me, all I know is that I know nothing."[6]

WHAT IS ASTRO-GAIASOPHY?

Astro-Gaiasophy as presented in this article arises out of the phenomenological research into the mysteries of Astro-Gaia Sophia initiated by the author more than 30 years ago. Simply described, Astro-Gaiasophy contemplates *direct zenith-projection relationships between constellations of Stars and their positions on the surface of Earth*. The phrase "direct zenith-projection" refers to a *Star's position directly above a place on Earth*; that is, a person standing at that place could view that Star passing *directly overhead at the zenith position*. Zenith-projection relationships between the Stars and places on Earth can be visualized by examining the equivalent of the Star-Earth globe[7] described in this article. Astro-Gaiasophy considers that lofty spiritual Beings dwelling in the periphery of the celestial sphere form and condense the Earth, and that radial lines projecting inwardly from Stars at the periphery of the celestial sphere converge and are mirrored *at the exact geographical center of the Earth, as well as upon Earth's surface*.

Rudolf Steiner articulated the basis for Astro-Gaiasophy very clearly in 1922 as he described understandings that arose within the Egyptian Mysteries:

> If you had been able to participate in many a scene in the Mysteries during a certain epoch of Egyptian development, in times when the custom of the mummification of bodies was at its height, you would have experienced something

---

5 Ibid., p. 397 (capitalization added by author).

6 Plato, *Republic*, conclusion of book 1.

7 Celestial Globe CG 616, Trippensee Planetarium, 1967. See figure 6 in this article.

like the following. The Priest-Instructor in the Mysteries would have tried, first, to explain to his pupils that in the human head all the mysteries of the world lie concealed, in a very special sense. *He would have bidden them regard the Earth, the dwelling-place of the human being, as a mirror, a reflection of the whole Cosmos.* In very truth, *everything that exists in the Cosmos is also to be found in the Earth itself.* Looking upward to the world of Stars, we see the Moon as our nearest neighbor among the heavenly bodies. Think of the Earth and the Moon circling around the Earth. We can picture the course taken by the Moon as it moves around the Earth and all that lies between the Earth and the orbit of the Moon. Those who rightly understand how to interpret what they find when they dig down into the Earth, will say: What is present in the environment is mirrored, and condensed, in an outermost layer of the Earth itself.

And now take another planet, which together with the Earth, circles round the Sun. We can picture this planet, Venus, and its path. This sphere is filled with delicate, aeriform, etheric substance. Again a lower layer in the Earth must be pictured as a reflection of what is outside in the Cosmos. Proceeding in this way we have **the whole Earth as a mirror image of the Universe**, remembering that what exists out yonder in a state of extremely delicate, ethereal volatility is *condensed and still further condensed when it is found in the Earth's strata.* **Thus at the center of the Earth, the outermost periphery of the Universe would be condensed into a single point.**[1]

This passage given by Rudolf Steiner in 1922 establishes the cognitive foundation for Astro-Gaiasophy and describes its central approach. Although the author only recently (in 2013) discovered this passage, it independently anchors and characterizes three decades of research into the mysteries of Astro-Gaia Sophia. This approach to Astro-Gaiasophy feels inspired by and aligned with Rudolf Steiner's description; for that I am most grateful.

One way to picture the relationships between the Stars in the Heavens and the places on the Earth presented through Astro-Gaiasophy is to imagine all points on the periphery of the entire celestial sphere "condensed" inwardly and contracted until they exactly touch the spherical surface of the Earth. This "condensing" brings the activity from the periphery of the celestial sphere to *focus upon the exact center of the Earth*. Astro-Gaiasophy considers the *direct zenith-projection of each Star on the celestial sphere as raying spiritual influences toward a place on the Earth's surface*, where on the Earth's surface each Star maintains its positional relationships with the celestial sphere. *The Earth's surface bears the imprint of the Zodiac and fixed Stars.* In this way the description *"the whole Earth as a mirror image of the Universe"* arises for our contemplation through Astro-Gaiasophy.

Three Planes of Reference

Three distinct planes of reference are helpful to establish a cognitive framework for Astro-Gaiasophy: the **ecliptic plane**, the **equatorial plane**, and the **galactic plane**. The *ecliptic plane* and *galactic plane* arise by observing the Sun, planets, and stars motions and positions on the celestial sphere from the Earth. Thus the *ecliptic plane* and *galactic plane* are primarily of interest to *Astrosophy*. On the other hand, the *equatorial plane* arises by observing the Earth's rotation about its North-South axis and the daily rising and setting of the Sun and stars. Thus the *equatorial plane* is primarily of interest to *Gaiasophy*. But for us to grasp dynamic interactions between Star Wisdom and Earth Wisdom, *all three planes* are the concern of *Astro-Gaiasophy*. It is important to keep these three distinct planes in mind, for each plays a significant but different role.

The **ecliptic plane** is the *path of the Sun through the twelve constellations of the Zodiac* as viewed from Earth. The ecliptic plane is considered important for Star Wisdom because it locates the Sun's plane of movement against the background of the *celestial sphere*. Initially it might seem that the ecliptic plane is of minor importance to Earth Wisdom, because the Earth makes a complete rotation

---

[1] Steiner, *Supersensible Influences in the History of Mankind.* Sept. 29, 1922.

within the celestial sphere on its north-south axis every 23 hours and 56 minutes. Since the *ecliptic plane* is tilted 23½° in relation to the Earth's *equator*, at any given moment of the day the *ecliptic plane* and Zodiac stand directly above and intersect some part of Earth in that region called the "tropics"—that is, between 23½° north latitude (the "Tropic of Cancer") through the equator to 23½° south latitude (the "Tropic of Capricorn").

Since the *ecliptic plane* continually appears to "move" during the course of the day as viewed from the rotating Earth, the *ecliptic plane* is not usually sought on the Earth's surface. But Astro-Gaiasophy identifies and contemplates *the ecliptic plane and Zodiac imprinted into the surface of the Earth* at a particular moment of alignment each day. Astro-Gaiasophy asks the question, *"Where on Earth is the Zodiac?"* Hence the *imprint of the Zodiac and fixed-star constellations upon the surface of the Earth* is of major concern. The *ecliptic plane* extending the Zodiac from the celestial sphere through the center of the Earth presently *imprints the Earth* at a tilt of 23½° off the Earth's equator (see figure 2).

The *ecliptic plane imprinted on Earth* currently intersects the *equatorial plane—the plane of the Earth's equator*—at two places on the Earth's surface: A) near the mouth of the Amazon River at the north coast of South America, and B) near the islands of Indonesia. Astro-Gaiasophy traces the *imprinted ecliptic plane* from its crossing the equator A) near the Amazon River and continues to the northeast across the Atlantic Ocean to northern Africa, where it "levels out" at 23½° north latitude in the Red Sea. The *imprinted ecliptic plane* turns southeastward across the Arabian Peninsula and through southern India and Malaysia to cross the equator B) in Indonesia near the island of Halmahera. The ecliptic continues southeastward across New Guinea and through several island clusters to southern culmination at 23½° south latitude in the South Pacific, below French Polynesia. It gradually turns northeastward across Peru and the Amazon Basin and returns to cross the equator A) near the mouth of the Amazon River. This paper presents further details about the ecliptic and Zodiacal

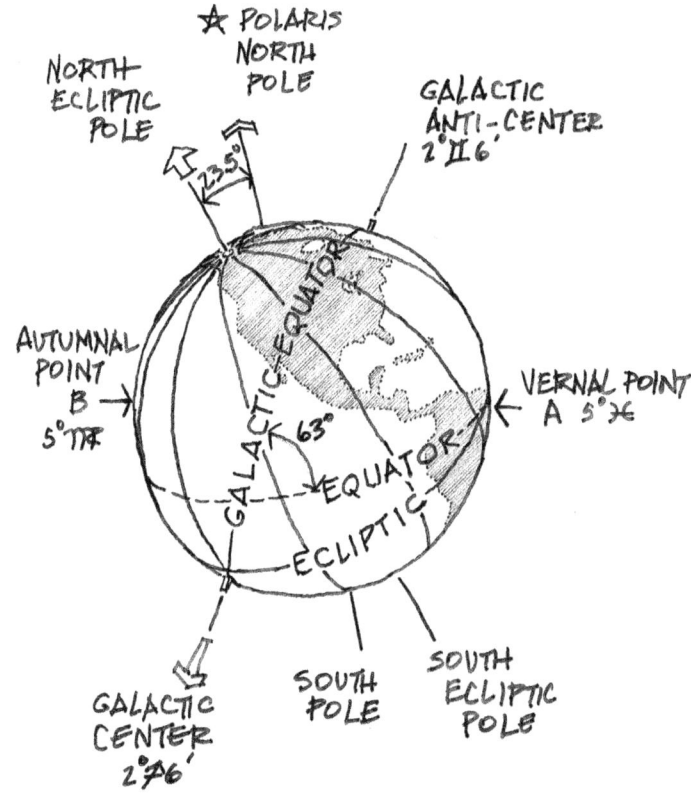

Figure 2

positions and illustrates other star constellations imprinted upon the Earth at the present time. Published here for the first time is the *Zodiac imprinted on Earth* as revealed through research into the mysteries of *Astro-Gaiasophy*.

On the celestial sphere, the ecliptic plane through the Zodiac has its "north ecliptic pole" in the constellation of Draco and its "south ecliptic pole" in the southern-hemisphere constellation of Dorado, near the Large Magellenic Cloud. In exactly the same way *on the Earth*, the ecliptic **plane of the Zodiac imprinted on Earth** has its *"north ecliptic pole" in Alaska* on the Arctic Circle and its *"south ecliptic pole" just off the coast of Antarctica* (far south of Madagascar) on the Antarctic Circle.

Astro-Gaiasophy recognizes as significant the **lines of ecliptic longitude (ecliptic meridians)** extending between the *north pole of the ecliptic* and the *south pole of the ecliptic* as **imprinted on the Earth's surface**. These *imprinted ecliptic meridians* divide the Earth's surface into *12*

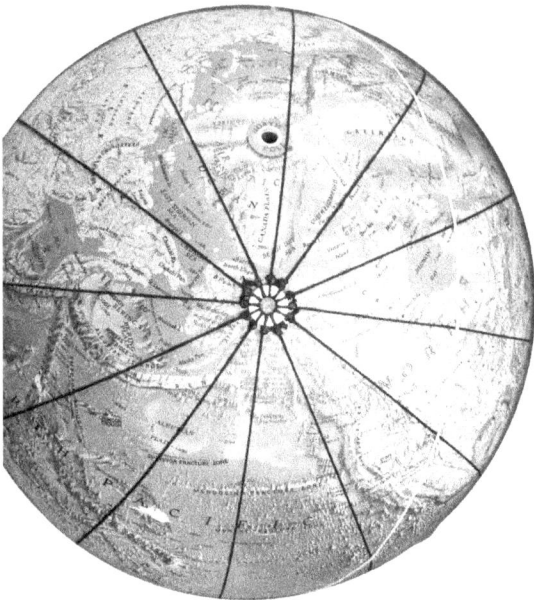

Figure 3   *Figure 4*

distinct Zodiacal sectors. Each *Zodiacal sector of the Earth* bears and reflects the spiritual influences of its celestial Zodiacal counterpart. Throughout each *Zodiacal sector* on Earth, a constellation of the Zodiac radiates its spiritual influences *between the poles of the ecliptic* (see figure 3).

The *equatorial plane* is a second plane of importance when describing the phenomena of Astro-Gaiasophy. As its name implies, the "equator" of the Earth is the plane located equidistant between the geographic North Pole and the South Pole, which mark the *Earth's axis of rotation*. On the Earth, the geographic *north and south rotational pole of the Earth* (the "North Pole" and "South Pole") are currently tilted 23½° off the *poles of the ecliptic*, and the Earth's equator is tilted 23½° off the ecliptic plane (see figure 4). Ptolemy and other cartographers in Alexandria established the *equator* and the *North and South poles* as frameworks for mapping the Earth's surface. Lines parallel with the equator are called *geographic latitudes*, and lines extending between the North Pole and South Pole are lines of *geographic longitude*. The *equatorial plane* is most frequently used when mapping the Earth by latitude and longitude. Most maps of the Earth and Earth globes designate t*he Earth's equator* as a key plane of reference.

But the **Earth's equatorial plane** can also be extended out to intersect the celestial sphere. The plane where the Earth's **equatorial plane** *intersects the celestial sphere* is called the **celestial equator.**

Please notice that the **ecliptic plane** *on the celestial sphere* is very different than the **equatorial plane** extended as the **celestial equator**; the ecliptic plane and equatorial plane are currently tilted off away from each other by 23½°. The **ecliptic plane** and the **celestial equator** are different planes of reference. On the Earth, the *imprinted ecliptic plane* is tilted off the equator by 23½°.

A *third significant plane* considered by Astro-Gaiasophy is the *galactic plane*—the term used to refer to the approximate center of the **Milky Way Galaxy**, the local galaxy to which our Sun and solar system belong. The Milky Way Galaxy forms the mysterious glowing band of light of variable width that wraps across the celestial sphere and encircles the Earth. *On the celestial sphere*, the **galactic plane** is tilted off both the **ecliptic plane** and the **celestial equator**. In the ancient Egyptian mysteries the Milky Way was considered the pathway taken by the soul and spirit into the spiritual world after death, as well as the pathway leading the soul and spirit back toward a new incarnation on Earth. In Astro-Gaiasophy, the *galactic plane* of the Milky Way is recognized as being very significant. The Milky Way divides the heavens into two parts, and its band of light mediates between the two as a third element. The galactic plane of the encircling Milky Way also imprints the Earth. The ***imprinted galactic plane*** divides the Earth into two portions while mediating between them as a third element. Its role and significance on Earth will be discussed later in this article.

BECOMING AWARE OF ASTRO-GAIA SOPHIA

Where on Earth is the Zodiac? How are the starry heavens related to the different regions of the Earth? The author began actively studying, mapping, observing, contemplating, meditating on, and discussing these questions with others in 1982. Astro-Gaia Sophia often reveals her mysteries artistically, through imaginations and inspirations, rather than through abstract theories and mathematical calculations, from which she shyly retreats. Because her mysteries manifest directly in the corresponding phenomena between the Stars and the Earth, her revelations arise most directly in us by *beholding these phenomena* with an open mind and *thinking about their correspondences* with wonder, reverence, wisdom-filled harmony, and devoted self-surrender.[1] It can be difficult to let go of pre-judgments and favorite theories when seeking her, yet Astro-Gaia Sophia can best reveal her mysteries if we surrender our preconceptions and let her guide us through attentive receptivity to her phenomena. She has wonderful things to teach us.

Finding an "exact" point of the present Star-Earth alignment to "lock everything in place" is not easy. *Astro-Gaia Sophia* resists our efforts to pin down her alignments with mathematical precision, and she deflects our attempts to define them too narrowly. Her Star-Earth relationships are living, mobile, and artistic rather than static,

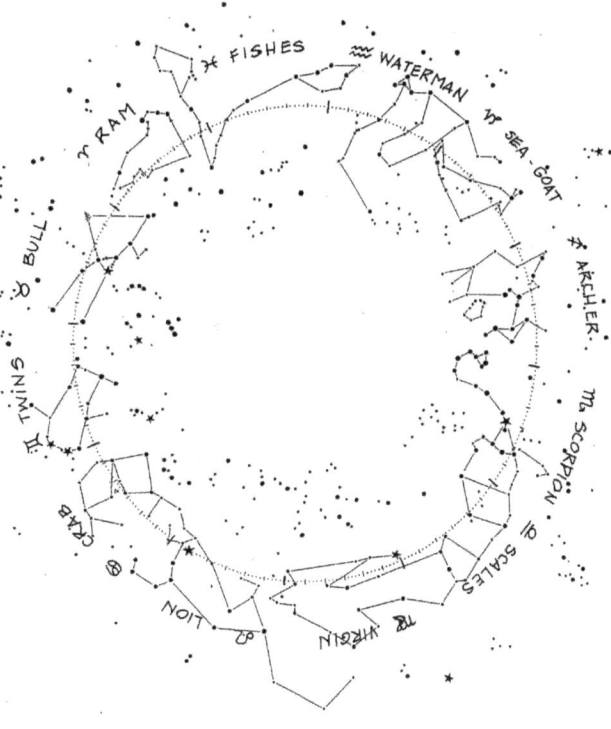

Figure 5

"dead," and calculable. *Astro Sophia* is the cosmic living being who mildly tolerates our human attempts to "plot," calculate, and predict her celestial phenomena. *Gaia Sophia* is the dynamic living Earth who rotates beneath the celestial sphere in the course of the day and year while slowly shifting her rotational axis relative to the celestial sphere through the *precession of the equinoxes*. *Gaia Sophia* is far less tolerant of our attempts to plot, calculate, and predict her earthly phenomena than is *Astro Sophia*. Thus when we approach *Astro-Gaia Sophia*, our approach must be artistic, living, and adaptable.

Having some practical skills can facilitate our search for Astro-Gaia Sophia and help prepare our souls to receive her secrets. My background training in architecture, landscape architecture, and environmental planning prepared me to work with large scale maps of the Earth and geometric drawing, and my interest in the Stars led to my constructing a map of the Babylonian Sidereal Zodiac in 1982 (see figure 5). Practicing Astrology since 1967 and studying Steiner's descriptions of cosmic and human evolution since 1976 attuned

---

[1] Steiner, *The World of the Senses and the World of the Spirit,* December 27, 1911.

Figure 6: Star-Earth globe

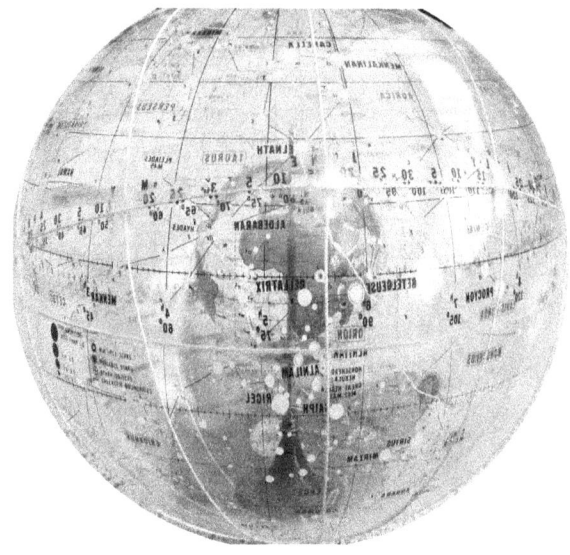

Figure 7: Orion over Africa

me to subtle mysteries of the Heavens, the Earth, and the human Being. Anthroposophy became my spiritual path in 1976, and entering Rudolf Steiner College as a student of René Querido and Willi Sucher in 1979, becoming an active teacher there since 1981, and finding other colleagues who are interested in these mysteries profoundly changed my life.

But by 1982 I had not yet encountered Rudolf Steiner's statements (some quoted in this article) that point toward specific correlations between the Stars in the Heavens and particular places on the Earth. Hence my imagination was stirred and awakened when (in 1982) I first read this vivid passage written by Moira Timms in her 1980 book, *Prophecies and Predictions*:

> If a star map is superimposed over the Earth with the pole star placed over the terrestrial North Pole, we have a celestial clock making one revolution daily. The noon point of that map (like Greenwich) is the Great Pyramid of Giza referred to by the prophet Isaiah, "There shall be a pillar at the borders of Egypt for a sign and for a witness."[1] Thousands of years ago Egypt was known as the Land of Khem, and the Pleiades, a group of seven stars in the constellation of Taurus, were known as the Khema. If the map is placed with the Khema over the Land of Khem (Egypt) then Taurus falls over the Taurus Mountains of southern Turkey; Ursa Major, the Great Bear, rambles over Russia; the head of Draco the Dragon rears itself over China; Orion over Iran; Aries the Ram over Rome, and Capricorn (identified with the god Pan) falls over Panama, Panuco and Mayapan, the old name of Yucatan. Aquila the Eagle spans the United States. The analogies are obvious, and quite impressive. This is one of the clearest examples of "As Above, So Below."[2]

Reading this somewhat fanciful description awakened me (like a "destiny call") to actively search for Astro-Gaia Sophia. This description of Star-Earth correspondences was provocative but also somewhat troubling. Was it accurate and true? If such ideas had emerged from ancient mystery wisdom, did this description still apply to today's alignments between Stars and Earth? I immediately wanted to test these alignments for myself but did not have the necessary maps. I felt the need to be patient, calm, and faithful to this destiny call from Astro-Gaia Sophia. I recognized that mine would not be a quick journey; I could only approach her *gradalis*—slowly, step-by-step.

1

2 Timms, *Prophecies and Predictions*, pp. 51–52.

I vowed to pursue her and develop my understanding of Astro-Gaiasophy at moments when I could do so, consider the insights she provided, and wait until the next steps toward her became clear.

EARLY INTIMATIONS

Affirmation of my "destiny call" from Astro-Gaia Sophia in 1982 came several months later, in 1983. Clifford Monks, a beloved colleague teaching at Rudolf Steiner College, approached me holding a large sixteen-inch transparent plastic globe depicting the Stars on the celestial sphere encircling a rotating transparent Earth (see figure 6). Clifford no longer needed his Star-Earth globe[3] and he kindly offered it to me to assist my teaching classes in Star Wisdom at Rudolf Steiner College. My heart leapt with joy! Gratefully I accepted Clifford's generous gift, knowing it would prove to be invaluable for research. The Star-Earth globe allows one to examine *how stars pass directly above different portions of the rotating Earth*—exactly what was needed to test the provocative description published by Moira Timms!

I immediately rotated the Earth inside the starry sphere to test the Star-Earth alignments described above. A few alignments she described generally "worked," but most did not "fit" the phenomena at all. But my interest had been awakened, so I began searching for a more "accurate" alignment between the Stars and Earth—one faithful to the phenomena given us for our observation and contemplation that could be embodied in Astro-Gaiasophy.

Exploring possible patterns of alignment between the Stars and the Earth raises many questions. "What patterns would one look for between the Stars and the Earth? How could one recognize a "proper alignment" between Stars and Earth? Since the Earth completely rotates on her axis every 23 hours and 56 minutes, is there an "archetypal alignment" imprinting spiritual exchanges between the Stars and Earth at a particular moment each day? How would such an "archetypal alignment" reveal itself to our observation and contemplation? Would such an alignment gradually shift over time with the precession of the equinoxes? What "clues" would confirm or cast doubt upon the validity of a particular alignment between Stars and Earth?"

So many questions; yet with the Star-Earth globe I could observe and test possible current alignments and contemplate as time allowed with open-mindedness, patience, and trust that answers would be found. While it was very tempting to conjecture about how earlier stages of Earth were placed in relation to the Stars, I tried to remain *faithful to the present phenomena presented by Astro-Gaia Sophia* and truthful to what she reveals as the basis for contemplation. Moira Timms had stirred up my interest, and Clifford Monks had given me an instrument to facilitate further investigation.

The outer plastic sphere of the Star-Earth globe consists of two bowl-shaped hemispheres depicting "fixed stars" on the celestial sphere. One hemisphere displays stars of the northern heavens, and the other displays stars of the southern hemisphere. The two plastic hemispheres are conveniently seamed along the *celestial equator*, the Earth's equator extended out to the celestial sphere. Inside the sixteen-inch transparent celestial sphere is a small six-inch plastic Earth globe that can easily be rotated on its north/south axis within the celestial sphere. The Earth's axis is conveniently tilted by 23½°, so that the Earth's North Pole points toward Polaris, the current "north star." The ecliptic—the Sun's path through the Zodiac—and the stars of the Zodiac are designated on the plastic celestial sphere. I modified the Star-Earth globe by locating the north and south ecliptic poles and running strings between them to help reveal the Zodiacal sectors on the celestial sphere (see figure 7).

DISCOVERING AN *ORION–AFRICA ALIGNMENT*

Observing the night sky as well as the layout of constellations depicted on the Star-Earth globe, *Orion* stands out vividly from all other major constellations on the celestial sphere. For hundreds of years past and into the future, *the three bright*

---

[3] Celestial Globe CG 616, Trippensee Planetarium Co., 1967.

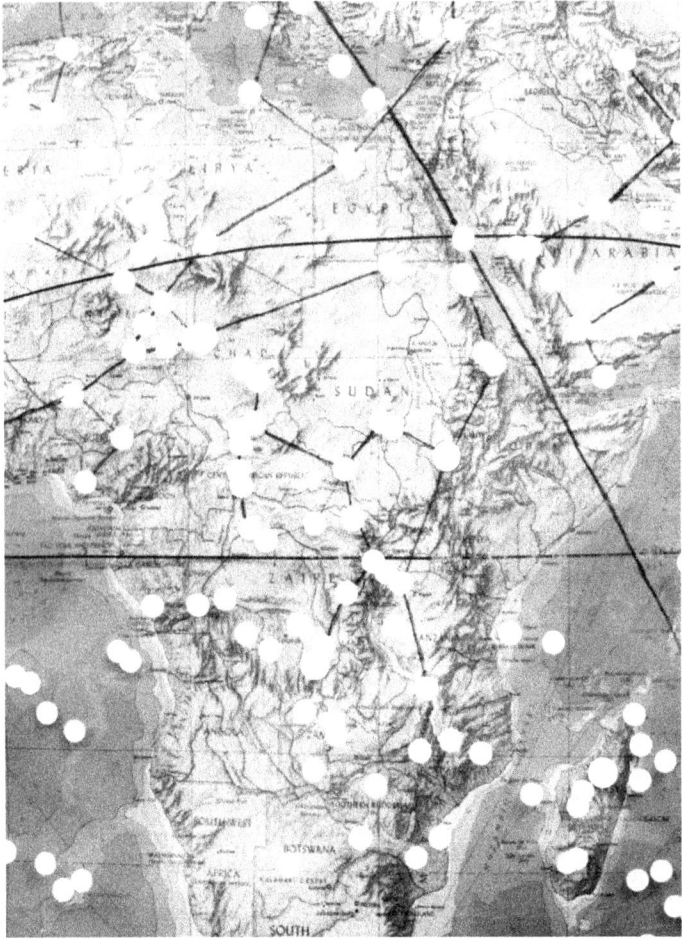

Figure 8

In 1983, while contemplating the Star-Earth globe and considering the Hermetic maxim "As above, so below," a question arose: Might Orion's unique form and position near the *celestial equator* be mirrored anywhere near the *Earth's equator*? Immediately the answer emerged: *Yes—Africa* straddles Earth's equator in a similar way that *Orion* straddles the celestial equator! Is *Africa* is a possible counterpart to the constellation *Orion*? As I rotated the Earth globe within the celestial sphere searching for other possible candidate alignments between Orion and the Earth, it readily became apparent that *Orion and Africa belong together*—they "fit" beautifully! (see figure 8). The next question is, at the moment when Orion aligns with Africa, how do other Star constellations "fit" above the Earth? Their resulting Star-Earth alignments might confirm or lead one to dismiss an Orion-Africa correspondence.

Astro-Gaiasophy and the Cultural Ages of Post-Atlantis

The Star-Earth globe allows one to conveniently identify possible correlations between each constellation of the Zodiac and regions of the Earth's surface that lie directly below. Searching in 1983 for possible evidence to support or dismiss an Orion-Africa correspondence, I examined the resulting Zodiacal alignments. To my amazement, *when Orion stands directly above eastern Africa*, Cancer the Crab stands directly above India, Gemini the Twins stand directly above the Mid-East (Iran/Iraq and the Arabian Peninsula), Taurus the Bull stands directly above Egypt and North Africa, Aries the Ram stands over the western part of Africa, Pisces the Fishes swim northward and westward across the Atlantic Ocean, Aquarius the Water-Carrier stands above northwestern South America, and Capricorn (the Goat with the fish's tail) swims away from the Andes out into the Pacific Ocean. Along with Capricorn, Sagittarius the Archer, Scorpio the Scorpion/ Eagle, Libra the Scales, and Virgo the Virgin (which stands above New Guinea) hover above the large expanse of the Pacific Ocean (see figure 9).

stars of Orion's belt are positioned very close to the *celestial equator*—the plane of the Earth's equator extended out to the *celestial sphere*. This means that some part of Orion is visible to viewers on Earth in both hemispheres from North Pole to South Pole. Orion's belt stars currently rise along the Eastern horizon and set along the Western horizon as viewed from nearly everywhere on Earth.[1] Orion's seven bright stars form a distinctive overall shape, and its three belt stars form a nearly straight line and are spaced almost equally apart. Orion's visibility from all parts of Earth makes it well-known to people of all cultures. Orion is currently the only major constellation of bright stars that straddles the celestial equator.

---

1 All three stars of the belt of Orion are not visible to viewers between 88° to 90° north latitude, near the North Pole.

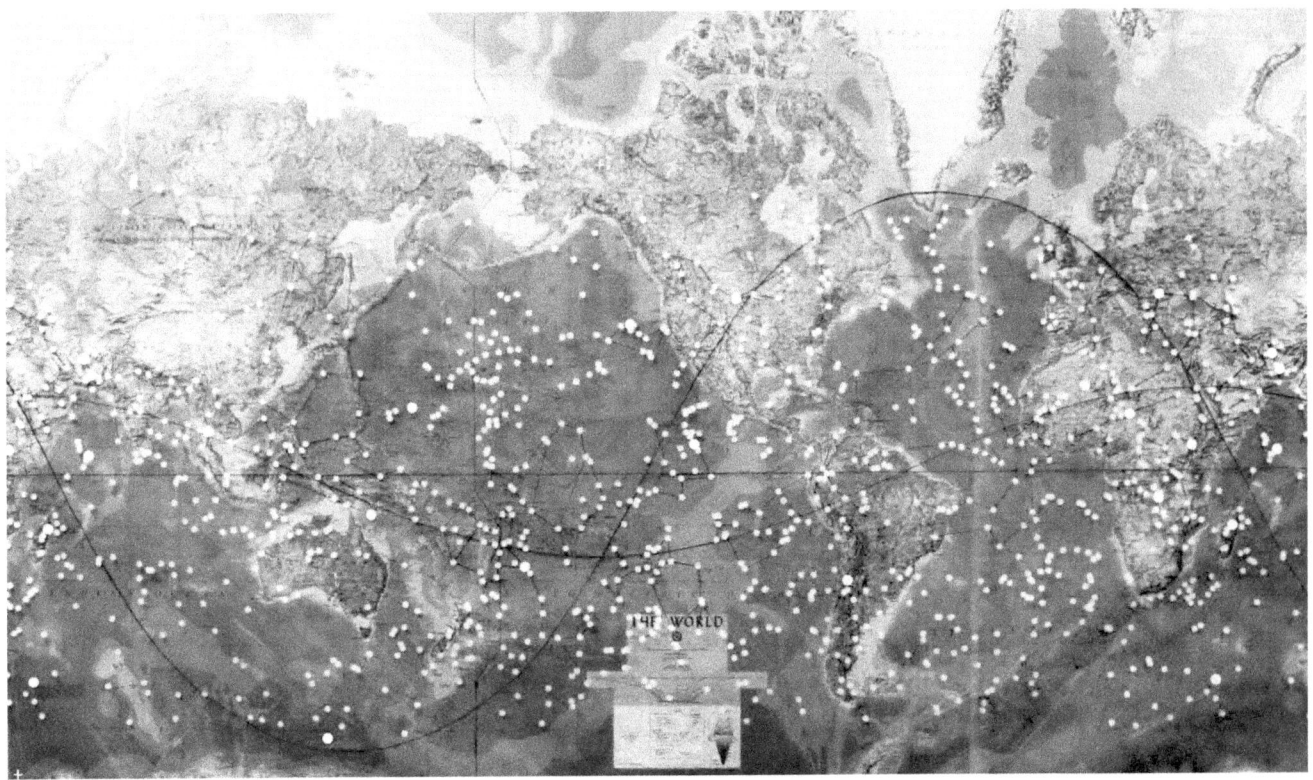

Figure 9: Astro-Gaiasophy Map of Stars above the Earth

The above sequence of Zodiac-Earth alignments closely agrees with Rudolf Steiner's depictions of the *cultural ages* of Post Atlantis, which correspond to the precession of the vernal point "backward" through the Zodiac. Rudolf Steiner describes seven "cultural ages" of Post-Atlantis as sequential periods of 2,160 years apiece that correspond with the position of the vernal point (the position of the Sun at the first day of spring in the northern hemisphere) as it slowly falls backward through the Zodiac. This gradual "falling back" of the vernal point is part of the phenomena known as the *precession of the equinoxes*. Without going into greater detail about precession or about the 1,199-year "lag period" that occurs between the dates of the astronomical ages and the corresponding human cultural ages, here is a list of the cultural ages as Rudolf Steiner designated them, their approximate dates, their association with the Sun's precession through the Zodiac, and the focal part or member of the human being brought further in development through spiritual Beings guiding human evolution in each cultural age (see table 1, next page).

What is remarkable about the *Orion-Africa alignment* is how closely it brings the stars of the Zodiac to align directly above the corresponding region of Earth in which the forefront of human and cultural development was taking place. These Star-Earth correlations hold true primarily for the first five periods of Post-Atlantis: Ancient India (Cancer), Ancient Persia (Gemini), Ancient Egypt (Taurus), Ancient Greece, Rome and their cultural extensions (Aries). Our present age, the Age of Pisces, was initiated in part by European explorers sailing west across the Atlantic Ocean toward the Americas who (re)-discovered a "New World" lying between Europe and Asia. Human development in the present cultural age (Pisces) is not focused strongly upon only one particular geographic region nor is it limited to that region, but rather becomes taken up by striving individuals who seek spiritual development within the consciousness soul (spiritual soul) out of their own initiative.

Cultural Age	Dates	Zodiacal Age	Part of the Human Being
Ancient India	7227–5067 BC	Cancer	etheric body
Ancient Persia	5067–2907 BC	Gemini	sentient body
Ancient Egypt	2907–747 BC	Taurus	sentient soul
Greco-Roman	747 BC – AD 1413	Aries	heart and mind soul
Present Age	AD 1413–3573	Pisces	consciousness soul
Sixth Age	AD 3573–5733	Aquarius	(spirit self)
Seventh Age	AD 5733–7893	Capricorn	(life spirit)

Table 1: Cultural Ages of Post-Atlantis

This "discovery" in 1983—of direct correspondences between certain Zodiacal constellations and their geographic counterparts where human beings were participating at the "leading edge" of human development and cultural evolution—astonished and humbled me. This discovery arose through examining apparent *correspondences between Orion and Africa*, which indirectly finds agreement with Steiner's work through these correspondences. This revelation assured me that Astro-Gaia Sophia was guiding my research, and I am eternally grateful for her generous and insights; they encouraged me to proceed further along this path of inquiry.[1]

Mapping the Zodiac and Starry Heavens on the Earth

The next steps in developing Astro-Gaiasophy required entering more deeply into the details of the possible Star-Earth correspondences. I painstakingly plotted individual star positions onto Mercator maps scaled to fit available maps of Earth.[2] I pasted stars (as circle dots) onto a large clear acetate overlay and slid it back and forth across physiographic Mercator maps of the world at the same scale, searching for specific places on the Earth where significant stars or constellations might imprint cosmic forces every 23 hours 56 minutes in a great rhythmic "pulse" as the Earth rotated on her axis. I included the galactic equator, the celestial equator, and the ecliptic plane and Zodiac on the Star overlay map. This tedious and ambitious Star effort took many years to complete, with lots of interruptions and gaps in between. Even when all the stars were accurately plotted, it took time to find the "right" correspondence between Stars and Earth (see figure 9).

I was primarily searching for physiographic features on Earth that might hold clues to Star-Earth correspondences: significant mountain peaks, bodies of water, volcanic craters, perhaps "hot spots" where magma leaked through the upper crust of the earth, edges of tectonic plates, and earthquake zones, places where unusual mineral or metal deposits might be found, unusual features and conditions on the ocean floor, landmass shapes reflecting on Earth the positions of the ecliptic and the Milky Way—any phenomena that might clearly show in the Star-Earth interactions the revelations of Astro-Gaia Sophia came under consideration. I also strung a physiographic

---

1   In 1983, quite independent from my "discovery" concerning an Astro-Gaiasophical correspondence between Orion and Africa, Robert Bauval began to explore correspondences between the three Giza Pyramids and the three stars in Orion's belt. Bauval published his research as *The Orion Mystery* eleven years later, in 1994.

2   My friend Robert Freehling initiated using Mercator maps to compare Star positions with Earth positions.

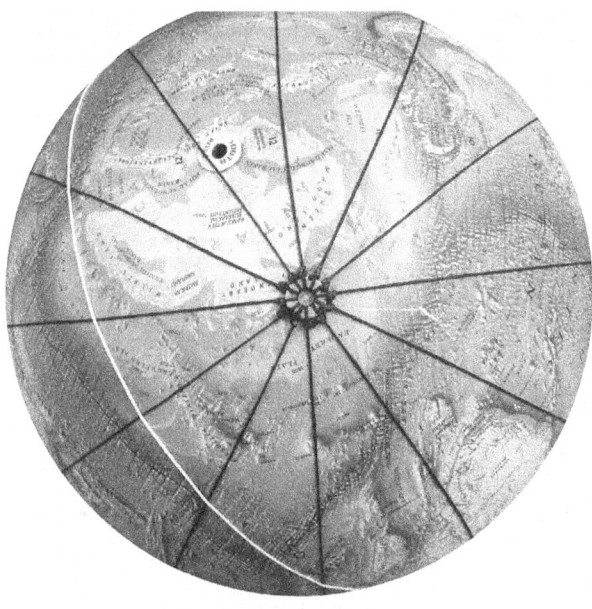

Figure 10: South Eliptic Pole

globe of the Earth with 12 *ecliptic meridian lines* between likely positions of the *north ecliptic pole* and *south ecliptic pole* along the Arctic Circle and the Antarctic Circle (see figures 4 and 10). This research work proceeded slowly over many years. However, I kept coming back to examine Orion's position over Africa more carefully.

While Orion and Africa clearly "fit" together, how did the Star-Earth alignments appear more precisely? Orion's belt stars presently lie within less than 2° south of the *celestial equator*. As the Earth turns on its axis each day, Orion's belt stars *pass directly overhead* across a narrow band of the Earth's surface within 2° south of the *Earth's equator*. Are any distinctive geographical features found in Africa just south of the equator? Yes—*Lake Victoria, the source of the Nile River*, lies directly beneath the *zenith passage* of the three stars of Orion's belt! (The term *zenith passage* refers to *a star's crossing directly overhead above a place on the Earth's surface*.) The Great Rift Valley and several volcanoes and craters can be found in close proximity to the west and east of Lake Victoria. Just to the east stands Mount Kilimanjaro, a triple-peaked volcano that is the highest point in Africa. The three stars of the belt of Orion make zenith passages over this part of equatorial Africa every day. Is there an obvious correlation between the belt stars of Orion and the Lake Victoria/ Mount Kilimanjaro area on the Earth?

Positioning Orion's three belt stars at their *zenith passage* above Lake Victoria in eastern Africa, I examined the *zenith passages* of the Stars above regions of the Earth at that very same moment, trying to "fine tune" the *direct zenith-projection alignments* to be able to map them. The result is shown in a series of maps and photos of the Zodiacal sectors on the Earth globe. [See figure 9.] Please note there are three continuous dark lines depicted: the horizontal line depicting the *equatorial plane* passing through the *Earth's equator* extends out to the celestial sphere; the gently sinuous line of the *ecliptic plane* along which the Sun travels through the 12 constellations of the Zodiac over the course of the year; and the higher and lower sinuous line representing the *galactic equator* that represents the central plane of the Milky Way Galaxy encircling our Earth and solar system.

STUDYING THE EARTH-STAR MAPS OF ASTRO-GAIASOPHY

First, let's look at the divisions of the Earth more generally. The **Earth's equator** divides the Earth in northern and southern hemispheres; the **North Pole** found in the northern hemisphere points toward the star Polaris in Ursa Minor, and the **South Pole** in the southern hemisphere points toward Octans, a dim constellation.

The **Zodiac** is depicted along the sinuous **ecliptic plane** shown as a dark line intersecting the equator. The ecliptic plane also divides the Earth into two hemispheres, and the ecliptic has a **north ecliptic pole in Alaska** and a **south ecliptic pole in the South Indian Ocean below Madagascar**. The north ecliptic pole points toward **Draco**, and the south ecliptic pole points toward the constellation of **Dorado**.

At this present time (2014) the ecliptic intersects the equator at about **5° of Pisces the Fishes** very **near the mouth of the Amazon River**, at about 52° 45" West longitude. (The Earth's equator is

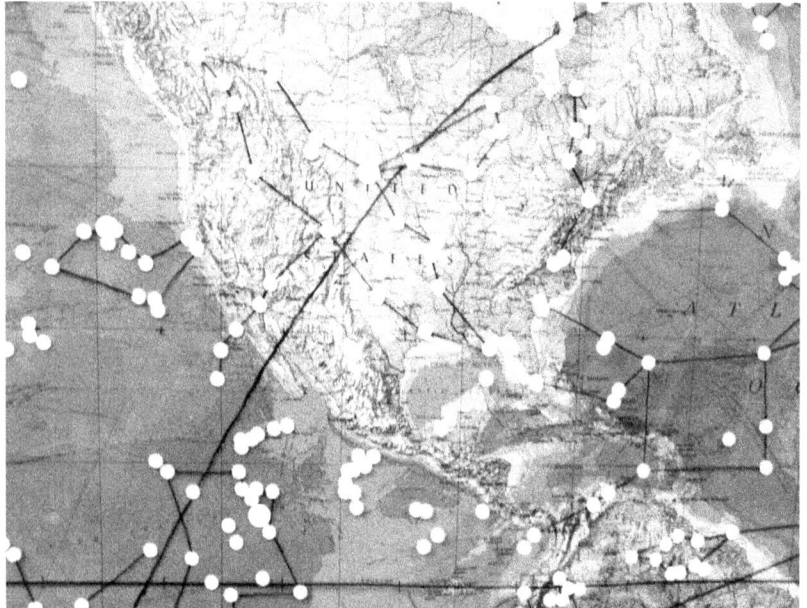

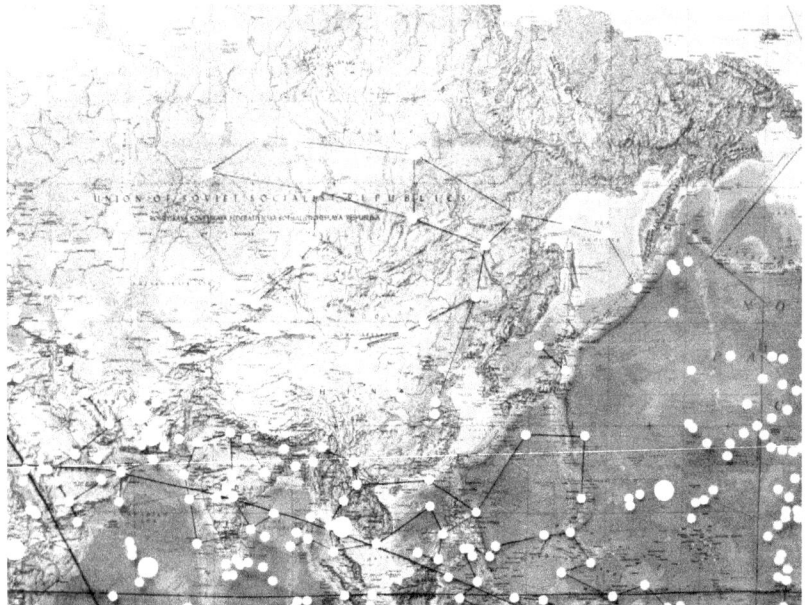

*Figure 11: Cygnus the Swan above North America (above);
Figure 12: The Great Bear above Russia*

0° latitude.) Around March 21ˢᵗ the Sun crosses this position (the vernal point in the northern hemisphere).

The ecliptic extends up into the Northern hemisphere until it reaches 23½° North latitude at about **5° of Gemini the Twins** as it **crosses the Red Sea at 37° 15" East longitude.** Around June 21, the Sun reaches this position (summer solstice in the northern hemisphere).

From there the ecliptic slowly turns southeastward and crosses the equator once again at about **5° of Virgo the Virgin** near the **Indonesian island of Halmahera**, west of New Guinea, at 127°15" East longitude. Around September 21, the Sun reaches this position (autumnal equinox in the northern hemisphere).

The ecliptic continues southward to reach 23.5° South latitude at about **5° of Sagittarius the Archer just south of the Tuamoto Islands in the South Pacific** at 142°45" West longitude. The Sun crosses this position around December 22. From there the ecliptic moves northward toward its crossing point on the equator on March 21.

Before we study the Zodiac positions in more detail, please note that there is a great heavenly bird flying across much of western North America—not an eagle as suggested by Moira Timms, but rather **Cygnus the Swan** (see figure 11). The wings of Cygnus extend diagonally from the Canadian Rocky Mountains southeastward through the Great Plains and appear to terminate in the Gulf of Mexico. The body of Cygnus the Swan flies near the Milky Way Galaxy; his tail feathers extend above Lake Superior and Lake Michigan, and the bright star Deneb imprints above western South Dakota. His neck extends southwest past the Gulf of California and Baja as Cygnus flies out into the Pacific Ocean.

When we observe eastern Asia, just as Moira Timms had suggested, we find the **Great Bear** lumbering over the Russian Federation as well as above parts of Mongolia and China (see figure 12). We have already discussed the significance of **Orion** imprinting over eastern Africa above and below the equator.

The **Galactic Equator**—the central plane of the Milky Way—imprints the Earth in a striking way. The Galactic Equator is tilted off the equatorial plane by about 63°. As we examine figure 9 and certain detailed maps, we will find that the Galactic Equator passes right **through the Red Sea** and continues across the Eastern Mediterranean up **through the Aegean Sea** and into central Europe and the North Sea across northern Scotland, across the North Atlantic to touch the southern tip of Greenland and the northern tip of Labrador and Quebec through the southeastern corner of Hudson Bay, descending southwest across Ontario and Minnesota out into the Great Plains and out through the northwest tip of Mexico into the Pacific Ocean. The Galactic Equator continues southward below New Zealand and Australia, turning northwest through the Indian Ocean and on through the Red Sea.

What is the significance of the **Galactic Equator**—the plane of the Milky Way galaxy—as it imprints mother Earth? Please note that the Milky Way itself is a band of varying width that extends hundreds of miles along either side of the Galactic Equator. The Milky Way serves as a kind of threshold for human beings, linking the *not yet born*, the *living*, and *those who have died*. The Milky Way's imprint upon the Earth seems to divide the Earth into different cultures that could very roughly be termed "Eastern" and "Western" cultures. And those parts of the Earth that lie several hundred miles on either side of the Galactic Equator—that is, those regions above which the Milky Way imprints the Earth—tend to be places where cultural mixing is taking place—sometimes easily, sometimes with great tensions. Much more research needs to be done to characterize the imprinted Milky Way's influence upon the Earth and human beings.

EXPLORING THE ZODIAC IMPRINTED ON THE EARTH: A BRIEF EASTWARD JOURNEY

On figure 13, **Capricorn, the Goat** with a fish's tail, appears to be swimming away from the Andes out into the Pacific Ocean. Why else would a mountain goat need a fish's tail? Capricorn climbs high mountain peaks that plunge directly into the Pacific. On figure 14, the Zodiacal Sector

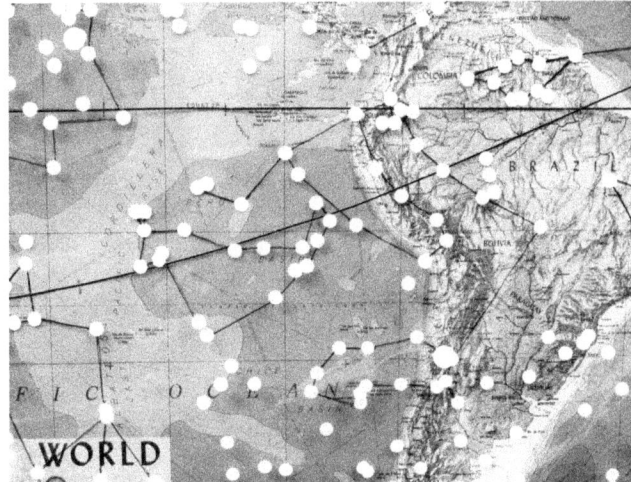

Figure 13: Capricorn and Aquarius (above);
Figure 14: Capricorn and Aquarius Sectors

of Capricorn includes all the western mountain ranges of North America and the southern tip of the Andes in South America, but a large portion of the **Capricorn Sector** is the eastern edge of the Pacific Ocean. Directly above the horns of Capricorn is the bright star Altair, part of Aquila the Eagle which flies above his head. This is an active tectonic zone along the eastern Rim of Fire.

The **Capricorn Sector** includes: e. Alaska, sw. Yukon, British Columbia, Washington, Oregon, Idaho, w. Montana, w. Wyoming, California, Nevada, Utah, w. Colorado, Arizona, w. New

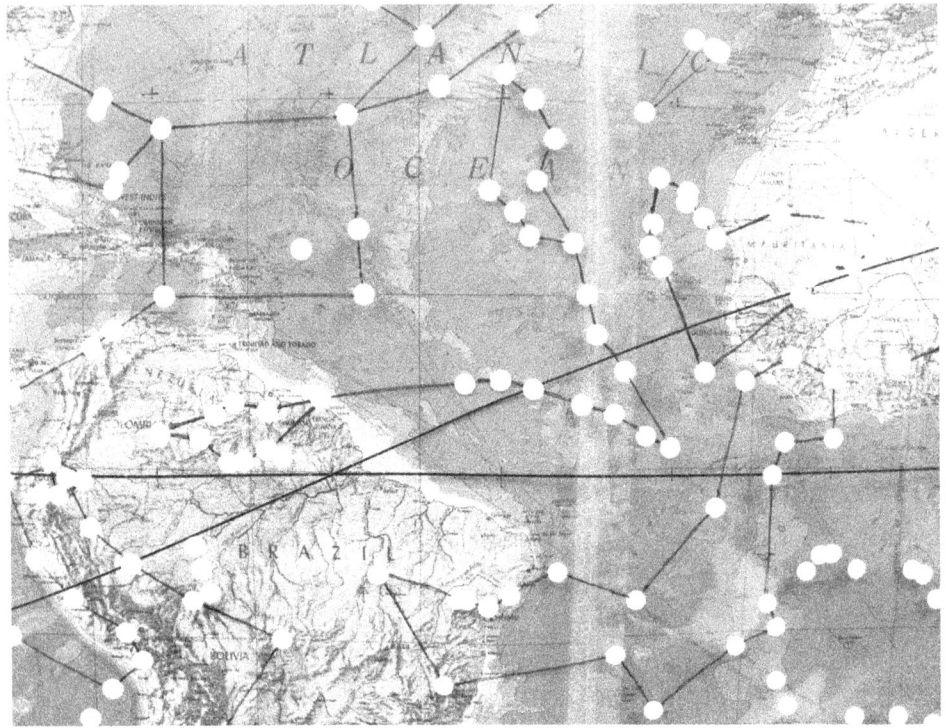

Figure 15: Pisces and Aries

Gaia breathes life through the realm of Aquarius the Water-Carrier.

The **Aquarius Sector** includes: ne. Alaska, central Yukon, sw. Northwest Territories, Alberta, w. Saskatchewan, sw. Manitoba, sw. Ontario, e. Montana, North Dakota, Minnesota, w. Lake Superior, w. Michigan, Lake Michigan, South Dakota, Nebraska, Iowa, Illinois, Indiana, Ohio, e. Colorado, Kansa, Kentucky, West Virginia, w. Virginia, Oklahoma, Texas, Arkansas, Tennessee, w. North Carolina, Mississippi, Alabama, Georgia, South Carolina, Louisiana, Florida, e. Mexico, Gulf of Mexico, Cuba, Caribbean Sea, Bahamas, Guatemala, Belize, El Salvador, Honduras, Nicaragua, Costa Rica, Panama, Jamaica, Haiti, Dominican Republic, w. Puerto Rico, e. Pacific Ocean, e. Galapagos Islands, Colombia, Ecuador, Venezuela, w. Guyana, w. Brazil, Peru, Bolivia, n. Chile, Paraguay, n. Argentina, Uruguay, Falkland Islands, sw. Atlantic Ocean. Mexico, sw. Texas, Baja California, w. Mexico, e. Pacific Ocean, s. Chile, s. Argentina, Tierra del Fuego, n. Antarctic Peninsula, Queen Maud Land.

Aquarius the Water-Carrier extends his right arm above Capricorn as if gathering the waters of the Pacific, but he pours water out of his pitcher at the equator just to the east of the Andes Mountains into the western headwater region of the Amazon River basin near Ecuador (see figures 13 and 14). It is remarkable how the north-south trending Andes Mountains "jog" to the northwest along the length of the body of Aquarius. Looked at as a whole, the **Aquarius Sector** covers some of the largest basins of water in the world: many of the Canadian lakes, most of the Missouri-Mississippi River basin, the western Great Lakes, the Gulf of Mexico, the Caribbean Sea, the area around Panama where the Pacific and Atlantic nearly join together, most of the Amazon Basin, and the southern river basins of South America into the South Atlantic Ocean. The rainforests, freshwater basins, and prime agricultural lands covered by Aquarius Sector reveal that

On figure 15, **Pisces the Fishes** are swimming in the Atlantic Ocean. The easternmost Fish is swimming northward toward Labrador Bay and Greenland, into the region where Andromeda is chained to a rock. The westernmost Fish has achieved landfall along the northern shores of South America just above the equator. Both Fishes appear to be bound by a common cord that is anchored in the mid-Atlantic close to the equator, and below the equator is Cetus the Sea Monster. Above the equator is the square of Pegasus, the Flying Horse. The ecliptic plane crosses the equator near the mouth of the Amazon Basin, where the vernal Sun crosses in Pisces. Most of the Pisces Sector covers portions of the North Atlantic and South Atlantic Oceans, along with the northeastern portions of South America (see figure 16).

The **Pisces Sector** includes: Alaska, n. Yukon, e. Northwest Territories, Nunavut, Hudson Bay, ne. Saskatchewan, ne. Manitoba, ne. Ontario, Quebec, Labrador, Newfoundland, New Brunswick, Prince Edward Island, Nova Scotia, Maine, e. Lake Superior, Lake Huron, Lake Erie, ne. Michigan, New York, Vermont, New Hampshire, Massachusetts, Connecticut, Rhode Island, Pennsylvania, New Jersey, Delaware, Maryland, e. West Virginia, e. Virginia, e. North Carolina, Bermuda, w. North Atlantic Ocean, e. Puerto Rico, Antigua and Barbuda, Dominica, Saint Lucia, Barbados, Saint Vincent and The Grenadines, Grenada, Trinidad and Tobago, ne. Venezuela, Guyana, Suriname, French Guiana, e. Brazil, Trinidad, w. South Atlantic Ocean.

Aries the Ram can also be viewed on figures 15 and 16. Aries leads with his head as he ventures offshore westward from Africa into the Atlantic Ocean. But the Ram is turning his head back over his shoulder as if to gaze upon northern Africa, Europe, and the Mediterranean. The body of Aries is firmly anchored in northwestern Africa. Rudolf Steiner conveys that there is deep meaning in the fact that the Ram looks backward over his shoulder; the head and brain carry out a reflective, contemplative activity while one is also fully engaged in moving forward through life. Below the Ram, the head of Cetus the Sea Monster raises its head, while above the Ram we find Andromeda.

The **Aries Sector** includes: Alaska, Yukon, Nunavut (Baffin Island), w. Greenland, coastal Newfoundland, Labrador Sea, North Atlantic Ocean, Azores, Portugal, w. Spain, Gibraltar, Canary Islands, w. Morocco, w. Algeria, Mauritania, w. Mali, Senegal, Cape Verde, Gambia, Guinea-Bissau, Guinea, Upper Volta, Sierra Leone, Liberia, Ivory Coast, Ghana, Togo, Benin, South Atlantic Ocean, Ascension Islands, St. Helena Islands.

Taurus the Bull can be seen on figures 17 and 18 (next pages). Taurus dominates northern Africa. The Pleiades cluster stands above south-central Algeria, while the Hyades—the stars that form the "V" of the face of the Bull—stand over eastern

Figure 16 Pisces and Aries Sectors

Nigeria and Chad. Aldebaran, the bright Eye of the Bull, stands above western Chad, and the horns of the Bull extend through Libya and Sudan into Egypt and the Nile River. The Bull's horns touch into the Milky Way near the Nile River and Red Sea. Below Taurus the Bull we find the bright stars of Orion, whose belt stars straddle the equator. Orion dominates south-central Africa just as the Taurus the Bull dominates northern Africa. Unlike most regions, the Taurus Sector extends over the greatest landmass of all the Zodiacal Sectors—much of Greenland, Europe, and the length of Africa is under the guidance of Taurus the Bull. Much of Western Europe is covered by the hero Perseus, from the British Isles down through France and Spain across the western Mediterranean into northwestern Africa. Perseus has cut the head off the Medusa and is on his way to saving Andromeda from being consumed by Cetus the Sea Monster. There are many wonderful legends about these starry figures among the peoples whose lands bear their imprint. This entire Taurus Sector bears amazing landscapes and habitats, including Scandinavia and the British Isles, most of Europe including the Alps, the Carpathians and Pyrenees, the Mediterranean landscapes, and the

Figure 17: Taurus and Gemini

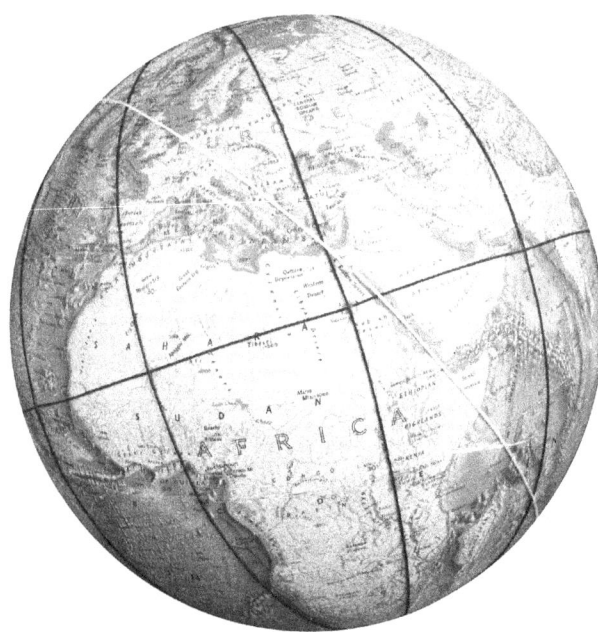

Figure 18: Taurus and Gemini Sectors

bulk of Africa—the Great Rift Valley, the Congo Basin, the Sahara and Kalahari Deserts, thousands of miles of shorelines and remarkable monuments left by ancient civilizations and empire-builders. One could spend a lifetime exploring the landscapes and places covered by the Taurus Sector.

The **Taurus Sector** includes: Alaska, Yukon, Queen Elizabeth Islands, n. Greenland, Greenland Sea, w. Spitsbergen, Iceland, Norwegian Sea, Norway, Sweden, Baltic Sea, w. Finland, Estonia, Latvia, Denmark, Lithuania, Scotland, England, Ireland, Wales, North Sea, Byelorussia, San Marino, Poland, Luxembourg, Germany, Liechtenstein, Netherlands, Belgium, France, Montenegro, Czech Republic, Hungary, Austria, Switzerland, w. Ukraine, Monaco, Italy, Sicily, Adriatic Sea, Vatican City, Bosnia and Herzegovina, Serbia, Romania, Bulgaria, Croatia, Greece, Macedonia, Albania, Moldova, Mediterranean Sea, Sardinia, Slovakia, Slovenia, Spain, w. Turkey, e. Morocco, e. Algeria, Tunisia, Libya, w. Egypt, e. Mali, Niger, Chad, w. Sudan, Nigeria, Cameroon, Central African Republic, w. Uganda, Burundi, Rwanda, Equatorial Guinea, Sao Tome and Principe, Gabon, Congo, Zaire, Angola, w. Zambia, Angola, Namibia, Botswana, Zimbabwe, South Africa, Swaziland, Lesotho, nw. Mozambique, South Atlantic Ocean.

Gemini the Twins can also be viewed on figures 17 and 18. The Twins stand northeast of the Bull, on the eastern side of the Galactic Equator that runs through the center of the Milky Way. The Galactic Equator imprints the Earth here along the length of the Red Sea. The Galactic anti-center (pointing away from the center of the Milky Way Galaxy) imprints its position in the

Sinai Peninsula, about 29° North latitude. The Twins appear to be wading in the Milky Way with their feet planted just east of the Red Sea, and their bodies extend across the lower Arabian Peninsula across the Persian Gulf into Iran and Pakistan. **Castor**, the head of one Twin, stands above Iran, and **Pollux**, the head of the other Twin, stands above western Pakistan. Gemini the Twins have a great deal to do with relationships, symmetries and asymmetries. Many cultures within the Gemini Sector undergo dramatic extremes through their relationships with others, and this sector is a dynamic region.

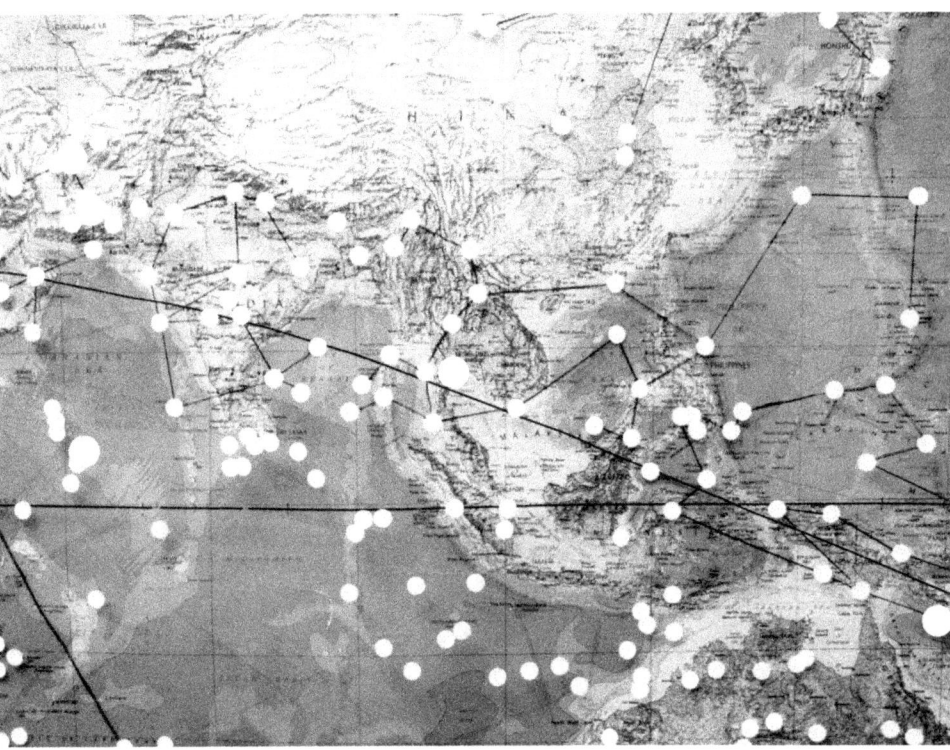

Figure 19: Cancer and Leo

The **Zodiacal Sector of Gemini** includes: Alaska, Arctic Ocean, North Pole, Barents Sea, e. Spitsbergen, ne. Norway, e. Finland, w. Russian Federation, e. Ukraine, Black Sea, Georgia, e. Turkey, w. Kazakhstan, Caspian Sea, Armenia, Turkmenistan, Uzbekistan, Iran, Iraq, Kuwait, Syria, e. Mediterranean Sea, Cyprus, Lebanon, Israel, Pakistan, Jordan, e. Egypt, w. Afghanistan, w. Pakistan, Saudi Arabia, Persian Gulf, Red Sea, Qatar, United Arab Emirates, Oman, Yemen, Arabian Sea, e. Sudan, Ethiopia, Somalia, e. Uganda, Kenya, e. Tanzania, e Zambia, e. Mozambique, Malawi, Madagascar, sw. Indian Ocean.

Cancer the Crab stands directly above India, as shown on figure 19. The Crab has a hard shell to protect is tender interior organs, and in the human form the Crab forms our rib cage that protects our heart and lungs. It is remarkable to see on figure 20 how the subcontinent of India is bounded by the steep Himalayan Mountains to the north and by the Arabian Sea, Bay of Bengal,

Figure 20: Cancer and Leo Sectors

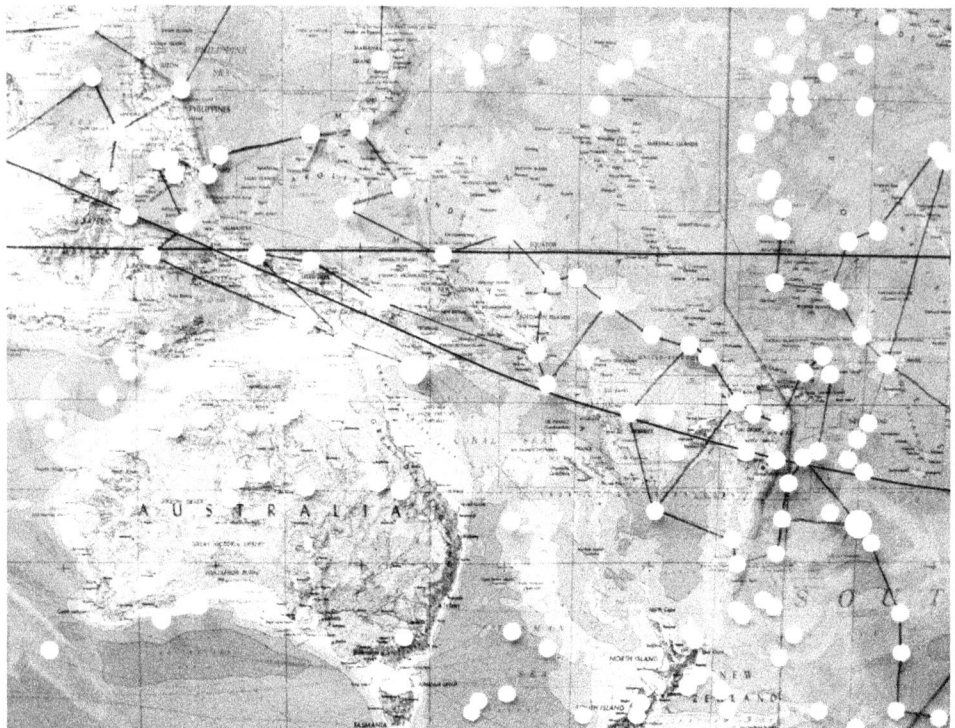

Figure 21: Virgo and Libra

Figure 22: Virgo, Libra, and Scorpio Sectors

and Indian Ocean along its southern shorelines. Beyond the Himalayas are the Plateau of Tibet and a series of mountain ranges, plateaus, and basins extending north to the Central Siberian Plateau. The Cancer Sector includes dynamic and varied landscapes.

The **Cancer Sector** includes: nw. Alaska, Arctic Ocean, Russian Federation, e. Kazakhstan, w. Mongolia, w. Gobi Desert, w. China, Tibet, e. Afghanistan, e. Pakistan, India, Bhutan, Nepal, Kamchatka Peninsula, Japan, Sea of Japan, e. China, Yellow Sea, East China Sea, e. Gobi Desert, North Korea, South Korea, Taiwan, Vietnam, Laos, e. Myanmar, Thailand, Cambodia, South China Sea, Philippines, Malaysia, Indonesia, Sumatra, Borneo, Java, Christmas Island, se. Indian Ocean.

Leo the Lion can also be seen on figures 19 and 20. Regulus, the Heart of the Lion, imprints into the region west of the Indochina Peninsula, in the Andaman Sea in southern Myanmar, southeast of Yangon and southwest from Bangkok in Thailand. The Lion's head and mane extend northwesterly toward southern China and Bangladesh. The Lion's forepaws reach into the Bay of Bengal, and the stars marking his hindquarters stand over the South China Sea below Hong Kong and the Philippines Islands. The Leo Sector extends northward through Japan and southward through Borneo, Sumatra, and Java into the southern Indian Ocean. This region of the Far East has remarkable dynastic cultures whose wisdom can be traced back into the ending periods of Atlantis. Residents of the Leo Sector feel that they are living in the Heart of the World, and they possess a regal heart quality that can be courageous and strong-willed, as well as gracious.

The **Leo Sector** includes: nw. Alaska, Chukchi Sea, Russian Federation, Sea of Okhotsk, Kamchatka Peninsula, Japan, Sea of Japan, e. China, Yellow Sea, East China Sea, e. Gobi Desert, North Korea, South Korea, Taiwan, Vietnam, Laos, e. Myanmanr, Thailand, Cambodia, South China Sea, Philippines, Malaysia, Indonesia, Sumatra, Borneo, Java, Christmas Island, se. Indian Ocean.

Virgo the Virgin imprints her Wisdom along the ecliptic as it crosses the equator in the Indonesian Islands and continues southeasterly through New Guinea. Ptolemy described the Virgin as lying down along the ecliptic, although in the Egyptian zodiac of Denderah she is pictured standing upright. Here in figure 21 we find the Virgin's head in the Phillipines and her body extending the length of New Guinea to the Solomon Islands. The bright star Spica imprints just below the southeastern tip of New Guinea. Most of the **Virgo Sector** seen in figure 22 stands above oceans, but western and central Australia is within her realm.

The **Virgo Sector** includes: w. Alaska, Bering Sea, w. Aleutian Islands, w. North Pacific Ocean, e. Philippine Sea, Bonin Islands, Volcano Islands/Iwo Jima, Northern Mariana Islands, Mariana Trench, Micronesia, Mindanao, Papua, New Guinea, Indonesian Islands, e. Lesser Sunda Islands, western and central Australia, Northern Territory, w. South Australia, Southeast Indian Ocean, w. Queensland, South Australia Basin.

Libra the Scales can also be seen in figures 21 and 22. Libra consists of two pans of scales, on one of which the Virgin stands while the Scorpion clasps the other pan. As imprinted along the ecliptic, Libra the Scales includes the Marshall Islands and Solomon Islands and the Libra Sector extends south to eastern Australia and Tasmania and western New Zealand. Most of the Libra Sector includes portions of the North and South

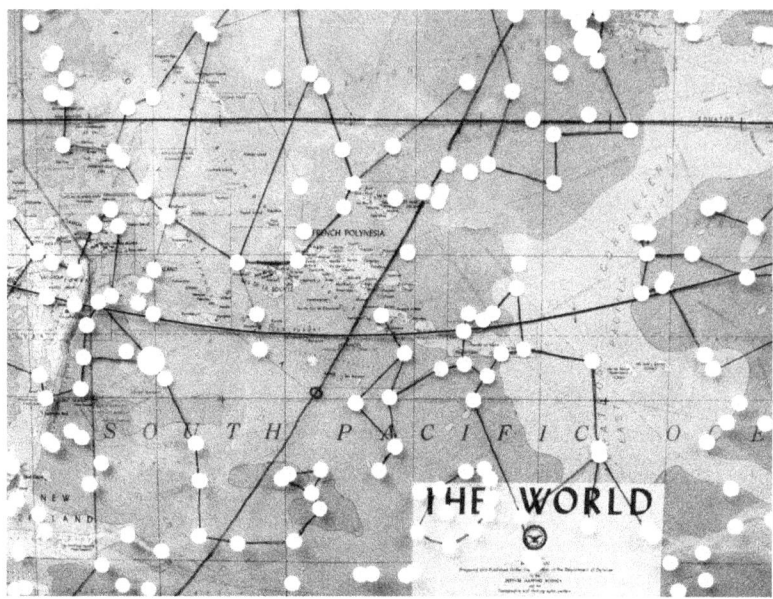

Figure 23: Scorpio and Sagittarius

Atlantic. The only other sectors that cover more water are those of Scorpio and Sagittarius.

The **Libra Sector** includes: Alaskan Peninsula, e. Aleutian Islands, Kodiak Island, North Pacific Ocean, Midway Island, Marshall Islands, Solomon Islands, Fiji, e. Australia, e. Queensland, New South Wales, Victoria, Tasmania, w. South Pacific Ocean, w. New Zealand, Wilkes Land, and Antarctica.

Scorpio the Scorpion (or Eagle) extends along and below the ecliptic as it continues southeastward into the South Pacific. See figure 23. Scorpio is only the lower half of a greater constellation that includes Ophiucus the Serpent-Bearer. Ophiucus is the healer who holds the Serpent of wisdom wrapped around his waist and keeps the Scorpion and its sting of death underfoot. The stinger of the Scorpion stands in the Milky Way, which may add spiritual insight to the role of the Milky Way as a path of the dead out into the spiritual world and of the unborn back into life. Ophiucus extends north across the equator toward the Hawaiian Islands, while the Scorpion reaches into the southern ocean depths east of New Zealand.

The **Scorpio Sector** includes: Alaska, North Pacific Ocean, Hawaiian Islands, South Pacific Ocean, Phoenix Islands, Samoa, Society Islands,

Tubuai Islands, Tonga, e. New Zealand, Antarctica, and Ross Sea.

Sagittarius the Archer guards and holds sway over the Galactic Center, the center of our Milky Way Galaxy. The tip of the Archer's arrow points toward the Galactic Center, which lays just a few degrees away. On figure 23 the Galactic Center is indicated by a black circle along the Galactic Equator.

The **Zodiacal Sector of Sagittarius** includes: Alaska, Yukon, North Pacific Ocean, Alexander Archipelago, Marquesas Islands, French Polynesia, South Pacific Ocean, Tuamoto Archipelago, Marie Byrd Land, Antarctica, South Pole.

Astro-Gaiasophy, Astroclimatology, Astrogeographia

The correspondences outlined above and illustrated in this article form part of the cognitive framework for the research in *Astro-Gaiasophy* undertaken by the author for over three decades. The cognitive framework underlying *Astro-Gaiasophy*—*direct zenith projections of Stars onto the Earth*—differs significantly from the approach taken by Dennis Klocek in developing *Astroclimatology*, and it differs even more from the approach taken by Robert Powell and David Bowden in developing *Astrogeographia*.

My early research into the mysteries of *Astro-Gaiasophy* preceded and in some small way helped guide Dennis Klocek's initial steps in developing his *Astroclimatology* and also Robert Powell's initial steps in developing his *Astrogeographia*. These friends and colleagues are creative researchers who found seed imaginations revealed in Astro-Gaiasophy (about the relationship between the Earth and the Zodiac) that they applied while pursuing their own original research.

While initiating his initial research into *Astroclimatology* in 1984 or 1985, Dennis Klocek approached the author with the question, *"Where on Earth is the Zodiac?"* I shared my Orion-Africa alignment discovery with Dennis, which he adapted and applied to his own research into weather patterns and planetary movements against the background of the Zodiac. Dennis Klocek has developed Astroclimatology into an extremely accurate method of weather forecasting, which he has successfully employed for many years. Dennis's work, along with that done by Brian Keats (Dennis's counterpart in the southern hemisphere) has become published and well known for accuracy and originality. The author feels grateful to have witnessed this remarkable and original research in Astroclimatology grow and become fruitful.

After viewing the author's maps of *Astro-Gaiasophy* over a period of several years and supportively encouraging their publication, in 2005 Robert Powell initiated his own independent research that developed into *Astrogeographia*. The maps produced by Astrogeographia differ considerably from those of Astro-Gaiasophy. Robert Powell has found remarkable correspondences between his star-projections and significant mystery centers and cultural sites on the Earth. In 2012 Robert Powell and David Bowden published their original research findings in the book, *Astrogeographia—Correspondences between the Stars and Earthly Locations*.[1]

Though I have shared the fruits of Astro-Gaiasophy with friends and have presented several lectures on this topic over the past 30 years, this article is the first time this research has been published. The author feels a deep moral responsibility toward Astro-Gaia Sophia to honor and protect her mystery wisdom, and thus I have been reluctant to reveal these findings. After contemplating these mysteries for more than 30 years, only now does it feel appropriate to begin publishing some portion of the findings of Astro-Gaiasophy.

Dennis Klocek and Robert Powell have each graciously acknowledged my work as helpful in stimulating their own independent research, which they have pursued vigorously and with wonderful results. My relationships with these colleagues are filled with respect, admiration, and gratitude; a great deal of my work has also been stimulated by their encouragement, support, and dedicated research, and I honor and acknowledge their significant gifts and contributions to humanity.

---

1 Powell and Bowden, *Astrogeographia*.

Each creative human being derives his/her own *moral intuitions* and *moral imaginations* from the spiritual world through the activity and initiative of the divine "I" dwelling within. Although our research approaches and the directions of interest differ from one another, as free human beings we celebrate one another's contributions and successes with great joy and appreciation. Our individual goals are related but distinct from one another, and I fully appreciate our mutual interests and the differences between our approaches. I am honored to share in our mutual striving to bring Star Wisdom and Earth Wisdom together and make it fruitful for our fellow human beings.

ASTRO-GAIASOPHY AND THE ROLE OF JERUSALEM

Astro-Gaiasophy attempts to stay true to the phenomena presented to human beings for our contemplation; but what is given for us to observe and think about is not limited to the realm of sense perceptions, but rather should be extended into living pictures—imaginations and inspirations. Steiner gave the following description of *how Jerusalem is perceived by the dead*:

> But it is particularly important to acquire not just abstract conceptions, but such *pictures* of the universe. We acquire a picture of the Earth when we imagine a Sphere floating in cosmic space, gleaming on one side in shades of blue and violet, on the other side burning, sparkling red and yellow; and between a belt of green. Conceptions which have the character of *pictures* gradually carry us over into the spiritual world. That is what matters. It is necessary to put forward such picture-conceptions, if one is speaking in an earnest sense about the spiritual worlds; and it is necessary too that such conceptions are not regarded as if they were arbitrary inventions, *but that something is made from them*—on this one depends. Let us consider it once more: the Eastern Earth, gleaming in blue and violet—the Western Earth, sparkling reddish-yellow. But other differentiations come in.
>
> If the soul of one who has died contemplates certain points in our present age, then he perceives at the place that is designated here as Palestine, as Jerusalem, out of the bluish-violet something of a golden form, a golden crystal form, which comes to life. That is Jerusalem, seen from the spirit! That is what also plays a part in the Apocalypse (in so far as I speak of Imaginations) as "heavenly Jerusalem." These are not things which are thought out. These are things which can be seen. Contemplated from the spirit, the Mystery of Golgotha was as it is in physical observation when the astronomer directs his telescope into cosmic space and then sees something that amazes him, for example the appearance of new stars. *Spiritually, observed from the cosmos, the event of Golgotha was the appearance of a golden star in the blue earth-aura of the eastern half of the earth.* Here you have the Imagination for what I described in conclusion the day before yesterday. It is really important that through such Imaginations conceptions of the Universe are acquired, which enable the human soul to find its place in feeling within the spirit of this Universe.
>
> Try to think this with someone who has died: the crystal form of the heavenly Jerusalem, building up in golden radiance, amid the blue-violet Earth-aura. This will bring you near. This is something which belongs to the Imaginations, into which the soul enters at death: *"Ex Deo nascimur, In Christo morimur!"* ...
>
> One approaches spiritual life the more one penetrates from external observation, and particularly from abstract conceptions, to picture conceptions. Copernicus brought men to calculate the universe; the opposite way of seeing things must bring men to form pictures of the universe again; to think of a universe, with which the human soul can identify itself—so that the Earth appears as an organism, shining out into the Cosmos: blue-violet, with the golden, shining heavenly Jerusalem on the one side, and on the other side sparkling reddish-yellow.
>
> From what does the **blue-violet** on one side of the Earth-aura originate? If you see this side of the Earth-sphere, what is physical of the earth disappears, seen from the outside; rather, the light-aura becomes transparent, and the dark of the Earth vanishes. The blue which shows brings this about. You can explain the

phenomenon from Goethe's Theory of Colour. But because the interior of the Earth sparkles out from the western half—sparkles out in such a way that it is true, as I described the day before yesterday, that *man is determined in America by the sub-earthly*; because of this **the interior of the Earth shines and sparkles as a reddish-yellow glow, as a reddish-yellow shooting fire out into the Universe.** This is only intended as a sketch, in quite feeble outlines; but it is meant to show you that it is possible to speak today not only in general abstract ideas about the World in which we live between death and a new birth, but in very concrete conceptions. All this is capable of preparing our souls to reach a connection with the spiritual world, a connection with the higher hierarchies, a connection with that World in which man lives between death and a new birth.[1]

This beautiful description of how the dead perceive the Earth as radiating colors from different sectors begins to offer substance to the divisions described in Astro-Gaiasophy, particularly the differences between East and West. One can awaken to the significance of Jerusalem through this pictorial description by Rudolf Steiner. Certainly the place where the Christ Event was enacted bears a very spiritual aura, and David Tresemer[2] has pointed out that the latitude of Jerusalem—31°47" north latitude—creates unique etheric conditions that are related to the position of the equinox Sun at noon. A shadow cast at noon during the spring equinox and the fall equinox will make visible the Golden Section relationship between the Sun and the Earth at Jerusalem. Rudolf Steiner speaks below about the how the etheric forces shape the physical body in accordance with the Golden Section's relationship:

Right into the second Post-Atlantean Age [Ancient Persia, the age of the Twins] one experienced the *number* qualitatively and into the third [Ancient Egypt, the age of the Bull] still the *measure* [was experienced qualitatively]. The Golden Section, a measure according to proportions, shows how one can measure without abstraction; the etheric body structures the physical body in accordance with cosmic relationships and follows the Golden Section.[3]

Closing Thoughts

Astro-Gaiasophy has been gestating for over 30 years, but it is still in its infancy, as the reader of this article will readily surmise. This article presents just a sketch of some of the direct zenith projections of the Stars upon the Earth that have evolved in the author's understanding and that continue to be fruitful year after year. The author does not claim these particular relationships to be the only valid approach to develop Astro-Gaiasophy. However, remaining faithful to the phenomena is certainly the best way to receive the imaginations, inspirations, and intuitions given by Astro-Gaia Sophia about her creative activity. There is a great deal more to be done.

A growing interest in sacred architecture, sacred geometry, astro-archaeology, ancient mythologies, biodynamic agriculture, cosmology—in other words, interest in Star Wisdom and Earth Wisdom—is evident in our time. If this paper stimulates readers to awaken to and develop sensitivities for the workings of Astro-Gaia Sophia, the author would be most grateful.

---

1 Steiner, "The Earth as Being with Life, Soul and Spirit; The Earth as Seen by the Dead," Mar. 30, 1918, and Apr. 1, 1918, Berlin.

2 Tresemer, "Finding Jerusalem, Part One," *Journal for Star Wisdom 2013*, pp. 34–37.

3 Steiner, "Measure, Number and Weight," April 4–23, 1921; in Husemann, *Knowledge of the Human Being Through Art*, p. 28, Mercury Press, 1990.

WORKING WITH THE STAR CALENDAR

Robert Powell, Ph.D.

In taking note of the astronomical events listed in the Star Calendar of the *Journal for Star Wisdom* (*JSW*), it is important to distinguish between long- and short-term astronomical events. Long-term astronomical events—for example, Pluto transiting a particular degree of the zodiac—will have a longer period of meditation than would the five days advocated for short-term astronomical events such as the new and Full Moon. The following describes, in relation to meditating on the Full Moon, a meditative process extending over a five-day period.

Sanctification of the Full Moon

As a preliminary remark, let us remind ourselves that the great sacrifice of Christ on the Cross—the Mystery of Golgotha—took place at Full Moon. As Christ's sacrifice took place when the Moon was full in the middle of the sidereal sign of Libra, the Libra Full Moon assumes special significance in the sequence of twelve (or thirteen) Full Moons taking place during the cycle of the year. In following this sequence, the Mystery of Golgotha serves as an archetype for *every* Full Moon, since each Full Moon imparts a particular spiritual blessing. Hence the practice described here of *Sanctification of the Full Moon* applies to every Full Moon. Similarly, there is also the practice of *Sanctification of the New Moon*, as described in *Hermetic Astrology, Volume 2: Astrological Biography*, chapter 10.

During the two days prior to the Full Moon, we can consider the focus of one's meditation to extend over these two days as *preparatory days* immediately preceding the day of the Full Moon. These two days can be dedicated to spiritual reflection and detachment from everyday concerns, as one prepares to become a vessel for the in-streaming light and love one will receive at the Full Moon, something that one can then impart further—for example, to help people in need, or to support Mother Earth in times of catastrophe. During these two days, it is helpful to hold an attitude of dedication and service and try to assume an attitude of receptivity that opens to what one's soul will receive and subsequently impart—an attitude conducive to making one a true *servant of the spirit*.

The day of the Full Moon is itself a day of *holding the sacred space*. In doing so, one endeavors to cultivate inner peace and silence, during which one attempts to contact and consciously hold the in-streaming blessing of the Full Moon for the rest of humanity. One can heighten this silent meditation by visualizing the zodiacal constellation/sidereal sign in which the Moon becomes full, since the Moon serves to reflect the starry background against which it appears.

If the Moon is full in Virgo, for example, it reminds us of the night of the birth of the Jesus child visited by the three magi, as described in the Gospel of St. Matthew. That birth occurred at the Full Moon in the middle of the sidereal sign of Virgo, and the three magi, who gazed up that evening to behold the Full Moon against the background of the stars of the Virgin, witnessed the soul of Jesus emerge from the disk of the Full Moon and descend toward Earth. They participated from afar, via the starry heavens, in the Grail Mystery of the holy birth.

In meditating upon the Full Moon and opening oneself to receive the in-streaming blessing from the starry heavens, we can exercise restraint by avoiding the formulation of what will happen or what one might receive from the Full Moon. Moreover, we can also refrain from seeking tangible results or effects connected with our attunement to the Full Moon. Even if we observe only the date but not the exact moment when the Moon is full, it is helpful to find quiet time to reflect alone or to use the opportunity for deep meditation on the day of the full moon.

We can think of the two days following the full moon as a *time of imparting* what we have received from the in-streaming of the full disk of the Moon against the background of the stars. It is now possible to turn our attention toward humanity and the world and endeavor to pass on any spiritual blessing we have received from the starry heavens. Thereby we can assist in the work of the spiritual world by transforming what we have received into goodwill and allowing it to flow wherever the greatest need exists.

It is a matter of *holding a sacred space* throughout the day of the full moon. This is an important time to still the mind and maintain inner peace. It is a time of spiritual retreat and contact with the spiritual world, of holding in one's consciousness the archetype of the Mystery of Golgotha as a great outpouring of Divine Love that bridges Heaven and Earth. Prior to the day of the full moon, the two preceding days prepare the sacred space as a vessel to receive the heavenly blessing. The two days following the day of the full moon are a time to assimilate and distribute the spiritual transmission received into the sacred space we have prepared.

One can apply the process described here as a meditative practice in relation to the full moon to any of the astronomical events listed in the *JSW*, especially as most of these *remember* significant Christ Events. Take note, however, whether an event is long-term or short-term and adjust the period of meditative practice accordingly.

"The shadow intellect that is characteristic of all modern culture has fettered human beings to the Earth. They have eyes only for earthly things, particularly when they allow themselves to be influenced by the claims of modern science. In our age it never occurs to someone that their being belongs not to the Earth alone but to the cosmos beyond the Earth. Knowledge of our connection with the cosmos beyond the Earth—that is what we need above all to make our own.... When someone says 'I' to themselves, they experience a force that is working within, and the [ancient] Greek, in feeling the working of this inner force, related it to the Sun;...the Sun and the 'I' are the outer and inner aspects of one being. The Sun out there in space is the cosmic 'I.' What lives within me is the human 'I'.... Human beings are not primarily a creation of Earth. Human beings receive their shape and form from the cosmos. The human being is an offspring of the world of stars, above all of the Sun and Moon.... The Moon forces stream out from a center in the metabolic system....[The] Moon stimulates reproduction.... Saturn works chiefly in the upper part of the astral body....Jupiter has to do with thinking...Mars [has] to do with speech.... The Mercury forces work in the part of the human organism that lies below the region of the heart...in the breathing and circulatory functions.... Venus works preeminently in the etheric body of the human being."

—Rudolf Steiner, *Offspring of the World of Stars*, May 5, 1921

SYMBOLS USED IN CHARTS

	PLANETS		ZODIACAL SIGNS		ASPECTS
⊕	Earth	♈	Aries (Ram)	☌	Conjunction 0°
☉	Sun	♉	Taurus (Bull)	✱	Sextile 60°
☽	Moon	♊	Gemini (Twins)	□	Square 90°
☿	Mercury	♋	Cancer (Crab)	△	Trine 120°
♀	Venus	♌	Leo (Lion)	☍	Opposition 180°
♂	Mars	♍	Virgo (Virgin)		
♃	Jupiter	♎	Libra (Scales)		
♄	Saturn	♏	Scorpio (Scorpion)		
⛢	Uranus	♐	Sagittarius (Archer)		
♆	Neptune	♑	Capricorn (Goat)		
♇	Pluto	♒	Aquarius (Water Carrier)		
		♓	Pisces (Fishes)		

OTHER

☊	Ascending (North) Node	☌⋅	Sun Eclipse
☋	Descending (South) Node	☍⋅	Moon Eclipse
P	Perihelion/Perigee	ⁱ☌	Inferior Conjunction
A	Aphelion/Apogee	ˢ☌	Superior Conjunction
⊥N	Maximum Latitude	⚷	Chiron
⊥S	Minimum Latitude		

TIME

To help readers work with the information given in the ephemerides, we are adding new information to last year's text—see "New."

The information relating to daily geocentric and heliocentric planetary positions in the sidereal zodiac is tabulated in the form of an ephemeris for each month, in which the planetary positions are given at 0 hours Universal Time (UT) each day.

Beneath the geocentric and heliocentric ephemeris for each month, the information relating to planetary aspects is given in the form of an aspectarian, which lists the most important aspects—geocentric and heliocentric/hermetic—between the planets for the month in question. The day and the time of occurrence of the aspect on that day are indicated, all times being given in Universal Time (UT), which is identical to Greenwich Mean Time (GMT). For example, zero hours Universal Time is midnight GMT. This time system applies in Britain; however, when summer time is in effect, one hour must be added to all times.

** In other time zones, the time has to be adjusted according to whether it is ahead of or behind Britain. For example, in Germany, where the time is one hour ahead of British time, an hour must be added; when summer time is in effect in Germany, two hours have to be added to all times.

Using the calendar in the United States, do the following subtraction from all time indications according to time zone:

- Pacific Time subtract 8 hours
  (7 hours for daylight saving time);
- Mountain Time subtract 7 hours
  (6 hours for daylight saving time);
- Central Time subtract 6 hours
  (5 hours for daylight saving time);
- Eastern Time subtract 5 hours
  (4 hours for daylight saving time).

This subtraction will often change the date of an astronomical occurrence, shifting it back one day. Consequently, since most of the readers of this calendar live on the American Continent, astronomical occurrences during the early hours of day x are sometimes listed in the Commentaries as occurring on days $x-1/x$. For example, an eclipse occurring at 03:00 UT on the 12th is listed as occurring on the 11/12th since in America it takes place on the 11th.[1]

NEW

The preceding procedure can be greatly simplified. Here is an example for someone wishing to know the zodiacal locations of the planets on Christmas Day, December 25, 2014. Looking at the December ephemeris, it can be seen that Christmas Day falls on a Thursday. In the upper tabulation, the geocentric planetary positions are given, with that of the Sun indicated in the first column, that of the Moon in the second column, and so on. The position of the Sun is listed as 8°09' Sagittarius.

For someone living in London, 8°09' Sagittarius is the Sun's position at midnight, December 24/25, 2014—noting that in London and all of the United Kingdom, the Time Zone applying there is that of Universal Time/Greenwich Mean Time—UT/GMT.

For someone living in Sydney, Australia, which on Christmas Day is eleven hours ahead of UT/GMT, 8°09' Sagittarius is the Sun's position at 11 a.m. on December 25.

For someone living in California, which is eight hours behind UT/GMT on Christmas Day,

---

1 See *General Introduction to the Christian Star Calendar: A Key to Understanding* for an in-depth clarification of the features of the calendar in the *Journal for Star Wisdom*, including indications as to how to work with it.

8°09' Sagittarius is the Sun's position at 4 p.m. on **December 24**.

For the person living in California, therefore, in order to know the positions of the planets on December 25, it is necessary to look at the entries for **December 26**. The result is:

For someone living in California, which is eight hours behind UT/GMT on Christmas Day, the Sun's position at 4 p.m. on December 25 is 9°10' Sagittarius and by the same token, the Moon's position on Christmas Day at 4 p.m. on December 25 is 2°34' Aquarius—these are the positions alongside December 26 at midnight UT/GMT—and eight hours earlier equates with 4 p.m. on December 25 in California.

From these examples it emerges that the **planetary positions as given in the ephemeris** can be utilized, but that according to the Time Zone one is in, **the time of day is different** and also for locations West of the United Kingdom **the date changes** (look at the date following the actual date).

Here is a tabulation in relation to the foregoing example of December 25 (Christmas Day).

UNITED KINGDOM, EUROPE, AND ALL LOCATIONS WITH TIME ZONES EAST OF GREENWICH

Look at what is given alongside December 25—these entries indicate the planetary positions at these times:

- 12:00 a.m. (midnight December 24/25) in London (UT/GMT)
- 01:00 a.m. in Berlin (CENTRAL EUROPEAN TIME, which is one hour ahead of UT/GMT)
- 11:00 a.m. in Sydney (AUSTRALIAN EASTERN DAYLIGHT TIME, which is eleven hours ahead of UT/GMT)

CANADA, USA, CENTRAL AMERICA, SOUTH AMERICA, AND ALL LOCATIONS WITH TIME ZONES WEST OF GREENWICH

Look at what is given alongside December 26—these entries indicate the planetary positions at these times:

- 7:00 p.m. in New York (EASTERN STANDARD TIME, which is five hours behind UT/GMT)
- 6:00 p.m. in Chicago (CENTRAL STANDARD TIME, which is six hours behind UT/GMT)
- 5:00 p.m. in Denver (MOUNTAIN STANDARD TIME, which is seven hours behind UT/GMT)
- 4:00 p.m. in San Francisco (PACIFIC STANDARD TIME, which is eight hours behind UT/GMT)
- **IF SUMMER TIME IS IN USE, ADD ONE HOUR**—FOR EXAMPLE:
- 8:00 p.m. in New York (EASTERN DAYLIGHT TIME, which is four hours behind UT/GMT)
- 7:00 p.m. in Chicago (CENTRAL DAYLIGHT TIME, which is five hours behind UT/GMT)
- 6:00 p.m. in Denver (MOUNTAIN DAYLIGHT TIME, which is six hours behind UT/GMT)
- 5:00 p.m. in San Francisco (PACIFIC DAYLIGHT TIME, which is seven hours behind UT/GMT)

Note that in the preceding tabulation, the time given in Sydney on Christmas Day, December 25, is in terms of Daylight Time. Six months earlier, on June 25, for someone in Sydney they would look alongside the entry in the ephemeris for June 25 and would know that this applies (for them) to...

- 10:00 a.m. in Sydney (AUSTRALIAN EASTERN TIME, which is ten hours ahead of UT/GMT).

In these examples, it is not just the position of the Sun that is referred to. The same applies to the zodiacal locations given in the ephemeris for *all* the planets, whether geocentric (upper tabulation) or heliocentric (lower tabulation). *All that is necessary to apply this method of reading the ephemeris is to know the Time Zone in which one is and to apply the number of hours difference from UT/GMT.*

The advantage of using the method described here is that it greatly simplifies reference to the ephemeris when studying the **zodiacal positions of the planets**. However, for applying the time indications listed under "Ingresses" or "Aspects" it is still necessary to add or subtract the time difference from UT/GMT as described in the above paragraph denoted **.

"Why does a feeling of grandeur, of reverent awe, come over us when we look up into the starry heavens? It is because without our knowing it the feeling of our soul's home awakens in us. The feeling awakens: Before you came down to earth to a new incarnation, you yourself were in those stars, and out of the stars have come the highest forces that are within you. Your moral law was imparted to you when you were dwelling in the world of stars. When you practice self-knowledge, you can behold what the starry heaven bestowed upon you between death and a new birth—the best and finest powers of your soul. What we behold in the starry heavens is the moral law that is given to us from the spiritual worlds, for between death and a new birth we live in these starry heavens. One should contemplate the starry heavens with feelings such as these.... If we then raise our eyes to the starry heavens, we will be filled with a feeling of reverence and will know that this is the memory of the human being's eternal home."

—Rudolf Steiner (*Life Between Death and Rebirth,* Nov. 18, 1912)

INTRODUCTION TO THE COMMENTARIES 2014
KASHYAPA IN THE LIGHT OF PENTECOST

Claudia McLaren Lainson

For most of this year Pluto will be at the same position it occupied during the event of Pentecost in AD 33 (16° Sagittarius). Pluto has been in Sagittarius since 2006 and will remain in this constellation until early 2021. Pluto in Sagittarius remembers the entire life of Jesus Christ and at 16° it remembers when, through Mary-Sophia, the Holy Spirit descended and brought the fire of the divine "I" into the hearts of the disciples. This memory creates a wonderful overlighting of "good news" that blesses this entire year. Valentin Tomberg and Robert Powell both address the World Pentecost prophesied by Steiner. This approaching reality is heightened this year with Pluto conjunct its position at the original Pentecost. With Uranus and Pluto square to each other during this year, we can imagine illuminating revelation descending upon all humanity. With the light, the darkness is also illumined; thus are we called to work diligently at the threshold to the spiritual worlds. Our task is to attend the light without ignoring the shadow.

In William Bento's excellent article in this journal, he writes about the Uranus–Pluto square, with these two planets ninety degrees from one another, applying it to historic events. The current square between these two planets has been occurring since 2012, and will continue into 2015, thus accompanying us through this year. Also writing in this journal, David Tresemer astutely addresses the 2010 Supreme Court ruling that gave corporations the status of personhood. And Robert Powell presents in these pages an essay relating to the prophecy of the individuality who is in the process of becoming the Maitreya Buddha.

As Powell indicates in his article, the Maitreya Buddha anticipated by Buddhists is the same as the Kalki Avatar awaited in Hinduism. Further, the article refers to a prophecy from an ancient Hindu text concerning the cosmic configuration announcing the coming of the Kalki Avatar. According to this Hindu text, he is to begin teaching when the New Moon in the Hindu *nakshatra Pushya*, which is in sidereal Cancer and contains the star cluster Praesepe at 12½° Cancer, occurs in conjunction with Jupiter. Just such a New Moon will occur in Pushya at 9° Cancer on July 27 of this year—with Jupiter close by at 7½° Cancer. The name *Kashyapa* is used in the subtitle of this article in relation to the Maitreya/Kalki individuality, since Kashyapa was the name of the future Maitreya Buddha in his incarnation some 2,500 years ago as a disciple of Gautama Buddha.[1]

Taking the focus of these three articles together, highlights for the year are announced. Bento attributes the following characteristics to the influence of Uranus: rebellion, freedom, liberation, reform/revolution, unexpected break-ups, surprise, revelations/awakening, lightning-like flashes of insight, creativity, originality and, we can add, a propensity to open to the future. And

---

[1] According to a classic text of Zen Buddhism, *The Transmission of the Light (Denkoroku)*, one day the Buddha silently raised a lotus blossom and blinked his eyes. At this, Kashyapa smiled. The Buddha said, "I have the treasury of the eye of truth, the ineffable mind of Nirvana. These I entrust to Kashyapa." He also passed his gold brocade robe to Kashyapa, thus indicating Kashyapa to be his successor in the Bodhisattva transmission—that is, the Bodhisattva who will become the next Buddha, the future Maitreya Buddha (http://www.ese-an.org/d/218-denko-roku.html).

to the influence of Pluto he assigns these attributes: elemental power, depth, intensity, compelling force, empowerment, catastrophic extremes, primordial instincts, destruction, regeneration, and cathartic transformations.

Since 2012 we have seen many of the above qualities in both their negative and positive expressions. The human soul, as Bento remarks, is longing for reunion with the divine; and since Uranus can be seen as a messenger of the thoughts of the Holy Spirit, the current position of this planet (aspecting Pluto's remembrance of Pentecost) brings this possibility closer. Uranus also can cause a collective anxiety in souls who have been severed from spiritual worlds. Here we see two attributes of Uranus: longing and/or anxiety. Rudolf Steiner spoke of the present age as that of the consciousness soul. He indicated the role of evil in awakening consciousness, pointing out that ours is an age in which human beings are able to develop and spiritually awaken by confronting evil. Thus it is in this age of the consciousness soul that we are collectively approaching the threshold to the spiritual world where the battle between good and evil is raging. It is Christ in his Second Coming who has gradually been calling us to this threshold. The esoteric prerogative is to stand with Christ and offer up one's personal will in order to become a vessel through which the will of Christ can become active. Powell speaks of the "magnification" that is now occurring in human souls. Magnification causes an increase of whatever it is that lives in us—for better or for worse. When the consciousness soul stands at the threshold with Christ it becomes the *conscience* soul. Without a connection to spiritual thoughts, the influence of Uranus, in aspect to Pluto, will perpetuate a collective anxiety.

Anxiety, as a collective phenomenon, will be rationalized personally by human beings as originating from the self. The origin of this ambient anxiety is not the self; in its current manifestation it is instead an all-pervasive presence spawned from the sub-earthly forces that we have allowed to permeate our world. We are to take up the truth of spiritual guidance at this time of the Second Coming; and through this we will find the peace that strengthens us to bear the intensity of standing at the threshold, where we will attune ourselves to Christ's divine presence and the protection afforded to us by our connection with him.

In this light it is urgently necessary that human beings develop a relationship with spiritual thoughts and spiritual realities. This is the antidote to anxiety. And in this year in particular, with Pluto remembering Pentecost, the longing for spiritual truth can strive toward its fulfillment. Through our openness to receive cosmic thoughts (Uranus), the soul is able to discriminate between ambient collective agitation and inner unrest. In turning toward the light of revelation that Uranus bestows, one can open to the cosmic thoughts now streaming from higher worlds. With Uranus square Pluto, a deepening into the cathartic intensity of what the light is bringing is supported. *To benefit from what the stars are speaking, human beings must direct their attention to what the stars are bringing.* In the words of Willie Sucher (1902–1985):

> Here we must come to be absolutely aware of the fact that in modern times man should receive consciously what the Cosmos offers as potential for positive response. If this does not happen, then the offerings of the Stars may be possessed by adverse forces and plunged into destructive events. Therefore it is of great importance that humanity meets cosmic events fully consciously, and with a constructive attitude.[1]

Sucher, the pioneer of Astrosophy and an enlightened forerunner in the new astrology, knew that forces are released as planets come into various aspects with each other. He knew also that these forces, if not freely breathed in, so to speak, by the consciousness of human beings, could then become inverted and used destructively against the good intentions of cosmic beings. *Cosmic beings speak through the movement of the stars. We listen when we give our attention to what they are speaking.* Sucher goes on to comment on the memories activated in the stars when they aspect

---

1 Willi Sucher, *Mercury Star Journal*, 1977.

positions that "remember" the three years in the life of Christ:

> This does not mean to suggest that we regard them [star memories of the life of Christ] as "nice" or "interesting" memories of the past, without much meaning for the present. We have experienced that such events can be of great significance for any later time, provided the human being revives these events in his inner spiritual life, and even identifies with them as much as he can. Thus the Christ events can become facts which are permanently present for the Earth and humanity, with all their healing and redeeming qualities. On such a Cosmic background they can be projected in the most positive sense into the present and future, and not just be seen as shadows of a long distant past.[2]

In the spirit of these words of Willie Sucher we can enter into the events of 2014 and muster the will to participate in cosmic stellar events. Toward this end are the commentaries offered.

Returning to the Uranus–Pluto square and its meaning for humanity, we look at the constellations in which this will be occurring between the years of 2012 and 2015. Uranus will be in Pisces—the constellation which, according to indications Steiner gave, is associated with the worldview of *psychism* and helps us to develop the virtue of *magnanimity*. Steiner noted, moreover, that through magnanimity one develops *love*. Uranus did not come into this constellation during the three years of the life of Christ, nor does its current location in Pisces oppose or square its position during the life of Christ, for it was then in the constellation of Leo. So what is the significance of Uranus in Pisces for the themes of 2014 that we are considering? It is undoubtedly of significance this year on account of its square to Pluto. Furthermore, we can gain a deeper understanding of Uranus in Pisces at the present time by considering historic events that occurred when Uranus was last at this year's positions in Pisces.

First, however, we will look at Pluto and its relevance to the life of Christ. Pluto was in Sagittarius during the entire life of Jesus Christ, and it has again been in Sagittarius over the past eight years. Pluto moved into Sagittarius in 2006 and will remain in this constellation until early 2021. Steiner indicated the virtue for Sagittarius to be *control of thought/control of speech*, i.e., minding one's tongue, and he noted that through control of speech one develops a sense for the truth. The worldview he attributed to this constellation is *monism*. One hundred years ago (1914) Steiner spoke of the beings that indwell words:

> Language does not contain only what modern, materialistic science believes it contains; there is something in language that, in many ways, is connected with our not-fully conscious experiences, which often occur in the subconscious realms of our being and are therefore interpenetrated by spiritual beings. Spiritual beings live and are active in human language, and when we form words, elemental spiritual beings pour into these words. When human beings converse together, spiritual beings fly about in the room on wings of the words. This is why it is so important that we pay attention to certain subtleties of language and do not simply let uncontrolled feelings get the better of us when we speak.[3]

Our speech engenders elemental beings of one sort or another and we are responsible for what our speech creates. With Pluto in Sagittarius, control of our own speaking will surely guide us to a feeling for the truth—despite the propaganda swirling through spiritless journalism and the media in general, not to mention the ceaseless barrage of untruths directed toward human beings from television, cinema, videos, computer games, blog spots, etc.

In 1917, Steiner indicated that the proclamation of Christ's second coming began already in 1909. In this year Pluto had just entered the constellation of Gemini (opposite Sagittarius). Steiner knew that the gradual descent of the Christ from spiritual heights made it possible for human beings to be very near to him in a quite different

---

2 Ibid.

3 Steiner, *Art as Seen in the Light of Mystery Wisdom*, p. 25.

way than had been hitherto possible.[1] It was in this same year that he gave his lectures on the *Spiritual Bells of Easter*, wherein he described the rising of the incorruptible body of Kashyapa. Powell quotes from these lectures in the second appendix of his book entitled *Christ and the Maya Calendar*:

> In Steiner's 1909 lectures he speaks of a legend "that when Kashyapa came to the point of death and on account of his mature wisdom was ready to pass into *nirvana*, he made his way to a steep mountain and hid himself in a cave. After his death his body did not decay but remained intact. Only initiates know of this secret and of the hidden place where the incorruptible body of the great initiate rests. But the Buddha foretold that one day in the future his great successor, the Maitreya Buddha, the new great teacher and leader of humankind, would come, and reaching the supreme height of existence to be attained during earthly life, would seek out the cave of Kashyapa and touch with his right hand the incorruptible body of the enlightened one. Whereupon a miraculous fire would stream down from heaven and in this fire the incorruptible body of Kashyapa, the enlightened one, would be lifted from earthly into spiritual existence."

Powell goes on to quote Steiner's comment that "Christ will be revealed to us in a spiritualized fire of the future." An intimate connection between the Etheric Christ and the being of Kashyapa is here indicated. The cave in which the incorruptible body of Kashyapa is preserved can be thought of as the etheric world. Transfigured etheric bodies of great initiates do not dissolve into the cosmic ether upon their death, but are etherically preserved, in their wholeness, from whence their disciples on earth can draw great strength. The legend tells us that when Kashyapa—Gautama Buddha's successor (see footnote 1)—will one day return as the Maitreya Buddha, he will meet his incorruptible body, and through the "spiritualized fire of the future," the etheric being of Kashyapa will be lifted into union with Christ.

Since the time of Gautama Buddha, Kashyapa has reincarnated many times. For example, according to Rudolf Steiner, Jeshu ben Pandira, the teacher of the Essenes, who lived about one hundred years before Christ, was an incarnation of the great teacher who will one day become the Maitreya Buddha. Moreover, closer to our time, as the Cosmic Christ came into the angelic spheres surrounding the earth, Kashyapa reincarnated. Rudolf Steiner indicated that the birth of this individuality, who had lived on earth as Jeshu ben Pandira, was around the year 1900. Steiner prophesied that it would be the individuality who was once Jeshu ben Pandira, born at the beginning of the twentieth century (and thus had already reincarnated at the time Steiner held this lecture in 1910), who would be the *actual* proclaimer of the Etheric Christ.[2]

The 1909 lectures on the Spiritual Bells of Easter[3] are significant. They were cosmically inspired as Pluto entered into the constellation of Gemini (opposite its position during the life of Christ), representing the mystery of "two becoming one." One hundred years after these lectures, in July of 2009, with Pluto at the same position it held at the Baptism in the Jordan River, the longest solar eclipse of the twenty-first century took place. Three 33⅓-year cycles after Steiner's subtle reference to the Etheric Christ, something inverse to Christ's manifestation in the etheric was afoot. It would be six months later that the person-hood of corporations would be decided. This year (2014), as indicated in Robert Powell's article, the July New Moon in Cancer on July 27 is evidently announcing the renewed teachings of Kashyapa. Pluto will be at 16° Sagittarius—where it was at Pentecost. An imagination is here offered whereby evil prepares to occult the good in 2009, resulting six months later in an economic *coup* delivered through Citizens United. The third temptation in the wilderness echoes from this decision. Ahriman becomes victorious through a new kind of being—a

---

1 See Powell and Dann, *Christ and the Maya Calendar*, appendix 2.

2 See Steiner, *According to Matthew*, lecture 10.

3 See Steiner, *Festivals and their Meaning*, for these two lectures.

corporation—and a new kind of government continues to threaten the viability of democracy.

The solar eclipse of 2009 was one hundred years after Steiner gave his account of the legend of Kashyapa and spoke of the return of Christ in the spiritualized fire of the future. Exactly three and one-half years after this eclipse a new presidential term began in the US. During the last term, corporations became persons. In the new term, what could be referred to as the children of corporations—predator drones[4]—will multiply; unforeseen new possibilities are developing as a result of the technology behind these predators and other advances in artificial intelligence now under development. The intention to create *singularity*—the merging of biological and non-biological intelligence—will, in the near future, create the possibility that humanity will transcend nature and embrace *transhumanistic* views. We are escalating toward the development of a superhumanity. But who will this new humanity of singularity serve?

The Pluto memory of the Baptism, where two became one as Christ entered the being of the Nathan Jesus, now shows its inversion of this enlightened union. The inversion is *possession*. The coldness of drones and the abstract intellectuality of singularity and other new "human enhancement" technologies will multiply the presence of Ahriman. *This multiplication is an inversion of the multiplying of the children of Abraham, for it is not the stars that artificial intelligence will multiply, but rather the mechanized reality of Ahriman's sub-earthly realms.* Citizens United was decided with Pluto at 9° Sagittarius. This was the same position of Pluto at the third temptation in the wilderness, where Jesus Christ was asked to turn stones into bread. The rule by the wealthy has escalated since this 2010 decision, therefore giving rise to a plutocracy that is trumping the last vestiges of a democracy. *Plutocracy* is a combination of *Pluto*: god of wealth and money (stones); and *autocrat/dictator* wielding undivided power (Ahriman). Just as Ahriman was behind the third temptation, so at the decision of corporate personhood was there a temptation by Ahriman, which in this case was victorious. With this decision the ahrimanic principle over-shadowed the spiritual principles set forth in Steiner's threefold social order, which Steiner began developing in the fateful year of 1917 as Pluto was opposing its position during the life of Christ. Three years prior to 1917 the "Great War" broke out, exposing the ever-advancing approach of Ahriman.

At the outbreak of World War I (July 1914), Pluto was at 7° Gemini, directly opposite its position when Christ, after the Baptism, had entered his forty days of continual temptation. This war began a period of temptation that continues today. A short few years after this outbreak, in 1917, the Russian October Revolution erupted with Pluto at 11° Gemini—reflecting a time during Christ's ministry when he was teaching and healing. Both of these events, the Great War and the Bolshevik Revolution most assuredly brought humanity into confrontation with evil, and with occult brotherhoods whose powers work specifically and directly against Christ. World War I and the Bolshevik Revolution were actions induced by the Antichrist against the unity of nations and the sanctity of human freedom and liberty. These events were also an assault targeted against the future location of the sixth cultural epoch, the Slavic countries. In 1934, after the rising of the beast a year earlier, Pluto left Gemini and entered Cancer, gradually making its way toward its position during the life of Christ that this year remembers.

Uranus was last in Pisces, very close to where it was last year and continues this year, during the disastrous years of the late twenties and early thirties of the nineteenth century. Stalin was imposing heinous restrictions in Russia, Hitler was gaining power in Germany, and the US stock market had crashed. It is not the life of Christ that Uranus is this year remembering, but rather the historical memories of war, hatred, genocide, extreme inflation, and economic collapse. At these mournful degrees Uranus is aspecting Pluto, where divine memories of the life of Christ are emphasized. This is what

---

4 See entry for Apr. 15: When drones operate as human beings, we are seeing the children of corporations in action. Just as a corporation is not a "being," a drone is not a soldier. See David Tresemer's article, page 39 in this journal.

makes this year profound—the contrast between the sublime memories of the life of Christ and the historic memories from the last time Uranus was at these degrees of the zodiac. Following the advice of Willie Sucher, we can read the articles in this journal, and also the monthly commentaries, in order to place our attention on the "good news" the stars are bestowing, even as we cast the knowing glance to dark agendas that have resulted from occult brotherhoods, which for centuries have gathered and inverted the stellar influences. It was eighty-four years ago (the orbital time for Uranus) that last saw Uranus at these degrees of Pisces.

It would be naive to think that occult brotherhoods are ignorant of the stars. They are not. It is incumbent upon all of us to remember the star wisdom of Egypt, now Christianized, so that our souls find fulfillment through receiving the *manna* that births free thinking (Uranus), and the divine love of the Father (Pluto) that purifies our will to do the good even in the face of evil. It will take active participation for humanity to bring the light of the stars into the trying times in which we live, yet it is just this light that is the antidote to the spreading darkness. The Uranus/Pluto square calls forth imaginative and intuitive capacities. As Bento writes in his article, Uranus–Pluto aspects have signified the work of great minds during great periods of our history, including the philosophic flowering of the Renaissance and the work of the "unknown ones"—the Rosicrucians. These memories can be the winds in the sails that steer us away from recapitulating the suffering that occurred in Germany and Russia in the thirties of the last century.

In order for our thinking to receive the light (Uranus) and our will to receive the life (Pluto), we need to open our hearts and nourish our feeling life with what brings peace and fosters love—this is Pentecost. The heart is the mediator between the head and the will. Christ is the supreme lord of the heart and the Second Coming is intrinsically interwoven with the being of the Maitreya.[1] In an excerpt of a vision offered by a contemporary seer, Estelle Isaacson, some of whose visions bear witness to the being of the Maitreya (Kashyapa),[2] the power of good thoughts and feelings is shown as what unites us to the being who will become the Maitreya Buddha. Steiner honors the Maitreya in his lectures on the *Spiritual Bells of Easter*. Here, now, with an excerpt from one of Estelle Isaacson's visions:

> The one who will become the Maitreya Buddha knows his small group of disciples and he is truly known only by his group of disciples. He is watching over the ones who know him, for he is preparing through them—through their hearts, for his life when he shall appear as the Maitreya. His disciples are doing the work to prepare for him. He appears to inner vision as a sitting Buddha, radiantly white, his head golden, filled with thoughts of the Good and all the Good thoughts of human beings. He holds for his disciples, and also for others, the ideals of the Good, the True, and the Beautiful, while here on the Earth there is the rumbling of degenerated thoughts and evil feelings plaguing the human condition.
>
> Human beings are now being told what to think in order to generate the most fear. Programs of anxiety are being sent around the globe, and not just general anxiety; for, these programs have the ability, once settling into the human field, to become personal to each individual, so that every person may begin to feel anxiety and may become trapped in his or her feelings. The Maitreya, however, offers a remedy.
>
> He says to all: Align with me, and think Good thoughts, feel Good feelings, and let Good will prevail.
>
> Through him—he who is aligned with Christ in the etheric—True and Good thoughts and Beautiful feelings are available as a remedy to those destructive programs being generated by the evil one. The evil one gains his power through fear and negative thinking and the ensuing forgetting of Love on the part of human beings. This is a process that contributes to the development of his body.

---

1 See *Hermetic Astrology,* vol. 1, appendix 2, "The Second Coming."

2 See also the article "The Bodhisattva Who Will Become the Maitreya Buddha" by Estelle Isaacson, page 34 in this issue of *Journal for Star Wisdom*.

Introduction to the Commentaries 2014: Kashyapa in the Light of Pentecost

Likewise, the Maitreya receives his body from the benevolent thoughts of those human beings who are able to awaken and say, "I will not think these thoughts; I will think the thoughts of the Good."

Some are called to see and behold what is truly happening in the world. These individuals must learn to think the Good thoughts even while beholding evil deeds.

May the peace that shines forth from the deeds of Christ be our guiding light in this dynamic year, as we await the presence of the Kashyapa–Maitreya individuality and the ever-increasing light of a World Pentecost. It is not yet known whether the teachings of Kashyapa will become public, or if instead they will need to remain in esoteric realms where those so directed will find him. Nonetheless, he will find those who seek him.

It is most probable that the ruling powers of the plutocracy will increase as this year progresses, and yet the results of this continuation of dominance are powerfully overlighted by the Pentecostal light bestowed by Christ and the presence of the enlightened one who is his proclaimer. Kashyapa is a source of strength for all who turn to him and find solace in his etheric vestments, which are deeply connected with the vestments of Christ. Through Christ, the Maitreya, and the discipline of constant positivity, ambient anxieties will not become part of our soul life, but rather will our peaceful souls be a solace to those who have succumbed to fear. The revelatory cosmic thoughts of Uranus and the depth of the cathartic transformation of Pluto are gifts bestowed by the stars, in this year when the remembrance of Pentecost bestows its fiery light.

"The shadow intellect that is characteristic of all modern culture has fettered human beings to the Earth. They have eyes only for earthly things, particularly when they allow themselves to be influenced by the claims of modern science. In our age it never occurs to someone that their being belongs not to the Earth alone but to the cosmos beyond the Earth. Knowledge of our connection with the cosmos beyond the Earth—that is what we need above all to make our own.... When someone says 'I' to themselves, they experience a force that is working within, and the [ancient] Greek, in feeling the working of this inner force, related it to the Sun;...the Sun and the 'I' are the outer and inner aspects of one being. The Sun out there in space is the cosmic 'I.' What lives within me is the human 'I'.... Human beings are not primarily a creation of Earth. Human beings receive their shape and form from the cosmos. The human being is an offspring of the world of stars, above all of the Sun and Moon.... The Moon forces stream out from a center in the metabolic system....[The] Moon stimulates reproduction.... Saturn works chiefly in the upper part of the astral body....Jupiter has to do with thinking...Mars [has] to do with speech.... The Mercury forces work in the part of the human organism that lies below the region of the heart...in the breathing and circulatory functions.... Venus works preeminently in the etheric body of the human being."

—Rudolf Steiner, *Offspring of the World of Stars*, May 5, 1921

COMMENTARIES AND EPHEMERIDES
JANUARY–DECEMBER 2014
Claudia McLaren Lainson and Sally Nurney

JANUARY 2014

We begin the year with a New Moon: Sun and Moon together in the middle of the Archer (Sagittarius). Mercury and Pluto are within the conjunction of Sun and Moon too, hidden in the Sun's glare. Half a constellation away, but still close enough to the Sun to be hidden is Venus, retrograde in Capricorn. Also kicking the year off is the Quadrantids Meteor Shower the evening of the 2nd and morning of the 3rd. This is an above average year, with as many as 40 meteors per hour. Best viewing is after midnight, with the "shooting stars" radiating from the direction of the constellation Bootes (Look off of the arc of the handle of the Big Dipper to the bright sacred star Arcturus who is at the "waist" of Bootes, the herder) but they can appear anywhere in the sky. Bundle up and get gazing! Mercury meets up with Venus on the 7th; they are invisible within the daylight, what might you sense here in your first "day gazing" opportunity of 2014? Venus conjuncts the Sun on the 11th and remains hidden with its radiant light until becoming visible as the morning star around the end of the month. The Sun moves in front of the constellation of Capricorn (the SeaGoat) late on the 14th while the almost full Moon is conjunct Retrograde Jupiter in Gemini (the Twins). They rise together in the east just before sunset. The Full Moon is the next evening of the 15th. The waning moon joins Mars in Virgo (the Virgin) and can be seen either rising in the east around midnight on the 22nd or in the hours before sunrise on the 23rd, depending on your own sleep cycles! The same applies to the Moon's conjunction with Mars in Virgo on the 23rd ~ visible rising in the east around midnight and visible until the sunrise. Two days later, on the 25th, the Moon joins Saturn rising a bit later (around 2 a.m.) and visible until the Sun hides Saturn within the new day (but we can still enjoy the waning moon's shape in the day sky.) Regardless of your sleep preferences, sunrise on the 29th should be worth getting up for, as the last slivers of the waning Moon rise with Venus (and Pluto, too far away to see) about 1 ½ hours before the Sun. To finish the month, a New Moon on the 30th in Capricorn.

January 1: New Moon 16° Sagittarius. Today's New Moon marks the anniversary of the birth of the Nathan Jesus (Dec/6/2 BC). A New Moon represents the beginning of a lunar cycle—a time for the sprouting of new life. This first New Moon of 2014, occurring on the first day of the year, silently stands in the darkness of this night, offering blessings for new beginnings. It was the pure and chaste Nathan Jesus who became Jesus Christ and walked among us. Since the event of the Mystery of Golgotha he is the spirit of the Earth; his sheaths are woven into the very fabric of our living, breathing Mother Earth. The entire future of humanity depends on human beings uniting with the unfathomable love and mercy of this first born Son of the Father. At this time of the Second Coming we are to relinquish egoistical "self-determination" in order to live into the words: "Not I, but Christ in me." In this way we will find our way through all trials.

The Jesus *being* is different from the Nathan Jesus we today commemorate. The Jesus being has renounced his higher rank in order to unite directly with humankind. In this way humanity has been strengthened to do the good through the renewal bestowed by sacrificial spiritual beings, such as the Jesus being, working on our behalf. Three such beings to whom we owe a great debt are Buddha, Elijah, and Jesus:

> Since the Lemurian Epoch, the Jesus *being*, who was partly embodied in the Nathan Jesus, has exercised a harmonizing influence on the human organism. He was an archangelic being who descended to the angelic hierarchy in order to be associated directly with humankind. Rudolf Steiner describes the effect of the threefold permeation of the Jesus being by Christ (during the Lemurian epoch, the first third of the Atlantean epoch, and the final third of the Atlantean epoch) as harmonizing, accordingly, the senses, the life processes, and the soul forces.[1]

Tomberg goes on to tell how the human being is held together as a complete being by the force of love. Extraordinary! The fourth deed of Christ that harmonized the "I" was only possible because of the work of Buddha, Elijah, and Jesus.

> Thus three beings worked together to prepare the birth of the conscience by means of which the Christ was able to descend to Earth. For the conscience which was to receive the Christ into itself must be fully awake; that is to say, it must be awake in the sentient soul, in the rational soul, and in the consciousness soul. But what does it mean when we say that the conscience must be fully awake in these three members of the soul? It means that the consciousness of *manas*, *buddhi*, and *atma* are all present. Before we can realize the true depth of the stirring spectacle of the three sheaths of the Nathan Jesus as he walked the path to baptism in the Jordan, we must first recognize the *atma* power, the *buddhi* life, and the *manas* light acting on the physical, etheric and astral bodies of the one who walked the path to the Jordan baptism. This wakefulness of the outer threefold conscience resulted from the collaboration of the three beings who had been preparing for this wonderful eventuality throughout long ages. The Buddha rays were active in it; the Elijah power prepared the way before it; and the Jesus life filled it. All of the sacred melodies of Orpheus, all the enlightenment of the Buddha, the wholehearted readiness of Jesus for willing, generous sacrifice—and, yes, even the ripest fruits of the great Zoroaster's experience—all lived in the figure of the awakened conscience of humanity as it walked the path to the Jordan.[2]

Tomberg goes on to describe how all places in creation have been occupied since the Fall, and that to create a new place is an accomplishment wrought through pain which culminates in the joy of Sun-lit conscience. It is the inner Sun that radiates outward from human souls living in alignment with Jesus Christ; for, through this all dark places are enlightened.

Christ in his Second Coming is creating this new place. It is the place wherein the "moral ether" is being born through the pain of the fifth sacrifice of Christ.[3] Through this newly forming ether we are able to unite with the source of revelation sounding from the pure intelligence of the Holy Spirit.

> What once existed as revealed wisdom will be the concrete life of future human beings. "To the one who is victorious, I will give the right to eat from the tree of life, which is in the paradise of God" (Rev. 2:7). This expresses the positive future of the endeavor that moves courageously forward into the future from a reminiscent longing for the comprehensive wisdom of the past. "Overcoming" here means to overcome the desire for the past. True, it means living by a longing that arises from the past, but it must seek satisfaction not in the past but in the future. The drift of the soul's desire toward the past must be overcome permanently, but the essence of that longing must not only be nurtured but even be strengthened to an energetic striving toward the future. It will then be possible for wisdom to become life and for the wisdom originally revealed from Heaven to live in human beings. This transformation indicates the future evolution of the "moral ether" in human nature, and this "moral ether" will be just as full of light as

---

1 Tomberg, *Christ and Sophia*, p. 73.

2 Ibid., pp. 78–79.

3 In the first four sacrifices of Christ harmony was brought into our physical, etheric, astral, and "I." The fifth sacrifice is new. It is the intrinsic gift of the Second Coming, which began in 1933 when Christ first appeared in the human atmosphere of the Earth. See Powell, *The Christ Mystery*, for the dating of this event, and Tomberg's *Christ and Sophia* for the mystery of the previous sacrifices of Christ.

was the original revelation of the wisdom of the Rishis. Moreover, it will not only give light, but also function as does the life force. "Eating of the tree of life" means that the human system will absorb the power to give life.[1]

The Second Coming marks a profound change in the relationship between humanity and the spiritual worlds. It is the future that is now bestowing the pure intelligence of wisdom upon all who turn from passive longing to *active cooperation* with the divinity that entered right into creation through the Nathan Jesus, whom the stars today remember. Those willing to participate in the great work of the salvation of the Earth are working for the cosmos itself. The future can only be created if seeds are planted in the present by those who have come specifically to fulfill this task, in support of the "moral ether" that is now being created:

> An esoteric pupil is actually doing something in anticipation of what will happen later. It is, in a certain sense, not yet quite timely. The physical body is not yet adapted for it. Esotericists thus live ahead of their time and work into the future.[2]

The moral ether, like all things in our world, has its inversion. Robert Powell long ago named the counterpoint to the "fifth ether (moral ether)" as the "fifth kingdom"—the kingdom of technology. As an esoteric teacher Powell is living in advance for a future that is in the process of becoming. In reading his book entitled *Inner Radiance and the Body of Immortality*, one is taken into the esoteric practices that are serving not only what is now happening, but also in anticipation of what will be escalating as we move forward.

Two great powers vie for the attention of human beings: the kingdom of technology spawned by ahrimanic designs, and the power born of Jesus Christ. We are to actively choose! Today another memory sounds from Pluto that is potentizing this New Moon:

New Moon conjunct Pluto 16° Sagittarius. Pluto at this degree remembers Pentecost (May/24/33).

Pluto will be within two degrees of Pentecost for this entire year. As a faithful servant to the Father spirit in the heights, Pluto (as Phanes) bestows the promise of Divine Love. At Pentecost the fire of the living spirit streamed down from above into the heart of the Virgin Mary, and through her into the hearts of the disciples. From this time forward it became possible for all humanity to know the higher worlds as an inner experience. Pluto is intensifying the birth we today commemorate by reminding us of the new revelation stream to which we are to turn as we strengthen our longing for the future. We are to be active participants in the healing of both nature and humanity. Pluto remembering Pentecost signifies the spiritual guidance that is leading us out of the limiting illusions of materialism.

> According to Rudolf Steiner the event of Pentecost, which took place over two thousand years ago, is to become a world event. He spoke of this as the coming World Pentecost. What does he mean by this? The World Pentecost is an event comparable to Pentecost two thousand years ago. However, it will be a world event, not just an event that impacts a relatively small group of people in a particular geographical location. At that time in AD 33 it was a matter of many thousands of people, initially the twelve disciples who became apostles, who then went out onto the streets of Jerusalem, to the pool of Bethesda, and baptized three thousand people that day (and thousands more subsequently). In contrast, the World Pentecost will be an event of the outpouring of Divine Love for the whole of humanity. Will humanity be sufficiently prepared to receive this? And when is the World Pentecost going to happen? And, further, what might this foretell concerning our primary question regarding the significance of the year 2012?[3]

Self-determination is a detriment to the path opening to the event of a World Pentecost, and today Mars remembers the progenitor of the will-to-power:

---

1 Tomberg, *Christ and Sophia*, p. 320.
2 Steiner, *The Secret Stream*, p. 33.
3 See *2012 and World Pentecost*, and article by Robert Powell available on the Sophia Foundation website. According to Dr. Powell, 2012 marks the transition point into a new outpouring of spiritual revelation.

SIDEREAL GEOCENTRIC LONGITUDES : JANUARY 2014 Gregorian at 0 hours UT

DAY	☉	☽	☊	☿	♀	♂	♃	♄	♅	♆	♇
1 WE	15 ♐ 33	8 ♐ 52	10 ♎ 36R	17 ♐ 10	1 ♑ 58R	16 ♍ 43	21 ♊ 11R	25 ♎ 26	13 ♓ 44	8 ♒ 18	16 ♐ 20
2 TH	16 34	24 11	10 26	18 47	1 32	17 9	21 3	25 31	13 45	8 20	16 22
3 FR	17 35	9 ♑ 30	10 16	20 24	1 5	17 36	20 55	25 36	13 46	8 21	16 24
4 SA	18 37	24 36	10 6	22 2	0 36	18 2	20 46	25 42	13 47	8 23	16 26
5 SU	19 38	9 ♒ 21	9 58	23 40	0 5	18 27	20 38	25 47	13 48	8 24	16 28
6 MO	20 39	23 39	9 53	25 18	29 ♐ 32	18 53	20 30	25 52	13 49	8 26	16 30
7 TU	21 40	7 ♓ 29	9 50	26 57	28 59	19 18	20 22	25 57	13 50	8 28	16 32
8 WE	22 41	20 51	9 49	28 36	28 24	19 43	20 14	26 2	13 51	8 30	16 34
9 TH	23 42	3 ♈ 48	9 49D	0 ♑ 15	27 48	20 8	20 6	26 7	13 52	8 31	16 36
10 FR	24 44	16 25	9 49R	1 55	27 12	20 33	19 58	26 12	13 53	8 33	16 38
11 SA	25 45	28 45	9 48	3 35	26 35	20 57	19 50	26 17	13 54	8 35	16 41
12 SU	26 46	10 ♉ 55	9 44	5 15	25 58	21 21	19 42	26 21	13 56	8 37	16 43
13 MO	27 47	22 56	9 37	6 55	25 21	21 45	19 34	26 26	13 57	8 38	16 45
14 TU	28 48	4 ♊ 52	9 27	8 36	24 45	22 8	19 26	26 30	13 58	8 40	16 47
15 WE	29 49	16 46	9 15	10 16	24 9	22 31	19 18	26 35	14 0	8 42	16 49
16 TH	0 ♑ 50	28 38	9 0	11 57	23 34	22 54	19 10	26 39	14 1	8 44	16 51
17 FR	1 51	10 ♋ 31	8 45	13 37	23 1	23 17	19 2	26 44	14 3	8 46	16 53
18 SA	2 52	22 25	8 30	15 17	22 29	23 39	18 55	26 48	14 4	8 48	16 55
19 SU	3 53	4 ♌ 23	8 18	16 57	21 58	24 1	18 47	26 52	14 6	8 50	16 57
20 MO	4 54	16 25	8 7	18 36	21 29	24 22	18 40	26 56	14 8	8 52	16 59
21 TU	5 55	28 34	8 0	20 14	21 2	24 44	18 32	27 0	14 9	8 54	17 1
22 WE	6 57	10 ♍ 53	7 56	21 51	20 37	25 5	18 25	27 4	14 11	8 56	17 3
23 TH	7 58	23 27	7 55	23 27	20 14	25 25	18 18	27 8	14 13	8 58	17 5
24 FR	8 59	6 ♎ 18	7 54	25 1	19 54	25 45	18 10	27 12	14 15	9 0	17 7
25 SA	10 0	19 32	7 54	26 33	19 35	26 5	18 3	27 15	14 16	9 2	17 9
26 SU	11 1	3 ♏ 13	7 53	28 2	19 20	26 25	17 56	27 19	14 18	9 4	17 11
27 MO	12 2	17 21	7 50	29 28	19 6	26 44	17 50	27 22	14 20	9 6	17 13
28 TU	13 3	1 ♐ 56	7 43	0 ♒ 50	18 56	27 3	17 43	27 26	14 22	9 8	17 15
29 WE	14 4	16 55	7 34	2 8	18 47	27 21	17 36	27 29	14 24	9 10	17 17
30 TH	15 5	2 ♑ 10	7 23	3 20	18 41	27 39	17 30	27 32	14 26	9 12	17 19
31 FR	16 6	17 30	7 12	4 27	18 38	27 56	17 24	27 35	14 29	9 14	17 21

INGRESSES :

2	☽ → ♑	9: 5	21	☽ → ♍	2:48
4	☽ → ♒	8:42	23	☽ → ♎	12:18
5	♀ → ♐	3:40	25	☽ → ♏	18:26
6	☽ → ♓	10:54	27	☿ → ♒	9:15
8	☽ → ♈	16:53		☽ → ♐	20:51
	☿ → ♑	20:21	29	☽ → ♑	20:36
11	☽ → ♉	2:26	31	☽ → ♒	19:40
13	☽ → ♊	14:12			
15	☉ → ♑	4:17			
16	☽ → ♋	2:45			
18	☽ → ♌	15:13			

ASPECTS & ECLIPSES :

1	☉ ☌ ☽	11:13	5	☉ ☍ ♃	20:59		☽ ☌ ♃	5: 4	24	☽ ☌ ☊	2:56
	☽ ☌ ♇	11:43	7	☽ ☌ ♅	11:18		☽ ☍ ♀	14:14		☉ □ ☽	5:18
	☽ ☌ ☿	14:32		☿ ☌ ♀	21:51	16	☽ ☌ A	1:53	25	☿ □ ♄	11:48
	☉ ☌ ♇	18:53		☽ ☍ ♂	21:53		☉ ☍ ☽	4:52		☽ ☌ ♄	13:41
	☽ ☍ ♃	19: 7	8	☉ □ ☽	3:39		♀ □ ♂	17: 6	29	☽ ☌ ♇	0:34
	☽ ☌ P	21: 0		♂ □ ♃	22:18		☽ (S) ☊	20:30		☽ ☍ ♃	1: 4
2	☽ ☌ ♀	11:10	9	☽ ☌ ☋	11:23	17	☽ ☍ ☿	7:17		☽ ☌ ♀	2:56
3	☉ □ ♂	0: 7	10	☽ ☍ ♄	19: 6	19	☽ ☍ ♆	8:55	30	☽ (N) ☊	8: 4
	☽ (N) ☊	1:11	11	☉ ⚻ ♀	12:17	22	☽ ☍ ♅	6:21		☽ ☌ P	10: 0
	☿ ☍ ♃	6:56	14	☿ □ ☊	11: 1		☉ □ ☊	22:50		☉ ☌ ☽	21:38
4	☽ ☌ ♆	22:26	15	☽ ☍ ♇	0: 6	23	☽ ☌ ♂	3:49	31	♃ ☍ ♇	8:16

SIDEREAL HELIOCENTRIC LONGITUDES : JANUARY 2014 Gregorian at 0 hours UT

DAY	Sid. Time	☿	♀	⊕	♂	♃	♄	♅	♆	♇	Vernal Point
1 WE	6:42:16	20 ♐ 41	9 ♊ 14	15 ♊ 33	10 ♌ 31	20 ♊ 7	21 ♎ 2	16 ♓ 33	9 ♒ 48	16 ♐ 21	5 ♓ 3'53"
2 TH	6:46:13	23 38	10 51	16 34	10 58	20 12	21 4	16 34	9 48	16 21	5 ♓ 3'53"
3 FR	6:50:10	26 38	12 28	17 35	11 24	20 17	21 6	16 34	9 48	16 21	5 ♓ 3'53"
4 SA	6:54: 6	29 40	14 6	18 36	11 50	20 22	21 8	16 35	9 49	16 22	5 ♓ 3'52"
5 SU	6:58: 3	2 ♑ 46	15 43	19 38	12 16	20 27	21 10	16 36	9 49	16 22	5 ♓ 3'52"
6 MO	7: 1:59	5 55	17 20	20 39	12 42	20 32	21 12	16 36	9 49	16 22	5 ♓ 3'52"
7 TU	7: 5:56	9 7	18 57	21 40	13 9	20 37	21 14	16 37	9 50	16 23	5 ♓ 3'52"
8 WE	7: 9:52	12 23	20 34	22 41	13 35	20 42	21 16	16 38	9 50	16 23	5 ♓ 3'52"
9 TH	7:13:49	15 44	22 11	23 42	14 1	20 47	21 17	16 38	9 51	16 23	5 ♓ 3'52"
10 FR	7:17:45	19 9	23 49	24 43	14 27	20 52	21 19	16 39	9 51	16 24	5 ♓ 3'52"
11 SA	7:21:42	22 39	25 26	25 44	14 53	20 57	21 21	16 40	9 51	16 24	5 ♓ 3'51"
12 SU	7:25:39	26 14	27 3	26 46	15 20	21 2	21 23	16 40	9 52	16 24	5 ♓ 3'51"
13 MO	7:29:35	29 54	28 41	27 47	15 46	21 7	21 25	16 41	9 52	16 25	5 ♓ 3'51"
14 TU	7:33:32	3 ♒ 41	0 ♋ 18	28 48	16 12	21 12	21 27	16 41	9 52	16 25	5 ♓ 3'51"
15 WE	7:37:28	7 33	1 55	29 49	16 38	21 17	21 29	16 42	9 53	16 25	5 ♓ 3'51"
16 TH	7:41:25	11 33	3 33	0 ♋ 50	17 4	21 22	21 31	16 43	9 53	16 26	5 ♓ 3'51"
17 FR	7:45:21	15 39	5 10	1 51	17 31	21 27	21 32	16 43	9 53	16 26	5 ♓ 3'51"
18 SA	7:49:18	19 52	6 47	2 52	17 57	21 32	21 34	16 44	9 54	16 26	5 ♓ 3'51"
19 SU	7:53:14	24 14	8 25	3 53	18 23	21 37	21 36	16 45	9 54	16 27	5 ♓ 3'50"
20 MO	7:57:11	28 43	10 2	4 54	18 49	21 42	21 38	16 45	9 55	16 27	5 ♓ 3'50"
21 TU	8: 1: 8	3 ♓ 21	11 40	5 55	19 16	21 47	21 40	16 46	9 55	16 27	5 ♓ 3'50"
22 WE	8: 5: 4	8 8	13 17	6 56	19 42	21 52	21 42	16 47	9 55	16 28	5 ♓ 3'50"
23 TH	8: 9: 1	13 3	14 55	7 57	20 8	21 57	21 44	16 47	9 56	16 28	5 ♓ 3'50"
24 FR	8:12:57	18 8	16 32	8 58	20 34	22 1	21 45	16 48	9 56	16 28	5 ♓ 3'50"
25 SA	8:16:54	23 21	18 10	9 59	21 1	22 6	21 47	16 49	9 56	16 29	5 ♓ 3'50"
26 SU	8:20:50	28 44	19 47	11 0	21 27	22 11	21 49	16 49	9 57	16 29	5 ♓ 3'49"
27 MO	8:24:47	4 ♈ 16	21 25	12 1	21 53	22 16	21 51	16 50	9 57	16 29	5 ♓ 3'49"
28 TU	8:28:43	9 58	23 2	10 2	22 19	22 21	21 53	16 50	9 57	16 30	5 ♓ 3'49"
29 WE	8:32:40	15 45	24 40	14 3	22 46	22 26	21 55	16 51	9 58	16 30	5 ♓ 3'49"
30 TH	8:36:37	21 41	26 17	15 4	23 12	22 31	21 57	16 52	9 58	16 30	5 ♓ 3'49"
31 FR	8:40:33	27 44	27 55	16 5	23 38	22 36	21 59	16 52	9 58	16 30	5 ♓ 3'49"

INGRESSES :

4	☿ → ♑	2:33
13	☿ → ♒	0:37
	♀ → ♋	19:35
15	⊕ → ♋	4:22
20	☿ → ♓	6:41
26	☿ → ♈	5:32
31	☿ → ♉	8:53

ASPECTS (HELIOCENTRIC +MOON(TYCHONIC)) :

1	☽ ☍ ♀	0:38	5	☽ ☌ ♆	0:46		☿ □ ♄	15: 6		☿ △ ♄	9:29		♀ ☌ P	4:15	30	☿ ☍ ♄	1: 3
	☿ ⚹ ♄	3: 0		☽ ☍ ♂	4:58	11	☿ (S) ☊	6:11		♃ △ ♄	20:35		☿ □ ♃	18:13		☿ ⚹ ♃	3:24
	♀ △ ♆	8:16		♀ ☍ ♇	9:45		♀ ☌ ⊕	12:17	19	☽ ☍ ♆	11: 2	25	☽ ☌ ♄	4: 0		☿ △ ♂	6:32
	☽ ☌ ♇	11:44		♀ □ ♅	13:10	14	♂ △ ♇	11:59	20	☽ ☌ ♂	4:57	26	♂ ⚹ ♄	21:55		☿ ☌ ☊	7:29
	☽ ☍ ♃	17:43		⊕ ☌ ♃	20:59		☽ ☍ ♇	23:19	21	☽ ☍ ☿	15:15	27	♀ □ ♄	6:37	31	☿ □ ♀	0:58
	⊕ ☍ ♇	18:53	6	⊕ △ ♄	13:24	15	☽ ☌ ♃	9:11		☿ △ ⊕	16:29	28	☿ ⚹ ♆	0: 4		☽ ☍ ♀	18:20
	☽ ☌ ☿	22:55	7	☽ ☌ ♅	16:19		☿ ☌ ♆	14: 5	22	☽ ☍ ♅	11:19		♂ ⚹ ♃	2:11		⊕ △ ♅	18:44
	⊕ □ ♅	23:52	8	♀ ☌ ♃	1:57	16	☽ ☌ ♀	11:29	23	☿ △ ♀	13: 2		☿ □ ⊕	15:36			
2	♀ ⚹ ♂	2: 7		♀ △ ♄	10:25	17	☿ ⚹ ♇	4:31		☿ □ ♇	16:13		☽ ☌ ♇	23:19			
	♂ ☌ A	23:11	9	☿ ⚹ ♅	6:25		☿ ☍ ♂	11:54		☿ ☌ ♅	17:45	29	☿ △ ♇	3: 3			
3	⊕ ☌ P	15:26	10	☽ ☍ ♄	9:30	18	☿ △ ♃	9:21	24	♀ △ ♅	3:53		☽ ☍ ♃	8:46			

Moon, Sun, Pluto square Mars 16° Virgo: Heliocentric Mars at this degree remembers the first temptation in the wilderness where Christ was tempted to bow to the prince of this world. This is the temptation for the will-to-power. Christ overcame this temptation by directing his gaze to his Father in heaven and letting the adversary know that it was God the Father whom he served. He relinquished self-determination in order to be infused with the love flowing into him from his Father in the heights (Phanes).

Dynamic star influences mark the beginning of 2014. Pluto, Sun, Moon, and Mercury are all in Sagittarius; and in five days, retrograde Venus will join some of them. Pluto will be in close square to Mars opposite Jupiter for the next week. For the entire year Pluto and Uranus will be square to each other.[1] As we remember the birth of the Nathan Jesus we can pray that we may find the purity that is ours to remember, and that the fire of Pentecost may enthuse us to welcome new revelation, and that our personal will finds its alignment with divine will. The tempter will surely seek to thwart us in our stalwart resolve, but we are to keep our eyes focused on the future no matter how much effort such a path entails. It is easier by far to avoid the work that is ours to do, but this New Moon beckons us to take the road less traveled and plant seeds of love. Such are the proclamations that begin our year. We can let these be a keynote for the next twelve months. There is much that needs healing in our human community and in the kingdoms of nature. Sacred Magic *is* the practice of aligning our personal will with divine will so that we become the allies of the spiritual worlds in the creation of a New Heaven and a New Earth. This is a good day to spend at least a few moments in contemplation of the Archer's aim (Sagittarius), which never wavers from attending the light, love, and life that continuously streams to us from the Central Sun. At this year's end another New Moon in Sagittarius will occur. In a certain sense the entire lunar cycle of the next twelve months is being seeded today and will culminate three days before Christmas with the Sagittarius New Moon that ends 2014. We have a year before us in which the fifth sacrifice of the Christ is inviting us into the *manna* of higher worlds.

January 3: Mercury 20° Sagittarius opposite Jupiter 20° Gemini: the Stilling of the Storm. Mercury was at this same degree at the Stilling of the Storm (Nov/21/30): At this time Christ raised his hand to still the upheaval of wind and waves that threatened the disciples in their little boat on the Sea of Galilee:

> When the party put out from shore the weather was calm and beautiful, but they had scarcely reached the middle of the lake before a violent tempest arose. I thought it very strange that, although the sky was shrouded in darkness, the stars were to be seen. The wind blew in a hurricane and the waves dashed over the boat, the sails of which had been furled. I saw from time to time a brilliant light glancing over the troubled waters. It must have been lightning. The danger was imminent, and the disciples were in great anxiety when they awoke Jesus with the worlds: "Master! Hast Thou no care for us? We are sinking!"[2]

In this scene, as described by Sister Emmerich, a battle of the soul is imaged: The lightning flashes proclaim cosmic thoughts that can agitate the mind (Mercury). The swelling waves threatened the little community (Jupiter) of disciples in their boat. Though the storm raged, the stars were visible above. Jesus calmed the storm and instructed the disciples to row back to Chorazin, named thus on account of the town Great Chorazin—a city Jesus cursed, for in spite of all the miracles they had witnessed, their hearts remained hardened to just who it was who stood before them as the Messiah:

> Then Jesus began to denounce the towns in which most of his miracles had been performed, because they did not repent. "Woe to you, Chorazin! Woe to you, Bethsaida! For if the miracles that were performed in you had been performed in Tyre and Sidon, they would have repented long ago in sackcloth and ashes." (Matt. 11:20–21)

---

1 See Bento, "Reuniting Psyche with Astro-Logos," in this Journal.

2 ACE, *LJC, Vol. 3*, pp. 46-47.

The cities Chorazin, Capernaum, and Bethsaida formed what is called the "Evangelical Triangle," the small area where most of Jesus' miracles were accomplished (Matt. 11:20). Yet, in spite of bearing witness to the power of Christ, this had little effect in the lives of these people. In the temple of Chorazin, there is what is called the "Moses seat." Jesus saw the people bowing to the laws of Moses, and to the Pharisees who hypocritically held up these laws and laid the burdens of these laws on the shoulders of their followers; and yet as the long-awaited Messiah worked in their midst, they knew him not.

As Mercury and Jupiter oppose each other today, the mind can reel as it experiences the agitation that is found when the wisdom flashing from cosmic intelligence meets the reality of a distracted and unawakened mind. To behold the wisdom, the mind is to become quiet. Nonetheless, during this event almost two thousand years ago, the stars shone despite the raging storm, odd as it appeared to Sister Emmerich. Individuals who are awake to the presence of Christ find they can calm storms in their communities and bring harmony in his name. A still mind receives the support of wisdom, and wisdom guides us to perceive the changes we are now experiencing as part of the shift we face. Many around us are in denial. Yet, small communities have formed and they are seeding a new future in spite of the naysayers who silently succumb to deceptive illusions.

The descendants of the people of Chorazin, after the time of Christ, allowed a Medusa to be built right into their synagogue wall. This is the fate of those who do not change: they are turned to stone. Humanity is increasingly facing the shriveled witch whose hair is a gnarled mass of snakes. These snakes represent the frenzied thoughts of a fractured mind driven by its own volition in ignorance of higher will.

Winds, waves, disturbances—and the stars above; and within, a certainty of who it is that supports us in times of change. In our times we are not to fearfully plead to be saved, but rather collaborate with the Savior in order to help save others as well as the kingdoms of our Mother.

Jupiter in Gemini invites "two to become one" within the sanctity of community. Our strengthened "I" can co-create with others to form community vessels for the new revelation. Mercury in Sagittarius asks us to stay awake and temper our words so they may give birth to the living truth now here with us.

January 5: Sun 20° Sagittarius opposite Jupiter 20° Gemini. Jupiter remembers the Virgin Mary receiving her first communion (Apr/23/33): Shortly after midnight the Blessed Virgin Mary received the holy sacrament from Peter (three weeks after the Last Supper). During this communion, Jesus appeared to her. Later she retired to her room to pray, and toward dawn the Lord appeared to her again and gave her power over the Church, a protective force, such that light flowed from him into her. The Virgin Mary could listen to the presence of the Christ. The assault on hearing from constant noise weakens the delicate organs of hearing, thereby encapsulating the human being in the coarser sounds of the material world. Yet, in living speech spiritual beings are active and the Sun in Sagittarius calls us to attend our words:

> Speech is by no means only what modern materialistic science conceives it to be; in speech there is something that is connected in many ways with a realm of not fully conscious human experiences, something that takes place in the subconscious regions and therefore teems with spiritual beings. Spiritual beings live and are active in human speech, and when humankind formulates words, elemental spiritual beings press into them. On the wings of words, spiritual beings fly through the area where people are conversing with one another. That is why it is so important to pay attention to certain subtleties of speech, and not to give way to the arbitrariness of passions and emotions when speaking.[3]

Today's Sun stands opposite Jupiter, asking us to speak consciously (Sun in Sagittarius) and listen quietly so as to discern the active work of spiritual beings who create according to our words. Mary listened and heard. High spiritual beings were

---

[3] Steiner, "Technology and Art" (*Art as Seen in the Light of Mystery Wisdom*, lect. 1).

activated through her words, and these beings helped her carry the task she would achieve at Whitsun, a mere four weeks from this time of her first communion. This is when a new community (Jupiter) of Apostles was born. Today we can exert care toward the words we speak and cultivate a sensitivity for the beings words engender and their effect upon our communities.

January 5: Venus (retrograde) enters Sagittarius. Venus in Sagittarius. "Becoming's power dies into existence."[1] Life dies into existence and is resurrected by the power of the spirit indwelling human beings. Venus was in Sagittarius as Jesus arrived at Mount Attarus where he would encounter the tempters. The tempters spoke words filled with fallen spirits. Christ spoke the Living Word. Venus will be in Sagittarius through February.

January 6: Epiphany. Today we close the door to the Holy Nights of 2013/14, and venture into the world with all we have gained through these sacred days and nights. A seedling star has been born within us. It will grow and ripen throughout the next twelve months. We are to protect this seedling, which represents a spark from our higher self that is striving to unite with our temporal self on Earth. This is the true gift of Christmas, and Epiphany marks the virginal beginnings of spirit-generated growth in the yearly cycle of time. Just as the three kings lost sight of the Star when they entered Herod's fallen realm, so too are we warned that Herodian materialism will predatorily stalk the occult truth of the fact that we have received a gift in these Holy Days and Nights. In this time of Epiphany, we are prudent to protect this new life and hold true to our ideals. As we journey through the new year this seed will mature into a fuller expression of who we truly are. What is now only a possibility, as this Christmas gift, will in nine months' time—at Michaelmas— arise with strength and power in order to help us battle the dragons that dwell within our individual souls and in the collective soul of the world that surrounds us. But this can happen only if we protect the light we bring from these depths of winter and successfully avoid the Herods of the world.

---
1 Steiner, *Twelve Cosmic Moods*.

Like the three kings before us, we are to avoid the enslaving limitations of false kings, false prophets, and false ideals.

January 7: Mercury conjunct Venus 28° Sagittarius. The Walking on Water (Dec/8/30). Today Venus remembers Jesus walking on the water to meet his disciples in their small boat, on the evening after the feeding of the five thousand.

The disciples' experience at the miracle of walking on water had five parts: the disciples experienced themselves as a group in the universe, united in one boat, driven over the waves by winds, and meeting with the Christ, who spoke to them. The whole night experience, culminating with the worlds "It is I," is thus made up of these elements:

1. awaking the disciples (self-awareness in sleep)
2. perceiving themselves as a group united in destiny (the boat)
3. threatened equilibrium (the waves)
4. forces pushing in a specific direction (the winds)
5. Christ speaking

These five experiences become an inner experience of the I AM and the sound that issues forth from the Word. Tomberg goes on to describe the effect recognition of Christ caused in the innermost being of the disciples in the night after the feeding of the five thousand. He describes how the elemental forces and waves from subconscious depths affected them, and how their consciousness was swept away by the blasts of conflicting cosmic forces:

At this moment, human beings have nothing to oppose that image of stupendous powers and raging cosmic waves in the subconscious, except the incomparable weaker force of their own personality; in this hour, heaven remains silent and veiled in darkness. Then everything depends on overcoming the fear evoked by that vision through the spring of one's inner forces. There is a force in this spring that will rush out at this moment, not manifesting as "personal" but as cosmic activity. Thus human beings must find within themselves a force of calm courage that can overcome the cosmic waves that assail the subconscious and the cosmic winds that sweep through one's consciousness. This force is contained in the words "I AM" once they have become a real experience of life. These words are the esoteric name of the Christ, who is the spring from which flows the strength of human "I" consciousness that can stand against the fear of cosmic forces.[2]

These images offer strong imaginations. The light that is coming will cause upheavals if we cannot find the wellspring within the heart that unites with the presence of Christ. The adversary that is most effectively working in the world now is Ahriman. It is not the individual that is his aim, but communities—for he works against groups, whereby he separates one from the other. In this way he is able to capsize the boats of destiny-communities in the stormy seas of change.

The planet of Love (Venus) and the planet of knowledge (Mercury) today bless us with the strength to meet all adversity. We are to do this in full consciousness, in devotion to Jesus Christ, so that we can play our part in calming the storms that threaten both personal and global equilibrium. We are called to awaken mental faculties of love-imbued clarity in order to actively and conscientiously serve as peacemakers in our time.

January 8: Mars 20° Virgo square Jupiter 20° Gemini. Mars today squares Jupiter at the zodiacal location of the Virgin Mary's first communion. Three days ago the Sun stood at this same place. Mars at this degree is a mere 2° from where it was when Christ began his forty days in the wilderness. Today a dynamic relationship is set up between higher communion (Jupiter) and egoistic drives and desires that seek to satisfy the self at the expense of others (lower aspect of Mars). It was not the sword, but the Word that Christ used to thwart his adversaries. If we take the [s] off "sword" we have "word." This can be seen as the transformation of the fallen word used by the serpent—the [s]word that wounds—to the living word used to silence the adversary.

The orbit of Mars marks the sphere of Old Moon evolution, a time when the human astral body was developing. It is the content of one's astral body that is revealed in the words we speak. The larynx is the focal point of the fifth chakra and this is the Mars chakra of the Word. In the Beatitudes of Christ, the seventh blesses the Peacemakers. *Blessed are the peacemakers for they will be called the Children of God* (Matt. 5:9):

> If the consciousness soul is filled with consciousness of the guilt and need of earthly life, it lifts it like a cup, interceding for the need of Earth. It can then encounter a current descending from above, one that absorbs the darkness of guilt and need into its own clear light, carried upward by the consciousness soul. It may happen then that the ascending darkness and the descending light unite, which leads to a "rainbow" of reconciliation between the two worlds.[3]

This can be our focus today, the rainbow of reconciliation between the natural laws propagating karma and the new law that carries the intercession of grace, whereby karma comes to balance. Whatever burdens we meet in the world, we can bear them in silence as our contribution to clearing the darkness of error that lays heavy on the shoulders of all humanity. We know we are on the path when we are assigned tasks to love. Evil comes with a heavy sense of duty, but spiritual tasks are given in the name of love, for love, through love.

January 11: Sun conjunct Venus (inferior) 26° Sagittarius. The Sun today remembers Jesus teaching in Carianthaim, located just outside the town of Saphet, north of Jerusalem. In the synagogue Jesus again taught the Beatitudes and—addressing the Levites—interpreted a passage from 1 Kings 6:15–19. This passage describes Solomon building the house of the Lord. Cedar wood is used, and he places the Ark of the Covenant in the holy of holies, the inner sanctuary. This holy sanctuary is overlaid with pure gold. So is the inner sanctuary of our heart to become the gold of ennobled virtue. With the planet of love in communion with the Sun this inner sanctuary of the heart is magnified, and one is invited to enter the path of the Grail.

---

2   Tomberg, *Christ and Sophia*, pp. 254–256.

3   Ibid., p. 220.

January 12: The waxing Moon is conjunct Aldebaran.

January 14: Sun enters Capricorn. "May the future rest upon the past" (Steiner, *Twelve Cosmic Moods*). William Bento illumines Steiner's mantra:

> Although this can be said to be a commonsense statement, it holds deeper mysteries into the streams of time. Implicit to this mood is how we all must bear the consequences and deeds of the past as seeds for the future. By being aware of this in the present we can affect the stream of time with conscious intent and not be laid a victim to the past as we step into and through the darkness of the unknown future.

Capricorn, the Goat, is the symbol of sacrificial death and the sign of atonement. Aquila the Eagle extends above the first decan of Capricorn, the main star of Aquila (Altair) being located at 7° Capricorn. The first decan of Capricorn is ruled by Jupiter (Zeus), to whom the Eagle was sacred. Capricorn signifies a special opportunity: Courage becomes the power to redeem, the power to develop conscience, and the insight to know what is right.

January 15: Full Moon 1° Cancer opposite Sun 1° Capricorn. Birth of John the Baptist (Jun/4/2 BC). This Full Moon occurs at midnight between the 15th and 16th. The Moon stands within 3° of where it was at the birth of John the Baptist. The Sun illumining this Moon remembers the birth of Martin Luther King. What links these two together is the power of the Word. It was the living force of the word that lent power to the speeches of Martin Luther King and his words changed the thinking of an entire generation. It was this same fullness of voice that gave John the Baptist the power to transfigure those who heard him speak. The star Procyon rests at 1° Cancer; it is the star that radiates the power of redemption. This Moon asks us to find the fullness of our voice and stand firmly before our "double" in order to govern our lower natures. Clothed in the Sun's power remembering King and the lunar forces remembering John we are well armed to suffer the soul trials that foreshadow redemption. Both King and John knew that it was the power of Jesus Christ through whom humanity would break through the iron gates of materialism in order to open to new vistas of understanding. In a certain sense all Full Moons recall the Full Moon of Golgotha and there are reports of those who met Christ under the influence of just such a Moon:

> As far as it is possible to judge from the selection of reports in *They Experienced Christ*, a large proportion of the appearances of Christ took place at night, with midnight often being referred to. One account describes that it was the night of the Full Moon:
>
>> It was a strange evening, Full Moon, and a tremendous storm. I stood at the window and looked at the clouds chasing across the heavens, and thought of a poem by Hjalmar Gullberg. After I had spoken the poem, someone came into my room. I knew instantly Who it was, and sank upon my knees at the window-sill, and did not dare to turn my head to look at Him. Light and peace radiated from Him, transcending all understanding. I distinctly felt the touch of His hand as He bent toward me and took away my burden, the burden that I am not fit to be His servant. How long I knelt at the window-sill I do not know. But outside, looking in through the window, there appeared out of the dark cross another Cross, which was bright and reached up to heaven. His voice explained to me the Mystery of the Cross. I did not hear a voice, but the meaning of the Cross became clear to me in a miraculous way. The whole question of sacrifice had been so difficult for me to grasp; now I suddenly understood, so I believe, the profound sense of Christ's deed of sacrifice and its significance for every single human being. A tremendously great perspective opened up. I saw the Cross between heaven and earth as an axis about which everything revolves, the innermost mystery of creation…Divine Love."

This account calls to mind that Christ's death on the Cross on Good Friday took place at the time of the Full Moon.

The foregoing descriptions translated from *They Experienced Christ* reveal that a number of people have had experiences of Jesus Christ in His second coming, since the onset of this event in the twentieth century. From these descriptions it is evident that Rudolf Steiner's prophecy is confirmed: appearances of the Etheric Christ can take place unexpectedly anywhere, at any time, to anyone. Who can tell just how many people in our time may have had such experiences? Common to all these appearances is the experience of Him as a comforter, helper, and source of healing strength. This profound, personal experience is unforgettable, a sacred memory, generally signifying not only a breakthrough to the religious dimension of existence but also being accompanied by a great strengthening of the soul and of the life forces. To use Rudolf Steiner's words, this is the "greatest mystery of the twentieth century," betokening the arising of a New Age, an Age of Light.[1]

Sun 1° Capricorn. Birth of Martin Luther King (Jan/15/29). In a speech directed against the Vietnam War, the words of King illumine us to perceive the beings and motives behind *all* wars:

> Now, let me make it clear in the beginning, that I see this war as an unjust, evil, and futile war. I preach to you today on the war in Vietnam because my conscience leaves me with no other choice. The time has come for America to hear the truth about this tragic war. In international conflicts, the truth is hard to come by because most nations are deceived about themselves.
>
> Rationalizations and the incessant search for scapegoats are the psychological cataracts that blind us to our sins. But the day has passed for superficial patriotism. He who lives with untruth lives in spiritual slavery. Freedom is still the bonus we receive for knowing the truth. "Ye shall know the truth," says Jesus, "and the truth shall set you free." Now, I've chosen to preach about the war in Vietnam because I agree with Dante, that the hottest places in Hell are reserved for those who in a period of moral crisis maintain their neutrality. There comes a time when silence becomes betrayal.[2]

The virtue of Capricorn is "Courage becomes the power to redeem." May we find the courage to stand with the truth as redeemers. Today we remember a mighty voice who gave his life for the redemptive power of truth.

January 16: ASPECT: Venus 23° Sagittarius square Mars 23° Virgo. Power on the twelve (Dec/4/30). Venus was here when Jesus gave the twelve the power to cast out unclean spirits:

> Jesus continued the Sermon on the Mount near Bethsaida-Julias. He spoke on the fourth Beatitude. Afterward, he went with the twelve to a place on the east shore of the lake. There he gave the twelve authority to cast out unclean spirits (Matt. 10:1–4). Jesus then sailed with the twelve and about five other disciples to Magdala, where he exorcised some people who were possessed. Peter, Andrew, James, and John also cast out unclean spirits. Jesus and the disciples then spent the night on board the boat.[3]

The duality of "unclean spirits" (possession) creates convulsions that toss one from one extreme to another. This can tear the soul apart. This can happen within individuals, in groups, in communities, in nations and in the world itself. Stark contrasts are becoming increasingly prevalent in politics, in economic inequality, and in the cultural life. The center is being lost, and the center is the place where equilibrium is maintained. Convulsions can reach a tearing point—a point in which the middle tears open from the intensity of two forces striving against each other. Through the tear, "unclean spirits" can enter into the individual and/or into various aspects within the threefold social order. We witness this in the rise of derisive ridicule in politics, in increasing economic fears and anxieties, and in atrocities born of psychosis in the social spheres. When the middle has been lost, all is in peril. As extremism is growing, it is imperative, from a spiritual perspective, that we bring down forces from spiritual realms in order to hold the balance of center between any two extremes. This acts to cast out what would otherwise rise from below and shatter the person, or group, community, or nation. Christ empowered the twelve to hold this absolute middle space of the heart in order to restore equilibrium to those being torn apart by unclean spirits.

---

1 See Powell, *Reflections of the Second Coming*.
2 Martin Luther King, "Why I Am Opposed to the War in Vietnam," April 30, 1967.

3 *Chron.*, p. 262.

In like manner we, too, are empowered, through Christ, to cast out the demons of the abyss and restore centeredness. The inversion of this power Christ bestowed upon the twelve is grasping power from sub-earthly realms where instead of equilibrium, tyrannical and unforgiving laws are enforced.

After casting out demons they spent the night aboard the boat. An image rises of a karmic group holding the dynamic center of balance on the vacillating waters of reality. The calm clear waters reflect the starry heaven above, and at the same time reveal what lies hidden beneath the surface. This is the way of the disciples of Christ—they rest in equilibrium before the trials of life, while at the same time do not refrain from seeing the causes of unrest that lie beneath superficial occurrences.

> The duality [convulsions] of the demon is also very vividly expressed in the description of the Evangelist Mark, where he writes: "And when the unclean spirit had torn him…" Between two extremes we are torn back and forth, paralyzed and rendered passive, so that we become incapable of maintaining self-control. This formulation shows the human soul condition in which, without the balancing, Trinitarian and mediating power of Christ, we find ourselves caught between the polarities of Lucifer and Ahriman. The influx of the Christ impetus into the human being always mediates between these two dark forces, placing itself between them as a wholesome and healing soul element and, by bringing the polarities back into equilibrium, not only halts their destructive power but also leads them toward redemption.[1]

The antidote to ridicule, fear, and hatred, is praise, courage, and love, which is the way of the twelve-fold community Venus today remembers. The model for this work is Rudolf Steiner's carving of the statue, the Representative of Man. For the middle is Christ! As Mars today remembers the arrival at Attarus, the mount Jesus climbed to begin his forty days of temptation, we can remember how Jesus never once looked at his tempters but instead held his center by devotion to his Father in heaven.

January 21: Sun 6° Capricorn. The Adoration of the Magi (Dec/26/6 BC) and the **Second Conversion of Mary Magdalene** (Dec/26/30). The magi were those who continued the Chaldean astrological tradition inaugurated in Babylon by Zoroaster in the sixth century BC. They were instructed to wait for the signs in Heaven that foretold the rebirth of their spiritual teacher, and they were to follow this sign (the Star of the Magi) to the birthplace of the new king. At the birth of Jesus they beheld the radiant star of the soul of their spiritual teacher, whose birth they beheld from the sign of the Virgin on the night of the Full Moon in Virgo, and they followed this star to Jerusalem.

> The three kings (magi) came as representatives of the soul of humankind—of humankind's powers of thought, feeling and will—faced with the choice between serving the higher Self or collaborating with the lower self in pitting itself against the higher Self. The meeting with Herod represented a temptation for the three kings, a temptation which was of significance for humanity. But with the help of divine intervention the temptation was rendered impotent, and the three magi did not betray their spiritual king.[2]

On the anniversary of this great event, decades later, Mary Magdalene experienced her second and last conversion. Magdalene, as the Apostle to the Apostles, was in mystical union with her teacher—and from this point onward she was therefore not spared from experiencing the trials of the God-Man in her heart. And, like the kings before her, Magdalene most certainly recognized Christ as the true king, one whose kingdom was not of this world.

The events of the Adoration and the Conversion, both occurring at this Sun degree, foretell how necessary is spiritual navigation in these times, when lies and deceit are everywhere. Today commemorates the birth of a true king, and the casting out of demons. May we too overcome the temptation of our lower self and rise to the mission of our higher self. We know not when we will find Herods along the way.

---

1 Von Halle, *Illness and Healing and the Mystery Language of the Gospels*, pp. 83–84.

2 CHA, "The Journey of the Three Kings and the Flight of the Holy Family to Egypt."

NOTE: Sun at this degree remembers the "Citizens United" ruling.

January 23: Moon conjunct Spica (29° Virgo) with Mars standing nearby.

January 25: Mercury 27° Capricorn square Saturn 27° Libra. Mercury is where it was when, after the feeding of the five thousand, Christ walked on the water (Jan/30/31). Saturn today is conjunct the Moon and both Moon and Saturn are (within one degree) opposite Saturn's position at the last Jupiter Saturn conjunction, which occurred in May 2000 at 28° Aries. This great conjunction marked the beginning of the new millennium and called for a new Christlike leadership. With Saturn and Moon standing opposite the great conjunction and in square to Mercury at the walking on water, a new call is sounding from the stars that ask us to forego the quantitative thinking of materialism in favor of the qualitative thinking that invites providence to act on our behalf in support of the good. In quantitative thinking money and worldly gain is often the bottom line. Judas thought in this way and was therefore capable of betraying Christ. Judas pitied the multitudes, thinking that they were incapable of knowing the "I AM" from within. He could not recognize the qualitative power of Christ surrounded by the little band of disciples and the effect this small group would have on the entire destiny of the earth. Judas opted to work for the many in neglect of the qualitative power of the few gathered around Christ, and through this choice he became a thief. Judas did not oppose Magdalene's waste of precious and expensive oil because he cared for the poor, but because he thought only in quantitative measure. Therefore, he stole from the larger community (the many) he thought he was serving, but he deprived that community of the presence of Christ.

> Thus, in the beginning Judas was a thief in the cosmic sense of *diabolos* (a term used for "Lucifer" in the Gospels), then he became a murdering thief when *Satan* entered him—that is, when Ahriman appeared as the karma of Lucifer. The destiny of Judas among the twelve was to fully bear the two crosses of human activity: the cross to the left and the cross to the right on Golgotha. His apostolic mission to humanity (what he proclaimed to humanity) was the bitter truth about the nature of human activity *without* Christ. The mission of the twelve apostles was to bring the message of Christ to humanity from twelve perspectives. Judas, however, had the terrible mission of imparting knowledge of what human activity becomes when it is without the Christ. Judas represented one aspect of the Christ mystery—the negative side in the sign of the Scorpion. This is why he belonged to the circle of the twelve, although right after the feeding of the five thousand, Jesus Christ stated that, although he had chosen all twelve, nonetheless, one among them in their circle had the mission that *diabolos* (Lucifer) has in the circle of the zodiac.[3]

If our decisions are based solely on the economic perspectives of spreadsheets, we renounce the qualitative actions of the spiritual world that bring the blessing of divine providence to serve our earthly activities when they are aligned with the good. As Saturn and Moon stand opposite the great conjunction of 2000 we can beware of quantitative thinking and the trap of falling prey to Ahrimanic deceit as did Judas. Judas was situated between two streams of will—that of the many who wanted a king, and those of the disciples who experienced Christ as the "I AM" as he walked on the water the night after the feeding of the five thousand. We are to become one with the "I AM" and receive the warmth of living life force supporting us in our quest for understanding. Conversely, a quantitative view, based only on materialistic concerns, will cause us to sink in seas of doubt and uncertainty before the change now upon us. The qualitative comes to us in the night. It marks the turning point from doubt to faith. Our will is not to follow either Lucifer or Ahriman, but is to serve a balanced (Saturn in Libra) and forward thinking mind (Mercury in Capricorn).

Sun 10° Capricorn: The Sun enters the second decan of Capricorn, in conjunction with the mega star 9° Sagitta in the Arrow, above the Goat. Heliocentric Mercury was in conjunction with this mega

---

3 Tomberg, *Christ and Sophia*, p. 255.

star at the Resurrection. Sagitta extends above most of this decan, which is ruled by Mars.

January 28: Moon conjunct Pluto 17° Sagittarius opposite Jupiter 17° Gemini. The Mystery of Golgotha. Today's opposition between Pluto and Jupiter exactly mirrors where these two planets were at the death of Christ on the cross. This star alignment gives us the picture of the frozen wisdom (Jupiter) that stands as the laws and universal facts behind all creation—a wilderness dumb and cold in itself, but when questions of the human soul enliven this wisdom, love is born as the life that frees the force of created wisdom from its entombment in matter. The dumb and cold wilderness of frozen wisdom is like a transparent coffin. The human soul is to awaken from this coffin to find its true majesty in love. On the hill of Golgotha Christ was nailed upon the cross of this frozen world; and from this place of isolation he gave his life, after which love poured into creation. His life gave each of us the opportunity to awaken from the icy presence of Satan (Pluto) into the life eternal promised by this deed of Christ.

> Thus, the immensely meaningful fairy tale of Snow White—the crystal tomb with a dead maiden guarded by dwarfs—arises before the souls of those who see the universe as a "moral impression." This image expresses the fact that the present cosmos is one of wisdom, but one in which love is absent. This is the essential result of contemplating the universe from the outside as it appears to the consciousness between birth and death. Human beings can also come to understand the universe from the other perspective, the state of consciousness between death and a new birth. In either condition, human beings no longer experience the universe as merely rigidified wisdom, or as the expression of wisdom; rather, they have the sense of being submerged in a surging blood of wisdom. That flooding, flowing wisdom encircles and overwhelms the human soul so that, for the soul, it is not a matter of allowing wisdom to enter (as one does in the case of earthly consciousness); rather, it is important for the soul to assert itself as a soul, with the content of a soul, in this sea of purposeful wisdom.[1]

With Moon and Pluto opposing Jupiter we remember Golgotha and the glass coffin from which our souls are released from their imprisonment in matter to awaken to love. As Venus stands close by Pluto and the Moon, it is love that rays to us from the starry heavens today. We are called to love wisdom into life through the power invested in us by Christ. This influence continues for the next few weeks.

Venus is standing with the Moon in tonight's sky.

January 29: Sun 14° Capricorn. Death of John the Baptist. John the Baptist is the great individuality of whom Rudolf Steiner foretold that he would be with us again at the end of the twentieth century, to lead humanity past the great crisis it would then be facing. As John was there to behold the Light at the First Coming, so is this individuality here again to meet those witnessing the true Light of the Second Coming. When Lazarus was paralyzed in the shadowland of the dead, it was John who united with him, and it was Christ who freed Lazarus from his entombment, by raising him from the dead.

> John the Baptist was one who held the Mysteries of the death initiation. And because of his love for Lazarus, he had been drawn to him as the death initiation commenced. Lazarus's angel turned him over to John the Baptist, who was to guide him now in his descent.
>
> As the descent commenced I saw below us a "lake of light," which I knew to be a "portal" to another realm. This also is difficult to describe.
>
> It was as though we were standing in a light-filled lake; and as we prepared to descend through this "lake," light gathered around us at its surface wherever we touched it. Then, as we began our descent, light burst out all around us.
>
> We passed through many spheres of this light, which I understood represented angelic realms, descending further and further until we came at last to the sphere of humanity, of which there were many levels. We descended through each of these levels.

---

[1] Ibid., p. 292.

Having reached the lowest level of the human sphere, we continued down through the kingdoms of Nature, of which there were also many.

I could hear Nature singing the "One Song of Nature." I do not know how I knew it was the one song of nature, but it was a song of Earth, and very different from anything I have ever heard in the music of the spheres.

We passed through the many levels of Nature, continuing lower and lower until we reached its lowest kingdom. I began to feel a heaviness, intermingled with fear. It became clear to me that I was feeling fallen Nature's pain and sadness.[2]

John and Lazarus work together. The initiation of the Lazarus-John being uniquely prepared him to be our guide as we now endure the meeting with our individual shadow nature; he prepares us as well for the meeting with the collective shadow nature of all humanity. This is the signature of the Rosicrucian stream Lazarus later founded in his incarnation as Christian Rosenkreutz.

After his beheading, John became the guardian of the circle of Christ's disciples and was therefore aware of the plight of Lazarus—the beloved friend of Jesus. It was John who went to rescue Lazarus. In like manner John is now the guardian of the communities working with Michael and Sophia in the name of Christ. He can lead us out of any darkness that entraps us individually or collectively, but first we must open to his ministration. The Sun in the middle of the constellation of Capricorn empowers us to transform darkness into light—to steadfastly meet resistance from rigid thought-forms that are holding on to the past. This is our work: to transform the limitations of the brain-bound intellect into forces born of our heart's cognition. The heart will lead us into our intended future, and to find this future we call upon John. The disciples of John are now forming communities that can be recognized in the fact that they love one another. Can we live into the redeeming presence of John's spiritual guidance?

January 30: New Moon 15° Capricorn. Death of John the Baptist (Jan/4/31). As the sanctification of the New and Full Moon is experienced three days before and after its exact alignment, we can immerse ourselves in this New Moon as the Moon of John's death. At his death John's new mission was bequeathed—the mission to guard the Sophia mysteries and the communities of eternal Israel that would be gathering into the far distant future. These communities are devoted to John and Sophia and carry the task of turning to the Church of John as the fountain from whence new revelations are flowing into time. What does this mean? It means that the mysteries of the "night" can be found in the clear light of day. This was the mission of Valentin Tomberg:

> Planting the seeds for the opening of the Church of John was Tomberg's task, given to him by Christ. The adversaries to Christ, who are serving the imminent incarnation of Ahriman, will thwart all who are faint of heart. How could it be otherwise? If the Church of John is recognized, people will be raised to new levels of understanding. They will experience Christ, and through the teachings of Spiritual Science they will come to understand the presence of evil. This is part of the Rosicrucian path: to know evil and bring forth the good. This is what Steiner called the stage of *mystic death*, in which one experiences "…the curtain still covering the spiritual world, but then also…how it is rent asunder and you look into the spiritual world. In this way, you learn to behold the depths of evil: the descent into hell." Here is echoed the third verse of the Foundation Stone Meditation: Spirit Beholding. This is the verse of sacred magic by which, out of free will, one sees—and then must do—the deeds that counter the forces that evil is bringing into the world.[3]

This is a Moon of sacred magic. New revelations are sounding from behind the curtain covering the spiritual worlds. As we hear these messages, may we have the courage to do what is called for by the bearers of these new mysteries.

---

2 Isaacson, *Through the Eyes of Mary Magdalene*, vol. 1, p.187.

3 McLaren Lainson, *The Fruits of Valentin Tomberg's Life and Work in the Endeavors of Robert Powell*.

January 31: Jupiter 17° Gemini opposite Pluto 17° Sagittarius. Today the opposition between these two planets (with Venus within one degree) is exact. See entry for January 28.

FEBRUARY 2014

The Sun starts the month mid Capricorn (the SeaGoat) and shifts into Aquarius (the Water-Carrier) on the 14th (a Full Moon). Mercury begins its first Retrograde cycle of the year on the 6th and stations Direct on February 28th. The waxing Moon joins Jupiter in Gemini on the 10th; look for them in the south east after sunset. The Full Moon rises in the first degrees of Leo (the Lion) at sunset on the 14th. The waning Moon is next to (and slightly below) Mars on the 19th—look for the sacred star Spica just to their right at 29° Virgo (the Virgin). The Moon then passes literally across Saturn in Libra (the Scales). Look to the eastern horizon just after midnight on the 21st to see the Moon to the right of Saturn, who sits within the left pan of the scales. By the next evening, they will have shifted positions, with the Moon now to the left of Saturn and rising an hour later than the night before. By the 26th, the waning Moon will have caught up with the morning star of Venus; watch them rise together in the east about 2 hours before sunrise. The next day's pre-dawn brings the Moon together with Mercury (who is stationing direct the next day), but they are only 19° from the Sun and will be most likely hidden from your outer eye's view—seek to cultivate your inner eyes!

February 1: Neptune conjunct Moon at Fomalhaut (9° Aquarius). Neptune at this degree remembers the gold rush of 1849, the defeat of the Aztecs by Cortez in 1519, and—going even further back, to 1189—the construction of the cathedral of Chartres. Neptune remains at this degree through the 21st of this month and then retrogrades back to this degree again at the end of October, staying there through the first week of December.

In the life of Christ, the Moon was at this degree at the summons of Matthew (Nov/19/30). Matthew was the evangelist who represented the constellation of Aquarius where stands the angel-human being.

With Neptune at this powerful degree in the heavens, and conjunct Moon, we can remember the coming age of Sophia in the sixth cultural epoch of Aquarius, and set our sights on the inspirations Sophia brings as the Goddess Night who inspires through the sphere of Neptune. Inversely it is Ahriman who seizes the human soul and inspires an intelligence that is hostile and destructive against humanity and nature. Neptune's inspiration in the hands of Ahriman seeks to ensnare whole groups, and mass communication systems easily and unwittingly fall into his control.

NOTE: Neptune will be close to this degree throughout this year.

February 2: Candlemas. The seed for our future spiritual potential, which we brought out of the Holy Nights, now quickens with new life. Today Mars transits Spica bestowing messages from realms of wisdom from whence Sophia speaks.

February 5: Sun enters the third decan of Capricorn, ruled by the Sun, and associated with the constellation of the Dolphin.

February 8: Mars enters Libra. Having just passed Spica (29° Virgo), Mars ingresses into the constellation of the scales: "And Beings give rise to Beings" (*Rudolf Steiner's Twelve Cosmic Moods*). Mars marks the sphere of ancient Moon evolution, representing the time when we received our astral bodies. With Mars in Libra, our astral forces are to find balance in relationship with others. We are to find the eternal being within ourselves so as to perceive the eternal being in others. Through this discipline we enact deeds that serve what is striving to become. In contrast to this, self-inflation is the tendency to elevate the self at the expense of others. Humility is the force of powerlessness that offers equilibrium to the personal will; and in this equilibrium the fulcrum of truth becomes the light that strengthens us to bear what is ours to bear, while allowing us to help others bear what is theirs to bear.

The Moon is conjunct Aldebaran.

SIDEREAL GEOCENTRIC LONGITUDES: FEBRUARY 2014 Gregorian at 0 hours UT

DAY	☉	☽	☊	☿	♀	♂	♃	♄	⚴	♆	♇
1 SA	17 ♉ 6	2 ♒ 43	7 ♎ 1R	5 ♑ 27	18 ♐ 37	28 ♍ 13	17 ♊ 17R	27 ♎ 38	14 ♓ 31	9 ♒ 16	17 ♐ 23
2 SU	18 7	17 39	6 51	6 20	18 39	28 30	17 11	27 41	14 33	9 19	17 24
3 MO	19 8	2 ♓ 10	6 44	7 4	18 43	28 46	17 5	27 44	14 35	9 21	17 26
4 TU	20 9	16 11	6 40	7 39	18 49	29 2	17 0	27 47	14 37	9 23	17 28
5 WE	21 10	29 42	6 39	8 5	18 57	29 17	16 54	27 49	14 40	9 25	17 30
6 TH	22 11	12 ♈ 45	6 39D	8 20	19 8	29 32	16 49	27 52	14 42	9 27	17 32
7 FR	23 12	25 25	6 39R	8 24R	19 21	29 46	16 43	27 54	14 45	9 29	17 34
8 SA	24 12	7 ♉ 45	6 38	8 17	19 36	0 ♎ 0	16 38	27 57	14 47	9 32	17 35
9 SU	25 13	19 52	6 36	8 0	19 53	0 13	16 33	27 59	14 49	9 34	17 37
10 MO	26 14	1 ♊ 50	6 30	7 32	20 12	0 26	16 29	28 1	14 52	9 36	17 39
11 TU	27 15	13 42	6 22	6 54	20 33	0 38	16 24	28 3	14 54	9 38	17 41
12 WE	28 15	25 33	6 11	6 7	20 56	0 49	16 20	28 5	14 57	9 41	17 42
13 TH	29 16	7 ♋ 25	5 59	5 12	21 20	1 1	16 15	28 7	15 0	9 43	17 44
14 FR	0 ♒ 17	19 21	5 46	4 11	21 46	1 11	16 11	28 9	15 2	9 45	17 46
15 SA	1 17	1 ♌ 20	5 33	3 6	22 14	1 21	16 7	28 10	15 5	9 47	17 47
16 SU	2 18	13 26	5 21	1 57	22 44	1 31	16 4	28 12	15 8	9 50	17 49
17 MO	3 18	25 38	5 12	0 48	23 15	1 40	16 0	28 13	15 10	9 52	17 51
18 TU	4 19	7 ♍ 59	5 6	29 ♑ 40	23 48	1 48	15 57	28 15	15 13	9 54	17 52
19 WE	5 19	20 29	5 3	28 35	24 22	1 55	15 54	28 16	15 16	9 56	17 54
20 TH	6 20	3 ♎ 10	5 2	27 33	24 57	2 2	15 51	28 17	15 19	9 59	17 55
21 FR	7 20	16 7	5 2D	26 37	25 34	2 9	15 48	28 18	15 22	10 1	17 57
22 SA	8 21	29 21	5 3	25 47	26 12	2 15	15 46	28 19	15 24	10 3	17 58
23 SU	9 21	12 ♏ 55	5 3R	25 3	26 51	2 20	15 43	28 20	15 27	10 5	18 0
24 MO	10 22	26 52	5 2	24 27	27 32	2 24	15 41	28 21	15 30	10 8	18 1
25 TU	11 22	11 ♐ 11	4 58	23 58	28 13	2 28	15 39	28 21	15 33	10 10	18 3
26 WE	12 22	25 50	4 53	23 36	28 56	2 31	15 37	28 22	15 36	10 12	18 4
27 TH	13 23	10 ♑ 44	4 45	23 22	29 39	2 33	15 36	28 22	15 39	10 15	18 5
28 FR	14 23	25 46	4 37	23 15	0 ♑ 24	2 35	15 34	28 23	15 42	10 17	18 7

INGRESSES:

2 ☽→♓ 20:22   22 ☽→♏ 1: 9
5 ☽→♈ 0:32   24 ☽→♐ 5:18
7 ☽→♉ 8:51   26 ☽→♑ 6:45
8 ♂→♎ 0:45   27 ♀→♑ 11:12
9 ☽→♊ 20:19   28 ☽→♒ 6:46
12 ☽→♋ 9: 0
13 ☉→♒ 17:27
14 ☽→♌ 21:19
17 ☽→♍ 8:31
☿→♉ 16:59
19 ☽→♎ 18: 2

ASPECTS & ECLIPSES:

1 ☽☌☿ 4:37   12 ☽☌A 4:54   22 ☉□☽ 17:14
  ☽☌♆ 10:29   ☽☿☊ 21: 8   23 ☉☌♆ 18:19
3 ☽☌⚴ 21:16   14 ☉☌☽ 23:52   25 ☽☍♃ 7:22
4 ☽☍♂ 23:13   15 ☽☍☿ 3:11   ☽☌♆ 11:19
5 ☽☌♃ 12:40   ☽☍♀ 16:50   26 ☽☌♀ 5:16
6 ☉□☽ 19:21   ☉♀☿ 20:14   ♃△♄ 5:50
7 ☽☍♄ 4:48   18 ☽☍⚴ 13:59   ☽☌P 19:47
11 ☽☌♃ 5:25   19 ☿□♄ 7: 2   27 ☽☌P 19:47
  ☽☍♆ 8: 4   ☽☌♂ 21:51   ☽☌♀ 20: 0
  ☽☍♀ 14:18   20 ☽☌☊ 3:27   28 ☽☌♆ 23:17
  ☉□♄ 19:50   21 ☽☌♄ 22: 8

SIDEREAL HELIOCENTRIC LONGITUDES: FEBRUARY 2014 Gregorian at 0 hours UT

DAY	Sid. Time	☿	♀	⊕	♂	♃	♄	⚴	♆	♇	Vernal Point
1 SA	8:44:30	3 ♉ 53	29 ♋ 32	17 ♌ 6	24 ♌ 5	22 ♊ 41	22 ♎ 0	16 ♓ 53	9 ♒ 59	16 ♐ 31	5 ♓ 3'49"
2 SU	8:48:26	10 6	1 ♌ 10	18 7	24 31	22 46	22 2	16 54	9 59	16 31	5 ♓ 3'48"
3 MO	8:52:23	16 23	2 47	19 8	24 57	22 51	22 4	16 54	10 0	16 31	5 ♓ 3'48"
4 TU	8:56:19	22 42	4 25	20 9	25 24	22 56	22 6	16 55	10 0	16 32	5 ♓ 3'48"
5 WE	9: 0:16	29 1	6 2	21 10	25 50	23 1	22 8	16 56	10 0	16 32	5 ♓ 3'48"
6 TH	9: 4:12	5 ♊ 19	7 40	22 11	26 16	23 6	22 10	16 56	10 1	16 32	5 ♓ 3'48"
7 FR	9: 8: 9	11 35	9 17	23 11	26 43	23 11	22 12	16 57	10 1	16 33	5 ♓ 3'48"
8 SA	9:12: 6	17 47	10 55	24 12	27 9	23 16	22 13	16 58	10 1	16 33	5 ♓ 3'48"
9 SU	9:16: 2	23 53	12 32	25 13	27 36	23 21	22 15	16 58	10 2	16 33	5 ♓ 3'47"
10 MO	9:19:59	29 54	14 10	26 14	28 2	23 26	22 17	16 59	10 2	16 34	5 ♓ 3'47"
11 TU	9:23:55	5 ♋ 46	15 47	27 14	28 28	23 31	22 19	17 0	10 2	16 34	5 ♓ 3'47"
12 WE	9:27:52	11 31	17 25	28 15	28 55	23 36	22 21	17 0	10 3	16 34	5 ♓ 3'47"
13 TH	9:31:48	17 6	19 2	29 16	29 21	23 41	22 23	17 1	10 3	16 35	5 ♓ 3'47"
14 FR	9:35:45	22 32	20 39	0 ♌ 16	29 48	23 46	22 25	17 1	10 4	16 35	5 ♓ 3'47"
15 SA	9:39:41	27 49	22 17	1 17	0 ♍ 14	23 51	22 27	17 2	10 4	16 35	5 ♓ 3'47"
16 SU	9:43:38	2 ♌ 56	23 54	2 18	0 41	23 56	22 28	17 3	10 4	16 36	5 ♓ 3'47"
17 MO	9:47:35	7 53	25 32	3 18	1 7	24 1	22 30	17 3	10 5	16 36	5 ♓ 3'46"
18 TU	9:51:31	12 41	27 9	4 19	1 34	24 6	22 32	17 4	10 5	16 36	5 ♓ 3'46"
19 WE	9:55:28	17 19	28 46	5 19	2 0	24 11	22 34	17 5	10 5	16 37	5 ♓ 3'46"
20 TH	9:59:24	21 49	0 ♍ 23	6 20	2 27	24 16	22 36	17 5	10 6	16 37	5 ♓ 3'46"
21 FR	10: 3:21	26 9	2 1	7 20	2 53	24 21	22 38	17 6	10 6	16 37	5 ♓ 3'46"
22 SA	10: 7:17	0 ♍ 22	3 38	8 21	3 20	24 26	22 40	17 7	10 6	16 38	5 ♓ 3'46"
23 SU	10:11:14	4 27	5 15	9 21	3 46	24 31	22 41	17 7	10 7	16 38	5 ♓ 3'46"
24 MO	10:15:10	8 25	6 52	10 21	4 13	24 36	22 43	17 8	10 7	16 38	5 ♓ 3'45"
25 TU	10:19: 7	12 15	8 29	11 22	4 40	24 41	22 45	17 9	10 8	16 39	5 ♓ 3'45"
26 WE	10:23: 4	16 0	10 6	12 22	5 6	24 46	22 47	17 9	10 8	16 39	5 ♓ 3'45"
27 TH	10:27: 0	19 38	11 43	13 22	5 33	24 50	22 49	17 10	10 8	16 39	5 ♓ 3'45"
28 FR	10:30:57	23 10	13 20	14 23	6 0	24 55	22 51	17 10	10 9	16 40	5 ♓ 3'45"

INGRESSES:

1 ♀→♌ 6:48
5 ☿→♊ 3:43
10 ☿→♋ 0:25
13 ⊕→♌ 17:31
14 ♂→♍ 11: 8
15 ☿→♌ 10:10
19 ♀→♍ 18:13
21 ☿→♍ 21:51

ASPECTS (HELIOCENTRIC + MOON(TYCHONIC)):

1 ☽☌♆ 11:35   ☿△⚴ 17:57   13 ☿☍♄ 23:26   18 ☽☍⚴ 17:30   26 ☿□♆ 4:16
  ☿□♆ 23:33   7 ♀☌♆ 10:47   14 ☿☌☊ 4:36   ☿△♀ 20:17   ☿☌⚴ 7:36
2 ☽☌♂ 11:36   ☿♀ 19:12   ☽☌♄ 11:30   20 ☿△♄ 4:19   28 ☿□♃ 12:24
3 ☿✱⚴ 1:59   ☿□♆ 20:47   ♀☌⚴ 17:55   ☿✱♃ 13:42   ☽☌♀ 23: 0
  ☿✱⊕ 12:28   8 ☿△♄ 17:30   15 ♀✱⚴ 2:25   21 ☽☌☿ 11:54
4 ☿☌P 0: 9   ☿☌♃ 21:50   ☽☌♆ 17:20   ♀☌♂ 17:54
  ☽☌⚴ 1:16   9 ☿✱♂ 15:54   ☿☌⊕ 20:14   22 ☿☌♀ 19:27
  ☿□♄ 11: 0   11 ☽☌♄ 5:48   16 ♀✱♃ 23:44   23 ☿✱♀ 8: 1
5 ⊕□♄ 23:38   ♀△♆ 11:33   ☽☌⚴ 23:44   ⊕☍⚴ 18:19
6 ☿✱♀ 12: 4   12 ☿△⚴ 23:37   17 ☿✱♆ 10:54   25 ☽☌♀ 9: 1
  ☽☍♄ 17:48   ☿☌♂ 11: 5   ☽☌♃ 22:15

February 10: Sun 26° Capricorn. Presentation in the Temple (Jan/15/1BC). According to Jewish Law, the sanctification of the firstborn should take place traditionally upon the fortieth day after birth. This was also a naming day for the infant. The Holy Family traveled to Jerusalem and stayed in the outskirts of town. The following day they set off for the temple. It was still dark when Mary and Joseph arrived with their infant son. Simeon, the old priest of the temple, had been told in a dream the previous night that the first child presented that morning would be the Messiah. When Simeon saw the infant Jesus he was taken up in rapturous joy. Rudolf Steiner tells us that Simeon was the reincarnation of Asita, who was a sage at the time of Buddha. Asita wept when he saw the little Bodhisattva who was to become Buddha, for he knew he would not live to see the day when the Bodhisattva would walk the Earth as Buddha. But now, in his incarnation as Simeon, he was granted witness to the Buddha. The astral sheath of the Nathan Jesus was filled with the presence of the Buddha. In the words of Rudolf Steiner: "When the Buddha appeared to the shepherds in the image of the 'heavenly hosts,' he was present not in a physical body, but in an astral body through which he continued to influence the Earth."[1] Thus, Simeon saw the further stages of development of his beloved little Bodhisattva when he blessed the Jesus child in the temple. The next day Simeon died in peace. On this naming day in 1 BC, the name of him who would bear the One was pronounced. Now this name lives in each of us. Christ is in us! Hallowed be Thy Name! May this serve as a reminder to hold respectfully each Name in the community and see the One in each other.

February 11: Sun 28° Capricorn square Saturn 28° Libra. The Sun was at 28° Libra when Jesus arrived at Mount Attarus to enter his forty days of temptation. Hell itself would there tempt him. These forty days prepared him for the Pharisees he would later meet—men who had lost the balance (Libra) between macrocosm and microcosm through the rigidity of their laws. They were entrapped in the quantitative strategies of power; and when they sentenced love to death, they revealed their lovelessness. For, to be without love is to be in Hell:

> The following is the answer we arrive at when we abandon a quantitative correlation between time and eternity: whoever enters the region of eternity without an ounce of love, enters it without an ounce of love, i.e., he enters eternal hell. For to live without love—this is hell. And to live without love in the region of eternity—this is to live in eternal hell.
>
> > Hell is the state of the soul powerless to come out of itself, absolute self-centeredness, dark and evil isolation, i.e., final inability to love. (Nicolas Berdyaev, *The Destiny of Man*, London, 1937, p. 351).
>
> This subjective state of soul is neither long nor short—it is as *intense* as eternity is. Similarly, the blessedness that a saint experiences in the vision of God is as intense as eternity—although it could not so last, since someone present at the ecstasy of a saint would time it as a few minutes. The "region" of eternity is that of *intensity*, which surpasses the measure of quantity that we employ in time and space. "Eternity" is not a duration of infinite length; it is the "intensity of quality" which, when compared with time and thus translated into the language of quantity, is comparable with an infinite duration.[2]

With Saturn in Libra the intensity of eternity stands in the balance between left and right. At the fulcrum point of absolute center the "I" aligns with the cosmic "I" and eternity becomes an illumining blessedness. In the case of absolute self-centeredness this same eternity becomes a hellish state where the soul is imprisoned in itself by the iron bars of rigidity to which it clings. This was the case with the Pharisees. With Sun square to Saturn at the memory of the period of temptations, we can sense any tension between love and rigid dogmas that we may hold. The former opens the gates of heaven, the latter eventually opens to the underworld. The opposite of self-centeredness is selfless interest in others. What keeps us from selflessness shows us what imprisons us. Michael guards the threshold of knowledge, waiting until

---

1 Steiner, *According to Luke*, p. 77.

2 Anonymous, *Meditations on the Tarot*, p. 180

we have found this point of balance at the center of the scales of justice. Today we can hope to free ourselves from attachments and open ourselves to new thinking and perspectives. Hostility to the perspectives of others is a sign of attachment.

February 13/14: Sun enters Aquarius. "May what is bounded yield to the boundless" (*Rudolf Steiner, Twelve Cosmic Moods*). William Bento illumines this mantra:

> All that finds its existence into forms, including all our thoughts, feelings and actions, remains bounded. The bounded are boundaries that too often confine and define who we are. Yielding to the boundless is not a given. It requires a willingness to let go and trust in the boundless, which is full of new possibilities. And the new possibilities, after all, are what allow us to continue our development and become free from the forms and patterns of our lives that tend to be static and inert.

Discretion becomes silence, becomes meditative force, and becomes power. The first decan of Aquarius is ruled by Mercury, the planet of movement, and is associated with the Southern Fish, whose main star Fomalhaut is 9° Aquarius.

Full Moon: Sun 1° Aquarius Moon 1° Leo: The Raising of Lazarus (July/26/32). The Moon was at this degree when Jesus Christ enacted the last of his seven healing miracles: the raising of Lazarus from the dead:

> The raising of Lazarus was an archetypal event for humanity, demonstrating the possibility in the future, following Golgotha, for the human being to receive the breath of life from the creative source of the living Word, received as an initiatory breath from the etheric life body of Jesus Christ. This was the octave of the baptism in the Jordan, wherein a new consciousness was to be born of water, understanding water as the physical agent of cleansing and the faithful bearer of vibratory imprint.
>
> The importance of the desert experience for the Israelites was a movement forward away from the Egyptian mystery tradition where the spiritual aspirant left the physical body during the three-day temple sleep to unite with the spiritual world, which could be born as an imprint thereafter as a source of inspiration throughout life. In contrast, the Israelite's mission under the guidance of Yahweh, was to make a step forward, undertaking the work of calling down the spiritual world into the physical body—with the goal of bringing an imprint of the spiritual world into the "I" of the individual.[3]

Dr. Powell goes on to explain how the miracle of the Raising of Lazarus was a baptism by air, which denotes a rebirth, after which the transformed consciousness of the one initiated develops the ability to work with conscience (a bestowal from the beings of Saturn), which means working with the spiritual world. How does this apply to us?

The miracle of The Raising of Lazarus works irrespective of time and place, where what is forgotten is remembered, where what sleeps is awakened, and where what is dead is brought to life. Lazarus, according to Rudolf Steiner, was the individuality who became Christian Rosenkreutz, he who brought the Rose Cross and founded Rosicrucianism. The mysteries of the depths open as the heights are revealed; and as the heights are opened, so also are the depths. This is the work before us: facing the darkness in pursuit of the Light, as "Knights of the Threshold."

This Full Moon calls us to awaken from our sleep in the increasingly ominous illusions of materialism. Are we willing to be called from the grave of our entombment?

February 15: Inferior conjunction of Sun and Mercury 2° Aquarius. Mercury at this degree remembers Christ teaching on the road that led into Bethsaida (Feb/2/31). As evening approached marking the start of the Sabbath, he went into the synagogue and continued his teaching. Three days previously, Jesus had taught about the Eucharistic bread of life but had not then said that he himself was this bread. On this occasion, however, he did call himself the bread of life come down from heaven, and this caused an uproar. "The Pharisees cried out: How can he give us his body (flesh) to eat? Jesus replied

---

[3] Powell, *Elijah Come Again*, p. 133.

that he would give them the food of which he spoke 'in its own time' (in 113 weeks)."[1]

Many of his disciples turned from him due to this statement, for they could not comprehend this teaching. Christ was bringing something entirely new, and few around him had concepts to understand what he was saying. The mind (Mercury) needs to understand, and yet new imaginations have no precedent and therefore no ready concepts. We are to form new concepts to fit the new revelations. If we turn away from the influences of the Etheric Christ, as did many of the larger circle of disciples at the first coming, we are in danger of succumbing to the second fall whereby we become worshippers of the golden calf, which represents the double of humanity—Ahriman.

The past must be overcome to make way for the future. We are to walk into the wilderness of the unknown as did the people following Moses, in order to receive the heavenly *manna* that is now bringing moral forces of life into all things of this Earth. Eating the bread of life (body) is communion with love, through which we will find the moral cosmic forces that prepare us to *give* to others and nature. Eating of this bread restores our purity and gives us the strength to overcome our double. With Sun and Mercury radiating the memory of Jesus Christ announcing himself as the "bread of life come down from heaven," we can today practice silence in our astral bodies in order to receive the imaginations an inferior conjunction between Mercury and Sun bestows. To hold onto what is familiar can cause us to miss the unfamiliarity of what is striving to become. Three Beatitudes are directed to the heart chakra (Sun/bread of life): Blessed are those who hunger and thirst for righteousness; blessed are the merciful; and blessed are the pure in heart. These can be our contemplations today.

February 19: Mercury 28° Capricorn square Saturn 28° Libra. The Sun was at 28° Libra during the Battle of White Mountain (November 8, 1620) where Frederick V was defeated by the mounting Catholic armies of the Counter Reformation: Frederick V was a key figure involved in the Thirty Years War. He was inspired by Christian Rosenkreutz, but again something went seriously wrong. I mentioned yesterday the mother of the youth of Nain, Maroni, who was a rich widow. She reincarnated at the time of the Grail events, and had the name Schoysiane. She was the sister of Herzeloyde and Repanse de Schoye. Her brothers were Trevrizent and Amfortas. She married Kyot, but she died giving birth to their daughter Sigune. Schoysiane had a later incarnation as one who lived in Heidelberg and lived historically as the Winter King (he was king for only one winter), or Frederick V. Frederick V was the grandson of William of Orange. He was a mystic, and at his court in Heidelberg, there was a great deal of interest in esotericism.[2]

This battle was part of the Thirty Years War (1618-1648) that decimated much of Europe. This war was a counter-move by adversary forces to blunt the effect of the Rosicrucian wisdom that was then surfacing through the manuscripts *The Chymical Wedding of Christian Rosenkreutz* and the *Pharma Fraternitas*. The influence these books could have wielded would have offered a counterbalance to the rising up of modern materialistic science. Instead, a war occurred that wrested attention to matters of divisiveness. Just as the Catholics and Protestants were fighting against each other in the seventeenth century, so does this conflict materialize in the twenty-first century in the Anthroposophic Society. The hostility toward Catholicism is an inversion of the free Christian spirituality emblematic of Rosicrucianism. From what are we being diverted?

With Mercury (intelligence) in tension with Saturn in the constellation of relationships (Libra), where the battle between Protestants and Catholics is remembered, we can ask: What stands behind religious intolerance in this new age when brotherly/sisterly collaboration is the mark of those bringing to fruition the freedom inherent in the consciousness soul? This is a good day to practice tolerance in spite of the examples contrary to this held by persons in positions of authority.

---

1 *Chron.*, p. 277.

2 Powell, *Great Teachers of Humanity*, chap. 13.

February 23: Sun conjunct Neptune at Fomalhaut 9° Aquarius. One of the four Royal Stars of Persia, Fomalhaut is the Watcher in the South, who stands with Tat—the loyal student of Hermes:

> (turning to the South): Holy Gabriel, thou who carries the spirit-light of the Age of the Moon, whence radiates the fount underlying the life of thought, help illumine our thinking that it be raised to knowledge of the cosmic mystery of the Logos who is the Salvation of humankind and the Earth.[3]

The Age of the Moon (when our astral bodies first manifested) is resurrected in the Age of Jupiter (when the purification of our astral bodies into Spirit Self will be attained), the fifth manifestation of the body of the Earth as depicted in Occult Science: Saturn, Sun, Moon, Earth, future Jupiter, future Venus, future Vulcan. The Aquarian mind thirsts for the wisdom of future Jupiter evolution, which is in its esoteric dawning in our Age of the consciousness soul. This will intensify through the resurrection of the Egyptian mysteries in our time. May we remember the call of star wisdom—the rising gnosis of Egypt.

With the Sun conjunct Neptune at this powerful degree of the zodiac we can remember the last time Neptune was at this degree, which was the time of the California gold rush of 1849. It takes 165 years for Neptune to orbit the Sun. The gold fever that overtook the human soul during the gold rush was the same illness that laid seize upon Philip the Fair, who was responsible for the torture and death of the Knights Templar in 1312. At that time Neptune was square today's degree (9° Scorpio).

> A highly gifted personality, Philip the Fair, who was equipped with an extraordinary degree of cunning and the most evil ahrimanic wisdom, had access to such inspiration through gold. Philip IV, who reigned in France from 1285 to 1314, can really be said to have had a genius for avarice. He felt the instinctive urge to recognize nothing else in the world but what can be paid for with gold, and he was willing to concede power over gold to no one but himself. He wished to bring forcibly under his control all the power that can be exercised through gold.[4]

Ahrimanic cunning and avarice is the mark of the military industrial economic complex and the 1% whose desire for the power of gold is ruthless. After 168 years Neptune returns to Fomalhaut and the good power of gold can be remembered. What is this? It is the power of wisdom that shines from a soul devoted to higher truths. Those following the stream of John, which is leading us into the cultural epoch of Aquarius, are learning how to swallow gold (become inwardly wise) in order to cross the bridge of the green snake and receive the *manna* flowing from the urns of Aquarius. Today Neptune and Sun stand together in Aquarius promising the golden wisdom of Sophia's light, which is the gold that ahrimanic forces cannot claim.

February 24: Sun 10° Aquarius. Feeding of the Five Thousand and the Walking on Water. "Deneb, seen by the Greeks as marking the tail of the Swan, is at the head of the Northern Cross. It is remarkable to consider that the cross is the symbol of Christ, and that—in the sense of 'as above, so below'—his central miracles (the feeding of the five thousand and the walking on the water) were aligned via the sun with Deneb at the head of the cross..." (Robert Powell and Kevin Dann, *Astrological Revolution*, p. 151).

These two miracles signify a day side (Feeding of the Five Thousand) and a night side (Walking on Water). Christ feeds five thousand with moral-sensory impressions, and these impressions echo into the night for the twelve disciples.

Rudolf Steiner frequently spoke of spiritualizing sensory impressions; "moral impressions" was the term he gave to sensory impressions of moral and spiritual phenomena.[5] Christ, whose heart was in union with the twelve constellations of the zodiac, filled the twelve senses of the multitude with moral impressions. This satisfied their hunger. They sought to crown him king in this world, whereby they could continue to passively receive spiritual

---

3 CHA, "A Discourse of Hermes to Tat, The Mystery of the Zodiac."

4 Steiner, *The Knights Templar*, p. 52.

5 On the twelve senses, see Steiner, *Anthroposophy (A Fragment)*, chap. 2, "The Human Being as a Sensory Organism."

nourishment. His disciples, on the other hand, bore witness to his spiritual kingliness when, later that night, he approached their boat as he walked on water, saying, "It is I; don't be afraid" (John 6:20). These words contain the revelation of Christ's kingly nature.

> [This kingly nature] does not call the Christ to govern (as the five thousand wished), but bestows on the human being the spiritual force of self-determination. The kingly nature of the Christ is his capacity not only to give humankind freedom, but also to give the needed strength to assert that freedom. In the spiritual-moral sense, it would be proper to say that the royal nature of Christ involves giving kingly dignity to human beings.[1]

In the night comes the recognition of the kingly dignity that Christ gives to human beings. His words—"It is I; be not afraid"—remind us of who it is that brings us certainty when the winds of change and the waves of uncertainty threaten our equilibrium. We are also reminded of the different natures of sense impressions. Moral impressions echo into the higher hierarchies by night, strengthening the human "I"—whereas immoral impressions, impressions man-made to imitate creation, echo into the sphere of materialism by night, thereby capturing the ego in its *maya*. *What is taken in by day determines which school we enter at night—the school of the Greater Guardian who is Christ, or the school of materialism that is ruled by the tempters. This is a good day to ponder the quality of impressions we place before our senses and, more importantly, the quality of impressions we allow to enter our children's senses. For the nature of these impressions by day will determine who, or what, it is they will meet in the night.*

The Sun at 10° Aquarius enters the second decan of Aquarius, ruled by Venus and associated with the Swan (sacred to Venus). Sun at 10 1/2° Aquarius is conjunct the mega star Deneb, marking the tail of the Swan (the head of the Northern Cross). The Sun was conjunct Deneb at the Feeding of the Five Thousand.

February 25: Moon and Venus stand together in Sagittarius.

February 26: Jupiter 15° Gemini square Uranus 15° Pisces. Jupiter was here during Holy Week of AD 33, two weeks before the Mystery of Golgotha. During this week Jesus cursed the fig tree, drove the money changers from the temple, gave parables to parry the aggressive blows of the Pharisees, was anointed by Magdalene (setting up the betrayal by Judas), and gathered his disciples together for a last supper. Then, he went to Gethsemane where he was arrested and thus began his Passion. All these events are enlivened today through Jupiter. As Jupiter is square to Uranus we can imagine that the Etheric Christ is offering us his spiritual touch in order to comfort us as we face the demons over which he was victorious. Uranus brings new revelation; and to receive these imaginations one must have courage to bear what the light illumines, loyalty toward the mission of the earth and humanity, and the will to develop righteousness born of self-control. These can be our contemplations for the next few weeks. Each of us has a passion to endure in order to prepare our souls for the trials now being revealed in preparation for the sixth cultural epoch—the culture of Sophia. Such work is the task of those choosing to become part of a new knighthood:

> When you follow the teaching of the Templars, there at the heart of it is a kind of reverence for something of a feminine nature. This femininity was known as the Divine Sophia, the Heavenly Wisdom. *Manas* is the fifth principle, the spiritual self of the human being, that must be developed and for which a temple must be built.[2]

In his article in this Journal, William Bento references another quote from Steiner in which he refers to the fifth principle as *manas*. *Manas* builds a spiritual temple within and without—in the realm of nature. We build this temple through the practice of the three Rosicrucian mantras: *Ex Deo Nascimur* (from the divine humanity is born); *In Christo Morimur* (in Christ death becomes life); *Per Spiritum Sanctum Reviviscimus* (through the Holy Spirit our souls awaken). The successors of

---

[1] Tomberg, *Christ and Sophia*, p. 254.

[2] Steiner, *The Knights Templar*, pp. 127–128.

the Templars are the Rosicrucians and both of these orders dedicated themselves to building the great temple of humanity. May we find our readiness to work at the side of this knighthood.

The deeds of Holy Week are our guide; and they set a precedent for all cycles of change. 1) First we receive the new; 2) next we must cast out and curse all that would thwart the new; 3. then we parry the blows of adversaries to our striving; 4) then we must overcome restlessness and find stillness in order to let the change seat itself in time; 5) then a quietude comes over us as we begin to partake of the *manna* the new is bestowing; 6) it then becomes necessary to suffer our karma in order to make room for the new in the depths of our being; 7) finally we rise with the new into a fresh expression of our selfhood. The effects of this Jupiter-Uranus square, remembering Holy Week, will be with us throughout the coming spring into June.

Note: Uranus at 15° Virgo (opposite today's position) marks its position at the birth of Ralph Waldo Emerson. In an editorial commentary Thomas Meyer remarks on this individuality, he states:

> In the end, Emerson will persevere longer than all the occultists of his home continent who have narrowed their horizon with their egoistic goals. His thinking and feeling reach into the realm of the eternal laws of humankind and the universe, such as every man and woman can grasp and experience; they transcend the temporal interests of the few who have been seduced by the temptation of power. [3]

February 28: Sun 14° Aquarius. Birth of Rudolf Steiner and Valentin Tomberg. Jesus taught on the same theme as the Sermon on the Mount. the Beatitudes and the Lord's Prayer (Matt. 5:3–12; 6:9–13).

Both Rudolf Steiner and Valentin Tomberg gave close attention to the Lord's Prayer and the Beatitudes.

> [Valentin Tomberg] can be viewed in the line of the great teachers of humanity. He is one such teacher in our time in the post-Christian era, who is bringing the teaching for the ascending phase of this great movement of Christ on his path of return to the heavenly Father, leading humanity stage by stage on the ascending path leading to the Resurrection. He connected onto the great teacher Rudolf Steiner—this connection shows in their horoscopes, where the Sun's location (14 1/2° Aquarius) at his birth aligned exactly with the position of the Sun (14 1/2° Aquarius) at Rudolf Steiner's birth. Whereas Rudolf Steiner's task was to prepare for the onset of Christ's Second Coming in the etheric aura of the Earth in 1933, the task of the author of *Meditations on the Tarot* was to help humanity align with the Etheric Christ in the period after 1933.
>
> As through antiquity Christ descended from the heights of our galaxy down to the Earth, so now he is uniting with the etheric aura of the Earth all the way down to the golden heart of the Earth (Shambhala), from there to begin his ascending movement from the depths in the spiritualization of the Earth, creating the "New Earth."[4]

As true initiates all work together, coming into incarnation in various cultures at various times in order to continue the work of spiritually guiding humanity, it would follow that one of the tasks of an initiate is to assure his successor is recognized. Rudolf Steiner fulfilled this task, without trespassing upon the freedom of his successor, who was still under the age of thirty-three at the time of Steiner's death. (Before this age an individuality may not as yet have accepted the responsibility of a foreordained mission.) Rudolf Steiner said the individuality in the process of becoming the next Buddha was born in 1900 and would begin teaching in the 1930's.

It was more discreetly, and without putting a particular person in the limelight as candidate, that Dr. Rudolf Steiner, founder of the Anthroposophical Society predicted the manifestation—again in the first half of the twentieth century—not of the new Maitreya Buddha or Kalki Avatar, but rather of the Bodhisattva, i.e., the individuality in the process of becoming the

---

3 From http://www.perseus.ch/PDF-Dateien/fundamental.pdf.

4 Powell, *Cultivating Inner Radiance and the Body of Immortality*, p. 192.

next Buddha, whose field of activity he hoped the Anthroposophical Society would serve.[1]

Aquarius is future-oriented and brings something new into the present. Aquarian teachers bear witness to the future. Aquarius is leading us into the next zodiacal age (beginning in 2375)—in which the Slavic cultural epoch will open new possibilities for *manas* cognition. We are on the doorstep to this Aquarian Age. Both of these great teachers brought change based on the traditions of the past, but not limited by these traditions. For, to be limited is to become rigidified. *The sanctity of humanity's freedom allows each of us to discern for ourselves whom we recognize as bearers of revelation. Error occurs when those in positions of authority misuse their positions by imposing personal opinions as objective truths, thereby transgressing upon the freedom of others.*

Venus enters Capricorn: "The past, feel the future." Venus represents the etheric body and the subtle intelligence of the heart. Between the past and the future rests the present moment. In this place of centeredness we are to increase our vigilance so that the forces moving toward us from the etheric periphery imbue our life-work with a might to meet what the future is asking. Venus was in Capricorn at the conception of the Solomon Mary, through the temptations of Christ, and during the first miracle of changing water into wine at the wedding in Cana.

MARCH 2014

The Sun begins the month in Aquarius (the Water-Carrier) conjunct the Moon: a New Moon. Mars and Saturn, both in Libra station Retrograde: Mars on the 2nd (until May 21) and Saturn on the 3rd (through the middle of July). Jupiter in Gemini stations Direct on the 6th and the waxing Moon joins it on the 9th. You can see the Moon all day, rising just after midday. Look to the south at and after sunset to watch for Jupiter to "pop out" above and to the left of the Moon as the dusk darkens into night. The Sun journeys into Pisces (the Fishes) on the 15th and is opposite the Moon in Virgo on the 16th, forming a Full Moon. We can observe the Moon moving past Mars and Spica in Virgo on the evenings of the 18th and 19th. Spica is the star beneath Mars, while Mars is to the left of the Moon on the 18th and to the right of the Moon on the 19th. From here, the Moon continues its rhythmic conjunctions with Saturn, Venus, and Mercury: the New Moon on the 30th will hide the conjunction with Mercury on the 29th, but Moon and Saturn can be seen from just before midnight on the 21st until sunrise the next morning and Moon and Venus can be spotted rising in the east 1½ hours before the sunrise on the 27th for you early risers!

March 1: New Moon 15° Leo. Third Temptation in the Wilderness (Nov/29/29). The Moon was here at this third and last temptation of Jesus Christ. This third temptation is now the temptation of all humanity, according to the Apocalypse Code of Dr. Powell.[2] The temptation to turn bread into stones and stones into bread is everywhere around us, and it is Ahriman's intention that we fail to notice his handiwork. He spoke to Jesus Christ:

> Look at the dead earthly phenomena, the stones; they can come to life as bread if you only command them to do so. They will become as bread because, from the earth's interior, I can supply a lifelike force to all dead matter. You must simply will what is dead to live.[3]

Christ rejected the temptation by pointing to the Word of God as the true source of life—the life that gives both nature and humanity the ability to move with evolution toward its fifth manifestation—future Jupiter existence. Today remembers this miracle and the anti-life that today threatens humanity from sub-earthly realms. During this Full Moon we can be reminded to say "no" to manipulations that fulfill Ahriman's continual drive to remove *Life* from our daily bread and to render chaos in the etheric sheath of our planet. Instead of participating in the treacherous debasing of our Mother

---

1 Anonymous, *Meditations on the Tarot*, p. 614.

2 See Powell and Dann, *Christ and the Maya Calendar*.

3 Tomberg, *Christ and Sophia*, p. 174.

SIDEREAL GEOCENTRIC LONGITUDES : MARCH 2014 Gregorian at 0 hours UT

DAY	☉	☽	☊	☿	♀	♂	♃	♄	♅	♆	♇
1 SA	15 ♒ 23	10 ♒ 46	4 ♎ 29R	23 ♑ 14	1 ♑ 9	2 ♎ 36	15 ♊ 33R	28 ♎ 23	15 ♓ 45	10 ♒ 19	18 ♐ 8
2 SU	16 23	25 34	4 23	23 20	1 56	2 36R	15 32	28 23	15 48	10 21	18 9
3 MO	17 24	10 ♓ 4	4 18	23 32	2 43	2 35	15 31	28 23R	15 51	10 24	18 11
4 TU	18 24	24 8	4 16	23 50	3 31	2 34	15 31	28 23	15 55	10 26	18 12
5 WE	19 24	7 ♈ 45	4 16D	24 13	4 20	2 32	15 30	28 23	15 58	10 28	18 13
6 TH	20 24	20 56	4 17	24 41	5 10	2 29	15 30	28 22	16 1	10 30	18 14
7 FR	21 24	3 ♉ 42	4 18	25 14	6 1	2 25	15 30D	28 22	16 4	10 33	18 15
8 SA	22 24	16 7	4 19	25 51	6 52	2 21	15 31	28 21	16 7	10 35	18 17
9 SU	23 24	28 17	4 19R	26 32	7 44	2 16	15 31	28 21	16 10	10 37	18 18
10 MO	24 24	10 ♊ 16	4 18	27 18	8 36	2 10	15 32	28 20	16 14	10 39	18 19
11 TU	25 24	22 9	4 14	28 6	9 29	2 3	15 32	28 19	16 17	10 42	18 20
12 WE	26 24	4 ♋ 1	4 9	28 58	10 23	1 55	15 33	28 18	16 20	10 44	18 21
13 TH	27 24	15 54	4 3	29 53	11 17	1 47	15 35	28 17	16 23	10 46	18 22
14 FR	28 24	27 53	3 56	0 ♒ 51	12 12	1 38	15 36	28 16	16 27	10 48	18 23
15 SA	29 24	9 ♌ 59	3 50	1 52	13 8	1 28	15 37	28 15	16 30	10 50	18 24
16 SU	0 ♓ 23	22 15	3 44	2 55	14 4	1 18	15 39	28 14	16 33	10 53	18 25
17 MO	1 23	4 ♍ 40	3 39	4 1	15 0	1 7	15 41	28 12	16 37	10 55	18 26
18 TU	2 23	17 17	3 36	5 9	15 57	0 55	15 43	28 11	16 40	10 57	18 26
19 WE	3 22	0 ♎ 6	3 35	6 19	16 55	0 42	15 46	28 9	16 43	10 59	18 27
20 TH	4 22	13 6	3 36D	7 31	17 53	0 28	15 48	28 8	16 47	11 1	18 28
21 FR	5 22	26 20	3 37	8 45	18 51	0 14	15 51	28 6	16 50	11 3	18 29
22 SA	6 21	9 ♏ 47	3 38	10 1	19 50	29 ♍ 59	15 54	28 4	16 54	11 5	18 30
23 SU	7 21	23 27	3 40	11 19	20 49	29 44	15 57	28 2	16 57	11 8	18 30
24 MO	8 20	7 ♐ 23	3 40	12 39	21 49	29 27	16 0	28 0	17 0	11 10	18 31
25 TU	9 20	21 32	3 40R	14 0	22 49	29 10	16 3	27 58	17 4	11 12	18 32
26 WE	10 19	5 ♑ 53	3 38	15 23	23 49	28 53	16 7	27 56	17 7	11 14	18 32
27 TH	11 19	20 23	3 36	16 48	24 50	28 34	16 11	27 53	17 11	11 16	18 33
28 FR	12 18	4 ♒ 58	3 33	18 14	25 51	28 16	16 15	27 51	17 14	11 18	18 33
29 SA	13 17	19 31	3 30	19 42	26 52	27 56	16 19	27 48	17 17	11 20	18 34
30 SU	14 17	3 ♓ 56	3 28	21 11	27 54	27 36	16 23	27 46	17 21	11 22	18 34
31 MO	15 16	18 8	3 27	22 42	28 56	27 16	16 28	27 43	17 24	11 24	18 35

INGRESSES :

2 ☽ → ♓ 7:16	♂ → ♍ 22:40
4 ☽ → ♈ 10:13	23 ☽ → ♐ 11:19
6 ☽ → ♉ 16:58	25 ☽ → ♑ 14:11
9 ☽ → ♊ 3:24	27 ☽ → ♒ 15:49
11 ☽ → ♋ 15:53	29 ☽ → ♓ 17:24
13 ☿ → ♒ 2:51	31 ☽ → ♈ 20:27
14 ☽ → ♌ 4:13	
15 ☉ → ♓ 14:39	
16 ☽ → ♍ 15: 1	
18 ☽ → ♎ 23:49	
21 ☽ → ♏ 6:35	

ASPECTS & ECLIPSES :

1 ☉ ☌ ☽ 7:59	☽ ☌ A 19:53	24 ☉ □ ☽ 1:45	31 ☽ ☍ ♂ 15:19
2 ♀ □ ♂ 19:57	12 ☽ ☿ ☊ 0:17	☽ ☍ ♃ 14:43	
3 ☽ ☌ ♅ 9:49	☽ ☍ ♀ 13:56	☽ ☌ ♇ 18:56	
4 ☽ ☍ ♂ 14:42	14 ☽ ☍ ☿ 6:27	25 ☽ ♅ ☊ 20:16	
☽ ☌ ☋ 17:45	15 ☽ ☍ ♆ 1:41	27 ☽ ☌ ♀ 7:51	
♀ □ ☊ 21:41	16 ☉ ☍ ☽ 17: 8	☽ ☌ P 18:18	
6 ☽ ☍ ♄ 13:53	17 ☽ ☍ ♅ 22:49	28 ☽ ☌ ♆ 10:27	
8 ☉ □ ☽ 13:26	19 ☽ ☌ ♂ 1: 5	29 ☽ ☌ ☿ 0:19	
10 ☽ ☌ ♃ 10:36	☽ ☌ ☊ 6:28	♀ □ ♄ 21: 4	
☽ ☍ ♇ 16:15	21 ☽ ☌ ♄ 3:10	30 ☉ ☌ ☽ 18:44	
11 ☿ □ ♄ 6: 5	22 ☿ ☌ ♆ 20:18	☽ ☌ ♅ 22:44	

SIDEREAL HELIOCENTRIC LONGITUDES : MARCH 2014 Gregorian at 0 hours UT

DAY	Sid. Time	☿	♀	⊕	♂	♃	♄	♅	♆	♇	Vernal Point
1 SA	10:34:53	26 ♍ 37	14 ♍ 57	15 ♌ 23	6 ♍ 26	25 ♊ 0	22 ♎ 53	17 ♓ 11	10 ♒ 9	16 ♐ 40	5 ♓ 3'45"
2 SU	10:38:50	0 ♎ 0	16 34	16 23	6 53	25 5	22 55	17 12	10 9	16 40	5 ♓ 3'45"
3 MO	10:42:46	3 18	18 11	17 23	7 20	25 10	22 56	17 12	10 10	16 41	5 ♓ 3'44"
4 TU	10:46:43	6 31	19 48	18 24	7 46	25 15	22 58	17 13	10 10	16 41	5 ♓ 3'44"
5 WE	10:50:39	9 41	21 25	19 24	8 13	25 20	23 0	17 14	10 10	16 41	5 ♓ 3'44"
6 TH	10:54:36	12 47	23 1	20 24	8 40	25 25	23 2	17 14	10 11	16 41	5 ♓ 3'44"
7 FR	10:58:33	15 50	24 38	21 24	9 7	25 30	23 4	17 15	10 11	16 42	5 ♓ 3'44"
8 SA	11: 2:29	18 51	26 15	22 24	9 34	25 35	23 6	17 16	10 11	16 42	5 ♓ 3'44"
9 SU	11: 6:26	21 48	27 51	23 24	10 0	25 40	23 8	17 16	10 12	16 42	5 ♓ 3'44"
10 MO	11:10:22	24 44	29 28	24 24	10 27	25 45	23 9	17 17	10 12	16 43	5 ♓ 3'44"
11 TU	11:14:19	27 37	1 ♎ 5	25 24	10 54	25 50	23 11	17 18	10 13	16 43	5 ♓ 3'43"
12 WE	11:18:15	0 ♏ 28	2 41	26 24	11 21	25 55	23 13	17 18	10 13	16 43	5 ♓ 3'43"
13 TH	11:22:12	3 18	4 17	27 24	11 48	26 0	23 15	17 19	10 13	16 44	5 ♓ 3'43"
14 FR	11:26: 8	6 6	5 54	28 24	12 15	26 5	23 17	17 20	10 14	16 44	5 ♓ 3'43"
15 SA	11:30: 5	8 53	7 30	29 23	12 42	26 10	23 19	17 20	10 14	16 44	5 ♓ 3'43"
16 SU	11:34: 2	11 40	9 7	0 ♍ 23	13 9	26 15	23 21	17 21	10 14	16 45	5 ♓ 3'43"
17 MO	11:37:58	14 25	10 43	1 23	13 36	26 20	23 22	17 21	10 15	16 45	5 ♓ 3'43"
18 TU	11:41:55	17 10	12 19	2 23	14 3	26 25	23 24	17 22	10 15	16 45	5 ♓ 3'42"
19 WE	11:45:51	19 55	13 55	3 22	14 30	26 30	23 26	17 23	10 15	16 46	5 ♓ 3'42"
20 TH	11:49:48	22 40	15 31	4 22	14 57	26 34	23 28	17 23	10 16	16 46	5 ♓ 3'42"
21 FR	11:53:44	25 24	17 7	5 21	15 24	26 39	23 30	17 24	10 16	16 46	5 ♓ 3'42"
22 SA	11:57:41	28 9	18 43	6 21	15 51	26 44	23 32	17 25	10 17	16 47	5 ♓ 3'42"
23 SU	12: 1:37	0 ♐ 55	20 19	7 21	16 18	26 49	23 34	17 25	10 17	16 47	5 ♓ 3'42"
24 MO	12: 5:34	3 41	21 55	8 20	16 46	26 54	23 36	17 26	10 17	16 47	5 ♓ 3'42"
25 TU	12: 9:31	6 29	23 31	9 20	17 13	26 59	23 37	17 27	10 18	16 48	5 ♓ 3'41"
26 WE	12:13:27	9 17	25 7	10 19	17 40	27 4	23 39	17 27	10 18	16 48	5 ♓ 3'41"
27 TH	12:17:24	12 7	26 43	11 18	18 7	27 9	23 41	17 28	10 18	16 48	5 ♓ 3'41"
28 FR	12:21:20	14 58	28 19	12 18	18 35	27 14	23 43	17 29	10 19	16 49	5 ♓ 3'41"
29 SA	12:25:17	17 51	29 55	13 17	19 2	27 19	23 45	17 29	10 19	16 49	5 ♓ 3'41"
30 SU	12:29:13	20 46	1 ♏ 30	14 17	19 29	27 24	23 47	17 30	10 19	16 49	5 ♓ 3'41"
31 MO	12:33:10	23 43	3 6	15 16	19 56	27 29	23 49	17 30	10 20	16 50	5 ♓ 3'41"

INGRESSES :

2 ☿ → ♎ 0: 2
10 ♀ → ♎ 7:57
11 ☿ → ♏ 20: 2
15 ⊕ → ♍ 14:43
22 ☿ → ♐ 16: 2
29 ♀ → ♏ 1:21

ASPECTS (HELIOCENTRIC +MOON(TYCHONIC)) :

2 ♀ □ ♇ 1:30	8 ⊕ ⚹ ♄ 17:11	♀ △ ♆ 16:57	25 ♀ ☌ ♄ 1:32	31 ☿ ⚹ ♄ 0:41
⊕ △ ♇ 6:47	9 ☿ ☌ ♄ 10:55	17 ☽ ☌ ♂ 17:38	☽ ☍ ♃ 9:12	☽ ☍ ♂ 3:11
♀ ☍ ♅ 9:22	☿ ☌ ☋ 14:23	18 ☽ ☍ ♅ 0: 9	♂ ☍ ♅ 12:29	
☽ ☍ ♂ 19:16	☿ ⚹ ⊕ 19:53	☿ △ ♅ 1:44	26 ☿ ⚹ ♆ 8:40	
3 ☽ ☌ ♅ 12: 5	10 ☿ △ ♃ 8:43	20 ☿ ☌ A 0:41	☿ □ ⊕ 13:33	
☽ ☍ ♀ 15:32	☽ ☍ ♇ 13: 0	☽ ☌ ♀ 5: 1	27 ♀ △ ♃ 6:52	
5 ☿ △ ♆ 3:45	11 ☽ ☌ ♃ 7:29	♀ ⚹ ♇ 18:42	28 ☽ ☌ ♆ 8:48	
☽ ☍ ☿ 4:31	⊕ ⚹ ♃ 11:20	☽ ☌ ♄ 18:53	☿ ☌ ♇ 15:24	
6 ☽ ☍ ♄ 3:54	15 ☽ ☍ ♆ 0:29	23 ☽ ☌ ☿ 16: 6	☿ □ ♅ 20:59	
7 ☿ ⚹ ♇ 6:48	☿ □ ♆ 11:38	24 ♂ □ ♇ 1:33	29 ☿ □ ♂ 11:33	
♀ □ ♃ 13:36	16 ☿ ⚹ ♂ 15:26	☽ ☌ ♇ 16: 0	30 ☽ ☌ ♅ 22:55	

Earth's bountiful gifts, we can spend time in nature taking notice of her every expression with grateful hearts. We are to actively choose the bread of life over the stones of materialism and all the entrapments caused by augmented realities, weather modification techniques, and genetic manipulations. We are surrounded by what is dead masquerading as the living. May we find the holiness of Life this day, and open our eyes to the activity of the usurper, who causes what is dead to appear as if living.

March 2: Venus 2° Capricorn square Mars 2° Libra. Venus was here at the commissioning of the twelve (Dec/10/30).

> Today there occurred—for the first time—the sending out of the disciples. At about ten o'clock in the morning, with the twelve and about thirty other disciples, Jesus left Capernaum and went north in the direction of Saphet and Hanathon, accompanied by a large crowd. Around three in the afternoon, they approached Hanathon. Here Jesus and the disciples climbed a mountain used in former times by the prophets. Jesus had taught there less than one year ago. This time, however, the crowd did not go up the mountain. On the mountain, Jesus addressed the disciples, giving them instructions and sending them out into the world with the words found in Matthew 9:36–10:16. Each of the twelve had a small flask of oil, and Jesus taught them how to use it for anointing and also for healing. Afterward, the disciples knelt in a circle around Jesus, and he prayed and laid his hands upon the head of each of the twelve.[1]

Jesus as the healing power of the Word, speaks from high on the mountain, where only disciples were allowed to be present. When the Bible tells us of teachings given on the mountains, we can rightly imagine this means "high" teachings given to those prepared to receive them. Today with Venus square Mars such high teachings are potentized, for this aspect promises an in-streaming of the cosmic Word, seeking to manifest through the spoken word of human beings on Earth. The mountains of the prophets are calling to those who have been given a small flask of oil. This is the property of all who have made themselves ready to heal through the power of Christ. This requires love (Venus), receptivity, and a willingness to kneel in humility before the profundity of cosmic wisdom. Inversely, it is the lower nature that speaks through a jealous heart (lower Venus) with cloaked hatred, close mindedness, and flaring egoism that spills the poison of the antiLogos—a force of destruction toward what Venus yearns to birth. May we choose our words carefully.

Saturn stations at 28° Libra before moving retrograde. When a planet stations it adds particular emphasis to the zodiacal memory of the given degree of the station. Saturn at this degree stands opposite its position at the great conjunction of 2000 between Jupiter and Saturn. The ideals born at the centuries beginning are being assessed by the planet of cosmic memory. This continues until the 24th of this month and will return at the end of October. The Christlike leadership heralded in Aries, is now ripe for its interweaving in human communities (Libra). We must decide who to follow.

March 4: Sun 19° Aquarius. Raising an Essene girl from the dead (Feb/7/30) (*Chron.* p. 219). The Sun is aligned with the mega star 68 Cygnus in the Swan—the second most luminous star visible to us.

> This girl was born into an Essene family, whom Jesus Christ visited at their home in Phasael, six weeks after the wedding at Cana. At that time she was about sixteen years old, and her father's name was Jairus. Jesus warned those present not to speak of what they had witnessed, and this—which took place less than five months into his 3 1/2-year ministry—was therefore not recorded in the Gospels. It is remarkable that this raising from the dead took place when the Sun was aligned with a star which the Hipparcos satellite identified as one of the most luminous stars in our galaxy.[2]

Rejoicing in the glorious brilliance of this mega star, we can seek to heal what in us is "dead" in order to free our souls from influences we may have long outgrown. A jealous heart breeds ill will; a

---

[1] *Chron.*, p. 263.

[2] Powell and Dann, *The Astrological Revolution*, p. 155.

righteous heart radiates a peace that surpasses all understanding.

March 6: Jupiter stations direct at 15° Gemini. The Woe upon the Pharisees (Mar/24/33). Ten days before his Passion, Christ gave seven woes to the teachers who uphold the law—the Pharisees. These warn of things that are as applicable to our time as they were at the time of Christ's first coming. One of the seven woes addresses money: "Woe to you, blind guides! You say, 'If anyone swears by the temple, it means nothing; but whoever swears by the gold of the temple is bound by the oath.' You blind fools! Which is greater: the gold, or the temple that makes the gold sacred?" (Matt. 23:16). With Jupiter stationed at the memory of the Woes, a warning goes out to all who are involved in the feverish greed that increases profits and power, and are thus destructive to the holy temple of the human body and the body of the Mother. This would include GMOs, weather modifications techniques, and the encroaching new developments of augmented realities. Until morality is the bottom line, the illness of materialism will continue to spawn destruction through the inverted wisdom of guile and avarice. We can intervene on behalf of goodness through the meditative exercises brought forth by Robert Powell in his book entitled *Inner Radiance and the Body of Immortality*.

March 10: Sun 24° Aquarius. Healing of the Syrophoenician Woman (Feb/12/31). Here Jesus is approached by a crippled woman who begs him to come and heal her daughter who is possessed. Concerned about giving offense, Jesus cannot heal the woman's pagan daughter before he heals the Jews. Later that day Jesus exorcises the unclean spirit from the daughter (Matt 15:21–28). Jesus also heals the crippled woman: "Jesus asked her whether she herself wished to be healed, but the Syrophoenician woman replied that she was not worthy, and that she asked only for her daughter's cure. Then Jesus laid one hand upon her head, the other on her side, and said: 'Straighten up! May it be done to you as you also will it to be done!'" (*Chron.*, p. 279).

This is a story about faith and one's willingness to be healed. The shepherding hand of our angel rests upon our head, and the guiding hand of destiny gently rests upon our side, leading us forward. Feeling into the presence of Christ-imbued spiritual forces makes faith a fact. Our willingness to be healed is foreshadowed by our courage to face the forces that have caused our diminishment:

> Should we inquire as to the reason why most people fail to do something, we find that the answer invariably is: love of ease. Whether we consider the most important things of life or mere trifles, we find that love of ease is ubiquitous. To hold on to the old and outdated, not being able to shake it off, is a form of love of ease. Steiner mentions in this connection that people are not always as wicked as they may appear. For instance, those who were responsible for the burning at the stake of Giordano Bruno, or the maltreatment of Galileo, did not necessarily act out of wickedness, but rather out of love of ease. They could not accept the new. It often takes a long time for people to be able to think and feel along new lines and the reason for this tardiness is love of ease! It is those who were prone on earth to love of ease who have to serve Ahriman in the life after death. For Ahriman, apart from his many other functions, is the "spirit of obstacles." Wherever obstacles arise to true progress there Ahriman is to be found. He applies the brakes to life and to the spiritual development of human beings. "Those who are subject to love of ease on earth will become agents to the slowing down process of everything that comes into the world from the supersensible. So love of ease fetters human souls between death and rebirth to spirits who, under Ahriman, are compelled to serve the powers of opposition and hindrance."[3]

Love of ease is the trial of our times. Where are we harboring an unwillingness to shake off the past in order to receive new paradigms of possibility? These are the places where the ease of disease is a greater yearning in the soul than is the daring it would take to become a vessel through which new inspirations may sound. Are you worthy to collaborate with angels? Dare to become an open book on whose pages the future may inscribe its miracles.

---

3 Nesfield-Cookson, *Rudolf Steiner's Vision of Love*, p. 118.

The alternative is the crucifixion of those whose courage outshines us.

March 10: Mercury 28° Capricorn square Saturn 28° Libra. Saturn continues to rest opposite its position at the Jupiter-Saturn great conjunction that began this century in the year 2000. Venus, too, was at this same degree (28° Aries) in 1801 at the death of Novalis (the last incarnation of John the Baptist until the present incarnation). Thus a John/Novalis memory is kindled when any planet aspects this zodiacal degree as do both Mercury and Saturn today. One hundred years ago (March 7, 1914), Rudolf Steiner gave two lectures entitled *Pre-Earthly Deeds of Christ*. One hundred years marks three cycles of 33⅓ years. This is the rhythm of Christ's etheric body. What Steiner spoke then, can be received now as a ripened renewal of what he then brought.

> We will be able to say that Christ is in our inner soul life. Many of us will feel it to be so if we learn to unite ourselves with the Christ impulse, even as the human child learns to stand upright and to speak because he has united himself with the Christ impulse. Viewing our present faculty of memory as a preparatory stage, many of us also realize that it must fall into disorder in the future unless it has the will to allow itself to be permeated with the Christ impulse. Should there be a state of materialism on Earth in which the Christ is denied, the power of memory would fall into disorder. More and more people would appear whose memory is chaotic; they would become duller and duller in their darkened "I"-consciousness if memory were not to shine into this darkness of the "I."
>
> Our power of memory can develop in the right way only if the Christ impulse is perceived correctly. History will then be a living memory because a true understanding of events has entered the memory; human memory will understand the central point of world evolution [the Mystery of Golgotha]. A perceptive faculty will then arise in people and their ordinary memory, which is presently directed only to one life, will extend over former incarnations. Memory at the present is in a preparatory stage, but it will be endowed through the Christ. Whether we look outward and see how we as children have as yet developed unconsciously, or through an intensive deepening of our soul forces look within to what remains in our memory as our inner being—everywhere we see the living force and activity of the Christ impulse.
>
> The Christ event that is now approaching us—not in the physical but in the etheric, and connected with the first kindling of the power of memory, with the first kindling of the Christ-permeated memory—will be such that Christ will approach humanity as an angel-like being. We must prepare ourselves for this event.[1]

In December of 2020 a new great conjunction will occur in Capricorn. We are in the autumn period of the last conjunction; its fruits have ripened; its seeds are being prepared for winter's sleep, awaiting the next conjunction between Jupiter and Saturn. And, Michael is battling the dragon—the adversary to the Christlike leadership the conjunction of 2000 announced, for this is the task during the Michaelmas season. The autumnal period of the great conjunctions are decisive in the seasons of the year as well as in the seasons of a human life. The autumn answers the question: What has come to being from the potential given? This is a question we can hold. What has become of the Christlike leadership and new cultural inspiration that the last great conjunction announced? Despite the work of sinister agendas over the past fourteen years, the sprouting, blooming, fruiting Christ impulse is bearing the gift of a new memory—clairvoyant in its nature—that is bringing us understanding for what underlies the developments now taking form in our political, economic, and social sectors. The bountiful harvest for the next six years will be the awakening of a Christ-imbued memory so as to honor what was brought at the beginning of the millennium. If we choose instead to sleep, the human soul may be what is harvested by adversarial powers. We may contemplate these thoughts as Saturn (since the 10th of last month through the 23rd of this month) rests at this degree of the heavens. It will return to this degree again in October before moving into Scorpio. Our minds

---

1 Steiner, *Background of the Mystery of Golgotha*, lect. 7 (trans. revised).

(Mercury) can awaken to new memories when we actively open our consciousness soul to see the battle for the human soul now occurring in our global community.

March 15: Sun enters Pisces: "In what is lost, may the loss find itself" (Steiner, *Twelve Cosmic Moods*). William Bento illumines this mantra:

> Regardless of the nature of what is let go of there is a sense of accompanying loss. With those losses that have been treasured and valued (such as a loved one), there lives the hope that the object or being that is lost will not be forgotten or forlorn, but will find new life in an entirely new realm. The plea that states, "may the loss find itself" is really a statement of hope in the eternal cycle of life.

Above the first decan is the Square of Pegasus, hence the association of this decan with the body of Pegasus, the Winged Horse, also called the Horse of the Fountain. This decan is ruled by Saturn. Pisces bestows Magnanimity born of Love. The challenge is to stay grounded in reality in the inclination toward the mystical.

March 16: Full Moon. Sun 1° Pisces Moon 1° Virgo. Start of the forty days of temptation (Oct/21/29). Today's Moon remembers the beginning of Christ's period of temptation. The Sun on this day was within one degree of today's Saturn—the planet of memory (29° Libra). According to the Apocalypse Code developed by Robert Powell, one day in the life of Christ equates to 29.5 years in the unfolding of history. Christ's ministry lasted for 1,290 days, culminating with the Resurrection. This number multiplied by 29.5 equals 38,000 years, which coincides with the end of Earth evolution (after which evolution transitions to the Jupiter stage). This is a remarkable discovery by Dr. Powell. It means that each day of Christ's life gives the "bread of life" for the entire remaining years of Earth's evolution. A Pisces/Virgo Full Moon calls forth the imagination of the loaves (Virgo) and fishes (Pisces) that fed the multitudes at the feeding of the five thousand. Today's New Moon can be celebrated as a time of recognition of Christ and the strength he gives to all who face trials. We are living in the period of a collective temptation and it is the experience of temptation that awakens us to actively decide the path we will take. Temptations are not a problem in and of themselves; a problem occurs only when they go unnoticed. The Prophet Daniel also speaks of 1,290 years: "From the time that the daily sacrifice is abolished and the abomination that causes desolation is set up, there will be 1,290 days" (Daniel 12:11).

The time between the Baptism and the Resurrection amounts to exactly 1,290 days. The rule of the adversary of Christ is said to be of this same duration. The Book of Revelation also mentions this number and the number 2,160 days:

> They will trample on the holy city for 42 months. (Rev. 11:2)

> And I will appoint my two witnesses, and they will prophesy for 1,260 days. (Rev. 11:3)

> The woman fled into the wilderness to a place prepared for her by God, where she might be taken care of for 1,260 days. (Rev. 12:6)[2]

> The beast was given a mouth to utter proud words and blasphemies and to exercise its authority for forty-two months. (Rev. 13:5)

The two witnesses of God are able to prophesy for three and one-half years. Dr. Powell names these two witnesses as the first and third great teachers of the twentieth century—Moses and John.[3] Alongside the three and one-half years from the Baptism to the Resurrection and the dates mentioned by Daniel and Revelation, are the three and one-half years given to Anne Catherine Emmerich: "Anne Catherine Emmerich began to communicate her day-by-day account of the ministry of Christ to Clemens Brentano on July 29, 1820. Counting the days from then till her death on February 9, 1824, yields 1,290 days, the same period of approximately 3½ years again!"[4] Owing to Brentano's absence and Emmerich's times of illness, the account she offers is just short of three years. It is astonishing

---

2 In *The Book of Revelation: And the Work of the Priest*, Steiner calls this number (1,260) a "printer's error." Indicating that the correct number should have been recorded as 2,160 (p. 199).
3 See Powell, *The Most Holy Trinosophia*.
4 *Chron.*, p. 41.

to realize that she was given the same time of 1,290 years despite her inability to relate the full content. This content will come through others who are working in the future-oriented stream of the second witness—John.

This Full Moon calls us to find peace with the *fact* that the three and one-half years of Christ's ministry will be with us until the end of Earth evolution. First, of course, we must choose to follow him.

March 18: Moon transits both Spica and Mars.

March 20: Vernal Point 5° Pisces: Spring Equinox. The earth is breathing out her soul. Her breath is half within the earth and half without. The little seed of our future spiritual potential, which we carried out of the Holy Nights last January, is also breathing outward. Both microcosmically (human being) and macrocosmically (the Earth) an exhalation is taking place. The Earth Mother is going to sleep, and her dream body engenders the sprouting enlivening of Nature's springtide. Nature is the soul of the Mother out-breathed in sleep. Just as our soul leaves our body in sleep, so too does the great Earth soul leave her body in sleep, and this manifests as the beauty and majesty of Natura. Our Christmas seed is preparing to take flight. It will begin its gradual ascent with the Earth soul into the heights of summer where creative forces will fill what has since Christmas been only a dream, with the creativity needed to develop into a full reality. This will come into form later at Michaelmas. Today marks a sprouting, quickening within and without. It will not be until the first Sunday, after the first Full Moon following this equinox, that the inner spirit of the Earth—Christ—will begin the ascent to meet the warmth of the Sun. This will be on the 20th of April following the Full Moon of April 15: "While in December the Christ withdrew the Earth-soul element into the interior of the Earth, in order to be insulated from cosmic influences, now with the out-breathing of the Earth, He begins to let His forces breathe out, to extend them to receive the forces of the Sun which radiate toward Him."[1]

We wait with expectant longing for the Full Moon to come, as well as for the Sunday following the Full Moon.

This restraint is the meaning behind the Lenten and Easter mystery. Until the time of the first Sunday after the First Full Moon following the equinox, malevolent elementals can impede the delicate unfolding of our Christmas gift. We are to be vigilant. The Easter Sun, having tamed the lunar forces at the time of Full Moon, is a benediction that harkens the handing of humanity over from lunar forces to the custodianship of solar forces, for it is at this time of year when the Sun-filled day becomes longer than the Moon-filled night.

March 22: Mercury conjunct Neptune 11° Aquarius: Mercury at this degree remembers Jesus speaking of Jonah (Feb/7/31):

> After healing the sick of Cydessa, Jesus taught in the synagogue. He spoke of the duration of the descent of the Son of Man into the earth's womb, saying it was the same as Jonah had endured in the whale's belly (Matt. 12:38-40). Continuing northward, Jesus then conferred new power upon the twelve and the disciples for healing the sick and exorcising the possessed. Anne Catherine saw rays of different colors streaming out from Jesus into each disciple according to his disposition.[2]

With Mercury conjunct Neptune three different Jonah experiences are possible. One is the three-day initiation, a temple sleep of sorts, where golden wisdom illumines the inner spirit; the other is one in which Ahriman cloaks the soul with a darkness that separates one from the blessings of true illumination. Between the two is the soul who humbly treads the path in devotion toward a future possibility. Spiritual seekers who walk the middle path in consciousness of their Angel find interest in all things. To succumb to apathy signifies one has forgotten one's angel and this forgetting renders the angel motionless:

> But—and this is the tragic side of Angelic existence—this geniality shows up only when the human being has need of it, when he or she

---

[1] Steiner, *The Cycle of the Year*, p. 7.

[2] *Chron.*, p. 278.

makes room for the flashing forth of its illumination. The angel depends on human beings in his creative activity. If the human being does not ask for it, if he turns away from him, the angel has no motive for creative activity. He can then fall into a state of consciousness where all his creative geniality remains in potential and does not manifest.[3]

Forgotten angels are rendered into a twilight existence comparable to sleep, and this leaves their human protégés susceptible to Ahriman. Apathy is a sign of Ahriman's approach. It is a signature of being swallowed by darkness. Tomberg calls apathy one of the three primal illnesses into which human beings can fall. Interest in others, in nature, and in all things engenders an awakening in the human soul and, as consequence, for the angel of that soul. With Ahriman slinking through the world, our interest in all things becomes our shield against his sinister approach: "But what appears initially as sheer lack of interest and also of the capacity to wonder can in time become a kind of psychic illness—that of *apathy* toward all and sundry."[4]

Neptune calls forth the inspirations of Sophia and inversely the machinations of Ahriman. In wakefulness (Mercury) we can today seek interest in all we meet. A ray from the Etheric Christ is waiting to illumine each of us according to our disposition.

Retrograde Mars enters Virgo: "Work out of life powers." Mars in Virgo calls us to trust Nature's becoming and exert our wills to cooperate with her needs, in clear understanding of the world beings who stand with her. Mars was in Virgo as Jesus began his forty days of continual temptation.

March 25: Sun enters the second decan of Pisces, ruled by Jupiter. This decan is associated with Cepheus, the Crowned King located high above, whose head is surrounded and illuminated by the Milky Way.

March 27: Moon transits Venus.

---
3 Anonymous, *Meditations on the Tarot*, p. 378.
4 Tomberg, *Studies on the Foundation Stone Meditation*, p. 66.

March 29: Venus 27° Capricorn square Saturn 27° Libra: The summons of Philip (Dec/24/29). On this eve of a New Moon Venus recalls the summons of Phillip:

> Jesus taught again, morning and afternoon, in the synagogue. At the close of the Sabbath, he and his disciples went for a walk in the little vale nearby. Philip, who was modest and humble, hung back. Jesus turned and said to him: "Follow me" (John 1:43), whereupon Philip, filled with joy, joined the other disciples.[5]

This was on the New Moon festival, which Jesus celebrated that evening. Venus in Capricorn asks that we find the courage to redeem our inner nature through the humility of soul that grants us perception of what can be improved.

March 30: New Moon 15° Pisces. Birth of the Solomon Jesus (Mar/5/6 BC). The great teacher Zarathustra reincarnated as the Solomon Jesus, who was visited by the Three Kings. The kings brought the wisdom gathered by initiates in the three preceding cultural ages: Myrrh from Ancient India, Frankincense from Ancient Persia, and Gold from Ancient Egypt. The influence of this great teacher, called the Master Jesus, is always present on Earth. It takes discernment to hear his teachings through the cacophony of distractions, but he is always here. There is always an initiate who is working with him, even if he himself is not physically incarnated. The ideal of Pisces, the Sun sign at this birth, is "Not I, but Christ in me." To find this alignment is to supplicate oneself to the force of "celestial gravitation" where the personal will follows the dictums of spiritual will:

> The law of terrestrial gravitation, evolution and earthly life in general is *enfoldment*, i.e., the coagulation of mental, psychic and physical stuff around relative centers of gravitation, such as the earth, the nation, the individual, the organism—whilst the law of celestial gravitation, evolution, and spiritual life in general is *radiation*, i.e., the extension of mental, psychic and physical stuff rising up to an absolute center of gravitation. "Then the righteous will

---
5 *Chron.*, p. 212.

shine like the sun in the kingdom of the Father" (Matt. 13:43)—this is a precise and comprehensive characterization of the law of celestial gravitation.[1]

This New Moon calls us to radiate from our innermost center, for in this place of centeredness we will eventually become one with the radiance of the Sun of all Suns at the center of the Milky Way. Enfoldment comes from selfishness just as radiance comes from selflessness. The mantra for Pisces is "Magnanimity becomes Love." We can plant new intentions to love with greater measure under the influences of this New Moon. The Solomon Jesus so loved the Nathan Jesus that he sacrificed his life in order that the mission of Jesus Christ could be accomplished. In the final account it is our ability to love that matters most.

March 31: Sun 16° Pisces. Conception of the Nathan Jesus (Mar/6/2 BC). The Nathan Jesus is the immaculate soul who physically incarnated for the first time as Jesus of Nazareth. It is profound that the birth of the Solomon Jesus and the conception of the Nathan Jesus were so beautifully interwoven in the stars, just as was their interweaving upon the Earth. The Nathan Jesus was a representative of the Indian spiritual stream—in contrast to the Persian spiritual stream of Zarathustra (Solomon Jesus).

> Just as the Solomon Jesus, the reincarnated Zarathustra, was the leader of the "wisdom stream" stemming back to the Persian culture of the Magi, so the Nathan Jesus was the leader of the Hindu spiritual stream exemplified by Krishna in the Bhagavad Gita, the stream that later brought forth the great teacher of compassion, Gautama Buddha. According to Rudolf Steiner, however, whereas the individuality of the Solomon Jesus had incarnated repeatedly, the individuality of the Nathan Jesus had never incarnated before, apart from an "embodiment" in Krishna.[2]

Today we celebrate the conception of this pure and self-sacrificing soul who carried to Earth the holiness of the un-fallen image through which we will restore our fallen likeness.

In July of this year, when the stars fulfill the prophecy of the return of the Kalki (Hindu name) Avatar, there will be a potentization of the Nathan Jesus being, who—as the Avatar Krishna—is revered in heaven as a leading deity in the spiritual stream of humanity.[3]

APRIL 2014

The month begins with the Sun shining forth and amplifying the gifts of Pisces (the Fishes) and shifting into Aries (the Ram) on the 14th, the same day that Pluto stations Retrograde (until turning Direct in late September). The waxing Moon joins Jupiter again in Gemini on the 6th, Mars on the 14th and is Full (i.e., opposite the Sun), on the 15th in Libra. This will be a total lunar eclipse visible over east Australia, the Pacific, and North and South America. As the Moon moves past full, it meets up with Saturn on the 17th visible all evening, beginning about an hour after sunset in the east and crossing the night sky as our earth turns. The 22nd and 23rd bring us the Lyrids Meteor Shower: while only about 20 meteors per hour, they are worth seeking as they can produce bright dust trails. Unfortunately this year, the waxing moon may get in our way. Look toward the constellation of Lyra (the Lyre, which holds the sacred star Vega) after midnight. By the end of the month, the almost-new moon joins Venus in Aquarius on the 25th, while the Sun embraces Mercury in Aries on the 26th (and therefore not visible to the outer eyes). The month concludes with another eclipse at the New Moon—this one an annular solar eclipse in Aries on the 29th.

April 2: Sun conjunct Uranus 17° Pisces. Death of Novalis (1772–1801): the North Node was at this degree when Novalis reentered the spiritual world at his death. He died suddenly at the age of 28 from tuberculosis. His life work as a genius of the Word was evident in his birth chart where the planet Mars

---

1 Anonymous, *Meditations on the Tarot*, p. 314.
2 *Chron.*, p. 62.

3 See Robert Powell's article in this journal.

SIDEREAL GEOCENTRIC LONGITUDES : APRIL 2014 Gregorian at 0 hours UT

DAY	☉	☽	☊	☿	♀	♂	♃	♄	⛢	♆	♇
1 TU	16 ♓ 15	2 ♈ 2	3 ♎ 26R	24 ♒ 14	29 ♑ 58	26 ♍ 55R	16 ♊ 32	27 ♎ 40R	17 ♓ 28	11 ♒ 26	18 ♐ 35
2 WE	17 14	15 34	3 27D	25 48	1 ♒ 0	26 34	16 37	27 38	17 31	11 28	18 36
3 TH	18 14	28 44	3 28	27 23	2 3	26 13	16 42	27 35	17 34	11 30	18 36
4 FR	19 13	11 ♉ 32	3 29	29 0	3 6	25 51	16 47	27 32	17 38	11 31	18 37
5 SA	20 12	24 2	3 30	0 ♓ 38	4 10	25 28	16 53	27 29	17 41	11 33	18 37
6 SU	21 11	6 ♊ 15	3 31	2 17	5 13	25 6	16 58	27 26	17 45	11 35	18 37
7 MO	22 10	18 17	3 31	3 58	6 17	24 43	17 4	27 22	17 48	11 37	18 37
8 TU	23 9	0 ♋ 12	3 31R	5 41	7 21	24 21	17 10	27 19	17 52	11 39	18 38
9 WE	24 8	12 5	3 31	7 24	8 25	23 58	17 16	27 16	17 55	11 41	18 38
10 TH	25 7	24 0	3 30	9 10	9 30	23 35	17 22	27 12	17 58	11 42	18 38
11 FR	26 6	6 ♌ 1	3 29	10 57	10 34	23 12	17 28	27 9	18 2	11 44	18 38
12 SA	27 5	18 12	3 28	12 45	11 39	22 48	17 34	27 5	18 5	11 46	18 38
13 SU	28 4	0 ♍ 36	3 27	14 35	12 44	22 26	17 41	27 2	18 9	11 48	18 38
14 MO	29 2	13 14	3 27	16 26	13 50	22 3	17 48	26 58	18 12	11 49	18 38
15 TU	0 ♈ 1	26 8	3 26	18 19	14 55	21 40	17 54	26 54	18 15	11 51	18 38R
16 WE	1 0	9 ♎ 18	3 26D	20 14	16 1	21 17	18 1	26 50	18 19	11 53	18 38
17 TH	1 59	22 43	3 27	22 10	17 7	20 55	18 9	26 47	18 22	11 54	18 38
18 FR	2 57	6 ♏ 22	3 27	24 7	18 13	20 33	18 16	26 43	18 25	11 56	18 38
19 SA	3 56	20 13	3 27R	26 6	19 19	20 11	18 23	26 39	18 29	11 57	18 38
20 SU	4 54	4 ♐ 13	3 27	28 7	20 25	19 50	18 31	26 35	18 32	11 59	18 38
21 MO	5 53	18 20	3 26	0 ♈ 9	21 32	19 29	18 38	26 31	18 35	12 1	18 38
22 TU	6 52	2 ♑ 31	3 26	2 12	22 38	19 9	18 46	26 27	18 39	12 2	18 37
23 WE	7 50	16 45	3 26D	4 16	23 45	18 48	18 54	26 23	18 42	12 4	18 37
24 TH	8 49	0 ♒ 59	3 26	6 22	24 52	18 29	19 2	26 18	18 45	12 5	18 37
25 FR	9 47	15 9	3 27	8 29	25 59	18 10	19 10	26 14	18 49	12 6	18 37
26 SA	10 45	29 14	3 27	10 36	27 6	17 51	19 19	26 10	18 52	12 8	18 36
27 SU	11 44	13 ♓ 11	3 28	12 44	28 14	17 33	19 27	26 6	18 55	12 9	18 36
28 MO	12 42	26 56	3 28	14 53	29 21	17 16	19 36	26 1	18 58	12 11	18 36
29 TU	13 41	10 ♈ 27	3 28R	17 2	0 ♓ 29	16 59	19 44	25 57	19 1	12 12	18 35
30 WE	14 39	23 43	3 28	19 11	1 36	16 43	19 53	25 53	19 5	12 13	18 35

INGRESSES :

1	♀ → ♒	0:47	20	☿ → ♈	22:18
3	☽ → ♉	2:20	21	☽ → ♑	19:44
4	☿ → ♓	14:49	23	☽ → ♒	22:21
5	☽ → ♊	11:40	26	☽ → ♓	1:18
7	☽ → ♋	23:35	28	☽ → ♈	5:24
10	☽ → ♌	12: 1		♀ → ♓	13:47
12	☽ → ♍	22:51	30	☽ → ♉	11:31
14	☉ → ♈	23:32			
15	☽ → ♎	7: 5			
17	☽ → ♏	12:50			
19	☽ → ♐	16:48			

ASPECTS & ECLIPSES :

1	☽ ☌ ☋	2:27	11	☽ ☍ ♀	9:54		☽ ● T	7:46	22	☽ N ☊	1:32		☽ ☌ ⛢	10: 0
	☉ □ ♃	7:33		☽ ☍ ♆	11:20		☽ ☌ ☊	13:22		☉ □ ☽	7:51	28	☽ ☌ ☋	11:33
2	☉ ☌ ⛢	7: 7	12	♀ ☌ ♆	2:29	16	☿ ☍ ♂	11: 4		☿ ☍ ☊	14:23	29	☉ ● T	6: 3
	☽ ☍ ♄	21:52	13	☉ □ Π	14:58	17	☽ ☌ ♄	7: 8		♂ □ ♃	19: 8		☉ ☌ ☽	6:14
3	☉ □ ♇	9: 9	14	☽ ☍ ☿	7: 2	18	☉ ☍ ☊	12: 5	23	☽ ☌ P	0:35		☽ ☌ ☿	14: 7
6	☽ ☌ ♃	21:32		☽ ☍ ⛢	9:20		☉ □ Π	19:20		♂ ☍ ⛢	6:41	30	☽ ☍ ♄	3:55
7	☽ ☍ ♇	0:40		☽ ☌ ♂	15:58	20	♃ □ ⛢	7:52		♂ □ ♇	13:48			
	☉ □ ☽	8:30		☿ □ ♃	18:22		♃ ☍ ♇	21:58	24	☽ ☌ ♆	18:49			
8	☽ S ☊	6:42		☿ ☌ ⛢	23: 7	21	☽ ☌ ♇	0:30	25	☽ ☌ ♀	20: 2			
	☽ ☌ A	14:53	15	☿ □ ♇	3:59		☽ ☍ ♃	0:31	26	☉ S ☿	3:13			
	☉ ☍ ♂	20:55		☉ ☍ ☽	7:42		⛢ □ ♇	15:34	27	☽ ☍ ♂	7:26			

SIDEREAL HELIOCENTRIC LONGITUDES : APRIL 2014 Gregorian at 0 hours UT

DAY	Sid. Time	☿	♀	⊕	♂	♃	♄	⛢	♆	♇	Vernal Point
1 TU	12:37: 6	26 ♐ 43	4 ♏ 42	16 ♍ 15	20 ♍ 24	27 ♊ 34	23 ♎ 50	17 ♓ 31	10 ♒ 20	16 ♐ 50	5 ♓ 3'40"
2 WE	12:41: 3	29 46	6 17	17 14	20 51	27 39	23 52	17 32	10 20	16 50	5 ♓ 3'40"
3 TH	12:45: 0	2 ♑ 52	7 53	18 14	21 19	27 44	23 54	17 32	10 21	16 51	5 ♓ 3'40"
4 FR	12:48:56	6 1	9 28	19 13	21 46	27 49	23 56	17 33	10 21	16 51	5 ♓ 3'40"
5 SA	12:52:53	9 13	11 4	20 12	22 14	27 53	23 58	17 34	10 22	16 51	5 ♓ 3'40"
6 SU	12:56:49	12 30	12 39	21 11	22 41	27 58	24 0	17 34	10 22	16 52	5 ♓ 3'40"
7 MO	13: 0:46	15 50	14 14	22 10	23 9	28 3	24 2	17 35	10 22	16 52	5 ♓ 3'40"
8 TU	13: 4:42	19 15	15 50	23 9	23 36	28 8	24 3	17 36	10 23	16 52	5 ♓ 3'40"
9 WE	13: 8:39	22 45	17 25	24 8	24 4	28 13	24 5	17 36	10 23	16 52	5 ♓ 3'39"
10 TH	13:12:35	26 20	19 0	25 7	24 32	28 18	24 7	17 37	10 23	16 53	5 ♓ 3'39"
11 FR	13:16:32	0 ♒ 1	20 36	26 6	24 59	28 23	24 9	17 38	10 24	16 53	5 ♓ 3'39"
12 SA	13:20:29	3 48	22 11	27 5	25 27	28 28	24 11	17 38	10 24	16 53	5 ♓ 3'39"
13 SU	13:24:25	7 40	23 46	28 3	25 55	28 33	24 13	17 39	10 24	16 54	5 ♓ 3'39"
14 MO	13:28:22	11 40	25 21	29 2	26 22	28 38	24 15	17 39	10 25	16 54	5 ♓ 3'39"
15 TU	13:32:18	15 46	26 56	0 ♎ 1	26 50	28 43	24 16	17 40	10 25	16 54	5 ♓ 3'39"
16 WE	13:36:15	20 0	28 31	1 0	27 18	28 48	24 18	17 41	10 26	16 55	5 ♓ 3'38"
17 TH	13:40:11	24 22	0 ♐ 7	1 58	27 46	28 53	24 20	17 41	10 26	16 55	5 ♓ 3'38"
18 FR	13:44: 8	28 52	1 42	2 57	28 14	28 58	24 22	17 42	10 26	16 55	5 ♓ 3'38"
19 SA	13:48: 4	3 ♓ 30	3 17	3 56	28 42	29 2	24 24	17 43	10 27	16 56	5 ♓ 3'38"
20 SU	13:52: 1	8 17	4 52	4 54	29 10	29 7	24 26	17 43	10 27	16 56	5 ♓ 3'38"
21 MO	13:55:58	13 12	6 27	5 53	29 38	29 12	24 28	17 44	10 27	16 56	5 ♓ 3'38"
22 TU	13:59:54	18 17	8 2	6 51	0 ♎ 6	29 17	24 29	17 45	10 28	16 57	5 ♓ 3'38"
23 WE	14: 3:51	23 31	9 37	7 50	0 34	29 22	24 31	17 45	10 28	16 57	5 ♓ 3'37"
24 TH	14: 7:47	28 54	11 12	8 48	1 2	29 27	24 33	17 46	10 28	16 57	5 ♓ 3'37"
25 FR	14:11:44	4 ♈ 26	12 47	9 47	1 30	29 32	24 35	17 47	10 29	16 58	5 ♓ 3'37"
26 SA	14:15:40	10 7	14 22	10 45	1 58	29 37	24 37	17 47	10 29	16 58	5 ♓ 3'37"
27 SU	14:19:37	15 56	15 56	11 44	2 26	29 42	24 39	17 48	10 29	16 58	5 ♓ 3'37"
28 MO	14:23:33	21 52	17 01	12 42	2 55	29 47	24 41	17 49	10 30	16 50	5 ♓ 3'37"
29 TU	14:27:30	27 55	19 6	13 40	3 23	29 52	24 43	17 49	10 30	16 59	5 ♓ 3'37"
30 WE	14:31:27	4 ♉ 4	20 41	14 39	3 51	29 57	24 44	17 50	10 31	16 59	5 ♓ 3'36"

INGRESSES :

2	☿ → ♑	1:50
10	☿ → ♒	23:53
14	⊕ → ♎	23:35
16	♀ → ♐	22:20
18	☿ → ♓	5:57
21	♂ → ♎	19: 7
24	☿ → ♈	4:48
29	☿ → ♉	8: 9
30	♃ → ♋	16:47

ASPECTS (HELIOCENTRIC +MOON(TYCHONIC)) :

1	☿ ☍ ♃	6:51	9	♀ △ ⛢	2:50		♀ ⚹ ♂	21:48	21	☿ □ ♇	17:43		☿ △ ♇	4:15
	⊕ □ ♇	14: 9		☿ S ☊	5:27	15	☽ ☌ ♂	1:20		☽ ☍ ♃	18:30		☽ ☌ ⛢	8: 1
2	⊕ ☍ ⛢	7: 7		☿ □ ♄	9: 5		☿ ⚹ ♇	6:30		☿ ☌ ⛢	21:27		♀ ☌ ♇	15:41
	☽ ☍ ♄	15: 5		☿ △ ♂	10: 9	16	☿ △ ♄	23:50	23	♀ ⚹ ♆	13: 1	28	♀ □ ⛢	4:22
3	☽ ☍ ♀	19:31		☿ △ ⊕	12:49	17	☽ ☌ ♄	2:51	24	☿ □ ♃	2:26		☿ ☌ ☊	6:45
4	♀ □ ♆	13:23	10	☽ ☍ ☿	6:45	18	☿ △ ♃	0:31		☿ ☍ ♂	10: 9		☽ ☍ ♂	10:56
6	☿ ⚹ ♀	2:12	11	☽ ☍ ♆	8:40		☿ □ ♀	22:18		☽ ☌ ♆	16: 4		☿ ☍ ♄	11:15
	☽ ☍ ♇	21: 9		♀ ☌ ☋	19:17	19	♂ □ ♃	21:35	25	⊕ △ ♆	17:18	29	☿ ⚹ ♃	7:42
7	☿ ⚹ ⛢	12:22	13	⊕ □ ♃	13: 6	20	☽ ☌ ♀	1:15	26	☿ ⚹ ♆	1:33	30	☽ ☍ ♄	1:51
	☽ ☌ ♃	19:48		☿ ☌ ♆	16:32		♀ ⚹ ⊕	1:41		☿ ☍ ⊕	3:13			
8	⊕ ☌ ♂	20:55	14	☽ ☍ ⛢	8:17		☽ ☌ ♇	21:38	27	☿ △ ♀	0: 4			

(13° Pisces) stood at the Midheaven, close to today's conjunction: "The placement of a planet close to the Ascendant or to the Midheaven often indicates that it is of primary significance in the person's life. The planet Mars, therefore, was extremely important in the life of Novalis, albeit the higher aspect of Mars, which is concerned with the word, since the Mars center in the human being is located in the region of the larynx."[1]

With Sun conjunct Uranus where the portal to the angels opened (north node) at the death of Novalis, we can meditate on the power of the Word, which from out of future's might inspired Novalis after the death of his beloved Sophie, who was thereafter his muse from spiritual realms. Uranus can bring sudden and unexpected change; and when united with the Sun, this change can be infused with the moral forces of the heart, bringing penetrating insights into new imaginations. This was the case for Novalis, whose words were illumined with wisdom. He wrote his *Hymns to the Night* in celebration of the profound understanding he gained through his spiritual perceptions. This being is here with us now:

> Again, Rudolf Steiner gave a clear indication concerning the teacher who would bear the central impulse relating to the unfolding of the Christ impulse during the latter part of the twentieth century. This is revealed in his *Last Address* to members of the Anthroposophical Society, where he said that the individuality of John the Baptist had reincarnated as the German Romantic poet Novalis (1772–1801). Steiner indicated that at the time he was speaking, Michaelmas 1924, the individuality John the Baptist–Novalis was in the spiritual world. However, he hinted that this individuality would be incarnated for the struggle to be fought out in the last part of the century:
>
> > And we see in Novalis a radiant and splendid forerunner of that Michael stream which is now to lead you all, my dear friends, while you live; and then, after you have gone through the gate of death, you will find in the spiritual, supersensible worlds all those others—among them also the being of whom I have been speaking to you today—all those with whom you are to prepare the work that shall be accomplished at the end of the century and that shall lead humankind past the crisis in which it is involved.[2]

It can be a comfort to us that this being in now incarnated and we can turn to this individuality for help in times of trial.

Conversely, Uranus at this degree remembers the Gulag established in Russia in 1930. These prison camps are symbolic of attempts to imprison and break the minds of dissenters. Meanwhile, in Germany, the Hitler Youth movement was establishing branches for boys ages 10 to 14 years and for girls aged 10 to 18 years. These examples are inversions of the freedom in thinking Uranus seeks to ignite.

Venus enters Aquarius: "May what is lacking bounds, establish bounds" (Rudolf Steiner, *Twelve Cosmic Moods*). Venus was in Aquarius at the death of John the Baptist. In our deepest soul we know what is needed to attain our destiny task. It takes discipline to create boundaries, yet it is just this that helps us find the stream of spiritual guidance that is seeking our attention.

April 3: Sun 18° Pisces square Pluto 18° Sagittarius. Pluto at this degree remembers the entire Passion of Christ. With Sun and Pluto square, a tension can develop between revolutionary ideals and the art of compromise. Christ was revolutionary and his conception Sun stood within two degrees of today's Sun, but the spirit of compromise was not granted to him. A tension between love (Pisces) and power (Pluto) is created when we remember the conception of Nathan Jesus and the power mongers who condemned him resulting in his sorrowful Passion. In the higher planes of Phanes this tension brings a deepening and an awakening of intuitive capacities.

April 5: The Sun enters the third decan of Pisces, the Mars decan, associated with the constellation Andromeda, the Chained Woman, who—threatened by the sea monster Cetus from below—was rescued by Perseus.

---

1 Powell, *Elijah Come Again*, p. 38.

2 Powell, *The Most Holy Trinosophia*, pp. 65–66.

April 8: Sun 24° Pisces opposite Mars 24° Virgo. Mars was at this same degree on the third day after Christ arrived at Mt. Attarus to enter his forty days in the wilderness: "During this period he was subjected daily to temptation, but this culminated in three definite temptations toward the end of the forty days. Jesus Christ underwent these temptations—the confrontation with evil—on behalf of the whole of humankind, but especially for those who became his disciples and for the twelve who later became apostles."[3]

Mars represents the astral body, and as we transform our astral bodies we become united with our Angels. In the astral body is the Luciferic double that Tomberg writes about in his *Inner Development* lectures, and in more depth in his *Lord's Prayer Course*. The Luciferic double wants to destroy the continuity of the flow of memory from life to life. The human being's angel is the guardian of this memory. As the astral body redeems its fallen state, it regains this memory. As this occurs one's actions (Mars) reveal that one has become more and more a peacemaker. As one remembers the continuity of memory, one no longer seeks for power from the prince of this world (first temptation), but rather bows in humble modesty before the intelligence revealed in angelic realms of imagination. With Sun opposite Mars we can drink in the loving presence of the Virgin Sophia whose ministrations Mars amplifies when in the constellation of Virgo. This brings joy that elevates the soul:

> Joy is more profound than pleasure. It is still an index, but what it indicates is deeper than the relationship between a desire and the event of its being satisfied. Joy is the state of soul which participates most intensely in life and experiences it in appreciating its value. Joy is the spreading of the soul beyond the limits of conscious awareness. It signifies an augmentation of the soul's vital élan.[4]

In this passage we see the true augmentation that humanity is to develop—augmentation bestowed by uniting with the realities lying beyond the limits of conscious awareness. Behind the augmented realities of technology is the hidden intention of thwarting just what has now become possible from realms of spirit. In the technological augmentation the soul contracts and circles endlessly for its own pleasure:

> Pleasure is therefore most peripheral and superficial on the scale of blessedness. Yet, in the technique of temptation it plays the same role with regard to the soul as doubt does with regard to the spirit. For just as doubt reduces the spirit to impotence, so does pleasure (or sterile enjoyment) reduce the soul to impotence, to a state of passivity. It enslaves it and changes it from the subject into an object of action.[5]

Indeed virtual realities *play the soul,* though the soul is usually unaware of this. This weakens the soul at a time when it can, instead, become strengthened by what is newly developing at this period of our evolution. Ahriman imitates what spirit is bringing and offers humanity a cheap caricature in place of what is noble. When we realize the "game" that is being played at our expense, we are able to turn to the source of joy whereby we soar on wings of spirit into new vistas of imagination. Turning to the augmentation that ennobles the astral body, we begin to grow toward the threshold behind which our angel waits. These thoughts can be our contemplation as we move through the coming days. A still and quiet mind becomes an ocean of light in which higher thoughts are reflected.

April 11: Venus conjunct Neptune 11° Aquarius. Venus represents the etheric body. This was seeded during ancient Sun existence (the second incarnation of our Earth). When we reach future Venus evolution (fifth incarnation of Earth) we will be forming our transfigured etheric body, which is referred to by Steiner as *Buddhi*. In our etheric lives, the second manifestation is the "double." This double is an etheric being that is filled with astrality and is comprised of both luciferic and ahrimanic influences. This double is called the "karmic double," for it accompanies one through all lives until it is cast out and brought under control by the "I." As one strives to cross the threshold, the

---

3 CHA, "The Temptations in the Wilderness."
4 Anonymous, *Meditations on the Tarot*, p. 285.
5 Ibid., p. 285.

Lesser Guardian of the Threshold (Michael) shows this intruder to us and we then battle in order to uncover our resolve to master it. With Venus conjunct Neptune (which in its lower aspect represents Ahriman), we are strengthened to bring love to our selves so as not to be distracted by the self-hatred Ahriman can conjure from within toward the self and others. We can cast the knowing glance to this double who lives in the collective as well as the personal subconscious. Through the discipline of attending what is loving, we open ourselves to Sophia, called in Orphic mythology the *Goddess Night* (higher aspect of Neptune). Sophia guides us, through love, helping us cast out this being.

Heliocentric Venus was at this same degree when Mary Magdalene experienced her second conversion (Dec/26/30). She had been brought by her sister Martha to where Jesus was teaching:

> Many listeners, including Magdalene, were deeply moved by this [Christ's words]. Jesus then spoke the words recorded in Matthew 12:43. Magdalene was truly shocked. Turning to different parts of the crowd, Jesus commanded the devils to depart from all those who sought freedom from their possession. As the devils departed, many, including Mary Magdalene, sunk to the ground. Three times in all, as she took in Jesus's powerful and moving words, Mary Magdalene fell unconscious to the ground. Coming to, after the third occasion, she wept bitterly and asked Martha to bring her to join the holy women.[1]

When we seek to find freedom from possession (the karmic double), it is wise to surround ourselves with others who are doing this work. This is a kind of protection. Another form of protection is practicing meditative verses and sacred prayer eurythmy as offered in Dr. Powell's book entitled *Inner Radiance and the Body of Immortality*. Today's aspect asks us to love ourselves so as not to be afraid of the "thing" in us that is not us, and yet has been created by us. This is the riddle our angel can help us resolve.

April 12: Sun 28. Pisces. Peter receives the keys (Mar/19/31). Four days after the Feeding of the Four Thousand, Jesus and the disciples had withdrawn to a mountain. At dawn, Jesus went to them and asked, "Who do you say that I am?" Peter saw the majesty of Jesus, and proclaimed his divinity by saying, "You are the Messiah, the Son of the living God" (Matt. 16:15–16). Jesus replied:

> Blessed are you, Simon son of Jonah, for this was not revealed to you by flesh and blood, but by my Father in heaven. And I tell you that you are Peter, and on this rock I will build my church, and the gates of Hades will not overcome it. I will give you the keys of the kingdom of heaven; whatever you bind on earth will be bound in heaven, and whatever you loose on earth will be loosed in heaven. (Matt. 16:17–19)

We can only wonder about what has been loosed on Earth because of humanity's failure to hold the gates of Hell in check. In January of 2010 it was Citizens United; in April of 2010, oil was pouring into the waters of the Gulf of Mexico; in April of 2011, radiation from the Fukushima meltdown was pouring into the ocean off the eastern shores of Japan. In 2012 it was laws that breeched the sovereignty of freedom in the U.S. through the National Defense Appropriations Act, the July Aurora Theater shooting, hurricane Sandy, and the Sandy Hook massacre. Last year (2013) is still expressing its history, and as of the date of this commentary (April 2014), many months are yet to come. The keys to the kingdom of Heaven signify the power, drawn from the kingdom of the Father, to be able to hold in check the forces of the underworld arising through the gates of Hell. This realm of Hell is guarded by the "gate" of the first chakra, the Moon chakra. "The two keys laid one over the other form a cross, and it is precisely the sign of the cross to which the Father had lent power to banish the evil forces back into the underworld. This can only be achieved in purity and in faith, qualities which Peter had" (*CHA*, The Transfiguration).

It is time to become like Peter and restore our faith in Christ so that we can hold in check the forces of the underworld. First we face our inner underworld, and only then are we ennobled to serve

---

1 *Chron.*, p. 267.

April 13: Sun 29° Pisces. Triumphant entry into Jerusalem (Mar/19/33). Exactly two years after Peter is given the keys to guard the gates of Hell, he who would pass through the gates of Hell and descend into the underworld, for the salvation of all humanity, entered Jerusalem as the sacrificial lamb. This was two weeks before his Passion and death.

April 14: Sun enters Aries. "Arise, O shining light" (Rudolf Steiner, *Twelve Cosmic Moods*). William Bento illumines this mantra:

> A call is heard as the Sun enters the sign of Aries. It is a call to not merely arise, but to awaken. The Sun effortlessly does this every morning, bestowing light upon us all. Should we not follow the Sun in this way? In the heart of every human being there lives this light that can be made available to others every day. It is our mandate to make it available to all, every day and in every way that aids an awakening to the many miracles that take place daily.

Aries and "The Lamb and his Bride" signify the process of spiritualization (Christ) and interiorization (Sophia). The teachings of Hermes in ancient Egypt contained a pre-Christian understanding of the relationship between the Lamb and his Bride through the mystery teachings of Isis and Osiris. The first decan is ruled by Mars and is associated with the Girdle of Andromeda, symbolizing the power of unity and purity worn by the Mystic Woman representing the soul of humanity.

ASPECT: Mercury conjunct Uranus 18° Pisces (square Jupiter, square Pluto). Uranus and Pluto will be in close square to each other for this entire year. Today this square tightens[2] and Mercury joins Uranus in Pisces, as Jupiter and Pluto oppose each other. Mars completes the cross in the heavens today as it stands approximately within 3° of its exact opposition with Uranus. In short, a cosmic cross stands in the heavens involving Jupiter, Pluto, Uranus/Mercury, and Mars/Moon, revealing a very dynamic set of circumstances.

The first beam of the cross—opposition between Uranus/Mercury and Mars:

> Mercury is remembering Gethsemane, the betrayal by Judas and the trial by Caiaphas. Across the sky, Mars 21° Virgo remembers the start of the forty days.
> The second beam of the cross—opposition between Jupiter and Pluto:
> Jupiter remembers Christ appearing to his disciples after his resurrection; Pluto remembers the entire Passion of Christ.

The last square between Uranus and Pluto was between 1932 and 1934, years ripe with trial in Germany, Russia, and the United States. In 1933 (the mid-point of this square) Christ was appearing in the etheric aura surrounding the Earth and the prophecy of his Second Coming was fulfilling itself, as it continues to do. So too does the prophecy of Rudolf Steiner fulfill itself, for he stated that this would be the year in which the beast would rise from the abyss. This is a day to remember the presence of Christ and call forth the goodness and moral will that serves as an antidote to dark forces that continually strive to obscure this Good News. With tomorrow's total lunar eclipse, these potent memories remain active.

April 15: Full Moon. Sun 0° Aries opposite Moon 0° Libra: Total Lunar Eclipse. This eclipse will be visible in western Asia, most of North America, and the western edge of South America. Today's eclipse occurs where the Moon remembers the dynamic events of the Walking on Water (Moon 0° Libra) and the Baptism in the Jordan (Sun 0° Libra). The miracle of walking on water was the fifth miracle of Christ. In this deed he manifested the victory we will celebrate when we have overcome our "karmic double" that weighs us down and strives to pull us under. The fifth miracle is connected to the fifth chakra—the larynx. This is the chakra where the third petition of the Lord's Prayer eternally sounds into the world: Thy will be done on Earth as it is in Heaven. *Thy will be done* takes us into the realms of the Eternal Apocalypse, which sounds from the astral sheath of the Earth. In this realm

---

2 See William Bento's article in this journal.

the judgment of Christ comes as an awakening force that helps us turn to his will over and above our personal will and/or the will of another who is prophesied will come and must be recognized. Powell addresses these themes in an article entitled *The Second Coming and the Approaching Trial of Humanity*:

> Just as Christ's etheric body is the bearer of the Eternal Gospel mirrored (in part) in the Four Gospels, so Christ's astral body is the bearer of the Eternal Apocalypse, part of which is mirrored in the Apocalypse of St. John (Book of Revelation). There Christ appeared to St. John with "seven stars in His right hand" (Rev. 1:16), symbolizing the seven planetary forces underlying the astral body. The entire symbolism of the Book of Revelation relates to the "night consciousness" that awakens through purification of the astral body, which then is able to enter into communion with Christ's astral body—as exemplified by St. John.
>
> Now, the moment of the baptism in the Jordan can be likened to the conception of Christ, and the resurrection on Easter Sunday morning can be thought of as the moment of birth of the Risen One. By way of analogy, the period from the baptism to the resurrection, which lasted 1290 days, was the embryonic period of the Christ Impulse which has been at work since the Mystery of Golgotha. And just as human destiny unfolds in seven-year periods from the moment of birth onward, so the Christ Impulse is unfolding historically according to a certain rhythm. What is this rhythm?
>
> It is a much longer rhythm than the seven-year rhythm underlying the unfolding of human destiny. Let us recall that there is a correspondence between each 27⅓-day lunar sidereal month of the embryonic period and each seven-year period of human life. Similarly, there is a correspondence between the "embryonic period" of 1290 days of the ministry of Christ and the rhythm underlying the unfolding of the Christ Impulse historically. This correspondence is such that one day of Christ's ministry corresponds to 29½ years historically. Those readers who are familiar with astronomy will recognize here the Saturn rhythm, this being the period required by Saturn to complete one orbit of the sidereal zodiac, just as the Sun's period is one year and Jupiter's period is twelve years. In fact, 29½ years is the rhythm of Christ's astral body.

In this article Dr. Powell goes on to describe the signs of the time of trial. The Beatitude today's Moon calls to mind is the seventh: *Blessed are the peace-makers for theirs is the kingdom of heaven.* For this Beatitude is the antidote to the seventh sub-earthly sphere in which Christ is now working.[1] And the temptation sounding forth from apocalyptic realms is the third: Turning stones to bread. When drones operate as human beings we are seeing the children of corporations in action. Just as a corporation is not a "being," a drone is not a soldier. (See David Tresemer's article in this issue.)

The new definition of "beings" and the mechanizations of warfare are leading us into dark waters. We walk upon these waters when we recall the presence of Christ and align our will with his will, that it be done on Earth as it is willed in Heaven. A choice is before us:

> This is a choice between good and evil, between a spiritual outlook and materialism. In the last analysis it is a question of whether humanity will recognize and choose Christ as the Risen One, who through the Resurrection celebrated the triumph of the spiritual. In the words of Soloviev: "We have only one firm support: the true Resurrection." We know that the struggle between good and evil is being fought; and not only in the soul and in society, but also deeper—in the physical world. And from the past we know already of a victory of the Good—the personal resurrection of One.... The kingdom of God is the kingdom of victorious life, triumphant through the resurrection, and here—in this triumphant life—lies also the true and ultimate good that has to be brought to realization. Herein lies the entire power and the whole work of Christ.[2]

This Full Moon and total lunar eclipse connects us to the astral worlds of the Eternal Apocalypse and the awakening to divine will. Contemplation

---

1 See Powell, *The Christ Mystery*.
2 See Powell "The Second Coming and the Approaching Trial of Humanity."

of the Baptism and the Walking on Water[3] offers countermeasures to certain forces emblematic of a lunar eclipse:

> The other safety valve, the lunar eclipse, exists for the purpose of allowing the evil thoughts that are present in the cosmos to approach those human beings who desire to be possessed by them. In matters of this kind people do not, as a rule, act in full consciousness, but the facts are nevertheless real—just as real as the attraction of a magnet for small particles of iron. Such are the forces at work in the cosmos—forces no less potent than the forces we analyze and investigate today in our chemical laboratories.[4]

Note: On this date last year the Boston marathon bombing occurred. Later that same week shots were fired at a gathering in Denver, Colorado. It is sobering to see that our right to assemble may be dismantled, not by an outer force, but voluntarily from within as the consequence of the fear caused by increasing acts of violence in places where the public assembles. This internalization of tyranny whereby within the inner landscape of the human soul self-restrictions is actioned, is an ingenious victory for the ahrimanic powers.

April 18: Christian Celebration of Good Friday. Commemoration of Christ's Passion and Death on the Cross. The stars and planets, which bore witness to the events of this day, show us the interconnectedness between Heaven and Earth. It is a profound mystery that the seven classical planets rose in their respective order between Thursday night through Friday afternoon: Moon, Venus, Mercury, Sun, Mars, Jupiter and Saturn (See *Chron.*, The Stages of the Passion). This order also reflects the *ascending* order of the chakras. The Moon rose on the evening of the Last Supper, Venus rose at Peter's first denial, Mercury with Peter's second denial. As the Sun rose that morning, judgement was passed on the Son of Man. As Mars rose he was scourged. Jupiter rose as he was crowned with thorns, and as Saturn rose he was carrying the cross up Mt. Calvary. The rising planets were a perfect prophesy for the different stages of the passion. As the Cross was raised upon the hill of Golgotha, Leo was rising—the Lion of Judah, out of unfathomable love and mercy, was hung on a cross between two criminals. It is the star beings working from the constellation of Leo that form the heart as conception begins in a mother's womb. At the crucifixion of Christ, it was the cosmic heart that was being formed—a heart of eternal love and forgiveness. The primal forces of Divine Love rayed forth from the heart of Christ, the Son of God, and the Earth was illumined with grace.

> Hanging there on the holy cross, the crucified Jesus Christ signified the new Tree of Life, raised up for the first time on Earth since the expulsion of man from Paradise. The blood flowed from his wounds for the regeneration of the Earth and humankind, for the restoration of a new paradise, the heavenly Jerusalem—in place of the earthly city of Jerusalem—away from which, facing North-West, his gaze was now directed. Thus he could say to the repentant criminal crucified to his right: "Today you will be with me in Paradise." For, on that Good Friday the new Paradise began, a new afterlife for all who unite themselves with Christ. And the repentant criminal was the first human being to die in proximity to Christ, to be taken up by Christ, since the New Era denoted by the Mystery of Golgotha began.[5]

The death of Jesus on the cross marked the descent of Christ into the underworld. Before he died he was taunted, mocked, and rejected by those he came to redeem. In the subearthly realms, however, he was greeted as the king he truly was. On this Good Friday we remember the Lamb of God who died so that we may find the eternal nourishment of Heaven. It was fulfilled!

April 19: Christian Celebration of Holy Saturday. Holy Saturday—Commemoration of Christ's Descent into Hell. The descent of Christ to the Mother in the heart of the earthly realm was for the redemption of Nature and the entire Earth. In Paradise the kingdom of the Father and the realm of the Mother were interpenetrated. After the Fall,

---

3 See *CHA*.
4 Steiner, *Astronomy and Astrology*, p. 200.
5 *CHA*, "The Mystery of Golgotha."

the two kingdoms fell further and further from each other. Christ descended into the depths of the inner Earth and planted his spirit as a seed in the womb of the Earth. As he began his descent, Virgo was rising in the East. This is the constellation connected to the womb, and to the sowing of seeds that will birth new impulses into the womb of all creation (see *CHA*, The Mystery of Golgotha):

> The descent into Hell fulfilled the sixth stage of the Passion. In Hell Christ encountered the Antichrist: The power of the Antichrist is, or is almost, equal to that of Christ. The feather that tips the balance is the powerlessness Christ voluntarily takes upon himself in his self-sacrificing deed; and this powerlessness, of which the Antichrist is incapable, ultimately leads to the hair's breadth more power that Christ possesses.[1]

It is incumbent upon each of us to render the Antichrist powerless—through recognizing and resisting his presence in the world. For if left unnamed, this presence causes fear, uncertainty, and denial that such a force even exists. The presence of the Antichrist leads people to seek worldly power and worldly things in a vain attempt to out-run their fear. Avoidance, however, does not work; instead it divides people and sets each against the other through wars and other inequities. In "powerlessness" we stand together with Christ, and thereby bring the strength of love and courage that pushes fear into the underworld from whence it came.

Sun 4° Aries: Woe Upon the Pharisees: (24/Mar/33). In this address to the crowds and disciples, Jesus Christ threw down the gauntlet before the Pharisees (Matt. 23:2–39). Powerful words echo from this "woe" into our own time. The powerful princes of the material world have nothing but loathing for anything spiritual, and these words from Matthew are words to all that is vainglorious. Jesus, before the Pharisees had gathered around him, had been teaching his disciples of humility, giving these instructions: "They should never boast: 'I have driven out devils in your name!' or 'I have done this and that!' Also, they should not carry out their work publicly" (*Chron.*, p. 345). The moment we forget humility we are vulnerable to inflation, as were the Pharisees. In the seventh Arcanum of *Meditations on the Tarot*, the Chariot, the unknown author speaks of the danger of the fourth temptation—the temptation to come in one's own name—which is the subtlest temptation of all. He calls this "inflation"—a condition fraught with risk. "Here, then, are the principal dangers of inflation: exaggerated importance attached to oneself, superiority complex tending toward obsession and, lastly, megalomania. The first degree signifies a practical task for work upon oneself; the second degree is a serious trial; whilst the third is a catastrophe."[2] It is also interesting to note that in this Arcanum reversed inflation is described as negation of the self.

Today we can focus on humility, which from one perspective can be summarized as being *all* that we are and *nothing* that we are not.

April 20: Christian celebration of Easter Sunday. The spiritual worlds held their breath at the descent of Christ into Hell. A world unknown to the higher hierarchies was being penetrated by Jesus Christ:

> The "gardener" who appeared to the woman made clairvoyant by grief was not a "gardener" from only her perspective. In a deeper sense, he was truly a gardener, because he had acquired the power to cause the Earth's soil to produce the fruits of goodness. From that time forward, the highest human initiates have likewise become "gardeners"; they work for the well-being of humanity—and not just the direct concerns of humanity, but also those that reach indirectly through nature and Earth's soil.[3]

What now occurred was the Resurrection of our Savior and this takes place as a real rhythm of the Earth and as a spiritual power, creating substance every Sunday anew in every single human being. At this moment the Savior of the world revealed the whole immeasurable grandeur of his love to the world with which he had completely united himself, as well as with the human beings living on it. At this moment, as the Christ Spirit arises from the grave in the first

---

1 Von Halle, *Descent into the Depths of the Earth*, p. 108.

2 Anonymous, *Meditations on the Tarot*, p. 153.

3 Tomberg, *Christ and Sophia*, p. 299.

Resurrection body, he merges into the innermost heart of every human soul. It is now up to us in humility, in devotion and in joy, to celebrate daily this inner core of holiness by becoming aware that we ourselves bear him—the highest and most precious—in us.[4]

Today we celebrate the Risen One and the work of his "gardeners," as we remember the Sabbath and keep it holy—for the Sabbath Sunday is a day to rest from the toil of daily life, in memory of spiritual worlds and spiritual beings. The fact that materialistic culture has intruded upon this holy day of rest does not mean we need comply.

Sun 6° Aries: Jesus speaks of his Second Coming (Mar/26/33).

> Watch out that no one deceives you. For many will come in my name, claiming, "I am the Messiah," and will deceive many. You will hear of wars and rumors of wars, but see to it that you are not alarmed. Such things must happen, but the end is still to come. Nation will rise against nation, and kingdom against kingdom. There will be famines and earthquakes in various places. All these are the beginning of birth pains.
>
> Then you will be handed over to be persecuted and put to death, and you will be hated by all nations because of me. At that time many will turn away from the faith and will betray and hate each other, and many false prophets will appear and deceive many people. Because of the increase of wickedness, the love of most will grow cold. (Matt. 24:4–12)

We are living in a "New Age." This is an expression first used by Rudolf Steiner to describe the time of the Second Coming of Christ. We cannot attribute a time or place for the beginning of this Age, any more than we can appoint a certain leader or sect as its inaugurator. It has been called an inevitable evolutionary leap that cannot be silenced. It seems to be something that cannot stop happening. This shift is a great threat to those who wield power *over* others. The prophet Daniel saw that there would be teachers who would understand the times and preach the kingdom as a witness unto all nations. "Those who are wise shall shine like the brightness of the heavens, and those who lead many to righteousness, like the stars for ever and ever" (Daniel 12:3).

We are to know we are in changing times and we are to seek the righteous prophets of our age, whose light ennobles others in order to unify people toward a single ideal: Love. With Sun in Aries, idealism engenders devotion. While the world lowers the bar in order to avoid guilt and maintain comfort, the righteous are to keep the bar high and ever strive to achieve the ideals sounding from the one heart—the heart of eternal love and devotion that beats in harmony with the mission of Earth and humanity.

ASPECT: Jupiter 18° Gemini square Uranus 18° Pisces opposite Pluto 18° Sagittarius. Again we encounter the cosmic cross between Uranus and Pluto involving Jupiter. (See commentary for April 14.) Over the period of the next few days this cosmic cross will reach its exact oppositions and squares. The influence from this aspect can be felt long after its exactitude. In a certain sense, the entire year is an expression of the Uranus/Pluto square and the next month an expression of the Jupiter/Pluto opposition.

April 21: Uranus 18° Pisces square Pluto 18° Sagittarius. Today there is an exact square between these two planets. Pluto, in opposition to its position today (18° Gemini), recalls the Hamburg Uprising. This was an insurrection that began in October 1923 during the Weimar Republic in Germany. Hyperinflation was at its peak and a series of nationwide strikes against Chancellor Willhelm Cuno had taken place. In the words of historian Peter Schwarz:

> But the workers were not the only ones ruined by hyperinflation. Those living on a pension lost all means of subsistence. Those who had saved some money lost everything overnight. In order to survive, many had to sell their house, their jewelry and everything else they had saved in the course of their lives—only to find out the next day that the revenue was worthless.

Arthur Rosenberg, who wrote the first authoritative history of the Weimar Republic in 1928, states: "The systematic expropriation

---

4 Von Halle, *And If He Had Not Been Raised*, p. 127.

of the German middle classes, not by a socialist government but in a bourgeois state dedicated to the defense of private property, was one of the biggest robberies in world history" (Arthur Rosenberg, *Entstehung und Geschichte der Weimarer Republik*).

On the other side of the social gap there was a group of speculators, profiteers, and industrialists who made a fortune out of inflation. Whoever had access to foreign currency or gold was able to export German commodities abroad and reap super-profits due to the low wages. These were the forces behind the Cuno government. The most famous of them was Hugo Stinnes, who bought 1,300 factories and made billions in this period. He was also a major political operator behind the scenes.

The social polarization and the collapse of the middle classes brought about a sharp political polarization.[1]

The author of the preceding text goes on to state that the far-reaching implications of this uprising eventually led to the fateful events that culminated in the coming to power of Hitler and strengthened the rise of Stalinist bureaucracy. It is important for us all to understand historic precedents as we navigate through the economic, political, and social upheavals of our time. With Pluto remembering the Passion of Christ, our path forward is clearly one of confronting evil forces that lead to revolutions and tyranny before they become unstoppable. Christ did not shy away from Ahriman but instead found his strength to endure extraordinary trial by aligning his will with the will of his Father in Heaven.

April 22: Mars 18° Virgo square Jupiter 18° Gemini. The Cosmic Cross continues to stand in the heavens as the four planets (Pluto opposite Jupiter; and Mars opposite Uranus) bring this cross into form. It is the square between Mars and Jupiter that today is exact. Heliocentric Mars was here at both the second and third temptations of Christ in the wilderness. Jupiter was here as Christ appeared to his disciples after his resurrection. With the planet of cosmic wisdom (Jupiter) in square to Mars remembering the second and third temptations, a dynamic

---

[1] See the article by Peter Schwartz, "The German October: The Missed Revolution of 1923."

tension expresses itself. World events will help us understand which octave of possibilities humanity will manifest. A square between Jupiter and Mars can bring inclinations of extremism, fanaticism, and a lack of moderation. On the other hand we have the memory of Christ in the wilderness, victorious over the forces of evil. This victory leads to self-sacrifice on behalf of the greater community, as was exemplified in the entire life of Christ. We can send love into our global community and into the interior of the Earth, thus sending our blessings to the heights and the depths along with the prayer that the Words (Mars) of peace and justice fill our communities (Jupiter) and the world with good will.

April 23: Mars 18° Virgo square Pluto 18° Sagittarius and Mars opposite Uranus 18° Pisces are exact today. The cross continues to sound through the stars today with exact alignments to the influences we have been referencing since the 14th of this month. Pluto is within two degrees of where it was during the Passion, Resurrection, Ascension, and Pentecost. Strong memories are kindled with the Cosmic Word (Mars) squaring these memories and square to Uranus, which in its highest aspects brings illumination, new revelation, and futuristic direction. A World Pentecost is upon us as one aspect of the Second Coming of Christ:

> Expressed in a positive way, we have to raise our level of vibration in order to come into and receive the approaching wave of Divine Love. Let us remember that this is an event that is happening on a global scale. Throughout the whole world human beings have to come to terms with the shadow, the lower side of human nature, and at least begin to work upon transforming the negative into something positive. Hence the importance of knowing the deeper level of significance of the year 2012. This also helps us to understand why some people write of 2012 as a kind of "stepping into paradise," because in a certain respect—at least, potentially—this is true. It also helps us understand why others write of tremendous catastrophes associated with the end date of the Maya calendar in 2012, which could also be true if humanity does not prepare to receive the great wave of Divine Love, preparation for which entails undergoing

purification. Purification can be undertaken voluntarily. On the other hand, catastrophe brings with it the necessity of new orientation and, correspondingly, purification.[2]

Since December of 2012 a new paradigm is striving to be born. It will have its adversaries, but we are called to focus on the positive signs and there direct our will. Active participation is called for. We can contemplate what today we can contribute to world wellness.

April 24: Sun 10° Aries. The Visitation (Mar/30/2 BC). The Nathan Mary, pregnant with Jesus, visited her cousin Elizabeth, who was pregnant with John the Baptist. During that meeting all four of them were filled with holy awe as the Old Adam, John the Baptist in Elizabeth's womb was quickened by the presence of the New Adam, the Jesus child in Mary's womb. Rudolf Steiner describes how an "I" like that of John's was directly guided by the great mother lodge of humanity, the center of spiritual life on Earth. Both the John-I and the soul of the Luke Jesus originated in this mystery center, although the qualities Jesus received were not yet pervaded by the egoistic "I"—for, the being guided toward incarnation as the New Adam was a young soul.

> The reality of this situation, strange as it may seem, was that the great mother lodge sent out a soul unaccompanied by an actual developed "I," for the same "I" that was reserved for the Jesus of the Luke Gospel was bestowed on the body of John the Baptist, and these two elements—the soul being that lived in the Luke Jesus and the "I" that lived in the Baptist—were intimately related from the very beginning.[3]

The great mystery of the Visitation is the mystery of how the old Adam—who fell from Paradise—is visited by the New Adam, the being holding the forces of purity and love held back at the time of the Fall. The celestial part of John approached him from without, as the child in Mary's womb. Through the immaculate Jesus being, John was enabled to take hold of his incarnation in spite of the conditions on Earth at that time. Through the Jesus child he was quickened to take up his destiny as the forerunner of Christ. This Visitation points us to the fact of heredity becoming subservient to destiny forces in-streaming from Christ. What John experienced at the Visitation is now possible for each human being. Our higher Christ-imbued self shall quicken our lower "I" just as the Jesus child quickened the John child. The Sun today remembers the reunion between the lower and higher self.

This is a good day to serve the quickening in others. Through questions we can ask today, may we practice the art of drawing forth the higher in others.

Sun enters the second decan of Aries, ruled by the Sun. This decan is associated with Cassiopeia, the Enthroned Woman, a figure of matchless beauty called "the daughter of splendor" or the "glorified woman clothed with the Sun."

April 25: Superior conjunction Sun and Mercury 11° Aries. Mercury was here at the Transfiguration and the Sun was here just before the Last Anointing, which is remembered tomorrow. The Sun asks Mercury to gather intuitions of revelation—as is the case in superior conjunctions, when Mercury is on the far side of the Sun; and Mercury shares with the Sun what has thus been gathered. As Sun and Mercury remember respectively the last anointing and the transfiguration, we can imagine our minds receiving revelation that assists us in our inner work of transforming our astral drives and desires into selfless service to the ideals streaming to humanity from the future. At the last anointing by Magdalene, she played the part of a mediator between heaven and earth, through which sacred messages came into time:

> Magdalene was in line with a force radiating from the heavens and directing it into the body of Jesus Christ. At the same time she was somehow directing certain symbols into his body through the light center at the crown of his head.
>
> I could see the symbols. They were golden and shining. They were symbolic keys to a spiritual script. The beings of the cosmos were working through her to bless him. At that moment she was acting as priestess, directed in her

---

2 Powell, *2012 and World Pentecost*.
3 Steiner, *According to Luke*, p. 112.

ministrations by spiritual beings. Seen spiritually, Magdalene was like a fiery, brilliant rose-red angel. Her presence was suffused with great power, augmented now by that instreaming from the spiritual world.[1]

Steiner speaks of the symbols of the Rosicrucians, noting that they were messages of high teachings from the stars: "The [Rosicrucian] brothers whose destiny it was to bring the symbols from the spiritual worlds could only transcribe them and say, when they returned again into their ordinary consciousness, 'We have been among the stars and among the spirits of the stars, and have found the old teachers of the esoteric knowledge.'"[2]

Receiving esoteric teachings involves a mastery with symbols, for the highest revelation is expressed most genuinely when clothed in symbols. At the last anointing, the contemporary seer (quoted above) witnesses the descent of revelation in symbol, as Christ —meaning *anointed one*—is being recognized, by Magdalene as the High Priest he was. Witness to this anointing was Judas, the one who would later betray him. Judas was greatly agitated by this deed of Magdalene, and because of this deed the demons in him rallied him to set the betrayal in motion. Christ was becoming reviled and hated by the spirit of Ahriman, who peered at him through the eyes of Judas.

Moon conjunct Venus.

April 26: Sun 12° Aries. Cosmic memory of The Last Anointing (Apr/1/33). Mary Magdalene's last anointing of Christ set the betrayal by Judas in motion. "Truly I tell you, wherever this gospel is preached throughout the world, what she has done will also be told, in memory of her" (Matt. 26:13). Magdalene's devotional understanding stands in opposition to Judas's inability to see what was right before him—Christ. It takes courage to represent the new in the face of those muttering against its possibility, as Judas muttered against Magdalene. Now Christ is present in the etheric realms surrounding the Earth; he is with us. Will we know him? Are we Judas—or Magdalene?

April 28: Sun 13° Aries. Cosmic memory of the Last Supper through the Nailing on the Cross (Apr/2–3/33). The Sun today remembers the most wretched moments in the life of Christ up to his final victory on the hill of Golgotha. All that Christ then *experienced from* humanity, allows him to *give to* humanity now. The deeds done to him during the Passion created the opening in the laws of karma that allows him now, in this time of the Second Coming, to spiritually touch us. Christ gives all his love to humanity, as humanity once gave all of its hatred to him. Each step of the way must be contemplated as the greatest mystery of Earth evolution. The Passion of Christ is the path of the initiate. We may pray for the strength to willingly carry the cross of our own burdens, for this lightens the Cross of Christ. In the words of Judith von Halle:

> There can be no fantasy or even wish on the part of the spiritual pupil of entering upon a path of cognition that would be broad and well trodden, easy and without effort. The path of cognition that one takes is one's own. Hence no one has entered upon it before. At the beginning of the journey, at the time of one's decision to commit, it actually does not exist at all. It is one's task to direct oneself through the morass of one's soul urgings, and to direct one's I through the "soul emptiness of space," through the "destruction of time."[3]

The sacred freedom that Christ brought to all humanity is a force of guidance directing each of us to find our *own way*, upon *our own untrodden path*, to realize *our own initiation*. This demands sobering sanctification for the preservation of free impulses as intended by Rudolf Steiner, in devotion to his founding of the School for Spiritual Science. He could only have founded this school as an affirmation for the necessity of independent research. This is the sacred ground upon which Anthroposophy has been founded.

April 29: ASPECT: New Moon and Annular Solar Eclipse 14° Aries. This eclipse will be visible in Asia, Australia, the Pacific, Indian Ocean, and Antarctica. The Crucifixion of Christ (Apr/3/33). The narrow

---

1 Isaacson, *Through the Eyes of Mary Magdalene*, pp. 96–97.
2 Steiner, *The Secret Stream*, p. 221.
3 Von Halle, *The Descent into the Depths of the Earth*, p. 20.

way of the cross is the way of initiation that each of us will eventually encounter. When the two beams of the cross we carry—the bright spirit cross and the dark earth cross—unite without a splinter of light showing between them, then we have entered the stage of crucifixion. Tomberg describes this as a moment when "personal consciousness becomes a single point that collects its whole force, and from that it is poured into the cross. It dies by becoming a cross itself; it no longer carries the cross, but unites with the human spirit and body. Thus its "spiritual duty," or higher human being, becomes flesh and blood; the human blood system becomes the organ of spiritual truth."[4] Tomberg goes on to describe the meaning of the words *Today you shall be with me in Paradise* as an expression of complete and true *presence* with and in Christ, and like the criminal to the left we experience guilt as we look upon the crucifixion of innocence:

> This "looking on the innocent" is the essence of meeting the Greater Guardian of the Threshold as the crucified conscience of the world. This meeting is, at the same time, the experience of the reality of the presence, the reality of "today in paradise."
>
> The "today" experienced in paradise is the present awaking of conscience to a sense of human responsibility for the whole past and future. The conscience, as a present knowing of the past and the future, is the "great secret of initiation" that can never be betrayed. It cannot be betrayed because it cannot be expressed; it is absolutely incommunicable, whether in human language, that of suprasensory thought transference, or through signs and symbols. That "today" can rise only as a soul experience. It cannot in any way be given by a teacher. Consequently, the purpose of Christian Rosicrucian teachers is limited to helping students find a direction leading to this experience; the actual experience and the progression toward that goal must be left to the student. Rosicrucian students must live through this experience alone, just as they must pass through the gate of death alone.[5]

---

4 Tomberg, *Christ and Sophia*, p. 285.
5 Ibid., pp. 285–286.

The mystery of the proclaimer of the Etheric Christ is here touched upon. Steiner called Tomberg the *actual* proclaimer and yet in *Meditations on the Tarot*, his anonymously written magnum opus, there is no mention of the Etheric Christ. Tomberg instead set out a course for moral-spiritual development that would lead human beings to their *own* inner recognition of the Christ in the etheric. This can only be proclaimed from within. Tomberg gave the schooling necessary for the students of Rosicrucianism in the twentieth and twenty-first centuries. This mighty deed has unfortunately gone unnoticed by many, and therefore the mission of Tomberg has been seriously misunderstood.

In these same lectures, Tomberg goes on to write of the encounter with the Lesser Guardian of the Threshold that meets us at this stage of initiation, and how Plato spoke of the "crucified world soul." The soul of the world will be on this cosmic cross until we, through our own volition, take up the weight that is ours to bear. After taking up our personal cross, we then take up the cross on behalf of others, and on behalf of nature. As today the Moon eclipses the Sun at the memory of the crucifixion, we can contemplate the cross of innocence and the love of Christ that streams now from this profound degree of the zodiac.

Venus enters Pisces: "In winning may gain be lost" (Rudolf Steiner, *Twelve Cosmic Moods*). Venus was in Pisces throughout the entire Passion of Christ. We must lose ourselves in gain so that we may continue to grow. If we attach to gain, we attach to the temporal and thereby sacrifice our willingness to be one with the flowing stream of eternal growth.

April 30: Sun 15° Aries. Cosmic memory of the Descent into Hell. (See entry for April 19.)

Sun 15 1/2° Aries. Resurrection (Apr/5/33). The depth of this mystery holds the promise that each human being may become a Christ Bearer. The words of the Risen Christ, to Mary Magdalene, sound throughout time: "Do not hold on to me, for I have not yet ascended to the Father. Go instead to my brothers and tell them, 'I am ascending to my Father and your Father, to my God and your God'" (John 20:17). These words contain the powerful fact that Christ, following his descent to the Mother on Holy Saturday, would then, following the Resurrection, ascend to his Father, thereby restoring the unity between the Mother in the depths and the Father in the heights. The coming Ascension (forty days from now) was a deed that would also unite fallen humanity with its divine archetype—an archetype sacrificed at the time of the Fall. From the moment of the Resurrection onward he has been within us. This eternal oneness with Christ interconnects the whole of humanity into brother- and sisterhood. The actual awakening of the disciples to the reality of this oneness came only later at the Holy Whitsun Festival. During the forty days between the Resurrection and the Ascension, the disciples were in a kind of sleep. Images from their daily life with Christ during his three and one half years on Earth rose into their consciousness (etheric images). These images helped them understand the cosmic teachings Christ was giving during these forty days after the Resurrection. It is just these cosmic teachings that were culled from mainstream Christianity, and these cosmic teaching are resurrecting in this time of the Second Coming through great teachers now working with us.

Valentin Tomberg, in his summary of the last four stages of the Passion brought the image of the Rose Cross:

> This picture is the Rose Cross, which epitomizes not only the higher stages of the Passion but also, in fact, the whole path of Christian initiation. It is the symbol of the narrow way of sacrifice and the forces of resurrection that flower on this path. Death and resurrection are the two fundamental themes of the Christian spiritual path, and the two are united in the symbol of the Rose Cross.
>
> Thus the black cross with the glowing red roses can summarize all we have said here about Christian initiation; it can stand, if only for a moment, before the inner eye of the reader's soul as a token of the solemn spirit world and, at the same time, as the author's Easter greeting to his readers.[1]

MAY 2014

We begin May with the Sun in the constellation of Aries (the Ram), shifting into Taurus (the Bull) on the 15th /16th. Mars and Saturn are still moving Retrograde in Virgo and Libra, respectively. They are easily visible in the night sky, along with Jupiter in Gemini who is joined by the waxing moon on the 4th. The 5th and 6th are the peak of the Eta Aquarids Meteor Shower, with up to 30 meteors per hour. The Moon should set just after midnight, leaving dark skies for viewing. Look eastward toward the constellation of Aquarius (the Water-Carrier). The Moon can be seen joining Mars in Virgo on the 11th and Saturn in Libra on the 14th which is also the Full Moon. Mars stations Direct on the 21st halfway through Virgo. The waning Moon swings past Venus in Pisces on the 25th on her way to the New Moon in Taurus on the 28th and ends the month as a just barely-there crescent with Mercury on the 30th in Gemini (the Twins).

May 2: Sun 17° Aries. Appearance in Emmaus (Apr/6/33). These days, following the Resurrection, specifically mark the communion of the disciples and holy women with the resurrection body of Christ. There are several different kinds of communion with Christ, of which four are primary:

1. Communion with Christ's physical body—Bread (resurrection body/forty-days)
2. Communion with Christ's "I"—Wine (descent into hell)
3. Communion with Christ's etheric body—the Eternal Gospel (Life Tableau of Christ)
4. Communion with Christ's astral body—the Eternal Apocalypse (Book of Revelation is a portion of this body)[2]

The day after the Resurrection, Luke and Cleophas were traveling to Emmaus when suddenly a third person joined them. That evening the three went to a guesthouse, where they were served food. The third person took the bread, blessed it and broke it into small pieces. Through this act

---

1 Tomberg, *Christ and Sophia*, p. 290.

2 CHA, "The Forty Days After the Mystery of Golgotha."

SIDEREAL GEOCENTRIC LONGITUDES : MAY 2014 Gregorian at 0 hours UT

DAY	☉	☽	☊	☿	♀	♂	♃	♄	♅	♆	♇
1 TH	15 ♈ 37	6 ♉ 43	3 ♎ 27R	21 ♈ 20	2 ♓ 44	16 ♍ 28R	20 ♊ 2	25 ♎ 48R	19 ♓ 8	12 ♒ 14	18 ♐ 34R
2 FR	16 35	19 26	3 25	23 28	3 52	16 14	20 11	25 44	19 11	12 16	18 34
3 SA	17 34	1 ♊ 53	3 23	25 35	5 0	16 0	20 20	25 39	19 14	12 17	18 33
4 SU	18 32	14 6	3 21	27 42	6 8	15 47	20 29	25 35	19 17	12 18	18 33
5 MO	19 30	26 9	3 19	29 46	7 17	15 34	20 39	25 30	19 20	12 19	18 32
6 TU	20 28	8 ♋ 5	3 18	1 ♉ 49	8 25	15 23	20 48	25 26	19 23	12 20	18 32
7 WE	21 26	19 58	3 18	3 50	9 33	15 12	20 58	25 21	19 26	12 21	18 31
8 TH	22 24	1 ♌ 53	3 18D	5 49	10 42	15 2	21 7	25 17	19 29	12 22	18 30
9 FR	23 22	13 54	3 19	7 45	11 50	14 53	21 17	25 12	19 32	12 23	18 30
10 SA	24 20	26 6	3 20	9 39	12 59	14 45	21 27	25 8	19 35	12 24	18 29
11 SU	25 18	8 ♍ 34	3 22	11 29	14 8	14 37	21 37	25 3	19 38	12 25	18 28
12 MO	26 16	21 20	3 23	13 17	15 17	14 30	21 47	24 59	19 41	12 26	18 27
13 TU	27 14	4 ♎ 27	3 23R	15 1	16 26	14 24	21 57	24 54	19 44	12 27	18 27
14 WE	28 12	17 55	3 23	16 43	17 35	14 19	22 7	24 50	19 47	12 28	18 26
15 TH	29 10	1 ♏ 44	3 21	18 21	18 44	14 15	22 18	24 45	19 50	12 29	18 25
16 FR	0 ♉ 8	15 50	3 18	19 55	19 53	14 11	22 28	24 41	19 52	12 30	18 24
17 SA	1 6	0 ♐ 9	3 14	21 26	21 2	14 9	22 39	24 36	19 55	12 31	18 23
18 SU	2 3	14 35	3 10	22 54	22 12	14 7	22 49	24 32	19 58	12 31	18 22
19 MO	3 1	29 4	3 7	24 18	23 21	14 6	23 0	24 28	20 1	12 32	18 21
20 TU	3 59	13 ♑ 30	3 4	25 38	24 30	14 5	23 11	24 23	20 3	12 33	18 20
21 WE	4 57	27 48	3 2	26 54	25 40	14 5D	23 22	24 19	20 6	12 33	18 19
22 TH	5 54	11 ♒ 56	3 2D	28 7	26 50	14 7	23 33	24 14	20 9	12 34	18 18
23 FR	6 52	25 52	3 3	29 16	27 59	14 8	23 44	24 10	20 11	12 35	18 17
24 SA	7 50	9 ♓ 37	3 5	0 ♊ 21	29 9	14 11	23 55	24 6	20 14	12 35	18 16
25 SU	8 48	23 9	3 6	1 23	0 ♈ 19	14 14	24 6	24 1	20 16	12 36	18 15
26 MO	9 45	6 ♈ 28	3 6R	2 20	1 29	14 18	24 17	23 57	20 19	12 36	18 14
27 TU	10 43	19 36	3 5	3 13	2 39	14 23	24 29	23 53	20 21	12 37	18 13
28 WE	11 40	2 ♉ 31	3 2	4 3	3 49	14 29	24 40	23 49	20 24	12 37	18 12
29 TH	12 38	15 14	2 57	4 48	4 59	14 35	24 51	23 44	20 26	12 37	18 11
30 FR	13 36	27 45	2 50	5 28	6 9	14 42	25 3	23 40	20 29	12 38	18 10
31 SA	14 33	10 ♊ 4	2 43	6 5	7 19	14 49	25 15	23 36	20 31	12 38	18 8

INGRESSES :

2	☽ → ♊	20:20	23	☽ → ♓	7:10
5	☿ → ♉	2:38		☿ → ♊	15:55
	☽ → ♋	7:43	24	♀ → ♈	17:28
7	☽ → ♌	20:13	25	☽ → ♈	12:18
10	☽ → ♍	7:33	27	☽ → ♉	19:18
12	☽ → ♎	15:55	30	☽ → ♊	4:22
14	☽ → ♏	21: 1			
15	☉ → ♉	20:44			
16	☽ → ♐	23:45			
19	☽ → ♑	1:32			
21	☽ → ♒	3:43			

ASPECTS & ECLIPSES :

3	☿ ☍ ♄	0:42		☽ ☍ ♀	11:34		☽ ☍ ♃	13:48	28	☉ ☌ ☽	18:39
	☉ □ Π	10:23		☿ □ ♆	12:30		♀ □ ♃	15:28		☉ □ ♆	23:43
4	☽ ☍ ♇	8:48		☽ ☍ ♅	20:55	19	☽ N□ ☊	6:41	30	☽ ☌ ☿	15:48
	☽ ☌ ♃	12:50	12	☽ ☌ ☊	22: 4	21	☉ □ ☽	12:58	31	☽ ☍ ♇	15:53
5	☽ □S ☊	14:22	14	☽ ☌ ♄	12: 0	22	☽ ☌ ♆	1: 4			
6	☽ ☌ A	10:17		♀ □ ♇	17:32	24	☽ ☍ ♂	8: 5			
7	☉ □ ☽	3:14		☉ ☍ ☽	19:15		☽ ☌ ♅	18:51			
8	☽ ☍ ♆	21: 0	15	♀ ☌ ♅	23:49	25	☽ ☌ ♀	14: 6			
10	☉ ☍ ♄	18:14	16	☽ ☍ ☿	7:43		☽ ☌ ☋	17:54			
11	♀ ☍ ♂	9:17	18	☽ ☌ ♇	6:15	27	☽ ☍ ♄	7:52			
	☽ ☌ ♂	11:21		☽ ☌ P	11:45		♀ ☍ ☊	8:36			

SIDEREAL HELIOCENTRIC LONGITUDES : MAY 2014 Gregorian at 0 hours UT

DAY	Sid. Time	☿	♀	⊕	♂	♃	♄	♅	♆	♇	Vernal Point
1 TH	14:35:23	10 ♉ 18	22 ♐ 16	15 ♎ 37	4 ♎ 19	0 ♋ 1	24 ♎ 46	17 ♓ 50	10 ♒ 31	17 ♐ 0	5 ♓ 3'36"
2 FR	14:39:20	16 35	23 51	16 35	4 48	0 6	24 48	17 51	10 31	17 0	5 ♓ 3'36"
3 SA	14:43:16	22 53	25 26	17 34	5 16	0 11	24 50	17 52	10 32	17 0	5 ♓ 3'36"
4 SU	14:47:13	29 13	27 1	18 32	5 45	0 16	24 52	17 52	10 32	17 1	5 ♓ 3'36"
5 MO	14:51: 9	5 ♊ 31	28 35	19 30	6 13	0 21	24 54	17 53	10 32	17 1	5 ♓ 3'36"
6 TU	14:55: 6	11 47	0 ♑ 10	20 28	6 42	0 26	24 56	17 54	10 33	17 1	5 ♓ 3'36"
7 WE	14:59: 2	17 58	1 45	21 26	7 10	0 31	24 57	17 54	10 33	17 2	5 ♓ 3'36"
8 TH	15: 2:59	24 5	3 20	22 24	7 39	0 36	24 59	17 55	10 33	17 2	5 ♓ 3'35"
9 FR	15: 6:56	0 ♋ 5	4 55	23 22	8 8	0 41	25 1	17 56	10 34	17 2	5 ♓ 3'35"
10 SA	15:10:52	5 57	6 30	24 20	8 36	0 46	25 3	17 56	10 34	17 3	5 ♓ 3'35"
11 SU	15:14:49	11 41	8 5	25 18	9 5	0 51	25 5	17 57	10 35	17 3	5 ♓ 3'35"
12 MO	15:18:45	17 16	9 39	26 16	9 34	0 55	25 7	17 58	10 35	17 3	5 ♓ 3'35"
13 TU	15:22:42	22 42	11 14	27 14	10 3	1 0	25 9	17 58	10 35	17 3	5 ♓ 3'35"
14 WE	15:26:38	27 58	12 49	28 12	10 31	1 5	25 10	17 59	10 36	17 4	5 ♓ 3'35"
15 TH	15:30:35	3 ♌ 5	14 24	29 10	11 0	1 10	25 12	18 0	10 36	17 4	5 ♓ 3'34"
16 FR	15:34:31	8 2	15 59	0 ♏ 8	11 29	1 15	25 14	18 0	10 36	17 4	5 ♓ 3'34"
17 SA	15:38:28	12 49	17 34	1 6	11 58	1 20	25 16	18 1	10 37	17 5	5 ♓ 3'34"
18 SU	15:42:25	17 28	19 9	2 3	12 27	1 25	25 18	18 1	10 37	17 5	5 ♓ 3'34"
19 MO	15:46:21	21 57	20 44	3 1	12 56	1 30	25 20	18 2	10 37	17 5	5 ♓ 3'34"
20 TU	15:50:18	26 17	22 19	3 59	13 25	1 35	25 22	18 3	10 38	17 6	5 ♓ 3'34"
21 WE	15:54:14	0 ♍ 30	23 54	4 57	13 54	1 40	25 23	18 3	10 38	17 6	5 ♓ 3'34"
22 TH	15:58:11	4 35	25 29	5 54	14 24	1 45	25 25	18 4	10 38	17 6	5 ♓ 3'33"
23 FR	16: 2: 7	8 32	27 4	6 52	14 53	1 49	25 27	18 5	10 39	17 7	5 ♓ 3'33"
24 SA	16: 6: 4	12 23	28 38	7 50	15 22	1 54	25 29	18 5	10 39	17 7	5 ♓ 3'33"
25 SU	16:10: 0	16 7	0 ♒ 13	8 47	15 51	1 59	25 31	18 6	10 40	17 7	5 ♓ 3'33"
26 MO	16:13:57	19 44	1 48	9 45	16 21	2 4	25 33	18 7	10 40	17 8	5 ♓ 3'33"
27 TU	16:17:54	23 17	3 24	10 43	16 50	2 9	25 35	18 7	10 40	17 8	5 ♓ 3'33"
28 WE	16:21:50	26 44	4 59	11 40	17 20	2 14	25 36	18 8	10 41	17 8	5 ♓ 3'33"
29 TH	16:25:47	0 ♎ 6	6 34	12 38	17 49	2 19	25 38	18 9	10 41	17 9	5 ♓ 3'33"
30 FR	16:29:43	3 24	8 9	13 36	18 19	2 24	25 40	18 9	10 41	17 9	5 ♓ 3'32"
31 SA	16:33:40	6 37	9 44	14 33	18 48	2 29	25 42	18 10	10 42	17 9	5 ♓ 3'32"

INGRESSES :

4	☿ → ♊	2:59
5	♀ → ♑	21:23
8	☿ → ♋	23:41
14	☿ → ♌	9:25
15	⊕ → ♏	20:46
20	☿ → ♍	21: 6
24	♀ → ♒	20:35
28	☿ → ♎	23:17

ASPECTS (HELIOCENTRIC +MOON(TYCHONIC)) :

1	☿ □ ♆	0:50	6	♀ ☍ ♃	4:11		♀ □ ♂	21:55	17	⊕ △ ♃	6:33	24	☽ ☍ ☿	6:44
	☽ ☌ ☿	13:12		☿ ☍ ♇	20:18	12	☿ △ ♅	3: 0		♀ ✶ ♅	6:50		☽ ☌ ♅	15: 0
2	☿ ✶ ♅	4:51		☿ □ ♅	23:44	13	☿ N□ ☊	3:51		☿ △ ♇	22: 1	25	☿ □ ♇	6:38
	⊕ ✶ ♇	10:10	7	☿ △ ⊕	16: 7		☽ ☌ ♂	10:24	18	☽ ☌ ♇	4: 8		☿ ☍ ♅	13: 6
	♀ ✶ ♄	14:45	8	☿ △ ♄	3:37		☿ □ ♄	11: 5	19	☽ ☍ ♃	4: 3	26	☽ ☍ ♂	18:43
	☿ ☌ P	23:25		☽ ☍ ♆	17:22	14	☿ □ ⊕	1:17		☿ ✶ ♄	18:44		⊕ □ ♆	22:59
4	☽ ☍ ♇	5:45	9	☿ ☌ ♃	2:28		♂ △ ♆	3:33	20	☽ ☌ ♀	16:36	27	☽ ☍ ♄	11: 5
5	☿ △ ♂	2:54	10	☿ ☍ ♀	3: 6		☽ ☌ ♄	12:42	21	☿ ✶ ♃	6:53		♂ ✶ ♇	14:40
	☽ ☍ ♀	5:38		☿ □ ♂	12: 2	16	♀ ☌ A	12:46		☽ ☌ ♆	21:47	29	☿ □ ♃	16:29
	☽ ☌ ♃	8:29		⊕ ☌ ♄	18:14		☿ ☍ ♆	12:48		♀ □ ♄	23: 9	31	☽ ☍ ♇	13:58
	☿ △ ♆	19:15	11	☽ ☍ ♅	17:42		☿ ✶ ♂	19:10	22	☿ ✶ ⊕	10:31		♀ ☌ ♆	14:41

the disciples recognized their traveling companion, who was Christ.

The bread communion is communion with the resurrection body of Christ, given to Luke and Cleophas and accompanied by Christ's words, "I am the bread of life" (John 6:35). This bread of life is the substance of the Word of God living in all pure nourishment, as the antidote to destructive manipulation of the Mother's archetypes in seeds. Christ throughout the forty days was ministering the bread of life to his disciples. Through his wounds and from his mouth flowed pure light, giving them the power to forgive sins, to baptize, to heal, and to lay on hands. As communion with the resurrection body was the forty days between the Resurrection and the Ascension, so is communion with the Self of Christ, the wine communion, connected to Christ's descent into hell. It was the "I" (or self) of Christ that descended after Jesus died on the cross. Christ descended toward the heart of the Mother at the Earth's center. And it was from communion with the Self of Christ that the Grail Knights were schooled to develop the courage to descend into hell, meet evil, confront and overcome this evil. Parsifal took up this battle with evil for the sake of human beings and the Mother Earth. He is the human being of the future, the future Jupiter human being.

The Self of Christ follows the twelve-year rhythm of Jupiter. In 1945 Christ began his penetration of the sub-earthly layers of the Earth on behalf of the Mother in the heart of the Earthly realm. Christ is currently working in the seventh interior sphere, the Earth Mirror (July 23, 2004 - June 3, 2016), connected with the *manas* cognition of the spirit self (see Robert Powell's book, *The Christ Mystery*). The Beatitude that is the antidote to the evil of this sphere is *Blessed are the peacemakers for they shall be called the Children of God*. Valentin Tomberg speaks of the peacemakers:

> If the consciousness soul is filled with consciousness of the guilt and need of earthly life, it lifts it like a cup, interceding for the need of Earth. It can then encounter a current descending from above, one that absorbs the darkness of guilt and need into its own clear light, carried upward by the consciousness soul. It may happen then that the ascending darkness and the descending light unite, which leads to a "rainbow" of reconciliation between the two worlds. For example, Goethe, in his soul, carried knowledge of this process of reconciliation and peace between the two worlds. Such knowledge became not only the basis of his theory of color, but also of his fairytale, The Green Snake and the Beautiful Lily.[1]

The fruition of Earth evolution is the ripening of the consciousness soul to receive into itself the angelic sphere. We reach this fruition through partaking in communion with Christ as did the disciples Luke and Cleophas. If Christ, or an ambassador of Christ, were among us—would we know this? Or, would we persecute such a one in this Second Coming as we did in the first? This is food for thought during these days, remembering the forty days of Christ's cosmic teachings. In remembrance of Christ's appearance in Emmaus, can we open our awareness to sense unseen beings moving among us? We are not alone!

ASPECT: Mercury 25° Aries opposite Saturn 25° Libra. Saturn was at this degree in AD 70, when the Romans destroyed the Temple at Jerusalem (Aug/29/70). This was two years after the death of the Emperor Nero. In their victory, the Romans slaughtered thousands, enslaved others to work in the mines of Egypt, and still others were sent to the public arenas throughout the Empire to be butchered for the amusement of the public. Jerusalem is mentioned in the Book of Daniel as well as in the work of Vladimir Solovyov:

> The reference to the prophet Daniel has to do with Daniel's prophecy regarding the city of Jerusalem (the "holy place"). Daniel speaks of "a prince who is to come [who] shall destroy the city and the sanctuary . . . desolations are decreed" (Daniel 9:26). Here Daniel refers to the "prince of this world" (Ahriman/Satan).

In Vladimir Solovyov's inspired work, *A Short Story of the Antichrist* (originally published in Russia at Easter 1900), he describes the false Christ (Antichrist) who, in league with a false prophet (the magician Apollyon), becomes emperor of the world and establishes

---

1 Tomberg, *Christ and Sophia*, p. 220.

his residence in Jerusalem. Among Apollyon's magical powers is the ability to make fire come down from heaven. This is a clear allusion to the two-horned beast referred to in the thirteenth chapter of the Book of Revelation. In fact, it is in Revelation that we find an account of the reign of the Antichrist (referred to there simply as "the beast"), who is aided by the two-horned beast:

> The two-horned beast exercises all the authority of the first beast in its presence, and makes the earth and its inhabitants worship the [first beast].... Men worshipped the first beast, saying, "Who is like the beast, and who can fight against it?" And the beast was given a mouth uttering haughty and blasphemous words, and it was allowed to exercise authority for forty-two months. (Rev. 13:12, 4–5)[2]

In two days' time the Sun will be square to where the Sun was at the prophesied birth of the Antichrist. This prophecy was given by the American clairvoyant Jean Dixon, who had a vision of this birth at sunrise on the morning of February 5, 1962. In private conversation Willie Sucher (an outstanding pioneer in astrosophy), shared with Robert Powell[3] his research findings:

> In this conversation Willi indicated to me that he had done research into Jeane Dixon's vision and that he had found it plausible. Based on his own inner perception, he had even identified the place of birth of the individual born on February 5, 1962—in Tobruk, Libya. This enabled him to cast the horoscope, showing the planetary alignment in Capricorn close to the Ascendant in Capricorn. When asked about the significance of the planetary alignment in Capricorn, he replied:
>
>> In antiquity Capricorn was called the "gateway to the gods," and what better moment could the Antichrist choose to be born than when all the planets are aligned in front of Capricorn, blocking the gateway to the spiritual world, in order to establish his rulership in a world of materialism, cutting off humanity from all spirituality.

---

2 *Journal for Star Wisdom, 2010,* pp. 19–20.
3 Robert Powell was a guest in Willi Sucher's home in Meadow Vista, California, in the summer of 1977, and then for four weeks during the summer of 1982.

Whether Jeane Dixon's vision comes true or not remains to be seen. What is striking for me is the confirmation of her vision by Willi Sucher, who even determined the place of birth of the individual born on February 5, 1962, and who spent time contemplating the horoscope of his birth. As I learned from a friend who was present at some of Willi's workshops at Hawkwood College in England during the 1970s, Willi had already spoken about this prophecy by Jeane Dixon on one occasion. In his conversation with me about it in California, he positively affirmed the validity of Jeane Dixon's vision and even added to it a geographical location (Tobruk) from his own perception. Moreover, he was certainly aware of Rudolf Steiner's words: "Before only a part of the third millennium of the post-Christian era has elapsed, there will be in the West an actual incarnation of Ahriman— Ahriman in the flesh."[4]

Today we remember the work of the resurrected Christ, the fall of Jerusalem, and the prophecy of the birth of a dark prince. It is Christ, now in the etheric, who is the antidote to evil. Communion with him provides protection, strength, and endurance for all trials. This day we can contemplate the materialistic values that are driving the masses and find our willingness to align with the noble values of love, brother/sisterhood, and peace.

In January of 2015 we will celebrate the 66⅔ birthday of the founding of Israel (May 14, 1948). This marks the completion of two cycles of 33⅓-year rhythms (the rhythm of the etheric body of Christ). In the historic biography of our time, significant events are being orchestrated commensurate with this milestone. Jerusalem is considered, by some, to be the heart of the Earth, and there are forces striving to destroy the new Temple that is now being formed in the heart of all who seek the mystery of the Holy Grail. We are urged to participate in founding new mysteries so that the memory of the Fall of Jerusalem 1,944 years ago will not recapitulate itself as another Fall, whereby humanity becomes entrapped in the cunning agenda's of anti-Grail magicians.

---

4 Powell, "In Memory of Willi Sucher," *Journal for Star Wisdom 2010.*

May 4: Sun 19° Aries. Conversation with the Pharisee Nicodemus (Apr/9/30). "The wind blows wherever it pleases. You hear its sound, but you cannot tell where it comes from or where it is going. So it is with everyone born of the Spirit" (John 3:8). In the second arcanum of *Meditations on the Tarot*, The High Priestess, the unknown author describes the "pure act of intelligence": Like the wind, "the pure act in itself cannot be grasped; it is only its reflection which renders it perceptible, comparable and understandable or, in other words, it is by virtue of the reflection that we become conscious of it."[1]

This seems to fit the nighttime conversations between Jesus and Nicodemus. Three times it is reported in the Bible that Nicodemus comes to Jesus in the night. Rudolf Steiner says this:

> Let us accustom ourselves to accuracy in dealing with words. We are told that Nicodemus came to Jesus "by night"; this means that he received outside of the physical body what Jesus Christ had to communicate to him. "By night" means that, when he uses his spiritual senses, he comes to Jesus Christ.[2]

Jesus approaches Nicodemus in the night. The original forces of the world are living in Jesus—he is bringing not only new teachings, but a kind of teaching that comes from his astral body into the consciousness of others who are prepared to receive these apocalyptic teachings. Jesus makes the preparation for receiving these cosmic teachings clear: "Very truly I tell you, no one can enter the kingdom of God unless they are born of water and the Spirit" (John 3:5).

The "pure act of intelligence" comes like the wind—no one knows whence it comes or whither it goes. It is the spirit of Jesus's teaching in the night. Nicodemus is able to receive these teachings as reflections, and through the reflections he can grasp the wind that blows where it will as the cosmic teachings of Christ. Nicodemus was born of Water and of Spirit, as was John—they entered the kingdom of God by letting go of the lower human being and reviving the higher human being. This is the second birth—to be born into spirit consciousness. This is to be "born of Water and the Spirit."

This day calls forth the memory of Nicodemus who communed with Christ's astral body in the night, when the Sun was in the constellation of Aries—whose virtue is devotion—dedicated to the higher ideals that we are all striving toward knowingly or unknowingly. "This nightly conversation was in fact an initiation of Nicodemus. The task is to be able to read the language spoken by the movements of the heavenly bodies, to grasp their significance intuitively."[3] What material attachments block us from receiving the wind of spirit or believing in the language of the stars?

Sun enters third decan of Aries, ruled by Mercury and associated with Cassiopeia's outstretched legs seated on her throne, so that this decan is sometimes known as Cassiopeia's Throne or Cassiopeia's Chair.

May 10: Sun 25° Aries. The appearance of the Risen One to the seven disciples (Apr/15/33). This occurred at the northeast end of the Sea of Galilee (John 21:1–23). Here Peter is bid three times to "Feed my Sheep." He is given the task to be the spiritual leader of the Church, to ensure that the sacraments, Holy Communion above all, continue to be celebrated for all time. Peter asks what will become of John, and the Risen One answers: "If it is my will that he remain until I come, what is that to you?" Implicit here is the task of the Church of John to wait until the Second Coming of Christ in the etheric realm. The Church of Peter has the task to lead human beings to the threshold of the spiritual world, and the Church of John has the task of leading them across the threshold *into* the spiritual world. John and Peter work together, united in their service to Christ and Sophia. The Church of John is centered in the heart, and those who choose to join this Church are summoned by the call of the Grail. Corresponding to the Mass in the exoteric church is the Grail Mystery in the esoteric church. Grail communion is communion with the Beings of the stars, which requires a crossing of the threshold—which in turn requires a meeting with the fallen

---

1 Anonymous, *Meditations on the Tarot*, p. 30.
2 Steiner, *The Gospel of St. John*, pp. 90–91 (trans. revised).
3 CHA, "Jesus' First Visit to Jerusalem Since the Baptism."

nature of the soul in the depths of the underworld. This is why it is the John being that Rudolf Steiner claims will be with us at the end of the century. For, it was John who accompanied Lazarus through the underworld after his death and before he was raised by Christ. We live now in the time of the Second Coming, a time when the Church of John is opening, and this is a time when humanity is both collectively and individually crossing the threshold. Moreover, we live in a time when star wisdom is being reborn as communion with the beings of the Heavens. With the Sun in Aries, the constellation of self-sacrifice, spiritual strength, and leadership, we may feel inspired to open to the vastness of the mysteries surrounding us in our everyday life. Alternatively we may find we are excessively caught up in the small story of our "little" biography. As our interest in others and in the vastness of other worlds that interact with us increases, new possibilities are revealed. We may ask ourselves: What about John? Where do I stand before the Hermetic mysteries?

ASPECT: Sun 25° Aries opposite Saturn 25° Libra: Now the Sun comes into opposition with Saturn at this degree (25° Libra), where the fall of Jerusalem is remembered, as did Mercury a week ago. The Sun at this degree remembers Christ's promise that it would be John whose time would come as Christ returned in the etheric. We can contemplate the Church of John and the work of Valentin Tomberg, who entered the Catholic Church in order to water the seeds of John's Church that lay at its heart. This deed by Tomberg has profound meaning in the revelatory stream coming to us from the future. It will be through John that the New Jerusalem will be built, by those coming to serve his work.

May 11: Venus 14° Pisces opposite Mars 14° Virgo. Mars was at this degree approximately two weeks before Jesus went into the wilderness for his forty-day period of fasting and prayer. This was shortly after his baptism by John. He was in the town of Gilgal where he had caused great jubilation. As Mars came to today's degree, agents for the Sanhedrin warned them of the excitement caused by Jesus—the storm clouds were already gathering: Agents reported back to the Sanhedrin in Jerusalem about the jubilation Jesus evoked at Gilgal and his baptizing activity there. The Sanhedrin, composed of seventy-one priests and scribes, appointed a committee of twenty to investigate Jesus. They concluded that Jesus was in league with the devil. On this day, Jesus and about twenty followers left Gilgal. Traveling eastward, they crossed the Jordan on a large raft. Coming to a place where many tax collectors lived— they had already been baptized by John—Jesus taught them the parable of the sower (Matt. 13).[4]

Today Venus listens to the words (Mars) sounding forth from all humanity, for Venus loves to create space for the creative Word. In her higher aspects she makes space for love, in her lower aspects she makes space for jealousies and rivalries. We are invited to speak with consciousness and cast out the temporal agitations born of egoism. When words are in service to peace, we propagate the joy of togetherness that overcomes the fears of those under the influence of aggression (lower Mars).

Tonight the Moon stands with Mars.

Also today: Mercury 12° Taurus square Neptune 12° Aquarius: Neptune was opposite today's degree when, in the early 1930's in Russia, thousands of people were sentenced to death and hundreds of thousands were sent to prison camps.

With Mars remembering the Sanhedrin opposition to Jesus, and the spies they sent to watch over his activities, and Neptune remembering times when non-conformists were imprisoned, or killed, we are encouraged to honor freedom and speak out against all restraints to this blessed gift.

May 14: Full Moon 28° Libra opposite Sun 28° Aries. The Great Conjunction of 2000 (May/14/2000). Aries is the first sign of the zodiac standing for innovation, pioneering efforts and leadership. Under this sign Jesus died on the cross. Christ, as the leader of the entire evolution of the Earth, is the archetype inherent in the Jupiter/Saturn great conjunction that began our millennium. Robert Powell called the arrival of Pentecost, just following this great conjunction, the beginning of 2,400 years of a new era of Christianity dedicated

---

4 *Chron.*, p. 204.

to the mysteries of the Divine Feminine. He writes that during the time of the waxing and waning of this twenty-year Jupiter/Saturn cycle, the new etheric forces with which Nature has been impregnated, will cause many to experience a new relationship with the Mother. Cultural renewal is generated by these great conjunctions, and when colored by the influences of the constellation of Aries, the above mentioned qualities of Christlike leadership is heralded. In the first thirteen years we have witnessed many power struggles as well as new communities forming in the name of peace, creating pioneering developments like "slow food," "slow money," and "fair trade." Increasingly groups are gathering who share similar ideals, in order to bring healing to both human beings and nature beings. These represent efforts of pioneering new leadership whereby the growing popularity of local movements are creating new paths forward, independent from corporate agendas.

Today's Full Moon at 28° Libra stands opposite this great conjunction. New ideals are coming to fruition through the illumined minds of devoted souls who are aligning their personal will with endeavors that serve higher will. This takes courage; and when courage works with obedience, peace is the result. Inversely, courage without obedience is aggressive and contributes to wars. It is obedience that tempers "self-will"—rendering integrity to courage. Another aspect today also calls for ennobled will:

Venus 18° Pisces square Pluto 18° Sagittarius: Venus at this degree finds Jesus in the town of Dan, called also Lais, or Leschem (Feb/11/31).

> On the way, Jesus instructed his followers—his subject always being prayer. He explained the Our Father. He told them that in the past they had not prayed worthily, but like Esau had asked for the fat of the earth; but now, like Jacob, they should petition for the dew of Heaven, for spiritual gifts, for the blessing of spiritual illumination, for the Kingdom according to the will of God, and not for one in accordance with their own ideas.[1]

Sister Emmerich continues to describe the city of Dan, situated at the base of a high mountain range, that covered a wide extent owing to the fact that every one of its houses was surrounded by a garden; but in spite of the fertility of this region, there were many who were sick.

With Venus square Pluto, forces are present that must be controlled by the free will. When human will and divine will strive against each other, the phenomenon of earthquakes can result. The priestly vow of poverty prepares the soul to relinquish attachment to "things" of this world, and the knightly vow of righteousness assures that the will seeks the righteousness of God. No matter how fertile the outer landscape, the inner landscape must also find its fertility through being nourished by the will of God moving through the human will.

Under this aspect we can contemplate the soul's thinking, feeling, and willing activated toward obedience, chastity, and poverty, so that it is the will of the higher that moves the lower. This asks that we do nothing out of self will, but discern the will of our higher nature and follow this as did Jacob before us. He wrestled to become a free personality, and in so doing kneeled in poverty before the Angel of Death, the necessities of karma, and the will of spirit. To practice these three virtues bestows the blessing this aspect promises when the soul (Venus) makes itself worthy of receiving the divine love of Phanes (higher Pluto).

Tonight the Moon stands with Saturn.

May 15: Venus conjunct Uranus 19° Pisces. With Uranus at this degree in 1930, the BIS (Bank for International Settlements) was established by the Rothschild Family in Basel, Switzerland. This private bank describes itself as *the central bank for central bankers*. It is the oldest international banking operation in the world, and it shuns all publicity and notoriety.

Venus at this degree still hovers over the memory of Jesus in the city of Dan, as mentioned above. Jesus there taught the difference between Jacob and Esau, saying: "Esau had asked for the fat of the earth" in juxtaposition to his brother Jacob who "petitioned for the dew of heaven." The autonomous will behind the world banking system

---

[1] *ACE*, vol. 3, p. 232.

seeks to secure the "fat of the earth," and directs its attention to worldly gains that can be likened to the principle of Esau. The principle of Jacob seeks spiritual treasures above worldly gain and will emerge as a new paradigm as we enter more deeply into consciousness of brotherly and sisterly love. Then we will be like unto Jacob. With Venus conjunct Uranus we can imagine future systems of exchange that serve the betterment of the world. Such systems will lovingly (Venus) serve the will of the living spirit (Uranus). The Jacob principle is evident in these words from Christ: "The kingdom of heaven is like treasure hidden in a field. When a man found it, he hid it again, and then in his joy went and sold all he had and bought that field" (Matt. 13:44).

May 15: Sun enters Taurus. Sun in Taurus: "Shine forth, O glory of being" (Steiner, *Twelve Cosmic Moods*): William Bento illumines this mantra:

> The shining light is here defined as a glorious being. It is not a phenomenon dissected as a scientific empirical fact. It is alive with being-ness. And surrounding this being is an aura of glory. Can you now gaze at the Sun with new eyes? Can you now look into another's eyes and see a glimmer of this glorious being? When this indeed occurs in our seeing we can experience the awe, wonder, and reverence of the sacredness of the "I/Thou" consciousness out of which each human being shines forth.

In Taurus, Inner Balance becomes Progress. It is a work of transforming the will. The first decan is ruled by Venus and is associated with Perseus, who was helped by Athena to overcome the Medusa.

May 17: Sun 2° Taurus. The Virgin Mary receives her first communion (Apr/23/33). Shortly after midnight the Blessed Virgin Mary received the holy sacrament from Peter (three weeks after the Last Supper). During this communion, Jesus appeared to her. Later she retired to her room to pray, and toward dawn the Lord appeared to her again and gave her power over the Church, a protective force, such that light flowed from him into her. In this we see a stage in the preparation for the event of Pentecost coming in the weeks that follow. The Virgin Mary could listen to the presence of the Christ. Taurus shapes the larynx and Eustachian tubes, mirrored by the form of the stethoscope. Through the organ of the larynx and its connection to the Eustachian tubes, we can listen to the heart of God. This is the kind of listening exemplified by the Virgin Mary. The assault on hearing from constant noise tends either to draw one into the outer world in covetousness of insatiable desire, or cause the soul to fall into indulgent apathy obliterating the inspirations sounding from the cosmic periphery. The sacred organs of hearing are being hardened, whereby we cease believing in spiritual thoughts—for we have lost the capacity to attune to these subtle frequencies.

The sense of hearing is a spiritual sense. The highest expression of hearing is through creating the stillness of inner balance. In this balance, point and periphery commune. This is the stillness of Mary—the stillness that could commune with the Risen One from the very center of her heart. It was into this still-point of centeredness that Mary would receive the Holy Spirit at Pentecost. Radiant inner stillness is the antidote to our tendency to become victims of the serpent's thoughts—thoughts that are empowered through avarice and work into the apathy of human souls separated from spirit; thus it is this very stillness that "noise" seeks to destroy. The preciousness of the organ of hearing can today be contemplated—as well as the centeredness of holding inner silence.

May 18: Venus 22° Pisces square Jupiter 22° Gemini. The Passion and Resurrection of Christ. Venus and Jupiter were square and very close to today's degree during the entire passion and through the beginning of the forty days after the resurrection. With Venus and Jupiter in this tension, karmic groups can awaken to an appreciation of the larger community in which they serve. Too often factionalism can tear groups asunder, yet this square can quicken an awareness of the greater good and one's place within it. Inversely, divisions can occur that are set in motion by jealousy and rivalry (lower Venus). These qualities weaken one's relationship to something higher (Jupiter's wisdom). We can find encouragement to rise above petty concerns of the personality in order to lift ourselves to realms of wisdom. Jupiter guides the soul to the promise of a Sun-filled countenance of radiant and joy-filled love. In the words of Pierre Teilhard de Chardin:

> Under the combined influence of human beings' thoughts and aspirations, the universe around us is seen to be knit together and convulsed by a vast movement of convergence. Not only theoretically, but experientially, our modern cosmogony is taking the form of a cosmogenesis…at the term of which we can distinguish a supreme focus of personalizing personality.… Just suppose that we identify (at least in his "natural" aspect) the cosmic Christ of faith with the Omega Point of science: then everything in our outlook is clarified and broadened, and falls into harmony.[1]

May 21: Mars stations before going direct at 14° Virgo. The Parable of the Sower (Matthew 13). In this parable Jesus speaks of preparing the soil into which seeds can take firm root in order that what is given may prosper and give forth abundantly. He says "those who do not have, even what they have will be taken from them." For if the soil is not prepared, then all else shall be swept away. These words speak to our times. We need have eyes to see and ears to hear so that the roots of our faith run deep, giving us fortitude before all trials. To superficially look at world events will render us deaf and blind. These words can be taken to heart:

> Though seeing, they do not see; though hearing, they do not hear or understand. In them is fulfilled the prophecy of Isaiah: You will be ever hearing but never understanding; you will be ever seeing but never perceiving.

As Mars stations where it was when Christ spoke these words, our consciousness is urged to wake up to what stands before us in these changing times. The alternative is the danger of being swept away when the truth of spiritual reality finally reveals itself—this will herald a time when we will most need deep-rootedness.

May 24: The Moon will today oppose Mars, and transit Uranus and Venus as it moves through Pisces: Thus it will activate the memories of the parable of the sower as well as the difference between Jacob and Esau (see commentary for May 15). The Moon is the gate to the underworld that we are to keep in check. When this is done, the Moon becomes a vessel for spiritual truths.

May 25: Venus enters Aries. "Take hold of growth's being" (Steiner, *Twelve Cosmic Moods*).

Venus was in Aries at the Ascension, Pentecost, the conception of the Nathan Jesus, and during the Flight into Egypt. We are urged to take hold of the cosmic forces of radiance and through these unite life forces that stream as cosmic ideals into devotional souls. This will foster a growing radiance to issue forth from our hearts into the whole of nature. In this way we will become participants in the evolving presence of Christ and Sophia.

Tonight the Moon stands with Venus.

May 28: New Moon 12° Taurus: Miraculous Draught (Nov/26/30). The Moon was at this degree when Christ asked Simon Peter to cast out his net, whereby he pulled up the miraculous draught of fishes. This is a guiding imagination that can help us overcome doubt, no matter how tested our spiritual will. We have taken the draught of forgetfulness; and having done this, we have been led further and further into materialism, all the while becoming increasingly severed from higher worlds. It is the Miraculous Draught that Christ gives, and this is the draught of remembrance. We can cast our nets into etheric realms and he will show us an abundance of protection and grace that is the spiritual nourishment known by his followers. We are to put on Christ's armor of light in order to preserve our integrity as we progress through world changes now upon us. The horns of the bull listen to spirit and gradually learn to read the highest of all chronicles—the moral chronicle wherein the essential holds sway over the temporal:

> And it is the third Akasha chronicle, or the "book of life," which is the essence of karma. Since the incarnation of Christ, karma has become the affair of the Lord of Karma, who is

---

[1] Anonymous, *Meditations on the Tarot*, p. 526.

Jesus Christ. For Jesus Christ not only *preached* the new law which must replace the old law of "eye for eye, tooth for tooth" (Ex. 21:24), but also *realized* it on the cosmic level by elevating the "book of life" above the "book of accounts" of strict justice. Karma is therefore no more the law of cause and effect solely, which works from incarnation to incarnation—it is now, above all, the means of salvation, i.e., the means of effecting new inscriptions in the "book of life" and of effacing other inscriptions from it.[2]

This New Moon in Taurus asks us to found an unshakable faith in the power of forgiveness so that we may work with the Lord of Karma in order to resurrect our souls from all enchainment to the past.

Jesus Christ waits with a miraculous draught for those who remember his name.

May 29: Christian Celebration of Ascension Thursday. Forty days after Easter Christ ascended to his Father. Today the teachings of the forty days since Easter come to an end. The little spark of our higher "I," which we brought out of the Holy Nights last January, now expands beyond our selfhood's limitation. Just as Christ ascended to his Father, so too does an aspect of our sprouting spirit-potential ascend to be infused with spirit. This expansion of new life moving through us, toward its full flowering, is utterly necessary for its later fruition. It seeks for the heights of heaven in order to be filled with creative power, thereby preparing it to become the sword of Michael that we will bear as it returns to us in autumn. This matured aspect of ourselves is exactly the power that will help us battle our inner dragons when the Earth again in-breathes her soul at summer's end. Something entirely new is striving to become one with us, but first it must make its ascent to the heights. May we let go of all limitation and joyfully dance our way into the communion with spirit that is the gift of summer, and the promise of the Ascension. (See entry for the cosmic remembrance of the Ascension on June 8.)

May 31: Sun 15° Taurus conjunct Aldebaran, the Bull's eye, known as the Watcher in the East. In a discourse of Hermes to Tat, the opening and closing invocations speak to the four directions and the royal stars of Persia who represent these primal directions: "(turning to the East): Holy Michael, thou who guards the Evolution of the Earth, during which the Mystery of Golgotha took place, whence comes the inner spirit birth of the true Self of man, may thy radiant Being guide the Self in freedom and love along the path of human existence which receives its meaning alone through Christ."[3] From the opening invocation: In the holy temple of the Sun, Hermes is standing at the altar in the East, Tat at the altar in the South, Asclepius at the altar in the West, and King Ammon at the altar in the North. Today, with Sun conjunct Aldebaran, we are invited to stand in the East with Hermes, under the watchful eye of Aldebaran.

JUNE 2014

June begins with the Moon conjunct Jupiter in Gemini on the 1st, but most of us will catch this after the new crescent Moon has continued on and is to the left and below Jupiter; look to the west after sunset. The Sun is in Taurus (the Bull) until the 15th, when it shifts into Gemini (the Twins). On the 7th, the growing Moon will join with Mars in Virgo; this will be easy to spot in the south at sunset and southwest as the dusk deepens into night. Mercury stations Retrograde on the 8th (turning Direct on July 1st) and Neptune also stations Retrograde (until November). By the evening of the 10th the almost full Moon will conjunct Saturn in Libra; look to the southeast after sunset and view Mars, too (to the right/in the south), and Jupiter (further right/in the western horizon). On the 13th, the Sun and Moon are opposite, forming the Full Moon: Sun in the constellation of Taurus and Moon in Scorpio. On the 19th, Retrograde Mercury is conjunct the Sun, now in Gemini. As the waning Moon moves closer to the Sun for the New Moon in Gemini on the 27th, it first joins up with Venus on the 24th (in Taurus) and Mercury on the 26th. And we end the month as we began: the new crescent Moon

---

2 Ibid., p. 566.

3 CHA, "A Discourse of Hermes to Tat, The Mystery of the Zodiac."

swings past Jupiter on the 29th now in Cancer (the Crab). By the time the Sun sets we may only be able to see the crescent to the left of Jupiter who brightly clings to the horizon or has sunk down out of view, just about 20° ahead of the Sun.

June 5: Sun enters the third decan of Taurus, ruled by Saturn, associated with Orion below and Auriga above.

June 7: Moon conjunct Mars in the evening sky.

June 10: Neptune stations 12° Aquarius before moving retrograde. Slow moving Neptune is close to this degree throughout the year. From March into September it is within 1° of today's position. Neptune was exactly opposite today's degree (12° Leo) in July of 1932. At that time the effects of the Great Depression were escalating. The Dow Jones Industrial Average closed at 41.63, down 91% from its level exactly three years earlier. Neptune in its lower octave represents ahrimanic inspirations, which infect masses. Propaganda is spun by ahrimanic influences as its intension is to put a "spin" on something in order to make facts palatable, or to lead mass consciousness to a pre-desired end. With this year remembering the failed economy of the early 1930s, we are given notice that the temporal gives no firm ground.

When the Sun stood at this degree, Jesus was challenged by the Pharisees for speaking he was the "bread of life." Hoarding coins and gold has become a choice for those who do not trust the stability of the economy. But what is this really? Aquarius is the sign under which the teachings of brother- and sisterhood are heard. If a great depression and economic instability are to become our future, it is important that we hold on to nothing, for attachments would eclipse the new paradigms that will become possible if we turn to the true bread that nourishes us. Inversely we may rather hoard things valuable to the old paradigm. The pneumatism (perception of revelation) of Aquarius calls us to open to entirely new possibilities.

> The coming tribulations will only come upon us as a "thief in the night" if we have something that can be stolen—if we are in possession of something. In other words, those who are attached to the material world, and love their possessions, have things that may be stolen. This includes whatever the ego may be attached to, including, potentially, everything that we identify ourselves with. positions of power, positions of weakness, the appearance of power or wealth, a victim mentality, relationships of influence, etc.— for all these take the self away from Christ. These are the things that may be taken away by the "thief in the night." Those who are empty vessels, identifying only with Christ, shall be given what they need when they need it; the grace of the Lord shall fill them.[1]

June 13. Full Moon 27° Scorpio opposite Sun 27° Taurus. The idol of the dragon (Sept/27/32). The Moon was at this same degree when Jesus, while visiting Mensor and Theokeno (the two remaining kings), found an idol of a dragon in the temple:

> As one of the women cast herself down before this idol to worship it, Jesus said, "Why do you cast yourself down before Satan? Your faith has been taken possession of by Satan. Behold whom you worship!" Instantly there appeared before her, visible to all, a slender, red fox-colored spirit with a hideously pointed countenance. All were horrified. Jesus pointed to the spirit and indicated that it was this spirit that had woken the woman from sleep each morning before the break of day. The woman had arisen each morning and cast herself down to pray in the direction of the dragon. Jesus said, "This awoke you. However, every person also has a good angel, who should wake you, and before whom you should cast yourself down and follow his advice." All then saw a radiant figure at the woman's side. At this approach of the good angel, the satanic spirit withdrew. Like the two kings, this woman later became baptized by the apostle Thomas and received the name Serena. Later, she suffered a martyr's death. [2]

This Full Moon gives us ample reason to summon the guidance of our guardian angel before going to sleep, and upon awakening. We can do this on behalf of our children as well. The angel offers

---

1 Isaacson, *The Coming Times*, chap. 1.
2 *Chron.*, p. 328.

SIDEREAL GEOCENTRIC LONGITUDES : JUNE 2014 Gregorian at 0 hours UT

DAY	☉	☽	☊	☿	♀	♂	♃	♄	♅	♆	♇
1 SU	15 ♉ 31	22 ♊ 13	2 ♎ 35R	6 ♊ 37	8 ♈ 29	14 ♍ 58	25 ♊ 26	23 ♎ 32R	20 ♓ 33	12 ♒ 38	18 ♐ 7R
2 MO	16 28	4 ♋ 13	2 28	7 4	9 40	15 7	25 38	23 28	20 35	12 39	18 6
3 TU	17 26	16 7	2 23	7 27	10 50	15 16	25 50	23 24	20 38	12 39	18 5
4 WE	18 23	27 59	2 18	7 46	12 0	15 26	26 2	23 20	20 40	12 39	18 4
5 TH	19 21	9 ♌ 52	2 16	7 59	13 11	15 37	26 14	23 17	20 42	12 39	18 2
6 FR	20 18	21 51	2 15	8 9	14 21	15 49	26 25	23 13	20 44	12 39	18 1
7 SA	21 16	4 ♍ 2	2 16D	8 13	15 32	16 1	26 38	23 9	20 46	12 39	18 0
8 SU	22 13	16 29	2 17	8 13R	16 42	16 14	26 50	23 5	20 48	12 40	17 58
9 MO	23 10	29 16	2 18	8 8	17 53	16 27	27 2	23 2	20 50	12 40	17 57
10 TU	24 8	12 ♎ 28	2 17R	8 0	19 4	16 41	27 14	22 58	20 52	12 40R	17 56
11 WE	25 5	26 6	2 15	7 47	20 14	16 55	27 26	22 55	20 54	12 40	17 54
12 TH	26 2	10 ♏ 10	2 11	7 30	21 25	17 10	27 38	22 51	20 56	12 40	17 53
13 FR	27 0	24 37	2 4	7 9	22 36	17 25	27 51	22 48	20 58	12 39	17 52
14 SA	27 57	9 ♐ 20	1 56	6 45	23 47	17 41	28 3	22 45	21 0	12 39	17 50
15 SU	28 54	24 14	1 48	6 18	24 58	17 58	28 16	22 42	21 1	12 39	17 49
16 MO	29 52	9 ♑ 7	1 40	5 49	26 9	18 15	28 28	22 39	21 3	12 39	17 48
17 TU	0 ♊ 49	23 53	1 34	5 17	27 20	18 32	28 41	22 35	21 5	12 39	17 46
18 WE	1 46	8 ♒ 25	1 29	4 44	28 31	18 50	28 53	22 32	21 6	12 38	17 45
19 TH	2 43	22 39	1 27	4 10	29 42	19 9	29 6	22 30	21 8	12 38	17 43
20 FR	3 41	6 ♓ 32	1 27D	3 36	0 ♉ 53	19 28	29 19	22 27	21 9	12 38	17 42
21 SA	4 38	20 7	1 27	3 2	2 4	19 47	29 31	22 24	21 11	12 38	17 40
22 SU	5 35	3 ♈ 24	1 28R	2 28	3 15	20 7	29 44	22 21	21 12	12 37	17 39
23 MO	6 32	16 25	1 27	1 56	4 27	20 27	29 57	22 19	21 14	12 37	17 37
24 TU	7 30	29 13	1 24	1 26	5 38	20 48	0 ♋ 10	22 16	21 15	12 36	17 36
25 WE	8 27	11 ♉ 49	1 18	0 59	6 49	21 9	0 22	22 14	21 16	12 36	17 34
26 TH	9 24	24 16	1 10	0 34	8 1	21 31	0 35	22 11	21 18	12 35	17 33
27 FR	10 21	6 ♊ 33	0 59	0 13	9 12	21 53	0 48	22 9	21 19	12 35	17 31
28 SA	11 19	18 42	0 47	29 ♉ 55	10 24	22 15	1 1	22 7	21 20	12 34	17 30
29 SU	12 16	0 ♋ 44	0 34	29 41	11 35	22 38	1 14	22 5	21 21	12 34	17 28
30 MO	13 13	12 39	0 22	29 32	12 47	23 1	1 27	22 3	21 22	12 33	17 27

INGRESSES :

1 ☽ → ♋ 15:32
4 ☽ → ♌ 4: 5
6 ☽ → ♍ 16: 6
9 ☽ → ♎ 1:20
11 ☽ → ♏ 6:43
13 ☽ → ♐ 8:49
15 ☽ → ♑ 9:17
16 ☉ → ♊ 3:31
17 ☽ → ♒ 10: 2
19 ♀ → ♉ 6: 5
☽ → ♓ 12:38
21 ☽ → ♈ 17:48
23 ♃ → ♋ 6: 1
24 ☽ → ♉ 1:28
26 ☽ → ♊ 11:10
27 ☿ → ♉ 16:26
28 ☽ → ♋ 22:32

ASPECTS & ECLIPSES :

1 ☽ ☌ ♃ 6:31
☽ S ☊ 20:32
3 ☽ ☌ A 4:27
5 ☽ ☍ ♆ 5:36
☉ □ ☽ 20:38
7 ☽ ☌ ♂ 23:30
8 ☽ ☍ ♅ 8:12
9 ☽ ☌ ☊ 5:34
10 ☽ ☍ ♀ 12:48
☽ ☌ ♄ 18:29
13 ♀ ☍ ♄ 3:54
☉ ☍ ☽ 4:11
☽ ☍ ☿ 19:55
14 ♂ □ ♇ 12: 0
☽ ☌ ♇ 13:41
15 ☽ ☌ P 3:18
☽ ☍ ♃ 6:34
☽ N ☊ 12: 4
18 ☽ ☌ ♆ 7: 4
19 ☉ □ ☽ 18:38
☉ i☌ ☿ 22:42
20 ☽ ☍ ♂ 23:23
21 ☽ ☌ ♅ 1:54
☽ ☌ ☋ 20:28
23 ☽ ☍ ♄ 10:57
24 ☽ ☌ ♀ 13:26
25 ♂ ☍ ♅ 8:21
26 ☽ ☌ ☿ 11:55
27 ☉ ☌ ☽ 8: 8
♃ □ ☊ 10: 7
☽ ☍ ♇ 21:37
28 ☽ S ☊ 23:40
29 ☽ ☌ ♃ 1: 2
♀ □ ♆ 19:23
30 ☽ ☌ A 19: 4

SIDEREAL HELIOCENTRIC LONGITUDES : JUNE 2014 Gregorian at 0 hours UT

DAY	Sid. Time	☿	♀	⊕	♂	♃	♄	♅	♆	♇	Vernal Point
1 SU	16:37:36	9 ♎ 47	11 ♒ 19	15 ♏ 31	19 ♎ 18	2 ♋ 34	25 ♎ 44	18 ♓ 10	10 ♒ 42	17 ♐ 10	5 ♓ 3'32"
2 MO	16:41:33	12 53	12 54	16 28	19 48	2 38	25 46	18 11	10 42	17 10	5 ♓ 3'32"
3 TU	16:45:29	15 56	14 29	17 26	20 17	2 43	25 48	18 12	10 43	17 10	5 ♓ 3'32"
4 WE	16:49:26	18 56	16 4	18 23	20 47	2 48	25 49	18 12	10 43	17 11	5 ♓ 3'32"
5 TH	16:53:23	21 54	17 39	19 21	21 17	2 53	25 51	18 13	10 44	17 11	5 ♓ 3'32"
6 FR	16:57:19	24 49	19 15	20 18	21 47	2 58	25 53	18 14	10 44	17 11	5 ♓ 3'31"
7 SA	17: 1:16	27 42	20 50	21 15	22 17	3 3	25 55	18 14	10 44	17 12	5 ♓ 3'31"
8 SU	17: 5:12	0 ♏ 33	22 25	22 13	22 47	3 8	25 57	18 15	10 45	17 12	5 ♓ 3'31"
9 MO	17: 9: 9	3 23	24 0	23 10	23 17	3 13	25 59	18 16	10 45	17 12	5 ♓ 3'31"
10 TU	17:13: 5	6 11	25 36	24 8	23 47	3 18	26 1	18 16	10 45	17 13	5 ♓ 3'31"
11 WE	17:17: 2	8 59	27 11	25 5	24 17	3 22	26 2	18 17	10 46	17 13	5 ♓ 3'31"
12 TH	17:20:58	11 45	28 46	26 2	24 47	3 27	26 4	18 18	10 46	17 13	5 ♓ 3'31"
13 FR	17:24:55	14 30	0 ♓ 22	27 0	25 17	3 32	26 6	18 18	10 46	17 13	5 ♓ 3'30"
14 SA	17:28:52	17 15	1 57	27 57	25 47	3 37	26 8	18 19	10 47	17 14	5 ♓ 3'30"
15 SU	17:32:48	20 0	3 32	28 54	26 18	3 42	26 10	18 20	10 47	17 14	5 ♓ 3'30"
16 MO	17:36:45	22 45	5 8	29 51	26 48	3 47	26 12	18 20	10 48	17 14	5 ♓ 3'30"
17 TU	17:40:41	25 29	6 43	0 ♐ 49	27 18	3 52	26 14	18 21	10 48	17 15	5 ♓ 3'30"
18 WE	17:44:38	28 15	8 19	1 46	27 49	3 57	26 15	18 21	10 48	17 15	5 ♓ 3'30"
19 TH	17:48:34	1 ♐ 0	9 54	2 43	28 19	4 1	26 17	18 22	10 49	17 15	5 ♓ 3'30"
20 FR	17:52:31	3 46	11 30	3 41	28 50	4 6	26 19	18 23	10 49	17 16	5 ♓ 3'29"
21 SA	17:56:27	6 34	13 5	4 38	29 20	4 11	26 21	18 23	10 49	17 16	5 ♓ 3'29"
22 SU	18: 0:24	9 22	14 41	5 35	29 51	4 16	26 23	18 24	10 50	17 16	5 ♓ 3'29"
23 MO	18: 4:21	12 12	16 16	6 32	0 ♍ 22	4 21	26 25	18 25	10 50	17 17	5 ♓ 3'29"
24 TU	18: 8:17	15 3	17 52	7 30	0 52	4 26	26 27	18 25	10 50	17 17	5 ♓ 3'29"
25 WE	18:12:14	17 56	19 28	8 27	1 23	4 31	26 28	18 26	10 51	17 17	5 ♓ 3'29"
26 TH	18:16:10	20 52	21 3	9 24	1 54	4 36	26 30	18 27	10 51	17 18	5 ♓ 3'29"
27 FR	18:20: 7	23 49	22 39	10 21	2 25	4 41	26 32	18 27	10 51	17 18	5 ♓ 3'29"
28 SA	18:24: 3	26 49	24 15	11 19	2 56	4 45	26 34	18 28	10 52	17 18	5 ♓ 3'28"
29 SU	18:28: 0	29 52	25 50	12 16	3 27	4 50	26 36	18 29	10 52	17 19	5 ♓ 3'28"
30 MO	18:31:56	2 ♑ 57	27 26	13 13	3 58	4 55	26 38	18 29	10 53	17 19	5 ♓ 3'28"

INGRESSES :

7 ☿ → ♏ 19:18
12 ♀ → ♓ 18:32
16 ⊕ → ♐ 3:34
18 ☿ → ♐ 15:17
22 ♂ → ♏ 7: 4
29 ☿ → ♑ 1: 5

ASPECTS (HELIOCENTRIC +MOON(TYCHONIC)) :

1 ☿ △ ♆ 7: 5
☽ ☌ ♃ 20:49
2 ☿ △ ♀ 0:14
3 ☿ ✶ ♇ 9:50
⊕ △ ♅ 19:28
4 ♀ ✶ ♇ 16:46
☿ ☌ ♂ 17:57
5 ☽ ☍ ♆ 1:44
☿ ☌ ☋ 13:38
☽ ☍ ♀ 18: 0
6 ☿ ☌ ♄ 8:57
7 ♀ S ☊ 15:40
♀ □ ⊕ 16:11
8 ☽ ☍ ♅ 3:21
♀ △ ♂ 7:51
☿ △ ♃ 22:28
10 ♀ △ ♄ 6:23
☽ ☌ ♂ 20:42
☽ ☌ ♄ 23:53
11 ☿ □ ♆ 15:29
♂ ☌ ☋ 21:31
12 ☽ ☌ ☿ 3:17
14 ☿ △ ♅ 9:17
☽ ☌ ♇ 12:44
♂ ☌ ♄ 17:31
15 ♀ △ ♃ 2:31
☽ ☍ ♃ 15:19
☿ ☌ A 23:56
18 ☽ ☌ ♆ 3:59
19 ☿ ☌ ⊕ 22:42
20 ☽ ☌ ♀ 9:50
☽ ☌ ♅ 20:54
22 ☿ ✶ ♆ 12:25
23 ♀ □ ♇ 15:11
☽ ☍ ♄ 18:44
24 ☽ ☍ ♂ 3:15
♀ ☌ ♅ 8:24
☿ ☌ ♇ 18:36
25 ☿ □ ♅ 4: 5
26 ☿ □ ♀ 3:29
27 ⊕ ✶ ♆ 12:42
☽ ☍ ♇ 21:14
☿ ✶ ♄ 21:59
28 ☽ ☍ ☿ 21:40
29 ☽ ☌ ♃ 8:18
30 ☿ ✶ ♂ 9:15
☿ ☍ ♃ 15:23

protecting forces from those "other" beings who would like very much to gain our attention and have us bow to them. When we practice communion with our angel, we begin to grow wings born of the collaboration between our efforts and the response of grace from above, which meets these efforts:

> Wings are formed only when the two currents—that of human endeavor and that of grace—meet and unite.[1]

ASPECT: Venus 22° Aries opposite Saturn 22° Libra. Jesus warns about the Pharisees and Sadducees (Mar/16/31). Jupiter was at 22° Aries, where Venus stands today, when Jesus taught the disciples concerning the persecution and suffering that he would endure. The day before, Jesus had given the so called Sermon on the Mount, signifying the conclusion of his Beatitude teachings. Today he prepared his disciples for the coming trials he would endure as one who would be hated and reviled as a "Christ-bearer" (ninth Beatitude). During this discourse he spoke warnings:

> When they went across the lake, the disciples forgot to take bread. "Be careful," Jesus said to them. "Be on your guard against the yeast of the Pharisees and Sadducees."
>
> They discussed this among themselves and said, "It is because we didn't bring any bread."
>
> Aware of their discussion, Jesus asked, "You of little faith, why are you talking among yourselves about having no bread? Do you still not understand? Don't you remember the five loaves for the five thousand, and how many basketfuls you gathered? Or the seven loaves for the four thousand, and how many basketfuls you gathered? How is it you don't understand that I was not talking to you about bread? But be on your guard against the yeast of the Pharisees and Sadducees." Then they understood that he was not telling them to guard against the yeast used in bread, but against the teaching of the Pharisees and Sadducees. (Matt. 16:5–12)

Venus today reminds us to have faith and know the power of metaphor. Whatever teachings are coming toward us from restrictive perpetuators of worn-out paradigms (negative Saturn), we can remain untouched in remembrance of the warnings the "new teacher" gave to his disciples at the turning point in time, when he warned them of the entrapments "party politics" can set up when threatened by the unfamiliarity of the new. This is a day to maintain harmonious relationships, while holding onto the truth we are to defend.

June 14: Mars 17° Virgo square Pluto 17° Sagittarius. Pluto remains at its position during the Passion of Christ. In square to Mars, aggression can result. Mars was opposite Pluto during the Passion of Christ, which is an example of soul-wrenching aggression. When, out of a hidden will-to-power, we allow demons to occupy our lower nature, the results are destructive. C. G. Jung regarded demons as parasitic entities [psychological complexes] living in the subconscious. Tomberg quotes Jung in the fifteenth Arcanum of the Tarot (The Devil):

> It appears as an autonomous formation intruding upon consciousness...It is just as if the complex were an autonomous being capable of interfering with the intentions of the ego ["I"]. Complexes do indeed behave like secondary or partial personalities possessing a mental life of their own.[2]

Today asks us to bear witness to any forcefulness we may find in our nature that seeks to impose, on others, ideas, feelings, or actions that are not in keeping with our conscious intentions. Bringing this aspect to light gives birth to a penetrating depth of concentration that can be turned toward progressive action.

June 15: Sun enters Gemini the Twins. "Reveal thyself, Sun life" (Rudolf Steiner, *Twelve Cosmic Moods*). William Bento characterized this mantra:

> Within this phrase there is a hidden mystery. How does the Sun hide from our view? It is certainly not the physical Sun we see daily that is being referred to here—but the living, etherically permeated Sun, felt and experienced, though rarely perceived. Within this Sun exist the threefold sources of health, life, and goodness. How easily we forget to place our trust in

---

1 Anonymous, *Meditations on the Tarot*, p. 384.

2 Ibid., p. 407.

this ever-present stream of divinity when we are faced with illness, death, and evil! For this reason alone, it is well worth reminding ourselves to see beyond appearances and behold the true revelation of the Sun, which reveals itself to our hearts, where its life resides.

The first decan of Gemini is ruled by Jupiter and associated with Orion, whose bright star Betelgeuse is located at 4 degrees Gemini.

June 18/19: Sun 3° Gemini. June 19: Mercury in superior conjunction with the Sun 3° Gemini.

Cosmic Pentecost (May/24/33). The Sun was 2 1/2° Gemini at Pentecost, when Sophia descended, through the Holy Spirit, and entered into the being of the Blessed Virgin Mary. At this degree, the Sun is directly opposite the Galactic Center (2° Sagittarius). The Galactic center, also known as the Central Sun, is the Divine Heart of the galaxy, which is the source of the Holy Spirit. The Blessed Virgin Mary, who was presented by Jesus Christ (before the Ascension) as the center of the community, served here—at Pentecost—as this heart-center and as the bearer of Divine Sophia.

> Because of extremely complicated influences and experiences coming from the spiritual world, Mary had an astral body that was so purified it could receive the revelations of Sophia and pour them out again as inspirations of the soul. This faculty was the very reason why, at the time of Pentecostal revelation, the Virgin Mary occupied the central position in the circle of the twelve. Without her, the revelation would have been only spiritual; there would have been twelve prophets, united in the Holy Spirit as was ancient prophecy. Through the cooperation of Mary, however, something more could happen; the disciples' hearts beat in harmony with hers while they experienced the Pentecostal revelation as *personal* human conviction. Through this experience, they became not prophets but specifically apostles.[3]

The difference between prophets and apostles is that prophets proclaim revelations impersonally, whereas apostles reveal the Holy Spirit *within* their own souls. This was possible only because the Virgin Mary transmitted *ensouled* revelation to the disciples—through her, revelation became personal and yet maintained its objective spiritual truth.

From the moment of Pentecost onward, the silence imposed on Sophia through Lucifer's intervention in human destiny was released. Sophia became free to reach down into groups of earthly human beings. This was a great event for both the earthly and spiritual worlds.

The sparks of fire that issued from her blessed soul were the ensouled manifestation of Christ's cosmic I AM. This eternal "I" of the world was born into the disciples through the immaculate heart of the divine Mary-Sophia, who was standing at the heart of their community. Since that first Pentecost, the Christ spirit has lived within human souls on Earth. Pentecost was the awakening of Christ's disciples from a dreamlike state, whereby they united with the principle of Christ's love as an experience within their own being. We also are to awaken from our dream-like sleep to meet the challenge of our time with hearts filled with wakeful awareness.

Emanations from the heart of the galaxy are increasing in our time, leading up to a Pentecost on a world scale.[4] In remembrance of this profound moment, which today quickens as Mercury conjuncts Sun, we are encouraged to live into this Sophianic awakening to Christ. It is our "I" that receives the new revelation, and it is the sense of one's ego (the "I") that is represented by the constellation of Gemini.

Can we find the strength of self to radiate from our center while all the while remaining open to the periphery?

June 20. Venus enters Taurus. "Feel growth's power" (Steiner, *Twelve Cosmic Moods*). With Venus in this earth sign we are called to take hold of our feeling for the power of growth, and radiate its light as the weaving thread of etheric life that we have been given. As we shine forth as life imbued being, we weave into the world etheric. Venus was in Taurus as Peter received the keys, and at the Transfiguration.

---

3 Tomberg, *Christ and Sophia*, p. 306.

4 See Powell, "World Pentecost," *Journal for Star Wisdom 2010* (also at www.sophiafoundation.org).

June 24. Jupiter enters Cancer. "Toward spiritual self-permeation" (Steiner, *Twelve Cosmic Moods*). With Jupiter moving into the sign where catharsis becomes selflessness, the giant planet calls us to expand our efforts to pass through the eye of the needle of our inner transformation in order to selflessly serve the needs of the earth and humanity. As we accomplish our inner work, we become permeated with spirit, and as spirit permeates our being we gain strength to care for others.

St. John's Day: As we follow the seed we brought out of the Holy Nights last January, we can know that at this mid-point of the year, just following the summer solstice, our Christmas gift is in full flower, gathering the creative forces from the cosmos that it will need in order to return to us life-filled in the coming time of Michaelmas. The Earth Mother is deep in her summer's sleep. Her soul having reached the greatest point of out-breath, she will now ever so gradually begin her inhalation, carrying to earth all that she has gained during her communion with the stars. Our soul, too, is being imbued with spirit, wherein something entirely new is being fructified.

Moon conjunct Venus in the evening sky.

June 25: Mars 21° Virgo opposite Uranus 21° Pisces. Mars squared Pluto on the 14th and now it opposes Uranus. Uranus was transiting Gemini (square to Pisces and near this degree) in the year 1616. According to William Bento's article in this Journal, this was the time when *The Chymical Wedding of Christian Rosenkreutz* was published. This work was the last of a trilogy revealed at this time. We yearn for a renaissance of wisdom-filled guidance, and the hermetic stream of Rosenkreutz gives just this sustenance to quench the thirst of all who are living in these materialistic times. With Mars opposed Uranus, revolutionary ideals can come to light—not the destructive revolutions of history, but rather the re-evolution of thinking to embrace the good, the beautiful, and the true. Today calls us to awaken to restrictions and break the bands that bind our hearts from knowing the new revelation as the peaceful power of the word (Mars). It is the word, not the sword, that cuts through the webs of deceit that materialism has spun.

June 27: New Moon 10° Gemini. Little Transfiguration (Sept/16/29). Here we find Jesus walking with Eliud, who was one of the best-instructed of the Essenians.

> Around midnight, Jesus said to Eliud that he would reveal himself, and—turning toward heaven—he prayed. A cloud of light enveloped them both and Jesus became radiantly transfigured. Eliud stood still, utterly entranced. After a while, the light melted away, and Jesus resumed his steps, followed by Eliud, who was speechless at what he had beheld.[1]

In this "Little Transfiguration" Jesus reveals himself to his friend and confidant, Eliud, who did not live to see the Crucifixion. The light encompasses Eliud as well as Christ. Perhaps there is a story here for us—by which we ourselves are encouraged to be Eliuds and walk with Christ. In small steps this will lead us toward the light. In the darkness of this moonless night we can water the seeds of love still slumbering in the light of our Sunlit hearts.

June 29: Venus 12° Taurus square Neptune 12° Aquarius: The inspirations of Sophia coming into time. Venus in dynamic relationship with Neptune (Sophia) can radiate wisdom into the human soul life (Venus), thus bringing to harmony the forces of thinking, feeling, and willing in relationship to the body, soul, and spirit. Venus was at this degree when Christ exasperated the Pharisees to a state of frenzy. In spite of their disharmony, he went on teaching: "The Pharisees asked scornfully whether he—the prophet—would do the honor of eating the paschal lamb with them. Jesus replied: 'The Son of Man is himself a sacrifice for your sins!' In the end, as Jesus continued teaching, the Pharisees became so exasperated that they made a great commotion. But Jesus managed to slip away and disappear into the crowd."[2]

The clamor of the nonbelievers will continue to work against divine inspiration. We are encouraged to continue in harmony, obediently serving the truth we have had the privilege of hearing: "True obedience is not at all the subjugation of the will to another will, but rather the moral clairaudience

---

1 *Chron.*, pp. 197–198.
2 Ibid., p. 287.

of the will—the faculty of knowing and recognizing the voice of truth. And it is this which renders the soul inaccessible to the lures of the sphere of mirages [illusions]."³

June 28: Sun 12 1/2° Gemini. Birth of John the Baptist (Jun/4/2 BC). John the Baptist was revealed by Christ to be the reincarnated Elijah, and later came to Earth as the Renaissance painter Raphael, and still later as Novalis. John fulfilled his mission when he baptized Jesus in the Jordan River in the year AD 29, when he bore witness to the incarnation of Christ—the true Light of the World and the Lamb of God. After the fulfillment of this mission, his new mission began, which was in service to Sophia. Just as John was the guide and preparer for those who would recognize the incarnated Christ, so too is he the preparer and guide for those working on behalf of Sophia, in recognition of the etheric return of Christ. This is a day to open our eyes and ears to the truth ringing through the world—a truth enlightened by wisdom and born of love. John works in the apocalyptic realms where the *Book of Revelation* lives eternally. He needs us to wake up to the presence of adversaries and to face this truth as would the Grail Knights. To know evil, is to bring forth the good. This is true for those following a Christ-centric Grail path. For those who do not know Christ, such knowledge regarding evil is imprudent. John is the bearer of strength and works through the power of the Word. May we find our fullness of voice and proclaim the Light, lest we become swallowed in the shadows of illusion!

JULY 2014

July opens with the Sun in Gemini and Mercury stationing Direct in the last degrees of Taurus. The evening sky this year has offered Jupiter (in Cancer), Mars (in Virgo) and Saturn (in Libra) but now Jupiter starts to be hard to see in the glare of the Sun catching up. Now sunsets offer a view of Mars and Saturn only and the waxing Moon joins each of them: Mars and Moon on the 6th and Saturn and Moon on the 8th. The Full Moon follows on the 12th, with the Moon reaching the constellation of Sagittarius (the Archer) opposite Gemini (the Twins). Saturn stations Direct on the 21st (Retrograde since March). Uranus turns Retrograde on the 23rd and will be for the rest of 2014. The Sun moves into Cancer on the 18th and finally does catch Jupiter, on the 24th. The same day, the waning Moon is conjunct Venus who is visible as the morning star. Early risers will catch this pretty sight about 1½ to 2 hours before sunrise: look to the east! By the 26th, we have the New Moon which includes Jupiter hidden alongside the Moon in Cancer. The end of the month brings the Delta Aquarids Meteor Shower: 20 meteors per hour, peaking on the night of the 28th and morning of the 29th. Best viewing is from a dark location after midnight; meteors will radiate from the constellation Aquarius in the southeast/south, but can appear anywhere in the sky.

July 1: Sun 14° Gemini. Death of the Solomon Jesus (June/5/12). Robert Powell refers to the death of the Solomon Jesus shortly after the Union in the Temple between the two Jesus children:

In the case of a highly developed individuality such as Zarathustra, who reincarnated as the Solomon Jesus, death signifies merely a translation of activity from one realm to another. This individuality worked on, after the death of the body on June 5, AD 12, in union with the Nathan Jesus. Thus, the Solomon Jesus was active in preparing the way for the unfolding of the earthly mission of Jesus Christ—the mission which began with the Baptism in the Jordan and culminated in the death on the cross on Golgotha.⁴

Today we are reminded of the presence of initiates working from behind the veil of sense existence. Faithfulness and perseverance (Gemini) are virtues that guide us to develop our "I." As our "I" develops we become more aware of the continuous interaction between ourselves and with beings in the spiritual worlds. Today we can bring our attention to the weaving between worlds and how this vertical communion increases the harmony between all beings—inclusive of the beings of nature.

---

3 Anonymous, *Meditations on the Tarot*, p. 640.

4 *Chron.*, p. 91.

July 2: Sun 16° Gemini. Conception of Solomon Jesus (June/7/7 BC). Two years ago we commemorated the Union in the Temple between the two Jesus children. This continues to sound through time. The Jesus being, after the union, traveled and taught, learning the deepest truths. His soul suffered from all that he saw. He saw people were afflicted with all kinds of terrible diseases that affected their souls and also their bodies. After an encounter at the altar of the pagans he heard words sounding within his soul from the spheres of Sun existence:

> Amen.
> The evils hold sway,
> Witness of egoism freeing itself.
> Selfhood guilt through others incurred,
> Experienced in the daily bread,
> Wherein the will of the heavens does not rule,
> Because human beings separated themselves
>   from your realm,
> And forgot your names,
> You Fathers in the heavens.[1]

This prayer came as he witnessed the decadence that had come into the different streams of worship, and this prayer was an inversion of what would later come (after the Baptism in the Jordan) as the Lord's Prayer. Through this prayer human beings would find protection from evil forces that would continue to prey upon them—until the end of Time. We have been told: "Heaven and Earth shall pass away but my words shall not pass away." Turning to this prayer creates a connection to Christ.

July 4: Sun 17° Gemini opposite Pluto 17° Sagittarius. Pluto continues to stand where it was during the Passion of Christ. The Sun at this degree is within a degree of where it was at the conception of the Solomon Jesus (Jun/7/7 BC). Pluto and Sun were opposite each other at the birth of this being nine months later. The Sun represents our higher "I" and Pluto in its highest expression represents the love of the Father. Inversely, egoism and hatred represent the lower influence of this aspect. Today we can find the strength of our "I" in the interior of our heart and find our "wonder" for what we may not readily understand. For, in times of change we will need to form new concepts.

July 6: Sun 19° Gemini. This position is aligned exactly with the most radiant star in our heavens, Sirius, known as the star of the Master Jesus and revered by the Egyptians as the star of Isis (a pre-Christian manifestation of Sophia). Today we celebrate Sun conjunct Sirius, which closely follows the commemoration of the conception of the Master Jesus (he who would bear the Christ).

There is a mysterious connection among the star Sirius, our Sun, and Shambhala—the golden realm at the heart of the Earth. When Sun aligns with Sirius we can imagine a conversation amplifying between the Daughter in the heights and the Mother in the depths, born through the interweaving of the Holy Soul. In our Sun-heart we can witness this communion. Sun in Gemini proclaims: "Reveal thyself, Sun life" (Steiner, *Twelve Cosmic Moods*). The inversion to the radiance of the cosmic Sun/Son, is well known, and the puppets of this anti-Son demon fill too many pages in the darker remembrances of history. Today, however, the power of great spiritual beings and great masters can illumine our hearts.

Sun enters third decan of Gemini, ruled by the Sun and associated with the constellation of the Lesser Dog, Canis Minor. The second star in this constellation, Gomeisa, signifying redemption, marks the neck of the dog at 27 1/2° Gemini. The Lesser Dog was seen by the Egyptians in connection with Horus, just as the Greater Dog was seen to be the dwelling place of Isis, and Orion was seen as the cosmic abode of Osiris.

July 12: Full Moon 25° Sagittarius opposite Sun 25° Gemini. Healing of the ten lepers (Jun/12/32). At this healing the Moon was full at this same degree. Only one of the lepers ran after him to thank him. This man became a disciple. Shortly after this healing of the ten lepers, Jesus was summoned to the house of a shepherd in order to raise the man's daughter from the dead. He told the three disciples who accompanied him—Peter, James, and John—that in his name they should do the same (see *Chron.* p. 313).

---

[1] Steiner, *The Fifth Gospel*, p. 51 (trans. revised).

SIDEREAL GEOCENTRIC LONGITUDES : JULY 2014 Gregorian at 0 hours UT

DAY	☉	☽	☊	☿	♀	♂	♃	♄	♅	♆	♇
1 TU	14 ♊ 10	24 ♋ 31	0 ♎ 11R	29 ♉ 27R	13 ♉ 58	23 ♍ 25	1 ♋ 40	22 ♎ 1R	21 ♓ 23	12 ♒ 32R	17 ♐ 25R
2 WE	15 8	6 ♌ 21	0 3	29 27D	15 10	23 49	1 53	21 59	21 24	12 32	17 24
3 TH	16 5	18 13	29 ♍ 58	29 32	16 22	24 13	2 6	21 57	21 25	12 31	17 22
4 FR	17 2	0 ♍ 11	29 55	29 41	17 34	24 38	2 19	21 56	21 26	12 30	17 21
5 SA	17 59	12 19	29 54	29 56	18 45	25 3	2 33	21 54	21 27	12 29	17 19
6 SU	18 57	24 43	29 53	0 ♊ 15	19 57	25 29	2 46	21 53	21 28	12 29	17 18
7 MO	19 54	7 ♎ 27	29 53	0 40	21 9	25 54	2 59	21 51	21 28	12 28	17 16
8 TU	20 51	20 37	29 52	1 10	22 21	26 20	3 12	21 50	21 29	12 27	17 15
9 WE	21 48	4 ♏ 15	29 49	1 44	23 33	26 47	3 25	21 49	21 30	12 26	17 13
10 TH	22 45	18 23	29 43	2 24	24 45	27 14	3 39	21 48	21 30	12 25	17 12
11 FR	23 42	2 ♐ 58	29 35	3 9	25 57	27 41	3 52	21 47	21 31	12 24	17 10
12 SA	24 40	17 55	29 25	3 58	27 9	28 8	4 5	21 46	21 31	12 23	17 9
13 SU	25 37	3 ♑ 6	29 14	4 52	28 21	28 36	4 18	21 45	21 32	12 22	17 7
14 MO	26 34	18 19	29 4	5 52	29 33	29 4	4 32	21 44	21 32	12 21	17 6
15 TU	27 31	3 ♒ 24	28 55	6 55	0 ♊ 45	29 32	4 45	21 44	21 33	12 20	17 5
16 WE	28 28	18 13	28 49	8 4	1 57	0 ♎ 0	4 58	21 43	21 33	12 19	17 3
17 TH	29 26	2 ♓ 38	28 45	9 17	3 9	0 29	5 11	21 43	21 33	12 18	17 2
18 FR	0 ♋ 23	16 39	28 44	10 34	4 22	0 58	5 25	21 42	21 33	12 17	17 0
19 SA	1 20	0 ♈ 14	28 44	11 56	5 34	1 28	5 38	21 42	21 34	12 16	16 59
20 SU	2 17	13 26	28 44	13 23	6 46	1 57	5 51	21 42	21 34	12 15	16 57
21 MO	3 15	26 19	28 42	14 53	7 59	2 27	6 5	21 42D	21 34	12 14	16 56
22 TU	4 12	8 ♉ 56	28 39	16 28	9 11	2 57	6 18	21 42	21 34R	12 12	16 54
23 WE	5 9	21 19	28 33	18 6	10 24	3 28	6 31	21 42	21 34	12 11	16 53
24 TH	6 7	3 ♊ 33	28 23	19 48	11 36	3 58	6 45	21 43	21 34	12 10	16 52
25 FR	7 4	15 39	28 12	21 34	12 49	4 29	6 58	21 43	21 34	12 9	16 50
26 SA	8 1	27 39	27 59	23 23	14 1	5 0	7 11	21 43	21 33	12 7	16 49
27 SU	8 59	9 ♋ 34	27 45	25 15	15 14	5 32	7 25	21 44	21 33	12 6	16 47
28 MO	9 56	21 27	27 32	27 10	16 27	6 4	7 38	21 45	21 33	12 5	16 46
29 TU	10 53	3 ♌ 17	27 21	29 7	17 39	6 35	7 51	21 45	21 33	12 3	16 45
30 WE	11 51	15 8	27 12	1 ♋ 7	18 52	7 8	8 5	21 46	21 32	12 2	16 43
31 TH	12 48	27 1	27 6	3 8	20 5	7 40	8 18	21 47	21 32	12 1	16 42

INGRESSES :

1 ☽ → ♌	11: 7	16 ☽ → ♓	19:33
2 ☊ → ♍	12:53	17 ☉ → ♋	14:22
3 ☽ → ♍	23:38	18 ☽ → ♈	23:35
5 ☿ → ♊	5:44	21 ☽ → ♉	6:57
6 ☽ → ♎	10: 2	23 ☽ → ♊	16:59
8 ☽ → ♏	16:36	26 ☽ → ♋	4:43
10 ☽ → ♐	19:10	28 ☽ → ♌	17:20
12 ☽ → ♑	19: 7	29 ☿ → ♋	10:38
14 ♀ → ♊	9: 3	31 ☽ → ♍	6: 0
☽ → ♒	18:33		
15 ♂ → ♎	23:43		

ASPECTS & ECLIPSES :

2 ☽ ☍ ♆ 12:29	12 ☉ ☍ ☽ 11:24	☉ □ ♂ 6:23	28 ☽ ☌ A 3:13
4 ☉ ☍ ♇ 7:42	☽ ☊ ☊ 17:58	20 ☽ ☍ ♄ 15:19	☿ □ ☊ 4: 8
5 ☉ □ ☽ 11:58	13 ☽ ☍ ♃ 1:56	22 ☿ ☍ ♇ 6:32	♀ ☍ ♇ 6:17
☽ ☍ ♅ 17:45	☽ ☌ P 8:25	24 ☽ ☌ ♀ 17:43	29 ☽ ☍ ♆ 17:45
6 ☽ ☌ ♂ 1:30	14 ♂ ☌ ☊ 0: 2	☉ ☌ ♃ 20:48	
☽ ☌ ☊ 9:50	15 ☽ ☌ ♆ 14:23	☿ □ ♅ 23:55	
8 ☽ ☌ ♄ 2:10	16 ☉ □ ☊ 7:55	25 ☽ ☍ ♇ 2:21	
☉ □ ♅ 16:13	18 ☽ ☌ ♅ 8:35	☽ ☌ ☿ 13:54	
10 ☽ ☍ ♀ 11:30	☽ ☌ ☋ 21:18	26 ☽ ☋ ☊ 0:39	
11 ☽ ☍ ☿ 0:18	19 ☉ □ ☽ 2: 8	☽ ☌ ♃ 19:33	
☽ ☌ ♇ 22:46	☽ ☍ ♂ 2:17	☉ ☌ ☽ 22:41	

SIDEREAL HELIOCENTRIC LONGITUDES : JULY 2014 Gregorian at 0 hours UT

DAY	Sid. Time	☿	♀	⊕	♂	♃	♄	♅	♆	♇	Vernal Point
1 TU	18:35:53	6 ♑ 6	29 ♓ 2	14 ♐ 10	4 ♏ 29	5 ♋ 0	26 ♎ 40	18 ♓ 30	10 ♒ 53	17 ♐ 19	5 ♓ 3'28"
2 WE	18:39:50	9 19	0 ♈ 38	15 8	5 0	5 5	26 41	18 30	10 53	17 20	5 ♓ 3'28"
3 TH	18:43:46	12 36	2 14	16 5	5 31	5 10	26 43	18 31	10 54	17 20	5 ♓ 3'28"
4 FR	18:47:43	15 56	3 49	17 2	6 3	5 15	26 45	18 32	10 54	17 20	5 ♓ 3'28"
5 SA	18:51:39	19 22	5 25	17 59	6 34	5 20	26 47	18 32	10 54	17 21	5 ♓ 3'27"
6 SU	18:55:36	22 52	7 1	18 56	7 5	5 24	26 49	18 33	10 55	17 21	5 ♓ 3'27"
7 MO	18:59:32	26 27	8 37	19 54	7 37	5 29	26 51	18 34	10 55	17 21	5 ♓ 3'27"
8 TU	19: 3:29	0 ♒ 8	10 13	20 51	8 8	5 34	26 53	18 34	10 55	17 22	5 ♓ 3'27"
9 WE	19: 7:25	3 55	11 49	21 48	8 40	5 39	26 54	18 35	10 56	17 22	5 ♓ 3'27"
10 TH	19:11:22	7 48	13 25	22 45	9 11	5 44	26 56	18 36	10 56	17 22	5 ♓ 3'27"
11 FR	19:15:18	11 47	15 1	23 42	9 43	5 49	26 58	18 36	10 57	17 23	5 ♓ 3'27"
12 SA	19:19:15	15 54	16 37	24 40	10 15	5 54	27 0	18 37	10 57	17 23	5 ♓ 3'26"
13 SU	19:23:12	20 8	18 13	25 37	10 47	5 58	27 2	18 38	10 57	17 23	5 ♓ 3'26"
14 MO	19:27: 8	24 30	19 49	26 34	11 18	6 3	27 4	18 38	10 58	17 23	5 ♓ 3'26"
15 TU	19:31: 5	29 0	21 26	27 31	11 50	6 8	27 5	18 39	10 58	17 24	5 ♓ 3'26"
16 WE	19:35: 1	3 ♓ 39	23 2	28 28	12 22	6 13	27 7	18 40	10 58	17 24	5 ♓ 3'26"
17 TH	19:38:58	8 26	24 38	29 26	12 54	6 18	27 9	18 40	10 59	17 24	5 ♓ 3'26"
18 FR	19:42:54	13 22	26 14	0 ♑ 23	13 26	6 23	27 11	18 41	10 59	17 25	5 ♓ 3'26"
19 SA	19:46:51	18 27	27 50	1 20	13 58	6 28	27 13	18 41	10 59	17 25	5 ♓ 3'25"
20 SU	19:50:47	23 41	29 27	2 17	14 30	6 33	27 15	18 42	11 0	17 25	5 ♓ 3'25"
21 MO	19:54:44	29 4	1 ♉ 3	3 15	15 3	6 37	27 17	18 43	11 0	17 26	5 ♓ 3'25"
22 TU	19:58:41	4 ♈ 37	2 39	4 12	15 35	6 42	27 18	18 43	11 0	17 26	5 ♓ 3'25"
23 WE	20: 2:37	10 18	4 16	5 9	16 7	6 47	27 20	18 44	11 1	17 26	5 ♓ 3'25"
24 TH	20: 6:34	16 7	5 52	6 6	16 40	6 52	27 22	18 45	11 1	17 27	5 ♓ 3'25"
25 FR	20:10:30	22 3	7 29	7 4	17 12	6 57	27 24	18 45	11 2	17 27	5 ♓ 3'25"
26 SA	20:14:27	28 7	9 5	8 1	17 45	7 2	27 26	18 46	11 2	17 27	5 ♓ 3'25"
27 SU	20:18:23	4 ♉ 16	10 42	8 58	10 17	7 7	27 28	18 47	11 2	17 28	5 ♓ 3'24"
28 MO	20:22:20	10 29	12 18	9 56	18 50	7 11	27 30	18 47	11 3	17 28	5 ♓ 3'24"
29 TU	20:26:16	16 46	13 55	10 53	19 22	7 16	27 31	18 48	11 3	17 28	5 ♓ 3'24"
30 WE	20:30:13	23 5	15 31	11 51	19 55	7 21	27 33	18 49	11 3	17 29	5 ♓ 3'24"
31 TH	20:34:10	29 25	17 8	12 48	20 28	7 26	27 35	18 49	11 4	17 29	5 ♓ 3'24"

INGRESSES :

1 ♀ → ♈	14:32
7 ☿ → ♒	23: 8
15 ☿ → ♓	5:12
17 ⊕ → ♑	14:26
20 ♀ → ♉	8:17
21 ☿ → ♈	4: 3
26 ☿ → ♉	7:24
31 ☿ → ♊	2:14

ASPECTS (HELIOCENTRIC +MOON(TYCHONIC)) :

2 ♂ △ ♃ 4:16	8 ♀ ⚹ ♆ 10:37	14 ⊕ ⚹ ♄ 12:52	21 ☽ ☍ ♄ 1:48	☿ ☌ ☊ 6: 0	☽ ☍ ♆ 15:45
☽ ☍ ♆ 9:11	☽ ☌ ♄ 11: 9	☿ △ ♄ 13:49	☽ ☌ ♀ 10:15	☿ ☍ ♄ 21:19	☿ ☌ P 22:40
4 ⊕ ☌ ♇ 7:42	9 ☽ ☌ ♂ 7:52	☿ ⚹ ⊕ 14: 3	☿ □ ⊕ 21:51	26 ☽ ☌ ♃ 18:59	
☿ ⚹ ♅ 18:16	10 ☿ □ ♂ 9:44	15 ☽ ☌ ♆ 12:11	22 ☿ □ ♃ 9: 2	27 ♀ □ ♆ 5:10	
♀ □ ♃ 22:28	☿ ☌ ♆ 18:56	16 ☿ △ ♃ 13:13	☽ ☍ ♂ 13:25	☿ ⚹ ♃ 11: 9	
5 ⊕ ☌ A 6:30	11 ☽ ☌ ♇ 23: 8	17 ☽ ☌ ☿ 15: 8	23 ☿ ⚹ ♆ 3: 0	☿ △ ⊕ 21:28	
☽ ☍ ♅ 12: 8	12 ☿ ⚹ ♀ 6:38	18 ☿ △ ♂ 0:23	24 ☿ △ ♇ 5:26	♂ △ ♅ 22:11	
⊕ □ ♅ 14: 6	☿ ⚹ ♇ 8:27	☽ ☌ ♅ 3:33	♀ △ ⊕ 8:47	28 ☿ □ ♆ 2: 7	
6 ☿ ☋ ☊ 4:42	♀ △ ♇ 11:26	♀ ☍ ♄ 14:28	♀ ⚹ ♃ 15:40	☿ ☌ ♀ 9:19	
7 ☽ ☍ ♀ 2:27	13 ☽ ☍ ♃ 4:33	☿ □ ♇ 19:11	⊕ ☍ ♃ 20:48	29 ☿ ⚹ ♅ 7:43	
☿ □ ♄ 2:36	♂ □ ♆ 8: 8	19 ☿ ☌ ♅ 1: 7	25 ☽ ☍ ♇ 3:35	☿ ☍ ♂ 10:49	

On this Full Moon we can contemplate the virtue of Sagittarius: Control of Speech, which engenders a feeling for truth. When we speak in union with our conscience, we are speaking in unison with our angel; and our angel serves the great Spirits of Time, and these great beings serve Christ. Like Peter, James, and John, we too are urged to heal in Christ's name, and this we do as we learn to control our speech. We live in a world painfully intertwined with words that have woven lies and deception. Such words are carried by negative elementals and these captured beings are forced to serve disease and afflictions. This Moon asks that we raise ourselves from the sleep of forgetfulness and find a willingness to serve the good, the beautiful, and the true. May we find our way to freedom through truth. In this way we can raise our consciousness from the grave of denial that sees not the effects of materialism on the body, soul, and spirit of humanity and nature.

July 15: Venus enters Gemini. "Act upon reposing's urge" (Steiner, *Twelve Cosmic Moods*). This constellation opens to the mysteries of the cosmic heart—the central Sun—the origin of the Holy Spirit. We are to act in accordance with directives from above, while here below we are reposed in harmonious quietude of being.

July 16: Mars enters Libra. "And beings give rise to beings" (Steiner, *Twelve Cosmic Moods*). At the fulcrum of balance in the scales of Libra we find stillness. From this still-point conscience awakens to what weaves in our relationships that bear a karma from the past. Standing courageously before the realities we have created gives rise to consciousness of how to right all error. In so doing higher beings unite with us, and these beings of the heights give rise to our higher being.

July 18: Sun enters Cancer. "You resting, luminous glow" (Rudolf Steiner, *Twelve Cosmic Moods*). William Bento illumines this mantra:

> As the Sun reaches its zenith in the summer sky, it appears to rest and emit a luminous glow of warmth and light. This high point of the yearly cycle offers us the opportunity to express our gratitude for all the life we see around us, knowing that its existence is due to the Sun's luminosity. This phrase opens the breast and allows our heart to enter into dialogue with the mighty orb of warmth and light that bestows life to all.

In Cancer "Selflessness becomes Catharsis." The instinct to purify oneself is amplified. The Cathars were the "pure ones." The first decan is ruled by Mercury and is associated with the constellation of Argo the Ship—in which, according to Greek mythology, Jason and the Argonauts recovered the Golden Fleece.

July 19: Sun 2° Cancer square Mars 2° Libra. The Wedding at Cana (Dec/28/29). Heliocentric Mars was at this degree when Jesus turned water into wine at the wedding at Cana. This miracle reveals itself through a series of pictures. the exhaustion of the old wine, the filling of the empty vessels with water, and the turning of the water into new wine. In the exhaustion of the old wine, we see that the Yahweh function in the blood had been spent. Heredity alone would no longer represent the ties within a community; something more was needed. Through Christ's first miracle, community born of spirit came into being—the horizontal stream of heredity was raised into the vertical stream of spirit. In the filling of the vessels with water, we see the wine that stirs the blood being replaced by the clear, cool element that reflects what is above. The water element freed humanity from the stirring old forces in the blood and opened the possibility to love beyond the confines of blood relationships.

In the changing of the water into wine we see that the water is imbued with a force of pure love, which created a new wine—the wine of spirit descending into time—in contrast to the wine of ancestry, which had perpetuated itself to exhaustion. Through this miracle, humanity was given the capacity to form community based on spiritual blood—in contrast to being bound to hereditary blood. Thus Christ healed the future. From the stream of time moving toward us from the future, the radiant stream of descending eternal light will gradually transfigure our blood, freeing our soul for union with its higher self. This sacred union is to be mirrored in marriages—as the source of the new wine of karmic clairvoyance and respect toward the mission of each one.

With Mars square Uranus our will (Mars) can find obedience to our highest aim and seek to ray forth in order to illumine the highest in others. This is a day to practice the act of "presencing," and to honor the mystery of the forces that weave between Jesus and Mary for all time.

July 21. Sun 4° Cancer. Jesus teaches the significance of the word *Amen* (*Chron.*, p. 306). This is also where the Sun was at the July 2009 eclipse five years ago, when Pluto stood exactly where it was at the Baptism of Christ. The word "Amen" represents Christ and he is the one who calls us to take up our cross, and create the "new wine" yesterday remembers. Valentin Tomberg addresses the Amen:

"A: The risen head; M: The risen hands; E: The inner life of the resurrection body; N: The force of [the resurrection body's] denial of evil."[1]

The Amen is Christ in his cosmic robes. This is a day to experience the presence of the Amen and the power of the eurythmy gesture "N" as "No" to forces rising from the abyss. This is the gesture for the constellation of Pisces, making this the gesture of our time as we are living in the Piscean Age of the Consciousness Soul.

Saturn stations before going direct 21° Libra: Death of Rudolf Steiner (Mar/30/25). Saturn will be within two degrees of its position at Steiner's death. When a planet stations, it emphasizes what was inscribed at that point in the circle of the zodiac.

July 22: Mercury 17° Pisces opposite Pluto 17° Sagittarius. St. Thomas Aquinas is writing his *Summa Theologica* (1271). Pluto was at this degree in 1271 when Thomas Aquinas was working on his best-known work *Summa Theologica*. There he wrote that the effect of the sacraments is to infuse justifying grace into human beings. In December, two years later, while saying Mass, this noble-minded philosopher experienced a vision, and when urged to take up his pen again he replied: "Such things have been revealed to me that all that I have written seems to me as so much straw. Now I await the end of my life." He died three months later on March 7, 1274.

As Pluto continues to stand where it was at the Mystery of Golgotha, we can imagine that the vision experienced by Aquinas, with Pluto remembering this greatest mystery of Earth evolution, was so life-filled, that any intellectual pursuit dimmed in comparison.

With Mercury opposing Pluto, the human mind (Mercury) seeks the eternal love that governs all creation, and seeks to align the will (Pluto) with the forces of eternal life. Mercury was here at the last anointing of Christ by Magdalene, and two days later Jesus Christ would perform the sacrament of the Last Supper. Today we can seek the sacrament that infuses justifying grace into human beings. What is this? It is communion with love (Pisces)—the central focus of all sacramental celebration.

July 23: Uranus stations before going retrograde 21° Pisces. Conception of John the Baptist (Sept/9/3 BC). Uranus is within two degrees of where it was at this special event. With Uranus now turning retrograde, all the outer planets are retrograde (Uranus/Neptune/Pluto). Does this signify a cultural need for introspection?

July 24: Sun conjunct Jupiter 6° Cancer. Magdalene's Second Conversion (Dec/26/30). At 6° Capricorn, opposite to today's conjunction, Magdalene was healed of her demons by Jesus Christ. A contemporary modern seer describes the soul of Magdalene just before she was converted:

> Magdalene was restless, animated with a spirit of sarcasm. Then a sickly feeling of oppression overcame her. A heavy atmosphere enveloped and pressed down upon her. She grew lethargic, trapped in the darkness, seeming even to lose self-awareness.
>
> This apathy was a lower emotion even than fear or anger. It was a feeling of powerlessness, of being devoid of light, devoid of hope. With fear or anger there is still a will to act; but in the case of the kind of black apathy to which Magdalene was succumbing, the will forces were all

---

[1] Tomberg, *Christ and Sophia*, p. 300.

but snuffed out. She had no will to save herself, and no one else present had a will to save her.[1]

This scene calls to mind the emptiness that is afflicting so many today. We call it depression, or melancholia. It marks a lack of hope. The path to hopelessness is carved by doubt. Doubts become vessels through which demons can occupy the soul and thereby create hopelessness. Sun was at today's degree less than two and one half weeks before the death of Lazarus. In a sense we could call Magdalene's soul mood, before the second conversion, a kind of being lost amongst the dead—as was Lazarus before he was raised to new life. This state of lifelessness is the quandary that results when we have separated from the true light. With Sun and Jupiter conjunct in Cancer, we are called to the work of catharsis—a process whereby we muster the courage to meet our repressed emotions in order to release them, thus reentering alignment with the light. This can be a contemplation for today.

Mercury 21° Gemini square Uranus 21° Pisces. Heliocentric Uranus Remembers the Conception of John the Baptist (Sept/9/3 BC). With Mercury square Uranus there is a quickening in the receptivity of illumined thinking—the thinking that permeated John. Inversely, there is a possibility that illusory thinking leads to distortions of truth, leading to the veneration of false ideals and false authorities. This conjunction of Mercury/Uranus heightens perception in one way or another as the stars remember the conception of John. May we feel the presence of this great individuality.

July 26/27: New Moon 9° Cancer. The New Moon on the 26th will, by the 27th, be in conjunction with Praesepe, the Beehive (12 1/2° Cancer). Jupiter stands nearby at 7° Cancer. Therefore, Sun, Moon and Jupiter stand together in the heavens over the days leading up to and following this New Moon. This confluence reminds us that esoteric teachers have been proclaimed and will soon be speaking. We live in a critical time as the second Fall is happening—whereby the fall to earth becomes the fall into the sub-earth. The spiritual world will continually send esoteric teachers to guide us during this grave period of evolution. We are the religion of the gods; and if we do not take up the quest for goodness, all could be lost. Many significant individualities are still to come.

In his book *Christ and the Maya Calendar*, Powell has suggested that the Maitreya individuality—also known as the Kalki Avatar—has been prophesied to begin his teachings in July of 2014.[2]

> When the Supreme lord has appeared on Earth as Kalki, the maintainer of religion, Satya Yuga will begin, and human society will bring forth progeny in the mode of goodness...When the Moon, the Sun, and Brhaspati (Jupiter) are together in the constellation Karkata (Cancer), and all three enter simultaneously in the lunar mansion Pushya—at that exact moment the age of Satya, or Krita, will begin. (S'rimad Bhagavatam 12.2.22, 24)[3]

The prophesied conjunction of the Sun, Moon, and Jupiter in Cancer takes place today, possibly signifying the emergence of the Satya Yuga and the reemergence of the Kalki Avatar. This heavenly sign will inaugurate a new spiritual era. This being is also mentioned by Valentin Tomberg, who called the appearance of this individuality a fusion of revelation and knowledge:

> Since it is a question of the work of the fusion of revelation and knowledge, of spirituality and intellectuality, it is a matter throughout of the fusion of the Avatar principle with the Buddha principle. In other words, the Kalki Avatar awaited by the Hindus and the Maitreya Buddha awaited by the Buddhists will manifest in a single personality. On the historical planes the Maitreya Buddha and the Kalki Avatar will be one.[4]

Tomberg goes on to say:

> In other words, the Buddha-Avatar to come will not only speak of the good, but he will speak the good; he will not merely teach the way of salvation, but he will advance the course of this

---

[1] Isaacson, *Through the Eyes of Mary Magdalene*, vol. 1, pp. 96–97.

[2] See Robert Powell's article in this Journal.

[3] Powell and Dann, *Christ and the Maya Calendar*, p. 204.

[4] Anonymous, *Meditations on the Tarot*, p. 614.

way; he will not be solely a witness of the divine and spiritual world, but he will make human beings into authentic witnesses of this world; he will not simply explain the profound meaning of revelation, but he will bring human beings themselves to attain to the illuminating experience of revelation, of a kind that it will not be he who will win authority but rather He who is "the true light that enlightens every human being coming into the world" (John 1:9)—Jesus Christ, the Word made flesh, who is the way, the truth and the life.[5]

The one who came in the last century to continue the living stream of Anthroposophy, comes again (in every century) to continue the moral schooling that leads human beings to the place within whereby they proclaim out of their own "illuminating experience of revelation" through their connection to the Etheric Christ, the Light of the World. Having just celebrated a memory of the conception of John, we can be assured that the Church of John will make itself known in this age of the Satya Yuga. (See Robert Powell's article in this Journal for more on this theme.)

Sun enters second decan of Cancer, ruled by Venus. This decan contains the star cluster Praesepe, the Beehive (12 1/2 ° Cancer). According to Rudolf Steiner in his talks on beekeeping: "Bees surrender themselves entirely to Venus, unfolding a life of love through the whole beehive." This decan is associated with the neck of the Lesser Bear, Ursa Minor.

Praesepe, the beehive, is at the center of the spiraling arms of Cancer, the heart of the crab. It was through this gateway that the Greeks believed human souls entered earthly incarnation in order to gather the golden nectar of earthly experience to take back to Sophia, the Queen of the cosmic realm. Cancer marks a point of decision in our yearly journey through the zodiac: development or envelopment? The spiraling arms of Cancer invite us to breathe in the Light and to move forward with the evolution of life and consciousness. The opposite is envelopment, whereby we are arrested in our progress and are thus relegated to the dark corridors of rigidified convention—if we stay here too long, our atrophied forces may eventually turn toward the unrighteous.

July 28: Venus 16° Gemini opposite Pluto 16° Sagittarius. The death of the Solomon Jesus (Jun/5/12). Retrograde Pluto returns to its position at Pentecost, and Venus at this degree remembers the death of the Solomon Jesus shortly after the union between the two Jesus children in AD12. Yesterday the prophesied beginning of the Satya Yuga and the new teachings of the Maitreya/Kalki Avatar were heralded from the stars. The Satya Yuga lasts from 1899 to 4399 and is called the Age of the Fifth Sun. The World Pentecost that Steiner, Tomberg, and Powell all address may be at hand. We have been preparing in the "time-in-between" 1899 and our present moment in history. As today also remembers the death of the wisdom-filled Solomon Jesus and the influence of yesterday's New Moon continues, we can pay close attention to the wisdom of Jupiter showering us with a Praesepe-like golden nectar. The World Pentecost is an influence of great duration, extending over thousands of years.

AUGUST 2014

The outer (and not visible to the unaided eye) planets of Uranus, Neptune and Pluto remain Retrograde. The Sun begins August in Cancer (the Crab) and moves into Leo (the Lion) on the 18th. Mercury and Jupiter join on the 2nd, but we can only sense them with our inner capacities as the Sun's radiance will shield them from our 'normal' vision. On the 3rd the half Moon will cross past Mars and on the 4th, Saturn who are both in Libra (the Scales). Mars and Saturn are quite close together now, as Mars is more fleet of foot than Cosmic-Memory-Keeper Saturn. Look to the south/south west as the August warmth softens into sweet summer night. On the 8th, Mercury joins the Sun exactly. On the 10th the Moon is Full in Capricorn, opposing the Sun in Cancer. By the 18th, the Sun has passed Jupiter who is conjunct Venus as Morning Star. You might catch them just before sunrise on a flat, clear

---

5 Ibid., pp. 614–615.

eastern horizon, but they are still on the edge of too close to the Sun's power to be seen (only about 19° away.) August always brings the best known meteor shower. the Perseids. The meteor shower runs from July 17 to August 24, with the peak this year on the night of August 12th and morning of the 13th. The waning Moon's light may hide some but with up to 60 meteors per hour, this is a great show on a summer's eve! Best viewing after midnight; the meteors will radiate from the constellation of Perseus (look to the northeast) but can appear anywhere in the sky. On the two days preceding the Leo New Moon on the 25th, the Moon crosses Jupiter in Cancer (the 23rd) and Venus in Gemini (the 24th); again, it is the early risers who will have a look at this beautiful arrangement of expansive heart. The rest of us will need to sense it during the daylight hours, shining behind the glow of our nearest star. On the 25th, Mars catches up with Saturn , with Saturn 'stacked' above red shining Mars. To round out the month, the waxing Moon joins these two beginning the 30th ; keep your eyes on the southwest after sunset to watch their dance over the next 2 days.

August 1: Venus 21° Gemini square Uranus 21° Pisces. Uranus has been at this degree since mid-June and will remain here until the end of this month. Two previous memories of Uranus close to this degree are the publishing of Christian Rosenkreutz's *Chymical Wedding* in 1616, and the (heliocentric) conception of John the Baptist. It is interesting to note that Rosenkreutz, who was the reincarnated Lazarus, was and continues to be very closely aligned with John. With Venus in square to these memories, we are called to find harmony in our feeling life (Venus), which is the seat of our etheric body. Finding harmony with nature and with spirit helps bring us to balance. We are not to deny the body nor the spirit, but rather we are to balance the two harmoniously. Then can the revelations (Uranus) of Lazarus-John find us prepared.

Mars 8° Libra square Jupiter 8° Cancer. Heliocentric Mars was here at the flight into Egypt of the family of the Solomon Jesus (Mar/2/5 BC), **and also at the birth of the Nathan Jesus (Dec/6/2BC).** Mars in square to Jupiter calls us to temper extremist behaviors through applying the wisdom of Jupiter. Thus will a dynamic relationship occur between the two, where contemplative higher thinking (Jupiter) brings wisdom to the actions Mars seeks to do. With Mars remembering the flight and the birth of the Nathan Jesus, there is much to contemplate for the sake of hermetic wisdom (Jupiter) and peace-filled words (Mars).

August 7: Sun enters third decan of Cancer, ruled by the Moon and associated with the flank of the Great Bear (Ursa Major).

August 8: Mercury superior conjunction with the Sun 21° Cancer. Parsifal's first visit to the Grail Castle (July/15/32). The Sun was within two degrees of today's position at this first visit by Parsifal. The virtue of Cancer—*Selflessness becomes catharsis*—certainly applies to the path of initiation upon which Parsifal tread. Today calls forth this memory and the cross between two points of view that we are to master on our path to the Grail—the Cain stream of the dark beam of the cross and the Able stream of the light beam of the cross. When we make peace with the Cain and the Abel who within us dwell, we will be carriers of the Rose Cross—the Grail Cross.

August 9: Venus enters Cancer. "Engender Warmth of Life" (Steiner, *Twelve Cosmic Moods*)

Venus in Cancer asks that we feel into the full flowering of each day, each summer, and each lifetime. Every flowering is an expression of life's warmth, and this warmth is to be lovingly shared with others. Venus was in Cancer at the death of the Virgin Mary, at the conception of the Solomon Jesus and at the birth of John the Baptist.

August 10: Full Moon 23° Capricorn opposite Sun 23° Cancer. This Moon stands opposite where the Sun was at the Death of Lazarus (July/15/32). Lazarus lay in the sleep of initiation that led to his death and later to his resurrection through Christ. What happened in these eleven days between his sleep and his being raised from the dead? A contemporary seer speaks words that pierce many hearts with their truth. She speaks of the three days of an initiation trial that were to culminate in Lazarus returning to his body. But this was not to be. After having

SIDEREAL GEOCENTRIC LONGITUDES: AUGUST 2014 Gregorian at 0 hours UT

DAY	☉	☽	☊	☿	♀	♂	♃	♄	⚷	♆	♇
1 FR	13 ♋ 46	9 ♍ 0	27 ♍ 2R	5 ♋ 11	21 ♊ 18	8 ♎ 13	8 ♋ 31	21 ♎ 48	21 ♓ 31R	11 ♒ 59R	16 ♐ 41R
2 SA	14 43	21 9	27 1	7 15	22 31	8 45	8 45	21 49	21 31	11 58	16 39
3 SU	15 40	3 ♎ 31	27 1D	9 19	23 44	9 18	8 58	21 51	21 30	11 56	16 38
4 MO	16 38	16 13	27 1R	11 24	24 57	9 52	9 11	21 52	21 30	11 55	16 37
5 TU	17 35	29 18	27 0	13 29	26 10	10 25	9 24	21 53	21 29	11 54	16 36
6 WE	18 33	12 ♏ 51	26 58	15 34	27 23	10 59	9 38	21 55	21 28	11 52	16 34
7 TH	19 30	26 53	26 54	17 39	28 36	11 33	9 51	21 56	21 28	11 51	16 33
8 FR	20 28	11 ♐ 23	26 47	19 43	29 49	12 7	10 4	21 58	21 27	11 49	16 32
9 SA	21 25	26 18	26 38	21 47	1 ♋ 2	12 41	10 17	22 0	21 26	11 48	16 31
10 SU	22 23	11 ♑ 31	26 29	23 49	2 15	13 15	10 31	22 2	21 25	11 46	16 30
11 MO	23 20	26 50	26 20	25 51	3 28	13 50	10 44	22 4	21 24	11 45	16 29
12 TU	24 18	12 ♒ 5	26 13	27 51	4 42	14 25	10 57	22 6	21 23	11 43	16 28
13 WE	25 15	27 5	26 7	29 50	5 55	15 0	11 10	22 8	21 22	11 41	16 26
14 TH	26 13	11 ♓ 43	26 4	1 ♌ 48	7 8	15 35	11 23	22 10	21 21	11 40	16 25
15 FR	27 10	25 54	26 3	3 44	8 22	16 11	11 36	22 13	21 20	11 38	16 24
16 SA	28 8	9 ♈ 36	26 4D	5 39	9 35	16 46	11 49	22 15	21 19	11 37	16 23
17 SU	29 6	22 53	26 5	7 33	10 48	17 22	12 2	22 18	21 18	11 35	16 22
18 MO	0 ♌ 3	5 ♉ 46	26 5R	9 25	12 2	17 58	12 15	22 20	21 17	11 33	16 21
19 TU	1 1	18 19	26 3	11 16	13 15	18 34	12 28	22 23	21 15	11 32	16 20
20 WE	1 59	0 ♊ 38	25 59	13 5	14 29	19 10	12 41	22 26	21 14	11 30	16 19
21 TH	2 57	12 45	25 53	14 53	15 43	19 47	12 54	22 29	21 13	11 29	16 18
22 FR	3 54	24 44	25 45	16 40	16 56	20 23	13 7	22 32	21 11	11 27	16 18
23 SA	4 52	6 ♋ 38	25 36	18 25	18 10	21 0	13 20	22 35	21 10	11 25	16 17
24 SU	5 50	18 30	25 27	20 9	19 24	21 37	13 33	22 38	21 8	11 24	16 16
25 MO	6 48	0 ♌ 21	25 17	21 51	20 38	22 14	13 45	22 41	21 7	11 22	16 15
26 TU	7 46	12 13	25 9	23 32	21 51	22 51	13 58	22 45	21 5	11 21	16 14
27 WE	8 44	24 8	25 3	25 12	23 5	23 29	14 11	22 48	21 4	11 19	16 13
28 TH	9 42	6 ♍ 7	24 59	26 50	24 19	24 6	14 23	22 52	21 2	11 17	16 13
29 FR	10 40	18 13	24 57	28 27	25 33	24 44	14 36	22 55	21 0	11 16	16 12
30 SA	11 38	0 ♎ 29	24 57D	0 ♍ 3	26 47	25 22	14 48	22 59	20 59	11 14	16 11
31 SU	12 36	12 57	24 58	1 38	28 1	26 0	15 1	23 3	20 57	11 12	16 11

INGRESSES:
2 ☽→♎ 17:13   19 ☽→♊ 22:45
5 ☽→♏ 1:14   22 ☽→♋ 10:36
7 ☽→♐ 5:14   24 ☽→♌ 23:17
8 ♀→♋ 3:42   27 ☽→♍ 11:46
9 ☽→♑ 5:51   29 ☽→♎ 23:4
11 ☽→♒ 4:57   ☿→♍ 23:13
13 ☿→♌ 2:3
☽→♓ 4:43
15 ☽→♈ 7:6
17 ☽→♉ 13:11
☉→♌ 22:35

ASPECTS & ECLIPSES:
1 ♀□⚷ 4:26   ☉☌☿ 16:6   15 ☽☌♅ 0:16   25 ☉☌☽ 14:12
  ♂△♃ 23:5   9 ☽☍♂ 0:31   16 ☽☍♂ 13:27   ♂☌♄ 19:25
2 ☽☍⚷ 0:43   ♀□♄ 2:38   ☽☍♆ 22:55   ☽☍♆ 22:14
  ☽☌☊ 11:26   ☿☌♀ 8:9   17 ☉□☽ 12:25   26 ♀□♄ 18:11
  ☿☌♃ 19:26   ☉□♄ 15:3   18 ♀☌♃ 5:15   27 ☽☌☿ 2:29
  ☿□♄ 23:49   ☽☍♆ 22:24   19 ☿☌♆ 3:29   ♀☌⚷ 15:28
3 ☽☌♂ 11:31   10 ☽☌♇ 17:34   21 ☽☍♃ 7:5   29 ☽☍⚷ 5:28
4 ☉□☽ 0:49   ☉☍☽ 18:8   22 ☽⚹☊ 2:2   ☽☌☊ 13:13
  ☽☌♄ 10:28   ☽☍☿ 22:12   23 ☽☍♃ 13:46   ☉☍♆ 14:25
5 ♀□☊ 16:17   11 ☽☍♆ 23:24   24 ☽☌♀ 2:1   31 ☽☌♄ 19:9
8 ☽☌♆ 8:20   14 ☽☌⚷ 16:12   ☽☌A 5:47

SIDEREAL HELIOCENTRIC LONGITUDES: AUGUST 2014 Gregorian at 0 hours UT

DAY	Sid. Time	☿	♀	⊕	♂	♃	♄	⚷	♆	♇	Vernal Point
1 FR	20:38:6	5 ♊ 43	18 ♉ 44	13 ♑ 45	21 ♏ 1	7 ♋ 31	27 ♎ 37	18 ♓ 50	11 ♒ 4	17 ♐ 29	5 ♓ 3'24"
2 SA	20:42:3	11 58	20 21	14 43	21 34	7 36	27 39	18 50	11 4	17 30	5 ♓ 3'24"
3 SU	20:45:59	18 10	21 58	15 40	22 6	7 41	27 41	18 51	11 5	17 30	5 ♓ 3'23"
4 MO	20:49:56	24 16	23 35	16 38	22 39	7 45	27 43	18 52	11 5	17 30	5 ♓ 3'23"
5 TU	20:53:52	0 ♋ 16	25 11	17 35	23 13	7 50	27 44	18 52	11 5	17 31	5 ♓ 3'23"
6 WE	20:57:49	6 8	26 48	18 33	23 46	7 55	27 46	18 53	11 6	17 31	5 ♓ 3'23"
7 TH	21:1:45	11 52	28 25	19 30	24 19	8 0	27 48	18 54	11 6	17 31	5 ♓ 3'23"
8 FR	21:5:42	17 27	0 ♊ 2	20 27	24 52	8 5	27 50	18 54	11 7	17 32	5 ♓ 3'23"
9 SA	21:9:39	22 52	1 39	21 25	25 25	8 10	27 52	18 55	11 7	17 32	5 ♓ 3'23"
10 SU	21:13:35	28 8	3 16	22 22	25 59	8 14	27 54	18 56	11 7	17 32	5 ♓ 3'22"
11 MO	21:17:32	3 ♌ 14	4 53	23 20	26 32	8 19	27 56	18 56	11 8	17 32	5 ♓ 3'22"
12 TU	21:21:28	8 11	6 29	24 18	27 6	8 24	27 57	18 57	11 8	17 33	5 ♓ 3'22"
13 WE	21:25:25	12 58	8 6	25 15	27 39	8 29	27 59	18 58	11 8	17 33	5 ♓ 3'22"
14 TH	21:29:21	17 36	9 44	26 13	28 13	8 34	28 1	18 58	11 9	17 33	5 ♓ 3'22"
15 FR	21:33:18	22 5	11 21	27 10	28 46	8 39	28 3	18 59	11 9	17 34	5 ♓ 3'22"
16 SA	21:37:14	26 25	12 58	28 8	29 20	8 44	28 5	19 0	11 9	17 34	5 ♓ 3'22"
17 SU	21:41:11	0 ♍ 38	14 35	29 6	29 54	8 48	28 7	19 0	11 10	17 34	5 ♓ 3'21"
18 MO	21:45:8	4 42	16 12	0 ♒ 3	0 ♐ 28	8 53	28 8	19 1	11 10	17 35	5 ♓ 3'21"
19 TU	21:49:4	8 39	17 49	1 1	1 1	8 58	28 10	19 1	11 11	17 35	5 ♓ 3'21"
20 WE	21:53:1	12 30	19 26	1 59	1 35	9 3	28 12	19 2	11 11	17 35	5 ♓ 3'21"
21 TH	21:56:57	16 13	21 3	2 56	2 9	9 8	28 14	19 3	11 11	17 36	5 ♓ 3'21"
22 FR	22:0:54	19 51	22 41	3 54	2 43	9 13	28 16	19 3	11 12	17 36	5 ♓ 3'21"
23 SA	22:4:50	23 23	24 18	4 52	3 17	9 17	28 18	19 4	11 12	17 36	5 ♓ 3'21"
24 SU	22:8:47	26 50	25 55	5 50	3 52	9 22	28 20	19 5	11 12	17 37	5 ♓ 3'21"
25 MO	22:12:43	0 ♎ 12	27 33	6 48	4 26	9 27	28 21	19 5	11 13	17 37	5 ♓ 3'20"
26 TU	22:16:40	3 30	29 10	7 46	5 0	9 32	28 23	19 6	11 13	17 37	5 ♓ 3'20"
27 WE	22:20:37	6 43	0 ♋ 47	8 44	5 34	9 37	28 25	19 7	11 13	17 38	5 ♓ 3'20"
28 TH	22:24:33	9 53	2 24	9 42	6 9	9 42	28 27	19 7	11 14	17 38	5 ♓ 3'20"
29 FR	22:28:30	12 59	4 2	10 40	6 43	9 46	28 29	19 8	11 14	17 38	5 ♓ 3'20"
30 SA	22:32:26	16 2	5 39	11 38	7 17	9 51	28 31	19 9	11 15	17 39	5 ♓ 3'20"
31 SU	22:36:23	19 2	7 17	12 36	7 52	9 56	28 33	19 9	11 15	17 39	5 ♓ 3'20"

INGRESSES:
4 ☿→♋ 22:56
7 ♀→♊ 23:33
10 ☿→♌ 8:41
16 ☿→♍ 20:21
17 ♂→♐ 4:27
⊕→♒ 22:38
24 ☿→♎ 22:32
26 ♀→♋ 12:21

ASPECTS (HELIOCENTRIC +MOON(TYCHONIC)):
1 ♀⚹⚷ 1:20   ☽☌⚷ 19:30   ☽☌♄ 22:29   ☿⚹♃ 1:58   26 ☿⚹♂ 13:33
  ☽☍⚷ 19:28   7 ☽☌♀ 2:54   12 ☿☍♆ 14:43   ♀□⊕ 18:0   27 ☿△⊕ 21:56
  ☿△♆ 20:32   8 ☿△⚷ 6:25   13 ☿△♆ 23:46   20 ☽☍⚷ 1:58   ☿□♃ 22:32
2 ☿△♃ 9:57   ☽☌♆ 21:24   14 ☽☌⚷ 12:11   21 ☿□♀ 9:0   28 ☽☍♆ 10:25
  ♀☌☊ 22:34   ☿☌⊕ 16:6   ♀△♇ 21:9   ☽☌♆ 9:41   29 ☽☍⚷ 1:48
3 ☿□⚷ 2:41   9 ☿☍♅ 3:6   15 ⊕☌♄ 22:38   ☽☌♀ 19:13   ⊕☌♆ 14:25
  ♀☍♂ 3:15   ☿△♂ 12:54   16 ☿⚹♄ 9:25   ☽⚹⚷ 18:40   30 ☿⚹♆ 12:53
4 ☿△♄ 13:47   ☽☌♃ 18:50   ☿☍♇ 19:6   23 ☽☌♃ 5:23   31 ☽☌♇ 15:1
  ☽☌♄ 21:9   22:53   17 ☿☌♀ 9:41   ♀☌♆ 11:50
6 ☿☌♃ 7:31   11 ☿⚹♀ 11:39   18 ♀☌♇ 20:31   25 ♀△⚷ 12:17
  ⊕⚹⚷ 8:40   ☽☍☿ 14:54   19 ⊕⚹⚷ 0:25   ☽☍♆ 21:59

descended to the heart of the Mother in the depths of the Earth, Lazarus was dangerously distracted:

> But as he passed upward through the dark spheres of the sub-earthly world, he forgot to honor John's [the Baptist] admonitions to turn away his ears from the cries of the fallen souls.
>
> Having felt always a deep concern for humanity, he wanted only to save these lost souls. Poised for a time on the precipice of indecision, wondering how he might aid at least some few of these souls, he was swept away suddenly in a tornado of darkness.
>
> At first, just one soul reached out for him. But as he gave heed to this one soul's cry, others joined in, until Lazarus was overwhelmed and overtaken by their entreaties.
>
> Their cries were strange, as if sounding through mire. It was as if the depths of the Earth swallowed their cries. And yet, Lazarus could not turn his ears away. The souls could perceive his light, and they wanted that light for themselves.
>
> As Lazarus was swept away, I saw John reach out for him. But he reached in vain, for the dark forces had waxed too powerful—Lazarus was enshrouded in the darkness, and John could not retrieve him.
>
> And so was Lazarus lost in hell. He witnessed many horrors, the horrors of all humanity's works of darkness. Holocausts and wars passed before my spiritual eyes, just as they were being projected by the wretched souls at Lazarus. I saw the most degenerate of desires acted out, desires that would moreover remain always unfulfilled.
>
> Lazarus lost touch with the love of the Mother that he had come to know. His memory of Her love was being rapidly snuffed out in the darkness. I saw him grow rigid, lying in a spiritual grave surrounded by the spiritually dead. His light became as the guttering flame of a candle, about to expire for want of air.[1]

On this day, and for the next eleven days, we can imagine the magnetic spell of forces from beings working into our time from the darkness of the underworld. We are to follow the admonitions of John, and turn our ears from this. We are to "grail" for the light in spite of the presence of dark adversarial forces. We are not to be distracted.

This Full Moon calls us to face Ahriman's work in the world and find the courage to name his presence.

August 12: Sun 25° Cancer. Birth of the Nathan Mary (July/17/17 BC). The Nathan Mary bore the vessel for the Logos. Purity and gentleness are remembered today. At this birth, Venus, Mars and Moon were all conjunct Regulus, the heart of the Lion, providing a beautiful contemplation for the purity of heart we are all striving to attain—the purity of the Nathan Mary.

August 17: Sun enters Leo. "Invigorate with senses' might" (Rudolf Steiner, *Twelve Cosmic Moods*). William Bento illumines this mantra.

One of our most primal gifts we received from the Cosmos was the possibility to be endowed with senses, to have the capacity to witness the creation of all things upon the Earth. It is a gift we can so easily take for granted. Yet, when we ponder how the Sun being has gathered the forces of the entire zodiac and poured them down upon our uprightness in such a way as to create portals into the external world, we can sensitize ourselves to feel how this streaming of forces has never ceased. It is there in the infusion and invigoration of our senses' activity in grasping the world with all its beauty.

The first decan, ruled by Saturn, is associated with the faint constellation of Leo Minor, the Lesser Lion, above Leo and below the Great Bear. The virtue: *Compassion becomes Freedom*. This freedom is the foundation of the spiritualized "I."

August 18: Venus conjunct Jupiter 12° Cancer. Praesepe; the beehive in the middle of the spiraling arms of the constellation of Cancer. Jupiter is exalted at this degree of the zodiac.

We remember Praesepe, the "Beehive" cradled at the center of the spiraling in and spiraling out of Cancer, and ponder the words of Goethe, "When the inside is in order, the outside takes care of itself." Whereas Gemini's relational aspect is all about the "other," knowing oneself through the reflection of the other, clearly Cancer is about the inside-outside

---

1 Isaacson, *Through the Eyes of Mary Magdalene*, pp. 189–190.

relationship—understanding that what lives within is reflected outwardly. This calls forth the "inner work" of redeeming the outer reality.[2]

Clearly this Venus-Jupiter conjunction is filled with the powers of catharsis in order to redeem the fallen aspects of our soul and the fallen aspects of the world's soul. Today we can seek the joy of harmony and balance so that our souls may receive the light of wisdom.

August 22: Sun 5° Regulus; the Lion's Heart. In the closing invocation by Hermes to Tat on the mysteries of the zodiac, Hermes opens to the great beings who indwell the constellation of Leo:

(turning to the North): Holy Uriel, thou who bears the memory of the Golden Age of Saturn, whence streams the foundation of human will, pray strengthen the will of all who humbly seek to unite themselves with Christ and His Mission.[3]

Regulus is one of the four Royal Stars of Persia.

Already then in ancient Persia, Zarathustra spoke of the four royal stars as the four "foundation stones" of the zodiac—Aldebaran, the Bull's eye, the central star of the Bull; Regulus, the Lion's heart, shining from the breast of the Lion; Antares, the red-glowing Scorpion's heart, the central star of the Scorpion; and bright Fomalhaut in the mouth of the Southern Fish, beneath the stream of water flowing from the urn of the Water-Carrier.[4]

In the Foundation Stone Meditation, given by Rudolf Steiner, the spirits of the elements in the East, West, North and South are to hear the prayer, and the beings in the cosmos above are "trigger points" for the directions mirrored upon the Earth below.

- Aldebaran: The Bull's eye is the watcher in the East—15° Taurus.
- Antares: The Scorpion's heart is the watcher in the West—15° Scorpio.
- Regulus: The Lion's heart is the watcher in the North—5° Leo.
- Fomalhaut. The Southern Fish is the watcher in the South—9° Aquarius.

---

2 Paul and Powell, *Cosmic Dances of the Zodiac.*
3 CHA, "Closing Invocation; The Mystery of the Zodiac."
4 CHA, "The Mystery of the Zodiac."

August 25: New Moon 7° Leo. Four days after the raising of Lazarus Jesus finds a barren fig tree (July/30/32) (see *Chron.*, p. 318). After he teaches about repentance, Jesus tells a parable.

A man had a fig tree growing in his vineyard, and he went to look for fruit on it but did not find any. So he said to the man who took care of the vineyard, "For three years now I've been coming to look for fruit on this fig tree and haven't found any. Cut it down! Why should it use up the soil?" (Luke 13:6–7)

Repentance fertilizes the soil of the soul, making it ready to sacrifice itself by bequeathing fruits through which it and others will be nourished.

ASPECT: Mars conjunct Saturn 22° Libra: Mars conjunct Saturn calls us to obedience in the face of our destiny resolves. Mars was close to this degree when Anne Catherine Emmerich received the stigmata (20° Libra). At this time heliocentric Saturn was square to (h)Mars. The biography of Anne Catherine makes it self-evident that she had the will to carry forth her destiny task. For her, this was at a great cost.

August 26: Venus 22° Cancer square Saturn/Mars 22° Libra. The Transfiguration (Apr/4/31). Heliocentric Venus was within a degree of today's Venus when Christ manifested his purified astral body to Peter, James, and John: "A shining pathway of light reached down from heaven upon Jesus Christ, comprising the different choirs of Angelic beings in descending order from heaven down to the Earth. Among the shining figures that approached Jesus in the light were Moses and Elijah."[5] The disciples cast themselves upon the ground in fear and trembling before the power of this moment, and before the whispering voice that spoke: "This is my beloved Son in whom I am well pleased. Listen to him!." Such is the power of the light on humble beings of Earth.

With Venus remembering this moment in the life of Christ, and in square with Saturn/Mars, we can open to influences that bring life (Venus) to the power of the Word (Mars) in obedience to our highest spiritual resolves (Saturn).

---

5 CHA, "The Transfiguration."

August 27: Sun enters the second decan of Leo, ruled by Jupiter and associated with the tail of the Great Bear, Ursa Major.

August 28: Sun 10° Leo. The Healing of the Nobleman's Son (Aug/3/30) (John 4:46–54). In this second miracle of Christ, he healed the stream of heredity: The present worked back onto the past. Selathiel (the royal official) had given himself to his king. He came to Christ to beg that his son Joel be healed. Joel had been adopted by his King, Zorobabel; even this he had given away. Selathiel was a *kingsman*. This means he had to suppress his own "I" to serve his master's "I." This suppression weakens the "I." The weakness of the father's "I" created a physical weakness in the son's *body*. The boy's blood was too weak to carry an "I" and therefore his blood became inflamed. In his illness the boy constantly repeated: "Jesus, the prophet of Nazareth, alone can help me!" In desperation Selathiel rode to find Jesus. Jesus spoke: "Go, your son will live!" When Selathiel asked if this was really true, Jesus responded: "Believe me, in this very hour he has been cured."[1] The nobleman's faith in Christ restored his "I" to uprightness, and simultaneously healed his son. Jesus Christ gave the nobleman a new name. Instead of *basilikos* (King's Man) he was called *pater* (father); he became "father of his own house." This fatherhood involves not only responsibility in the physical world, but also the appointment of being a spiritual authority in the home. This story teaches the absolute necessity of fathering children with spiritual authority. This healing reveals the fact of the power of the vertically aligned, Christ centered "I" over any horizontal influence in the hereditary stream. We may contemplate today where we may be compromising our true self with excuses born of some hereditary story, or to gain favor with any powers of this world. Have we become a satellite of any person or bloodline, or collective body of thought? There is a great deal of reality being created by satellite-humans. Are we moons, or suns? Do we create, or are we puppets of another's creation? Are we taking up the responsibility of spiritually fathering our children?

August 29: Sun 11° Leo opposite Neptune 11° Aquarius. Neptune in its lower octaves represents ahrimanic activities such as mass communication and propaganda. Negative Neptune influences impose ideas on others—sometimes with great force. With Neptune in Aquarius, it is the *anti-Holy Spirit* that is working from lower Neptune as a caricature of the Holy Spirit that Aquarius represents. Through corrupting the inspiration from the Holy Spirit, ahrimanic beings launch attacks against the Son of God and those who follow him. They succeed when human beings choose ahrimanic *maya* over the presence of Christ now in the etheric of the Earth. Developments in augmented reality are winning the attention of the masses, and what of their souls? Horrible things were happening in Russia when Neptune was opposite its position today. While human beings entertain themselves to death, the loathsome technologies that seek to mechanize the human soul are winning overwhelming support. Today, however, the Sun draws near to the death Sun of the Nathan Mary. In Mary lived a soul in continual contemplation of the Goddess of Night (Sophia/higher Neptune). A choosing is upon us.

August 30: Sun 12° Leo. Death of the Nathan Mary (Aug/5/12). "Not long after the event in the Temple at the Passover of AD 12, the Nathan Mary died. Rudolf Steiner describes how, seventeen years later, at the baptism in the Jordan, the Nathan Mary was spiritually united with the Solomon Mary."[2]

At the moment of this baptism in the Jordan, the mother (the Solomon Mary) was aware of something like the climax of the change that had come about in her. She was then between her forty-fifth and forty-sixth years. She felt as though pervaded by the soul of that mother (the Nathan Mary) who had died, the mother of the Jesus child who in his twelfth year had received the Zarathustra individuality. Thus the spirit of the other mother had come upon the mother with whom Jesus had held that conversation [before the baptism]. And she felt herself as the young mother who had once given birth to the Jesus child of Saint Luke's Gospel.[3]

---

[1] *CHA*, p. 103.

[2] *Chron.*, p. 116.

[3] Steiner, *The Fifth Gospel*, p. 93.

The Nathan Mary comes as Grace for those who seek her.

SEPTEMBER 2014

The Sun begins September in Leo (the Lion) and moves into Virgo (the Virgin) on the 17th. The waxing Moon is finishing up what it started with Mars and Saturn in Libra, all visible beginning in the southwest after sunset until setting about 9 pm local time. The Full Moon is on the 8th: Sun in Leo, Moon in Aquarius (the Water-Carrier.) The waning Moon joins up with Jupiter for predawn viewing on the 20th now far enough from the Sun to give late nighters a chance to view their beauty as they rise about 4 hours before sunrise. On the 23rd the barely-there waning Moon meets up with Venus in Leo before joining the Sun in Virgo on the 24th for the New Moon. After that, the growing Moon conjuncts Mercury on the 26th, Saturn on the 28th and Mars on the 29th. Pluto will have stationed direct on the 24th.

September 7: Sun enters third decan of Leo, ruled by Mars and associated with the constellation of the Hunting Dogs (Canes Venatici).

Mars enters Scorpio: "In growth working persists" (Steiner, *Twelve Cosmic Moods*). Existence consumes us as we work with death forces in order to become conscious. This is necessary. These death forces are the very same forces that transfigure the material into spiritual substance, similar to how at death the corpse separates from the higher members of the human being. Though we grow old in life, our etheric being becomes younger. The etheric realms are to open more to the maturing human consciousness, so that growth persists in higher realms even as we are consumed by the world of matter into which our bodies work and die.

September 8: Full Moon 21° Aquarius opposite Sun 21° Leo. The end of the temptations in the wilderness (Nov/30/29). The Moon was at this position early in the morning of this 40th day in the wilderness when angels came to minister to Jesus:

Just as Jesus Christ triumphed in the confrontation with evil and emerged victorious on the fortieth day—to be consoled by the heavenly nourishment of the angels—so there is every hope that humankind as a whole will successfully navigate a course through the historical period of temptation [ending historically in 2018]. It is only after passing through this that the real unfolding of the Christ Impulse will come to manifestation. Then, for example, a historical mirroring of the miracle at the wedding at Cana will take place during the Aquarian age.[4]

May we all find the wings of the dove—the presence of the Holy Spirit—under the light of this Full Moon.

September 10: Sun 22° Leo. Death of the Virgin Mary (15/Aug/44). After the Ascension of Christ, John (the son of Zebedee) took the Blessed Virgin Mary to Ephesus where she lived until her death. This great being, the Virgin Mary, goes before us into future Jupiter evolution. She ascended at her death to take up this mission on behalf of all who are uniting into the stream of Eternal Israel. She who was Eve, the mother of all, prepares the way. It is the Blessed Virgin who helps all her children find their way home:

A short time before the Blessed Virgin's death, as she felt the approach of her reunion with her God, her Son, and her Redeemer, she prayed that there might be fulfilled what Jesus had promised to her in the house of Lazarus at Bethany on the day before his Ascension. It was shown to me in the spirit how at that time, when she begged him that she might not live for long in this vale of tears after he had ascended, Jesus told her in general what spiritual works she was to accomplish before her end on Earth. He told her, too, that in answer to her prayers the apostles and several disciples would be present at her death, and what she was to say to them and how she was to bless them... After the Blessed Virgin had prayed that the apostles should come to her, I saw the call going forth to them in many different parts of the world...I saw all, the

---

4 *CHA*, "The Temptation in the Wilderness."

farthest as well as the nearest, being summoned by visions to come to the Blessed Virgin.[1]

We are encouraged to keep our focus on the mission we have come to serve, and not be unduly burdened by the "vale of tears" that is the world in which we must continue our striving. Keep the light of goodness shining for all, and especially for the children. Today we remember to behold our common Mother, the Earth, and all her elemental beings—for her redemption rests upon each of us. In the still heart compassion pours from an eternal spring.

ASPECT: Venus 10° Leo opposite Neptune 10° Aquarius. Heliocentric Venus was here at the fall of Jerusalem (Aug/29/70). And, Neptune was where Venus is today during the turmoil of the year 1930 in Russia. Venus, the planet of love, stands before sorrowful memories inscribed in the Akashic chronicle. At this degree is recorded the establishment of the GULAG (Chief Administration of Corrective Labor Camps and Colonies), peasant uprisings, collectivization of farms, mass murders and the descent of very dark clouds upon an innocent people. She would, of course, oppose such tragedy. The fall of Jerusalem and the evil in Russia can give us pause as all of humanity stands before so much change and must sort through so much propaganda that seeks to mold public opinion. Where are we headed? The only firm ground is now *within* and through contemplation of the Virgin Mary, who was the Solomon Mary. She will guide us to the New Jerusalem, which she is helping us build now through all our spiritual efforts.

September 13: Mercury 20° Virgo opposite Uranus 20° Pisces. As Neptune comes into opposition with its position during the Russian revolution, Uranus returns to where it was during these painful years. Both of these outer planets are remembering very dark times in Russia, America, and Germany. Rudolf Steiner, in his lectures to the priests, saw that what was concentrated in a small area as the work of Bolshevism in Russia was a seed that would grow and become incorporated into the whole of human evolution on earth. This is a very sobering statement! He goes on to say:

That is why it is so important that all who are capable of doing so should strive for spirituality. What is inimical to spirituality will be there anyway, for it works not through freedom but under determinism. This determinism has already decreed that at the end of this century [20th] Sorat will be on the loose again, so that the intention to sweep away anything spiritual will be deep-seated in large numbers of earthly souls, just as the apocalyptist has foreseen in the beast-like countenance and the beast-like strength that will underlie the deeds of the adversary against the spiritual. Even today the rage against spiritual things is already immense. Yet it is still only in its very early infancy.[2]

The outer planets, Uranus, Neptune, and Pluto influence generations. This is what we must understand as we gaze back on the chronicles of history that these planetary positions evoke. What was seeded in Russia, will later rain down on the collective of humanity: "So today's revolutionary upheavals in Russia will one day manifest as mighty, thunderous revolutions taking place above the heads of human beings."[3]

Heliocentric Mercury was where Mercury is today when Christ was the recipient of the enmity of the Pharisees (Mar/26/31). The man he had healed at the pool of Bethesda, after having realized who it was that had healed him, made it his business to tell the Pharisees that it was Jesus who had healed him. Scornfully, the Pharisees approached Jesus with accusations (See *Chron.*, p. 287). Today, we can contemplate our discernment (Mercury) before the new revelations (Uranus) and hold compassion, and stalwart courage, before those who are hatefully reactive to the new paradigm now forming.

September 17: Sun enters Virgo. "Behold Worlds, O soul!" (Rudolf Steiner, *Twelve Cosmic Moods*)

William Bento illumines this mantra.

The more engaged we are with the phenomena of Natura, the accompanying rhythms of social life, and the planetary and starry celestial dances above us, the more awe and wonder arise in our soul. This

---

1 Emmerich, *LBVM*, pp. 363–364

2 Steiner, *The Book of Revelation: And the Work of the Priest*, p. 118.

3 Ibid., p. 205.

SIDEREAL GEOCENTRIC LONGITUDES : SEPTEMBER 2014 Gregorian at 0 hours UT

DAY	☉	☽	☊	☿	♀	♂	♃	♄	♅	♆	♇
1 MO	13 ♌ 34	25 ♎ 41	25 ♍ 0	3 ♍ 11	29 ♋ 15	26 ♎ 38	15 ♋ 13	23 ♎ 6	20 ♓ 55R	11 ♒ 11R	16 ♐ 10R
2 TU	14 32	8 ♏ 46	25 1	4 43	0 ♌ 29	27 16	15 26	23 10	20 53	11 9	16 9
3 WE	15 30	22 13	25 1R	6 13	1 43	27 55	15 38	23 14	20 52	11 7	16 9
4 TH	16 28	6 ♐ 6	24 59	7 43	2 57	28 33	15 51	23 18	20 50	11 6	16 8
5 FR	17 26	20 24	24 56	9 11	4 11	29 12	16 3	23 23	20 48	11 4	16 8
6 SA	18 24	5 ♑ 5	24 51	10 37	5 25	29 51	16 15	23 27	20 46	11 2	16 7
7 SU	19 22	20 4	24 46	12 3	6 40	0 ♏ 30	16 27	23 31	20 44	11 1	16 7
8 MO	20 21	5 ♒ 12	24 42	13 27	7 54	1 9	16 39	23 35	20 42	10 59	16 6
9 TU	21 19	20 21	24 38	14 49	9 8	1 49	16 51	23 40	20 40	10 57	16 6
10 WE	22 17	5 ♓ 21	24 35	16 11	10 22	2 28	17 3	23 44	20 38	10 56	16 5
11 TH	23 15	20 2	24 34	17 31	11 37	3 8	17 15	23 49	20 36	10 54	16 5
12 FR	24 14	4 ♈ 19	24 34D	18 49	12 51	3 47	17 27	23 54	20 34	10 53	16 5
13 SA	25 12	18 9	24 35	20 6	14 5	4 27	17 39	23 58	20 32	10 51	16 4
14 SU	26 10	1 ♉ 33	24 36	21 21	15 20	5 7	17 51	24 3	20 30	10 50	16 4
15 MO	27 9	14 31	24 38	22 34	16 34	5 47	18 2	24 8	20 27	10 48	16 4
16 TU	28 7	27 8	24 38R	23 46	17 49	6 27	18 14	24 13	20 25	10 46	16 4
17 WE	29 6	9 ♊ 27	24 37	24 56	19 3	7 8	18 26	24 18	20 23	10 45	16 3
18 TH	0 ♍ 4	21 33	24 36	26 4	20 18	7 48	18 37	24 23	20 21	10 43	16 3
19 FR	1 3	3 ♋ 30	24 33	27 10	21 32	8 29	18 48	24 28	20 19	10 42	16 3
20 SA	2 2	15 22	24 30	28 14	22 47	9 9	19 0	24 33	20 16	10 40	16 3
21 SU	3 0	27 12	24 26	29 16	24 1	9 50	19 11	24 39	20 14	10 39	16 3
22 MO	3 59	9 ♌ 4	24 23	0 ♎ 15	25 16	10 31	19 22	24 44	20 12	10 37	16 3
23 TU	4 58	21 1	24 20	1 11	26 31	11 12	19 33	24 49	20 9	10 36	16 3D
24 WE	5 56	3 ♍ 3	24 18	2 5	27 45	11 53	19 44	24 55	20 7	10 34	16 3
25 TH	6 55	15 13	24 17	2 55	29 0	12 35	19 55	25 0	20 5	10 33	16 3
26 FR	7 54	27 32	24 16D	3 42	0 ♍ 15	13 16	20 6	25 6	20 2	10 31	16 3
27 SA	8 53	10 ♎ 3	24 17	4 26	1 29	13 57	20 17	25 11	20 0	10 30	16 3
28 SU	9 52	22 45	24 18	5 6	2 44	14 39	20 28	25 17	19 58	10 29	16 3
29 MO	10 51	5 ♏ 42	24 19	5 41	3 59	15 21	20 38	25 23	19 55	10 27	16 3
30 TU	11 49	18 54	24 20	6 12	5 14	16 3	20 49	25 29	19 53	10 26	16 4

INGRESSES :

1	☽ → ♏ 7:59	18	☽ → ♋ 16:57
	♀ → ♌ 14:37	21	☽ → ♌ 5:39
3	☽ → ♐ 13:33		☿ → ♎ 17:51
5	☽ → ♑ 15:45	23	☽ → ♍ 17:56
6	♂ → ♏ 5:26	25	♀ → ♍ 19:16
7	☽ → ♒ 15:45	26	☽ → ♎ 4:45
9	☽ → ♓ 15:24	28	☽ → ♏ 13:29
11	☽ → ♈ 16:40	30	☽ → ♐ 19:46
13	☽ → ♉ 21:11		
16	☽ → ♊ 5:32		
17	☉ → ♍ 22:12		

ASPECTS & ECLIPSES :

1	☽ ☌ ♂ 1:50		☽ ☍ ☿ 19:25		☽ ☌ A 14: 1
2	☉ □ ☽ 11:10	11	☽ ☌ ♅ 0:56	22	☽ ☍ ♆ 3: 6
4	☽ ☌ ♇ 16:54		☽ ☌ ☋ 7:31		♂ □ ♆ 3:29
5	☽ N□ ☊ 7:26	13	☿ ☍ ♅ 8: 0	23	☽ ☌ ♀ 12:15
6	☽ ☍ ♃ 18:10		☽ ☍ ♄ 10:23	24	☉ ☌ ☽ 6:13
8	☽ ☌ P 3:11	14	☽ ☍ ♂ 6:53	25	☽ ☍ ♅ 9:28
	☽ ☍ ♀ 4:37	16	☉ □ ☽ 2: 4		☽ ☌ ☊ 17:39
	☽ ☌ ♆ 9: 7		☿ ☌ ☊ 17:35	26	☽ ☌ ☿ 12:38
9	☉ ☍ ☽ 1:37	17	☽ ☍ ♇ 13: 3	28	☽ ☌ ♄ 4:46
	☿ □ ♇ 22:24	18	☽ □S ☊ 6: 5	29	☽ ☌ ♂ 18:33
10	♀ ☍ ♆ 10:37	20	☽ ☌ ♃ 7:29		

SIDEREAL HELIOCENTRIC LONGITUDES : SEPTEMBER 2014 Gregorian at 0 hours UT

DAY	Sid. Time	☿	♀	⊕	♂	♃	♄	♅	♆	♇	Vernal Point
1 MO	22:40:19	21 ♎ 59	8 ♋ 54	13 ♒ 34	8 ♐ 27	10 ♋ 1	28 ♎ 34	19 ♓ 10	11 ♒ 15	17 ♐ 39	5 ♓ 3'19"
2 TU	22:44:16	24 54	10 32	14 32	9 2	10 6	28 36	19 11	11 16	17 40	5 ♓ 3'19"
3 WE	22:48:12	27 47	12 9	15 30	9 36	10 11	28 38	19 11	11 16	17 40	5 ♓ 3'19"
4 TH	22:52: 9	0 ♏ 39	13 47	16 28	10 11	10 15	28 40	19 12	11 16	17 40	5 ♓ 3'19"
5 FR	22:56: 6	3 28	15 24	17 26	10 46	10 20	28 42	19 12	11 17	17 41	5 ♓ 3'19"
6 SA	23: 0: 2	6 17	17 2	18 24	11 21	10 25	28 44	19 13	11 17	17 41	5 ♓ 3'19"
7 SU	23: 3:59	9 4	18 39	19 22	11 56	10 30	28 46	19 14	11 17	17 41	5 ♓ 3'19"
8 MO	23: 7:55	11 50	20 17	20 20	12 31	10 35	28 47	19 14	11 18	17 41	5 ♓ 3'18"
9 TU	23:11:52	14 35	21 54	21 19	13 6	10 40	28 49	19 15	11 18	17 42	5 ♓ 3'18"
10 WE	23:15:48	17 20	23 32	22 17	13 41	10 44	28 51	19 16	11 19	17 42	5 ♓ 3'18"
11 TH	23:19:45	20 5	25 9	23 15	14 16	10 49	28 53	19 16	11 19	17 42	5 ♓ 3'18"
12 FR	23:23:41	22 50	26 47	24 14	14 51	10 54	28 55	19 17	11 19	17 43	5 ♓ 3'18"
13 SA	23:27:38	25 35	28 24	25 12	15 26	10 59	28 57	19 18	11 20	17 43	5 ♓ 3'18"
14 SU	23:31:35	28 20	0 ♌ 2	26 10	16 2	11 4	28 58	19 18	11 20	17 43	5 ♓ 3'18"
15 MO	23:35:31	1 ♐ 5	1 39	27 9	16 37	11 9	29 0	19 19	11 20	17 44	5 ♓ 3'18"
16 TU	23:39:28	3 52	3 17	28 7	17 13	11 13	29 2	19 20	11 21	17 44	5 ♓ 3'17"
17 WE	23:43:24	6 39	4 54	29 6	17 48	11 18	29 4	19 20	11 21	17 44	5 ♓ 3'17"
18 TH	23:47:21	9 27	6 32	0 ♓ 4	18 24	11 23	29 6	19 21	11 21	17 45	5 ♓ 3'17"
19 FR	23:51:17	12 17	8 9	1 3	18 59	11 28	29 8	19 21	11 22	17 45	5 ♓ 3'17"
20 SA	23:55:14	15 9	9 47	2 1	19 35	11 33	29 10	19 22	11 22	17 45	5 ♓ 3'17"
21 SU	23:59:10	18 2	11 24	3 0	20 10	11 38	29 11	19 23	11 22	17 46	5 ♓ 3'17"
22 MO	0: 3: 7	20 57	13 2	3 59	20 46	11 42	29 13	19 23	11 23	17 46	5 ♓ 3'17"
23 TU	0: 7: 4	23 55	14 39	4 57	21 22	11 47	29 15	19 24	11 23	17 46	5 ♓ 3'16"
24 WE	0:11: 0	26 55	16 17	5 56	21 58	11 52	29 17	19 25	11 24	17 47	5 ♓ 3'16"
25 TH	0:14:57	29 57	17 54	6 55	22 34	11 57	29 19	19 25	11 24	17 47	5 ♓ 3'16"
26 FR	0:10:50	3 ♑ 3	19 31	7 54	23 10	12 2	29 21	19 26	11 24	17 47	5 ♓ 3'16"
27 SA	0:22:50	6 12	21 9	8 53	23 46	12 6	29 22	19 27	11 25	17 48	5 ♓ 3'16"
28 SU	0:26:46	9 25	22 46	9 52	24 22	12 11	29 24	19 27	11 25	17 48	5 ♓ 3'16"
29 MO	0:30:43	12 42	24 24	10 50	24 58	12 16	29 26	19 28	11 25	17 48	5 ♓ 3'16"
30 TU	0:34:39	16 3	26 1	11 49	25 34	12 21	29 28	19 29	11 26	17 49	5 ♓ 3'15"

INGRESSES :

3	☿ → ♏ 18:33
13	♀ → ♌ 23:35
14	☿ → ♐ 14:32
17	⊕ → ♓ 22:15
25	☿ → ♑ 0:20

ASPECTS (HELIOCENTRIC +MOON(TYCHONIC)) :

1	☽ ☌ ♄ 5:21	7	♀ △ ♅ 8:35	16	☽ ☍ ☿ 16:53		☿ ☌ ♂ 22: 8	30	⊕ △ ♃ 13:58
	☿ ☌ ☋ 12:53		☿ △ ♃ 12:48		♂ ☌ ♇ 21:30	22	☽ ☍ ♆ 4:39		
	♀ ☌ ♃ 17:18		☿ □ ♆ 19:20		⊕ △ ♄ 23:16		☽ ☌ ♀ 9:13		
3	☿ ☌ ♄ 7: 8	8	☽ ☌ ♆ 9:38	17	☽ ☍ ♇ 16:25	24	☿ ⚹ ♄ 18:54		
4	☽ ☌ ♂ 7:13	10	☿ △ ♅ 16:50		☽ ☍ ♂ 17:23		♀ △ ♇ 22:15		
	☽ ☌ ♇ 19:29		☽ ☌ ♅ 22:44	18	☿ ⚹ ♆ 16: 9	25	☽ ☍ ♅ 8:14		
5	⊕ ⚹ ♇ 6: 2	11	☿ ☌ A 23:12	19	♂ □ ♅ 15:19	27	♀ N□ ☊ 10:39		
	♀ ☌ P 21: 2	12	☿ □ ⊕ 18:53		☽ ☌ ♃ 16:13	28	☿ ⚹ ⊕ 4:38		
	♂ ⚹ ♆ 21:28	13	♀ □ ♄ 8: 8	20	☿ ☌ ♇ 21:46		☽ ☌ ♄ 12:25		
6	☽ ☍ ♃ 8:38		☽ ☍ ♄ 19:19		♀ ☍ ♆ 23:33		☿ ☍ ♃ 20:47		
	☽ ☍ ♀ 21:29	15	☿ △ ♀ 11:50	21	☿ □ ♅ 11:10	29	♀ △ ♂ 13:26		

beholding is more than seeing; it is immersion into conscious participation—mystique. The mystery of worlds is precisely what the longing of the soul seeks to know; and so this beholding is indeed not a static event, but the movement of the soul into worlds known and unknown.

The first decan is ruled by the Sun, and associated with the constellation of the Cup (Crater): here we can think of the Grail chalice held by the Queen of Peace, represented by the Virgin. The virtue of Virgo: *Courtesy becomes tactfulness of heart*. The inner work of descent (Persephone) brings the awareness of self-knowledge. Hydra "the Serpent" stretches its undulating life force throughout the entire region beneath Virgo. To become self-aware, we must confront the serpent.

Sun 0° 19' Virgo. The Moon (portal to both angels and demons) stood here at the beginning of the forty days in the wilderness. In describing these forty days of continual temptation of Christ, Anne Catherine Emmerich depicts how Christ never once looked at his tempters. Instead he addressed himself directly to his Father in Heaven. This is a powerful example for humanity, who is now facing the united activity of the tempters on a global scale. May we remember to keep our attention on the in-streaming of spiritual Light and Love! This is what guides us through the changes so very necessary in our time. What we attend to will grow, and as the Sun enters Virgo, the sign of the Divine Sophia, we are to tend our garden gate. This means having proper boundaries. Our boundaries protect us and allow us to choose what shall enter and what shall not. The "B" in eurythmy is the gesture for the constellation of Virgo. This gesture characterizes the forming of our essential cloak of protection. May we thus practice wrapping ourselves in the protecting mantle of Sophia. And may we stand with the serpent underfoot!

September 21: Mars 10° Scorpio square Neptune 10° Aquarius: Flight into Egypt (Mar/2/5 BC). Mars was at this same location when the family of the Solomon Jesus fled to Egypt to escape the murder of the innocent. In Egypt they were exposed to the Egyptian mystery stream inaugurated by Hermes. Johannes Kepler was a man who tapped into these same mysteries and used his profound hermetic understanding of the stars to reveal occult truths regarding both heaven and earth. Steiner seemed to revere this individuality:

> The individuality who once in the mystery places of Egypt raised the eyes of his soul up to the stars, and sought to unravel their secrets in celestial space after the manner of those days under the guidance of the Egyptian sages, lived again in our own epoch as Kepler. What had existed in another form in his Egyptian soul appeared in a newer guise as the great laws of Kepler, which today are such an integral part of astrophysics. It came to pass also that within the soul of this man there arose something that forced these words to be uttered—words that may be read in the writings of Kepler: "Out of the holy places of Egypt I have brought the sacred vessel; I have transported it to the present time, so that men may understand something in these days of those influences that are able to affect even the most distant future."[1]

These words by Steiner were spoken in 1914, one hundred years ago. Indeed, we, too, are to avoid the murderous activity of the adversaries by also finding sanctuary in the unfolding mysteries of Christ and Sophia, whose teachings are revealed through the stars—and this great wisdom has its origins in Egypt.

With Mars squaring Neptune where the latter remembers the evil times in Russia, we can contemplate the mystery of star wisdom and the enlightenment of revelation to which we are to awaken, as did Kepler before us. The stars offer an antidote to evil, as they are the abode of great and wondrous spiritual beings who yearn to help us. First we must pose the questions only they can answer.

September 24: New Moon 6° Virgo. The Sun remembers the fall of Jerusalem and the Moon remembers the feeding of the five thousand. As Jerusalem is a central focal point for prophecies regarding the Antichrist, when aspects kindle the memory of its fall in the year AD 70, we can call to mind the words in John's Gospel where Christ says, "Destroy this temple, and I will raise it again in three days." Then,

---

1 Steiner, *The East in the Light of the West*, p. 162.

in Revelation 3:14, we are guided to the powerful presence of the one who rebuilt the temple: "These are the words of the Amen, the faithful and true witness, the ruler of God's creation." Meditation on this verse brings us into contact with the mystery of the resurrection body. *Putting on the resurrection body* (This is a term used by St. Paul, who recognized immortality as *"putting on the resurrection body"*) is the goal of all humanity. Christ brought the bread of life as exemplified in his fourth miracle, the feeding of the five thousand. By finding our relationship to the stars, as Christ exemplified at the feeding of the five thousand, we begin the process of reclaiming the spiritual forces that rebuild our temple (physical body), a temple which leads us to participate in the creation of the New Jerusalem. This is the path of the Holy Grail, and as we mature on this path, we will gradually resurrect our consciousness to the vertically descending stream of nourishment that overcomes the *maya* of the serpent's horizontal world.

This New Moon asks us to protect all the beings within the kingdom of our Mother, and to nourish our bodies with the bread of life, which originates in the Word. Virgo bestows the gift of phenomenologically understanding the forces working in Nature and the story she is continuously weaving. Natura calls us to awaken to her pain, that we may work for her ennoblement. This work is the entire focus of Robert Powell's book entitled *Inner Radiance and the Body of Immortality*.

Pluto stations 16° Sagittarius before going direct: Pentecost (May/24/33). The light of spirit descending in waves of revelation has been highlighted since mid-July and will continue until the end of November of this year. Inverse to Pentecost, where the divine love of the Father worked through his only begotten son, is the plutocracy of greed. Taking this path separates one from the Pentecostal revelation. Pluto rules money and the turning of bread to stones and stones to bread; and an autocrat is a dictator wielding undivided power. If power through wealth continues to manipulate nations, impoverishment in body, soul, and spirit will continue. Yet, with this year highlighting the Pentecost of AD 33, we can lift ourselves out of the illusions of materialism and seek guidance from the wealth of spirit, under whose auspices all are loved as children of God.

September 26: Sun 9° Virgo. The Raising of Nazor (1/Sept/32). Jesus went to the field in which Nazor had died, and he there prayed. Returning to the house, Jesus and his followers found Nazor sitting upright in his coffin. Nazor was raised from a distance. Christ went to where his soul and spirit lingered over the field of his death. This is similar to how thoughts and words linger over locations in which they were expressed. We live in times when it is prudent to surround oneself with a protective sheath born of one's conscious attention to the etheric Christ:

May the outer sheath of my aura grow stronger.
May it surround me with an impenetrable
*   vessel against all impure, self-seeking*
*   thoughts and feelings.*
May it be open only to divine wisdom

This meditation is particularly significant in relation to the "radiant blue steam" of the Etheric Christ. Imagining a protective sheath of radiant blue aura thus links us directly to the in-streaming of the Etheric Christ.[2]

Wrapping oneself in this manner also invokes the mantle of Sophia's (Virgo) protection—the "B" gesture in eurythmy for the constellation of Virgo. As we become more skilled in creating this connection with Christ and Sophia, we are protected from corrupt thoughts, feelings, and deeds in our environment. Within such a conscientiously tended aura, the voice of spiritual guidance is more easily heard. This voice warns us to know when certain spaces and beings need to be cleared of ill will. By cleansing our environments, we help raise from the dead what is fallen. This can be done while in the location or even from a distance, as was the case in this healing of Nazor. New healing capacities are awakening as gifts from Sophia. Nazor was instructed, after his raising, to be kinder to his servants. We can remember to be more courteous in our words, thoughts and deeds, so as to preserve the environments of this kingdom of Our Mother (Virgo).

---

2 Powell, *Cultivating Inner Radiance and the Body of Immortality*, p. 124.

Elemental beings are longing to serve the good, and they look to us for their redemption. Today we can be particularly attentive to them as we surround ourselves in the radiant blue mantle whose source is Christ.

Venus enters Virgo: "May the soul fathom worlds" (Rudolf Steiner, *Twelve Cosmic Moods*). Venus was in Virgo at the conception of the Virgin Mary. This is an imagination of the purity we achieve when our souls unite with the World Soul. Venus in the Virgin seeks to comprehend the phenomenon of the world of nature in order to bring peace to the phenomena of the inner soul life. When inner and outer are in communion, the soul moves in harmony with Sophia—the World Soul—the Virgin.

September 27: Sun enters the second decan of Virgo, ruled by Mercury and associated with the constellation of Corvus the Raven, the messenger of Apollo and the bird that fed the prophet Elijah (1 Kings 17:4).

September 29: Michaelmas. This is the season of action, where we rid ourselves of old habits, thoughts, and images in order to make way for the new. What is the new? Autumn is morning for the Earth Mother; it is the time of year when the new is revealed as the Earth in-breathes her soul and she begins her awakening. The precious gift we received during the Holy Nights last winter, has sprouted, flowered, and is now bearing fruit. What was then given in the dark nights of winter as potential can now become realized through our deeds. We are to cast outworn dragons from our inner being in order to make room for new capacities. On a macrocosmic scale, the Earth herself is bearing new fruits that have been infused with creative force during summer, where her soul was impregnated with the dictums of Uriel; to make way for change, these fruits that have been ripened through the cycle of the year will also have macrocosmic dragons to dispel. Both microcosmically and macroscopically, deeds are called forth. As autumn progresses, these fruits will implant the earth with their seeds; and these seeds will become the beginning of yet another cycle when they are illumined by grace in the Holy days and nights to come.

OCTOBER 2014

The Sun begins October in Virgo and moves into Libra on the 18th. Mercury stations Retrograde on the 5th, and Direct again on the 26th. The Full Moon in Virgo (the Virgin) is the 8th and is a total lunar eclipse. It will be visible at least in part in Asia, Australia, parts of North America, and South America. Also at this time, peaking the 8th and 9th, is the Draconids Meteor Shower. With the Full Moon, we won't see much, but look toward the north after midnight and wish upon the falling stars! The Sun conjuncts Mercury again on the 16th, and Mercury and Venus join up on the 17th. The 18th brings the Moon together with Jupiter in Cancer, rising about 2 hours after midnight and visible in the east/south until sunrise hides Jupiter from view. On the 21st and 22nd, we get another chance at viewing "shooting stars" with the Orionids Meteor Shower, best viewing after midnight. Look toward the constellation of Orion as the origin point in the south high up, but these beauties can appear anywhere in the sky. (I'll meet you outside with a hot drink and some blankets!) On the 23rd the Moon catches back up with the Sun for the New Moon in Libra—a partial Solar Eclipse visible in Asia and much of North America. After that, the Sun takes Venus into its embrace on the 25th while the waxing new Moon joins Saturn in Libra most likely hidden within the Sun's light. The Moon joins quick paced Mars in Sagittarius on the 28th, visible in the southwest after the Sun's work is done for the day.

October 4: Sun 16° Virgo. Birth of Solomon Mary (Sept/7/21 BC). The Solomon Mary is the one referred to as the Blessed Virgin Mary; she is the mother of the Master Jesus (the reincarnated Zarathustra individuality who was called Zaratas in Babylon). It is the Virgin Mary who goes before us to future Jupiter existence in order to create a new star-temple for humanity, which will develop in the orbit currently inscribed by the planet called Venus. Her son, the great teacher of star wisdom, revealed the way:

> Zaratas's clairvoyance allowed him a panoramic vision of Time as well as Space, and he saw the

SIDEREAL GEOCENTRIC LONGITUDES : OCTOBER 2014 Gregorian at 0 hours UT

DAY	☉	☽	☊	☿	♀	♂	♃	♄	♅	♆	♇
1 WE	12 ♍ 48	2 ♐ 24	24 ♍ 21	6 ♎ 37	6 ♍ 29	16 ♏ 45	20 ♋ 59	25 ♎ 34	19 ♓ 50R	10 ♒ 25R	16 ♐ 4
2 TH	13 47	16 12	24 21R	6 58	7 43	17 27	21 10	25 40	19 48	10 23	16 4
3 FR	14 46	0 ♑ 18	24 20	7 12	8 58	18 9	21 20	25 46	19 46	10 22	16 4
4 SA	15 45	14 41	24 20	7 20	10 13	18 51	21 30	25 52	19 43	10 21	16 5
5 SU	16 45	29 18	24 19	7 22R	11 28	19 33	21 40	25 58	19 41	10 19	16 5
6 MO	17 44	14 ♒ 3	24 18	7 16	12 43	20 16	21 50	26 4	19 38	10 18	16 6
7 TU	18 43	28 51	24 17	7 3	13 58	20 58	22 0	26 10	19 36	10 17	16 6
8 WE	19 42	13 ♓ 34	24 17	6 42	15 13	21 41	22 10	26 17	19 33	10 16	16 6
9 TH	20 41	28 4	24 17D	6 12	16 28	22 24	22 19	26 23	19 31	10 15	16 7
10 FR	21 40	12 ♈ 17	24 17	5 35	17 43	23 7	22 29	26 29	19 29	10 14	16 7
11 SA	22 40	26 8	24 17	4 50	18 58	23 49	22 38	26 35	19 26	10 12	16 8
12 SU	23 39	9 ♉ 35	24 18	3 57	20 13	24 33	22 47	26 42	19 24	10 11	16 8
13 MO	24 38	22 38	24 18R	2 58	21 28	25 16	22 57	26 48	19 21	10 10	16 9
14 TU	25 38	5 ♊ 19	24 17	1 52	22 43	25 59	23 6	26 55	19 19	10 9	16 10
15 WE	26 37	17 42	24 17	0 43	23 58	26 42	23 15	27 1	19 16	10 8	16 10
16 TH	27 37	29 49	24 17D	29 ♍ 30	25 13	27 25	23 24	27 8	19 14	10 7	16 11
17 FR	28 36	11 ♋ 47	24 18	28 17	26 28	28 9	23 32	27 14	19 12	10 6	16 12
18 SA	29 36	23 39	24 18	27 5	27 43	28 52	23 41	27 21	19 9	10 5	16 13
19 SU	0 ♎ 35	5 ♌ 29	24 19	25 56	28 58	29 36	23 50	27 27	19 7	10 4	16 13
20 MO	1 35	17 23	24 19	24 53	0 ♎ 13	0 ♐ 20	23 58	27 34	19 5	10 4	16 14
21 TU	2 34	29 24	24 20	23 57	1 28	1 4	24 6	27 41	19 2	10 3	16 15
22 WE	3 34	11 ♍ 35	24 21	23 10	2 43	1 47	24 14	27 47	19 0	10 2	16 16
23 TH	4 34	23 58	24 21	22 33	3 59	2 31	24 22	27 54	18 58	10 1	16 17
24 FR	5 34	6 ♎ 34	24 21R	22 7	5 14	3 16	24 30	28 1	18 55	10 0	16 18
25 SA	6 33	19 25	24 20	21 52	6 29	4 0	24 38	28 8	18 53	10 0	16 19
26 SU	7 33	2 ♏ 29	24 19	21 49D	7 44	4 44	24 46	28 15	18 51	9 59	16 20
27 MO	8 33	15 48	24 17	21 57	8 59	5 28	24 53	28 21	18 48	9 58	16 21
28 TU	9 33	29 20	24 15	22 15	10 15	6 13	25 0	28 28	18 46	9 58	16 22
29 WE	10 33	13 ♐ 4	24 13	22 44	11 30	6 57	25 8	28 35	18 44	9 57	16 23
30 TH	11 33	26 58	24 11	23 21	12 45	7 42	25 15	28 42	18 42	9 56	16 24
31 FR	12 33	11 ♑ 1	24 11	24 7	14 0	8 26	25 21	28 49	18 40	9 56	16 25

INGRESSES :

2	☽ → ♑	23:29		♀ → ♎	19:46
5	☽ → ♒	1: 9	21	☽ → ♍	1:10
7	☽ → ♓	1:52	23	☽ → ♎	11:33
9	☽ → ♈	3:13	25	☽ → ♏	19:27
11	☽ → ♉	6:49	28	☽ → ♐	1:10
13	☽ → ♊	13:51	30	☽ → ♑	5:12
15	☿ → ♍	14:12			
16	☽ → ♋	0:21			
18	☉ → ♎	9:49			
	☽ → ♌	12:52			
19	♂ → ♐	13: 8			

ASPECTS & ECLIPSES :

1	☉ □ ☽	19:32		☽ ●● T	10:53		☉ □ ☽	19:11		☉ ● P	21:43
	☽ ☌ ♇	23:46		♀ □ ♇	17:16	16	☉ i☌ ☿	20:32		☉ ☌ ☽	21:56
2	☽ N□ ☊	13:55		☽ ☌ ☋	17:41	17	☿ ☌ ♀	17:44	25	☉ s☌ ♀	6:51
4	☉ □ ♇	7:53	9	☽ ☍ ☿	13: 6	18	☽ ☌ ♃	0: 4		☽ ☌ ♄	16:11
	☽ ☍ ♃	11:21	11	☽ ☍ ♄	0:48		☽ ☌ A	5:43	28	☽ ☌ ♂	12:45
5	☽ ☌ ♆	17:55		♀ ☍ ♅	8:48	19	☽ ☍ ♆	9:15	29	☽ ☌ ♇	5:45
6	☽ ☌ P	9:30	12	☉ ☌ ☊	15:37	20	☿ ☌ ☊	13:50		☽ N□ ☊	19:14
7	☉ ☍ ♅	20:40	13	☽ ☍ ♂	5:12	22	☽ ☍ ♅	14:22	31	☿ ☌ ☊	1:42
8	☽ ☍ ♀	2:58	14	☽ ☍ ♇	21: 0		☽ ☌ ☿	21:24		☉ □ ☽	2:48
	☽ ☌ ♅	9:50	15	♀ ☌ ☊	6:16	23	☽ ☌ ☊	0:45			
	☉ ☍ ☽	10:50		☽ □S ☊	13: 0		☽ ☌ ♀	21:12			

SIDEREAL HELIOCENTRIC LONGITUDES : OCTOBER 2014 Gregorian at 0 hours UT

DAY	Sid. Time	☿	♀	⊕	♂	♃	♄	♅	♆	♇	Vernal Point
1 WE	0:38:36	19 ♑ 28	27 ♌ 38	12 ♓ 48	26 ♐ 10	12 ♋ 26	29 ♎ 30	19 ♓ 29	11 ♒ 26	17 ♐ 49	5 ♓ 3'15"
2 TH	0:42:33	22 58	29 15	13 47	26 46	12 31	29 32	19 30	11 26	17 49	5 ♓ 3'15"
3 FR	0:46:29	26 34	0 ♍ 53	14 46	27 23	12 35	29 34	19 31	11 27	17 50	5 ♓ 3'15"
4 SA	0:50:26	0 ♒ 15	2 30	15 45	27 59	12 40	29 35	19 31	11 27	17 50	5 ♓ 3'15"
5 SU	0:54:22	4 2	4 7	16 44	28 35	12 45	29 37	19 32	11 28	17 50	5 ♓ 3'15"
6 MO	0:58:19	7 55	5 44	17 44	29 12	12 50	29 39	19 32	11 28	17 50	5 ♓ 3'15"
7 TU	1: 2:15	11 55	7 21	18 43	29 48	12 55	29 41	19 33	11 28	17 51	5 ♓ 3'14"
8 WE	1: 6:12	16 2	8 58	19 42	0 ♑ 25	12 59	29 43	19 34	11 29	17 51	5 ♓ 3'14"
9 TH	1:10: 8	20 16	10 35	20 41	1 1	13 4	29 45	19 34	11 29	17 51	5 ♓ 3'14"
10 FR	1:14: 5	24 39	12 12	21 40	1 38	13 9	29 47	19 35	11 29	17 52	5 ♓ 3'14"
11 SA	1:18: 2	29 9	13 49	22 40	2 15	13 14	29 48	19 36	11 30	17 52	5 ♓ 3'14"
12 SU	1:21:58	3 ♓ 48	15 26	23 39	2 51	13 19	29 50	19 36	11 30	17 52	5 ♓ 3'14"
13 MO	1:25:55	8 35	17 3	24 38	3 28	13 23	29 52	19 37	11 30	17 53	5 ♓ 3'14"
14 TU	1:29:51	13 31	18 40	25 38	4 5	13 28	29 54	19 38	11 31	17 53	5 ♓ 3'14"
15 WE	1:33:48	18 37	20 17	26 37	4 42	13 33	29 56	19 38	11 31	17 53	5 ♓ 3'13"
16 TH	1:37:44	23 51	21 54	27 36	5 18	13 38	29 58	19 39	11 31	17 54	5 ♓ 3'13"
17 FR	1:41:41	29 15	23 30	28 36	5 55	13 43	29 59	19 40	11 32	17 54	5 ♓ 3'13"
18 SA	1:45:37	4 ♈ 47	25 7	29 36	6 32	13 47	0 ♏ 1	19 40	11 32	17 54	5 ♓ 3'13"
19 SU	1:49:34	10 28	26 44	0 ♈ 35	7 9	13 52	0 3	19 41	11 33	17 55	5 ♓ 3'13"
20 MO	1:53:31	16 18	28 20	1 35	7 46	13 57	0 5	19 41	11 33	17 55	5 ♓ 3'13"
21 TU	1:57:27	22 14	29 57	2 34	8 23	14 2	0 7	19 42	11 33	17 55	5 ♓ 3'13"
22 WE	2: 1:24	28 18	1 ♎ 34	3 34	9 0	14 7	0 9	19 43	11 34	17 56	5 ♓ 3'12"
23 TH	2: 5:20	4 ♉ 27	3 10	4 34	9 37	14 11	0 11	19 43	11 34	17 56	5 ♓ 3'12"
24 FR	2: 9:17	10 41	4 46	5 34	10 15	14 16	0 12	19 44	11 34	17 56	5 ♓ 3'12"
25 SA	2:13:13	16 58	6 23	6 33	10 52	14 21	0 14	19 45	11 35	17 57	5 ♓ 3'12"
26 SU	2:17:10	23 17	7 59	7 33	11 29	14 20	0 16	19 45	11 35	17 57	5 ♓ 3'12"
27 MO	2:21: 6	29 36	9 35	8 33	12 6	14 31	0 18	19 46	11 35	17 57	5 ♓ 3'12"
28 TU	2:25: 3	5 ♊ 54	11 12	9 33	12 44	14 35	0 20	19 47	11 36	17 58	5 ♓ 3'12"
29 WE	2:29: 0	12 10	12 48	10 33	13 21	14 40	0 22	19 47	11 36	17 58	5 ♓ 3'11"
30 TH	2:32:56	18 21	14 24	11 33	13 58	14 45	0 23	19 48	11 37	17 58	5 ♓ 3'11"
31 FR	2:36:53	24 27	16 0	12 33	14 36	14 50	0 25	19 49	11 37	17 59	5 ♓ 3'11"

INGRESSES :

2	♀ → ♍	11: 0
3	☿ → ♒	22:23
7	♂ → ♑	7:45
11	☿ → ♓	4:27
17	☿ → ♈	3:18
	♄ → ♏	7: 4
18	⊕ → ♈	9:51
21	♀ → ♎	0:44
22	☿ → ♉	6:39
27	☿ → ♊	1:29
31	☿ → ♋	22:11

ASPECTS (HELIOCENTRIC +MOON(TYCHONIC)) :

1	☿ ⚹ ♅	0: 7		☿ ☌ ♆	21:20	14	♀ ☍ ♅	14:20		☿ □ ♃	14:16		☽ ☌ ♄	19:56		♀ □ ♃	5:30
2	☽ ☌ ♇	2:47	7	☽ ☍ ♀	15:33		☿ □ ♇	20:38	20	☿ △ ♇	6:36		☿ ☌ P	21:55		☿ □ ♅	5:39
	☿ □S ☊	3:57		⊕ ☌ ♅	20:40	15	☽ ☍ ♇	0:22	21	☿ ☌ ☊	5:15	28	♀ △ ♆	6: 1	31	☽ ☌ ♂	6:21
	♀ ⚹ ♄	4: 6	8	☽ ☌ ♅	9:53		☿ ☌ ♅	4:46	22	☿ ☍ ♄	7:16		☿ ⚹ ⊕	16:34		☽ ☍ ♃	6:31
	☽ ☌ ♂	18:50		☿ ⚹ ♇	10:23		☿ ☍ ♀	11:11		☽ ☍ ♅	15:49		☽ ☍ ☿	21:10		♂ ☍ ♃	10:22
3	☿ □ ♄	19:43	10	♀ ⚹ ♃	14:43	16	☽ ☍ ♂	11:34	23	☽ ☌ ♀	20: 7		☿ △ ♆	21:49			
	☽ ☍ ♃	20:38	11	☿ △ ♄	3:28		☿ ☌ ⊕	20:31		☿ △ ♂	22: 7	29	☿ △ ♀	3:17			
5	☽ ☌ ☿	10:27		☽ ☍ ♄	6:29	17	☽ ☌ ♃	3:55	24	☿ □ ♆	3:24		☽ ☌ ♇	8:30			
	☽ ☌ ♆	19:48		☿ ⚹ ♂	18:29	18	☿ □ ♂	8:21		☿ ⚹ ♃	13:53		♀ □ ♂	13:29			
6	⊕ □ ♇	2:49	13	♀ □ ♇	12:17	19	☿ ⚹ ♆	4:27	25	♀ ☍ ⊕	6:51		☿ ☍ ♇	22:29			
	♂ ⚹ ♄	18:59		☿ △ ♃	23:45		☽ ☍ ♆	12:13		☿ ⚹ ♅	10:34	30	⊕ ⚹ ♆	1:32			

imminent arrival of a period when humanity would no longer see these Holy Beings of the cosmos, nor even accept that such Beings existed. He understood that in this approaching period of spiritual darkness, humanity would need a science of the cosmos that would in veiled form express the cosmic mysteries, since the spiritual reality standing behind them would be lost. The mathematical exactitude that emerges from the astronomical texts of this period of ancient Babylon shows that Zaratas succeeded in this, the heart of his task as a teacher of the Babylonian astronomer-priests.[1]

Our awakening to the stars is thus necessary in order for us to be able to climb their stairway to the realms of future Jupiter existence that are being prepared for us by the Virgin Mary. The Virgin Mary's son revealed the way; and she prepares us through in-streaming moral forces that we are to take up on behalf of our brothers and sisters, the elemental beings, and in service to the entire evolution of the Earth. May we hear this as a serious call to follow the Morning Star (Venus).

ASPECT: Sun 16° Virgo square Pluto 16° Sagittarius: Mary Magdalene's first conversion and Pentecost. These two memories are kindled, respectively, by Sun and Pluto. How wonderfully they work together. It will be the light of spirit's power that will illumine what in us needs converting. This is a good day to contemplate any defensiveness in our soul that points to our self-limitation. These self-imposed limitations easily become projection. We contract in order to defend. As we mature we often carry these defensive soul postures long after their time of necessity has passed. Thus, we will find others falling into these contracted spaces; and rather than seeing the offender as the teacher pointing out our self-limitations, we often project our fear outwardly as antipathy toward the alleged offender. How foolish we can be when we fail to notice that the outer is a divine reflection of the inner! We can follow the example of the Virgin Mary who had achieved the purity of soul each of us is striving to attain.

October 7: Sun enters third decan of Virgo, ruled by Venus and associated with Hydra the Serpent. Here it is the tail of the Serpent, and the biblical image is the Woman standing on the serpent (Gen. 3:15). Likewise, the Chinese goddess of mercy, Kwan-Yin, is depicted riding upon a dragon. For the Chinese, Sophia *is* Kwan-Yin.

ASPECT: Sun 19° Virgo opposite Uranus 19° Pisces: The Sun was here eleven days before the Baptism when Jesus was approached by three youths from wealthy families in Nazareth. Their parents had sent them to hear a dispute between Jesus and some of the learned men of Nazareth—a dispute that had been set up by the Pharisees to test Jesus's wisdom:

> Jesus displayed such an extraordinary knowledge that all present were excited by this teaching. Urged on by their parents who thought that their sons could benefit from absorbing Jesus's wisdom, the three youths then sought to become Jesus's pupils; but Jesus rejected them, which incensed their parents.[2]

With Sun opposed Uranus at this memory, a teaching comes forth: The call to follow the new revelations (Uranus) is a call that comes from *within* one's heart (Sun). It is not one that can be imposed by others, nor is it one that is a self-seeking for what can be attained through knowledge. Sun in Virgo works toward developing the courteous heart, and this heart seeks what is beneficial for the work of redeeming the kingdoms of nature and humanity. A serving heart is the heart of a disciple—it disciplines itself to bring forth the good.

October 8: Full Moon 20° Pisces opposite Sun 20° Virgo—total lunar eclipse. This eclipse will be visible over North America, the Pacific, Australia, and East Asia. Moon at this degree remembers the appearance of the Risen one to seven disciples (Apr/15/33). This is when Peter asked Jesus what is to become of John, and the Risen One answered: "If it is my will that he remain until I come, what is that to you?" The Sun at this degree is within 3° of the Sun at the conception of John. The eclipse amplifies the warning that we are not to disregard

---

[1] Powell, "Origins of Star Wisdom" (http://www.astrogeographia.org).

[2] *Chron.*, p. 197.

John, or let the sterile bones of materialism occult his presence here with us now as a leader in the spiritual guidance of humanity. For, the Church of John is now calling its people from the realms of apocalyptic revelation.

The Church of John is centered in the heart, and those who choose to join this Church are summoned by the call of the Grail. Corresponding to the Mass in the exoteric church is the Grail Mystery in the esoteric church. Grail communion is communion with the Beings of the stars, which requires a crossing of the threshold—which in turn requires a meeting with the fallen nature of the soul. John is one who knows the power of the sub-earthly realms. He is the being that Rudolf Steiner prophesied would be with us at the end of the century. For it was John who accompanied Lazarus through the underworld after his death, and before he was raised by Christ. He knows the way to partake of the mysteries of bread (Virgo), and the mysteries of the fish communion (Pisces)—communion with the Mother in the depths of the Earth. We can contemplate John during this eclipse and our willingness to commune with the Father, through his Son, and with the Mother through her daughter, Sophia.

Venus 16° Virgo square Pluto 16° Sagittarius. Conception of the Nathan Mary (Oct/24/18BC). With Venus remembering this Holy conception and Pluto remembering Pentecost, we can open to Mary, in whom Divine Sophia dwelled:

> Thus, Pentecost was also a Sophianic event, inspiring the formation of a community on Earth that would unfold in the future toward the ideal of 'one human family'. And the continual in-streaming of Sophia, who is the bearer of the new heaven, is bringing about a World Pentecost which will enable every person on the planet to experience the power of divine love through the descent of the Holy Spirit, preparing us for the future culture of the Rose of the World, a worldwide culture of brotherly/sisterly love.[3]

Today we open to the memories of the Risen One, the Church of John, the conception of the Nathan Mary, and Pentecost. May we pray that nothing will eclipse the presence of spiritual guidance and new revelation that is leading us forward.

October 11: Venus 19° Virgo opposite Uranus 19° Pisces. Four days ago the Sun opposed Uranus. Today it is Venus, and at this degree the planet of love was very close to today's degree when Jesus was teaching and healing the pagans and their children—who were all suffering because of their parents' worship of Moloch. Jesus awakened them to the nature of their idolatry. Uranus represents fallen light (electrical forces), and we can be assured that by constant exposure to these forces we are offering our children to Moloch. This is a good day to contemplate the light that best nourishes the human soul. Fallen light is not a substitute for the cosmic light Venus lovingly receives when standing opposite Uranus (See *Chron.*, p. 248). Uranus at this degree remembers the electrical light of revolution that drove the Bolsheviks when last it was in Pisces:

> In order to arrive at Illumination, a subtle temptation must be met. Instead of thinking becoming a vehicle for divine truth, it can become "brilliant" and then "electrified." And there is a world of difference between an illumined person and a brilliant thinker. The brilliant thinker is able to combine thoughts to his own pleasing, to make everything conform to the way in which he wants to see things, whilst an illumined person is interested solely in divine truth, for which he sacrifices his personal viewpoints.[4]

Today Venus receives the cosmic light and we find benefit when contemplating this.

October 15: Sun 27° Virgo. The death of John the Baptist (Jan/4/31).

That night, during the festivities to celebrate Herod's birthday at Machaerus, John the Baptist was beheaded at the request of Herodias's daughter, Salome. After witnessing the spectacle of Salome dancing before him, Herod had said to her: "Ask what you will, and I will give it to you. Yes, I swear, even if you ask for half my kingdom, I shall give it to you." Salome hurriedly conferred with her

---

3 *Great Teachers of Humanity*, Pentecost: Jesus' Promise (a forthcoming book by Robert Powell).

4 Powell, *Hermetic Astrology*, vol. 2, p. 312.

mother, who told her to ask for the head of John the Baptist on a dish.[1]

Even after the death of John, Herod was uneasy, for he could still feel the mighty spirit of John, and this caused him great distress.

The Sun remembers Herod and the power of the desire nature, which has the ability to completely overwhelm us. If this were to happen, we would be given "half of Herod's kingdom" as was given to Salome. This is *not* the kingdom we are seeking. With the Sun in Virgo we can cast the knowing glance to the cunning of the serpent, Hydra, that stretches his undulating forces beneath this constellation. Crater—"the Cup" and a Grail symbol—is balanced on the serpent's back along with Corvus— "the Raven" and a symbol for intuitive feminine wisdom. The memory of John's death calls forth the Cup and the Raven: the Grail quest seeks the cup, and the Raven leads the Grail seeker to the mysterious and holy Castle of the Grail. It is in the realms where John is working that the Grail is preserved. John leads us to the Grail. Perhaps he speaks through the Raven. Inversely, Hydra can lead us into the dark castle of Klingsor, and once one is in this realm it is very difficult to get out—as exemplified with Herod and Herodias. *We can pay particular attention to the phenomena (Virgo) of nature in our surroundings and read the story the Mother is always telling. The headlines in our newsfeeds are ample evidence of the presence of Hydra amongst us. Seek the Grail wisdom in the living story of the stars; this is the greatest of the Virgin's phenomenological storytelling, for here she opens the book of Holy Wisdom Sophia—and the starry mantle worn by Sophia shows the path to the Holy Grail.*

October 16: ASPECT: Inferior conjunction Mercury and Sun 29° Virgo. The Sun was at this degree at the conversation between the Virgin Mary and Jesus before he left to be baptized by John at the Jordan River. Mercury was at this degree at the birth of the Virgin Mary. The healing truth representative of Mercury conjunct Sun today radiates the wisdom of Mary and the love of Jesus. As today's aspect occurs at the star Spica, there is emphasis on the feminine wisdom stream of Sophia. Mercury is the great healer, and when conjunct the Sun, this healing force is amplified.

October 17: Mercury conjunct Venus 27° Virgo. Jesus meets with the Karaites sect (Sept/27/30).

Less than a week after healing the Moloch worshippers, Jesus travels to Jogbeha:

> They went southward to Jogbeha, where lived members of the Karaites sect, descended from Jethro, the father-in-law of Moses. They led a plain, simple life. Because they rejected all oral traditions relating to the Law, the Karaites were the sworn enemies of the Pharisees. They lived in expectation of the coming of the Messiah, and regarded Jesus as a prophet. They received Jesus with great reverence. During his instruction, Jesus commended them for their charitable way of life.[2]

Under the influence of today's conjunction we can practice the ways of the Karaites. They renounced the old teachings and remained open to the the coming of the Messiah. It will take just this kind of openness to receive the Messiah at this time of the Second Coming. May we be true to the prophecy of Steiner, Tomberg, and Powell—conscious that the time of the Second Coming is now upon us.

October 18: Sun enters Libra. "Worlds are sustaining worlds" (Rudolf Steiner, *Twelve Cosmic Moods*). William Bento illumines this mantra:

> Everything is connected to everything, and so it is with any attempt to grasp how the Cosmos has given birth to worlds that sustain worlds. Nothing can be truly understood when it is taken out of the context of relatedness. Modern scientific thinking has unfortunately lost this understanding and continues to attempt to explain the complexity of nature, man and the heavens by abstracting it from its natural habitat. The result is a kind of lifelessness. The antidote to this edifice of abstractions is to apply the principles of a spiritual scientific thinking, which is based on the premise that "worlds sustain worlds."

The first decan is ruled by the Moon and associated with the constellation of Bootes the Ploughman. The deeper meaning of Bootes has to do with

---

1 *Chron.*, p. 270.

2 *Chron.*, pp. 248–249.

the Hebrew *Bo*, which means *coming*; hence Bootes is the Coming One. How appropriate that the Baptism of the *Coming One*, the Messiah, took place when the Sun entered this decan! Libra calls for balanced thought, which becomes balanced action, as well as a certain standard of uprightness that requires an alignment with higher consciousness. In Libra *contentment becomes equanimity*, whereby we enter the connectivity of all creation.

October 20: Venus enters Libra. "Being beholds itself within Being" (Steiner, *Twelve Cosmic Moods*). With Venus in Libra we seek the middle ground—the absolute fulcrum—where our soul finds its inner balance. Here is the place where Michaelic thoughts are found. Only in balance can we perceive the subtle, and in this quiet place we behold ourselves within the Beings of the spiritual worlds.

Venus was in Libra at the raising of Nazor and at the healing of the blind.

Mars enters Sagittarius: "In life's prevailing power of will" (Steiner, *Twelve Cosmic Moods*).

Mars materializes what has been conceptualized; and when Mars is in Sagittarius, it is through speech that life's prevailing power comes into form. Once formed, the word dies and must be resurrected through the prevailing power of the will; thereby its existence continues, through dying and becoming, in loyalty to the continuity between above and below. Mars was in Sagittarius when Jesus raised a pagan child from the dead.

October 23: New Moon and partial solar eclipse 5° Libra. This eclipse will be visible at sunrise in eastern Russia, and before sunset across most of North America. **The healing of Theokeno** (Sept/28/32). Theokeno was one of the three kings who visited the birth of the Solomon Jesus child. He was the king known as Caspar, whose name means "born of God." It was Theokeno who brought frankincense to the new born child. The three kings had been pupils of Zoroaster in their previous incarnations in Babylon, and Theokeno was famed in that incarnation for his reverence and piety as a mighty Persian king. His gift of frankincense was an offering from the Persian wisdom stream. The three kings reincarnated again in the eighth/ninth centuries AD as collaborators in the spiritual stream of the Holy Grail.

At this healing we find the Sun exactly square to where it was when the kings came to adore Jesus thirty-seven years earlier (6° Capricorn). Thirty-seven years marks the second nodal return;[3] this nodal point heralds the soul's need to fine-tune itself in order to meet its destiny task. This meeting between Jesus and Mensor (the gold king) was transfiguring to the souls of them both.

Jesus and Mensor then visited Theokeno in his tent, where he was confined to his bed. Jesus took Theokeno by the hand and raised him up. Thereafter, the three went to the local temple, where Jesus taught.

He explained that when the good angels withdraw, Satan takes possession of a temple service. He said that they should remove the various animal idols and teach love and compassion and give thanks to the Father in Heaven. Jesus now took bread and wine, which had been prepared beforehand. Having consecrated the bread and wine, he placed them upon a small altar. He prayed and blessed everyone. Mensor, Theokeno, and the four priests knelt before him with their hands folded across their chests.[4]

Satan not only takes possession of a temple service, but also of human beings if they allow animal instincts to rule in the temple of the human body. From the time of Christ forward, the "I" is to govern the animal forces in the astral body. Those who have animals on their altars will not attract good angels. It is no longer animals we offer for sacrifice, but our lower human passions instead. Christ now works in the "I." The "I" that governs the animal nature, in turn, shows compassion toward the animal kingdoms. The "I" enmeshed in the human animalistic nature will be deaf to the suffering of animals. Our hearts are the altars in our human temple; and upon this altar we give thanks, and partake in communion with the spiritual world. Human beings are now to rise from their beds of contentment and work for the salvation of the Earth and humanity. This will attract the good angels.

---

3 A nodal return of the Moon is a cycle of 18.6 years.
4 *Chron.*, pp. 328–329.

The square of the Sun's position between the Adoration of the Magi and Christ's visit to the kings, thirty-seven years later, exemplifies the awakening to a new relationship (Libra) in the mystery traditions. It is a relationship founded on a new covenant with the Sun mysteries. May we, too, rise from the illness of materialism in order to forge Michaelic resonances into a world gone deaf.

October 25: Superior conjunction Sun and Venus 7° Libra. Jesus leaves the kings (Sept/30/32): "Before daybreak, Jesus left the tent city of the kings. Mensor begged him to remain with them, and wept profusely at Jesus' departure. Jesus and the three shepherd youths traveled far and that evening reached a shepherd settlement where they stayed that night."[1] A poignant scene opens from the star chronicles today. Heliocentric Venus at this degree remembers Jesus teaching just two days after delivering his woe to the Pharisees. He spoke of the nearness of his delivery and of the coming betrayal. Peter assured him none of the twelve would ever betray him. He tells his disciples:

> He also spoke of the coming of a time of tribulation, when all would be filled with fear, and he referred to a woman in the pangs of giving birth. He spoke of the beauty of the human soul, created in God's image, and how wonderful it is to save souls and lead them to their salvation. He taught until late into the night. That night, Nicodemus and one of Simeon's sons came secretly from Jerusalem in order to see him.[2]

At this time of the Second Coming we can remember these words. Venus loves the human soul and serves it on behalf of Divine Sophia. As we too are in times of tribulation and know not where these trials will lead, it is important that we are loyal and chaste in order that we prepare a place for the guiding revelation now descending from above and, simultaneously, rising from the depths of the Mother. Mensor wept as Jesus left him. Rudolf Steiner indicated that Pythagoras was this king, and that these kings later were part of the Grail family. It is not difficult to understand that the members of this family have reincarnated and among us weave. For, the mysteries of the Grail are opening through John's Church to bring us the spiritual guidance needed in times of tribulation.

October 27: Sun enters the second decan of Libra, ruled by Saturn and associated with the constellations of Corona the Crown (above) and Crux the Southern Cross (below), representing the "life as your victor's crown" (Rev. 2:10) that is bestowed on those who "take up the cross" (Matt. 10:38) and follow the Anointed One, remaining "faithful, even to the point of death" (Rev. 2:10).

NOVEMBER 2014

The Sun begins the month in Libra and moves in front of Scorpio on the 18th. The Sun is opposite the Moon on the 6th for the Full Moon in Libra and Aries. By the 13th Venus and Saturn have come together, but they are very near the Sun (about 5° distant) and the Sun and Saturn are conjunct on the 18th. However, the Moon keeps giving beautiful views, joining Jupiter at the feet of the Lion (Leo) on the 14th. They rise in the east after midnight and cross the sky together until the dawn. Invisible-to-the-naked-eye- Uranus will station Direct on the 17th which is the same night as the peak of the Leonids Meteor Shower. Best viewed after midnight from a dark location, look toward the constellation of Leo as origin point (look southward and high up), but they can show up anywhere in the night sky. The last slivers of the Moon will join with Mercury on the 21st and slide into conjunction with the Sun for the New Moon in Scorpio on the 22nd and conjunction with Venus on the 23rd (hidden by the Sun.) On the 25th, Mercury and Saturn are together in the first degrees of Scorpio (also hidden by the Sun) while the waxing Moon joins Mars in Sagittarius. These two are visible at and after sunset, in the west with Mars to the left and below the sliver Moon.

November 1: Sun 13° Libra. Healing of the Blind (Oct/6/30 and 31). Twice at this Sun degree (one year apart) Christ healed the blind. The Earth and humanity are suffering from a systemic blindness that has brought about a conditioned belief that the information we are fed is showing us reality.

---

1 *Chron.*, p. 329.
2 Ibid., p. 346.

We are not to feign blindness in idle worship of a truth we are being handed, but are to open our eyes and find a willingness to encounter the truth that comes into vision as the pieces, intentionally separated, begin to form a story that is vastly different from what the severed pieces imply. This requires an awakened relationship (Libra) to world events in the light of a higher conscience. This is a good day to step away from our screens and find the images that the spiritual world needs us to see.

November 6: Full Moon 19° Aries opposite Sun 19° Libra. Conversation with Nicodemus (Apr/9/30). Three times it is reported in the Bible that Nicodemus came to Jesus *in the night*. Rudolf Steiner says this:

> Chapter after chapter of the Gospel reveals two things to us. First it shows that what was communicated was for those who were, in a certain way, able to comprehend occult truths. In our time, exoteric Spiritual Science is presented in lectures, but during that period spiritual-scientific truths could be understood only by those who had been in a sense actually initiated into this or that degree. Who were those who could understand some of what Jesus Christ was saying about profound truths? Only those who were able to perceive beyond the physical body—those who could withdraw from the body and become conscious in the spirit would. If Jesus Christ wanted to speak to those who could understand him, it had to be to those who were initiated in a certain way, those who could see spiritually. When he speaks about rebirth of the soul, for example, in the chapter on his conversation with Nicodemus, we see that he is revealing these truths to someone who perceives with spiritual senses.[3]

Jesus approaches Nicodemus in the night. The original forces of the world are living in Jesus—he is bringing not only new teachings, but a kind of teaching that comes from his astral body into the consciousness of others who are prepared to receive these teachings. Jesus makes the preparation for receiving these cosmic teachings clear: "Very truly I tell you, no one can enter the kingdom of God unless are born of water and the Spirit" (John 3:5).

At night we are reliving our previous day. If our day is filled with agitation and attention to primarily material concerns, we will find what comes out of us in sleep creates filmy clouds that obscure our ability to perceive the spiritual beings who are then striving toward us. The waters of our soul are to become still, for through stillness these waters become a surface that is able to reflect the above. Our spirits are to be actively attending what the waters of our soul are reflecting. This is the way of the Hermeticist. When one's consciousness bears witness to the perfect reflection of above and below, one is fulfilling the Hermetic axiom: as above, so also below. This is being born of water and spirit.

This Full Moon calls forth the memory of Nicodemus, who communed with Christ's astral body in the night. This was his initiation. His eagerness to learn and his ability to establish a new relationship with the realms of karmic judgment brought before his consciousness the Inspired teachings of Christ. This day reminds us of right preparation for sleep—for entering sleep is entering the great School of the Night.

Sun enters third decan of LIbra, ruled by Jupiter and associated with the constellation of Centaurus the Centaur. The most famous centaur was Chiron, to whom was ascribed great wisdom.

November 9: Venus 26° Libra square Jupiter 26° Cancer. Pentecost (Apr/5/33). Heliocentric Venus was within one degree of today's position at the first Pentecost. In square to Jupiter, this memory can find a dynamic relationship with wisdom Sophia. We can imagine Venus listening to the ensouling higher thoughts that ennoble matter (Cancer).

November 10: Mars conjunct Pluto 16° Sagittarius. Mars joins Pluto at Pentecost. Thomas Moore writes of the influence of Mars:

> In our world, too, one can go on to find the positive side of Mars only after facing the full potential of his other side. War and violence are still so widespread and are pursued with such self-righteous spirit as to threaten our very existence daily. Unrestrained heroism accompanies ideological fervor to such an extent that the religious

---

[3] Steiner, *The Gospel of St. John*, p. 90 (trans. revised).

nature of Mars-worship lies thinly concealed, especially in terrorism politically motivated.[1]

With Mars conjunct Pluto at Pentecost, we can strive to find the lofty strength of Mars when called to manifest the goodness inherent in peace.

November 11: Saturn enters Scorpio. "In avenging self-formation" (Steiner, *Twelve Cosmic Moods*).

Saturn stays in each constellation approximately two and one half years. Today Saturn moves into Scorpio; and its focus shifts from standing at the Michaelic fulcrum in Libra (having to do with our relationship to our conscience) and enters the sign of hidden dynamics. In this season of late autumn, Saturn calls us to penetrate into the depths to see what hidden causes lie beneath superficial reality. We are to relentlessly pursue the activity of forming ourselves in ever greater likeness to the higher "I" that strives to work with us, for us, and through us. Saturn was in Scorpio at the birth of the Nathan Mary.

November 12: Venus conjunct Saturn 0° 22 Scorpio. Two days before the summons of Judas (Oct/23/30). Venus at this degree remembers "Bartholomew and Simon recommending that Jesus accept Judas Iscariot as a disciple, whereupon Jesus sighed and appeared to be troubled" (*Chron.*, p. 253). Venus attracts us to love and when love is arrested, the jealous heart can surface, turning the cycle of love into a pit of bile. Ficino writes about the planet of love: "There is one continuous attraction, beginning with God, going to the world, and ending at last in God, an attraction which returns to the same place where it began as though in a kind of circle."[2] This is a strong contemplation for today. When Venus is free to travel from God to the world and back again to God, the power of love intensifies, the circle becomes a spiraling into higher love. Though jealousy and desire arrested this circle for Judas, his task was a great sacrifice allowed by Jesus on earth and by spiritual beings in heaven above. We can remember to love our enemies.

Mars 18° Sagittarius square Uranus 18° Pisces. Ouranos (Uranus in Orphic mythology), the sky God, offended his wife by shoving back into her womb the children she was bearing, causing her great pain and a desire for revenge. This is the low side of Uranus, the side that sparked the work of Stalin and Hitler when it last traversed this degree of the heavens. The embryonic seeds of future thoughts, incubating in the geographical location of the sixth Cultural Epoch, were pushed back into the womb of evolution by the looming clouds of hatred that sprang from the "social experiment" inaugurated through communism and fascism. It is the Holy Spirit who carries new thoughts to the right place in the right time. To work out of time is to work with regressive forces. The lingering etheric phantoms hovering as a consequence of the occult actions that occurred in the dark times following World War I are best rendered impotent when prudence accompanies courage, so as to temper the sword (Mars) of ideological fervor.

November 13: Venus enters Scorpio. "In Being, existence yet endures" (Steiner, *Twelve Cosmic Moods*). Venus in Scorpio represents the life forces that are consumed through Earth existence and yet endure within the human soul who is in communion with the source of all life—Christ. Here Venus asks us to seek the occult truths lying beneath the surface of all things, and to open our souls to find the maintaining growth that endures through all existence.

Venus was in Scorpio the birth of the Nathan Jesus, the Baptism, Magdalene's first conversion, and at the summons of both Judas and Thomas,.

November 16: Sun enters Scorpio. "Existence consumes being" (Steiner, *Twelve Cosmic Moods*). William Bento illumines this mantra:

> What a riddle this phrase proposes to us! *Existence* as a term expressing the state of life and the experience of living has a primary activity that cannot be denied. It does not preserve as much as it consumes. It is a force of changing all things. As the force empowering life it is always aiming at the inevitable end, death. And so it is, life begets death and in death springs forth new existence. This is a riddle that is equally valid in understanding the passage of human life on

---

1 Moore, *The Planets Within*, p.184.
2 Ibid., p. 139.

SIDEREAL GEOCENTRIC LONGITUDES : NOVEMBER 2014 Gregorian at 0 hours UT

DAY	☉	☽	☊	☿	♀	♂	♃	♄	♅	♆	♇
1 SA	13 ♎ 33	25 ♑ 12	24 ♍ 11	25 ♍ 1	15 ♎ 15	9 ♐ 11	25 ♋ 28	28 ♎ 56	18 ♓ 37R	9 ♒ 55R	16 ♐ 26
2 SU	14 33	9 ♒ 28	24 12	26 1	16 31	9 56	25 35	29 3	18 35	9 55	16 27
3 MO	15 33	23 47	24 14	27 7	17 46	10 40	25 41	29 10	18 33	9 54	16 28
4 TU	16 33	8 ♓ 7	24 15	28 18	19 1	11 25	25 48	29 17	18 31	9 54	16 30
5 WE	17 33	22 22	24 15	29 33	20 16	12 10	25 54	29 24	18 29	9 54	16 31
6 TH	18 33	6 ♈ 30	24 15R	0 ♎ 53	21 32	12 55	26 0	29 31	18 27	9 53	16 32
7 FR	19 33	20 25	24 13	2 15	22 47	13 40	26 6	29 38	18 25	9 53	16 33
8 SA	20 33	4 ♉ 5	24 10	3 40	24 2	14 25	26 11	29 45	18 23	9 53	16 35
9 SU	21 34	17 26	24 6	5 7	25 17	15 10	26 17	29 52	18 21	9 52	16 36
10 MO	22 34	0 ♊ 27	24 1	6 36	26 32	15 56	26 22	0 ♏ 0	18 19	9 52	16 38
11 TU	23 34	13 9	23 57	8 6	27 48	16 41	26 27	0 7	18 18	9 52	16 39
12 WE	24 34	25 33	23 53	9 38	29 3	17 26	26 32	0 14	18 16	9 52	16 40
13 TH	25 35	7 ♋ 42	23 50	11 11	0 ♏ 18	18 12	26 37	0 21	18 14	9 52	16 42
14 FR	26 35	19 41	23 48	12 44	1 34	18 57	26 42	0 28	18 12	9 51	16 43
15 SA	27 36	1 ♌ 32	23 48D	14 18	2 49	19 43	26 47	0 35	18 10	9 51	16 45
16 SU	28 36	13 23	23 49	15 53	4 4	20 28	26 51	0 42	18 9	9 51	16 46
17 MO	29 36	25 17	23 50	17 28	5 19	21 14	26 55	0 49	18 7	9 51D	16 48
18 TU	0 ♏ 37	7 ♍ 20	23 52	19 3	6 35	22 0	26 59	0 57	18 5	9 51	16 49
19 WE	1 37	19 36	23 53	20 38	7 50	22 45	27 3	1 4	18 4	9 52	16 51
20 TH	2 38	2 ♎ 8	23 53R	22 13	9 5	23 31	27 7	1 11	18 2	9 52	16 53
21 FR	3 39	14 59	23 51	23 49	10 21	24 17	27 10	1 18	18 1	9 52	16 54
22 SA	4 39	28 10	23 47	25 24	11 36	25 3	27 13	1 25	17 59	9 52	16 56
23 SU	5 40	11 ♏ 40	23 41	26 59	12 51	25 49	27 17	1 32	17 58	9 52	16 58
24 MO	6 40	25 27	23 34	28 34	14 7	26 35	27 20	1 40	17 57	9 52	16 59
25 TU	7 41	9 ♐ 26	23 27	0 ♏ 10	15 22	27 21	27 22	1 47	17 55	9 53	17 1
26 WE	8 42	23 35	23 19	1 45	16 37	28 7	27 25	1 54	17 54	9 53	17 3
27 TH	9 43	7 ♑ 48	23 14	3 20	17 53	28 53	27 27	2 1	17 53	9 53	17 4
28 FR	10 43	22 2	23 10	4 54	19 8	29 39	27 29	2 8	17 52	9 54	17 6
29 SA	11 44	6 ♒ 13	23 8	6 29	20 23	0 ♑ 26	27 31	2 15	17 50	9 54	17 8
30 SU	12 45	20 19	23 8D	8 4	21 39	1 12	27 33	2 22	17 49	9 55	17 10

INGRESSES :

1 ☽ → ♒ 8: 5	☽ → ♍ 9:25
3 ☽ → ♓ 10:24	19 ☽ → ♎ 19:57
5 ☿ → ♎ 8:10	22 ☽ → ♏ 3:17
☽ → ♈ 12:55	24 ☽ → ♐ 7:50
7 ☽ → ♉ 16:46	☿ → ♏ 21:35
9 ☽ → ♊ 23: 8	26 ☽ → ♑ 10:50
10 ♄ → ♏ 1:32	28 ♂ → ♑ 10:40
12 ☽ → ♋ 8:43	☽ → ♒ 13:28
♀ → ♏ 18: 9	30 ☽ → ♓ 16:32
14 ☽ → ♌ 20:52	
17 ☉ → ♏ 9:21	

ASPECTS & ECLIPSES :

1 ☽ ☍ ♃ 0:28	11 ☽ ☍ ♇ 6:43	18 ☉ ☌ ♄ 8:52	☽ ⊓ ☊ 23:33
2 ☽ ☌ ♆ 0:45	☽ ☍ ♂ 7:12	☽ ☍ ♅ 21: 1	26 ☿ ☌ ♄ 2:30
3 ☽ ☌ P 0:49	☽ ⊔ ☊ 20:44	19 ☽ ☌ ☊ 8:16	☽ ☌ ♂ 8: 6
4 ☽ ☌ ♅ 17:27	13 ♀ ☌ ♄ 0:55	20 ♂ □ ☊ 11: 0	27 ☉ □ ♆ 4:19
5 ☽ ☌ ☋ 3:11	♂ □ ♅ 1: 5	♀ □ ♆ 14:47	☽ ☌ P 23:10
☽ ☍ ☿ 13:24	14 ☉ □ ♃ 2:59	21 ☽ ☌ ☿ 18:19	28 ☽ ☍ ♃ 9:15
6 ☉ ☍ ☽ 22:22	☽ ☌ ♃ 14:17	22 ☽ ☌ ♄ 5:52	29 ☽ ☌ ♆ 6:16
7 ☽ ☍ ♀ 4:31	☉ □ ☽ 15:15	☉ ☌ ☽ 12:31	☉ □ ☽ 10: 6
☽ ☍ ♄ 16:16	15 ☽ ☌ A 1:32	23 ☽ ☌ ♀ 2:17	
9 ♀ □ ♃ 20:28	☽ ☍ ♆ 16:51	☿ □ ♃ 4:32	
10 ♂ ☌ ♇ 22:53	16 ☉ □ Π 23:44	25 ☽ ☌ ♇ 12:54	

SIDEREAL HELIOCENTRIC LONGITUDES : NOVEMBER 2014 Gregorian at 0 hours UT

DAY	Sid. Time	☿	♀	⊕	♂	♃	♄	♅	♆	♇	Vernal Point
1 SA	2:40:49	0 ♋ 27	17 ♎ 36	13 ♈ 33	15 ♑ 13	14 ♋ 55	0 ♏ 27	19 ♓ 49	11 ♒ 37	17 ♐ 59	5 ♓ 3'11"
2 SU	2:44:46	6 19	19 12	14 33	15 51	14 59	0 29	19 50	11 38	17 59	5 ♓ 3'11"
3 MO	2:48:42	12 2	20 48	15 33	16 28	15 4	0 31	19 51	11 38	17 59	5 ♓ 3'11"
4 TU	2:52:39	17 37	22 24	16 33	17 6	15 9	0 33	19 51	11 38	18 0	5 ♓ 3'11"
5 WE	2:56:35	23 2	24 0	17 33	17 43	15 14	0 35	19 52	11 39	18 0	5 ♓ 3'10"
6 TH	3: 0:32	28 18	25 36	18 33	18 21	15 19	0 36	19 52	11 39	18 0	5 ♓ 3'10"
7 FR	3: 4:29	3 ♌ 24	27 12	19 33	18 58	15 23	0 38	19 53	11 39	18 1	5 ♓ 3'10"
8 SA	3: 8:25	8 20	28 48	20 33	19 36	15 28	0 40	19 54	11 40	18 1	5 ♓ 3'10"
9 SU	3:12:22	13 7	0 ♏ 23	21 34	20 14	15 33	0 42	19 54	11 40	18 1	5 ♓ 3'10"
10 MO	3:16:18	17 45	1 59	22 34	20 51	15 38	0 44	19 55	11 40	18 2	5 ♓ 3'10"
11 TU	3:20:15	22 13	3 35	23 34	21 29	15 43	0 46	19 56	11 41	18 2	5 ♓ 3'10"
12 WE	3:24:11	26 33	5 10	24 34	22 7	15 47	0 47	19 56	11 41	18 2	5 ♓ 3'10"
13 TH	3:28: 8	0 ♍ 45	6 46	25 35	22 45	15 52	0 49	19 57	11 42	18 3	5 ♓ 3' 9"
14 FR	3:32: 4	4 50	8 21	26 35	23 22	15 57	0 51	19 58	11 42	18 3	5 ♓ 3' 9"
15 SA	3:36: 1	8 47	9 57	27 35	24 0	16 2	0 53	19 58	11 42	18 3	5 ♓ 3' 9"
16 SU	3:39:58	12 37	11 32	28 36	24 38	16 7	0 55	19 59	11 43	18 4	5 ♓ 3' 9"
17 MO	3:43:54	16 20	13 8	29 36	25 16	16 11	0 57	20 0	11 43	18 4	5 ♓ 3' 9"
18 TU	3:47:51	19 58	14 43	0 ♉ 37	25 54	16 16	0 59	20 0	11 43	18 4	5 ♓ 3' 9"
19 WE	3:51:47	23 30	16 18	1 37	26 32	16 21	1 0	20 1	11 44	18 5	5 ♓ 3' 9"
20 TH	3:55:44	26 56	17 54	2 38	27 10	16 26	1 2	20 2	11 44	18 5	5 ♓ 3' 8"
21 FR	3:59:40	0 ♎ 18	19 29	3 39	27 48	16 30	1 4	20 2	11 44	18 5	5 ♓ 3' 8"
22 SA	4: 3:37	3 36	21 4	4 39	28 25	16 35	1 6	20 3	11 45	18 6	5 ♓ 3' 8"
23 SU	4: 7:33	6 49	22 39	5 40	29 3	16 40	1 8	20 3	11 45	18 6	5 ♓ 3' 8"
24 MO	4:11:30	9 59	24 15	6 40	29 41	16 45	1 10	20 4	11 46	18 6	5 ♓ 3' 8"
25 TU	4:15:27	13 5	25 50	7 41	0 ♒ 19	16 50	1 11	20 5	11 46	18 7	5 ♓ 3' 8"
26 WE	4:19:23	16 7	27 25	8 42	0 57	16 54	1 13	20 5	11 46	18 7	5 ♓ 3' 8"
27 TH	4:23:20	19 7	29 0	0 42	1 35	16 59	1 15	20 6	11 47	18 7	5 ♓ 3' 7"
28 FR	4:27:16	22 5	0 ♐ 35	10 43	2 13	17 4	1 17	20 7	11 47	18 7	5 ♓ 3' 7"
29 SA	4:31:13	25 0	2 10	11 44	2 51	17 9	1 19	20 7	11 47	18 8	5 ♓ 3' 7"
30 SU	4:35: 9	27 53	3 45	12 45	3 30	17 14	1 21	20 8	11 48	18 8	5 ♓ 3' 7"

INGRESSES :

6 ☿ → ♌ 7:56
8 ♀ → ♏ 18: 9
12 ☿ → ♍ 19:37
17 ⊕ → ♉ 9:23
20 ☿ → ♎ 21:47
24 ♂ → ♒ 11:44
27 ♀ → ♐ 15: 9
30 ☿ → ♏ 17:48

ASPECTS (HELIOCENTRIC +MOON(TYCHONIC)) :

1 ☿ △ ♄ 0: 1	⊕ △ ♇ 10:56	13 ☿ ⚹ ♄ 0:23	19 ♀ △ ♃ 0:41	♂ □ ♄ 10:32
♀ ⚹ ♇ 5:38	⊕ □ ♂ 11: 5	☽ ☌ ♃ 16:26	☽ ☍ ♅ 0:48	☿ ⚹ ♇ 15:55
2 ☽ ☌ ♆ 3:37	6 ☿ □ ♄ 10:51	14 ☽ ☍ ♂ 7:53	☽ ☌ ☿ 10:24	27 ☽ ☍ ♃ 15:34
⊕ □ ♃ 11:39	7 ☽ ☍ ♀ 13:24	15 ☿ ⚹ ♀ 12:22	20 ☿ △ ♂ 1:54	28 ☿ ☌ ☋ 12: 8
3 ☿ ☌ ♃ 13:10	☽ ☍ ♄ 17:56	☽ ☍ ♆ 20:36	21 ♀ △ ♅ 8:26	☽ ☌ ♂ 18: 3
☿ □ ⊕ 18:19	8 ♂ ⚹ ♅ 11:27	16 ♀ □ ♆ 2:38	22 ☽ ☌ ♄ 5:16	29 ⊕ □ ♆ 1:19
☿ ☍ ♂ 21:27	☿ ☍ ♆ 16:39	♂ ⊔ ☊ 3:26	♀ ☌ ☋ 12: 3	☽ ☌ ♆ 9:28
4 ☿ △ ♅ 9:51	9 ♀ ☌ ♄ 4:46	☿ ⚹ ♃ 23: 0	23 ☽ ☌ ♀ 21:39	♀ ⚹ ♂ 17:25
☽ ☌ ♅ 19:45	10 ☿ △ ♇ 1:30	17 ☿ □ ♇ 11:22	24 ☿ △ ♆ 13:46	
5 ☿ ⊓ ☊ 2:22	11 ☽ ☍ ♇ 9:22	18 ☿ ☍ ♅ 0:16	25 ☽ ☌ ♇ 14:44	
☿ □ ♀ 6:14	☿ △ ⊕ 9:34	⊕ ☍ ♄ 8:52	26 ☿ □ ♃ 6:24	

Earth and in understanding the forces playing out through the course of nature.

The first decan is ruled by Mars and is associated with the constellation of Lupus the Wolf. Sun entering Scorpio began the forty days in the wilderness. With Sun in Scorpio, we are asked to be patient in order to gain insight.

November 17: Neptune 9ª Aquarius stations before going direct. Neptune at 9° Aquarius is conjunct the royal star Fomalhaut. The last time Neptune was at this degree (165 years ago), was the time of the California gold rush in 1949. Luciferic influences then caused what is now referred to as "gold fever." This fever is emblematic of economic greed. Neptune stationing at this degree intensifies the maniacal influence that captures those caught in the materialistic power of gold. The obsession with gold is the materialistic counterpart to reverence for God.

November 18: Sun conjunct Saturn 1° Scorpio. Attarus arrival (Oct/23/29). The Sun at this degree finds Jesus arriving at Mt. Attarus four weeks after his baptism in the Jordan River. Jesus Christ was faced with the iron necessity of confronting the tempters. What was then the temptation of one on behalf of the whole is now the temptation of all for the sake of the One. For, the second crucifixion of Christ is the result of ignoring the cross that at this time of the Second Coming is illumined for each of us as the *cross*, which when taken up, guides us—through temptation—into what can be called the theology of Grace. This, then, is reunion with the dharma of the Satya Yuga, the age of the fifth Sun.

November 20: Sun 3° Scorpio. Death of Johannes Kepler (Nov/5/1630). As the death horoscope is an expression of the fulfillment of an individuality's life, it is interesting to note Kepler's death horoscope with Sun, Mars, South Node, and Mercury in Scorpio. Kepler is one who penetrated into hidden realms to understand mysterious dynamics working in the movements of the planets and in the depths of the Earth. In his lecture cycle *Christ and the Spiritual World, the Search for the Holy Grail*[1], Rudolf Steiner spoke about Kyot, then wove in Kepler; and then he again wove back through the Grail, and wove into the hidden realms of Presbyter John, into which the Grail has been taken—realms beyond sense existence. Steiner called Kepler "a man in whom lived and pulsed the Christ-filled Astrology which draws after it, merely as its shadow, astrological superstition." The Kyot being led Steiner to "a thing called the Grail"; and Kepler worked with forces springing from the elemental world that maintain communication between the stars and the Earth. And as we follow the stars we find Presbyter John as the keeper of the Grail Mysteries. Such rich content to inbreathe! Mars was conjunct Kepler's death Sun in Scorpio at the birth of the Nathan Jesus, who later became Jesus Christ at the Baptism in the Jordan River. Jesus Christ is the highest manifestation of the work of reaching into realms of hidden dynamics, for it was he who descended into Hell. Steiner notes that the indications given by Kepler are spiritual revelations permeated by Christ.

Kepler did not view science and spirituality as mutually exclusive. His laws renewed the ancient Pythagorean concept of universal harmony. Today we can imagine the elemental beings rejoicing in the symphony of stars, and the stars rejoicing in the chorus of the elementals—and somewhere between the two we may find the mysteries of the Holy Grail. Kepler knew the harmony of the spheres as the music that sounds through Heaven and Earth: "The heavenly motions are nothing but a continuous song for several voices, perceived not by the ear but by the intellect, a figured music which sets landmarks in the immeasurable flow of time."[2]

The Grail Knight, Kyot, was trained to confront evil, as were all Grail Knights. These knights must be returning, for it is time to confront evil and unmask lies in order to restore harmony between Heaven and Earth. We can look into the eyes of the children we meet, and we may see that there are knights among them. This is a day to remember the harmony inherent in all archetypal life and to find the penetrating insight to notice forces working against divinity, the Grail, and harmony.

---

1 These lectures were given in 1914, one hundred years ago. Thus does the content therein find a new octave in this year.

2 Kepler *The Harmony of the World*.

The human being, as mediator between the stars above and the elemental beings below, has a sovereign, healing part to play in the drama of discord resounding throughout our world. What part can we play?

November 20: Venus 9° Scorpio square Neptune 9° Aquarius. Venus at this degree remembers Anne Catherine Emmerich receiving the stigmata; and in square to Neptune at Fomalhaut, this memory is potentized, becoming a source of inspiration for all. Neptune, as the Goddess Night, bestows Inspiration, to the soul whose soil has been well cultivated by attending to the movements of invisible worlds of spirit. On the other hand, if Venus tends the soil of the earthly soul alone, her inspirations become a self-centered dance into delusions born of truth's distortions.

November 22: New Moon 5° Scorpio. Conception of the Nathan Mary (Oct/24/18 BC). The immaculate conception of the pure and chaste Nathan Mary occurred at a New Moon 4° Scorpio. An immaculate conception is not only a conception free from the element of desire (which Lucifer implanted in the human astral body at the time of the Fall), but it is also immaculate in that the stream of heredity, moving from generation to generation, is held back in obedience to the spiritual stream moving downward from above. This New Moon heralds this triumph of spiritual forces over hereditary forces. We can contemplate this vertical stream of influence as we part the seas of materialism to make way for the new revelations assigning us our future tasks. It will be from this direction that purity will again be culturally created.

November 23: Mercury 27° Libra square Jupiter 27° Cancer. Conception of John the Baptist (Sept/9/3 BC). Heliocentric Jupiter was at this degree at John's conception and Mercury was at this degree as Jesus arrived at Mt. Attarus. Mercury is centered in the 10-petalled lotus flower—the solar plexus. The name "solar plexus" signifies the place toward which Mercury is to turn its attention—the Sun. When thinking is so oriented it can exercise "right judgement." This entails doing nothing without significant reason, and holding fast to what one has decided. The Jupiter center is the two-petalled lotus flower of the third eye, where "right thought" is practiced—to pay attention to one's ideas. John is the bearer of the apocalyptic future, calling humanity to forego the transitory and turn instead to the essential. Mercury's wing-footed speed, when concentrated on solar influences, can perceive and rightly judge what is meaningful. The dynamic interaction of these two planets can bring wise discernment to thinking.

November 25: Mercury conjunct Saturn 12° Scorpio. Judas becomes a disciple (Oct/24/30). The term *elders* refers to human beings working on the angelic level. "Rudolf Steiner gave an example of someone of this rank in the disciple Judas Iscariot. It is remarkable to consider that the individuality of Judas Iscariot was a very high being, and at the same time to behold how he fell prey to restlessness and betrayed Jesus Christ. Yet his rank—as an elder of humanity—comes to expression in his next incarnation as St. Augustine. Contemplating his life, we can understand that St. Augustine was one of the elders of humanity."[3]

Mercury remembers Judas joining the circle of twelve. In conjunction with Saturn, the mind deepens and has great resources for concentration. It is just this Saturnine influence that Judas lacked, and because of this he became the door through which evil entered the circle of disciples. Restlessness can cause one to become uncentered, and having lost center, one is vulnerable to being overtaken by influences coming from dubious sources. Today, concentration and stillness of mind are highlighted; and because this is occurring in Scorpio, penetrating insights may result.

November 26. Sun enters the second decan of Scorpio, ruled by the Sun and associated with the constellation of Hercules, the Mighty Sun Hero.

November 29: Mars enters Capricorn. "Within life's inner resistance" (Steiner, *Twelve Cosmic Moods*). It takes an inner resistance to avoid succumbing to the

---

[3] Powell, *Great Teachers of Humanity*. See footnote 3, page 199.

perpetuation of the past. Spiritual beings are ever-present with thoughts appropriate for any given time. Emptiness must be created—into which the thoughts of the present moment can be realized. If the continued presence of old thoughts prevails, such thoughts become a coffin of dogma arresting the continuity of change. The future finds its mooring when such effort to resist the past is practiced. The future is strongest when it properly rests upon a past that has not encroached beyond its rightful place.

DECEMBER 2014

The last month of the year begins with the Sun standing before the constellation of the Scorpion (Scorpio) and moving into Sagittarius on the 16th. The Full Moon with Sun in Scorpio, Moon in Taurus occurs on the 6th. The 8th brings the Sun into contact with Mercury again, and Jupiter stationing Retrograde once again and for what's left of 2014. Jupiter is joined by the waning Moon three days later on the 11th rising about 2 hours before midnight in the east, and visible until the dawn. The night of the 13th and morning of the 14th brings the peak of the Geminids Meteor Shower which is considered by many to be the best shower in the heavens, producing up to 120 multicolored shooting stars per hour at its peak! (The shower runs from the 7th—17th annually.) The waning Moon may block out some, but with such numerous and bright meteors, it is worth looking up (again: after midnight from a dark location!) Meteors radiate from the constellation of Gemini (look southward), but can appear anywhere in the sky. By the 19th, the Moon has journeyed around the wheel of the zodiac to join Saturn in Scorpio and then the Sun for the New Moon on the 21st. Continuing on, the Moon contacts Venus on the next day, the 23rd and Mars on the 25th. One last meteor opportunity is on the night of the 22nd: the Ursids Meteor Shower. It is a minor shower, with only about 5-10 an hour but this is a good year to catch them, as the Moon is tucked away and will not interfere with your viewing. Just after midnight, from a dark location, meteors will radiate from the constellation Ursa Minor (the Little Dipper; look to the North), but look all around you to catch these delightful gifts from the heavens streaming by.

December 1: Today is the first Sunday of Advent.
   ASPECT: Mercury 10° Scorpio square Neptune 10° Aquarius: The summons of Judas (Oct/24/30). As Advent begins we can pray to be shown all that stands in the way of our loyalty to each of our brothers and sisters. A shard from the archetypal betrayal can distort the Sophianic inspiration that so effortlessly blesses this season. We are to forgive all transgressions and pray that we be forgiven for those we have made. Embracing a state of reverent humility is a wonderful way to begin this preparation for the Holy Nights to come.

December 3: Sun 17° Scorpio. First conversion of Mary Magdalene (Nov/8/30). Jesus arrived at the mountain beyond Gabara, and delivered a powerful discourse with the words:

Come! Come to me, all who are weary and laden with guilt! Come to me, O sinners! Do penance, believe, and share the kingdom with me![1]

Magdalene was deeply moved by these words and experienced her first conversion. Later that evening, when Jesus was at a banquet at the home of a Pharisee named Simon Zabulon, Magdalene entered the room to anoint Jesus's head. This is a sure sign that she recognized him as a true King, and as the Messiah. It is astonishing, given the times, that Magdalene walked uninvited into a room where men were gathered. Women of those times were not allowed such privilege. The certainty of Magdalene is an example for us all. No matter where the old rules stultify, we are to walk in truth and without fear. This is a good day to contemplate where it is that we may allow ourselves to be limited due to soul contractions incurred long ago.

We contract in order to defend. As we mature we often carry these defensive soul postures long after their time of necessity has passed. Thus, we will find others falling into these contracted spaces; and rather than seeing the offender as the teacher pointing out our self-limitations, we often project our fear outwardly as antipathy toward the alleged

---
1   *Chron.*, p. 256.

SIDEREAL GEOCENTRIC LONGITUDES : DECEMBER 2014 Gregorian at 0 hours UT

DAY	☉	☽	☊	☿	♀	♂	♃	♄	♅	♆	♇
1 MO	13 ♏ 46	4 ♓ 21	23 ♍ 10	9 ♏ 38	22 ♏ 54	1 ♑ 58	27 ♋ 35	2 ♏ 29	17 ♓ 48R	9 ♒ 55	17 ♐ 11
2 TU	14 46	18 16	23 11	11 13	24 9	2 45	27 36	2 36	17 47	9 56	17 13
3 WE	15 47	2 ♈ 4	23 10R	12 47	25 24	3 31	27 37	2 43	17 46	9 56	17 15
4 TH	16 48	15 43	23 8	14 21	26 40	4 17	27 38	2 50	17 45	9 57	17 17
5 FR	17 49	29 14	23 3	15 56	27 55	5 4	27 39	2 57	17 44	9 58	17 19
6 SA	18 50	12 ♉ 32	22 55	17 30	29 10	5 50	27 40	3 4	17 44	9 58	17 21
7 SU	19 51	25 38	22 46	19 4	0 ♐ 26	6 37	27 40	3 11	17 43	9 59	17 23
8 MO	20 52	8 ♊ 29	22 35	20 38	1 41	7 23	27 41	3 18	17 42	10 0	17 25
9 TU	21 52	21 4	22 23	22 13	2 56	8 10	27 41R	3 25	17 41	10 0	17 26
10 WE	22 53	3 ♋ 25	22 13	23 47	4 11	8 56	27 41	3 32	17 41	10 1	17 28
11 TH	23 54	15 32	22 4	25 21	5 27	9 43	27 40	3 39	17 40	10 2	17 30
12 FR	24 55	27 30	21 58	26 55	6 42	10 30	27 40	3 46	17 40	10 3	17 32
13 SA	25 56	9 ♌ 20	21 54	28 30	7 57	11 16	27 39	3 53	17 39	10 4	17 34
14 SU	26 57	21 9	21 52	0 ♐ 4	9 13	12 3	27 38	3 59	17 39	10 5	17 36
15 MO	27 58	3 ♍ 2	21 52D	1 39	10 28	12 50	27 37	4 6	17 38	10 6	17 38
16 TU	28 59	15 3	21 53	3 14	11 43	13 36	27 36	4 13	17 38	10 7	17 40
17 WE	0 ♐ 0	27 19	21 53R	4 49	12 58	14 23	27 34	4 20	17 38	10 8	17 42
18 TH	1 1	9 ♎ 54	21 51	6 24	14 14	15 10	27 32	4 26	17 38	10 9	17 44
19 FR	2 3	22 51	21 47	7 59	15 29	15 57	27 31	4 33	17 37	10 10	17 46
20 SA	3 4	6 ♏ 14	21 41	9 34	16 44	16 44	27 28	4 39	17 37	10 11	17 48
21 SU	4 5	20 2	21 31	11 9	18 0	17 30	27 26	4 46	17 37	10 12	17 50
22 MO	5 6	4 ♐ 13	21 20	12 45	19 15	18 17	27 24	4 53	17 37D	10 13	17 52
23 TU	6 7	18 41	21 8	14 21	20 30	19 4	27 21	4 59	17 37	10 15	17 54
24 WE	7 8	3 ♑ 18	20 57	15 56	21 45	19 51	27 18	5 5	17 37	10 16	17 57
25 TH	8 9	17 59	20 47	17 32	23 1	20 38	27 15	5 12	17 37	10 17	17 59
26 FR	9 10	2 ♒ 34	20 40	19 8	24 16	21 25	27 12	5 18	17 38	10 18	18 1
27 SA	10 12	17 0	20 36	20 44	25 31	22 12	27 8	5 25	17 38	10 20	18 3
28 SU	11 13	1 ♓ 12	20 34	22 20	26 46	22 59	27 5	5 31	17 38	10 21	18 5
29 MO	12 14	15 10	20 34	23 56	28 2	23 46	27 1	5 37	17 38	10 22	18 7
30 TU	13 15	28 53	20 34	25 32	29 17	24 33	26 57	5 43	17 39	10 24	18 9
31 WE	14 16	12 ♈ 23	20 33	27 8	0 ♑ 32	25 20	26 53	5 49	17 39	10 25	18 11

INGRESSES :

2 ☽ → ♈ 20:24
5 ☽ → ♉ 1:22
6 ♀ → ♐ 15:50
7 ☽ → ♊ 8: 6
9 ☽ → ♋ 17:19
12 ☽ → ♌ 5: 3
13 ☿ → ♐ 22:53
14 ☽ → ♍ 17:53
16 ☉ → ♐ 23:50
17 ☽ → ♎ 5:11
19 ☽ → ♏ 12:54
21 ☽ → ♐ 16:55
23 ☽ → ♑ 18:35
25 ☽ → ♒ 19:45
27 ☽ → ♓ 21:56
30 ☽ → ♈ 1:58
♀ → ♑ 13:48

ASPECTS & ECLIPSES :

1 ☿ □ ♆ 4:20
☽ ☌ ♅ 23:10
2 ☽ ☌ ☋ 8:31
5 ☽ ☍ ♄ 6:44
6 ☽ ☍ ☿ 10:16
☉ ☍ ☽ 12:26
7 ☽ ☍ ♀ 9:52
8 ☉ ☋ ☿ 9:31
☽ ☍ ♇ 17: 1
9 ☽ ☋ ☊ 2:30
10 ☽ ☍ ♂ 11:37
12 ☽ ☌ ♃ 0:20
☽ ☌ A 22:43
13 ☽ ☍ ♆ 1:28
14 ☉ □ ☽ 12:50
15 ♅ □ ♇ 1:50
16 ☽ ☍ ♅ 5: 5
☽ ☌ ☊ 13:26
19 ☽ ☌ ♄ 21:10
20 ♀ □ ♅ 16:52
♀ ☌ ♇ 20:58
22 ☉ ☌ ☽ 1:35
☽ ☌ ☿ 15:57
☽ ☌ ♇ 22:43
23 ☽ ☌ ♀ 3:17
☽ ☊ ☊ 3:59
♀ □ ☊ 10:31
24 ☽ ☌ P 16:42
25 ☿ □ ♅ 1:18
☽ ☌ ♂ 4:35
☿ ☌ ♇ 6:44
☽ ☍ ♃ 15: 9
26 ☽ ☌ ♆ 12:50
☿ □ ☊ 21:58
28 ☉ □ ☽ 18:31
29 ☽ ☌ ♅ 4:18
☽ ☌ ☋ 9:24

SIDEREAL HELIOCENTRIC LONGITUDES : DECEMBER 2014 Gregorian at 0 hours UT

DAY	Sid. Time	☿	♀	⊕	♂	♃	♄	♅	♆	♇	Vernal Point
1 MO	4:39: 6	0 ♏ 44	5 ♐ 20	13 ♉ 46	4 ♒ 8	17 ♋ 18	1 ♏ 23	20 ♓ 9	11 ♒ 48	18 ♐ 8	5 ♓ 3' 7"
2 TU	4:43: 2	3 34	6 55	14 46	4 46	17 23	1 24	20 9	11 48	18 9	5 ♓ 3' 7"
3 WE	4:46:59	6 22	8 30	15 47	5 24	17 28	1 26	20 10	11 49	18 9	5 ♓ 3' 7"
4 TH	4:50:56	9 9	10 5	16 48	6 2	17 33	1 28	20 11	11 49	18 9	5 ♓ 3' 6"
5 FR	4:54:52	11 55	11 40	17 49	6 40	17 37	1 30	20 11	11 49	18 10	5 ♓ 3' 6"
6 SA	4:58:49	14 41	13 15	18 50	7 18	17 42	1 32	20 12	11 50	18 10	5 ♓ 3' 6"
7 SU	5: 2:45	17 26	14 50	19 51	7 56	17 47	1 34	20 12	11 50	18 10	5 ♓ 3' 6"
8 MO	5: 6:42	20 10	16 25	20 51	8 34	17 52	1 35	20 13	11 51	18 11	5 ♓ 3' 6"
9 TU	5:10:38	22 55	18 0	21 52	9 12	17 57	1 37	20 14	11 51	18 11	5 ♓ 3' 6"
10 WE	5:14:35	25 40	19 35	22 53	9 50	18 1	1 39	20 14	11 51	18 11	5 ♓ 3' 6"
11 TH	5:18:31	28 25	21 10	23 54	10 29	18 6	1 41	20 15	11 52	18 12	5 ♓ 3' 6"
12 FR	5:22:28	1 ♐ 10	22 44	24 55	11 7	18 11	1 43	20 16	11 52	18 12	5 ♓ 3' 5"
13 SA	5:26:25	3 57	24 19	25 56	11 45	18 16	1 45	20 16	11 52	18 12	5 ♓ 3' 5"
14 SU	5:30:21	6 44	25 54	26 57	12 23	18 20	1 46	20 17	11 53	18 13	5 ♓ 3' 5"
15 MO	5:34:18	9 33	27 29	27 58	13 1	18 25	1 48	20 18	11 53	18 13	5 ♓ 3' 5"
16 TU	5:38:14	12 23	29 4	28 59	13 39	18 30	1 50	20 18	11 53	18 13	5 ♓ 3' 5"
17 WE	5:42:11	15 14	0 ♑ 39	0 ♊ 0	14 17	18 35	1 52	20 19	11 54	18 14	5 ♓ 3' 5"
18 TH	5:46: 7	18 7	2 14	1 1	14 55	18 39	1 54	20 20	11 54	18 14	5 ♓ 3' 5"
19 FR	5:50: 4	21 3	3 48	2 2	15 33	18 44	1 56	20 20	11 55	18 14	5 ♓ 3' 4"
20 SA	5:54: 0	24 0	5 23	3 4	16 11	18 49	1 58	20 21	11 55	18 15	5 ♓ 3' 4"
21 SU	5:57:57	27 0	6 58	4 5	16 50	18 54	1 59	20 22	11 55	18 15	5 ♓ 3' 4"
22 MO	6: 1:54	0 ♑ 3	8 33	5 6	17 28	18 59	2 1	20 22	11 56	18 15	5 ♓ 3' 4"
23 TU	6: 5:50	3 9	10 8	6 7	18 6	19 3	2 3	20 23	11 56	18 15	5 ♓ 3' 4"
24 WE	6: 9:47	6 18	11 43	7 8	18 44	19 8	2 5	20 23	11 56	18 16	5 ♓ 3' 4"
25 TH	6:13:43	9 31	13 18	8 9	19 22	19 13	2 7	20 24	11 57	18 16	5 ♓ 3' 4"
26 FR	6:17:40	12 40	14 52	9 10	20 0	19 10	2 9	20 25	11 57	18 16	5 ♓ 3' 3"
27 SA	6:21:36	16 9	16 27	10 11	20 38	19 22	2 10	20 25	11 57	18 17	5 ♓ 3' 3"
28 SU	6:25:33	19 35	18 2	11 13	21 16	19 27	2 12	20 26	11 58	18 17	5 ♓ 3' 3"
29 MO	6:29:29	23 5	19 37	12 14	21 54	19 32	2 14	20 27	11 58	18 17	5 ♓ 3' 3"
30 TU	6:33:26	26 41	21 12	13 15	22 32	19 37	2 16	20 27	11 59	18 18	5 ♓ 3' 3"
31 WE	6:37:23	0 ♒ 22	22 47	14 16	23 10	19 41	2 18	20 28	11 59	18 18	5 ♓ 3' 3"

INGRESSES :

11 ☿ → ♐ 13:47
16 ♀ → ♑ 14:12
⊕ → ♊ 23:52
21 ☿ → ♑ 23:35
30 ☿ → ♒ 21:38

ASPECTS (HELIOCENTRIC +MOON(TYCHONIC)) :

1 ☿ ☌ ♄ 5:29
2 ☽ ☌ ♅ 3:16
☿ □ ♂ 13:16
4 ⊕ ⚹ ♃ 19: 7
☿ □ ♆ 23:11
5 ♀ ⚹ ♆ 2:23
☽ ☍ ♄ 4: 4
6 ☽ ☍ ☿ 4:54
7 ☿ △ ♃ 3:12
⊕ ⚹ ♅ 8:44
8 ☿ △ ♅ 0:24
☿ ☍ ⊕ 9:31
☽ ☍ ♀ 17:14
☽ ☍ ♇ 18:27
☿ ☌ A 22:27
9 ♀ ☌ ♇ 2:51
10 ♀ □ ♅ 10: 8
11 ☽ ☌ ♃ 5: 9
12 ♂ ☌ P 10:25
13 ♂ ☌ ♆ 4:50
☽ ☍ ♆ 5: 8
☽ ☍ ♂ 5: 9
15 ☿ ⚹ ♆ 19:54
16 ☽ ☍ ♅ 10:21
☿ ⚹ ♂ 13:49
17 ♀ ⚹ ♄ 18:55
18 ☿ ☌ ♇ 0:55
☿ □ ♅ 18:13
19 ☽ ☌ ♄ 16:23
22 ☿ ⚹ ♄ 15:26
☽ ☌ ♇ 23:18
23 ♂ ⚹ ♇ 6:12
24 ☽ ☌ ☿ 6:16
☽ ☌ ♀ 15:24
25 ☽ ☍ ♃ 2: 1
26 ☽ ☌ ♆ 15:34
27 ☿ ☌ ♀ 4: 2
♀ ☌ A 5:35
☽ ☌ ♂ 6:22
☿ ☍ ♃ 23: 6
28 ☿ ⚹ ♅ 5:56
⊕ △ ♆ 17:50
♀ ☍ ♃ 22:35
29 ☿ ☋ ☊ 3:12
☽ ☌ ♅ 9:11
♀ ⚹ ♅ 12:36
31 ☿ □ ♄ 12:25

offender. How foolish we can be when we fail to notice that the outer is a divine reflection of the inner! Magdalene, after being freed from a demon by Christ, redeemed her contracted soul that had allowed demons entrance, and she vowed to abstain from the behaviors of her past so that the presence of Christ could increase within her. For a time she experienced a greater expression of her full self and therefore could enter into places uninvited, in order to serve the One for whom she was making way in her heart. Where do we fear to enter, due to the limits we self-impose? Judgements often have their origin in selfhood's guilt. We must not be distracted by the limitations in others that cause them to cast aspersions toward us. May we walk with Christ in full expression of his presence within us!

On this first Sunday of Advent we may reflect upon our inner world and our openness for conversion. Magdalene fell after this first conversion and it was not until her second conversion, 2 1/2 weeks later, that she would find her ever-lasting peace and become the apostle to the apostles—the *spiritual sister* of Jesus.

December 5: Sun 19° Scorpio. Healing of the centurion's servant (Nov/10/30). Remarkable insights come to light with this healing. At the beginning of the new era in which Christ lived, there was a connection between the illness of a child and his parents, just as there was a connection between a master and his servant. A sick daughter meant a soul sickness in the parents, and a sick servant referred to an illness in the will of the master. This was understood in these days of old. At this time, humanity was in a transitional process in which it was still separating itself from the last effects of previous lives in ancient Lemuria and Atlantis. In these ancient cultures the will life was focused wholly outside the human being. Objects could be moved without being touched. Among the people at the time of Christ this was still found primarily amongst heathen peoples, who could dispatch their will into a servant.

The centurion's will inhabits the servant, so that when the former says: "Do this!" he does it. But now the servant has fallen ill, and cannot do what the master says; for, as we are told, he has "the palsy" (paralysis). He is incapable of acting, for the will is paralyzed. Then the centurion says: "Lord, I am not worthy that thou shouldest come under my roof; but speak the word only, and my servant shall be healed." This means that his roof covers and protects his house. But he is himself his house in which the will is sick. The centurion acknowledges this and asks the Christ to help him: to speak just *one* word so that his servant, his will, can recover. Through this one word the Lord will not enter physically into the centurion's house, but certainly will do so spiritually. This same process, already vouchsafed to the centurion before the Mystery of Golgotha, will come to every person on Earth through the Resurrection on Easter morning. The Word that is spoken and enters the "house" of the centurion is the same Word celebrated in the prologue to the St. John Gospel, the I AM. This I enters the habitation of the human being, enters the new house of the centurion, enlivening his sick servant—in other words, healing his sick will.[1]

With the Sun in Scorpio, the constellation that plummets the depths in order to reveal the heights, we can invite Christ into our house—our bodies—in order to experience a healing of our wills and our souls. This can happen only if we have faith: "I say to you that many will come from the east and the west, and will take their places at the feast with Abraham, Isaac, and Jacob in the kingdom of heaven. But the subjects of the kingdom will be thrown outside, into the darkness" (Matt. 8:11–12). The "outer darkness" refers to the fate of those in the community of ancient Israel who were children of the kingdom and yet placed not their faith in the Messiah who was sent into their kingdom at the Turning Point in Time. Again we face this situation—the Etheric Christ is here. Are we going to enter the community of Eternal Israel, or are we going to be "cast out into outer darkness." This is a day to make commitments to our spiritual practice.

December 6: Full Moon 19° Taurus opposite Sun 19° Scorpio. Meeting with Maroni, the widow of Nain (Nov/10/30). Today marks the place of the

---

1 Von Halle, *Illness and Healing and the Mystery Language of the Gospels*, pp. 119–120.

Sun when Jesus met Maroni (the mother of the Youth of Nain) in the Valley of the Doves, south of Capernaum. She begged him to come and heal her twelve-year-old son. As Jesus taught in the synagogue when the Sabbath began, a possessed man ran in, causing great commotion.[2] Images we can work with are: the Valley of the Doves, the widow, and the possessed man. The Holy Spirit (dove) can find us as we renew our relationship with the Father, thus becoming widows no more. This process sets us upon the path of deliverance from possessive forces in our lower nature (the Scorpion becomes the Eagle). As we begin to find Christ, as did Maroni, we will become worthy to encounter our higher self, for our souls will have found their purity. First we remember, then we awaken, then we are reborn. Where does our soul feel widowed from the divine love of our Father?

December 7: Sun enters the third decan of Scorpio, ruled by Mercury and associated with the constellation of Ophiucus the Serpent Holder. Ophiucus, sometimes also called Aesclepius, has a healing mission.

Venus enters Sagittarius: "In existence growth's power dies" (Steiner, *Twelve Cosmic Moods*). Venus was in Sagittarius during the forty days in the wilderness and during several of Christ's healing miracles up to the walking on the water. We are to prevail against the consuming forces of matter, and persevere through life-filled activity directed toward spiritual renewal. This renewal lifts the soul into its eternal becoming.

December 8: Superior conjunction Sun and Mercury 21° Scorpio. False teachers are addressed by Jesus (Nov/12/30). Jesus and his disciples were on their way to Nain. "Jesus taught how to distinguish true teachers from false teachers" (*Chron.*, p. 257):

> Watch out for false prophets. They come to you in sheep's clothing, but inwardly they are ferocious wolves. By their fruit you will recognize them. Do people pick grapes from thornbushes, or figs from thistles? Likewise, every good tree bears good fruit, but a bad tree bears bad fruit. A good tree cannot bear bad fruit, and a bad tree cannot bear good fruit. Every tree that does not bear good fruit is cut down and thrown into the fire. Thus, by their fruit you will recognize them. (Matt. 7:15–20)

December 9: Sun 22° Scorpio. Raising of the Youth of Nain (Nov/13/30). The Youth of Nain was the Son of the Widow, who is a significant figure for the entire history of humanity. We can follow the incarnations: Youth of Nain, Mani, Parsifal. Rudolf Steiner called Mani one of the greatest beings ever to incarnate upon the planet. Further, he indicates that this individuality will most likely incarnate again in the twenty-first century if conditions are right. (Has he perhaps incarnated already?) Parsifal was also a son of a widow. What does the "son of the widow" indicate? In this regard, Rudolf Steiner noted:

During the fifth Root Race*, the father withdraws. The soul is widowed. Humanity is thrown back onto itself. It must find the light of truth within its own soul in order to act as its own guide. Everything of a soul nature has always been expressed in terms of the feminine. Therefore this self-directing feminine element (which exists only in a germinal state today and will later be fully developed) is no longer confronted by the divine fructifier, and is called by Mani the "Widow." Therefore he calls himself "Son of the Widow."

Steiner then quotes the words of Mani:

> You must lay aside everything that you have acquired as outer revelation by means of the senses. You must lay aside all things that come to you via outer authority; then you must become ripe to gaze into your own soul.[3]

Clearly the teachings of Mani direct widowed souls to unite with the return of the Etheric Christ and the in-streaming wisdom of Divine Sophia. *We are now to become spiritual investigators in our own right through the inner ripening of our souls. Mani teaches the redemption of evil. The first step toward this great aspiration begins when one is able to confront evil in one's own nature.*

In following the continuous sequence of spiritual teachings, we develop greater abilities in

---

[2] *Chron.*, p. 256.

[3] Steiner, *The Temple Legend*, p. 62.

understanding the new language that is constantly forming. A deepening is occurring due to the effects of the Etheric Christ, wherein Platonic resonances are ensouling new dispensations. This is creating a renaissance of wisdom, and the language of wisdom is quite different from the abstractions of past theologies. *Just as we need to develop an organ for comprehending the wisdom of fairy tales, so too do we need to develop an organ for comprehending the wisdom streams now flowing from cosmic heights. Great teachers are preparing us. Each teacher brings a thread contributing to the masterpiece that is leading us toward the future. To renounce even one of these teachers hampers our ability to understand the next—renunciation can actually affect our ability to stay on course with the "spiritual trajectory" of Earth evolution.* The Youth of Nain is coming. Teachers are now preparing those who are to become his disciples. The new teachings may seem foolish at first; then they become obvious, but by that time there is already a new foolishness to follow in the continuous unfolding of time. We are to follow the Morning Star—Venus—and her pentagram of love!

Jupiter stations 27° Cancer before going retrograde: The conception of John the Baptist (Sept/9/3 BC). Heliocentric Jupiter was at this exact degree when the first Adam—John the Baptist—was conceived by his mother Elizabeth. Robert Powell calls John the third teacher of the twentieth century who is our guide in unmasking evil. John and Christian Rosenkreutz work together:

> The Johannine Stream is comprised of these two individualities, Lazarus John and John the Baptist, who are spiritually working together. They comprise the Johannine Stream. We can trace them back to the Primal Family. John the Baptist was Adam, and Lazarus-John was Cain— father and son. When one is incarnated, the other is almost always working inspiringly from the spiritual world and vice versa (like Master Jesus and Christian Rosenkreutz). This is why they can be seen together as a composite being. For example, John the Baptist, the reincarnated Adam, reincarnated as the painter Raphael in 1483, one year before the death of Christian Rosenkreutz in 1484. In 1484 Christian Rosenkreutz passed into the spiritual world and worked as the inspirer of Raphael from above. Rudolf Steiner describes how the soul of Raphael was opened to Christian Rosenkreutz, who was guiding him from the spiritual world. Out of this came one beautiful painting after another, paintings that had to do with the Divine Feminine, with the Madonna and child. This was the work of Raphael, but it was inspired from the spiritual realm by Christian Rosenkreutz.[1]

December 14: Sun 27° Scorpio. First raising of the daughter of Jairus (Nov/18/30). In biblical times a child might become ill as a result of a transgression (a moral failure) on the part of one of its parents—instead of the parent becoming ill. Children had great importance at this time, as they were links in the generational chain leading to the incarnation of the Messiah; and it was just this chain that caused such transference of illness from parent to child. After Christ performed his miracles he would offer a mantric prayer that was to help in sustaining the healing he had given, until the time when the Mystery of Golgotha would change everything:

> If we think back to the general condition of humanity shortly before the Mystery of Golgotha, we can gain a tangible sense of the reason for giving special mantras and prayers and urging people to remember these. The empty sheaths of the gods' dwelling places [chakras], which human beings had brought with them in their astral bodies through the succession of cultural epochs, had progressively been occupied by demons; and these could exert particularly destructive effects if those who led an immoral life supplied these demons improvident astral nourishment. At the moment a healing was performed and Christ had driven these demons out of the bodies of sick people, these sheaths of the dwelling places of the gods remained behind in an empty state, cleansed of the adversarial beings. Thus they were empty, and each person needed to fill them with something new to prevent them being reoccupied by the luciferic and ahrimanic spirits. They were therefore to fill them with the prayers and esoteric exercises that

---

1 Powell, *Great Teachers of Humanity*. See footnote 3, page 199.

Jesus Christ had given them, until the day when they would *behold the whole glory of the Son of the Father*; in other words, until the Mystery of Golgotha, when the divine spirit would itself enter and inhabit these sheaths of one's body.[2]

The family of Jairus fell into their old attitude of disrespect and disbelief toward Jesus—and so their daughter again fell ill and died two weeks later.

The special mantras and prayers that were to sustain soul health in those ancient times are applicable as well to our times. Due to humanity's disrespect and disregard of their spiritual well-being, demons again occupy the chakras. Materialism, false teachings, and immoral developments in all aspects of life have provided nourishment for demons. The vast amount of spiritual attention transferred to the world of mammon is engendering possessions in our chakras. We have forgotten our lofty origins and have given ourselves over to unholy alliances. *As a matter of spiritual hygiene in this time of the second coming of Christ, it is essential that we call the good powers again into our being through the practice of reciting prayers and mantras. This is no longer a mere option, for the adversary has grown too strong to be ignored. Our chakras need spiritual nourishment in order to maintain a connection, in freedom, to the divine-spiritual beings who would manifest within and through us.* In his book *Inner Radiance and the Body of Immortality*, Dr. Powell offers practices that bring from Heaven the *manna* that sustains us in maintaining our connection to Christ. We can counter the battle for the human soul now taking place on a global level by asking Christ to indwell us on a daily basis. Either we turn toward the spiritual world, or we will be taken up by the anti-spiritual beings that are rampantly swallowing many individuals and whole groups. Apathy toward this reality is a choice in and of itself.

December 15: Uranus 17° Pisces square Pluto 17° Sagittarius. Though this configuration has been with us all year, today this square is exact. Pluto was at this degree through the entire Passion of Christ and during the time after his resurrection when he was visiting certain of his disciples. At this time those who met Jesus Christ were in communion with his phantom body, which is represented in the bread communion during the Mass. With Pluto in this dynamic relationship with Uranus, we can expect the unexpected in this Advent season. The Earth is wide awake, her soul held within, and so, too, is Christ right here with us most especially at this inward time of the yearly cycle. May we find moments of quiet reflection, and wakefulness, that we may feel the presence of One who loves us dearly.

December 16. Sun enters Sagittarius. "Becoming achieves the power to be" (Steiner, *Twelve Cosmic Moods*). William Bento illumines this mantra:

When existence is regarded not merely as a noun, but as a verb, we enter the realm of becoming. It is being, in dynamic movement. Such movement is purposeful, for being seeks a state in which it can be a power of "presence," a reality of the here and now. This achievement "to be" is the drama of human potential. Each human being seeks "to be" what he or she has resolved to become. The arrival of that becoming is both a joyful and empowering experience where there is nothing to do but be.

Control of Speech becomes Feeling for Truth. Blessed are the self-disciplined, for they shall know the truth.

December 19: Sun 2° Sagittarius conjunct the Galactic Center. The Archer's arrow aims at the Galactic Center: the heart of the Milky Way. This is opposite to where the Sun was at Pentecost.

December 20: Venus conjunct Pluto 17° Sagittarius square Uranus 17° Pisces. The Passion and Resurrection of Jesus Christ. Venus comes with her empty cup to grail for the Father's divine love (Pluto). Pluto is remembering the Passion of Christ. Venus was at this degree at the beginning of the forty days in the wilderness; and now, with Pluto remembering the final days of the life of Christ that had begun shortly before the start of the forty days, she visits the heavenly Father who sent his only Son to save the people of Earth. There is great tenderness in this day. The gift of tears may flow from hearts receiving the gentleness of Venus as she remembers the beginning of the life that came to its

---

2 Von Halle, *Illness and Healing and the Mystery Language of the Gospels*, pp. 113-114.

end when Pluto stood where it does today. Today marks the beginning and the end, the alpha and the omega of the three and one half years in the life of Christ. May we spread peace and love to one another and turn our hearts to the new revelations (Uranus) guiding us forward.

December 21: New Moon 5° Sagittarius and Winter Solstice 2014. The year began on January 1st with a New Moon in Sagittarius, and now the lunar year comes to an end. Twelve New Moons have graced the heavens. It takes three days for the lunar influences to fully ebb, which takes us to Christmas Eve and the beginning of the Holy Nights. Sun and Moon stand conjunct the galactic equator at this, the darkest time of the year. The Sun at this degree remembers the miraculous draught (Nov/26/30) and the Moon remembers the healing of Theokeno (Sept/28/32). He was the king who brought frankincense to the newborn Solomon Jesus. Frankincense is an ancient medium of aromatherapy that already had scented the Egyptian Temples to honor Ra and Horus, and it is said that Queen Sheba brought a great number of Frankincense trees as a special gift for King Solomon. The miraculous draught of fishes, under the influence of this New Moon in Sagittarius, likewise offers us a miraculous draught of etheric images as well as the life forces that strengthen us for our future tasks. This leads us to the healing of the king in us—our higher "I"— which longs to be drawn from our entrapment in *maya* in order to find the spiritual thoughts that seek our opened minds and guide us to the magic of miracles. It is time to begin a new quest. May we find the one path that is ours to take (the monism of Sagittarius) so that we may begin the quest that leads us toward our true home.

December 22: Uranus stations 17° Pisces before going direct. We can recall (at this degree) the year of 1762, three Uranus cycles past, when Wolfgang Amadeus Mozart was touring Europe as a six year old child prodigy. Particularly important was his meeting in London with Johann Christian Bach (Johann Sebastian Bach's youngest son), who had a strong influence on Wolfgang. Mozart died at the age of 35, the cause of death uncertain, after having composed over 600 works. Beethoven (fifteen years his junior) was deeply influenced by the works of Mozart. With Uranus remembering this brilliant composer we can, in this Advent season, fill our minds and hearts with music that resounds with the harmony of the spheres.

December 23: Sun 6°51 Sagittarius. First Temptation in the Wilderness (Nov/27/29): There are forces that originated in cosmic aeons prior to that of the human being. Remnants of these forces live in densified forms within the interior of the Earth, and from here they work negatively against the human being. The remnants from previous aeons that work negatively with the will-nature of human beings are those of "trapped life." Through the transformation of the will, whereby it becomes obedient to Divine Will, "trapped life" becomes united with cosmic love (Pluto/Phanes). The first temptation in the wilderness was the temptation to bow to the Prince of this World. This is the temptation to use the personal will in service of self-gain—a temptation that continues in our time through all forms of tyranny.

Humanity has the task of bringing to realization what Nature does not bring to realization. Nature becomes conscious in us, and we have to create further. The kingdoms of Nature are beneath the human being. The ideal to strive for is the kingdom of God (*regnum Dei*)—as in the Lord's Prayer: "Thy kingdom come!" To bring this to realization—this is the task which the human being has to fulfill on Earth, following his/her highest ideal. This world that is not yet there is what the human being has to learn to build.[1]

May we become the "handmaids of the Lord" so that our deeds reflect what is best for all of humanity and all of Earth's creatures. In this way we become builders of the "world that is not yet there." The brick and mortar of this building are not those sculpted on Earth, but rather the forces that are freed when moral will holds sway in our deeds.

December 24: Christmas Eve and the opening to the Holy Nights. May we consciously enter through

---

[1] *Starlight*, vol. 10 (translations of unpublished works of Valentin Tomberg).

the wonder of this portal that leads us into the mysteries of the Holy Days and Nights that begin at sunset.

Sun 7°53 Sagittarius: The Second Temptation in the Wilderness (Nov/28/29). Forces from past aeons that work negatively against the feeling nature of human beings are the forces in the inner Earth that work from "trapped sound" (Neptune/Night). *Through the transformation of our heart, our feeling life becomes permeated with cosmic sound, whereby we hear spiritual beings working with us.* The second temptation in the wilderness was the temptation to plunge from the pinnacle of the temple, with the assurance that angels would catch us. This is the temptation to fall from consciousness, forsaking the angels, and instead become pawns in magnetic attractions to fallen, and, densified forces. This can result in terrible polarization in the feeling life, as happened with those who were behind the communist revolution of 1917 in Russia.

Circumstances are always influenced by the subconscious if the human being is not active. If he does not strive continually with respect to his subconscious, he succumbs to some kind of inertia, which leads to a darkening of the subconscious. Thus, the human being can find himself in complete darkness. "The pinnacle of the temple" (Luke 4:9) is the superconscious. The temptation [of casting oneself from the pinnacle of the temple] of Jesus Christ in the wilderness is that of believing in the wisdom of the subconscious.[2]

May our heart beat as one with the hearts of others, in spirit awareness. And may we reach for the true pinnacle of our temple!

December 25: Christian Celebration of the Birth of Christ. This day a seed is planted in the inner sanctuary of our heart. May we believe in this gift and tend it through the coming weeks. It will quicken at Candlemas, and then sprout, revealing its new life at Easter. We can follow the flowering as we move through the coming summer, and this will come to fruition at Michaelmas (nine months from this time of our conceiving). This is the seed of our future spiritual potential for the coming year. What in childhood came from without as gifts becomes, in our adulthood, our recognition of a new aspect of our eternal being that is born from the depths of winter's night, and seeks to become one with us as the year unfolds.

Sun 8°54 Sagittarius: The Third Temptation in the Wilderness (Nov/29/29). Forces from past aeons that work negatively against the thinking life of human beings are the forces in the inner Earth that work out of "trapped light" (Uranus/Ouranos). These forces can cause a poverty of thought, whereby thinking is torn from cosmic thoughts. Through the transformation of our thinking we can become a vehicle for cosmic light. The third temptation in the wilderness was the temptation to turn stones to bread:

The temptation of "turning stones to bread" is that of "producing" the living and organic from the dead and material. For example, one does precisely this if one conceives of thinking as a mechanical process in the brain. That is, if one supposes that the brain produces thoughts just as the glands produce secretion. Thus, the third temptation has to do with materialism, just as the second temptation has to do with the force of moral irresponsibility, and the first temptation with the will to power.[3]

May our thinking be illumined by truth, and our contemplation ennobled through spirit beholding.

Mercury conjunct Pluto 17° Sagittarius square Uranus 17° Pisces: With both Venus and Mercury in Sagittarius, both transit Pluto and square the tempestuous Uranus. Venus transited Pluto earlier this month and now Mercury is transiting. These two aspects offer intensity of thought and illuminated cognition. As we celebrate the birth of Jesus, the stars offer us depth so that we may contemplate the One who did the greatest deed in the history of Earth's evolution.

December 26: Sun enters the second decan of Sagittarius, ruled by the Moon and associated with the constellation Corona Australis, the Southern Crown, forming a moonlike chalice beneath the central part of the Archer.

---

2 Ibid.

3 Ibid.

Sun 9°58 Sagittarius: End of the forty days in the wilderness. In 2010 Pluto's transit of 8°54 Sagittarius was of special significance. It recalled Pluto's actual position at the climax of the temptation period in the wilderness, when the Sun and Pluto were in conjunction—reflecting the time when Ahriman approached Christ with the third temptation. This was the year in which corporations were crowned with the status of personhood. Yet today the Sun marks the end of the forty days, and we can remember that it is the sovereign "I" that reveals to us the possessing anti-"I" of the Antichrist. On this fortieth day in the wilderness the tempters withdrew, and many angels came to minister to Christ:

Just as Jesus Christ triumphed in the confrontation with evil and emerged victorious on the fortieth day—to be consoled by the heavenly nourishment of the angels—so there is every hope that humankind as a whole will successfully navigate a course through the historical period of temptation [ending historically in 2018]. It is only after passing through this that the real unfolding of the Christ Impulse will come to manifestation. Then, for example, a historical mirroring of the miracle at the wedding at Cana will take place during the Aquarian age.[1]

May we all find the wings of the dove—the presence of the Holy Spirit—during these blessed days and nights we have now entered. Let this peace enfold and envelop us.

December 27: Sun 11° Sagittarius. Second raising of the daughter of Jairus (Dec/1/30) Thirteen days after her first raising from the dead, Salome was again close to death. At this second raising from the dead, Salome was deeply moved and shed tears:

Jesus exhorted the parents to receive God's mercy thankfully, to completely renounce vanity and worldly pleasure, to do penance, and to beware of again compromising their daughter's life, now restored for the second time. Jesus told Salome that in the future she should no longer live according to the dictates of her flesh and blood, but that she should eat the Bread of Life—the Word of God—and she should repent, believe, pray, and do good deeds. Salome's parents became inwardly transformed and expressed their determination to change their ways.[2]

There is a universal teaching in this miracle:

In this example of Jairus's daughter is contained a teaching concerning the Second Coming of the Lord. Many are those who received the grace of Jesus Christ through his First Coming, but in later incarnations have forgotten it. Like Jairus and his wife, they have lived frivolous lives based on worldly concerns, even mocking the memory of the Holy One of Israel, the Saviour of mankind. But misfortune is bound to strike whosoever turns away from the Source of all Goodness. And this is the situation in which many find themselves in their incarnations in the Age of the Second Coming. Salvation can be found only by turning to Jesus Christ, and as in the case of Jairus, a second opportunity will be given to all who sincerely seek him. And in the case of those who have missed the grace of Jesus Christ in their incarnations up until now, there is now another opportunity—as in the case of the pagan woman Enue[3]—to seek out Jesus Christ and make contact with him. However great the throng, he notices each one, and his healing power of love and compassion goes forth to each who seeks it and needs it.[4]

Pagans, Jews, Christians, Buddhist, Hindus—and all the other religious groups devoted to the various petals of the *Rose of the World*—can touch him now. Christ, the being of Love, is the center of all groups of people until the end of time. Where Christ has been usurped, the soul of the person (also: the circle, the organization, or society) is dying, just as Salome died when her father dismissed the presence of Christ. We too, however, are given a second chance.

As the year comes toward its end, we can contemplate how we may strive to change our ways to become more of who we truly are. May we

---

1 *CHA*, "The Temptation in the Wilderness."

2 Ibid. "The Raising of the Youth of Nain and of the Daughter of Jairus."

3 Enue was the woman healed of the issue of blood whose destiny was intricately intertwined with that of Salome.

4 Ibid.

receive the blessed nourishment of these holy days and nights.

December 31: Venus enters Capricorn. "May the past feel the future" (Steiner, *Twelve Cosmic Moods*). When, with courageous loyalty to the past, the future moors itself to the present, we are in harmony with world beings; and in vigilance we can weave the continuity of time. Venus was in Capricorn at the three temptations in the wilderness as well as at the turning of water into wine at the wedding in Cana.

"The stars are the expression of love in the cosmic ether…To see a star means to feel a caress that has been prompted by love.… To gaze at the stars is to become aware of the love proceeding from divine spiritual beings.… The stars are signs and tokens of the presence of gods in the universe." (*Karmic Relationships,* vol. 7, June 8, 1924)

"We must see in the shining stars the outer signs of colonies of spirits in the cosmos. Wherever a star is seen in the heavens, there—in that direction—is a colony of spirits." (*Karmic Relationships,* vol. 6, June 1, 1924)

"They looked up above all to what is represented by the zodiac. And they regarded what the human being bears within as the spirit in connection with the constellations, the glory of the fixed stars, the spiritual powers whom they knew to be there in the stars." (*Karmic Relationships,* vol. 4, Sept. 12, 1924)

"All the stars are colonies of spiritual beings in cosmic space, colonies which we can learn to know when, having passed through the gate of death, our own soul lives and moves among these starry colonies…with the beings of the hierarchies.… To understand karma, therefore, we must return once more to a wisdom of the stars. We must discover spiritually the paths of human beings between death and a new birth in connection with the beings of the stars.… There has come forth a certain stream of spiritual life which makes it very difficult to approach with an open mind the science of the stars, and the science of karma.… We can nevertheless go forward with assurance and approach the wisdom of the stars and the real shaping of karma." (*Karmic Relationships,* vol. 4, Sept. 18, 1924)

GLOSSARY

This glossary of entries relating to Esoteric Christianity lists only some of the specialized terms used in the articles and commentaries of the *Journal for Star Wisdom*. For reasons of space, the entries are very brief, and the reader is encouraged to read the works of Rudolf Steiner for a more complete understanding of these terms.

Ahriman: An adversarial being identified by the great prophet Zarathustra during the ancient Persian cultural epoch (5067–2907 BC) as an opponent to the Sun God, *Ahura Mazda,* or *Ahura Mazdao* (obs.), ("Aura of the Sun"). Also called Satan, Ahriman represents one aspect of the Dragon. Ahriman's influence leads to materialistic thinking devoid of feeling, empathy, and moral conscience. Ahriman helps inspire science and technology, and works through forces of sub-nature such as gravity, electricity, magnetism, radioactivity—forces that are antithetical to life. The influence of Ahriman's activity upon the human being limits human cognition to what is derived from sense perception, hardens thinking (materialistic thoughts), attacks the etheric body by way of modern technology (electromagnetic radiation, etc.), and hardens hearts (cold and calculating).

ahrimanic beings: Spiritual beings who have become agents of Ahriman's influences.

Angel Jesus: A pure immaculate Angelic being who sacrifices himself so that the Christ may work through him. This Angelic being is actually of the status of an Archangel, who has descended to work on the Angelic level in order to be closer to human beings and to assist them on the path of confrontation with evil.

Ascension: An unfathomable process at the start of which, on May 14, AD 33, Christ united with the etheric realm that surrounds and permeates the earth with Cosmic Life. Thus began his cosmic ascent to the realm of the heavenly Father, with the goal of elevating the Earth spiritually and opening pathways between the Earth and the spiritual world for the future.

astral body: Part of the human being that is the bearer of consciousness, passion, and desires, as well as idealism and the longing for perfection.

Asuras: Fallen Archai (Time Spirits) from the time of Old Saturn, whose opposition to human evolution comes to expression through promoting debauched sexuality and senseless violence among human beings. So low is the regard that the Asuras have for the sacredness of human life, that as well as promoting extreme violence and debauchery (for example, through the film industry), they do not hold back from the destruction of the physical body of human beings. In particular, the activity of the Asuras retards the development of the consciousness soul.

bodhisattva: On the human level a bodhisattva is a human being far advanced on the spiritual path, a human being belonging to the circle of twelve great teachers surrounding the Cosmic Christ. One who incarnates periodically to further the evolution of the Earth and humanity, working on the level of an angelic, archangelic, or higher being in relation to the rest of humanity. Every 5,000 years, one of these great teachers from the circle of bodhisattvas takes on a special mission, incarnating repeatedly to awaken a new human faculty and capacity. Once that capacity has been imparted through its human bearer, this Bodhisattva then incarnates upon the earth for the last time, ascending to the level of a Buddha in order to serve humankind from spirit realms. See also Maitreya Bodhisattva.

Central Sun: Heart of the Milky Way, also called the Galactic Center. Our Sun orbits this Central Sun over a period of approximately 225 million years.

chakra: One of seven astral organs of perception through which human beings develop higher

Glossary

levels of cognition such as clairvoyance, telepathy, and so on.

Christ: The eternal being who is the second member of the Trinity. Also called the *Divine I AM*, the Son of God, the Cosmic Christ, and the Logos/Word. Christ began to fully unite with the human vessel (Jesus) at the Baptism in the Jordan, and for 3½ years penetrated as the *Divine I AM* successively into the astral body, etheric body, and physical body of Jesus, spiritualizing each member. Through the Mystery of Golgotha Christ united with the Earth, kindling the spark of Christ consciousness (*Not I, but Christ in me*) in all human beings.

Jesus Christ: The Divine-Human being; the God-Man; the union of the Divine with the Human. The presence of the Cosmic Christ in the physical body of the human being called the Nathan Jesus during the 3½ years of the ministry.

consciousness soul: The portion of the human soul in which "I" consciousness is awakening not only to its own sense of individuality and to the individualities of others, but also to its higher self—spirit self (Sanskrit: *manas*). Within the consciousness soul, the "I" perceives truth, beauty, and goodness; within the spirit self, the "I" becomes truth, beauty, and goodness.

crossing the threshold: a term applicable to our time, as human beings are increasingly encountering the spiritual world—in so doing, crossing the threshold between the sense-perceptible realm and non-physical realms of existence. To the extent that spiritual capacities have not been cultivated, this encounter with non-physical realms beyond the sense world signifies a descent into the subconscious (for example, through drugs) rather than an ascent to knowledge of higher worlds through the awakening of higher levels of consciousness.

Decan: The zodiac of 360° is divided into twelve signs, each of 30°. A decan is 10°, thus one third of one sign or $1/36$ of the zodiac.

Devil: Another name for Lucifer.

Dragon: As used in the Apocalypse of John, there are different appearances of the dragon, each one representing an adversarial being opposed to Michael, Christ, and Sophia. For example, the great red dragon of chapter 12 opposes Sophia, the woman clothed with the Sun (Sophia is the pure Divine-Cosmic Feminine Soul of the World). The imagery from chapter 12 of Revelations depicts the woman clothed with the Sun as pregnant and that the great red dragon attempts to devour her child as soon as it is born. The child coming to birth from the woman clothed with the Sun represents the Divine-Cosmic "I AM" born through the assistance of the pure Divine Feminine Soul of the World. The dragon is cast down from the heavenly realm by the mighty Archangel Michael. Cast down to the Earth, the dragon continues with attempts to devour the cosmic child (the Divine-Cosmic "I AM") coming to birth among humankind.

ego: The soul sheath through which the "I" begins to incarnate and to experience life on Earth (to be distinguished from the term *ego* used in Freudian and Jungian psychology—hence written capitalized "Ego" to make this distinction). The terms *ego*, *"I,"* and *soul* are often used interchangeably in Spiritual Science. The ego maintains threads of integrity and continuity through memory, while experiencing new sensations and perceptions through observation and thinking, feeling, and willing. The ego is capable of moral discernment and also experiences temptation. Thus, it is often stated that the "I" comprises both a higher nature ("Ego") and a lower nature ("ego").

Emmerich, Anne Catherine (also "Sister Emmerich"): A Catholic stigmatist (1774–1824) whose visions depicted the daily life of Jesus, beginning some weeks before the event of the descent of Christ into the body of Jesus at the Baptism in the River Jordan and extending for a period of several weeks after the Crucifixion.

Ephesus: The area in Asia Minor (now Turkey) to which the Apostle John (also called John Zebedee, the brother of James the Greater) accompanied the Virgin Mary approximately three years after the death of Jesus Christ. Ephesus was a very significant ancient mystery center where cosmic mysteries of the East found their way into the West. Initiates at Ephesus were devoted to the goddess Artemis, known as "Artemis of Ephesus," whose qualities are more those of a Mother goddess than is the case with the Greek goddess Artemis, although there is a certain degree of overlap between Artemis and Artemis of Ephesus with regard to many of their respective characteristics. A magnificent Ionic mystery temple was built in honor of Artemis of Ephesus at a location close to the Aegean Sea. Mary's house, built by John, was located high up above, on the nearby hill known as Mount Nightingale, about six miles from the temple of Artemis at Ephesus.

etheric body: The body of life forces permeating and animating the physical body. The etheric body was formed during Ancient Sun evolution. The etheric body's activity is expressed in the seven life processes permeating the seven vital organs. The etheric body is related to the movements of the seven visible planets.

Fall, The: A fall from oneness with spiritual worlds. The Fall, which took place during the Lemurian period of Earth evolution, was a time of dramatic transition in human evolution when the soul descended from "Paradise" into earthly existence. Through the Fall the human soul began to incarnate into a physical body upon the earth and experience the world from "within" the body, perceiving through the senses.

Fifth Gospel: The writings and lectures of Rudolf Steiner based on new spiritual perceptions and insights into the mysteries of Christ's life on earth, including the second coming of Christ—his appearance in the etheric realm in our time, beginning in the twentieth century.

Golgotha, Mystery of: Rudolf Steiner's designation for the entire mystery of the coming of Christ to the Earth. Sometimes this term is used more specifically to refer to the events surrounding the Crucifixion and Resurrection. In particular, the Crucifixion—the sacrifice on the cross—marked the birth of Christ's union with the Earth. Also referred to as the "Turning Point of Time," whereby at the Crucifixion Christ descended from the sphere of the Sun and became the "Spirit of the Earth."

Grail: An etheric chalice into which Christ can work to transform earthly substance into spiritual substance. The term *Grail* has many deep levels of meaning and refers on the one hand to a spiritual stream in service of Christ, and on the other hand to the means by which the human "I" penetrates and transforms evil into good. The power of transubstantiation expresses something of this process of transformation of evil into good.

Grail Knights: Those trained to confront evil and transform it into something good, in service of Christ. Members of a spiritual stream that existed in the past and continues to exist—albeit in metamorphosed form—in the present. Every human being striving for the good can potentially become a Grail Knight.

I AM: One's true individuality, that—with few exceptions—never fully incarnates but works into the developing "I" and its lower bodies (astral, etheric, and physical). The **Cosmic I AM** is the "I AM" of Christ, through which—on account of the Mystery of Golgotha—we are all graced with the possibility of receiving a divine spark therefrom.

Jesus (see Nathan Jesus and Solomon Jesus): The pure human being who received the Christ at the Baptism in the River Jordan.

Jesus Christ: See Jesus Christ.

Jesus of Nazareth: The name of the human being whose birth is celebrated in the Gospel of Luke, also referred to as the Nathan Jesus. When Jesus of Nazareth reached the age of twelve, the spirit of the Solomon Jesus (Gospel of Matthew) united with the body and sheaths of the pure Nathan Jesus. This union lasted for about 18 years, until the Baptism in the River Jordan. During these eighteen years, Jesus of Nazareth was a composite being comprising the Nathan Jesus and the spirit ("I") of the Solomon Jesus. Just before the Baptism, the spirit of the Solomon Jesus withdrew, and at the Baptism Jesus became known as "Jesus Christ" through the union of Christ with the sheaths of Jesus.

Jezebel: Wife of King Ahab, approximately 900 BC, who worked through the powers of black magic against the prophet Elijah.

Kali Yuga: Yugas are ages of influence referred to in Hindu cosmography, each yuga lasting a certain numbers of years in length (always a multiple of 2,500). The Kali Yuga is also known as the Dark Age, which began with the death of Krishna in 3102 BC (-3101). Kali Yuga lasted 5,000 years and ended in AD 1899.

Kingly Stream: Biblically, the line of heredity from King David into which the Solomon Jesus (Gospel of Matthew) was born. The kings (the three magi) were initiates who sought to bring the cosmic will of the heavenly Father to expression on the Earth through spiritual forces working

Glossary

from spiritual beings dwelling in the stars. The minds of the wise kings were enlightened by the coming of Jesus Christ.

Krishna: A cosmic-human being, the sister soul of Adam that overlighted Arjuna as described in the Bhagavad Gita. The overlighting by Krishna of Arjuna could be described as an incorporation of Krishna into Arjuna. An incorporation is a partial incarnation. The cosmic-human being known as Krishna later fully incarnated as Jesus of Nazareth (Nathan Jesus—Gospel of Luke).

Lazarus: The elder brother of Mary Magdalene, Martha, and Silent Mary. At his raising from the dead, Lazarus became the first human being to be fully initiated by Christ (see Lazarus–John).

Lazarus–John: At the raising of Lazarus from the dead by Christ, the spiritual being of John the Baptist united with Lazarus. The higher spiritual members of John (Spirit Body, Life Spirit, Spirit Self) entered into the members of Lazarus, which were developed to the level of the consciousness soul.

Lucifer: The name of a fallen spiritual being, also called the Light-Bearer, who acts as a retarding force within the human astral body and also in the sentient soul. Lucifer inflames egoism and pride within the human being, often inspiring genius and supreme artistry. Arrogance and self-importance are stimulated, without humility or sacrificial love. Lucifer stirs up forces of rebellion, but cannot deliver true freedom—just its illusion.

luciferic beings: Spiritual beings who have become agents of Lucifer's influences.

magi: Initiates in the mystery school of Zarathustra, the Bodhisattva who incarnated as Zoroaster (Zaratas, Nazaratos) in the sixth century BC and who, after he came to Babylon, became a teacher of the Chaldean priesthood. At the time of Jesus, the magi were still continuing the stargazing tradition of the school of Zoroaster. The task of the magi was to recognize when their master would reincarnate. With their visit to the new-born Jesus child in Bethlehem (Gospel of Matthew), to this child who was the reincarnated Zarathustra/Zoroaster, they fulfilled their mission. The three magi are the "priest kings from the East" referred to in the Gospel of Matthew.

Maitreya Bodhisattva: The bodhisattva individuality that is preparing to become the successor of Gautama Buddha and will be known as the Bringer of the Good. This bodhisattva was incarnated in the second century BC as Jeshu ben Pandira, the teacher of the Essenes, who died about 100 BC. Rudolf Steiner indicated that Jeshu ben Pandira reincarnated at the beginning of the twentieth century as a great bodhisattva individuality in order to fulfill the lofty mission of proclaiming Christ's coming in the etheric realm, beginning around 1933: "He will be the actual herald of Christ in his etheric form" (lecture about Jeshu ben Pandira held in Leipzig on November 4, 1911). There are differing points of view as to who this individuality actually was in his twentieth century incarnation.

manas: Also called the Spirit Self; the purified astral body, lifted into full communion with truth and goodness by becoming the true and the good within the essence of the higher self of the human being. Manas is the spiritual source of the "I," and as it is the eternal part of the human being that goes from life to life, Manas bears the human being's true "eternal name" through its union with the Holy Spirit. The "eternal name" expresses the human being's true mission from life to life.

Mani: The name of a lofty initiate who lived in Babylon in the third century AD. The founder of the Manichean stream, whose mission is the transformation of evil into goodness through compassion and love. Mani reincarnated as Parzival in the ninth century AD. Mani/Parzival is one of the leading initiates of our present age—the age of the consciousness soul (AD 1414–3574). One of the highest beings ever to incarnate upon the earth, he will become the future Manu beginning in the astrological age of Sagittarius. This future Manu will oversee the spiritual evolution of a sequence of seven ages, comprising the seven cultural epochs of the Sixth Great Age of Earth evolution from the Age of Sagittarius to the Age of Gemini—lasting a total of 7 x 2,160 years (15,120 years), since each zodiacal age lasts 2,160 years.

Manu: Like the word Buddha, the word Manu is a title. A Manu has the task of spiritually overseeing one Great Age of Earth evolution, comprising seven astrological ages (seven cultural epochs)—lasting a total of 7 x 2,160 years (15,120 years), since each zodiacal age lasts 2,160 years. The present Age of Pisces AD 215–2375—with its corresponding cultural epoch (AD 1414–3574)—is the fifth epoch during the Fifth Great Age of Earth evolution. (Lemuria was the Third Great Age, Atlantis the Fourth Great Age, and since the great flood that destroyed Atlantis, we are now in the Fifth Great Age). The present Manu is the exalted Sun-initiate who guided humanity out of Atlantis during the ancient flooding that destroyed the continent of Atlantis formerly in the region of the Atlantic Ocean—the Flood referred to in the Bible in connection with Noah. He is the overseer of the seven cultural epochs corresponding to the seven astrological ages from the Age of Cancer to the Age of Capricorn, following the sequence: Cancer, Gemini, Taurus, Aries, Pisces, Aquarius, Capricorn. The present Manu was the teacher of the Seven Holy Rishis who were the founders of the ancient Indian cultural epoch (7227–5067 BC) during the Age of Cancer. He is known in the Bible as Noah, and in the Flood story belonging to the Gilgamesh epic he is called Utnapishtim. Subsequently this Manu appeared to Abraham as Melchizedek and offered Abraham an agape ("love feast") of bread and wine. Jesus "was designated by God to be high priest in the order of Melchizedek" (Heb. 5:10).

Mary: Rudolf Steiner distinguishes between the Nathan Mary and the Solomon Mary (see corresponding entries). The expression "Virgin Mary" refers to the Solomon Mary, the mother of the child Jesus whose birth is described in the Gospel of Matthew.

Mary Magdalene: Sister of Lazarus, whose soul was transformed and purified as Christ cast out seven demons who had taken possession of her. Christ thus initiated Mary Magdalene. Later, she anointed Jesus Christ. And she was the first to behold the Risen Christ in the Garden of the Holy Sepulcher on the morning of his resurrection.

megastar: Stars with a luminosity greater than 10,000 times that of our Sun.

Nain, Youth of: Referred to in the Gospel of Luke as the son of the widow of Nain. The Youth of Nain—at the time he was twelve years old—was raised from the dead by Jesus. The Youth of Nain later reincarnated as the Prophet Mani (third century AD) and subsequently as the Grail King Parzival (ninth century AD).

Nathan Jesus: From the priestly line of David, as described in the Gospel of Luke. An immaculate and pure soul whose one and only physical incarnation was as Jesus of Nazareth (Nathan Jesus).

Nathan Mary: A pure being who was the mother of the Nathan Jesus. The Nathan Mary died in AD 12, but her spirit united with the Solomon Mary at the time of the Baptism of Jesus in the River Jordan. From this time on, the Solomon Mary—spiritually united with the Nathan Mary—was known as the Virgin Mary.

New Jerusalem: A spiritual condition denoting humanity's future existence that will come into being as human beings free themselves from the *maya* of the material world and work together to bring about a spiritualized Earth.

Osiris: Osiris and Isis are names given by the Egyptians to the preincarnatory forms of the spiritual beings who are now known as Christ and Sophia.

Parzival: Son of Gahmuret and Herzeloyde in the epic *Parzival* by Wolfram von Eschenbach. Although written in the thirteenth century, this work refers to actual people and events in the ninth century AD, one of whom (the central figure) bore the name Parzival. After living a life of dullness and doubt, Parzival's mission was to seek the Castle of the Grail and to ask the question "What ails thee?" of the Grail King, Anfortas—moreover, to ask the question without being bidden to do so. Parzival eventually became the new Grail King, the successor of Anfortas. Parzival was the reincarnated prophet Mani. In the incarnation preceding that of Mani, he was incarnated as the Youth of Nain (Luke 7:11–15). Parzival is a great initiate responsible for guiding humanity during the Age of Pisces, which has given birth to the cultural epoch of the development of the consciousness soul (AD 1414–3574).

Pentecost: Descent of the Holy Spirit fifty days after Easter, whereby the cosmic "I AM" was birthed among the disciples and those individuals close to Christ. They received the capacity to develop Manas or Spirit Self within the community of striving human individuals, whereby the birth of the Spirit Self is facilitated through the soul of the Virgin Mary. See also World Pentecost.

phantom body: The pure spiritual form of the human physical body, unhindered by matter. The far-distant future state of the human physical body when it has become purified and spiritualized into a body of transformed divine will.

Presbyter John: Refers to Lazarus-John who moved to Ephesus about twenty years after the Virgin Mary had died there. In Ephesus he became a bishop. He is the author of the Book of Revelations, the Gospel of St. John, and the Letters of John.

Risen One: The initial appearance of Christ in his phantom body (resurrection body), beginning with his appearance to Mary Magdalene on Easter Sunday morning. Christ frequently appeared to the disciples in his phantom body during the forty days leading from Easter to Ascension.

Satan: The traditional Christian name for Ahriman.

Serpent: Another name for Lucifer, but sometimes naming a combination of Lucifer and Ahriman: "The great dragon was hurled down—that ancient serpent called the devil, or Satan, who leads the whole world astray" (Rev. 12:9).

Shepherd Stream: Biblically, the genealogical line from David the shepherd through his son Nathan. It was into this line that the Nathan Jesus was born, whose birth is described in the Gospel of Luke. Rudolf Steiner describes the shepherds, who—according to Luke—came to pay homage to the newborn child, as those servants of pure heart who perceive the good will streaming up from Mother Earth. The hearts of the shepherd were kindled with the fire of Divine Love by the coming of the Christ. The shepherds can be regarded as precursors of the heart stream of humanity that now intuits the being of Christ as the spirit of the earth.

Solomon Jesus: Descended from the genealogical line from David through his son Solomon. This line of descent is described in the Gospel of Matthew. The Solomon Jesus was a reincarnation of Zoroaster (sixth century BC). In turn, Zoroaster was a reincarnation of Zarathustra (6000 BC), the great prophet and founder of the ancient Persian religion of Zoroastrianism. He was a Bodhisattva, who as the founder of this new religion that was focused upon the Sun Spirit Ahura Mazdao, helped prepare humanity for the subsequent descent into incarnation of Ahura Mazdao, the cosmic Sun Spirit, as Christ.

Solomon Mary: The wise mother of the Solomon Jesus, who adopted the Nathan Jesus after the death of the Nathan Mary. At the time of the Baptism of Jesus in the River Jordan, the spirit of the Nathan Mary united with the Solomon Mary. Usually referred to as the Virgin Mary or Mother Mary, the Solomon Mary bore witness at the foot of the cross to the Mystery of Golgotha. She died in Ephesus eleven years after Christ's Ascension.

Sophia: Part of the Divine Feminine Trinity comprising the Mother (counterpart of the Father), the Daughter (counterpart of the Son), and the Holy Soul (counterpart of the Holy Spirit). Sophia, also known as the Bride of the Lamb, is the Daughter aspect of the threefold Divine Feminine Trinity. To the Egyptians Sophia was known as Isis, who was seen to belong to the starry realm surrounding the earth. In the Book of Proverbs, attributed to King Solomon, Sophia's temple has seven pillars (Proverbs 9:1). The seven pillars in Sophia's temple represent the seven great stages of Earth evolution (from Ancient Saturn to Future Vulcan).

Sorath: The great enemy of Christ who works against the "I" in the human being. Sorath is identified with the two-horned beast that rises up from the depths of earth, as described in the Apocalypse of St. John. Sorath is the Sun Demon, and is identified by Rudolf Steiner as the Antichrist. According to the Book of Revelations his number is 666.

Sun Demon: Another name for Sorath.

Transfiguration: The event on Mt. Tabor where Jesus Christ was illumined with Divine Light raying forth from the purified etheric body of Jesus, which the Divine "I AM" of Christ had penetrated. The Gospels of Matthew and Luke describe the Transfiguration. The sunlike radiance that shone forth from Jesus Christ on Mt. Tabor was an expression of the purified etheric body that had its origin during the Old Sun period of Earth evolution.

Transubstantiation: Sacramental transformation of physical substance—for example, the transubstantiation of bread and wine during the Mass to become the body and blood of Christ. During the Holy Eucharist the bread and wine are transformed in such a way that the substances of bread and wine are infused with the life force (body) and light (blood) of Christ. Thereby the bread and wine are reunited with their divine archetypes and are no longer "merely" physical substances, but are bearers on the physical level of a spiritual reality.

Turning Point of Time: Transition between involution and evolution, as marked by the Mystery of Golgotha. The descending stream of involution culminated with the Mystery of Golgotha. With the descent of the Cosmic Christ into earthly evolution, through his sacrifice on Golgotha an ascending stream of evolution began. This sacrifice of Christ was followed by the events of his Resurrection and Ascension, which were followed in turn by Whitsun (Pentecost)—all expressing the ascending stream of evolution. This path of ascent was also opened up to all human beings by way of the power of the divine "I AM" bestowed—at least, potentially—on all humanity by Christ through his sacrifice on the cross.

Union in the Temple: The event of the union of the spirit of the Solomon Jesus with the twelve-year-old Nathan Jesus. This union of the two Jesus children signified the uniting of the priestly (Nathan) line and the kingly (Solomon) line—both lines descended from King David.

Whitsun: "White Sunday"; Pentecost.

World Pentecost is the gradual event of cosmic revelation becoming human revelation as a signature of the end of the Dark Age (Kali Yuga). Anthroposophy (Spiritual Science) is a language of spiritual truth that could awaken a community of striving human beings to the presence of the Holy Spirit and the founding of the New Jerusalem.

Zarathustra: The great teacher of the ancient Persians in the sixth millennium BC (around 6000 BC). In the sixth century BC, Zarathustra reincarnated as Zoroaster. He then reincarnated as the Solomon Jesus (6 BC–AD 12), whose birth is described in the Gospel of Matthew.

Zoroaster: An incarnation of Zarathustra. Zarathustra–Zoroaster was a Bodhisattva. Zoroaster lived in the sixth century BC. He was a master of wisdom. Among his communications as a teacher of wisdom was his specification as to how the zodiac of living beings in the heavens comes to expression in relation to the stars comprising the twelve zodiacal constellations. Zoroaster subsequently incarnated as the Solomon Jesus, whose birth is described in the Gospel of Matthew, to whom the three magi came from the East bearing gifts of gold, frankincense, and myrrh.

REFERENCES

See "Literature" on page 10 for an annotated list of books on Astrosophy.

Andreev, Daniel. *Rosa Mira: Die Weltrose.* Frankeneck. Germany: Vega, 2009.

——. *The Rose of the World.* Great Barrington, MA: Lindisfarne Books, 1997.

Anonymous. *Meditations on the Tarot.* New York: Tarcher/Putman, 2002.

——. *The Mysterious Story of X7.* Berkeley, CA: North Atlantic Books, 2009.

Bento, William, Robert Schiappacase, and David Tresemer. *Signs in the Heavens: A Message for Our Time.* www.StarWisdom.org, 2001.

Blattmann, Georg. *Comets: Their Appearance and Significance.* Edinburgh: Floris Books, 1985.

Bock, Emil. *Moses.* Edinburgh: Floris Books, 1986.

Buber, Martin. *I and Thou.* New York: Scribner's, 1970.

Burne, Jerome. *Chronicle of the World.* Mount Kisco, NY: ECAM Publications, 1990.

Clements, Jeffrey. *Corporations Are Not People: Why They Have More Rights than You Do and What You Can Do about It.* San Francisco: Berrett-Koehler, 2012.

Der Europäer. Basel: Perseus Publishing, periodical.

Dorsan, Jacques. *The Clockwise House System: A True Foundation for Sidereal and Tropical Astrology.* Great Barrington, MA: Lindisfarne Books, 2011.

Edwards, Iorwerth. *The British Museum: Introductory Guide to the Egyptian Collections.* London: Trustees of the British Museum, 1964.

Fagan, Cyril. *Astrological Origins.* St. Paul, MN: Llewellyn, 1971.

——. *Zodiacs: Old and New.* Los Angeles: Llewellyn, 1950.

Grant, Joan. *So Moses Was Born.* London: Ariel Press, 1990.

Greenblatt, Stephen. *The Swerve: How the World Became Modern.* New York, Norton, 2011.

Greene, Liz. *The Astrological Neptune and the Quest for Redemption.* Boston: Weiser, 1996.

Hartmann Thom. *Unequal Protection: How Corporations Became "People"—and How You Can Fight Back* (2nd ed.). San Francisco, Berrett-Koehler, 2010.

Husemann, Armin. *Knowledge of the Human Being through Art. A Method of Anthroposophical Study.* Spring Valley, NY: Mercury Press, 1990.

Isaacson, Estelle. *Through the Eyes of Mary Magdalene,* 2 vols. Taos, NM: LogoSophia, 2012.

Kitchen, Kenneth. On the Reliability of the Old Testament. Cambridge, UK: William B. Erdmans, 2003.

LeGrice, Keiron. *The Archetypal Cosmos.* Edinburgh: Floris, 2010.

Madsen, Jon (ed.). *The New Testament: A Rendering.* Edinburgh: Floris Books, 1994.

Meyer, T. H., and Elisabeth Vreede. *The Bodhisattva Question: Krishnamurti, Rudolf Steiner, Valentin Tomberg, and the Mystery of the Twentieth-Century Master.* London: Temple Lodge, 2010.

Nesfield-Cookson, Bernard. *Rudolf Steiner's Vision of Love: Spiritual Science and the Logic of the Heart.* London: Ruldolf Steiner Press, 2011.

O'Leary, P. V. (ed.) *The Inner Life of the Earth: Exploring the Mysteries of Nature, Subnature, and Supranature.* Great Barrington, MA: SteinerBooks, 2008.

Powell, Robert. *The Christ Mystery.* Fair Oaks, CA: Rudolf Steiner College, 1999.

——. *Christian Hermetic Astrology: The Star of the Magi and the Life of Christ.* Great Barrington, MA: Lindisfarne Books, 2009.

——. *Chronicle of the Living Christ: The Life and Ministry of Jesus Christ: Foundations of Cosmic Christianity.* Hudson, NY: Anthroposophic Press, 1996.

——. *Cultivating Inner Radiance and the Body of Immortality: Awakening the Soul through Modern Etheric Movement.* Great Barrington, MA: Lindisfarne Books, 2012.

——. *Elijah Come Again: A Prophet for Our Time: A Scientific Approach to Reincarnation.* Great Barrington, MA: Lindisfarne Books, 2009.

——. *Hermetic Astrology,* vols. 1 and 2. San Rafael, CA: Sophia Foundation Press, 2006.

——. *History of the Zodiac.* San Rafael, CA: Sophia Academic Press, 2007.

——. *The Most Holy Trinosophia: The New Revelation of the Divine Feminine.* Great Barrington, MA: SteinerBooks, 2000.

——. *The Mystery, Biography, and Destiny of Mary Magdalene: Sister of Lazarus John & Spiritual Sister of Jesus.* Great Barrington, MA: Lindisfarne Books, 2008.

——. *The Sophia Teachings: The Emergence of the Divine Feminine in Our Time.* Great Barrington, MA: Lindisfarne Books, 2007.

Powell, Robert, and David Bowden. *Astrogeographia: Correspondences between the Stars and Earthly Locations: Earth Chakras and the Bible of Astrology.* Great Barrington, MA: SteinerBooks, 2012.

Powell, Robert, and Kevin Dann. *The Astrological Revolution: Unveiling the Science of the Stars as a Science of Reincarnation and Karma.* Great Barrington, MA: SteinerBooks, 2010.

——. *Christ and the Maya Calendar: 2012 & the Coming of the Antichrist.* Great Barrington, MA: SteinerBooks, 2009.

Powell, Robert, and Lacquanna Paul. *Cosmic Dances of the Planets.* San Rafael, CA: Sophia Foundation Press, 2006.

Sheen, A. Renwick. *Geometry and the Imagination* (revised ed.). Fair Oaks, CA: AWSNA, 2002.

Solovyov, Valdimir, *War, Progress, and the End of History: Three Conversaions.* Hudson, NY: Lindisfarne Press, 1990.

Steiner, Rudolf. *According to Luke: The Gospel of Compassion and Love Revealed.* Great Barrington, MA: SteinerBooks, 2006.

——. *According to Matthew: The Gospel of Christ's Humanity.* Great Barrington, MA: Anthroposophic Press, 2003

——. *Anthroposophical Leading Thoughts.* London: Rudolf Steiner Press. 1985.

——. *Anthroposophy (A Fragment): A New Foundation for the Study of Human Nature.* Hudson, NY: Anthroposophic Press, 1996.

——. *The Apocalypse of St. John: Lectures on the Book of Revelation.* Hudson, NY: Anthroposophic Press, 1993.

——. *Art as Seen in the Light of Mystery Wisdom.* London: Rudolf Steiner Press, 1996.

——. *Astronomy and Astrology: Finding a Relationship to the Cosmos.* London: Rudolf Steiner Press, 2009.

——. *Background to the Gospel of St. Mark.* London: Rudolf Steiner Press, 1968.

——. *The Book of Revelation: And the Work of the Priest.* London: Rudolf Steiner Press, 2008.

——. *Christ and the Spiritual World: And the Search for the Holy Grail.* London: Rudolf Steiner Press, 2008.

——. *Christianity as Mystical Fact: And the Mysteries of Antiquity.* Great Barrington, MA: SteinerBooks, 2006.

——. *Cosmic Memory: The Story of Atlantis, Lemuria, and the Division of the Sexes.* Great Barrington, MA: SteinerBooks, 2006.

——. *The Cycle of the Year: As Breathing Process of the Earth.* Great Barrington, MA: SteinerBooks, 1984.

——. *Deeper Secrets of Human History in the Light of the Gospel of St. Matthew.* London: Rudolf Steiner Press, 1985.

——. *The Destinies of Individuals and of Nations.* Hudson, NY: Anthroposophic Press, 1986.

——. *Esoteric Christianity and the Mission of Christian Rosenkreutz.* London: Rudolf Steiner Press, 2000.

——. *Esoteric Lessons 1904–1909.* Great Barrington, MA: SteinerBooks, 2007.

——. *Esoteric Develolpment: Selected Lectures and Writings.* Great Barrington, MA: SteinerBooks, 2003.

——. *Faculty Meetings with Rudolf Steiner.* Hudson, NY: Anthroposophic Press, 1998.

——. *The Festivals and Their Meaning.* London: Rudolf Steiner Press, 1996.

——. *The Fifth Gospel: From the Akashic Record.* London: Rudolf Steiner Press, 1998.

——. *"Freemasonry" and Ritual Work: The Misraim Service.* Great Barrington, MA: SteinerBooks, 2007.

———. *From Beetroot to Buddhism...: Answers to Questions*. London: Rudolf Steiner Press, 1999.

———. *The Gospel of St. John*. New York: Anthroposophic Press, 1962.

———. *How to Know Higher Worlds: A Modern Path of Initiation*. Hudson, NY: Anthroposophic Press, 1995.

———. *The Incarnation of Ahriman: The Embodiment of Evil on Earth*. London: Rudolf Steiner Press, 2006.

———. *Intuitive Thinking as a Spiritual Path: A Philosophy of Freedom*. Hudson, NY: Anthroposophic Press, 1995.

———. *The Karma of Untruthfulness: Secret Societies, the Media, and Preparations for the Great War*, vol. 1. London: Rudolf Steiner Press, 2005.

———. *Karmic Relationships: Esoteric Studies*, vol. 4. London: Rudolf Steiner Press, 1997.

———. *Materialism and the Task of Anthroposophy*. Hudson, NY: Anthroposophic Press. 1987.

———. *An Outline of Esoteric Science*. Hudson, NY: Anthroposophic Press, 1997.

———. *The Secret Stream: Christian Rosenkreutz & Rosicrucianism*. Great Barrington, MA: Anthroposophic Press, 2001.

———. *The Spiritual Hierarchies and the Physical World: Zodiac, Planets & Cosmos*. Great Barrington, MA: SteinerBooks, 2008.

———. *Supersensible Influences in the History of Mankind: With Special Reference to Cult in Ancient Egypt and in Later Times*. London: Rudolf Steiner Publishing, 1956.

———. *The Temple Legend: Freemasonry and Related Occult Movements: From the Contents of the Esoteric School*. London: Rudolf Steiner Press, 1997.

———. *Theosophy: An Introduction to the Spiritual Processes in Human Life and in the Cosmos*. Hudson, NY: Anthroposophic Press, 1994.

———. *The True Nature of the Second Coming*. London: Rudolf Steiner Press, 1971.

———. *Twelve Moods of the Zodiac*. Eschborn, Germany: Verlag Gerhold, 1987.

———. *The World of the Senses and the World of the Spirit*. N. Vancouver: Steiner Book Centre, 1979.

Steiner, Rudolf, and Édouard Schuré. *The East in the Light of the West/Children of Lucifer: A Drama*. Blauvelt, NY: Garber, 1986.

Sucher, Willi. *Isis Sophia I: Introducing Astrosophy*. Meadow Vista, CA: Astrosophy Research Center, 1999.

———. *Isis Sophia II: An Outline of a New Star Wisdom*. Meadow Vista, CA: Astrosophy Research Center, 1985.

Taft, John G. *Stewardship: Lessons Learned from the Lost Culture of Wall Street*. Hoboken, NJ: Wiley, 2012.

Tarnas, Richard. *Cosmos and Psyche*. New York: Viking, 2006.

Timms, Moira. *Prophecies and Predictions: Everyone's Guide to the Coming Changes*. Pacific Grove, CA: Orenda Unity Press, 1980.

Tomberg, Valentin, *Christ and Sophia: Anthroposophic Meditations on the Old Testament, New Testament, and Apocalypse*. Great Barrington, MA: SteinerBooks, 2006.

———. *Studies on the Foundation Stone Meditation*. Taos, NM: Logosophia, 2010.

von Halle, Judith. *Descent into the Depths of the Earth on the Anthroposophic Path of Schooling*. London: Temple Lodge, 2011.

———. *Illness and Healing: And the Mystery Language of the Gospels*. London: Temple Lodge, 2008.

Tresemer, David. *The Venus Eclipse of the Sun 2012*. Great Barrington, MA: Lindisfarne Books, 2011.

Tresemer, David, and Robert Schiappacasse. *Star Wisdom & Rudolf Steiner: A Life Seen through the Oracle of the Solar Cross*. Great Barrington, MA: SteinerBooks, 2007.

Vreede, Elizabeth. *Anthroposophy and Astrology: The Astronomical Letters of Elizabeth Vreede*. Great Barrington, MA: SteinerBooks, 2001.

Waddell, W. G. (tr.). *Manetho*. Cambridge, MA: Harvard University, 1940.

ABOUT THE CONTRIBUTORS

 **DANIEL ANDREEV** (1906-1959) was born in Berlin. His father was the well-known Russian writer Leonid Andreev. His mother Alexandra Veligorsky died during childbirth. Daniel's father, overcome with grief, gave up Andreev to Alexandra's sister Elizabeth Dobrov, who lived in Moscow. It was a critical event in Daniel Andreev's life, for in contrast to many of the Russian intelligentsia at the time, the family maintained its Russian Orthodox faith. Daniel's childhood included contact with persons such as his godfather Maxim Gorky. Daniel was conscripted as a noncombatant in the Soviet Army in 1942, and after the war he returned to writing fiction and poetry. He was arrested in 1947, along with his wife and many of his relatives and friends, and sentenced to twenty-five years in prison, while his wife received twenty-five years of labor camp. All of his previous writings were destroyed. With the rise of Khrushchev, Andreev's case was reviewed and his sentence reduced to ten years. He was released to his waiting wife in 1957, his health ruined following a heart attack in prison. While in prison, he had written the first drafts of *The Rose of the World* and *Russian Gods* (a collection of poetry), as well as *The Iron Mystery*, a play in verse. Andreev spent the last two years of his life finishing these works. Andreev's wife Alla, realizing the negative reception the books would get from the Soviet authorities, hid them until the mid-1970s and did not publish them until Gorbachev and glasnost. The first edition of *The Rose of the World* (100,000 copies) quickly sold out, and since then several editions have been equally popular in Russia.

 **WILLIAM BENTO**, Ph.D., has worked in the field of human development for more than thirty years. He is a recognized pioneer and a published author in psychosophy (soul wisdom) and astrosophy (star wisdom) and travels extensively as a speaker, teacher, and consultant. He currently resides in Rancho Cordova, California. Dr. Bento is the Associate Dean of Academic Affairs at Rudolf Steiner College, Fair Oaks, California and works as a transpersonal clinical psychologist at the Center for Living Health in Gold River, California, and is a clinical psychologist at Folsom State Prison Crisis Treatment Center. His involvement in guiding social therapy seminars for Camphill Communities has been well received over the last two decades. He is coauthor of *Signs in the Heavens: A Message for Our Time* and author of *Lifting the Veil of Mental Illness: An Approach to Anthroposophical Psychology*. His forthcoming book is *Psychosophy: A Primer for an Extended Anthroposophic Psychology,* to be published by SteinerBooks.

BRIAN GRAY trained an architect and environmental planner who also has deep interests in astrology, art, music and Anthroposophy. Since 1981, he has taught at Rudolf Steiner College in Fair Oaks, California. His research topics include cosmology, sacred architecture, the constitution of the human being, biography, life cycles, karma and reincarnation, esoteric Christianity and Astro-Gaiasophy. A student of astrology since 1967, Brian has interpreted astrological charts for thousands of people and offers classes in star wisdom and observation of the stars. He has discovered hidden astrological keys in Wolfram von Eschenbach's *Parzival* and in the Bible, particularly Genesis, the Gospel of St. John, and the Book of Revelation. Brian currently directs the Foundation Program in Anthroposophy Program at Rudolf Steiner College. Brian's lecture on compassion and forgiveness can be viewed on YouTube at "Compassion and Forgiveness by Brian Gray.mov."

ESTELLE ISAACSON is a contemporary mystic and seer whose first two books were published by LogoSophia in 2012: *Through the Eyes of Mary Magdalene: Early Years & Soul Awakening*. In this first book in a trilogy on the life of Mary Magdalene, Estelle Isaacson presents her visions of the life of "the Apostle to the Apostles" as seen through Magdalene's own eyes. The second book, *Through the Eyes of Mary Magdalene: From Initiation to the Passion*, enters the profound mysteries of Christ's Passion, culminating in the Resurrection.

CLAUDIA MCLAREN LAINSON is a teacher and Therapeutic Educator. She has been working in the field of Anthroposophy since 1982, when she founded her first Waldorf program in Boulder, Colorado. She lectures nationally on various topics related to Spiritual Science, human development, the evolution of consciousness and the emerging Christ and Sophia mysteries of the twenty-first century. Claudia is the founder of Windrose Farm and Academy near Boulder. Windrose is a biodynamic farm and academy for collaborative work in anthroposophic courses, therapeutic education, cosmic and sacred dance and nature-based educational programs. Claudia most recently founded the School for the Sophia Mysteries at Windrose.

 **PAUL MARX,** Ph.D., is a retired chemist whose interest in the Exodus story was sparked by a trip to Egypt in 1959 and travel through Goshen where the Israelites spent their Egyptian Sojourn. It was given further impetus through correspondence with Willi Sucher, a pioneer in Astrosophy. Paul's other interest is working with Nick Thomas whose book, *Science Between Space and Counterspace,* establishes a new scientific paradigm.

 **SALLY NURNEY** has been interested in astrology all her life, beginning her research with her "Sun sign" in elementary school. After several years of travel and exploration, she arrived at The StarHouse in Boulder, Colorado, in 1997 and quickly transitioned to the Sidereal perspective of reading the stars. Along with her studies in the Path of the Ceremonial Arts, she has deepened her direct understanding of the stars through research with David Tresemer at The StarHouse and study with Brian Gray at the Rudolf Steiner College in Fair Oaks, California. She currently lives in the Rocky Mountain foothills near the StarHouse of Boulder.

 **LAQUANNA PAUL** is a teacher of various forms of healing movement. As a graduate of the Choreocosmos School of Cosmic and Sacred Dance, Lacquanna has discovered astonishing correspondences between the ancient healing art of Qigong and the modern healing movements of Eurythmy, both working with the flow of etheric life force (prana, or chi). Her most recent work has centered on introducing the art of coming into connection with the vital realm of the etheric (life) body of the Earth, the mantle of Mother Earth, which bears the formative patterns of life on Earth. It is through our connection with the etheric realm of life forces that we can express our gratitude and take up a "response-able" life of service to one another and to Mother Nature. Together with Robert Powell, she has coauthored *Cosmic Dances of the Planets; Cosmic Dances of the Zodiac; The Foundation Stone Meditation in the Sacred Dance of Eurythmy;* and The Prayer Sequence in Sacred Dance (all available at Fields Bookstore/Sophia Foundation).

 **ROBERT POWELL,** Ph.D., is an internationally known lecturer, author, eurythmist, and movement therapist. He is founder of the Choreocosmos School of Cosmic and Sacred Dance, and cofounder of the Sophia Foundation of North America. He received his doctorate for his thesis *The History of the Zodiac,* available as a book from Sophia Academic Press. His published works include *The Sophia Teachings,* a six-tape series (Sounds True Recordings), as well as *Elijah Come Again: A Prophet for Our Time; The Mystery, Biography, and Destiny of Mary Madgalene; Divine Sophia—Holy Wisdom; The Most Holy Trinosophia and the New Revelation of the Divine Feminine; Chronicle of the Living Christ; Christian Hermetic Astrology; The Christ Mystery; The Sign of the Son of Man in the Heavens; The Morning Meditation in Eurythmy;* and the yearly *Journal for Star Wisdom* (previously *Christian Star Calendar*). He translated the spiritual classic *Meditations on the Tarot* and co-translated Valentin Tomberg's *Lazarus,*

Come Forth! Robert is also coauthor with Kevin Dann of *The Astrological Revolution: Unveiling the Science of the Stars as a Science of Reincarnation and Karma* and *Christ and the Maya Calendar: 2012 & the Coming of the Antichrist*; and coauthor with Lacquanna Paul of *Cosmic Dances of the Zodiac* and *Cosmic Dances of the Planets*. He teaches a gentle form of healing movement: the sacred dance of eurythmy, as well as the *Cosmic Dances of the Planets* and signs of the zodiac. Through the Sophia Grail Circle, Robert facilitates sacred celebrations dedicated to the Divine Feminine. He offers workshops in Europe, Australia, and North America, and with Karen Rivers, cofounder of the Sophia Foundation, leads pilgrimages to the world's sacred sites: Turkey, 1996; the Holy Land, 1997; France, 1998; Britain, 2000; Italy, 2002; Greece, 2004; Egypt, 2006; India, 2008; Turkey, 2009; the Grand Canyon, 2010; and South Africa, 2012. Visit www.sophiafoundation.org and www.astrogeographia.org.

ROBERT SCHIAPPACASSE has been a student of Rudolf Steiner's Anthroposophy for more than thirty years. He developed a deep interest in humanity's relationship to the world of the stars and, in 1977, began studies with Willi Sucher, a pioneer researcher in the field of Astrosophy, or star wisdom. He presents at conferences and workshops on star wisdom themes and other anthroposophic topics. He is coauthor with David Tresemer and William Bento of the book *Signs in the Heavens: A Message for our Time,* about the comets Hyakutake and Hale-Bopp and their crossing of the mysterious and ominous star Algol at the end of the twentieth century. Robert most recently worked with David Tresemer on the book *Star Wisdom and Rudolf Steiner: A life Seen through the Oracle of the Solar Cross*. He also coauthored with David Tresemer the articles "The Chain Reaction Experiment"; "The Signature of Saturn in Jesus Christ' Life"; and "The Signature of Pluto in the Events of Jesus Christ' Life."

DAVID TRESEMER, Ph.D., has a doctorate in psychology. In 1990, he cofounded the StarHouse in Boulder, Colorado, for community gatherings and workshops (www.TheStarHouse.org) and cofounded, with his wife Lila, the Healing Dreams Retreat Centre in Australia (www.MountainSeas.com.au). He has also founded the Star Wisdom website (www.StarWisdom.org), which offers readings from the Oracle of the Solar Crosses, an oracle relating to the heavenly imprint received on one's day of birth. Dr. Tresemer has written in many areas, including *The Scythe Book: Mowing Hay, Cutting Weeds, and Harvesting Small Grains with Hand Tools* and a book on mythic theater, *War in Heaven: Accessing Myth Through Drama*. With his wife, he also coauthored several plays produced in the U.S., including *My Magdalene* (winner of Moondance 2004, Best Script). With William Bento and Robert Schiappacasse, he wrote *Signs in the Heavens: A Message for Our Time*. He is also the author, with Robert Schiappacasse, of *Star Wisdom & Rudolf Steiner: A Life Seen through the Oracle of the Solar Cross,* and with his wife, the recent book, *One-Two-ONE: A Guidebook for Conscious Partnerships, Weddings, and Rededication Ceremonies*. He celebrated 2012 with his book *The Venus Eclipse of the Sun 2012.*

ASTROGEOGRAPHIA
CORRESPONDENCES BETWEEN THE STARS AND EARTHLY LOCATIONS
A BIBLE OF ASTROLOGY AND EARTH CHAKRAS

Robert Powell and David Bowden

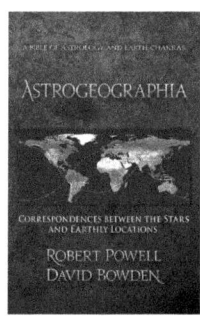

"As above, so below" is the foundation of all star wisdom. It was known in ancient times that there are correspondences between the macrocosm (heavenly realm) and the microcosm (human being) and the Earth. Astrogeographia is a modern form of that ancient star wisdom.

According to the astronomer Johannes Kepler:

"There radiates into the Earth soul an image of the sense-perceptible zodiac and the whole firmament as a bond of sympathy between Heaven and Earth.... This imprint into the Earth soul through the sense-perceptible zodiac and the entire sphere of fixed stars is also confirmed through observation."

Moreover, Rudolf Steiner said in his course on astronomy, "We can conceive of the active heavenly sphere mirrored in the Earth." The authors of *Astrogeographia* set out to determine the correspondences between the starry heavens and the earthly globe: *As above, so below.*

There are numerous books on the sacredness and the spirituality of our Earth. However, few books deal with the relationship between the Earth and the cosmos, which is the central theme for the research presented in *Astrogeographia*. Its point of departure is the one-to-one correspondence between the encircling starry heavens—the celestial sphere—and the sphere of the earthly globe. David Bowden has not only worked out the mathematics of this one-to-one correspondence, but has also written a computer program that applies it in practice. Thus, a new science has been born—Astrogeographia—concerning the one-to-one correspondence between the earthly sphere and the celestial sphere.

ISBN: 9781584201335 | 360 pages | pbk | $25.00

CULTIVATING INNER RADIANCE AND THE BODY OF IMMORTALITY
AWAKENING THE SOUL THROUGH MODERN ETHERIC MOVEMENT

Robert Powell

The human being is an expression of the ever-unfolding wisdom of the creative Logos, the Word. The whole of creation bears the imprint of the cosmic sounding. This book describes a way, through movement and gesture, to work with the creative, sounding principle that manifests in the Earth's enveloping life sphere. Today, the increasingly binding and hardening conditions of modern life now threatens the divine seed of life here on Earth, which has been fructified and developed over the millennia. Creation—coming to expression through the flowering of the cosmic breath—is losing its natural connection with humanity and with Mother Earth, which are increasingly given over to anti-life forces, comprising destruction, inversions, and lifeless replicas of creation's gifts.

The sacred movements described in this book arise from the modern art of movement known as eurythmy (Greek: "good movement"), which came into the world in 1912. These sacred gestures, when practiced with the words gifted to humanity by the incarnated Logos two thousand years ago, lead us back to our connection with the fullness of creation and toward the goal of developing the body of immortality, the resurrection body. In 2012, we celebrate the one-hundredth anniversary of the birth of eurythmy. This book invites us to partake of the richness of the sacred through life-enhancing movement and gesture as a path to reconnect with the cosmic formative forces that sound the call of resurrection.

The wealth of material included in this book educates the soul toward awaking to a conscious understanding of humanity's divine heritage and true calling. The exercises in this work provide a training that ennobles and refines the qualities of the human soul.

ISBN: 9781584201175 | 240 pages | pbk | $25.00

PROPHECY · PHENOMENA · HOPE
The Real Meaning of 2012
Christ and the Maya Calendar—An Update

Robert Powell

Robert Powell, explores what 2012 really means, updating the research presented in the ground-breaking book, *Christ and the Maya Calendar: 2012 and the Coming of the Antichrist* (coauthored with Kevin Dann). Here, Powell focuses on two significant prophecies by Rudolf Steiner. The first (from 1909) concerns the Second Coming of Christ, his appearance to humanity as the Etheric Christ. The second (from 1919) represents the shadow side of Christ's Second Coming—the incarnation in human form of Ahriman.

Powell points to the steady, multifaceted encroachment of ahrimanic forces today, especially as the harmful effects of modern technology on the etheric body. After looking into Steiner's prophetic remarks on the Book of Revelation, Powell looks into the prophecies of the Russian poet/mystic Daniel Andreev and examines the prophecy of the American clairvoyant Jeane Dixon concerning the human birth of the Antichrist. He also includes spiritual research by Judith von Halle regarding an earlier incarnation of Jospeh Stalin, as well as Andreev's indications relating to Stalin's earlier incarnations, which may be seen as preparation of this individuality for his role as "Mr. X," the human vessel for the incarnation of Ahriman.

Applying the astrological rules of reincarnation, Powell's research supports Jeane Dixon's prophecy, that Mr. X was born in 1962, a finding whose accuracy was also confirmed by Willi Sucher, Powell's mentor in Astrosophy. This finding, seen in relation to various contemporary phenomena, confirms Rudolf Steiner's prophetic statement that the incarnation of Ahriman into his human vessel would take place shortly after the year 2000.

Nonetheless, great hope for humankind is offered by the return of Christ in the etheric realm, an event to which human beings can connect, as humanity and the Earth pass through the great trials associated with 2012.

ISBN: 9781584201113 | 138 pages | pbk | $16.00

THE ASTROLOGICAL REVOLUTION
Unveiling the Science of the Stars as a Science of Reincarnation and Karma

Robert Powell & Kevin Dann

The reader is invited to question the basis of modern astrology—the tropical zodiac, which emerged through Greek astronomers from what was originally a calendar dividing the year into twelve solar months. Ninety-eight percent of Western astrologers use the tropical zodiac, meaning that it is based on a calendar system that no longer embodies the reality of the stars.

Astrology needs to be brought back into alignment with the stars in the heavens. The first step in this astrological revolution is to recognize the sidereal zodiac. In antiquity, the Babylonians, Egyptians, Greeks, Romans, and Hindus used the sidereal zodiac, and today Hindu (Vedic) astrologers still use the sidereal zodiac. Based on recognition—through the newly discovered rules of astrological reincarnation, that the sidereal zodiac presents an authentic astrological zodiac—a new practice of astrology is possible that offers tools to reestablish a wisdom-filled astrology in the modern world. This new astrology, based on the sidereal zodiac, is similar to the classic sidereal form but in a modern form, as that practiced by the three magi, who—prompted by the stars—journeyed to Bethlehem two thousand years ago.

Drawing on specific biographical examples, *The Astrological Revolution* reveals new understandings of how the starry heavens work into human destiny. The book points to the astrological significance of the entire celestial sphere, including all the stars and constellations beyond the twelve zodiacal signs. This discovery is revealed by studying the megastars, the most luminous stars of our galaxy, illustrating how megastars show up in an extraordinary way in Christ's healing miracles by aligning with the Sun at the time of those miraculous events.

KEVIN DANN, Ph.D., has taught history at SUNY Plattsburgh, the University of Vermont, and Rutgers University. He is also the coauthor of *Christ and the Maya Calendar* with Robert Powell.

ISBN: 9781584200833 | 254 pages | pbk | $25.00

THE CLOCKWISE HOUSE SYSTEM
A True Foundation for Sidereal and Tropical Astrology

Jacques Dorsan
Wain Farrants and Robert Powell, editors

Jacques Dorsan, a leading pioneer of sidereal astrology in France, uses more than eighty sidereal horoscopes to illustrate his clockwise house system. With charts from the original French edition and many added, this book embodies one of the most important astrological discoveries of twentieth and twenty-first centuries. Astrology normally views the twelve houses in astrology in a counterclockwise direction, the direction of the zodiac signs. According to Dorsan, however, we should view them in a clockwise direction.

By using this clockwise house system along with the sidereal zodiac, everything falls into place in a horoscope, unlocking the mystery of the horoscope. We are given access to a true form of astrology, enabling a giant leap forward in the practice of astrology. It allows us to recover the original astrology. Moreover, Rudolf Steiner's indications, as well as the research of the French statistician Michel Gauquelin, confirm that the astrological houses run in a clockwise direction.

This English translation includes more than eighty charts, both those in Dorsan's original work in French and more added by the editor of this edition.

JACQUES DORSAN was born December 22, 1912, in Orléans, France. In 1936, he moved to the Ivory Coast, where he drew his first horoscope. It was more than seven years before he began to do consultations. Fourteen years later, after intense practice in Brazil and before returning to France, he had become convinced that the houses actually move in the direction opposite the zodiacal signs. He put his idea to the test for more than twenty years before publishing the original version of this book *Le véritable sens des maisons astrologiques* (1984). Jacques Dorsan lived in Morocco, New York City, Monaco, Luxembourg, Belgium, Zaire, and New Caledonia. He died September 8, 2005, in Nice.

ISBN: 9781584200956 | 330 pages | pbk | $30.00

ELIJAH COME AGAIN
A Prophet for Our Time
A Scientific Approach to Reincarnation

Robert Powell

The research presented by Robert Powell in this book shows that a new science of the stars is possible, based on a study of reincarnation and karma. Willi Sucher did much to pioneer the development of a new star wisdom, or astrosophy, as a scientific tool for the investigation of karma. Powell has discovered that applying the science of astrosophy to the findings of karma research reveals—through the discovery of astrological reincarnation rules—the foundations underlying star wisdom. Once these foundational findings relating to astrological reincarnation research have been assimilated, a reformation of traditional astrology will inevitably take place. Once the new astrology is established, there will be a similar feeling in looking back upon traditional Western astrology that modern astronomers have when looking back upon the old geocentric astronomy.

The purpose of this book is to contemplate the incarnations of the prophet Elijah, with the goal of laying the foundation for a new "science of the stars" as the "science of karma." At the close of his last lecture, after discussing the sequence of incarnations of Elijah–John the Baptist–Raphael–Novalis, Rudolf Steiner spoke of this individuality as "a radiant and splendid forerunner...with whom you are to prepare the work that shall be accomplished at the end of the [twentieth] century, and will lead humankind past the great crisis in which it is involved." These words indicate that, from the end of the twentieth century and into the twenty-first century (that is, now), the Elijah-John individuality is to be a "radiant forerunner" for humanity in the next step underlying our spiritual evolution.

Elijah Come Again presents a scientific approach toward unveiling the mystery of human destiny. This theme is timeless in nature—yet timely, nevertheless, in the recounting of the unfolding destiny and mission of the Old Testament prophet Elijah.

ISBN: 9781584200703 | 260 pages | pbk | $35.00

The theme of this *Holy Nights Journal* focuses on finding resilience in a dark time. As we continue to face unexpected natural catastrophes, social and political unrest, global economic instability, and disruption in all aspects of our collective and individual lives, it becomes ever more imperative that we find both the strength and care of the soul that can maintain our sanity and sense of nobility. Resilience is an intrinsic capacity of the human being to endure and triumph over adversities. It does not belong to a chosen select few as once thought a century ago. With the emerging paradigm of salutogenesis, resilience has become an essential component to any holistic education. By identifying and cultivating a sense of coherence, we can build the healthy forces to withstand the onslaught of adversarial conditions shaping our postmodern life.

The *Holy Nights Journal* unfolds a threefold sequence of exercises to instill the powers of resilience we need as individuals, as families, as communities, as nations, and as humanity as a whole. Hygienic, psychological, and spiritual practices are introduced as a path of resilience for our time. Included is a guide for consciously working through meditations, questions, and journaling topics for each of the Holy Nights. In addition, correspondences of the Holy Nights to signs of the zodiac, human virtues, and dedications to the Saints accompany each journaling page.

This is a wonderful way to celebrate the Holy Nights and can be powerful gift for those who wish to enter more deeply into the significance of this sacred time.

The price per journal is $22.95 + shipping and handling
Available from the Rudolf Steiner College Bookstore
Ph. 916-961-8729 | Fax 877-782-1890
www.steinercollege.edu/bookstore
Email: orders@steinercollege.edu